Dedication

This volume is dedicated to Mary Ainsworth, whose clear theoretical vision, perceptive observations, and methodological ingenuity laid the foundations for programmatic empirical research on individual differences in attachment. Because she herself has been a "secure base" for subsequent theorists and researchers, her extraordinary gift has been multiplied many times.

Contents

Acknowledgments

In addition to the authors and the editors whose names appear in the "Contents," there are many unseen contributors to this volume. First, there are those who made the original conference possible. Without the inspired vision of Andrew Brink, there would have been no conference. The event was a joint project of the C.M. Hincks Institute, the University of Toronto, and the Ontario Institute for Studies in Education and received essential funding from the Ontario Mental Health Foundation, Trinity College, University of Toronto, Social Sciences and Humanities Research Council of Canada, Hannah Institute for the History of Medicine, Phoenix Community Works Foundation, the Hospital for Sick Children Foundation, Mr. and Mrs. Bram Appel, and RBC Holdings.

The conference committee, which consisted of Roy Muir (chair), Ken Adam, Andrew Brink, Susan Goldberg, Howell Gotlieb, Freda Martin, Mary Owens, and Otto Weininger worked long and hard to realize the vision of a gathering which would encourage wide-ranging discussion. Edythe Nerlich, the conference coordinator deserves a special mention, for she handled not only the administrative details, but the endless frustrations that accompanied them with an enthusiasm, grace, and dedication that enabled the others to rest assured that all was well (even when it was not!).

Individuals who chaired sessions and served as discussants for papers sessions made a substantial intellectual contribution to the volume you are about to read. These chapters are based on the conference presentations but often incorporate or respond to comments of the assigned discussants as well as the informal meetings and arranged participant discussions that took place over the three days of the conference. Thus, although you may not see their names in the Table of Contents, Andrew Brink, David Pederson, Gregory Moran, Morris Eagle, Roy Muir, Graeme Taylor, Susan Goldberg, Karin Grossmann, Diane Benoit, Erik Hesse, Malcolm West, Yvonne Gauthier, Dante Cicchetti, and John Kerr contributed to some of these chapters as did a number of participants from the audience.

When I joined the organizing committee of this conference, I had no idea that the task of editing this volume would fall primarily to me. My initial reaction to the assignment was disbelief and panic. I am pleased to report it has not been nearly as traumatic as I anticipated. Linda Citren, the secretary of my research unit assisted with many aspects of the project and her general support of the unit's daily work allowed me to focus on the task at hand. My fellow editors, Roy Muir and John Kerr, have not only shared much of the burden but made this an intellectually exciting and satisfying experience. I will not graciously credit them with all the fine points in this volume and excuse them from the errors and problems (a posture too reminiscent of the dismissing attachment pattern). It would be more realistic (and autonomous?) to indicate that this is a project for which we share and acknowledge full responsibility for the intellectual adventures that lie before you.

Susan Goldberg

Contributors

Kenneth S. Adam, M.D.–Professor of Psychiatry, University of Toronto.

Jay Belsky, Ph.D.–Professor of Human Development, Pennsylvania State University.

Inge Bretherton, Ph.D.–Professor of Child and Family Studies, University of Wisconsin-Madison.

Dante Cicchetti, Ph.D.–Director, Mt. Hope Family Center, and Professor of Psychology, Psychiatry, and Pediatrics, University of Rochester (New York).

Patricia M. Crittenden, Ph.D.–Family Relations Institute, Miami, Florida.

Keith Crnic, Ph.D.–Associate Professor of Psychology, Pennsylvania State College.

Morris Eagle, Ph.D.–Professor of Applied Psychology, Ontario Institute for Studies in Education; Professor, Derner Institute of Advanced Psychological Studies, Adelphi University, Garden City, New York.

Peter Fonagy, Ph.D.–Freud Memorial Professor of Psychoanalysis, Subdepartment of Clinical Health Psychology, Department of Psychology, University College, London; Research Coordinator, The Anna Freud Centre, London.

Susan Goldberg, Ph.D. (editor)–Research Scientist, Hospital for Sick Children, Toronto; Professor of Psychiatry and Psychology, University of Toronto.

Klaus E. Grossmann, Ph.D.–Professor of Psychology, Institut für Psychologie, University of Regensburg.

Myron A. Hofer, M.D.—Professor of Psychiatry, College of Physicians and Surgeons, Columbia University; Director, Developmental Psychobiology, New York State Psychiatric Institute.

Jeremy Holmes, M.B.B.Ch., (M.R.C.P., M.R.C., Psych., F.R.C. Psych.)—Psychiatrist/Psychotherapist, North Devon District Hospital, Devon, England.

Adrienne E. Sheldon Keller, Ph.D.—Assistant Professor of Psychiatric Medicine, University of Virginia.

Roger Kennedy, M.D.—Consultant Psychotherapist, Cassel Family Unit; Honorary Senior Lecturer in Psychiatry, Charing Cross and Westminster Medical Schools, London.

John Kerr (editor)—Associate editor, The Analytic Press; author, *A Most Dangerous Method: The Story of Jung, Freud, and Sabina Spielrein.*

Tom Leigh, MRc—Senior Registrar in Psychotherapy, Adult Department, Tavistock Clinic, London.

Giovanni Liotti, M.D.—Director of Training, Italian Association for Cognitive Psychotherapy; President, Roman Association for Research on the Psychopathology of the Attachment System (A.R.P.A.S.).

Mary Main, Ph.D.—Professor of Psychology, University of California, Berkeley.

Gretta Matoon, BSc—Research Assistant, Department of Psychology, University College, London.

Roy Muir, M.D. (editor)—Associate Professor of Psychiatry and Co-head, Infancy Program, Division of Child Psychiatry, University of Toronto.

Kate Rosenberger, M.S.—Graduate Student in Psychology, Pennsylvania State University.

Howard Steele, Ph.D.—Lecturer in Psychology, Subdepartment of Clinical Health Psychology, Department of Psychology, University College, London.

Miriam Steele, Ph.D.–Lecturer in Psychology, Subdepartment of Clinical Health Psychology, University College, London; Course Organizer for MSc in Psychoanalytic Developmental Psychology and Child Psychotherapist, The Anna Freud Centre.

Stephen J. Suomi, Ph.D.–Director, Laboratory of Comparative Ethology, National Institute of Child Health and Human Development, Bethesda, Maryland.

Mary Target, Ph.D.–Lecturer in Psychology/Senior Research Fellow, Subdepartment of Clinical Health Psychology, Department of Psychology, University College, London, and The Anna Freud Centre, London.

Sheree L. Toth, Ph.D.–Associate Professor of Psychology and Associate Director, Mt. Hope Family Center, University of Rochester.

Malcolm West, Ph.D.–Associate Professor of Psychiatry, University of Calgary.

Introduction

SUSAN GOLDBERG

John Bowlby, described as one of the "three or four most important psychiatrists of the twentieth century" (Storr, 1992), died in 1990. In October 1993 a conference was held in Toronto to honor Bowlby and to take stock of his theory of attachment, its origins, influences, and implications. Several previous conferences and volumes had focused on Bowlby's attachment theory, but the 1993 conference was unique in scope. Whereas prior conferences and volumes had concentrated on specific themes within attachment theory, research, and practice (e.g., attachment across the lifespan), this volume, which grew out of the 1993 conference, is designed to place attachment theory in its cultural and historical context (Holmes Bretherton, Grossmann, Eagle), evaluate its relation to clinical (Adam, Fonagy, Cichetti, Liotti) and to research endeavors (Belsky, Hofer, Suomi), and identify new directions in attachment work (Crittenden, Main).

This breadth of interest will appeal to clinicians and researchers alike. Indeed, the most remarkable aspect of the conference itself was the intense excitement generated among clinicians previously unaware of the extensive developmental research on attachment and its relevance to their work. Their enthusiasm was matched by corresponding enthusiasm from researchers whose view of attachment had been primarily academic without concern for clinical applications.

The chasm between researchers and clinicians, particularly clinicians from the psychoanalytic tradition, is not unusual. Each group has its own language, produces and reads its own journals, and generally communicates with professionals who share the same orientation. John Bowlby was a rare figure in the psychoanalytic community for his insistence on the importance of empirical and extraclinical validation of theory. To that end, he formed alliances with researchers in many disciplines and brought research-trained psychologists to the Tavistock clinic as collaborators.

The most important of these was Mary Ainsworth. It was Ainsworth's thoughtful observations, conceptual elaborations, and

1

development of a standardized laboratory procedure (known as the Strange Situation) for assessing individual differences in patterns of attachment that opened the door to programmatic empirical research. Ainsworth's own contributions initiated new directions in attachment theory and research. But her influence is multiplied many times because she nurtured a second generation of gifted researchers, who, in turn, trained major contributors.

Among Ainsworth's earliest intellectual descendants, Mary Main is the one most responsible for bridging the researcher–clinician gap. Main is one of several in her generation to explore attachment and its measurement beyond infancy. The Adult Attachment Interview, which she and her colleagues developed, proved to be an important touchstone for clinicians who recognized its content as familiar clinical material and the meticulous discourse analysis used to code it as an objective translation of important clinical intuitions. Indeed, it was in an adult attachment workshop led by Mary Main and Erik Hesse that Andrew Brink, then head of the Humanities and Psychoanalytic Thought Program at Trinity College, University of Toronto, conceived the idea for the 1993 Toronto conference as an opportunity to unite clinicians and researchers in a common endeavor.

Thus, this volume marks a new era in attachment theory and research, one in which attachment theory is being rediscovered by clinicians, especially analysts (who discarded it on the basis of Bowlby's early writings many years ago), and in which developmental researchers previously insulated from the front lines of clinical research are discovering the practical applications of attachment theory and research and thereby enriching theories of development.

It is our expectation that this volume will appeal to the same broad audience that enjoyed the conference. Like any specialized group, attachment researchers have developed a language and shorthand of their own to describe important behavioral patterns, a language that may not be familiar to this broader audience. Therefore, we have provided a guide to the labels for individual differences in attachment (attachment classifications) that are routinely used throughout the book. The appendices to this chapter summarize this information and may be used for quick reference. Readers who are already familiar with this material may want to skip this section and go directly to the next section.

ATTACHMENT AND ITS MEASUREMENT

This overview emphasizes observation and interview measures that are most germane to understanding the chapters in this volume. Other methods, such as the Water and Deane Q-sort (Waters and

Deane, 1985) and projective measures currently being developed, for example, the separation anxiety test and doll play stories (Bretherton, Ridgeway, and Cassidy, 1990) are discussed in individual chapters. Since the infancy scheme was first to develop and other schemes have been largely derivative, it is described in detail. Several chapters in this volume rely on the Adult Attachment Interview (AAI) and its associated scoring scheme, and it too is discussed in detail. Schemes for preschoolers and for five- to seven-year-olds are discussed more briefly, and the reader is referred to descriptions in relevant appendices. In addition, Appendix 1 provides an overview of the relations between different schemes.

The original classification scheme for infant–caregiver attachment was based on observation of behavior in the *Strange Situation* (a standardized laboratory procedure involving two separations and reunions between the caregiver and the infant) but was validated by showing that infant behavior in the Strange Situation was a good marker of the kind of caregiving infants had experienced at home over the first year (Ainsworth et al., 1978).

Ainsworth described three major patterns, each with two or more subtypes. The most common and most optimal major pattern was labeled *secure* (or Type B, with four subtypes). These were infants who clearly used their mothers as a secure base for exploration. That is, they explored freely in her presence, checked on her whereabouts and reactions periodically, and restricted exploration in her absence. They showed varying levels of distress in her absence (one feature that distinguishes subtypes), ranging from simple inhibition of play/exploration to extreme distress, but all greeted her positively on her return. Those who were more distressed sought physical contact, were comforted by it, and were soon able to return to exploration.

The next most common pattern was labeled *avoidant* (Type A, with two subtypes). These infants appeared to explore without interest in their mothers' whereabouts, were minimally distressed by her departure, and appeared to "snub" or ignore her when she returned.

The third pattern was labeled *ambivalent or resistant* (Type C, with two subtypes). These infants had difficulty separating from their mothers to explore, and their play was often impoverished. They were extremely distressed by their mothers' departure, and, although they sought contact with her on her return, they did not readily settle down or return to exploration.

A notable feature of this classification scheme is that the amount of distress shown during separation (previously considered to reflect the strength of infant–mother relationships) does not distinguish between secure and insecure relationships. Within the *secure* group, some infants (those in the B1 and B2 subgroups) show little distress and seek minimal contact with the mother at reunion. In this respect they are like *avoidant* infants, but their generally positive approach to their mothers, particularly at reunions, identifies them as *secure*. Other secure infants (those in the B3 and B4 subgroups) may be very distressed during separations, and some (those in the B4 subgroup), like *resistant* infants, may also be slow to settle down at reunions. Nevertheless, it is their competence in expressing their needs directly, and their unambivalent acceptance of maternal ministrations, that places them in the secure group. Thus, one of the most important lessons from Ainsworth's Baltimore study is that reunion behaviors are more telling than separation behaviors in revealing quality of attachment.

For many years, these three primary categories were adequate to capture individual differences in infant behavior in the *Strange Situation*. Research during this period documented the antecedents of these patterns in maternal and infant behavior in the home as well as the sequelae in the later social development of the child. The most notable example of the latter is a large longitudinal study by Sroufe and Egeland and their colleagues at University of Minnesota, which has followed infants for whom attachment was assessed at 12 and 18 months into late adolescence (e.g., Erickson, Sroufe, and Egeland, 1985; Sroufe et al., 1993). Two other major longitudinal studies, one at Berkeley led by Main and her colleagues (Main, Kaplan, and Cassidy, 1985) and one in Germany conducted by Klaus and Karin Grossmann and their colleagues (Wartner et al., 1994) have also made major contributions to this literature. In addition, numerous studies of normative and high-risk populations included attachment measures among other measures at discrete points in the life cycle. These studies occupied increasing space in leading developmental journals.

The original attachment classification scheme served these studies well, although there was always a small group of cases that were difficult to classify or that could not be readily assigned to one of the existing categories. As attachment studies expanded to include more clinical samples, such as maltreated children and infants of psychiatrically diagnosed mothers, it became evident that there were patterns of attachment behavior that could not be integrated into Ainsworth's original three-category scheme. A "mixed" avoidant/resistant (A/C) pattern was documented by Crittenden (1985) and by Radke-Yarrow and her colleagues (1985).

Subsequently, Main and Solomon (1986, 1990) reviewed a large number of "unclassifiable" tapes and developed criteria for identifying disorganized/disoriented (Type D) attachment. Unlike children in the three primary categories, which represented organized strategies for managing arousal in the context of the attachment relationship, infants classified as disorganized/disoriented did not appear to have an organized strategy. Furthermore, they engaged in odd behaviors (e.g., they were unable to approach the caregiver directly even when very distressed), which made sense only if they were assumed to be either frightened or confused by the caregiver.

Because the D classification did not provide information about attachment strategies, infants in this group were also assigned to a "forced" classification that represented the best fit of the ABC alternatives. Thus, the most widely used classification scheme for infants now includes four classifications: avoidant (A), secure (B), resistant (C), and disorganized (D). Appendix 2 summarizes this scheme. While the A/C patterns described by Crittenden (1985) and Radke-Yarrow et al. (1985) have sometimes been subsumed under the D category, Crittenden (1992, this volume) has argued convincingly that the A/C pattern can be an organized strategy and should be considered distinct from the disorganized category.

For many years after Ainsworth's development of the Strange Situation and the associated classification scheme, research focused on infants. Bowlby, however, clearly considered attachment to be a life-span construct, and it soon became evident that measures of attachment beyond infancy were needed.

One of the first steps in this direction was Main's development of the Adult Attachment Interview (AAI). For the purpose of instrument development, Main assumed that parents of infants exhibiting different attachment patterns would differ in their "states of mind" regarding intimate relationships. By grouping and using a "guess and uncover" method to examine transcripts of interviews from parents whose infants' attachment classification was known, Main and her colleagues established three primary adult attachment categories that corresponded to the infant scheme: dismissing (Ds, avoidant); autonomous or free to evaluate (F, secure); and preoccupied or enmeshed (E, resistant). It was also discovered that the parents of disorganized infants were likely to report salient loss or trauma with respect to attachment figures in childhood that had not been resolved. These parents were classified unresolved (U) and, as with the D classification of infancy, "forced" into one of the other categories that best captured their strategy for thinking about and discussing attachment experiences.

The method of classifying AAI transcripts is based on discourse analysis designed to assess one's ability to provide a coherent and relevant narrative regarding attachment experiences rather than an attempt to describe veridically the early experience of the person. Adults classified as *dismissing* minimize the effects of intimate relationships in their lives. They often idealize their relationships with parents and have difficulty providing concrete details to flesh out the generalizations they make about their childhood.

Those considered *autonomous* value intimate relationships and acknowledge the effects those relationships have had. Whether the specific experiences these people report are positive or negative, they are able to provide not only confirming details but also evidence of an ability to reflect on those experiences so as to understand both their own behavior and that of their parents and provide a coherent narrative.

Adults in the *preoccupied* group quickly become entangled in details of early experiences and are still engaged in struggles with their parents. They often appear to lack an identity independent of these struggles and have little reflective understanding of the issues.

The *unresolved* category is based on specific references to loss or trauma that reveal disorganization of thought such as would normally occur at the time of the actual experience (e.g., reference to a deceased parent as if he or she were still alive; preoccupation with guilt over one's role in loss or abuse). Appendix 3 summarizes the AAI classification system.

Because the scoring of the AAI is so labor intensive, there have also been efforts to develop questionnaire measures of adult attachment. Some of these are specifically derived from the AAI and are intended to be more cost-effective strategies for duplicating AAI classifications. Others have evolved independent of the AAI and assess somewhat different aspects of adult attitudes toward close relationships. At present there is no published validated questionnaire that can satisfactorily substitute for the AAI.

Classification systems for preschoolers and five- to seven-year-olds have been introduced more recently. Two different schemes have been proposed for preschoolers, both based on adaptations of the Strange Situation procedures. Both take account of newly emerging skills, such as children's understanding of social conventions and independent parent agendas, as well as ability to discuss and negotiate attachment related goals.

That of Cassidy and Marvin (1987) is closely related to an earlier scheme (Main and Cassidy, 1988) for five- to seven-year-olds. Each of these schemes retains the four categories of the infant and adult schemes described above [avoidant (A), secure (B), dependent (C), disorganized or controlling (D)] and adds a fifth (insecure-other), which includes a mixture of insecure strategies or accommodates cases that clearly are insecure but do not fit any of the existing categories. (See Appendix 4 for a more detailed description.)

Crittenden's (1992) preschool scheme retains the three primary classifications (avoidant (A), secure (B), and coercive (C), as well the mixed A/C pattern previously discussed. This scheme is illustrated in more detail in Crittenden's chapter in this volume. At present, the period from age seven to adulthood is relatively uncharted territory as far as attachment assessment is concerned. There have been some efforts to use the AAI with teenagers (e.g., Kobak and Sceery, 1988) and at least one effort to develop procedures unique to adolescents (Cobb, 1993).

Attachment researchers frequently use the shorthand alphabetical labels for classifications and speak of A's, F's, or C's, or, even more confusing, B4's, E3's, and so on. In this volume, we try to minimize confusion for nonexperts in two ways. First, whenever possible, we use descriptive, rather than alphabetical, labels in the text (e.g., "avoidant" rather than "A"). Sometimes, however, it is not evident that different descriptive labels refer to related patterns (e.g., resistant, dependent, preoccupied). The main purpose of Appendix 1 is to indicate such matches in a systematic way.

THIS VOLUME AND THE STATE OF THE ART

This volume captures current work in attachment theory at an important juncture in its history, one where theory, research, and practice unite to create new directions in a rapidly evolving field. At the interface between clinical and developmental science, there are several major issues. First, a number of contributors consider the implications of attachment theory for psychoanalytic theories of development and psychopathology (Bretherton, Eagle, Grossmann, Holmes, Main). Although attachment theory is rooted in the psychoanalytic tradition, it is primarily the programmatic empirical research of developmental psychologists that has enabled it to return to those roots to realize Bowlby's initial vision.

A second group of contributors are concerned with the processes that underlie formation of early attachments (Belsky, Fonagy, Hofer, Suomi). Nearly 30 years of developmental research have provided only the outlines of the underlying processes, which are yet to be studied in detail. Full understanding of these processes is invaluable to those who undertake to overcome the damaging effects of inappropriate early caregiving such as maltreatment (Cicchetti and Toth).

Individual patterns of attachment develop as adaptations to experience with caregivers. Patterns labeled "insecure" are conventionally thought to have less adaptive value when generalized to the wider social environment. Adam and Crittenden, however, press us in their chapters to consider the adaptive implications of insecure attachment patterns.

These implications may be particularly relevant for comprehending the origins and treatment of psychiatric disorders. Thus, patterns of attachment may have unique associations with specific diagnoses including psychopathy (Crittenden), borderline disorder (Adam, Fonagy), dissociation and multiple personality (Main, Liotti), and depression (Crittenden, Liotti). An understanding of internal working models and the manner in which they normally change may provide clinicians with the foundations of new psychotherapeutic techniques (Liotti).

An understanding of attachment and attachment patterns can also be of broad use to clinicians in understanding the therapeutic process (Holmes, Main, Liotti). The manner in which a person forms (or fails to form) a therapeutic alliance and the nature of transference, resistance, and dependency within treatment can also be viewed as reflecting attachment history (i.e., pattern). Furthermore, the therapist brings an attachment history of his or her own to the process and thus may enhance or limit effectiveness.

These are domains in which we can expect exciting new developments in the near future. Of course, no single volume can adequately represent the breadth and depth of any rapidly developing field. We think of this volume as a tantalizing sampler—one that can be a reference for workers in the field yet lure the novice into further exploration.

APPENDIX 1

ATTACHMENT TERMINOLOGY ACROSS THE LIFE SPAN*

Age	Reference	Method	Classifications			
			Secure	Avoidant (A)	Ambivalent or Resistant (C)	Other
Infancy	Ainsworth et al., 1978	Observation: Strange Situation (reunions)	Secure (B)	Avoidant (A)	Ambivalent or Resistant (C)	
	Crittenden, 1985	"				Avoidant-Resistant (A/C)
	Main & Solomon, 1986	"				Disorganized/ Disoriented (D)
Preschool	Cassidy & Marvin, 1987, 1992, (see also Shouldice & Stevenson-Hinde, 1992; Greenberg et al., 1991)	Strange Situation other reunions	Secure (B)	Avoidant (A)	Dependent (C)	Controlling (D) Insecure-other
	Crittenden, 1992	"	Secure/ Balanced (B)	Defended (A)	Coercive (C)	Defended-coercive (A/C) Disorganized (D) Anxious Depressed Insecure-other

Age	Reference	Method	Classifications			
			Secure	Insecure		
5–7 yrs.	Main & Cassidy, 1988	Observation: Reunions	Secure (B)	Avoidant (A)	Dependent (C)	Controlling (D) Insecure-other
7–11 yrs.	No classification scheme available					
Adolescence	Cobb, 1993	Observation: Revealed differences or Reunions	Balanced (B)	Limiting (A)	Preoccupied (C)	Disorganized (D)
Adult	Main, Kaplan & Cassidy, 1985	Discourse analysis: Adult Attachment Interview	Autonomous (F)	Dismissing (Ds)	Preoccupied (E)	Unresolved about loss or trauma (U)

*This table lists the methods originally used to generate the classification schemes at each age period. In addition to the methods listed, researchers have employed numerous other techniques to investigate attachment. These include Q-sort methodology, figure drawings, doll play, story stems, and questionnaires. These methods may or may not yield the detailed classification scheme outlined in the table.

APPENDIX 2
PATTERNS OF ATTACHMENT IN INFANCY

Secure (B)   Uses caregiver as a "secure base," explores freely when the caregiver is available, may or may not be distressed at separation but greets positively on reunion, seeks contact if distressed, settles down, returns to exploration. 55–65% of normative population.

Avoidant (A)   Appears minimally interested in caregiver, explores busily, minimal distress at separation, ignores or avoids caregiver on reunion. 20–25% of normative population.

Resistant/
Ambivalant (C)   Minimal exploration, preoccupied with caregiver, has difficulty settling down, both seeks and resists contact on reunion, may be angry or very passive. 10–15% of normative population.

Disorganized/
Disoriented (D)   Disorganized and/or disoriented behavior in the caregiver's presence (e.g., approach with head averted, trancelike freezing, anomalous postures). Infants placed in this category are also "forced" into the best fit of the preceding categories. 15–20% of normative population.

Other (cannot
classify)   Some children may not fit any of the other patterns. Extremely rare, except in combination with D classification.

APPENDIX 3
PATTERNS OF ATTACHMENT—PRESCHOOL/5–7 YEARS OLD

Secure (B)   Happy but casual greeting, fluent conversation, appropriate eye contact. Coordinated attention to child's ongoing activity and the parent. Child may initiate casual physical contact.

Avoidant (A)   Polite greeting with little welcoming initiative toward parent. Minimal response to parent overtures, minimal eye contact, neutral affect. Busy with other activities.

Dependent (C)   In preschool years, child is whiny and contentious; parent and child struggle for most of the episode. OR the child acts inappropriately coy and helpless. Not well defined in the 5–7-year-old group.

Controlling (D)   In early preschool years there may be some signs of disorganization. The child has taken control of relationship either by working hard to entertain the parent (being overly bright and enthusiastic-caregiving) OR by treating the parent in a condescending and humiliating manner. Also given an alternative ABC classification.

Insecure-Other   In both age periods, this classification is used for children who are clearly insecure but do not fit any other category. They may use a combination of the other insecure strategies. Also given the best fitting ABC alternative.

APPENDIX 4
ADULT ATTACHMENT CLASSIFICATIONS

Secure/ autonomous (F)
Coherent and collaborative in discussing attachments. Dialogue is fresh and thoughtful. May have had positive or negative childhood experiences but has perspective and understanding of own and other contributions to these experiences. (45–55% in normative samples)

Dismissing (Ds)
Attachment concerns dismissed from active consideration. Some insistence on lack of memory for childhood experiences. May idealize but be unable to support with details. May provide details but be cut off from related feelings or dismiss their significance. Transcripts often short. (20–35% in normative samples)

Preoccupied (E)
Confused and preoccupied with details of past experiences without objective perspective. May seem passive and vague or angry, conflicted or unconvincingly analytical. Transcripts often long and incoherent. (10–15% in normative samples)

Unresolved/ disorganized (U)
Lapses in monitoring of reasoning or discourse when discussing events concerning attachment loss or trauma (e.g. disbelief in death, confused or incomplete statements, change to inappropriate tense). (15–20% in normative populations. Also assigned an alternative from F, Ds, E).

Cannot classify (CC)
Does not fit any of the other categories.

REFERENCES

Ainsworth, M. D. S., Blehar, M. Waters, E. & Wall, S. (1978), *Patterns of Attachment*. Hillsdale, NJ: Lawrence Erlbaum Associates.

Bretherton, I., Ridgeway, D. & Cassidy, J. (1990), Assessing internal working models of the attachment relationship: An attachment story completion task for 3-year-olds. In: *Attachment in the Preschool Years*, ed. M. T. Greenberg, D. Cicchetti & E. M. Cummings. Chicago: University of Chicago Press, pp. 273–308.

Cassidy, J. & Marvin, R. S. with the Attachment Working Group of the MacArthur Network on the Transition from Infancy to Early Childhood (1987), Attachment organization in three- and four-year-olds: Coding guidelines. Unpublished manual, Psychology Dept. of University of Virginia, Charlottesville (revised 1992).

Cobb, C. (1993), Patterns of attachment and family paradigms. Unpublished doctoral dissertation, Department of Sociology, York University, Downsview, Ontario.

Crittenden, P. (1985), Maltreated infants: Vulnerability and resilience. *J. Child Psychol. Psychiat.*, 26:85–96.

—— (1992), Quality of attachment in the preschool years. *Devel. Psychopathol.*, 4:209–241.

Erickson, M. F., Sroufe, L. A. & Egeland, B. (1985), The relationship between quality of attachment and behavior problems in a preschool high risk sample. In: *Growing Points of Attachment Theory and Research*, ed. I. Bretherton & E. Waters. *Monographs of the Society for Research in Child Development*. Serial No. 209, Vol. 50, Nos. 1–2, pp. 147–166.

Greenberg, M. T., Speltz, M. L., DeKlyen, M. C. & Endriga, M. C. (1991), Attachment security in preschoolers with and without externalizing problems: A replication. *Devel. Psychopathol.*, 3:413–430.

Kobak, R. R. & Sceery, A. (1988), Attachment in late adolescence: Working models, affect regulation, and representations of self and others. *Child Devel.*, 59:135–146.

Main, M. & Cassidy, J. (1988), Categories of response to reunion with the parent at age six: Predicted from attachment classifications and stable over a one-month period. *Devel. Psychol.*, 24:415–426.

—— Kaplan, N. & Cassidy, J. (1985), Security in infancy, childhood and adulthood: A move to the level of representation. In: *Growing Points of Attachment Theory and Research*, ed. I. Bretherton & E. Waters. *Monographs of the Society for Research in Child Development*. Serial No. 209, Vol. 50, Nos. 1–2. pp. 66–104.

—— & Solomon, J. (1986), Discovery of an insecure-disorganized/disoriented attachment pattern. In: *Affective Development in Infancy*, ed. T. B. Brazelton & M. W. Yogman. Norwood, NJ: Ablex pp. 95–124.

—— —— (1990), Procedures for identifying infants as disorganized/disoriented during the Ainsworth Strange Situation. In: *Attachment in the Preschool Years*, M. T. Greenberg, D. Cicchetti & E. M. Cummings. Chicago: University of Chicago Press, pp. 121–160.

Radke-Yarrow, M., Cummings, E. M., Kuczinski, L. & Chapman, M. (1985), Patterns of attachment in two- and three-year-olds in normal families and families with parental depression. *Child Devel.*, 56:519–615.

Shouldice, A. & Stevenson-Hinde, J. (1992), Coping with security and distress: The separation-anxiety test and attachment classification at 4.5 years. *J. Child Psychol. Psychiat.*, 33:331–348.

Sroufe, L. A., Bennett, C., Englund, M., Urban, J. & Shulman, S. (1993), The significance of gender boundaries in preadolescence: Contemporary correlates and antecedents of boundary violation and maintenance. *Child Devel.*, 64:455–466.

Storr, A. (1992), John Bowlby. *Munks Roll*. London: Royal College of Physicians.

Wartner, U. G., Grossmann, K., Femmes-Bombik, E. & Suess, G. (1994), Attachment patterns at age six in south Germany: Predictability from infancy and implications for preschool behavior. *Child Devel.*, 65:1014–1027.

Waters, E. & Deane, K. E. (1985), Defining and assessing individual differences in attachment relationships. Q-methodology and the organization of behavior in infancy and early childhood. In: *Growing Points of Attachment Theory and Research*, ed. I. Bretherton & E. Waters. *Monographs of the Society for Research in Child Development*. Serial No. 209, Vol. 50, Nos. 1–2, pp. 45–61.

Part I

Origins and Context of Attachment Theory

2

"Something There Is That Doesn't Love a Wall"

John Bowlby, Attachment Theory, and Psychoanalysis

JEREMY HOLMES

At Trumpan on the Waternich peninsula of the Scottish island of Skye stands a remote and wild hillside graveyard. There John Bowlby lies buried, among the hills and coast where for half a century he loved to walk and where he spent his holidays and, after retirement, the spring and summer months of the year. Much of his writing was done there, and he and his wife, Ursula, were familiar figures on the Kyle of Lochalch ferry, their car filled to the brim with books, a few personal possessions perched precariously in suitcases on the roofrack. The contrast with the busy sophistication of Hampstead and the Tavistock clinic where Bowlby spent the other half of his year could hardly be greater, and this split—or creative tension—between town and country, wildness and civilization, culture and nature, forms the background to this chapter.

Bowlby's headstone is a simple granite slab, with the inscription "To be a pilgrim," taken from John Bunyan's famous hymn. The choice was apt: Bunyan the puritan, the dissenter, the rebel, who spent many years imprisoned for his radical views and who used simple, profound, and powerful words:

> There's no discouragement
> Shall make him once relent
> His first avowed intent . . .

Bowlby had a stubborn, determined streak, which meant that he was prepared to follow his ideas, however unpopular, to their logical and detailed conclusion.

Who so beset him round
With dismal stories
Do but themselves confound
His strength the more is . . .

[Harrison, 1977]

The pilgrim's prescription "'gainst all disaster" is to "follow the Master." Whatever his difficulties with the psychoanalytic world, especially with the "dismal stories" of Kleinian psychoanalysis, Bowlby's admiration for Freud never wavered. But his first and most abiding master was Darwin, with whom I believe he strongly identi-fied. At a time when most men and women of achievement might have been resting on their laurels, Bowlby devoted the final years of his life to writing his biography of Darwin, perhaps his most personal and accessible work.

The quest for Bowlby has, for me, centered on three main issues. First is the attempt to understand the origins of attachment theory in Bowlby's own character and life history, and second is to look at Bowlby's break with psychoanalysis, which meant that attachment theory was for two decades virtually airbrushed out of the psycho-analytic record—rather like some dissident in Stalinist times—despite Bowlby's avowed intent to direct his theoretical work "primarily towards my colleagues in the International [Psychoanalytic] Associa-tion" (Bowlby, 1991). The third issue is to track the reattachment of Bowlbian and post-Bowlbian ideas within psychoanalytic psycho-therapy and to show how they can contribute to, and enrich the emergence of, a new relational perspective within psychoanalysis in both theory and practice (Mitchell, 1988).

PSYCHOBIOGRAPHY

Born in 1907, Bowlby was contemporary with the younger Darwin grandchildren. Good family therapist that he was, Bowlby begins his Darwin story with the grandparental generation, and we shall follow his example (Holmes, 1993b). Bowlby's paternal grandfather was a successful journalist, "Bowlby of the *Times*," who was killed in 1861 in Bejing during the opium wars, which he was covering as a foreign correspondent; he left a widow and several children, of whom Bowlby's father, Anthony, was the eldest. Anthony, able, single-minded, and very hardworking, eventually became a fashionable London surgeon and, having successfully operated on one of Queen Victoria's numerous children and spent almost the entire 1914–18 war at the front as a surgeon general, was duly knighted, becoming president of the Royal College of Surgeons in 1920. He died in 1927, late enough to sanction Bowlby's career switch from naval cadet to medical student, early enough not to oppose his choice of psychiatry and psychoanalysis as a career.

Sir Anthony felt his duty was to support his widowed mother, and only after her death, when he was 40, did he feel free to marry. May Mostyn's wedding dress was embroidered with violets in deference to her mother-in-law, for whom the statutory year of mourning had not yet passed. May herself was not young, 30 years old, the oldest daughter of a country parson, the Honorable Hugh Mostyn, who, as "Grampy," was to play an important part in the lives of the Bowlby children. He loved country pursuits—walking, shooting, fishing, hunting—and, during the long Bowlby holidays, would join them in Scotland and, with infectious enthusiasm, teach them his skills.

John Bowlby's parents were thus both well into middle age by the time he, the fourthborn, arrived. His father worked very hard, and John saw little of him during his childhood, but perhaps enough to alert him to the way in which childhood bereavement can lead to emotional suppression—Sir Anthony's remote and rather frightening manner was no doubt, in part, typical of his class and occupation but also perhaps connected with the loss of his father at an early age. Bowlby appears to have grieved little when he died; but the death of his closest friend, the Labor politician Evan Durbin, in a drowning accident in the 1940s put him in touch with his feelings of sadness and loss. The negative effects of suppressed mourning were a central theme for Bowlby. His theory about Darwin's mysterious illness centers on the death of Darwin's mother when he was eight and on the refusal of the family—especially his workaholic doctor father—to speak about this, so much so that when Darwin was playing a Victorian word completion game, he insisted there was no such word when his fellow player added the letter "m" to Charles's "other" (Bowlby, 1990)!

Bowlby's mother was also a product of her era. The oldest of numerous children, she was released by her marriage from looking after her younger brothers and sisters. She seems to have rather despised her own mother but revered her father, and "Grampy's" views were adduced as the final word in any discussion. She certainly favored boys: her youngest daughter, Evelyn, recalled in her 80s with miserable and furious tears the feelings of neglect and favoritism of her early years, while her older brother Tony remembered "a generally happy childhood"—each respectively, perhaps, illustrating the enmeshed and avoidant narrative styles delineated by the Adult Attachment Interview (Bretherton, 1991).

A possible explanation for this different perception lies in the pattern of family holidays, which played a very important part in the

Bowlby household (as they did for John's family in the next generation). May Mostyn had vowed that she would never marry a "city
man," and, when she did, she insisted that they spend long holidays
away from her husband's practice in Manchester Square in the West
End of London. In London, May saw little of her children, whose
care was left mainly to nannies and nursemaids. The children were
ushered into the drawing room from five until six o'clock in the
evening, where May would sometimes read to them her favorite
adventure stories, *Children of the New Forest* and *Treasure Island*.
But things were very different when they were on holiday. Each year
they spent the Easter holidays in the New Forest and long summer
holidays in Scotland. Here May shared her love of nature and country activities with the children. A boyhood naturalist and beetle
collector, John became a lifelong hill walker and clearly understood
Darwin's ecstatic feeling that "[n]o poet ever felt more delight at
seeing his first poem published than I did at seeing in Stephen's
Illustrations of British Insects the magic words 'captured by
C. Darwin esq'" (quoted in Bowlby, 1990, p. 99).

John was sandwiched between two brothers. Tony, like himself,
was a highly intelligent and vigorous little boy with whom there was
an intense but generally amicable rivalry—only 13 months separated
them, and they were dressed and treated almost as twins. Jim, his
younger brother, was, by Bowlby standards, considered backward,
which worried John and may well have influenced his eventual
choice of career. He was very excited when, in his teens, he read
about "monkey gland extract" (thyroxine) and hoped that the
answer to Jim's difficulties had been found.

John started his training as a naval cadet but, chafing against the
narrow intellectual and political service horizons, just as he felt constrained within the psychoanalytic society three decades later, as
well as suffering badly from seasickness, changed to study medicine
at Cambridge. But the naval values of probity, order, punctuality,
and a love of the sea remained with him for a lifetime.

Prematurely self-possessed, John knew his own mind and, his
preclinical studies completed, decided to take a year off to work in a
progressive school for maladjusted boys run along the lines of the
Reichian A. S. Neill. There he found his vocation as a child psychiatrist, and when he returned to his medical studies in London (which
he found desperately dull and alleviated his boredom by running a
highly successful sandwich stall, Bogey's-Bar, for fellow students), he
simultaneously started his training in psychoanalysis.

The impact of Bowlby's psychoanalytic training is something of a
mystery. Bowlby himself was deeply reticent, eschewed gossip, and
could well have been classified as "avoidant" on the Adult Attach-

ment Interview. The British Psychoanalytic Society, which Bowlby joined in the 1930s, was in turmoil riven between Klein and her mostly British followers, and the Viennese refugees who clustered around Anna Freud and her father after their arrival in London in 1938. Freud was clearly not immortal, and the question of who was to succeed him was in everybody's mind. Bowlby's analyst was the leading Kleinian Joan Riviere, who was also Winnicott's analyst, and one of his supervisors was Klein herself. Bowlby, like everyone else, was caught up in this struggle. He emerged from his training as a non-Kleinian "Kleinian," which stood him good stead when, after the "gentleman's agreement" between Klein and Anna Freud in 1944, he became training secretary of the psychoanalytic society—in part, a recognition of his exceptional organizational skills but also of his status as a compromise candidate who was acceptable to both sides (Grosskurth, 1986).

How, then, did Bowlby resist the force field of the Klein-Freud polarization—how did he keep his head while all about him were losing theirs? An obituarist stated, "It is a tribute to his independence to point out that neither of these two formidable ladies [Riviere and Klein] appears to have had the slightest effect on his subsequent development" (Storr, 1992). This is not entirely true, since one of Bowlby's abiding projects was to challenge what he saw to be the defects in psychoanalytic thinking, especially the Kleinian *weltanschauung*. He had four main objections to the attitudes that he encountered in the British society in the 1930s and 1940s. First, he was troubled by the dogmatism and cultism of the psychoanalytic world and argued strongly for open scientific debate and inquiry. Flowing from this was his feeling that psychoanalysis had sequestered itself from contemporary science and clung needlessly to an ossified metapsychology and arcane vocabulary. Third, he was suspicious of theories of childhood that were essentially extrapolations from the couch to the crib and not based on observations of normal development. Above all, he felt that psychoanalysis neglected the role of real environmental trauma in the genesis of neurosis and emphasized, instead, the part played by infantile fantasy. A paper by Bowlby's analyst Riviere contains the following passage: "Psychoanalysis is Freud's discovery of what goes on in the imagination . . . it has no concern with anything else, it is not concerned with the real world. . . . [I]t is concerned simply and solely with the imaginings of the childish mind" (Rayner, 1992, p. 8). Bowlby penciled in the margin: "role of the environment=zero."

Bowlby's Darwinism, his leftish sympathies and friendships, and his direct experiences in the London Child Guidance Clinic in the 1930s combined to make him a firm believer in the central importance of environmental influence in psychological development. With hindsight, it seems curious that the psychoanalysts, especially the Kleinians, took such an extreme antienvironmentalist position. This was, in part, due to the needs of a new discipline struggling to define itself, to mark out a territory of discourse. Perhaps, too, the idea that an inner world could be separated from external reality was a necessary defense for a generation of displaced European intellectuals whose world had been shattered by the rise of fascism. Bettelheim (1960) and Levi (1958) have recorded how those with firm belief systems who were able to detach themselves from what was going on around them were the most likely to survive in the concentration camps. Whatever the reason, a certain detachment from external reality existed within psychoanalysis in the 1930s through the 1960s, especially in its Kleinian form—an issue with which Bowlby struggled over the ensuing decades.

Bowlby's Englishness—his reticence, formal manner, upper-class voice, and gentile origins—meant that he was viewed with some suspicion in inner analytic circles. But his energy, efficiency, and intellectual originality could hardly be ignored, and by the mid-1950s he was prominent in the British Psychoanalytic Society and became deputy to Winnicott's presidency in 1956.

Meanwhile, he had made his reputation with his World Health Organization (WHO) report *Maternal Care and Mental Health* (Bowlby, 1951). The views he expressed in that report on the impact of environmental failure on child development gained wide acceptance even within the highly conservative British medical establishment, where, in contrast to the psychoanalytic society, Bowlby's conventional background and mannerisms helped to give his ideas credibility. The completion of the WHO book left a vacuum, and Bowlby was searching for a new project when, while on holiday in Scotland, his friend and neighbor Julian Huxley, the biologist and grandson of Darwin's "bulldog," T. H. Huxley, lent him a prepublication copy of Lorenz's (1953) *King Solomon's Ring*. Bowlby suddenly saw in the new science of ethology the framework he had been looking for in which to recast psychoanalysis in a contemporary scientific idiom. Attachment theory was born.

Attachment theory was launched in the psychoanalytic community in three key papers, all published in the *International Journal of Psycho-Analysis*, each of which prefigures a volume of his famous trilogy: "The Nature of the Child's Tie to His Mother" (Bowlby, 1958), "Separation Anxiety" (Bowlby, 1960), and "Processes of Mourning" (Bowlby, 1961). Each of these papers was later expanded into an entire volume: *Attachment* (Bowlby, 1969), *Separation* (Bowlby, 1973), and *Loss* (Bowlby, 1980). Each paper, although typically scholarly and rigorous in its presentation, makes a simple but, in the face of the prevailing Kleinian orthodoxy, revolutionary point. First, there is a primary attachment bond between mother and child, "wired in" (Mitchell, 1988) from birth, which does not depend on "oral drive" or reward by feeding and whose evolutionary function was protection from predation. Although this view met with violent opposition, it was, in fact, no more than an extension of ideas already prevalent among the object relations analysts in the 1950s—Balint's "primary clinging," Winnicott's concept of an "environment mother" as well as an "object mother," and Fairbairn's view that drives are "signposts to the object" rather than vice versa. Similarly, Bowlby's ideas on separation anxiety were closely related to Freud's mature view of anxiety, which he saw as an affective response to threat (conceived mainly as the threat of castration) but also as the threat of separation from a loved one (Freud, 1926). Third, the idea that separated or bereaved infants and small children could experience grief and mourning no less intensely than could adults, strongly supported by the evidence of Bowlby's film made with the Robertsons, *A Two Year Old Goes to Hospital*, was rejected by a psychoanalytic community wedded to the idea that mental pain had its origins in the internal, rather than the external, world. When the film was shown at the British society, Bion insisted that the little girl's misery was a manifestation of her envy of her mother's pregnancy, rather than a response to the separation itself.

As well as fulfilling Bowlby's "Koch's postulates" of developmental psychology—observability, testability, use of the ideas of contemporary science, and a basis in observations of normal, rather than disturbed, development—attachment theory differed from prevailing psychoanalytic ideas at a deep level, which was, I believe, why it met with such profound resistance among psychoanalysts. First, it is an *interpersonal*, rather than an intrapersonal, theory. Second, it implies an essentially *harmonious*, rather than conflictual, model of mother–infant interaction, unless the interaction is disturbed by external difficulty; the implication of this is that therapy should concentrate not so much on *conflict* as on *deficiency*. The Freudian view of civilization as a thin and fragile veneer superimposed on an untamed and self-seeking monad is implictly challenged. Third, in keeping with the previous point, the role of sexuality in infant life is downplayed: pleasure is related to proximity, play, and nurturance rather than orgasmic discharge. Fourth, the key issue in infantile experience becomes not so much power (the power of the phallus, the breast, the logos) but *space*: attachment theory is a spatial theory, in which where I *am* in relation to my loved one becomes the key issue, rather than what I can do or have done to me.

Bowlby hoped that his new ideas would reconcile the warring factions within the Psychoanalytic Society and bring about a new openness and wide-ranging debate. By bringing together psychoanalysis and ethology, I believe, he was also at an unconscious level hoping to reconcile his "town mother"—remote and self-centered and now projected onto his Kleinian analyst and supervisor—with his "country mother"—warm and child-centered and now represented by the Darwinian discipline of ethology. As an aside, it is interesting to find Klein's famous "Richard" trying to instill in her the basic principles of ethology and telling her that he is Mum's "chick" and that "chicks do run after their Mums" (Klein, 1961, p. 58). By going back to Freud, Bowlby was also, perhaps, appealing to his absent father, away at the battlefront, over the heads of the mother and her nannies in the "patriarchal but father-absent" (Leupnitz, 1988) world in which, like so many children of his generation, he had found himself growing up.

Whatever the truth of these speculations, the outcome was not as Bowlby had hoped. He *did* succeed in unifying the analytic world: they closed ranks against him in what Grotstein (1990, p. 62) has described as "one of the most dreadul, shameful and regrettable chapters in the history of psychoanalysis." Bowlby became for nearly two decades almost a nonperson in analytic circles, a fate he accepted with dignity and, apart from the occasional venerable jibe, without retaliation, until his rehabilitation in the 1980s began with his appointment as Freud Memorial Professor of Psychoanalysis at University College in London. A system of mutual projection had been set up in which each side expelled into the other a feared aspect of its own experience. For Bowlby this aspect was the inner world of fantasy; for the British psychoanalysts, it was common sense, outer reality, and the need to reconsider their basic beliefs in the "madness" of infancy and the universality of the Oedipus complex in the light of contemporary science.

BOWLBY AND THE INNER WORLD

Psychoanalysis's loss was developmental psychology's gain. The explosion in mother–infant research that has taken place since the 1970s can be traced, in large part, to the inspiration of Bowlby and his collaborators and coworkers, especially Mary Ainsworth. These workers were determined to establish an account of infancy and childhood that was based on experimental evidence and was interpersonal, rather than intrapsychic, and in which the unconscious was seen not so much as a cauldron of fantasy but as containing a representation of the interpersonal world.

Out of this work a detailed map of mother–infant interaction is beginning to emerge. A key question concerns the pathways by which "character" and, for the clinician, character pathology or neurotic disposition emerge from the interactive matrix of the early years of life. The research evidence suggests that the influence of parental handling, especially maternal responsiveness to the growing child's affective states, can have a critical influence on subsequent adaptation. The links that have been demonstrated between secure attachment at one year of age and narrative competence (Holmes, 1993a) in midchildhood and, conversely, between insecure attachment and avoidant or enmeshed narrative styles are of enormous clinical importance (Main, 1991). Equally striking are the similar connections between maternal performance on the Adult Attachment Interview during pregnancy and attachment status of children at one year (Fonagy et al., 1991).

Bowlby has been accused of neglecting the inner world and therefore of missing the heart of the psychoanalytic project. It is certainly true that he was wary of straying into a realm in which he felt ill at ease, both personally and as a researcher. He admitted:

I am not strong on intuition . . . perhaps my saving graces have been that I am a good listener and not too dogmatic about theory. . . . I often shudder to think how inept I have been as therapist. . . . Clearly the best therapy is done by a therapist who is naturally intuitive and also guided by the appropriate theory [Bowlby, 1991, p. 16].

The psychoanalytic reader will find little in the trilogy about free association, dreams, fantasies, the Oedipus complex, or other staple psychoanalytic fare. Toward the end of *Attachment*, Bowlby introduces a disclaimer:

To follow this theme further would be to broach the large, difficult and profound questions of how a child gradually builds up his own "internal world." . . . [These] are matters, however, that raise too many giant problems (and giant controversies) for it to be sensible to deal with them here. In any case systematic research has only just begun and little that is firm is yet known [Bowlby, 1969, p. 418].

In his repeated use of the word "giant" (and he was not a tall man), Bowlby was perhaps reacting against the omnipotent strivings of the psychoanalytic project. He certainly knew his own limitations, as well as his strengths. We can at this point usefully contrast the differing perspectives of attachment theory and Kleinian psychoanalysis, against which attachment theory was, to some extent, reacting. Each is, in a sense, a mirror image of the other—albeit separated for many years by an ideological iron curtain. First, attachment theory focuses primarily on how the inner world is influenced by the environment, how, in Freud's famous phrase (Bolas, 1987), "the shadow of the object" falls on the subject. Kleinian psychoanalysis is concerned with the converse—how external reality is perceived and, by projective identification, shaped by the inner world of the subject. Second, following from this, attachment theory sees infant and parent as psychologically separate and interacting from birth, while Kleinian theory remains a derivative of Freud's "egg" model (Hamilton, 1982), in which the space between subject and object is both obliterated and populated by projected, innate "internal objects" (Hinshelwood, 1989). Third, the two viewpoints approach the distinction between normal and abnormal development quite differently. To oversimplify, Klein, like Freud, tries to derive the normal from the abnormal—"normality" is finally achieved when the paranoid-schizoid position is transcended by the "depressive position." Bowlby, perhaps more logically, tries to understand abnormality in the context of normal development and postulates primary nurturance at the heart of sanity (Gallwey, 1993). In this model, awareness of the object (a "depressive position" function) *precedes* projective identification and omnipotence, which are responses to loss and environmental failure. Finally, following from the latter, Klein places aggression and destructiveness much more centrally in her map of the human heart than does Bowlby and so can perhaps more easily account for the intractability, resistance, and masochism that psychoanalysis so often reveals.

In the space between these two positions I believe that, both theoretically and clinically, the future of psychoanalytic psychotherapy is to be found. Inspired by the strange bedfellows of Klein and Bowlby and based on the work of Bion, Winnicott, Kohut, and, more recently, among others, Benjamin (1988), Mitchell (1988), and Alvarez (1992), a truly interpersonal or intersubjective psychoanalytic psychotherapy is beginning to evolve. The remainder of this chapter is devoted to discussing some of the social, theoretical, and clinical implications of this emerging paradigm.

ATTACHMENT THEORY AND PRIMARY INTERSUBJECTIVITY: THE CULTURAL CONTEXT OF A PARADIGM SHIFT

One way of approaching the emergence of intersubjective psychoanalytic theories, which occupy the middle ground between Bowlby and Klein, is to see them as emerging from social concerns, especially around femininity and the inner space of solitude, that have been central themes of modernism in the postwar world. We begin by examining the fate of Bowlby's most famous concept, maternal deprivation, to which he remained faithful right to the end of his life. In 1988, he wrote:

> Man and woman power devoted to the production of material goods counts a plus in all our economic indices. Man and woman power devoted to the production of happy, healthy, self-reliant children in their own homes does not count at all. We have created a topsy turvy world. . . . Just as a society in which there is a chronic insufficiency of food takes a deplorably inadequate level of nutrition as the norm, so may a society in which parents of young children are left on their own with a chronic insufficiency of help take this state of affairs as its norm [Bowlby, 1988, p. 4].

When Bowlby first introduced the concept of maternal deprivation, he was championing the rights to love and care for children who were innocent victims of the horrors of war, social disruption, and emotional poverty. He was also advocating the rights of mothers to *be* mothers to their children, to devote themselves to their care and protection, rather than the mothers' being victims of an economic system that forced them into long hours of debilitating factory work, while subjecting their children to the draconian regimes of institutional care. He was similarly reproaching a state whose hygienic drive led it to separate children from parents it deemed "inadequate."

New and David (1985) comment that in the aftermath of World War II, Bowlby

> got an audience: women who had been working in munitions factories obliged to send their children for nine or ten hours daily into indifferent nurseries, men who had for years been equating peace with the haven of the family, governments who saw the social and financial potential of idealising motherhood and family life [p. 55].

The collective sense of guilt and loss and the desire for reparation both found an answer in the idea of maternal deprivation. Children had suffered terribly as a result of the war, as had the repressed, childlike aspects of the adults who had witnessed and perpetrated the horrors of war. This valuation and, at times, sentimentalizing of

the mother–child relationship in postwar Europe can be compared
with a similar sentiment that emerged in the 19th century in the face
of the brutality of the Industrial Revolution. Bowlby's tenderness
toward little children carries echoes of Blake and Wordsworth; his
outrage is a continuation of the tradition of Dickens and Kingsley.
There had to be a safe place that could be protected from the violent
intrusion of the modern world, and the Christian imagery of mother
and child reappears in Bowlby's work as an icon for a secular
society.

But, as the historical and social context has changed, so has
maternal deprivation come to be seen as a shackle rather than a
liberation. Terrified that even brief separations from their children
would produce irreparable emotional damage, mothers began to feel
oppressed by the influence of Bowlby and turned with relief to
Winnicott, who reassured them that it was good-enough to be
"good-enough." Bowlby's concept of "monotropism" was misunderstood to mean that *only* mother would do. This ignored the
evidence that what is anthropologically normal is for child care to be
shared by a stable *group* of adults of whom the mother is only one;
maternal deprivation, in Margaret Mead's (1962, p. 43) famous statement, became a "reification into a set of universals of a set of ethno-
centric observations of our own society."

The problem facing the modern family is not so much maternal
deprivation as paternal deprivation due to weak, absent, or abusive
fathers and the "implosion" of children onto unsupported mothers.
Ironically, the dangers that Bowlby in later work identified as among
the most damaging for the growing child—role reversal between
mother and child, threats of sending the child away or of parental
suicide (often later denied), and physical abuse (like the rest of the
psychological world, Bowlby came late to appreciating the extent of
sexual abuse of children)—may well be made more, rather than less,
likely for mothers thown into 24-hour constant proximity with their
children than for those for whom temporary respite is available.

As Margaret Mead's remark indicates, Bowlby was highly sensitive
to the lineaments of patriarchy, of which he was, in some ways,
such a typical example. Many of the revolutionary changes in child
care of the postwar period—the transformation of pediatric practice
by allowing parents into hospitals with their sick children; the
emphasis on foster rather than institutional care, for children at risk,
political acceptance of the need for universal child benefits paid to
the mother (now under threat in Britain for the first time in 40
years)—can be traced, in part at least, to Bowlby's efforts to counter
the patriarchal assumptions of a society that undervalues the
"female" principles of nurturance and care.

BOWLBY AND PATRIARCHY

Bowlby's difficulties with psychoanalysis can also be seen in terms of an intuitive, antipatriarchal perspective. For Freud, the phallus reigned supreme: every growing child has to accommodate to its law. The little boy has to master his castration anxiety in order to identify with the paternal standard-bearer; the little girl has to over-come her disappointment at its lack and await her consolation prize—the baby. This world of male omnipotence was, with Freud's death, transformed in the Kleinian vision into its mirror image—a world of female omnipotence based on the supremacy of the breast (Benjamin, 1988). Confronted by the all-powerful patriarchal princi-ple of conventional society and the equally intimidating prospect of an inner world dominated by ferocious drives and an all-powerful mother, Bowlby escaped into a space between, the hitherto undis-covered country of mother–infant *interaction*. Here he could observe and stalk his intellectual prey without anxiety, just as he could hunt and fish and walk with his country mother as a child. Attachment theory is a theory about the spatial relations of mother and child. The securely attached child seeks proximity when threat-ened, explores when safe; the avoidantly insecure child hovers in the proximity of the parent in a compromise between proximity seeking and fear of getting close; the ambivalent child clings and tries to bury himself in the unpredictable parent. Bowlby's own patriarchal inhibitions (based, perhaps, on his never really having had the chance to get close to his father and so be released from the fantasy of his omnipotence) meant that he held back from transpos-ing attachment from the outer to the inner world, where he would have encountered *inner space*—the female principle that can balance the phallus and transform its omnipotent strivings into real potency (Erikson, 1968). In inner space are found Freud's "dark continents"—the mysteries of female desire and creativity. Bowlby's "internal working models," although a useful bridge between psy-chodynamics and cognitive science, are too masculine and mechani-cal to capture adequately the world of affective experience.

But by opening the space between parent and child for scrutiny, Bowlby paved the way for a fully interpersonal psychotherapy. Freud and Klein showed how the apparently coherent self of adult-hood can, if traced back ontogenetically, be unpacked into an assembly of intrapsychic components—drives, part-objects, repres-sive forces, critical agencies, and so on. Bowlby saw, and contempo-rary psychoanalytic psychotherapy would agree, to paraphrase Winnicott (1965), that "there is no such thing as an individual": what is found if the adult self is traced back is not an individual assemblage, but a *society* of parent and child whose interactions are gradually internalized to form the intrapsychic structures that psychoanalysis has delineated.

BOWLBY, WINNICOTT, AND BION

While Bowlby boldly abandoned Kleinian metapsychology, his fellow Darwinian (Phillips, 1987) and, in a sense, alter ego, Donald Winnicott, much more cautiously and ambivalently attempted through the invocation of paradox to remain loyal to the Kleinian tradition while at the same time undermining it. What is paradoxical about Winnicott's concepts is their attempt to create an interpersonal perspective out of an intrapsychic model. His paper "The Capacity to Be Alone" (Winnicott, 1965) is based on the paradox that successful solitude in adult life (including, in another paradox, the sense of completeness and unconflictual solitude that accompanies the merging of sexual union) requires an experience of having been watched over in childhood by an unobtrusive parent. There is a direct parallel between the notion of an external, secure base that facilitates the capacity to explore and this Winnicottian paradigm of inner exploration. In "The Use of an Object" and "Hate in the Counter-Transference" (Winnicott, 1971), he argues that the mutual *recognition* of infant and parent depends on an active interaction in which the infant repeatedly negates or "destroys" the parent in fantasy, with the parent's task being to survive in reality so that the child can say: "Hello object! I destroyed you" (Winnicott, 1971). As Bateson (1971, p. 6) put it more abstractly, "information is difference" (Hamilton, 1982). For Bowlby, loss, especially in the early years of life, is potentially catastrophic and can at best be coped with by appropriate mourning; for Winnicott, dealing with the inevitable discontinuities of nurturance is a spur to creativity and an essential part of growing up.

In "The Location of Cultural Experience" Winnicott (1971, p. 163) quotes a favorite line from Tagore: "On the seashore of endless worlds children play." Here, too, as Benjamin (1988) points out, there is the paradoxical tension between limit and infinite possibility, *endless* worlds on a sea *shore*. Only if one can contain oneself, one's feelings and desires, can one truly let go. Only if one has had the experience of secure attachment, can one allow oneself to undergo the rhythm of loss and rediscovery that is at the heart of creativity.

In a similar vein, in Bion's notion of maternal reverie and containment, the mother "invites" the child into her own inner space, and, on the basis of this, the child's inner world begins to open up.

But, as Hamilton (1982) has argued, compared with the mutual, Einsteinian "holy curiosity" of Bowlby's model of mother and baby, Bion's mother is a more passive, gnomic bearer of the painful truth of forever being separated from prelinguistic, pure experience.

Psychoanalysis itself was also adjusting to the postwar world of modernism and searching for a role and definition for itself. Both Winnicott and Bion—and, to a lesser extent, Bowlby—were, in their models of infant development, also reaching toward an understanding of their position as psychoanalysts. Broadly speaking, there are two polar views of the nature of the psychoanalytic process. In what might be called the *esoteric vision*, the analytic task is the uncovering of a hidden reality to which the analyst, through his or her training and initiation, is privy and of which, with analytic help, the patient may begin to get a glimpse. The transference here is a vehicle for elucidating and eliminating the distortions of this reality that neurosis throws up, with the analyst a priestly guide into the mysterious underworld. In the *constructivist vision*, to which, had he conceived it in these terms, Bowlby would, I believe, have subscribed, the task of therapy is deepening existing reality, rather than replacing it with some secret truth. Transference here is, in Levenson's (1984, p. 266) words, "[a] slice of life, intensified yet made manageable by the constraints of the analytic frame," with the analyst a coexplorer of a shared psychic space.

ATTACHMENT THEORY AND CONTEMPORARY PSYCHOANALYTIC PSYCHOTHERAPY

Thus far we have considered attachment theory and psychoanalysis in their social and historical context. But psychoanalysis is an autonomous discipline, with its own internal logic and preoccupations, detached—perhaps, I have argued, too detached—from such wider concerns. Yet, patients need help and understanding. I therefore turn now, albeit schematically, to the implications of attachment theory for the practice of psychotherapy, and consider four main themes: the secure base phenomenon, narrative, affect and defense, and sexuality. I conclude with a case example that illustrates some of the theoretical points.

The Secure Base Phenomenon

Attachment research has shown that a school-age child's sense of security is greatly influenced by the consistency, responsiveness, and attunement he or she experienced with his or her parents in infancy. Similar behaviors—many of them nonverbal—may influence the establishment of a secure therapeutic bond and thereby affect subsequent outcome in psychotherapy. There is firm evidence that early, positive therapeutic alliance is the best predictor of good outcome in therapies of all types and that "nonspecific factors" (i.e., not based on any one theory or practice)—usually subsumed under the Rogerian triad of empathy, nonpossessive warmth, and honesty— play a decisive role in outcome (Holmes and Lindley, 1989). Research is needed to identify the therapeutic homologues of successful maternal behaviors. For example, responsive mothers with securely attached offspring pick up their babies more rapidly and frequently than mothers of insecure children; similarly, the effective therapist "picks up" the cues of his patient and responds appropriately. In Stern's (1985) picture of affective attunement, the mother acts as a modulator to the minute-by-minute line of her child's moods; she stimulates when activity drops, calms when the child becomes overexcited. The rhythms of psychotherapy sessions can be analyzed in a similar way, with effective therapists intervening enough to keep the patient's thought-bubbles airborne, but not puncturing them with premature or intrusive comments. Just as the secure infant scans his environment until he finds the familiar face, to which he responds with smiling and the beginnings of playful interaction, so the good therapist creates conditions in which the patient can find an interpretation for himself and respond with a comparable "aha" of excitement and relief.

Narrative

Psychoanalysis is based on narrative. The patient tells her *story*, and the therapist listens and, tries to make sense of it, to find *meaning* in its inchoate swirls, to fill in its gaps and lacunae, to shape its eruptions and collapses. Attachment theory provides the link between the hermeneutic slant of the consulting room and the empirical world of developmental psychology. Vygotsky (1962) shows how the mother, working at the "zone of proximal development," gives meaning to the infant's innate physiology: the grasp reflex becomes, under her tutelage, a *gesture* of pointing, and babble becomes the beginnings of meaningful speech.

Meaning enables separation to occur without irremediable loss. The secure base is never entirely safe. Breaks, gaps, losses are as intrinsic to the rhythm of life as are attachment and connectedness. Narrative bridges these inevitable discontinuities in experience, the capacity to survive major losses in later life being built on the overcoming of the minor fissures that appear in the course of normal development. An obsessional avoidance of cracks in the pavement is a poor preparation for the abysses of adulthood. The Adult Attachment Interview has enabled links to be made between the attachment status of infants and narrative patterns—"autobiographical competence" (Holmes, 1993a)—in later life. The clinical resonance of this work is very strong. The patient's narrative is the raw material of therapy and provides clues to the interactional matrix out of which it emerged. Discontinuities in the way a person tells his story reflect breaks in the holding environment in childhood. Dismissive narratives (avoidant attachment), overwhelming, unprocessed feelings (enmeshed, ambivalent attachment), and disorganized narratives (childhood trauma) at present remain hypotheses, but the evidence in favor of them is impressive (Main, 1991; Holmes, 1993b). The therapeutic process can be evaluated by the emergence of a more fluent, yet emotionally charged, coherent narrative. Just as literary narrative can be "deconstructed" into a dialogue between writer and reader, so, as therapy unfolds, is a shared narrative forged to which both patient and therapist contribute, the former mainly through his words and affects, the latter by his responsiveness and attunement.

Affect and Defense

Bowlby, perhaps in a rather simplistic way, saw the suppression of negative affect, as opposed to its being expressed or worked through, as a central cause of neurotic difficulty. Infant research suggests that the modulation of infant affect by an attuned and responsive mother is the essential precursor of secure attachment. The patterns of insecure attachment represent compromises in which an infant is forced to trade off the pain of unmodulated affect against the discomfort of incompetent modulation, defenses designed to maintain contact with the object at all costs. The "avoidant" infant, who attends to the mother's comings or goings but conceals its distress in favor of maintaining a distal, minimized relationship, treads a thin line between the loneliness of abandonment and the pain of rebuff. The "ambivalent" infant, whose mother inconsistently neglects or overwhelms him and whose pain on parting is matched by its conflicted response to reunion, cannot risk "destroying" (in a Winnicottian sense) his mother with anger for fear she will either actually disappear or invade his inner space.

Hamilton (1985) has pointed out that the notion of "defense" implicit in this interpersonal account is radically different from the classical, Freudian view of defense mechanisms designed to reduce potentially overwhelming levels of psychic excitation arising from *within* the organism. This view goes some way, for example, to explain the extraordinary loyalty of the abused child to her abuser. Attachment theory suggests that the psychobiological response to threat is to turn to an attachment figure. But when the threat originates with an abusive attachment figure, a vicious circle is set up in which the greater the abuse, the more the child clings, a response that may, in turn, be used by the abuser to license further abuse, and so on. Similar patterns can easily be observed in the transference when working therapeutically with abused patients. As Fairbairn (1952) stated, better to cling to a bad object than to have none at all.

Sex and Sexualization in Therapy

Bowlby conceived of attachment as a primary behavioral system in its own right, distinct from feeding and sexuality. Just as this enabled him to dispense with explanations of mother–infant bonding that depended on feeding, so attachment theory presents a challenge to explanations of the emotional life of toddlers and young children that are based on oedipal theory. The triangular rivalries of family life do not necessarily need to be understood in classical oedipal terms, since family members can equally be seen as vying with one another for attachment as well as for sexual possession, although, as we shall see in the case example, attachment is a bodily experience, as Freud (1923, p. 19) hinted in his famous remark that "ultimately the ego is a bodily ego." Bowlby was also critical of the "orgasm-is-all" theories of adult psychic health (Balint, 1968) and saw consummation as only one part of adult bonding.

This discarding of Oedipus played its part in putting Bowlby beyond the psychoanalytic pale in the 1950s and 1960s, when a belief in the Oedipus complex was an unchallengeable part of the psychoanalytic credo. (Klein was obliged to insist that oedipal conflicts occurred in early infancy in order to retain her psychoanalytic credibility.) Recent views, however, tend to support the Bowlbian position (Slavin and Kriegman, 1992; Erickson, 1993). Many pschoanalytic writers (Hamilton, 1982) have pointed out that Oedipus was an abused child, physically attacked ("oedipus"= swollen feet) and banished by his parents, a victim of Laius's fear of the oracle's prediction that he would be killed by his child, and that his "infantile sexuality" was a consequence of this rejection. Both anthropological and ethological evidence suggests that sexual behavior in immature organisms and incest is much more likely to occur when there has been some weakening of the attachment bonds between adults and children, when for example, children have been reared apart or reared by nonkin, that is, stepparents. Observations of kin and reciprocal altruism in contemporary evolutionary theory suggest a much less conflictual model of the human psyche than Freud and Klein imagined. Rather than an inherent opposition between "primitive" instinctual forces of sexuality and aggression and the guilt-inducing, civilizing forces of socialization, selective pressure toward group bonding in order to enhance inclusive fitness means (1) that the interests of the parental and infant "selfish genes" coincide in the early months of life and (2) that where they begin to diverge in the "oedipal" phase, guilt is secondary to affiliation, a marker of reciprocal altruism rather than a cause of it. The overwhelming guilt of neurosis is, in this perspective, an insistent cry for empathy and attachment, not a manifestation of uncontrollable drives.

Sexualization in therapy is most likely to arise when the secure base of attachment is at its weakest, for example, at times of breaks or when there have been countertransferential "frame-violations" (Langs, 1978) by the therapist, such as lateness and forgetting appointments. This needs to be differentiated from more mature erotic feelings that may arise and need to be confronted in therapy. This more complex and multileveled approach to sexuality and "sexualization" in therapy is especially important if one component of desire—especially "female" desire—is conceived in terms of the erotics of inner space. As Benjamin (1988) puts it:

> Psychoanalytic valorisation of genital sexuality has obscured the equal importance of erotic pleasure of the early attunement and mutual play of infancy. When the sexual self is represented by the sensual capacities of the whole body, when the totality of space, between, outside, and within our bodies becomes the site of pleasure, then desire escapes the borders of the imperial phallus and resides on the shore of endless worlds [p. 152].

I now bring some of these theoretical points together with a case example that illustrates how a Bowlbyan perspective may influence adult work in psychoanalytic psychotherapy.

CASE EXAMPLE: "BREATHING THE SAME AIR"

Margaret was in her middle 40s when she sought help for feelings of depression, panic, and futility, focused around her inability to decide whether to settle in England, where her elderly mother lived, or to return to Australia, where she had lived for several years. She had had an unusual childhood, as she grew up in her parent's progressive, private children's home where the regime was much given to nudity and cold showers and where, from the age of three,

she was expelled from her parents' domain into the dormitory with
the other children. Her father, who was something of a Laius, ran
the home in a tyrannical fashion, resented his children's relationship
with their mother, and subjected Margaret to physical, verbal, and
sexual abuse. Her mother was depressed and responded to
Margaret's attempts to alert her to her distress—deliberately falling
down stairs, swallowing poison berries and, on one occasion, a nut
and bolt—by vaguely telling her to go and swallow some bread or
"go and see matron."

*Pathological Organization and Omnipotence as Defenses
against Insecure Attachment*

Margaret dealt with the intense miseries and insecurities of her
childhood by developing an elaborate fantasy, akin to Steiner's
(1985) "pathological organization," in which she would, each night,
with erotic excitement and then relief, systematically inflict pain on
herself while she '"turned" herself into a horse. She saw horses as
free from individual feelings, group creatures with no personal pain
or anxiety. Since she actually believed herself to *be* a horse, this was
a "symbolic equation" (Segal, 1957), rather than a true symbol, and
matched the split she later felt between her cheerful, efficient, and
well-liked group self and the intense fear and discomfort she felt
when threatened with intimacy with one other person. Unsurpris-
ingly, she had married and divorced a man who was similarly unable
to get close, but she had managed to combine working as a teacher
with some success as a painter.

The intimacy of therapy was utterly terrifying to her. She dealt
with her terror by an instant and intensely sexualized attachment to
therapy. Breaks were particularly difficult for her, and she would
desperately ask for reassurance around the time of separation: "Tell
me that you like me," "Tell me it is not surprising I am like I am with
a father like that," "Give me something to have from this room while
you are away." For the most part, I resisted these entreaties and
interpreted her separation anxiety. During a break she contacted a
former lover and rushed rapidly into marriage, which was in difficulties within a few weeks. She had begged to be advised whether or
not to marry. I should perhaps have said, "If I advise you not to
marry, then, like your father, I will be giving a message that I want
you for myself; if I advise you to marry, I shall be like your mother,
fobbing you off with someone else." But, afraid that any such comment would have been taken as a seduction (and in any case having
not yet reached such a formulation), I said nothing.

Separation Protest as the First Stirrings of a Secure Base

In the early months of therapy, she was compliant and submissive—
in one dream she pictured herself as a servant to the therapist and
his wife—but early in the third year began to be much more
assertive. She demanded more frequent sessions, a request that,
while acknowledging that this would be desirable, I was logistically
—and possibly as a countertransferential response to the intensity of
her ambivalent attachment—unable to grant. She arrived at a session
one day and read out a furious letter in which she accused me of
being cruel and punitive like her father, neglectful and indifferent
like her mother. By reading, rather than directly expressing anger,
and by preempting my response through the parental comparison,
she was still pulling her punches—but this was a definite advance. In
the next few sessions, she became increasingly anxious, trembling
and shaking and having difficulty in breathing. She described for the
first time the horse fantasy and spoke of how naked and helpless she
felt on the couch and wondered if the horse "magic" that had saved
her as a child from complete madness and disintegration but that
now entrapped her could be put somehow into reverse so that she
could be released.

Intense Separation Anxiety as Insecure Attachments Are
Relinquished and Before Secure Ones Have Been Formed

As the defensive structures of insecure attachments are relinquished,
it becomes possible, for the first time, to form a secure base. For
Margaret, this meant giving up the horse fantasy and deciding to
separate from her unhappy second marriage. At this point, a
patient's vulnerability—like a free radical in search of a bond or an
animal that has just shed its skin—is often also at its height. In one
session around this time Margaret developed a frank panic attack,
and I felt under great pressure to provide some modulatory response
—to reassure her and perhaps even take her hand, but I held back,
feeling that to do so would be to reproduce, albeit in benign form,
the abuse she had suffered at her father's hands. Her demand that I
do something was intense. Eventually, searching for a metaphor that
would be powerful enough to hold her, I said: "You want me to
hold you so that you feel connected and safe—but we *are* attached:
we are breathing the same air, the air you breathe out I take in, the
air I breathe out comes into you." She calmed a little and said that
she had composed a poem recently that was on her mind all the
time, an invocation to me. She felt, she said, that her mouth and
genitals had been irreparably dirtied by the abuse and wanted me to

Make them clean of nastiness and shame
Neither top nor bottom
But somewhere in between
With my breath, through my skin, come in
Knowing me, naming me.

The Necessity and Dangers of Reassurance

The "breathing the same air" comment could be criticized as being essentially a reassurance, failing to get in touch with her intense *anxiety* about being held, although some such intervention seemed to be necessary at the time if she were to survive the gaps between sessions—breathing being *both* a symbolic equation *and* a true symbol. It could perhaps be understood as a "transference reassurance" and served the function of protecting the therapeutic alliance at a critical moment, when, as with so many borderline patients, the therapeutic bond was under threat. When, later, she arrived at a session with something in her eye, she was able to describe her simultaneous longing for me to examine her and so touch her and her enormous fear of my doing so.

The Emergence of Narrative, As Separation Can Increasingly Be Tolerated in the Context of a Secure Base

The importance of seeing the secure base as a psychosomatic phenomenon—involving body and mind—was further reinforced some months later, when, now making good progress in therapy and, in a playful way, much more able to differentiate reality and fantasy in her narrative style, Margaret described a waking dream or self-guided fantasy in which she had imagined herself lying on a bed and my looking into her eyes, lifting each of her limbs in a calm and gentle manner, touching her stomach, and, in a completely nonsexual way, parting her legs, "looking," she said, "at the whole of me." In this fantasy she realized, to her surprise, that her body was preadolescent.

Attachment as a Bodily Experience

I responded by saying that as she described this fantasy, I had pictured the careful and almost mystic examination of newborn babies by their mothers. This made immediate sense to Margaret, who spoke of her genitals and how she was normally unable to think of them other than with disgust or sexuality, but how, in this fantasy, she was "perfect" and "complete." I pointed to the double meaning of "the (w)hole of me" and contrasted the loving bond of a parent to a newborn baby with the hollow attachment that resulted from penetrative abuse. Here we can see the contrast between an insecure base characterized by the omnipotent, sexualized narcissism of her attempts to get me to admire or fall in love with her and the healthy adoration of a parent for a newborn child. I suggested that what had pushed her father to intrude and smash up his children's relationship with their mother (mirrored by Margaret's fantasies of doing the same to my family and so have me all to herself) was intense envy of this first, all-important bond, since, in Bowlby's (1979) words, "the most intense of all human emotions arise during the formation, the maintenance, the disruption and the renewal of affectional bonds. . . . [T]he formation of a bond is described as falling in love" (p. 176).

EPILOGUE

Margaret's turning point occurred when she disengaged from her defensive attachments and survived the extreme vulnerability of her new state. In this chapter I have showed how Bowlby's capacity to survive the disruption of his ambivalent relationship with psychoanalysis led to the development of attachment theory, and I pointed to the possibility of a renewal of that relationship through the emerging psychoanalytic paradigm of primary intersubjectivity. The nature of that relationship is a central theme of this volume.

I started with John Bunyan. I end with another poet. Robert Frost, like Bowlby, was vigorous, long lived, and much feted, a man of action in a world of contemplation who turned his back on the obscurities of modernism and sought instead the poetry of the everyday, the commonplace, the observable:

> Two roads diverged in a wood and I—
> I took the one less travelled by,
> And that has made all the difference.

Bowlby's less traveled road—an initial tentativeness followed by the decisive stride of the repeated "I"—has become a broad highway, and, as this volume testifies, many people are to be found journeying there. The roads of attachment theory and psychoanalysis are increasingly and excitingly convergent. In Frost's (1952) *Mending Wall*, he says:

> Something there is that doesn't love a wall
> That sends the frozen-ground-swell under it

And spills the upper boulders in the sun . . .
I let my neighbour know before the fall
And on a dry day we meet to walk the line
And set the wall between us once again . . .
There where it is we do not need the wall:
He is all pine and I am apple orchard
My apple trees will never get across
To eat the cones under his pines, I tell him.
He only says, "good fences make good neighbors."

Frost's tantalizing juxtaposition—"good fences make good neigh-
bours," but "[s]omething there is that doesn't love a wall"—evokes
many opposing echoes: the security of attachment poised against
the call of the wild, boundary and space, defense and exploration,
liminal shores and infinite worlds, epitomizing the Bowlbyian capacity to reconcile discordant elements and to create from them a
secure, yet creative, whole.

REFERENCES

Alvarez, A. (1992), *Live Company*. London: Routledge.
Balint, M. (1968), *The Basic Fault*. London: Tavistock.
Bateson, G. (1973), *Steps towards an Ecology of Mind*. London: Paladin.
Benjamin, J. (1988), *The Bonds of Love*. London: Virago.
Bettelheim, B. (1960), *The Informed Heart*. New York: Free Press.
Bolas, C. (1987), *The Shadow of the Object*. London: Free Association Books.
Bowlby, J. (1951), *Maternal Care and Mental Health*. WHO Monograph Series No. 2.
    Geneva: World Health Organization.
—— (1958), The nature of the child's tie to his mother. *Internat. J. Psycho-Anal.*,
    39:350–373.
—— (1960), Separation anxiety. *Internat. J. Psycho-Anal.*, 41:89–113.
—— (1961), Processes of mourning. *Internat. J. Psycho-Anal.*, 42:317–340.
—— (1969), *Attachment*. London: Penguin.
—— (1973), *Separation*. London: Penguin.
—— (1979), *The Making and Breaking of Affectional Bonds*. London: Tavistock.
—— (1980), *Loss*. London: Penguin.
—— (1988), *A Secure Base*. London: Routledge.
—— (1990), *Charles Darwin*. London: Hutchinson.
—— (1991), The role of the psychotherapist's personal resources in the therapeutic
    situation. *Tavistock Gazette* (autumn).
Bretherton, I. (1991), Pouring new wine into old bottles: The social self as internal
    working model. In: *Self Processes and Development*, ed. M. Gunnar & L. Sroufe.
    Hillsdale, NJ: Lawrence Erlbaum Associates, pp. 26–53.
Erickson, M. (1993), Rethinking Oedipus. *Amer. J. Psychiat.*, 150:411–416.
Erikson, E. (1968), *Identity: Youth and Crisis*. London: Faber.
Fairbairn, W.R.D. (1952), *Psychoanalytic Studies of the Personality*. London:
    Routledge.
Fonagy, P., Steele, M., Moran, G. Steele, H. & Higgitt, A. C. (1991), The capacity for
    understanding mental states. *Infant Ment. Health J.*, 12:201–218.

Freud, S. (1923), The ego and the id. *Standard Edition*, 19:12–59. London: Hogarth Press, 1961.
—— (1926). *Inhibitions, Symptoms and Anxiety. Standard Edition*, 20:87–172. London: Hogarth Press, 1959.
Frost, R. (1952), *Selected Poems*. London: Penguin.
Gallwey, P. (1993), The Concept of a Person. Unpublished manuscript.
Grosskurth, P. (1986), *Melanie Klein: Her World and Her Work*. Cambridge, MA: Harvard University Press.
Grotstein, J. (1990), Introduction. In: *Psychotic Anxieties and Containment* by M. Little. Northvale, NJ: Aronson.
Hamilton, V. (1982), *Oedipus and Narcissus*. London: Routledge.
—— (1985), John Bowlby: An ethological basis for psychoanalysis. In: *Beyond Freud*, ed. J. Reppen. New York: The Analytic Press.
Harrison, M. ed. (1977), *New Dragon Book of Verse*. New York: International Universities Press.
Hinshelwood, R. (1989), *A Dictionary of Kleinian Thought*. London: Free Association Books.
Holmes, J (1993a), *Between Art and Science*. London: Routledge.
—— (1993b), *John Bowlby and Attachment Theory*. London: Routledge.
—— & Lindley, R. (1989), *The Values of Psychotherapy*. Oxford: Oxford University Press.
Klein, M. (1959), *Narrative of a Child Analysis*. London: Hogarth Press.
Langs, R. (1978), *The Listening Process*. New York: Aronson.
Leupnitz, D. (1988), *The Family Interpreted*. New York: Basic Books.
Levenson, P. (1984), Interpersonal theory. In: *Models of the Mind*, ed. A. Rothstein. New York: International Universities Press.
Levi, P. (1958), *If This Be a Man*. London: Paladin.
Lorenz, K. (1953), *King Solomon's Ring*. London: Methuen.
Main, M. (1991), Metacognitive knowledge, metacognitive monitoring, and singular vs. multiple models of attachment. In: *Attachment across the Life Cycle*, ed. P. Harris, S. Stevenson-Hinde & C. Parkes. London: Routledge, pp. 127–159.
Mead, M. (1962), A cultural anthropologist's approach to maternal deprivation. In: *Deprivation of Maternal Care*. Geneva: WHO.
Mitchell, S. (1988), *Relational Concepts in Psychoanalysis*. Cambridge, MA: Harvard University Press.
New, C. & David, M. (1985), *For the Children's Sake*. London: Penguin.
Phillips, A. (1987), *Winnicott*. London: Fontana.
Rayner, E. (1992), John Bowlby's contribution. *Bull. Brit. Psychoanal. Soc.*, 20–32.
Segal, H. (1957), Notes on symbol formation. *Internat. J. Psycho-Anal.*, 38:391–397.
Slavin, M. & Kriegman, D. (1992), *The Adaptive Design of the Human Psyche*. New York: Guilford.
Steiner, J. (1985), The interplay between pathological organisations and the paranoid-schizoid and depressive positions. *Internat. J. Psycho-Anal.*, 68:69–80.
Stern, D. (1985), *The Interpersonal World of the Infant*. New York: Basic Books.
Storr, A. (1992), John Bowlby. *Munks Roll*. London: Royal College of Physicians.
Vygotsky, L. (1962), *Thought and Language*, ed. & trans. E. Haufmann & G. Vakav. Cambridge, MA: MIT Press.
Winnicott, D. (1965), *The Maturational Process and the Facilitating Environment*. London: Hogarth Press.
—— (1971), *Playing and Reality*. London: Penguin.

3

The Origins of Attachment Theory

John Bowlby and Mary Ainsworth

INGE BRETHERTON

Attachment theory is the joint work of John Bowlby and Mary Ainsworth (see Ainsworth and Bowlby, 1991). Drawing on concepts from ethology, cybernetics, information processing, developmental psychology, and psychoanalysis, John Bowlby formulated the basic tenets of the theory. He thereby revolutionized our thinking about a child's tie to the mother and its disruption through separation, deprivation, and bereavement. Mary Ainsworth's innovative methodology not only made it possible to test some of Bowlby's ideas empirically but also helped expand the theory itself and is responsible for some of the new directions it is now taking. Ainsworth contributed the concept of the attachment figure as a secure base from which an infant can explore the world. In addition, she formulated the concept of maternal sensitivity to infant signals and its role in the development of infant–mother attachment patterns.

The ideas now guiding attachment theory have a long developmental history. Although Bowlby and Ainsworth worked independently of each other during their early careers, both were influenced by Freud and other psychoanalytic thinkers—directly in Bowlby's case, indirectly in Ainsworth's. In this chapter, I document the origins of ideas that later became central to attachment theory. I then discuss the subsequent period of theory building and consolidation. Finally, I review some of the new directions in which the theory is currently developing and speculate on its future potential. In taking this retrospective developmental approach to the origins of attachment theory, I am reminded of Freud's (1920) remark:

An earlier version of this chapter appeared in *Developmental Psychology* (28:759–775). ©1992 by American Psychological Association. Adapted by permission.

45

So long as we trace the development from its final outcome backwards, the chain of events appears continuous, and we feel we have gained an insight which is completely satisfactory or even exhaustive. But if we proceed in the reverse way, if we start from the premises inferred from the analysis and try to follow these up to the final results, then we no longer get the impression of an inevitable sequence of events which could not have otherwise been determined [p. 167].

In elucidating how each idea and methodological advance became a stepping-stone for the next, my retrospective account of the origins of attachment theory makes the process of theory building seem planful and orderly. No doubt this was the case to some extent, but it may often not have seemed so to the protagonists at the time.

ORIGINS

John Bowlby

After graduating from the University of Cambridge in 1928, where he received rigorous scientific training and some instruction in what is now called developmental psychology, Bowlby performed volunteer work at a school for maladjusted children while reconsidering his career goals. His experiences with two children at the school set his professional life on course. One was a very isolated, remote, affectionless teenager who had been expelled from his previous school for theft and had no stable mother figure. The second child was an anxious boy of seven or eight who trailed Bowlby around and who was known as his shadow (Ainsworth, 1974). Persuaded by this experience of the effects of early family relationships on personality development, Bowlby decided to embark on a career as a child psychiatrist (Senn, 1977b).

Concurrently with his studies in medicine and psychiatry, Bowlby undertook training at the British Psychoanalytic Institute. During this period Melanie Klein was a major influence there (the institute had three groups: Group A sided with Freud, Group B sided with Klein, and the Middle Group sided with neither). Bowlby was exposed to Kleinian (Klein, 1932) ideas through his training analyst, Joan Riviere, a close associate of Klein, and eventually through supervision by Klein herself. Although he acknowledges Riviere and Klein for grounding him in the object relations approach to psychoanalysis, with its emphasis on early relationships and the pathogenic potential of loss (Bowlby, 1969, p. xvii), he had grave reservations about aspects of the Kleinian approach to child psychoanalysis. Klein held that children's emotional problems are almost entirely due to fantasies generated from internal conflict between aggressive and libidinal drives, rather than to events in the external world. She hence forbade Bowlby to talk to the mother of a three-year-old whom he analyzed under her supervision (Bowlby, 1987). This was anathema to Bowlby, who, in the course of his postgraduate training with two psychoanalytically trained social workers at the London Child Guidance Clinic, had come to believe that actual family experiences were a much more important, if not the basic, cause of emotional disturbance.

Bowlby's plan to counter Klein's ideas through research is manifest in an early theoretical paper (Bowlby, 1940) in which he proposes that, like nurserymen, psychoanalysts should study the nature of the organism, the properties of the soil, and their interaction (p. 23). He goes on to suggest that, for mothers with parenting difficulties,

a weekly interview in which their problems are approached analytically and traced back to childhood has sometimes been remarkably effective. Having once been helped to recognize and recapture the feelings which she herself had as a child and to find that they are accepted tolerantly and understandingly, a mother will become increasingly sympathetic and tolerant toward the same things in her child [p. 23].

These quotations reveal Bowlby's early theoretical and clinical interest in the intergenerational transmission of attachment relations and in the possibility of helping children by helping parents. Psychoanalytic object relations theories later proposed by Fairbairn (1952) and Winnicott (1965) were congenial to Bowlby, but his thinking had developed independently of them.

Bowlby's first empirical study, based on case notes from the London Child Guidance Clinic, dates from this period. Like the boy at the school for maladjusted children, many of the clinic patients were affectionless and prone to stealing. Through detailed examination of 44 cases, Bowlby was able to link their symptoms to histories of maternal deprivation and separation.

Although World War II led to an interruption in Bowlby's budding career as a practicing child psychiatrist, it laid further groundwork for his career as a researcher. His assignment was to collaborate on officer selection procedures with a group of distinguished colleagues from the Tavistock Clinic in London, an experience that gave Bowlby a level of methodological and statistical expertise then unusual for a psychiatrist and psychoanalyst. This training is obvious in the revision of his paper, "Forty-Four Juvenile Thieves: Their Characters and Home Lives" (Bowlby, 1944), which includes statistical tests as well as detailed case histories.

At the end of World War II, Bowlby was invited to become head of the Children's Department at the Tavistock Clinic. In line with his earlier ideas on the importance of family relationships in child therapy, he promptly renamed it the Department for Children and Parents. Indeed, in what is credited as the first published paper in family therapy, Bowlby (1949) describes how he was often able to achieve clinical breakthroughs by interviewing parents about their childhood experiences in the presence of their troubled children.

To Bowlby's chagrin, however, much of the clinical work in the department was done by people with a Kleinian orientation who, he says, regarded his emphasis on actual family interaction patterns as not particularly relevant. He therefore decided to found his own research unit whose efforts were focused on mother–child separation. Because separation is a clear-cut and undeniable event, its effects on the child and the parent–child relationship were easier to document than more subtle influences of parental and familial interaction.

Mary Ainsworth

Mary Ainsworth (née Salter), six years younger than Bowlby, finished graduate study at the University of Toronto just before World War II. Courses with William Blatz had introduced her to security theory (Blatz, 1940), which both reformulated and challenged Freudian ideas, though Blatz chose not to recognize his debt to Freud because of the anti-Freudian climate that pervaded the University of Toronto at that time (Blatz, 1966; Ainsworth, 1983).

One of the major tenets of security theory is that infants and young children need to develop a secure dependence on parents before launching out into unfamiliar situations. In her dissertation, entitled "An Evaluation of Adjustment Based on the Concept of Security," Salter (1940) elaborates on this idea:

Familial security in the early stages is of a dependent type and forms a basis from which the individual can work out gradually, forming new skills and interests in other fields. Where familial security is lacking, the individual is handicapped by the lack of what might be called a *secure base* from which to work [p. 45; italics added].

Interestingly, Salter's dissertation research included an analysis of students' autobiographical narratives in support of the validity of her paper-and-pencil self-report scales of familial and extrafamilial security, an approach that foreshadowed her later penchant for narrative methods of data collection. Indeed, few researchers realize the enormous experience in instrument development and diagnostics she brought to attachment research.

Like Bowlby's, Mary Salter's professional career was shaped by her duties as a military officer during World War II (in the Canadian Women's Army Corps). After the war, as a faculty member at the University of Toronto, she set out to deepen her clinical skills in response to the request to teach courses in personality assessment. To prepare herself for this task, she signed up for workshops by Bruno Klopfer, a noted expert in the interpretation of the Rorschach test. This experience led to a coauthored book on the Rorschach technique (Klopfer et al., 1954), which is still in print.

In 1950 Mary Salter married Leonard Ainsworth and accompanied him to London, where he completed his doctoral studies. Someone there drew her attention to a job advertisement in the *London Times* that happened to involve research, under the direction of John Bowlby, into the effect on personality development of separation from the mother in early childhood. As Mary Ainsworth acknowledges, joining Bowlby's research unit reset the whole direction of her professional career, though neither Bowlby nor Ainsworth realized this at the time.

THE EMERGENCE OF ATTACHMENT THEORY

In 1948, two years before Ainsworth's arrival, Bowlby had hired James Robertson to help him observe hospitalized and institutionalized children who were separated from their parents. Robertson had had impeccable training in naturalistic observation, obtained as a conscientious objector during World War II, when he was employed as a boilerman in Anna Freud's Hampstead residential nursery for homeless children. Anna Freud required that all members of the staff, no matter what their training or background, write about the children's behavior on note cards (Senn, 1977a), which were then used as a basis for weekly group discussions. The thorough training in child observation that Robertson thus obtained at the Hampstead residential nursery is Anna Freud's lasting personal contribution to the development of attachment theory.

After two years of collecting data on hospitalized children for Bowlby's research projects, Robertson protested that he could not continue as an uninvolved research worker but felt compelled to do something for the children he had been observing. On a shoestring budget, with minimal training, a hand-held cinecamera, and no artificial lighting, he made the deeply moving film *A Two-Year-Old Goes to Hospital* (Robertson and Bowlby, 1952; Robertson, 1953a, b). Foreseeing the potential impact of this film, Bowlby insisted that it be carefully planned to ensure that no one would later be able to accuse Robertson of biased recording. The target child was randomly selected, and the hospital clock on the wall served as proof that time sampling took place at regular periods of the day. Together with Spitz's (1947) film, *Grief: A Peril in Infancy*, Robertson's first film helped improve the fate of hospitalized children all over the Western world, even though it was initially highly controversial among the medical establishment.

When Mary Ainsworth arrived at Bowlby's research unit late in 1950, others working there (besides James Robertson) were Mary Boston and Dina Rosenbluth. Rudolph Schaffer, whose subsequent attachment research is well known (Schaffer and Emerson, 1964), joined the group somewhat later, as did Christoph Heinicke (1956; Heinicke and Westheimer, 1966), who undertook additional separation and reunion studies, and Tony Ambrose (1961), who was interested in early social behavior. Mary Ainsworth, who was charged with analyzing James Robertson's data, was tremendously impressed with his records of children's behavior and decided that she would emulate his methods of naturalistic observation were she ever to undertake a study of her own (Ainsworth, 1983).

At this time, Bowlby's earlier writings about the familial experiences of affectionless children had led Ronald Hargreaves of the World Health Organization (WHO) to commission him to write a report on the mental health of homeless children in postwar Europe. Preparation of the WHO report gave Bowlby an opportunity to pick the brains of many practitioners and researchers across Europe and the United States who were concerned with the effects of maternal separation and deprivation on young children, including Spitz (1946) and Goldfarb (1943, 1945). The report was written in six months and translated into 14 languages, with sales of 400,000 copies in the English paperback edition; it was published as *Maternal Care and Mental Health* (Bowlby, 1951). A second revised edition was entitled *Child Care and the Growth of Love*, with review chapters by Mary Ainsworth (Bowlby, 1965).

It is interesting to examine the 1951 report from today's perspective. At that time Bowlby still used the terminology of traditional psychoanalysis (love object, libidinal ties, ego, and superego), but his ideas were little short of heretical. Perhaps following Spitz, he used embryology as a metaphor to portray the maternal role in child development:

> If growth is to proceed smoothly, the tissues must be exposed to the influence of the appropriate organizer at certain critical periods. In the same way, if mental development is to proceed smoothly, it would appear to be necessary for the undifferentiated psyche to be exposed during certain critical periods to the influence of the psychic organizer—the mother [Bowlby, 1951, p. 53].

Then, seemingly doing away with the idea that the superego has its origin in the resolution of the Oedipus complex, Bowlby (1951) claims that during the early years, while the child acquires the capacity for self-regulation, the mother is a child's ego and superego:

> It is not surprising that during infancy and early childhood these functions are either not operating at all or are doing so most imperfectly. During this phase of life, the child is therefore dependent on his mother performing them for him. She orients him in space and time, provides his environment, permits the satisfaction of some impulses, restricts others. She is his ego and his superego. Gradually he learns these arts himself, and as he does, the skilled parent transfers the roles to him. This is a slow, subtle and continuous process, beginning when he first learns to walk and feed himself, and not ending completely until maturity is reached. . . . Ego and superego development are thus inextricably bound up with the child's primary human relationships [p. 53].

This sounds more Vygotskian than Freudian. Moreover, despite his disagreements with Kleinian therapy, I detect remnants of Kleinian ideas in Bowlby's discussions of children's violent fantasies on returning to parents after a prolonged separation and "the intense depression that humans experience as a result of hating the person they most dearly love and need" (p. 57).

Bowlby's major conclusion, grounded in the available empirical evidence, was that to grow up mentally healthy, "the infant and young child should experience a warm, intimate, and continuous relationship with his mother (or permanent mother substitute) in which both find satisfaction and enjoyment" (p. 13). Later summaries often overlook the reference to the substitute mother and to the partners' mutual enjoyment. They also neglect Bowlby's emphasis on the role of social networks and on economic as well as health factors in the development of well-functioning mother–child relationships. His call to society to provide support for parents is still not heeded today:

> Just as children are absolutely dependent on their parents for sustenance, so in all but the most primitive communities, are parents, especially their mothers, dependent on a greater society for economic provision. If a community values its children it must cherish their parents [Bowlby, 1951, p. 84].

True to the era in which the WHO report was written, Bowlby emphasized the female parent. In infancy, he comments, fathers have their uses, but normally they play second fiddle to mother. Their prime role is to provide emotional support to their wives' mothering.

The proposition that, to thrive emotionally, children need a close and continuous caregiving relationship called for a theoretical explanation. Bowlby was not satisfied with the then-current psychoanalytic view that love of mother derives from sensuous oral gratification, nor did he agree with social learning theory's claim that dependency is based on secondary reinforcement (a concept that was itself derived from psychoanalytic ideas). Like Spitz (1946) and Erikson (1950), Bowlby had latched on to the concept of critical periods in embryological development and was casting about for similar phenomena at the behavioral level when, through a friend, he happened upon an English translation of Konrad Lorenz's (1935) paper on imprinting.

From then on, Bowlby began to mine ethology for useful new concepts. Lorenz's (1935) account of imprinting in geese and other precocial birds especially intrigued him, because it suggested that social bond formation need not be tied to feeding. In addition, he favored ethological methods of observing animals in their natural environment, because this approach was so compatible with the methods Robertson had already developed at the Tavistock research unit.

One notable talent that stood Bowlby in great stead throughout his professional life was his ability to draw to himself outstanding individuals who were willing and able to help him acquire expertise in new fields of inquiry that he needed to master in the service of theory building. To learn more about ethology, Bowlby contacted Robert Hinde, under whose "generous and stern guidance" (see Bowlby, 1980b, p. 650) he mastered ethological principles to help him find new ways of thinking about infant–mother attachment. Conversely, Hinde's fascinating studies of individual differences in separation and reunion behaviors of group-living rhesus mother–infant dyads (Hinde and Spencer-Booth, 1967) were inspired by the contact with Bowlby and his coworkers (Hinde, 1991).

Bowlby's first ethological paper appeared in 1953. Somewhat surprisingly, however, various empirical papers on the effects of separation, published with his own research team in the very same period, show little trace of Bowlby's new thinking, because his colleagues were unconvinced that ethology was relevant to the mother–child relationship (Bowlby, personal communication, October 1986). Even Mary Ainsworth, though much enamored of ethology, was somewhat wary of the direction Bowlby's theorizing had begun to take. It was obvious to her, she said, that a baby loves his mother because she satisfies his needs (Ainsworth, personal communication, January 1992). A paper coauthored with Ainsworth and others dating from this period (Bowlby, Ainsworth, Boston, and Rosenbluth, 1956) is nevertheless important, because it prefigures Ainsworth's later work on patterns of attachment. Her contribution to the paper was a system for classifying three basic relationship patterns in school-age children who had been reunited with parents after prolonged sanatorium stays: those with strong positive feelings toward their mothers; those with markedly ambivalent relationships; and a third group with nonexpressive, indifferent, or hostile relationships with their mothers.

THE FORMULATION OF ATTACHMENT THEORY AND THE FIRST ATTACHMENT STUDY

Theoretical Formulations

Bowlby's first formal statement of attachment theory, building on concepts from ethology and developmental psychology, was presented to the British Psychoanalytic Society in London in three now-classic papers: "The Nature of the Child's Tie to His Mother" (Bowlby, 1958), "Separation Anxiety" (Bowlby, 1959), and "Grief and Mourning in Infancy and Early Childhood" (Bowlby, 1960). By 1962 Bowlby (1962a, b) had completed two further papers on defensive processes related to mourning that were never published. These five papers represent the first basic blueprint of attachment theory.

The Nature of the Child's Tie to His Mother. This paper reviews and then rejects those contemporary psychoanalytic explanations for the child's libidinal tie to the mother in which need satisfaction is seen as primary and attachment as secondary or derived. Borrowing from Freud's (1905) notion that mature human sexuality is built up of component instincts, Bowlby proposed that 12-month-olds' unmistakable attachment behavior is made up of a number of component instinctual responses that have the function of binding the infant to the mother and the mother to the infant. These component responses (among them sucking, clinging, and following, as well as the signaling behaviors of smiling and crying) mature relatively independently during the first year of life and become increasingly integrated and focused on a mother figure during the second six months. Bowlby saw clinging and following as possibly more important for attachment than sucking and crying.

To buttress his arguments, Bowlby reviewed data from existing empirical studies of infants' cognitive and social development, including studies by Piaget (1951, 1954), with whose ideas he had become acquainted during a series of meetings by the Psychobiology of the Child study group, organized by the same Ronald Hargreaves at the World Health Organization who had commissioned Bowlby's 1951 report. These informative meetings, also attended by Erik Erikson, Julian Huxley, Baerbel Inhelder, Konrad Lorenz, Margaret Mead, and Ludwig von Bertalanffy, took place between 1953 and 1956. For additional evidence, Bowlby drew on many years of experience as weekly facilitator of a support group for young mothers in London.

After his careful discussion of infant development, Bowlby introduced ethological concepts, such as sign stimuli or social releasers that "cause" specific responses to be activated and shut off or terminated (see Tinbergen, 1951). These stimuli could be external or intrapsychic, an important point in view of the fact that some psychoanalysts accused Bowlby of behaviorism because he supposedly ignored mental phenomena. Bowlby also took great pains to draw a clear distinction between the old social learning theory concept of dependency and the new concept of attachment, and noted that attachment is not indicative of regression but, rather, performs a natural, healthy function even in adult life.

Bowlby's new instinct theory raised quite a storm at the British Psychoanalytic Society. Even Bowlby's own analyst, Joan Riviere, protested. Anna Freud, who missed the meeting but read the paper, politely wrote: "Dr. Bowlby is too valuable a person to get lost to psychoanalysis" (Grosskurth, 1987).

Separation Anxiety. The second seminal paper (Bowlby, 1959) builds on observations by Robertson (1953b) and Heinicke (1956; later elaborated by Heinicke and Westheimer, 1966), as well as on Harlow and Zimmermann's (1958) groundbreaking work on the effects of maternal deprivation in rhesus monkeys. Traditional theory, Bowlby claims, can explain neither the intense attachment of infants and young children to a mother figure nor their dramatic responses to separation.

Robertson (Robertson and Bowlby, 1952) had identified three phases of separation response: protest (related to separation anxiety), despair (related to grief and mourning), and denial or detachment (related to defense mechanisms, especially repression). Again drawing on ethological concepts regarding the control of behavior, Bowlby maintained that infants and children experience separation anxiety when a situation activates both escape and attachment behavior, but an attachment figure is not available.

The following quote explains, in part, why some psychoanalytic colleagues called Bowlby a behaviorist: "For to have a deep attachment for a person (or a place or thing) is to have taken them as the terminating object of our instinctual responses" (Bowlby, 1959, p. 13). The oddity of this statement derives from mixing, in the same sentence, experiential language ("to have a deep attachment") with explanatory language representing an external observer's point of view (the attachment figure as the terminating object).

In this paper Bowlby also takes issue with Freud's claim that maternal overgratification is a danger in infancy. Freud failed to realize, says Bowlby, that maternal pseudoaffection and overprotection may derive from a mother's overcompensation for unconscious hostility. In Bowlby's view, excessive separation anxiety is due to adverse family experiences—such as repeated threats of abandonment or rejection by parents—or to a parent's or sibling's illness or death for which the child feels responsible.

Bowlby also points out that, in some cases, separation anxiety can be excessively low or altogether absent, giving an erroneous impression of maturity. He attributes pseudoindependence under these conditions to defensive processes. A well-loved child, he claims, is quite likely to protest separation from parents but will later develop more self-reliance. These ideas later reemerged in Ainsworth's classifications of ambivalent, avoidant, and secure patterns of infant–mother attachment (Ainsworth et al., 1978).

Grief and Mourning in Infancy and Early Childhood. In the third, most controversial paper, Bowlby (1960) questions Anna Freud's contention that bereaved infants cannot mourn because of insufficient ego development and therefore experience nothing more than brief bouts of separation anxiety if an adequate substitute caregiver is available. In contrast, Bowlby (citing Marris, 1958) claims that grief and mourning processes in children and adults appear whenever attachment behaviors are activated but the attachment figure continues to be unavailable. He also suggests that an inability to form deep relationships with others may result when the succession of substitutes is too frequent.

As with the first paper, this paper drew strong objections from many members of the British Psychoanalytic Society. One analyst is said to have exclaimed: "Bowlby? Give me Barrabas" (Grosskurth, 1987). Controversy also accompanied the published version of this paper in the *Psychoanalytic Study of the Child*. Unbeknownst to Bowlby, rejoinders had been invited from Anna Freud (1960), Max Schur (1960), and René Spitz (1960), all of whom protested various aspects of Bowlby's revision of Freudian theory. Spitz (1960) ended his rejoinder by saying:

> When submitting new theories we should not violate the principle of parsimony in science by offering hypotheses which in contrast to existing theory becloud the observational facts, are oversimplified, and make no contribution to the better understanding of observed phenomena [p. 93].

Despite this concerted attack, Bowlby remained a member of the British Psychoanalytic Society for the rest of his life, although he never again used it as a forum for discussing his ideas. At a meeting of the society in memory of John Bowlby, Eric Rayner (1991) expressed his regret at this turn of events: "What seems wrong is when a theorist extols his own view by rubbishing others; Bowlby received this treatment. . . . Our therapeutic frame of mind is altered by theory. John Bowlby was a great alterer of frames of mind."

Bowlby's controversial paper on mourning attracted the attention of Colin Parkes, now well known for his research on adult bereavement. Parkes saw the relevance of Bowlby's and Robertson's work on mourning in infancy and childhood for gaining insight into the process of adult grief. On joining Bowlby's research unit at the Tavistock Institute in 1962, Parkes set out to study a nonclinic group of widows in their homes to chart the course of normal adult grief, about which little was known at the time. The findings led to a joint paper with Bowlby (Bowlby and Parkes, 1970) in which the phases of separation response delineated by Robertson for young children were elaborated into four phases of grief during adult life: (1) numbness, (2) yearning and protest, (3) disorganization and despair, and (4) reorganization (see also Parkes, 1972).

Before the publication of the 1970 paper, Parkes had visited Elizabeth Kubler-Ross in Chicago, who was then gathering data for her influential book *On Death and Dying* (Kubler-Ross, 1970). The phases of dying described in her book (denial, anger, bargaining, depression, and acceptance) owe much to Bowlby's and Robertson's thinking. Bowlby also introduced Parkes to the founder of the modern hospice movement, Cicely Saunders. Saunders and Parkes used attachment theory and research in developing programs for the emotional care of the dying and bereaved. What they found particularly helpful in countering negative attitudes to the dying and bereaved was the concept of grief as a process toward attaining a new identity, rather than as a state (Parkes, personal communication, November 1989).

The First Empirical Study of Attachment: Infancy in Uganda

Let us now return to Mary Ainsworth's work. In late 1953, she left the Tavistock Clinic and was obviously quite familiar with Bowlby's thinking about ethology but not convinced of its value for understanding infant–mother attachment. The Ainsworths were headed for Uganda, where Leonard Ainsworth had obtained a position at the East African Institute of Social Research at Kampala. With help from the same institute, Mary Ainsworth was able to scrape together funds for an observational study, but not before writing Bowlby a letter in which she called for empirical validation of his ethological notions (Ainsworth, personal communication, January 1992).

Inspired by her analyses of Robertson's data, Ainsworth had initially planned an investigation of toddlers' separation responses during weaning, but it soon became obvious that the old tradition of sending the child away "to forget the breast" had broken down. She therefore decided to switch gears and observe the development of infant–mother attachment.

As soon as she began her data collection, Ainsworth was struck by the pertinence of Bowlby's ethological ideas. Hence, the first study of infant–mother attachment from an ethological perspective was undertaken several years before the publication of the three seminal papers in which Bowlby (1958, 1959, 1960) laid out attachment theory.

Ainsworth recruited 26 families with unweaned babies (ages 1–24 months), whom she observed every two weeks for two hours per visit over a period of up to nine months. Visits (with an interpreter) took place in the family living room, where Ganda women generally entertain in the afternoon. Ainsworth was particularly interested in determining the onset of proximity-promoting signals and behaviors and noted carefully when these signals and behaviors became preferentially directed toward the mother.

On leaving Uganda in 1955, the Ainsworths moved to Baltimore, where Mary Ainsworth began work as a diagnostician and part-time

clinician at the Sheppard and Enoch Pratt Hospital and further consolidated her already considerable assessment skills. At the same
time, she taught clinical and developmental courses at the Johns
Hopkins University, where she was initially hired as a lecturer.
Because of her involvement in diagnostic work and teaching, the
data from the Ganda project lay fallow for several years.

REFINING ATTACHMENT THEORY AND RESEARCH: BOWLBY AND AINSWORTH

Before the publication of "The Nature of the Child's Tie to His
Mother" (Bowlby, 1958), Mary Ainsworth received a preprint of the
paper from John Bowlby. This event led Bowlby and Ainsworth to
renew their close intellectual collaboration. Ainsworth's subsequent
analysis of data from her Ganda project (Ainsworth, 1963, 1967)
influenced and was influenced by Bowlby's reformulation of attachment theory (published in 1969). In this sharing of ideas,
Ainsworth's theoretical contribution to Bowlby's presentation of the
ontogeny of human attachment cannot be overestimated.

Findings from Ainsworth's Ganda Project

The Ganda data (Ainsworth, 1963, 1967) were a rich source for the
study of individual differences in the quality of mother–infant interaction, the topic that Bowlby had earlier left aside as too difficult to
study. Of special note, in light of Ainsworth's future work, was an
evaluation of maternal sensitivity to infant signals, derived from
interview data. Mothers who were excellent informants and who
provided much spontaneous detail were rated as highly sensitive, in
contrast to other mothers who seemed imperceptive of the nuances
of infant behavior. Three infant attachment patterns were observed:
securely attached infants cried little and seemed content to explore
in the presence of mother; insecurely attached infants cried frequently, even when held by their mothers, and explored little; and
not-yet attached infants manifested no differential behavior to the
mother.

Attachment quality was significantly correlated with maternal sensitivity. Babies of sensitive mothers tended to be securely attached,
whereas babies of less sensitive mothers were more likely to be classified as insecure. Mothers' enjoyment of breast-feeding also correlated with infant security. These findings foreshadow some of
Ainsworth's later work, although the measures are not yet as sophisticated as those developed for subsequent studies.

Ainsworth presented her initial findings from the Ganda project at meetings of the Tavistock Study Group organized by Bowlby during the 1960s (Ainsworth, 1963). Participants invited to these influential gatherings included many now-eminent infant researchers of diverse theoretical backgrounds (in addition to Mary Ainsworth, there were Genevieve Appell, Miriam David, Jacob Gewirtz, Hanus Papousek, Heinz Prechtl, Harriet Rheingold, Henry Ricciuti, Louis Sander, and Peter Wolff), as well as renowned animal researchers such as Harry Harlow, Robert Hinde, Charles Kaufmann, Jay Rosenblatt, and Thelma Rowell. Their lively discussions and ensuing studies contributed much to the developing field of infant social development in general. Important for Bowlby, they also enriched his ongoing elaboration of attachment theory. Bowlby had always believed that he had much to gain from bringing together researchers with different theoretical backgrounds (e.g., learning theory, psychoanalysis, and ethology), whether or not they agreed with his theoretical position. Proceedings of these fruitful meetings were published in four edited volumes entitled *Determinants of Infant Behaviour* (Foss, 1961, 1963, 1965, 1969).

The Baltimore Project

In 1963, while still pondering the data from the Ganda study, Mary Ainsworth embarked on a second observational project whose thoroughness no researcher has since equaled. Again, she opted for naturalistic observations, but with interviews playing a somewhat lesser role. The 26 participating Baltimore families were recruited prenatally, with 18 home visits beginning in the first month and ending at 54 weeks. Each visit lasted 4 hours to make sure that mothers would feel comfortable enough to follow their normal routine, resulting in approximately 72 hours of data collection per family.

Raw data took the form of narrative reports, jotted down in personal shorthand, marked in five-minute intervals, and later dictated into a tape recorder for transcription. Typed narratives from all visits for each quarter of the first year of life were grouped together for purposes of analysis.

A unique (at the time) aspect of Ainsworth's methodology was the emphasis on meaningful behavioral patterns in context, rather than on frequency counts of specific behaviors. This approach had roots in her dissertation work, in which she classified patterns of familial and extrafamilial dependent and independent security, in her expertise with the Rorschach test, and in her work at the Tavistock Institute with Bowlby and Robertson.

Close examination of the narratives revealed the emergence of characteristic mother–infant interaction patterns during the first three months (see Ainsworth et al., 1978; see also Ainsworth, 1982, 1983). Separate analyses were conducted on feeding situations (Ainsworth and Bell, 1969), mother–infant face-to-face interaction (Blehar, Lieberman, and Ainsworth, 1977), crying (Bell and Ainsworth, 1972), the attachment exploration balance (Ainsworth, Bell, and Stayton, 1971), obedience (Stayton, Hogan, and Ainsworth, 1973), close bodily contact (Ainsworth et al., 1971), approach behavior (Tracy, Lamb, and Ainsworth, 1976), and affectionate contact (Tracy and Ainsworth, 1981).

Striking individual differences were observed in how sensitively, appropriately, and promptly mothers responded to their infants' signals. For some mother–infant pairs, feeding was an occasion for smooth cooperation. Other mothers had difficulties in adjusting their pacing and behavior to the baby's cues. In response, their babies tended to struggle, choke, and spit up, hardly the sensuous oral experience Freud had had in mind. Similar distinctive patterns were observed in face-to-face interactions between mother and infant during the period from 6 to 15 weeks (Blehar et al., 1977). When mothers meshed their own playful behavior with that of their babies, infants responded with joyful bouncing, smiling, and vocalizing; however, when mothers initiated face-to-face interactions silently and with an unsmiling expression, ensuing interactions were muted and brief. Findings on close bodily contact resembled those on feeding and face-to-face interaction, as did those on crying. There were enormous variations in how many crying episodes a mother ignored and how long she let the baby cry. In countering those who argued that maternal responsiveness might lead to "spoiling," Bell and Ainsworth (1972) conclude that "an infant whose mother's responsiveness helps him to achieve his ends develops confidence in his own ability to control what happens to him" (p. 1188).

Maternal sensitivity in the first quarter was associated with more harmonious mother–infant relationships in the fourth quarter. Babies whose mothers had been highly responsive to crying during the early months now tended to cry less, relying for communication on facial expressions, gestures, and vocalizations (Bell and Ainsworth, 1972). Similarly, infants whose mothers had provided much tender holding during the first quarter sought contact less often during the fourth quarter, but when contact occurred, it was rated as more satisfying and affectionate. Ainsworth et al. (1978) explain these findings by recourse to infants' expectations, based on prior satisfying or rejecting experiences with mother.

All first-quarter interactive patterns were also related to infant behavior in a laboratory procedure known as the Strange Situation (Ainsworth and Wittig, 1969). This initially very controversial laboratory procedure for one-year-olds was originally designed to examine the balance of attachment and exploratory behaviors under conditions of low and high stress, a topic in which Harlow (1961) had aroused Ainsworth's interest during meetings of the Tavistock group but also a topic that reminded her of an earlier study by Arsenian (1943) on young children in an insecure situation and of her dissertation work on security theory.

The Strange Situation is a 20-minute miniature drama with eight episodes. Mother and infant are introduced to a laboratory playroom, where they are later joined by an unfamiliar woman. While the stranger plays with the baby, the mother leaves briefly and then returns. A second separation ensues during which the baby is completely alone. Finally, the stranger and then the mother return.

As expected, Ainsworth found that infants explored the playroom and toys more vigorously in the presence of their mothers than after a stranger entered or while the mother was absent (Ainsworth and Bell, 1970). Although these results were theoretically interesting, Ainsworth became much more intrigued with unexpected patterns of infant reunion behaviors, which reminded her of responses Robertson had documented in children exposed to prolonged separations, and about which Bowlby (1959) had theorized in his paper on separation.

A few of the one-year-olds from the Baltimore study were surprisingly angry when the mother returned after a three-minute (or shorter) separation. They cried and wanted contact but would not simply cuddle or "sink in" when picked up by the returning mother. Instead, they showed their ambivalence by kicking or swiping at her. Another group of children seemed to snub or avoid the mother on reunion, even though they had often searched for her while she was gone. Analyses of home data revealed that those infants who had been ambivalent toward, or avoidant of, the mother on reunion in the Strange Situation had a less harmonious relationship with her at home than those (a majority) who sought proximity, interaction, or contact on reunion (Ainsworth, Bell, and Stayton, 1974). Thus originated the well-known Strange Situation classification system (Ainsworth et al., 1978), which, to Ainsworth's chagrin, has stolen the limelight from her observational findings of naturalistic mother–infant interaction patterns at home.

The First Volume in the Attachment Trilogy:
Attachment and Ethology

While Ainsworth (1967) wrote up the findings from her Ganda study for *Infancy in Uganda* and was engaged in collecting data for the Baltimore project, Bowlby worked on the first volume of the attachment trilogy, *Attachment* (published in 1969). When he began this enterprise in 1962, the plan had been for a single book; however, as he explains in the preface: "As my study of theory progressed it was gradually borne in upon me that the field I had set out to plough so light-heartedly was no less than the one Freud had started tilling sixty years earlier" (p. xi). In short, Bowlby realized that he had to develop a new theory of motivation and behavior control, built on up-to-date science rather than the outdated psychic energy model espoused by Freud.

In the first half of *Attachment*, Bowlby lays the groundwork for such a theory and takes pains to document each important statement with available research findings. He begins by noting that organisms at different levels of the phylogenetic scale regulate instinctive behavior in distinct ways, ranging from primitive, reflex-like "fixed action patters" to complex plan hierarchies with subgoals. In the most complex organisms, instinctive behaviors may be "goal-corrected" with continual on-course adjustments (such as a bird of prey's adjusting its flight to the movements of the prey). The concept of cybernetically controlled behavioral systems organized as plan hierarchies (Miller, Galanter, and Pribram, 1960) thus came to replace Freud's concept of drive and instinct. Behaviors regulated by such systems need not be rigidly innate but—depending on the organism—can adapt in greater or lesser degrees to changes in environmental circumstances, provided these do not deviate too much from the organism's environment of evolutionary adaptedness. Such flexible organisms pay a price, however, because adaptable behavioral systems can more easily be subverted from their optimal path of development. For humans, Bowlby speculates, the environment of evolutionary adaptedness probably resembles that of present-day hunter-gatherer societies.

The ultimate functions of behavioral systems controlling attachment, parenting, mating, feeding, and exploration are survival and procreation. In some cases, the predictable outcome of system activation is a time-limited behavior (such as food intake); in others it is the time-extended maintenance of an organism in a particular relation to its environment (e.g., within its own territory or in proximity to particular companions).

Complex behavioral systems of the kind proposed by Bowlby can work with foresight in organisms that have evolved an ability to construct internal working models of the environment and of their own actions in it (a concept taken over from Craik, 1943, through the writings of the biologist J. Z. Young, 1964). The more adequate an organism's internal working model, the more accurately the organism can predict the future; however, adds Bowlby, if working models of the environment and self are out-of-date or are only half revised after drastic environmental change, pathological functioning may ensue. He speculates that useful model revision, extension, and consistency checking may require conscious processing of model content. In humans, communicative processes—initially limited to emotional or gestural signaling and later including language—also permit the intersubjective sharing of model content. On an intrapsychic level, the same processes are useful for self-regulation and behavioral priority setting.

In mammals and birds, behavioral systems tend to become organized during specific sensitive developmental periods. As initial reflexlike behavior chains come under more complex, cybernetically controlled organization, the range of stimuli that can activate them also becomes more restricted. This is the case in imprinting, broadly defined as the restriction of specific instinctive behaviors to particular individuals or groups of individuals during sensitive phases of development, as in filial, parental, and sexual imprinting.

Having laid out this general theory of motivation and behavior regulation in the first half of the volume, Bowlby goes on, in the second half, to apply these ideas to the specific domain of infant–mother attachment. He defines attachment behavior as behavior that has proximity to an attachment figure as a predictable outcome and whose evolutionary function is protection of the infant from danger; that attachment has its own motivation and is in no way derived from systems subserving mating and feeding.

Although human infants initially direct proximity-promoting signals fairly indiscriminately to all caregivers, these behaviors become increasingly focused on those primary figures who are responsive to the infant's crying and who engage the infant in social interaction (Schaffer and Emerson, 1964). Once attached, locomotor infants are able to use the attachment figure as a secure base for exploration of the environment and as a safe haven to which to return for reassurance (Schaffer and Emerson, 1964; Ainsworth, 1967). How effectively the attachment figure can serve in these roles depends on the quality of social interaction, especially the attachment figure's sensitivity to the infant's signals, although child factors also play a role. Building on Ainsworth's (1967) Ganda study and preliminary findings from her Baltimore project, Bowlby (1969) comments that

> when interaction between a couple runs smoothly, each party manifests intense pleasure in the other's company and especially in the other's expression of affection. Conversely, whenever interaction results in persistent conflict each party is likely on occasion to exhibit intense anxiety or unhappiness, especially when the other is rejecting. . . . Proximity and affectionate interchange are appraised and felt as pleasurable by both, whereas distance and expressions of rejection are appraised as disagreeable or painful by both [p. 242].

During the preschool years the attachment behavioral system, always complementary to the parental caregiving system, undergoes further reorganization as the child attains growing insight into the attachment figure's motives and plans. Bowlby refers to this stage as *goal-corrected partnership*. In emphasizing infant initiative and sensitive maternal responding, however, Bowlby's (1951) earlier theorizing on the mother as the child's ego and superego was regrettably lost.

Consolidation

The publication of the first volume of the attachment trilogy in 1969 coincided with the appearance in print of initial findings from Ainsworth's Baltimore project (reviewed earlier). Many investigators, however, strongly contested Ainsworth's claims regarding the meaning of Strange Situation behavior, often because they failed to note that Strange Situation classifications had been validated against extensive home observations. Some interpreted avoidant infants' behavior as independence. The controversy lessened somewhat after the publication of *Patterns of Attachment* (Ainsworth et al., 1978), which drew together the results from the Baltimore project and presented findings from other laboratories on the sequelae of attachment classifications in toddlerhood and early childhood (e.g., Main, 1973; Matas, Arend, and Sroufe, 1978).

During this period, many of Ainsworth's graduate students began to publish their own work. Silvia Bell (1970) examined the relationship between object permanence and attachment. Mary Main (1973) studied secure and insecure toddlers' capacity to become invested in play activities and problem solving. Mary Blehar (1974) undertook the first study of attachment and nonmaternal care, and Alicia

Lieberman (1977) investigated attachment and peer relationships in preschoolers. Mary Ainsworth's influence is also evident in the fact that many Johns Hopkins undergraduate students who had helped with the analysis of data from the Baltimore project later produced innovative dissertations on attachment-related topics at their respective graduate institutions; among these students were Robert Marvin (1972, 1977), who wrote on the goal-corrected partnership; Milton Kotelchuck (1972), who studied father attachment; Mark Cummings (1980), who investigated attachment and day care; Mark Greenberg (Greenberg and Marvin, 1979), who examined attachment in deaf children; and Everett Waters (1978), who documented the longitudinal stability of attachment patterns from 12 to 18 months.

Everett Waters's entry into graduate study at the University of Minnesota in 1973 had a profound effect on Alan Sroufe, who had read Mary Ainsworth's (1968) theoretical article about object relations and dependency but had not heard of the Strange Situation of the Baltimore project (Sroufe, personal communication, 1988). Sroufe's contact with Waters led to significant empirical and theoretical collaborations. In 1977, Sroufe and Waters wrote an influential paper that made attachment an organizational construct accessible to a much larger audience. At the same time, Sroufe and Egeland, together with many of their students, undertook a large-scale longitudinal study of attachment with an at-risk population (disadvantaged mothers). The Minnesota study, summarized in Sroufe (1983) but still ongoing, stands as the second major longitudinal study of the relationship between quality of caregiving and security of attachment.

Elsewhere across the United States, much time was spent testing the predictive validity of Strange Situation reunion classifications. Many researchers sought to train with Mary Ainsworth or her former students to learn the procedure and classification system. Hundreds of studies using the Strange Situation appeared in print. It often seemed as if attachment and the Strange Situation had become synonymous.

ATTACHMENT THEORY AND MENTAL REPRESENTATION

Separation (Bowlby, 1973) and *Loss* (Bowlby, 1980a), the second and third volumes in Bowlby's attachment trilogy, were slower to make an impact on the field of developmental psychology than the first volume, in part because relevant empirical studies lagged behind. Like *Attachment*, these two volumes cover much more theoretical ground than their titles imply.

Separation

In this book, Bowlby (1973) revises Freud's (1926) theory of signal anxiety, lays out a new approach to Freud's (1923, 1940) motivational theories, and presents an epigenetic model of personality development inspired by Waddington's (1957) theory of developmental pathways.

Elaborating on his seminal 1959 paper, Bowlby notes that two distinct sets of stimuli elicit fear in children: the *presence* of unlearned, and later of culturally acquired clues to danger or the *absence* of an attachment figure or both. Although escape from danger and escape to an attachment figure commonly occur together, the two classes of behavior are governed by separate control systems (observable when a ferocious dog comes between a mother and her young child).

Although Bowlby regards the systems controlling escape and attachment as conceptually distinct, he considers both to be members of a larger family of stress-reducing and safety-promoting behavioral systems, whose more general function is maintaining an organism within a defined relationship to his or her environment. Rather than seeing humans as striving for stimulus absence, as Freud had suggested, Bowlby posits that humans are motivated to maintain a dynamic balance between familiarity-preserving, stress-reducing behaviors (attachment to protective individuals and to familiar home sites, retreat from the strange and novel) and antithetical exploratory and information-seeking behaviors.

After revising Freud's theories of fear and motivation, Bowlby reexamined Freud's concept of the "inner world" in light of modern cognitive theory. In *Separation*, he expands ideas proposed in *Attachment* by suggesting that, within an individual's internal working model of the world, working models of self and attachment figure are especially salient. These working models, acquired through interpersonal interaction patterns, are complementary. If the attachment figure has acknowledged the infant's needs for comfort and protection while simultaneously respecting the infant's need for independent exploration of the environment, the child is likely to develop an internal working model of self as valued and self-reliant. Conversely, if the parent has frequently rejected the infant's bids for comfort or for exploration, the child is likely to construct an internal working model of self as unworthy or incompetent. With the aid of working models, children predict the attachment figure's likely behavior and plan their own responses. What type of model they construct is therefore of great consequence.

In *Separation*, Bowlby also elucidates the role of internal working models in the intergenerational transmission of attachment patterns. Individuals who grow up to become relatively stable and self-reliant, he postulates, normally have parents who are supportive when called upon but who also permit and encourage autonomy. Such parents tend not only to engage in fairly frank communication of their own working models of self, of their child, and of others but also to indicate to the child that these working models are open to questioning and revision. For this reason, says Bowlby, the inheritance of mental health and of ill health through family microculture is no less important, and may well be far more important than, genetic inheritance (Bowlby, 1973, p. 323).

Loss

In the third volume of the attachment trilogy, Bowlby (1980a) uses information-processing theories to explain the increasing stability of internal working models as well as their defensive distortion. The stability of internal working models derives from two sources: (1) patterns of interacting grow less accessible to awareness as they become habitual and automatic, and (2) dyadic patterns of relating are more resistant to change than individual patterns because of reciprocal expectancies.

Given that old patterns of action and thought guide selective attention and information processing in new situations, some distortion of incoming information is normal and unavoidable. The adequacy of internal working models can be seriously undermined, however, when defensive exclusion of information from awareness interferes with their updating in response to developmental and environmental change.

To explain the workings of defensive processes, Bowlby cites evidence that incoming information normally undergoes many stages of processing before reaching awareness (see Dixon, 1971; Erdelyi, 1974). At every stage, some information is retained for further processing, and the remainder is discarded. That this may happen even after information has already undergone very advanced levels of encoding is shown by dichotic listening studies. In these studies, individuals who are presented with different messages to each ear through headphones are able to attend selectively to one of them. That the unattended message is nevertheless receiving high-level processing becomes obvious when the person alerts to a word of personal significance (e.g., the person's name) that has been inserted into the unattended message.

Bowlby proposes that *defensive* exclusion of information from awareness derives from the same processes as *selective* exclusion, although the motivation for the two types of exclusion differs. Three situations are believed to render children particularly prone to engaging in defensive exclusion: situations that parents do not wish their children to know about, even though the children have witnessed them; situations in which the children find the parents' behavior too unbearable to think about; and situations in which children have done or thought about doing something of which they are deeply ashamed.

Although defensive exclusion protects the individual from experiencing unbearable mental pain, confusion, or conflict, it is bound to interfere with the accommodation of internal working models to external reality. Indeed, a number of clinical studies reviewed in *Separation* (e.g., Cain and Fast, 1972) suggest that defensive exclusion leads to a split in internal working models. One set of working models—accessible to awareness and discussion and based on what a child has been told—represents the parent as good and the parent's rejecting behavior as caused by the "badness" of the child. The other model, based on what the child has experienced but defensively excluded from awareness, represents the hated or disappointing side of the parent.

In *Loss*, Bowlby attempts to shed further light on these repressive and dissociative phenomena with the aid of Tulving's (1972) distinction between episodic and semantic memory. According to Tulving, autobiographical experience is encoded in episodic memory, whereas generic propositions are stored in semantic memory, with each memory system possibly using distinct storage mechanisms. Generic knowledge may derive from information supplied by others and from actual experience. Bowlby surmises that severe psychic conflict is likely to arise when the two sources of stored information (generalizations built on actual experience and on communications from others) are highly contradictory. In such cases, defensive exclusion may be brought to bear on episodic memories of actual experience. According to Bowlby, such processes are especially likely in bereaved children under three years of age.

Finally, in *Loss*, Bowlby also considers a more complex, related problem, namely, the control of simultaneously active behavioral systems. In *Attachment* and *Separation*, the interplay of behavioral systems was implicitly treated as competition, not as higher-level regulation (see also Bretherton and Ainsworth, 1974). In *Loss*, Bowlby posits an executive structure that takes the place of Freud's (1923) concept of ego. The central nervous system, Bowlby suggests, is organized in a loosely hierarchical way, with an enormous network of two-way communications among subsystems. At the top of the hierarchy, he posits one or perhaps several principal evaluators or controllers, closely linked to long-term memory. Their task is to scan incoming information for relevance. If evaluated as relevant, it may be stored in short-term memory to select aspects thereof for further processing.

Conscious processing is likely to facilitate high-level activities such as categorizing, retrieving, comparing, framing plans, and inspection of overlearned, automated action systems. In a unified personality, Bowlby claims, the principal system or systems can access all memories in whatever type of storage they are held. In some individuals, however, the principal system or systems may not be unified or capable of unimpeded intercommunication with all subsystems. In these individuals, particular behavioral systems may not be activated when appropriate, or signals from these behavioral systems may not become conscious, although fragments of defensively excluded information may, at times, seep through.

Some of the dissociative or repressive phenomena involved in the deactivation of the attachment system occur during pathological mourning. For example, complete or partial disconnection of an emotional response from its cause is frequent. When the disconnection is only partial, emotional responses may be directed away from the person who caused them to third persons or to the self. Hence, a bereaved person may become morbidly preoccupied with personal reactions and sufferings rather than attributing his or her feelings to the loss of a close relationship. Similarly, in disordered mourning, a bereaved person's disposition toward compulsive caregiving may derive from the redirection of attachment behavior. The individual may be taking the role of attachment figure instead of seeking care.

Attachment and Therapy

This discussion of defensive processes leads into the topic that preoccupied Bowlby during the last ten years of his life: the uses of attachment theory in psychotherapy (Bowlby, 1988). Under attachment theory, a major goal in psychotherapy is the reappraisal of inadequate, outdated working models of self in relation to attachment figures, a particularly difficult task if important others, especially parents, have forbidden their review. As psychoanalysts have repeatedly noted, a person with inadequate, rigid working models of attachment relations is likely to impose these models inappropriately on interactions with the therapist (a phenomenon known as *transference*). The joint task of therapist and client is to understand the origins of the client's dysfunctional internal working models of self and attachment figures. Toward this end, the therapist can be most helpful by serving as a reliable, secure base from which an individual can begin the arduous task of exploring and reworking his or her internal working models.

NEW DIRECTIONS

Currently, attachment theory and research are moving forward along several major fronts, inspired by the second and third volumes of Bowlby's attachment trilogy, by methodological advances, and by the infusion into attachment theory of complementary theoretical perspectives.

Attachment and Representation

As a result of Mary Main's Berkeley study (Main, Kaplan, and Cassidy, 1985) and, I think, the publication of the Society for Research in Child Development Monograph, *Growing Points of Attachment Theory and Research* (Bretherton and Waters, 1985), we are now beginning empirical explorations of the psychological, internal, or representational aspects of attachment, including the intergenerational transmission of attachment patterns that were at the center of Bowlby's interests since his beginnings in psychiatry but that are most clearly elaborated in volumes 2 and 3 of the attachment trilogy (see Bretherton, 1987, 1990, 1991).

Interestingly, an additional source of inspiration for the study of internal working models came from attempts to translate Ainsworth's infant–mother attachment patterns into corresponding adult patterns. In the Adult Attachment Interview (George, Kaplan, and Main, 1984; Main and Goldwyn, in press), parents were asked open-ended questions about their attachment relations in childhood and about the influence of these early relations on their own development. Three distinct patterns of responding were identified: *autonomous-secure* parents gave a clear and coherent account of early attachments (whether these had been satisfying or not); *preoccupied* parents spoke of many conflicted childhood memories about attachment but did not draw them together into an organized, consistent picture; and, finally, *dismissing* parents were characterized by an inability to remember much about attachment relations in childhood. In some of the dismissing interviews, parents' parents were idealized on a general level, but influences of early attachment experiences on later development were denied. Specific memories, when they did occur, suggested episodes of rejection.

Not only did the Adult Attachment Interview classifications correspond to Ainsworth's secure, ambivalent, and avoidant infant patterns at a conceptual level, but adult patterns were also empirically correlated with infant patterns (e.g., a dismissing parent tended to have an avoidant infant; Main and Goldwyn, in press). These findings have since been validated for prenatally administered interviews by Fonagy, Steele, and Steele (1991) and by Ward et al. (1990). Consonant findings were also obtained in a study of young adults in which Adult Attachment Interview classifications were correlated with peer reports (Kobak and Sceery, 1988).

In addition, representational measures of attachment have been devised for use with children. A pictorial separation anxiety test for adolescents, developed by Hansburg (1972), was adapted for younger children by Klagsbrun and Bowlby (1976) and more recently revised and validated against observed attachment patterns by Kaplan (1984) and Slough and Greenberg (1991). Likewise, attachment-based, doll-story completion tasks for preschoolers were validated against behavioral measures by Bretherton, Ridgeway, and Cassidy (1990) and Cassidy (1988). In these tests, emotionally open responding tended to be associated with secure attachment classifications.

Finally, several authors have created interviews that examine attachment from the parental as opposed to the filial perspective (e.g., Bretherton et al., 1989; George and Solomon, 1989). In addition, Waters and Deane (1985) developed a Q-sort that can be used to assess a mother's internal working models of her child's attachment to her.

Attachment Across the Life Span

A related topic, attachment relationships between adults, began in the early 1970s with studies of adult bereavement (Bowlby and Parkes, 1970; Parkes, 1972) and marital separation (Weiss, 1973, 1977). More recently, interest in adult attachments has broadened to encompass marital relationships (Weiss, 1982, 1991) and has taken a further upsurge with work by Shaver and Hazan (1988), who translated Ainsworth's infant attachment patterns into adult patterns and pointed out that adults who describe themselves as secure, avoidant, or ambivalent with respect to romantic relationships report differing patterns of parent–child relationships in their families of origin. Finally, Cicirelli (1989, 1991) has applied attachment theory to the study of middle-aged siblings and their elderly parents. Much future work will be needed to delineate more fully the distinct qualities of child–adult, child–child, and adult–adult attachment relationships (see Ainsworth, 1989), as well as their interplay within the family system, a task begun by Byng-Hall (1985) and Marvin and Stewart (1990).

Attachment and Developmental Psychopathology

Attachment theory and research are also making a notable impact on the emerging field of developmental psychopathology (Sroufe, 1988), with longitudinal, attachment-based studies of families with depres-sion (Radke-Yarrow et al., 1985), of families with maltreatment (e.g., Crittenden, 1983; Schneider-Rosen et al., 1985; Cicchetti and Barnett, 1991), and of clinical interventions in families with low social support (Lieberman and Pawl, 1988; Spieker and Booth, 1988) and with behavior-problem children (Greenberg and Speltz, 1988). Much of this work is represented in a volume on clinical implications of attachment (Belsky and Nezworski, 1988). These topics hark back to Bowlby's seminal ideas from the 1930s, but they have been greatly enriched by Mary Ainsworth's notions on the origins of individual differences of attachment patterns.

The Ecology of Attachment

Although we have made progress in examining mother–child attachment, much work needs to be done with respect to studying attachment in the microsystem of family relationships (Bronfenbrenner, 1979). Despite studies by Belsky, Gilstrap, and Rovine (1984), Lamb (1978), and Parke and Tinsley (1987) that show fathers to be competent, if sometimes less than fully participant, attachment figures, we still have much to learn regarding father attachment. Another important topic, sibling attachment, has been tackled by a few researchers (e.g., Stewart and Marvin, 1984; Teti and Ablard, 1989), but triadic studies of attachment relationships (modeled on Dunn, 1988) are sorely lacking. Especially crucial are attachment-theoretic studies of loyalty conflicts, alliances by a dyad vis-à-vis a third family member, and enmeshment of a child in the spousal dyad, as exemplified in a report by Fish, Belsky, and Youngblade (1991) in which insecure attachment in infancy was associated with inappropriate involvement in spousal decision making at four years of age. Finally, the interrelations of child temperament and developing attachment relationships with other family members remain conceptually unclear despite intensive research efforts (Sroufe, 1985; Belsky and Rovine, 1987).

The documentation of family and social network factors as they affect attachment relations (e.g., Belsky, Rovine, and Taylor, 1984;

Belsky and Isabella, 1988) has been more successful. In the Pennsylvania project, attachment quality at the end of the first year was predictable from relative changes in levels of marital satisfaction after the child's birth, as well as from parental satisfaction with social support, not its frequency.

An ecological perspective also calls for an examination of issues related to dual-worker families, especially in view of the continued sex-gender differentiation of parenting. Some feminist theorists have interpreted attachment theory as supporting the traditional view of women as primary caregivers (Chodorow, 1978; Johnson, 1988). This is not strictly justified, because attachment theory does not specify that caregiving must be done by mothers or be restricted to females (Marris, 1982). Most central to healthy development, according to attachment theory, is infants' need for a committed caregiving relationship with one or a few adult figures. Although the majority of attachment studies have focused on mothers because mothers tend most often to fill this role, we do have evidence that infants can be attached to a hierarchy of figures, including fathers, grandparents, and siblings (Schaffer and Emerson, 1964), as well as to day-care providers (Howes et al., 1988). Our knowledge about the range of societal options for successfully sharing the task of bringing up children is, however, still woefully inadequate. The recent spate of studies documenting an increased risk of insecure attachment if day care begins in the first year and is extensive in duration (Belsky and Rovine, 1988; Belsky and Braungart, 1991) is worrisome and needs resolution. Cross-cultural studies of attachment and non-parental care in countries such as Sweden or Israel may ultimately provide more reliable answers.

Cross-Cultural Studies

Moving from family and other social networks to the larger societal matrix, studies of Strange Situation classifications in other cultures have sparked a lively debate on their universal versus culture-specific meaning. In a North German study, avoidant classifications were overrepresented (Grossmann et al., 1985), whereas ambivalent classifications were more frequent than expected in Israeli kibbutzim (Sagi et al., 1985) and in Japan (Miyake, Chen, and Campos, 1985).

Initially, these findings were interpreted in purely cultural terms. Thus, Grossmann et al. (1985) proposed that the high incidence of avoidant infants in Germany should not be attributed to parental rejection, but rather to a greater parental push toward infants' independence. Similarly, the high frequency of ambivalent classifications observed in Israeli kibbutzim and Japan was attributed to underexposure to strangers (Miyake et al., 1985; Sagi et al., 1985). Though persuasive on the surface, these explanations were not based on systematic assessments of parental beliefs and culturally guided practices.

More recently, van IJzendoorn and Kroonenberg (1988) examined the frequency distributions of Strange Situation classifications from over a thousand U.S. and cross-national studies and pointed out that valid conclusions about cross-national differences should not be drawn from single samples. In addition, intercorrelational patterns of home and Strange Situation behavior in North Germany (Grossmann et al., 1985) closely resembled those in Ainsworth's Baltimore study, at least, in part, undermining a purely cultural interpretation. Likewise, Sagi et al. (1991) attribute the abundance of ambivalent classifications to specific nighttime caregiving arrangements in the kibbutzim they studied, rather than to fewer experiences with strangers. Taken in combination, these findings suggest that Strange Situation classifications and hence the concept of parental sensitivity may have more cross-cultural validity in industrialized nations than was initially believed, but the issue is by no means resolved.

Systematic work on the more fascinating topic of how different cultures—especially non-Western cultures—fit attachment behaviors and relationships into their overall social organization has barely begun. There are, however, some tantalizing hints in the ethnographic literature (see Bretherton, 1985, for a review). For example, the Micronesian society of Tikopia (Firth, 1936) deliberately fosters attachment between an infant and its maternal uncle by prescribing face-to-face talk with the infant on a regular basis. This maternal uncle is destined to play an important quasi-parental role in the life of the child. Along somewhat different lines, Balinese mothers control their infants' exploratory behavior by using fake fear expressions to bring the infants back into close proximity to them (Bateson and Mead, 1942). In both cultures, a biological system is molded to a particular society's purposes (by fostering specific relationships or controlling exploration).

A recent study of parent–infant attachment among the Efe begins to provide systematic information in this area. The Efe, a seminomadic people, live in the African rain forest and subsist on foraging, horticulture, and hunting (Tronick, Winn, and Morelli, 1985). Young Efe infants receive more care (including nursing) from other adult women than from their own mother, except at night. Despite this multiple mothering system, by six months, infants begin to insist on a more focalized relationship with their own mothers, although other female caregivers continue to play a significant role. Tronick et al. attributed Efe practices to their living arrangements, with closely spaced dwellings that offer little privacy and that make cooperation and sharing highly valued behaviors. In sum, attachment behavior is heavily overlaid with cultural prescriptions, even in a society that much more closely resembles the conditions of human evolution than our own. To better explore such cultural variations in attachment organization, attachment researchers need to develop ecologically valid, theory-driven measures, tailored to specific cultures and based on a deeper knowledge of parents' and children's culture-specific folk theories about family relationships and attachment.

Attachment and Public Policy

Cultural differences in the regulation of attachment behaviors raise important questions about the value diverse societies place on attachment relations. In a thought-provoking chapter, Marris (1991) points to the fundamental tension between the desire to create a secure and predictable social order and the desire to maximize one's own opportunities at the expense of others. A good society, according to Marris, would, as far as humanly possible, minimize disruptive events, protect each child's experience of attachment from harm, and support family coping. Yet, in order to control uncertainty, individuals and families are tempted to achieve certainty at the expense of others (i.e., by imposing a greater burden of uncertainty on them or by providing fewer material and social resources). When powerful groups in society promote their own control over life circumstances by subordinating and marginalizing others, they make it less possible for these groups to offer and experience security in their own families. Valuing of attachment relations thus has public policy and moral implications for society, not just psychological implications for attachment dyads. This brings me back to one of Bowlby's (1951) early statements: "If a community values its children it must cherish their parents" (p. 84).

CHALLENGING TASKS FOR ATTACHMENT THEORY

In the preceding section I outlined the many new directions into which attachment research is branching out. It is difficult to predict which of these efforts will be most fruitful. No doubt, additions, revisions, and challenges to the theory will continue to arise out of future empirical studies.

In this final section, however, I focus briefly on some of the theoretical tasks that lie ahead. The idea that human motivation derives from an interplay of familiarity- and novelty-seeking systems needs further exploration, as does the notion that the human personality can be conceptualized as a hierarchy of interlinked systems. New theoretical treatments of defensive processes in the construction of internal working models of attachment need to be worked out in relation to insights from representational theories and research, and clinical attachment theory requires the development of an experiential language akin to that used by other psychoanalytic theories of interpersonal relatedness, such as Winnicott's (1965) and Sullivan's (1953). Most important, in my view, the development of internal working models of self and other within-attachment relations should be studied in conjunction with new approaches to the "dialogic" or "narrative" self, integrating the mental health perspective of attachment theory with the perspective of theorists interested in the social construction of reality (Hermans, Kempen, and van Loon, 1992).

These theoretical developments must go hand in hand with, or be followed by, new methodological developments. Without Mary Ainsworth's work on patterns of attachment in the Strange Situation and Mary Main's Adult Attachment Interview, which built on them, Bowlby's theoretical contributions to developmental and clinical psychology would not have had their current influence.

I predict that, in the future, attachment theory may provide the underpinnings of a more general theory of personality organization and relationship development, built on but going beyond Bowlby's reworking of Freud's ideas on motivation, emotion, and development (see also Ainsworth, 1991).

In formulating the basic tenets of attachment theory, Bowlby's strategy was, wherever possible, meticulously to test intuitive hunches against available empirical findings and concepts from related domains, thus keeping the theory open to change. In his last work—a biography of Charles Darwin—Bowlby (1991) might have been talking about himself when he said of Darwin: "Since causes are never manifest, the only way of proceeding is to propose a plausible theory and then test its explanatory powers against further evidence, and in comparison with the power of rival theories. . . . Since most theories prove to be untenable, advancing them is a hazardous business and requires courage, a courage Darwin never lacked" (p. 412). Bowlby and Ainsworth did not lack that courage either. To explore the full future potential of attachment theory, others will need to exercise similar courage in refining, extending, and challenging it.

REFERENCES

Ainsworth, M. D. S. (1963), The development of infant–mother interaction among the Ganda. In: *Determinants of Infant Behavior*, ed. B. M. Foss. New York: Wiley, pp. 67–104.

—— (1967), *Infancy in Uganda*. Baltimore, MD: Johns Hopkins University Press.

—— (1968), Object relations, dependency, and attachment: A theoretical review of the infant–mother relationship. *Child Devel.*, 40:969–1025.

—— (1974), Citation for the G. Stanley Hall Award to John Bowlby. Unpublished manuscript.

—— (1982), Attachment: retrospect and prospect. In: *The Place of Attachment in Human Behavior*, ed. C. M. Parkes & J. Stevenson-Hinde. New York: Basic Books, pp. 3–30.

—— (1983), A sketch of a career. In: *Models of Achievement*, ed. A. N. O'Connoll & N. F. Russo. New York: Columbia University Press, pp. 200–219.

—— (1989), Attachments beyond infancy. *Amer. Psychol.*, 44:709–716.

—— & Bell, S. M. (1969), Some contemporary patterns in the feeding situation. In: *Stimulation in Early Infancy*, ed. A. Ambrose. London: Academic Press, pp. 133–170.

—— & —— (1970), Attachment, exploration, and separation: Illustrated by the behavior of one-year-olds in a strange situation. *Child Devel.*, 41:49–67.

—— —— Blehar, M. C. & Main, M. (1971), Physical contact: A study of infant responsiveness and its relation to maternal handling. Presented at biennial meeting of the Society for Research in Child Development, Minneapolis.

—— —— & Stayton, D. J. (1971), Individual differences in strange situation behavior of one-year-olds. In: *The Origins of Human Social Relations*, ed. H. R. Schaffer. London: Academic Press, pp. 17–57.

—— —— & —— (1974), Infant–mother attachment and social development. In: *The Introduction of the Child into a Social World*, ed. M. P. Richards. London: Cambridge University Press, pp. 99–135.

—— Blehar, M.C., Waters, E. & Wall, S. (1978), *Patterns of Attachment*. Hillsdale, NJ: Lawrence Erlbaum Associates.

—— & Bowlby, J. (1991), An ethological approach to personality development. *Amer. Psychol.*, 46:331–341.

—— & Wittig, B. A. (1969), Attachment and the exploratory behaviour of one-year-olds in a strange situation. In: *Determinants of Infant Behaviour, Vol. 4*, ed. B. M. Foss. London: Methuen, pp. 113–136.

Ambrose, J. A. (1961), The development of the smiling response in early human infancy: An experimental and theoretical study of their course and significance. Unpublished doctoral dissertation, University of London.

Arsenian, J. M. (1943), Young children in an insecure situation. *J. Abn. Soc. Psychol.*, 38:225–229.

Bateson, G. & Mead, M. (1942), *Balinese Character*. New York: New York Academy of Sciences.

Bell, S. M. (1970), The development of the concept of the object as related to infant–mother attachment. *Child Devel.*, 41:291–311.

—— & Ainsworth, M. D. S. (1972), Infant crying and maternal responsiveness. *Child Devel.*, 43:1171–1190.

Belsky, J. & Braungart, J. M. (1991), Are insecure–avoidant infants with extensive day-care experience less stressed by and more independent in the strange situation? *Child Devel.*, 62:567–571.

—— Gilstrap, B. & Rovine, M. (1984), The Pennsylvania Infant and Family Development Project, 1: Stability and change in mother–infant and father–infant interaction in a family setting at one, three, and nine months. *Child Devel.*, 55:692–705.

—— & Isabella, R. (1988), Maternal, infant, and social-contextual determinants of attachment security. In: *Clinical Implications of Attachment*, ed. J. Belsky & T. Nezworski. Hillsdale, NJ: Lawrence Erlbaum Associates, pp. 41–94.

—— & Nezworski, T (1988), *Clinical Implications of Attachment*. Hillsdale, NJ: Lawrence Erlbaum Associates.

—— & Rovine, M. J. (1987), Temperament and attachment security in the strange situation: An empirical rapprochement. *Child Devel.*, 58:787–795.

—— & —— (1988), Nonmaternal care in the first year of life and the security of infant–mother attachment. *Child Devel.*, 59:157–167.

—— —— & Fish, M. (in press), The developing family system. In: *Systems and Development: Minnesota Symposia on Child Development, Vol. 22*, ed. M. Gunnar. Hillsdale, NJ: Lawrence Erlbaum Associates.

—— —— & Taylor, D. (1984), The Pennsylvania Infant and Family Development Project, 2: Origins of individual differences in infant–mother attachment: Maternal and infant contributions. *Child Devel.*, 55:706–717.

Blatz, W. (1940), *Hostages to Peace*. New York: Morrow.

—— (1966), *Human Security*. Toronto, Canada: University of Toronto Press.

Blehar, M. C. (1974), Anxious attachment and defensive reactions associated with day care. *Child Devel.*, 45:683–692.

—— Lieberman, A. F. & Ainsworth, M. D. S. (1977), Early face-to-face interaction and its relation to later infant–mother attachment. *Child Devel.*, 48:182–194.

Bowlby, J. (1940), The influence of early environment in the development of neurosis and neurotic character. *Internat. J. Psycho-Anal.*, 21:1–25.

—— (1944), Forty-four juvenile thieves: Their characters and home lives. *Internat. J. Psycho-Anal.*, 25:19–52.

—— (1949), The study and reduction of group tensions in the family. *Human Rel.*, 2:123–128.

—— J. (1951), Maternal care and mental health. *World Health Organization Monograph* (Serial No. 2).

—— (1958), The nature of the child's tie to his mother. *Internat. J. Psycho-Anal.*, 39:1–23.

—— (1959), Separation anxiety. *Internat. J. Psycho-Anal.*, 41:1–25.

—— (1960), Grief and mourning in infancy and early childhood. *The Psychoanalytic Study of the Child*, 15:3–39. New York: International Universities Press.

—— (1962a), *Defences that follow loss: Causation and function.* Unpublished manuscript, Tavistock Child Development Research Unit, London.

—— (1962b), *Loss, detachment and defence.* Unpublished manuscript, Tavistock Child Development Research Unit, London.

—— (1965), *Child Care and the Growth of Love*. Harmondsworth, England: Pelican Books.

—— (1969), *Attachment and Loss, Vol. 1*. New York: Basic Books.

—— (1973), *Attachment and Loss, Vol. 2*. New York: Basic Books.

—— (1980a), *Attachment and Loss, Vol. 3*. New York: Basic Books.

—— (1980b), By ethology out of psycho-analysis: An experiment in interbreeding. *An. Behav.*, 28:649–656.

—— (1987), Colloquium presented at the University of Virginia.

—— (1988), *A Secure Base*. New York: Basic Books.

—— (1991), *Charles Darwin*. London: Hutchinson.

—— Ainsworth, M., Boston, M. & Rosenbluth, D. (1956), The effects of mother–child separation: A follow-up study. *Brit. J. Med. Psychol.*, 29:211–247.

—— & Parkes, C. M. (1970), Separation and loss within the family. In: *The Child in His Family*, ed. E. J. Anthony & C. Koupernik. New York: Wiley, pp. 197–216.

Bretherton, I. (1985), Attachment theory: Retrospect and prospect. In: *Growing Points of Attachment Theory and Research*, ed. I. Bretherton & E. Waters. *Monographs of the Society for Research in Child Development*, Serial No. 209, Vol. 50, Nos. 1–2, pp. 3–35.

—— (1987), New perspectives on attachment relations: Security, communication, and internal working models. In: *Handbook of Infant Development*, ed. J. Osofsky. New York: Wiley, pp. 1061–1100.

—— (1990), Open communication and internal working models: Their role in attachment relationships. In: *Socioemotional Development (Nebraska Symposium 1987)*, ed. R. Thompson. Lincoln: University of Nebraska Press.

—— (1991), Pouring new wine into old bottles: The social self as internal working model. In: *Self Processes and Development: Minnesota Symposia on Child Psychology*, Vol. 23,, ed. M. R. Gunnar & L. A. Sroufe. Hillsdale, NJ: Lawrence Erlbaum Associates, pp. 1–41.

—— & Ainsworth, M. D. S. (1974), One-year-olds in the strange situation. In: *The Origins of Fear*, ed. M. Lewis & L. Rosenblum. New York: Wiley, pp. 134–164.

—— Biringen, Z., Ridgeway, D., Maslin, M. & Sherman, M. (1989), Attachment: The parental perspective. *Infant Ment. Health J.*, 10:203–220.

—— Ridgeway, D. & Cassidy, J. (1990), Assessing internal working models in the attachment relationship: An attachment story completion task for 3-year-olds. In: *Attachment during the Preschool Years*, ed. M. T. Greenberg, D. Cicchetti, & E. M. Cummings. Chicago: University of Chicago Press, pp. 272–308.

—— & Waters, E., ed. (1985), *Growing Points of Attachment Theory and Research. Monographs of the Society for Research in Child Develo*pment. Serial No. 209, Vol. 50, Nos. 1 & 2.

Bronfenbrenner, V. (1979), *The Ecology of Human Development*. Cambridge, MA: Harvard University Press.

Byng-Hall, J. (1985), The family script: A useful bridge between theory and practice. *J. Fam. Ther.*, 7:301–305.

Cain, A. C. & Fast, I. (1972), Children's disturbed reactions to parent suicide. In: *Survivors of Suicide*, ed. A. C. Cain. Springfield, IL: Charles C. Thomas, pp. 93–111.

Cassidy, J. (1988), The self as related to child–mother attachment at six. *Child Devel.*, 59:121–134.

Chodorow, N. (1978), *The Reproduction of Mothering*. Berkeley: University of California Press.

Cicchetti, D. & Barnett, D. (1991), Attachment organization in maltreated preschoolers. *Devel. Psychopathol.*, 3:397–411.

Cicirelli, V. G. (1989), Feelings of attachment to siblings and well-being in later life. *Psychol. Aging*, 4:211–216.

—— (1991), Attachment theory in old age: Protection of the attached figure. In: *Parent–Child Relations Across the Life Course*, ed. K. Pillemer & K. McCartney. Hillsdale, NJ: Lawrence Erlbaum Associates, pp. 25–42.

Craik, K. (1943), *The Nature of Explanation*. Cambridge: Cambridge University Press.

Crittenden, P. M. (1983), The effect of mandatory protective daycare on mutual attachment in maltreating mother–infant dyads. *Child Abuse Neglect*, 7:297–300.

Cummings, E. M. (1980), Caregiver stability and day care. *Devel. Psychol.*, 16:31–37.

Dixon, N. F. (1971), *Subliminal Perception*. London: McGraw-Hill.

Dunn, J. (1988), *The Beginnings of Social Understanding*. Cambridge, MA: Harvard University Press.

Erdelyi, H. M. (1974), A new look at the new look: Perceptual defense and vigilance. *Psychol. Rev.*, 81:1–25.

Erikson, E. (1950), *Childhood and Society*. New York: Norton.

Fairbairn, W. R. D. (1952), *An Object-Relations Theory of the Personality*. New York: Basic Books.

Firth, R. (1936), *We, the Tikopia*. London: Allen & Unwin.

Fish, M., Belsky, J. & Youngblade, L. (1991), Developmental antecedents and measurement of intergenerational boundary violation in a nonclinic sample. *Fam. Psychol.*, 4:278–297.

Fonagy, P., Steele, M. & Steele, H. (1991), Intergenerational patterns of attachment: Maternal representations during pregnancy and subsequent infant–mother attachments. *Child Devel.*, 62:891–905.

Foss, B. M. (1961), *Determinants of Infant Behaviour, Vol. 1*. London: Methuen.

—— (1963), *Determinants of Infant Behaviour, Vol. 2*. London: Methuen.

—— (1965), *Determinants of Infant Behaviour, Vol. 3*. London: Methuen.

—— (1969), *Determinants of Infant Behaviour, Vol. 4*. London: Methuen.

Freud, A. (1960), Discussion of Dr. John Bowlby's paper. *The Psychoanalytic Study of the Child*, 15:53–62. New York: International Universities Press.

Freud, S. (1905), *Three Essays on the Theory of Sexuality. Standard Edition*, 7:125–245. London: Hogarth Press, 1953.

—— (1920), *The Psychogenesis of a Case of Homosexuality in a Woman. Standard Edition*, 18:145–172. London: Hogarth Press, 1955.

—— (1923), The ego and the id. *Standard Edition*, 19:3–66. London: Hogarth Press, 1961.

—— (1926), *Inhibitions, Symptoms and Anxiety. Standard Edition*, 20:77–175. London: Hogarth Press, 1959.

—— (1940), An outline of psycho-analysis. *Standard Edition*, 23:141–207. London: Hogarth Press, 1964.

George, C., Kaplan, N. & Main, M. (1984), Adult attachment interview. Unpublished manuscript, University of California, Berkeley.

—— & Solomon, J. (1989), Internal working models of parenting and security of attachment at age six. *Infant Ment. Health J.*, 10:222–237.

Goldfarb, W. (1943), The effects of early institutional care on adolescent personality. *J. Exper. Ed.*, 14:441–447.

—— (1945), Psychological privation in infancy and subsequent adjustment. *Amer. J. Orthopsychiat.*, 15:247–255.

Greenberg, M. T. & Marvin, R. S. (1979), Attachment patterns in profoundly deaf preschool children. *Merrill-Palmer Quart.*, 25:265–279.

—— & M. Speltz, M. (1988), Attachment and the ontogeny of conduct problems. In: *Clinical Implications of Attachment*, ed. J. Belsky & T. Nezworski. Hillsdale, NJ: Lawrence Erlbaum Associates, pp. 177–218.

Grosskurth, P. (1987), *Melanie Klein*. Cambridge, MA: Harvard University Press.

Grossmann, K., Grossmann, K. E., Spangler, G. Suess, G. & Unzner, L. (1985), Maternal sensitivity and newborns' orientation responses as related to quality of attachment in northern Germany. *Growing Points of Attachment Theory and Research*, ed. I. Bretherton & E. Waters. *Monographs of the Society for Research in Child Development*, Serial No. 209, Vol. 50, Nos. 1–2, pp. 233–256.

Grossmann, K. E. & Grossmann, K. (1990), The wider concept of attachment in cross-cultural research. *Human Devel.*, 13:31–47.

Hansburg, H. G. (1972), *Adolescent Separation Anxiety*. Springfield, IL: Charles C. Thomas.

Harlow, H. F. (1961), The development of affectional patterns in infant monkeys. In: *Determinants of Infant Behaviour*, ed. B. M. Foss. London: Methuen, pp. 75–97.

—— & Zimmermann, R. R. (1958), The development of affective responsiveness in infant monkeys. *Proceedings Amer. Philosoph. Soc.*, 102:501–509.

Heinicke, C. M. (1956), Some effects of separating two-year-olds from their parents: A comparative study. *Human Rel.*, 9:105–176.

—— & Westheimer, I. (1966), *Brief Separations*. New York: International Universities Press.

Hermans, H. J. M., Kempen, H. J. G. & van Loon, R. J. P. (1992), The dialogic self. *Amer. Psychol.*, 47:23–33.

Hinde, R. A. (1991), Relationships, attachment, and culture: A tribute to John Bowlby. *Infant Ment. Health J.*, 12:154–163.

—— & Spencer-Booth, Y. (1967), The effect of social companions on mother–infant relations in rhesus monkeys. In: *Primate Ethology*, ed. D. Morris. London: Weidenfeld & Nicolson, pp. 267–286.

Howes, C., Rodning, C., Galluzzo, D. C. & Myers, L. (1988), Attachment and child care: Relationships with mother and caregiver. *Early Child. Res. Quart.*, 3:403–416.

Johnson, M. M. (1988), *Strong Mothers, Weak Wives*. Berkeley: University of California Press.

Kaplan, N. (1984), Internal representations of separation experiences in six-year-olds: Related to actual experiences of separation. Unpublished master's thesis, University of California, Berkeley.

Klagsbrun, M. & Bowlby, J. (1976), Responses to separation from parents: A clinical test for young children. *Brit. J. Proj. Psychol.*, 21:7–21.

Klein, M. (1932), *The Psycho-Analysis of Children*. London: Hogarth Press.

Klopfer, B., Ainsworth, M. D., Klopfer, W. F. & Holt, R. R. (1954), *Developments in the Rorschach Technique, Vol. 1*. Yonkers-on-Hudson, NY: World Book.

Kobak, R. R. & Sceery, A. (1988), Attachment in late adolescence: Working models, affect regulation, and perceptions of self and others. *Child Devel.*, 59:135–146.

Kotelchuck, M. (1972), The nature of the child's tie to his father. Unpublished doctoral dissertation, Harvard University.

Kubler-Ross, E. (1970), *On Death and Dying*. London: Tavistock.

Lamb, M. E. (1978), Qualitative aspects of mother–infant and father–infant attachments in the second year of life. *Infant Behav. Devel.*, 1:265–275.

Lieberman, A. (1977), Preschoolers' competence with a peer: Relations with attachment and peer experience. *Child Devel.*, 48:1277–1287.

—— & Pawl, J. H. (1988), Clinical applications of attachment theory. In: *Clinical Applications of Attachment*, ed. J. Belsky & T. Nezworski. Hillsdale, NJ: Lawrence Erlbaum Associates, pp. 327–351.

Lorenz, K. Z. (1935), Der Kumpan in der Umwelt des Vogels [The companion in the bird's world]. *Journal fuer Ornithologie*, 83:137–213. (Abbreviated English translation published 1937 in *Auk*, 54:245–273.)

Main, M. (1973), Exploration, play, and cognitive functioning as related to child-mother attachment. Unpublished doctoral dissertation, Johns Hopkins University.

—— & Goldwyn, R. (in press), Interview-based adult attachment classifications: Related to infant–mother and infant–father attachment. *Devel. Psychol.*

—— Kaplan, K. & Cassidy, J. (1985), Security in infancy, childhood and adulthood: A move to the level of representation. In: *Growing Points of Attachment Theory and Research*, ed., I. Bretherton & E. Waters. *Monographs of the Society for Research in Child Development*, Serial No. 209, Vol. 50, Nos. 1–2, pp. 66–104.

Marris, P. (1958), *Widows and Their Families*. London: Routledge.

—— (1982), Attachment and society. In: *The Place of Attachment in Human Behavior*, ed. C. M. Parkes & J. Stevenson-Hinde. New York: Basic Books, pp. 185–201.

—— (1991), The social construction of uncertainty. In: *Attachment across the Life Cycle*, ed. C. M. Parkes, J. Stevenson-Hinde, & P. Marris. London: Routledge, pp. 77–90.

Marvin, R. S. (1972), Attachment and cooperative behavior in 2-, 3-, and 4-year-olds. Unpublished doctoral dissertation, University of Chicago.

—— (1977), An ethological-cognitive model for the attenuation of mother–child attachment behavior. In: *Advances in the Study of Communication and Affect*, Vol. 3, ed. T. M. Alloway, L. Krames & P. Pliner. New York: Plenum Press, pp. 25–60.

—— & Stewart, R. B. (1990), A family system framework for the study of attachment. In: *Attachment beyond the Preschool Years*, ed. M. Greenberg, D. Cicchetti & M. Cummings. Chicago: University of Chicago Press, pp. 51–86.

Matas, L., Arend, R. A. & Sroufe, L. A. (1978), Continuity and adaptation in the second year: The relationship between quality of attachment and later competence. *Child Devel.*, 49:547–556.

Miller, G. A., Galanter, E. & Pribram, K. H. (1960), *Plans and the Structure of Behavior*. New York: Holt, Rinehart & Winston.

Miyake, K., Chen, S. & Campos, J. (1985), Infants' temperament, mothers' mode of interaction and attachment in Japan: An interim report. In: *Growing Points of Attachment Theory and Research*, ed. I. Bretherton & E. Waters. *Monographs of the Society for Research in Child Development*, Serial No. 209, Vol. 50, Nos. 1–2, pp. 276–297.

Parke, R. D. & Tinsley, B. J. (1987), Family interaction in infancy. In: *Handbook of Infant Development*, ed. J. D. Osofsky. New York: Wiley, pp. 579–641.

Parkes, C. M. (1972), *Bereavement*. New York: International Universities Press.

Piaget, J. (1951), *The Origin of Intelligence in Children*. New York: International Universities Press.

—— (1954), *The Construction of Reality in the Child*. New York: Basic Books.

Radke-Yarrow, M., Cummings, E. M., Kuczinsky, L. & Chapman, M. (1985), Patterns of attachment in two- and three-year-olds in normal families and families with parental depression. *Child Devel.*, 56:884–893.

Rayner, E. (1991), John Bowlby's contribution: A brief summary. Presented at meeting of the British Psychoanalytic Society, London.

Robertson, J. (1953a), *A Two-Year-Old Goes to Hospital* [Film]. Tavistock Child Development Research Unit, London (available through the Penn State Audiovisual Services, University Park, PA).

—— (1953b), Some responses of young children to loss of maternal care. *Nursing Care*, 49:382–386.

—— & Bowlby, J. (1952), Responses of young children to separation from their mothers. *Courrier Centre, Internationale Enfance, Paris*, 2:131–140.

Sagi, A., Aviezer, O., Mayseless, O., Donnell, F. & Joels, T. (1991), Infant-mother attachment in traditional and nontraditional kibbutzim. Presented at biennial meeting of the Society for Research in Child Development, Seattle.

—— Lamb, M. E., Lewkowicz, K. S., Shoham, R., Dvir, R. & Estes, D. (1985), Security of infant–mother, –father, and –metapelet among kibbutz reared Israeli children. In: *Growing Points of Attachment Theory and Research*, ed. I. Bretherton & E. Waters. *Monographs of the Society for Research in Child Development*, Serial No. 209, Vol. 50, Nos. 1–2, pp. 257–275.

Salter, M. D. (1940), *An Evaluation of Adjustment Based upon the Concept of Security*. Toronto, Canada: University of Toronto Press.

Schaffer, H. R. & Emerson, P. E. (1964), *The Development of Social Attachments in Infancy. Monographs of the Society for Research in Child Development*. Serial No. 94, Vol. 29.

Schneider-Rosen, K., Braunwald, K. G., Carlson, V. & Cicchetti, D. (1985), Current perspectives in attachment theory: Illustration from the study of maltreated infants. In: *Growing Points of Attachment Theory and Research*, ed. I. Bretherton & E.

Waters. *Monographs of the Society for Research in Child Development*, Serial No. 209, Vol. 50, Nos. 1–2, pp. 194–210.

Schur, M. (1960), Discussion of Dr. John Bowlby's paper. *The Psychoanalytic Study of the Child*, 15:63–84. New York: International Universities Press.

Senn, M. J. E. (1977a), *Interview with James Robertson*. Unpublished manuscript, National Library of Medicine, Washington, DC.

—— (1977b), *Interview with John Bowlby*. Unpublished manuscript, National Library of Medicine, Washington, DC.

Shaver, P. R. & Hazan, C. (1988), A biased overview of the study of love. *J. Soc. Pers. Rel.*, 5:473–501.

Slough, N. & Greenberg, M. (1991), 5-year-olds' representations of separation from parents: Responses for self and a hypothetical child. In: *Children's Perspectives on the Family*, ed. W. Damon, I. Bretherton & M. Watson. San Francisco: Jossey-Bass, pp. 67–84.

Spieker, S. & Booth, C. (1988), Maternal antecedents of attachment quality. In: *Clinical Implications of Attachment*, ed. J. Belsky & T. Nezworski. Hillsdale, NJ: Lawrence Erlbaum Associates, pp. 95–135.

Spitz, R. A. (1946), Anaclitic depression. *The Psychoanalytic Study of the Child*, 2:313–342. New York: International Universities Press.

—— (1947), *Grief: A Peril in Infancy* [Film]. University of Akron Psychology Archives, Akron, OH (available through the Penn State Audiovisual Services, University Park, PA).

—— (1960), Discussion of Dr. John Bowlby's paper. *The Psychoanalytic Study of the Child*, 15:85–208. New York: International Universities Press.

Sroufe, L. A. (1983), Infant–caregiver attachment and patterns of adaptation in preschool: The roots of maladaptation and competence. In: *Minnesota Symposium in Child Psychology, Vol. 16*, ed. M. Perlmutter. Hillsdale, NJ: Lawrence Erlbaum Associates, pp. 41–81.

—— (1985), Attachment classification from the perspective of infant–caregiver relationships and infant temperament. *Child Devel.*, 56:1–14.

—— (1988), The role of infant–caregiver attachment in adult development. In: *Clinical Implications of Attachment*, ed. J. Belsky & T. Nezworski. Hillsdale, NJ: Lawrence Erlbaum Associates, pp. 18–38.

—— & Waters, E. (1977), Attachment as an organizational construct. *Child Devel.*, 49:1184–1199.

Stayton, D. & Ainsworth, M. D. S. (1973), Development of separation behavior in the first year of life. *Devel. Psychol.*, 9:226–235.

—— Hogan, R. & Ainsworth, M. D. S. (1973), Infant obedience and maternal behavior: The origins of socialization reconsidered. *Child Devel.*, 42:1057–1070.

Stewart, R. B. & Marvin, R. S. (1984), Sibling relations: The role of conceptual perspective-taking in the ontogeny of sibling caregiving. *Child Devel.*, 55:1322–1332.

Sullivan, H. S. (1953), *The Interpersonal Theory of Psychiatry*. New York: Norton.

Teti, D. M. & Ablard, K. E. (1989), Security of attachment and infant–sibling relationships: A laboratory study. *Child Devel.*, 60:1519–1528.

Tinbergen, N. (1951), *The Study of Instinct*. London: Clarendon Press.

Tracy, R. L. & Ainsworth, M. D. S. (1981), Maternal affectionate behavior and infant–mother attachment patterns. *Child Devel.*, 52:1341–1343.

—— Lamb, M. E. & Ainsworth, M. D. S. (1976), Infant approach behavior as related to attachment. *Child Devel.*, 47:571–578.

Tronick, E. Z., Winn, S., & Morelli, G. A. (1985), Multiple caretaking in the context of human evolution: Why don't the Efe know the Western prescription to child care?

In: *The Psychobiology of Attachment and Separation*, ed. M. Reite & T. Field. San Diego, CA: Academic Press, pp. 293–321.

Tulving, E. (1972), Episodic and semantic memory. In: *Organization of Memory*, ed. E. Tulving & W. Donaldson. San Diego, CA: Academic Press, pp. 382–403.

Van IJzendoorn, M. H. & Kroonenberg, P. M. (1988), Cross-cultural patterns of attachment: A meta-analysis of the strange situation. *Child Devel.*, 59:147–156.

Waddington, C. H. (1957), *The Strategy of the Genes*. London: Allen & Unwin.

Ward, M. J., Carlson, E. A., Altman, S., Levine, L., Greenberg, R. H. & Kessler, D. B. (1990), Predicting infant-mother attachment from adolescents' prenatal working models of relationships. Presented at the Seventh International Conference on Infant Studies, Montreal.

Waters, E. (1978), The reliability and stability of individual differences in infant–mother attachment. *Child Devel.*, 49:520–616.

—— & Deane, K. E. (1985), Defining and assessing individual differences in attachment relationships: Q-methodology and the organization of behavior in infancy and early childhood. *Growing Points of Attachment Theory and Research*, ed. I. Bretherton & E. Waters. *Monographs of the Society for Research in Child Development*, Serial No. 209, Vol. 50, Nos. 1–2, pp. 41–65.

Weiss, R. S. (1973), *Loneliness*. Cambridge, MA: MIT Press.

—— (1977), *Marital Separation*. New York: Basic Books.

—— (1982), Attachment in adult life. In: *The Place of Attachment in Human Behavior*, ed. C. M. Parkes & J. Stevenson-Hinde. New York: Wiley, pp. 171–184.

—— (1991), The attachment bond in childhood and adulthood. In: *Attachment across the Life Cycle*, ed. C. M. Parkes, J. Stevenson-Hinde & P. Marris. London: Routledge, pp. 66–76.

Winnicott, D. W. (1965), *The Maturational Process and the Facilitating Environment*. New York: International Universities Press.

Young, J. Z. (1964), *A Model for the Brain*. London: Oxford University Press.

4

The Evolution and History of Attachment Research and Theory

KLAUS E. GROSSMANN

In the broadest sense, attachment theory is predicated on an investment in the psychological well-being of children and their parents. Such an investment cannot thrive in an atmosphere of indifference or despair. For adults to be motivated to interact sensitively with their infants, they must have a degree of respect for life–their own and that of significant others–based on a minimum of material and psychological security. Parents must possess a degree of self-confidence and optimism toward the future; they must be able to see life as worth pursuing beyond their own generation and beyond their own individual interests. Poverty, social isolation, a grim life perspective, unemployment, threats of war, epidemics and illnesses with little hope for cures, famine and pestilence–all these dramatically undercut the capacity for generating unconditional love toward oneself, one's partner, or one's children.

Child-rearing practices and the fate of children have been the subject of only minimal documentation over the course of human history. Perhaps the earliest recorded remarks on the subject of child rearing are those of Plato (1959) in his Dialogue on the "movements of the soul" over the life span (Laws, Book 7, 3). Plato postulates that training at a very early age can contribute to the "virtue" of the infant's soul. Caretakers should try to sense what the child wants, Plato writes, by evaluating the infant's response to their ministrations: "If the child is silent upon these offerings, then it is good; if, however, the child cries and screams, it is not good" (p. 162). Plato specifically notes that the communication by the infant that something feels teasing or unpleasant constitutes an important message to the caretaker. About this period in the child's development in general, Plato observes that it "lasts no less than three years, no small part of life to spend for better or worse" (p. 162).

I would like to thank my colleague and closest collaborator, Karin Grossmann, for her patience and support during my excursions into history.

Only recently have a few historians ventured to survey the available documentation in an attempt to reconstruct the realities of childhood over the course of the preceding centuries (see Ariès, 1975). Among them, deMause (1974) has emphasized the cruel treatment of infants and children during the Dark Ages. Similarly, Badinter (1984) has provided ample evidence for the sheer absence of "mother love" during the 17th and early 18th centuries, as a prelude to her attempt to outline how social changes subsequently allowed modern mother love to develop. Similarly, Shorter (1975) has attempted to trace the change in attitudes from a traditional indifference toward children and others to the sense of mutual concern between partners that led to the birth of the modern family. Imhof (1984), using demographic data, has documented a relationship between epochal traumas in different historical periods and a rise in indifference to close human relationships, most especially in regard to one's own family. All these studies have been forced to rely on deplorably inconclusive documentation that is biased in various ways. Nonetheless, there is considerable agreement among historians as to the facts of widespread neglect, indifference, maltreatment, sexual abuse, and abandonment of infants and children over the ages, particularly during the 18th and early 19th centuries.

In this general context, the recent emergence of attachment theory is embedded in the psychological consequences of modern cultural history. As a scientific discipline, however, attachment research is rooted in natural history, more specifically, in Darwinian evolutionary theory. Perspectives of both cultural and natural history must be kept in mind. What parents do to their offspring is an expression of their biological endowment, but it is also an expression of what they know and feel about themselves in any given period of history. Beyond biological factors, parenting is anchored in cultural and subcultural settings with culture-specific control mechanisms, plans, prescriptions, rules, and instructions designed to direct and control human behavior. These prescriptive rules and attitudes are shared by all, or at least most, of a society's members and, via parenting practices, are communicated to the next generation. Considered from an anthropological perspective, attachment relationships constitute the very foundation for the child's entry and socialization into the qualitatively specific type of engagements between people—emotional, communicative, and supportive—that is characteristic of a given culture.

It is important, obviously, to understand how negligence, hate, indifference, anxiety, and destructive selfishness could become cultural norms whose devastating and even fatal consequences for infants and children create a vicious chain of transmission across uncounted generations. It is perhaps even more important, however, to understand the necessary historical, cultural, and social conditions that allow loving relationships to emerge and thereby foster care, concern, and a sense of constructive meaning toward one's offspring—the preconditions for promoting their capacity for mutuality and for living well-balanced individual lives. In this respect, attachment theory potentially goes beyond being an academic discipline and acquires its own prescriptive social significance—and thus represents its own step in cultural evolution. To be sure, even in antiquity the value of living a well-balanced life was well understood, and the means of achieving it received great attention. But such wisdom was not based on a scientific understanding derived from empirical data, nor did it apply to infants, to those "unable to speak."

BIOLOGICAL FOUNDATIONS OF ATTACHMENT

John Bowlby conceptualized the attachment bond between infants and their caretakers as constituting part of a universal biological endowment that derived from the natural history of mankind. The infant's attachment bond develops through several stages. Individualized attachment to particular caretakers is clearly recognizable at around 6 months of age and appears to be fully developed around 12 months, being greatly enhanced by stranger anxiety, which is prominent by this age. Significant attachment figures serve as secure bases for the infant; with these figures he or she can seek refuge, and from them he or she can carefully and cautiously start exploring for knowledge. As Bowlby (1969) noted, the original selective pressure in evolution fostering this pattern of behavior in the infant was undoubtedly protection from predators.

Writing from an ethological perspective, the Tinbergens have provided compelling descriptions of infants oscillating between communication with, and physical closeness to, attachment figures and exploration of the environment, including investigation of objects and even strangers, during the latter half of the first year (Tinbergen and Tinbergen, 1972). Harry Harlow, working, in part, in collaboration with Bowlby, provided an empirical foundation for our understanding of the mechanisms involved, which create a balance between attachment and exploratory behaviors, from a naturalistic perspective as well as from comparative experiments. In an old film from the 1950s, Harlow showed what happens if a rhesus infant is frightened by a noisy toy car or by an oversized wooden grasshopper. In those days learning theory predicted that the infant should run away in panic, as rats do when shocked in electrically charged

runways. Moreover, according to theory, the infants would be motivated to learn to solve problems in order to escape. To the contrary,
however, Harlow demonstrated that in the presence of a "caretaker," the monkey infants would even venture to approach the fear-
eliciting stimulus if there was no other way to get close to, or in
touch with, their secure base, which in Harlow's experiments consisted only of terry-cloth cylinders with wooden heads. Harlow
(1971) described his findings in terms of an "affectionate system"
existing in rhesus between mother and infant.

Bowlby portrayed attachment behavior as "environmentally
stable" in an overall context of evolutionary adaptedness. As a biologist with a strong evolutionary bent, Bowlby was looking for universals. Yet, as a clinician, he was simultaneously on the lookout for
individual differences, and he remained keenly aware of deviations
from optimal biological norms that might result in individual maladjustment. The tension between these two perspectives runs like a
red thread throughout his scholarly writings, from his early retrospective study on 44 juvenile thieves in the 1940s (Bowlby, 1946) to
his late paper, "Developmental Psychiatry Comes of Age" (1988b).

Sensitivity to the Infant's Signals

Even prior to Bowlby's work, the Swiss biological anthropologist
Adolf Portmann (1956) had observed that the playful development
of preverbal communication between infant and mother during
physiologically immature stages provides the infant with a robust
ability, grounded in ever more differentiated emotions and emotional expressiveness, to communicate with adults. Colwyn
Trevarthen (1987) has put the matter succinctly: young brains are
designed to learn from older brains. This innate ability to learn, in
turn, interfaces with the availability of attachment figures who
respond promptly and appropriately to the baby's signals. The interaction between the infant's innate communicative abilities and
maternal responsiveness and the impact this interaction has on the
attachment system have been assessed by Mary Ainsworth in her
elegantly conceived and richly descriptive naturalistic studies.
Among the qualities in the mother that potentially impact upon the
attachment system for which Ainsworth derived assessment scales
are maternal sensitivity versus insensitivity, maternal cooperation
versus interference, and maternal acceptance versus rejection (Ainsworth et al., 1978).

The importance of Ainsworth's subsequent discovery of qualitative differences in attachment behavior among individuals at (only)
12 months of age cannot be overestimated. In the so-called Strange

Situation, the quality of attachment is assessed by what children do to restore a sense of security during reunion with their attachment figures after a brief separation. The children thereby reveal their emergent inner working model of the attachment system, based on what they have learned to expect from many communicative encounters throughout the first year of life. That there might be qualitative, as opposed to simply quantitative, differences in these behaviors upon reunion was unexpected. Yet, in contrast to secure infants, who showed the predicted attachment behaviors upon reunion with their mothers in the Strange Situation, some infants simply avoided their mothers, and others behaved with manifest ambivalence toward them. These surprising, unanticipated findings did not so much contradict Bowlby's postulate that there was a universal biological propensity toward attachment, as they provided a means for reconciling Bowlby's conception with empirical differences in sensitivity/insensitivity and other qualities among different mother-child dyads. In essence, Ainsworth and her coworkers had provided irrefutable evidence for the malleability of the attachment system, depending on the differential behavior of caretakers.

Ainsworth's contribution was thus a double one. Beyond the discovery of qualitative differences, her precise and richly descriptive prose describing caretakers' sensitivity to their babies opened a new way of viewing the intricacies of emotional communication. Forty years earlier, in 1925, Karl Bühler had emphasized the necessity for making the kind of disciplined, systematic observations later accomplished by Ainsworth. Bühler wrote of infant observation:

> How this is to be done cannot be told in two words and appropriately for all cases. Those interested in a deeper understanding of the most magnificent developmental drama, the becoming human of our children, must recognize that this is impossible to understand without preparation. One must, as in any science and art, learn to see first in order to understand more than a good nanny does. The time when conceptions from popular psychology were still sufficient is definitely over. Even today it seems poor what ingenious pioneers such as Comenius, Rousseau, and Pestalozzi had to say about the first year of life [Bühler, 1925, pp. 53–54].

Ainsworth's clear, precise descriptions of emotional communication within the infant–caretaker interaction provided the researcher with a powerful tool for understanding continuity and change in development. When her observations were combined with Bowlby's synthesis of findings from ethology, comparative psychology, psychiatry, and psychoanalysis, the juxtaposition of the two bodies of knowledge provided a new basis for insight into the critical conditions underlying emotional development from infancy into adulthood and old age.

Yet, caretakers' sensitivity, as we now know, is statistically strongly, but not perfectly, linked to the way 12-month-old babies resolve the arousal of their attachment systems by separation stress (Grossmann, and Grossmann, 1991). The dominance of the Strange Situation for the entire field of attachment research can be justified on the basis of methodological necessity; however, the statistically imperfect relationship between maternal sensitivity and the quality of the infant's attachment as revealed by the Strange Situation requires that we take more than a glance beyond the fence of current attachment research. After all, we may safely postulate that all attachment styles, whether secure, insecure, or frankly disoriented and disorganized, still must originate from the quality of the emotional communication between infants and their attachment figures.

Hence, we are led to broaden the inquiry in various ways, taking in biological factors, on one hand, and social and historical factors, on the other. What are the social and cultural circumstances under which babies thrive? What influence do historical or epochal conditions have? What role do differences in the babies' innate potentials for self-organization and emotional integration play? How do these differences respond under conditions of more or less external organization provided by attachment figures? These and other issues are presently waiting for a more cooperative interdisciplinary investigation by the scientific community. The complexities of interaction among genetic, cultural, and psychodynamic views need to be kept constantly in mind in order to avoid fruitless *pars-pro-toto* competition in research and theory, much as shown in a recent exchange between Fox (1995) and van IJzendorn (1995a, b).

Inborn Influences

I shall address inborn, presumably, genetic influences only briefly, because the field seems to be rapidly moving toward new conceptualizations as the data accumulate (Dunn and Plomin, 1990). Bowlby himself did not believe that inborn factors could satisfactorily explain the development of secure versus insecure attachments:

> Evidence points unmistakably to the conclusion that a lot of
> personal characteristics, traditionally termed temperamental
> and hitherto often believed to be inborn and unchangeable, are

environmentally induced. True, neonates differ from each other in many ways. Yet the evidence is clear from repeated studies that infants described as difficult during their early days are enabled by sensitive mothering to become easy toddlers. Contrarily, placid newborns can be turned into anxious, moody, demanding or awkward toddlers by insensitive or rejecting mothers [Bowlby, 1991, pp. 310–311].

Findings drawn from research directly into issues of temperament, however, sometimes invite alternative interpretations. Let me take an illustration from my own and my colleagues' data. In our original Bielefeld sample, which produced a high proportion of infants classified as insecure-avoidantly attached, there was a significant correlation between good orienting ability at birth and secure attachment classification at 12 months to mother and at 18 months to father (Grossmann, et al., 1985). Moreover, my coworker, Elisabeth Fremmer-Bombik, has recently reviewed the old data from 1977, and concentrated on those ten children classified as insecure-avoidant in the Strange Situation who had actually enjoyed sensitive mothering during the first year. The mothers of these children not only had been deemed reasonably sensitive during the first year but, when examined again five years later, were found to manifest secure attachment representations as measured by the Adult Attachment Interview (Grossmann et al., 1988). Fremmer-Bombik discovered that, as newborns, their children had been rated both as highly irritable and as far below average in orientation ability on the Brazelton Neonatal Assessment Scale; indeed, on the latter measure they constituted the lowest ten children in the entire sample (reported in Fremmer-Bombik and Grossmann, 1993). The data strongly suggest that the presence of these neonatal characteristics may have contributed to an insecure attachment by the end of the first year despite a reasonable degree of maternal sensitivity.

Then, too, it is possible that innate factors may play a role in shaping the kind of insecure attachment that a child manifests. In our combined Bielefeld-Regensburg sample (N = 88), security of attachment (secure versus insecure) correlated significantly with ratings of maternal sensitivity. The occurrence of disorganization/disorientation within the insecurely attached children, however, had no relation to ratings of maternal sensitivity. But it was significantly correlated with the infants' newborn orientation plus state regulation scores on the Brazelton Neonatal Assessment Scale (Spangler, Fremmer-Bombik, and Grossmann, in press).

Nonetheless, the overall data are still much in line with Bowlby's (1988b) summary evaluation of where attachment research stands:

"A major conclusion is that, whatever influence variations in genetic endowment may exert on personality development and psychopathology, an immense influence is unquestionably exerted by environmental variables of the kinds now being systematically explored" (p. 2).

CULTURAL CONTEXTS OF ATTACHMENT

Mary Ainsworth once admitted that her first empirical tests of Bowlby's ideas did not totally convince her until she started to work in Uganda in 1953–54. A pivotal reason for her determination to undertake a cross-cultural study is that attachment theory takes a very strong stand on optimal conditions for secure attachment with a specific subtype of secure babies (B3) considered to be most securely attached—regardless of culture.

Dunn (1993) has pointed out that attachment relationships are not the only important relationships the developing child has. Nor, from a cultural perspective, do relationships stand alone in shaping development. Relationships, play, art, aesthetics, and a host of other culturally shaped variables all need to be considered. This is obviously true. However, one need not concede that attachment relationships are but one type among many nor that they are superseded by other facets of a given culture in shaping development. To the contrary, the nature of the attachment bond contributes a distinct and fundamental psychological quality to experience that affects how many other experiences will be assimilated and integrated by the growing individual. Insofar as secure attachment favors autonomous and self-determined exploratory and playful behavior, it sets the stage for a smooth development into the world of cultural values—and as with the child, so with the adult. The ability to participate fully in cultural rituals and to take advantage of cultural assets is correlated, to no small degree, with one's esteem for the lives of others who belong to the same society. Minsky (1987) has written from an information-processing perspective that an important goal is to learn goals worth pursuing; attachment is such a superordinate, organizing goal. When basic attitudes toward attachment change, many other features of childhood are bound to change, too, including peer relationships, concentration, satisfaction, and coping (see Suess, Grossmann, and Sroufe, 1992; Grossmann et al., 1993). Wensauer (1994, in preparation) showed that, even in elderly people, social support and a pleasant perspective on the future are firmly tied to secure attachment representations. Viewed properly, attachment is the very foundation for a child's ability to understand and participate in the extended social and cultural world without undue emotional conflict.

In what follows I adopt an essentially diachronic perspective on issues bearing on the quality of attachment in different cultures. As a necessary corollary I also look at historical differences in the appreciation of the importance of attachment. Overall, my aim is a double one: within the history of culture, to explore the importance placed on attachment relationships in different periods; and within the history of psychology, to explore the gradual development of attachment theory.

History and (the Lack of) Attachment

From the perspective of attachment theory, historical data on the fate of children in past ages immediately present a critical question: does high infant mortality mean that attachment was of no concern?

There have been numerous attempts to reconstruct how children were treated from ancient times down to the present. Among the first was the psychohistorical study of Lloyd deMause, who attempted to interpret selected historical documents psychoanalytically (deMause, 1974). The German translation of the title of deMause's book—*Do You Hear the Children Cry?*—captures well his portrait of the tremendous psychological neglect, maltreatment, hostility, and general devaluation suffered by children over the ages; however, the historical documents used by deMause, after careful reanalysis, do not provide sufficient grounds for a definitive theory of the evolution of childhood (Nyssen, 1984). The psychoanalytic reflections offered by others (e.g., Schuster-Keim and Keim, 1988) likewise remain on shaky empirical grounds; moreover, they rely on formulations derived from classical psychoanalysis without any consideration of attachment research.

Philip Ariès has attempted to provide a more thorough point of departure built around two main hypotheses, which were first presented in his 1960 study on childhood and family life in the ancien régime (see Ariès, 1975). First, relying on a wealth of data, Ariès contends that traditional society possessed an underdeveloped understanding of the stages of childhood and adolescence. Instead, its view of family life was predicated on more immediate issues having to do with ensuring mutual survival in a world in which neither men nor, particularly, women could survive as individuals; among these issues were the transgenerational conservation of property, joint execution of handicraft, and, in critical times, the collective defense of honor and life. The family did not have any particular affective function, Ariès claims. Although love was sometimes reported, feelings between spouses and between parents and children where simply unnecessary for the existence and the stability of the family. Emotional attachments, if there were any at all, were chiefly made outside the family (Shorter, 1975), though a similar lack of concern for other individuals was apparently evident in communal affairs as well.

A historical story about a family from my home city of Regensburg may be relevant here (Schmuck, 1993). In 1713–14 pestilence killed about 8,000 inhabitants, one-third of the city's population. There were hunger and misery. The father of one family, a small retail dealer, had been expelled from the city because of a "lewd life." The family lived by dyeing linen. His wife, Isabella Philippina Gemeinhardt, stayed behind with their four children; the eldest child was ten years old, and the youngest, Justina Barbara, barely six months old. The city poverty or alms office granted the mother a monthly allowance until the fate of her children was decided. Then it was decreed that she should move into one small subrented room, while the oldest two children were sent to an orphanage, and the four-year-old son was sent to live with a foster mother. The family depended for its survival on the help of the older children in carrying out the dyed linen trade, but the city council insisted on their removal because the mother was accused of not educating them in a sufficiently "God-fearing" manner. When the mother stubbornly resisted, the city council responded by sending all three of her elder children to the orphanage. Next, because of quarrels with the women from whom she subrented her room, the mother received a notice to leave the home, and now even the baby, Justina Barbara, was taken away from her. The alms house reemployed the mother in taking care of people ill with pestilence; the job was fatally risky but well paid. She died on September 2 of the same year, and her husband, who had been allowed to rejoin her if he helped with the work, died four days later, on September 6. Justina Barbara, the baby, died on October 27. The youngest son survived four more years until he died at the age of nine; the fate of the eldest two children is unknown. The children's fate, as well as that of their parents, was from the moment of the breakup of the family as predictable as the almost certain death of infants given away to wet nurses during the same century, as depicted by Ariès (1975) and Badinter (1984).

Ariès's second hypothesis concerns the changing relationship between children and families brought about by the rise of higher education in modern industrial society, from about the end of the 19th century on. To be sure, school separated children from adults; this in itself helped make childhood and adolescence distinct from other periods in life. Moreover, at least according to Ariès, the investment in education would not have been possible without at least some affective attachment between spouses and between parents and their children. Perhaps the commitment to education did constitute a beginning. Children were no longer automatically put in the service of maintaining the family's property and honor; instead, parents were now engaged in monitoring and encouraging their children's progress. The family began to organize around the child, and the child thereby began to lose his or her anonymity and gained a measure of individuality and a status of his or her own. Such a child could no longer be easily lost or replaced without great pain. Moreover, the number of children being reared now had to be limited in order to be able to provide more care and—a new quality in many families—individual attention for each of them. The price paid for this social trend of fostering individuality and the beginnings of self-determination was the extended isolation of adolescents in school away from their families (Ariès, 1975, p. 49).

More generally, according to Ariès, one can find accounts of individual mourning for individual infants and small children during the first four centuries A.D. and again in the 15th and 16th centuries in families of high social standing. On the other side, as extensively documented by Elisabeth Badinter (1984), there are barely any recorded indications of mother love occurring during the 17th century. During this period, moreover, "excessive" marital life and sexual enjoyment were frankly suppressed; marriage was settled according to property and financial arrangements. There seems to have been great indifference between spouses, in life as well as after one of them died. Arguably, the two phenomena—the absence of mourning for children *and* spouses—are connected. Love, as Badinter points out, is possible only when one can identify with the other person, when one can be happy or sad with her or him. Seen in broad historical perspective, attachment theory constitutes an attempt to render on a scientific basis an ethic that is of relatively recent historical origin, that is, a commitment to a high quality of psychological life predicated not only on individualism but also on a transcendance of individualism that allows for tenderness and concern for others, most especially for one's children.

Surely the most thought-provoking data about children in the past three centuries come from historical demography. During this period, infant mortality was consistently extremely high. But that, arguably, is not the whole story. There was also printed and oral propaganda by "medical authorities" against any displays of tenderness toward children. Medical tracts fearfully decried such practices as "voluptuousness in breast-feeding," which was said to spoil the infant because "bodies were weakened by nothing more than by sensual pleasure" (Badinter, 1984, p. 38). To be sure, there were the occasional contrary reports of loving mothers who cried for the children when they lost them. In general, however, there is sufficient evidence to support Badinter's conclusion: "Mothers were disinterested not because infants died like flies, but, at least in part, they died in such great numbers because the mothers were not interested in them" (p. 63).

Interestingly, in our own day both popular and serious journalists and commentators have tendered similar hypotheses in which individually motivated behaviors give rise in the aggregate to great social costs. Sagan (1987), for example, has recently underscored the relevance of love and sympathy in families for the domain of health and illness generally, pointedly including in his review the comparatively high rate of infant mortality in the United States. Similarly, Sylvia Ann Hewlett (1991) has attempted to analyze the cost of child neglect, not merely in individual psychological terms but in terms of its economic impact on American society as a whole. The relevance of differences between individual households likewise emerges in the historical record of the last three centuries. According to Imhof (personal communication, 1992) some 50% of families appeared to have had no infant mortality at all, whereas 10% had multiple deaths. What was the difference?

Infant Mortality and Attachment

In today's world, a lack of care, support, and guidance by parents is likely to result chiefly in social and psychological maladjustment in the child, as well as in enhanced risk factors, most especially as regards health. In the past, however, many neglected children simply died early in life. The dramatic importance of attachment theory for understanding the modern age becomes clear from a brief look at a study of infant mortality from the late 18th century to the end of the 19th century conducted by A. Imhof, a historical demographer from Berlin. In his study, Imhof adopted H. V. Musham's contrasting concepts of a "system of wastage" and a "system of conservation of human life." Whereas Musham emphasized the historical transition from a system of wastage to a system of conservation of human life, Imhof ventured to show that both systems may actually coexist in the same country and at the same time, depending on local conditions and culture (Imhof, 1984). In some ways, his findings anticipate contemporary comparisons of the attachment status of children in the Minneapolis poverty sample with well-to-do children from other regions (Sroufe, Egeland, and Kreutzer, 1990).

Imhof compared demographic data from the period between 1780 and 1899 for two German villages: Hesel in Ostfriesland, close to the Dutch border, and Gabelsbach, west of Munich. Infant mortality in Hesel was low, 13%, but it was high, 33.9%, in Gabelsbach. Overall reproductive success was almost identical for the two villages—4.51 in Gabelsbach and 4.61 in Hesel—but the women in Hesel had to give birth to only 5.3 children to accomplish this degree of success, compared with 6.83 in Gabelsbach.

Economic hardship was reflected in high age at marriage: for women, 26.1 years of age in Hesel and 28.3 years in Gabelsbach; for men, 28.8 years of age in Hesel and 30.7 years in Gabelsbach. In both villages, fertility ended after only 12 years: at age 39 in Hesel and 39.9 in Gabelsbach, if both partners survived until at least the 45th year of the wife. In both villages intervals between births were short, 21.3 months in Hesel and 20.5 months in Gabelsbach, if the firstborn infant died within its first year. If the firstborn child survived, however, the birth interval was almost 3 years in Hesel (34.1 months) but only 22.9 months in Gabelsbach. Moreover, 87% of the infants survived in Hesel, but only 66.1% in Gabelsbach, which meant that, overall, women in Hesel had appreciably lower fertility rates independent of their ages. In Gabelsbach, by contrast, both infant mortality and fertility rates were higher, and the time interval between deliveries was shorter. (Birthrates in both villages were higher when fewer infants were breast-fed and when breast-feeding was short.)

Why were the conditions for infant survival better in Hesel and worse in Gabelsbach? The potential benefits of breast-feeding for enhancing infant survival, as well as for reducing the likelihood of a new conception and, thus, of a clear risk of death during delivery, were both well known at the time (Suessmilch, 1761, in Imhof, 1984). In Hesel mothers died in childbirth at the rate of 794 per 1,000, if the rate is calculated on the basis of the average number of births per mother per lifetime. But in Gabelsbach the rate of death among mothers climbed to 1,068 because they had to give birth to 1.53 more infants each to achieve the same reproductive success. In Gabelsbach both infants and mothers were "wasted," in Musham's terms; in Hesel both were "conserved." Different attitudes toward life must be seen in these demographic differences—toward children as well as toward spouses. The differences appear in other statistics as well. Among widowers in Gabelsbach fully 74% had remarried within 6.7 months after their spouse's death. But in Hesel only 53.6% of widowers had remarried after more than two years (27.7 months); and among widows in Hesel, the rate of 74% remarried was achieved only after 35.5 months, that is, almost three full years.

In a more descriptive vein Imhof (1984, p. 30) has provided a graphic medical topography of the system of human wastage in Gabelsbach for 1822, when infant mortality rose to 50%: heavy work until the last minute before birth and, immediately afterward, copulation as well; hardly any breast-feeding, only water soup; infants left at home crying while mothers worked in the fields; general resistance to vaccination; medical treatment of ill children frequently not sought; appalling hygiene; and so forth. Many medical observers at the time commented on the widespread indifference toward life, most especially on the widespread negligence toward infants and children.

It is still an open question what caused these differences: the frequent fatal threats to life by war, famine, and pestilence in Gabelsbach, threats that Hesel was spared, or a life perspective geared beyond death toward eternity. On the material plane, Imhof has demonstrated that the presence of continuing threats to survival lasted in Gabelsbach for several generations. Being overburdened with too many children in conditions of poverty was clearly a major determinant of infant mortality. In Gabelsbach infant mortality jumped from 29.4% for the first four children to 41.6% thereafter. In Hesel, by contrast, it jumped from about 13% to 18.4% only after the seventh child.

There was still another threat to attachment in a real world. In German Catholic cultures, "surplus" infants were routinely sent to "heaven." Imhof grimly describes in largely Catholic Gabelsbach "postnatal family planning and poorly veiled infanticide through conscious neglect of infants from a certain birth-rank on for the express purpose of ensuring an early demise" (p. 33). The motive, however, was "neither brutality nor a diminished love of parents for their children," as an observer, cited in Imhof, stated in 1855. Instead, in the parents' eyes, those children had not only been spared a miserable life on earth, but their chances to change to the heavenly fields from the vale of tears on earth were the more certain the earlier they died as innocent beings and were sent to heaven—provided they were baptized. Therefore, baptism took place as early after delivery as possible in order to facilitate the rapid succession of birth, to baptism, to handing over to a wet nurse, to death. In Bavaria at that time, a documented saying was, "Three deceased infants in heaven are so powerful a lobby that a mother's and father's souls are also saved." If the infant was already dead before it was baptized, it had to be brought to a church that specialized in arranging the wonder of restoring the child's life just briefly enough for baptism. Signs of life were red cheeks, a tear, a barely noticeable movement, and so on. The parents gave donations in return.

It is by no means clear what the feelings of these parents toward their infants and children were. Behind all the cruelty, planned and unplanned neglect, behind the abuse, disrespect, and fatal care, there were often indications of parental love, concern, and deeply felt relief and thankfulness if a child was saved for this life rather than the next. Still, we may assume that individual concern for infants, the prerequisite for care and attachment, was less likely to arise under conditions of extreme hardship. From a demographic viewpoint, wastage of human resources was a clear result.

The Historical Shift to Individuality and Romantic Feelings

If my excursions into cultural history have any merits at all, it is because they show that living conditions, perspectives on life, and the general cultural outlook are not always favorable for the development of secure attachments by infants and children. High esteem for the newborn individual child can arise in traditional cultures such as Japan (Benedict, 1946; Johnson, 1993), where infants are considered gifts from the gods who will be taken away again if they are not treated with unconditional love by their mothers. Or it can arise in cultures that develop a measure of esteem for human beings as self-determined individuals, as beings whose purpose lies within themselves, as Kant wrote in connection with his famous categorical imperative (Montada, 1987).

The key to understanding parental love and psychological investment in infants at different times and in different cultures is high esteem for significant others. When did individual feelings become a matter of public concern in modern Western society? What cultural developments led to an interest in individual development and welfare and, more recently, to an interest in child-rearing practices that foster autonomous individuality? In his not undisputed monograph on the origins of the modern family, Edward Shorter (1975) has contributed much to our present understanding of family life as it evolved in the 18th and 19th centuries. Again, the indications of widespread negligence, abuse, planned separation, and abandonment of infants are overwhelming. Yet, signs of individual love are also found in Shorter's survey. A typical note attached to the dress of an abandoned child read:

> Times are so hard and wretched, and misery is so great that we are forced against our will to abandon our dear three-year-old girl. We beg the good sisters of the foundling home to identify our poor girl by some sign and by the day and time of her abandonment, so that we may enjoy to recognize her and to

take her back [Shorter, German translation, 1977, pp. 202–
203].

The cultivation of such feelings of sympathy and concern toward
one's children and toward one's spouse, together with reflections on
these feelings, lay at the core of romance and romanticism. Romantic love is the term that Hazan and Shaver (1987) currently use in
their research on attachment relationships between spouses, but it
has a long history. Consideration of romanticism as the vehicle for
valuing individual experience in modern Western culture potentially
takes us beyond the issues raised by Shorter, Ariès, or Badinter. That
is, independent of the impact of captitalism, education, or state-
sponsored myths of mother love on child-rearing practices, a degree
of psychological individuation as a cultural value was essential for
attachment to become an important psychological variable, not only
in early development but across the whole life cycle (Ainsworth,
1985; Parkes, Stevenson-Hinde, and Marris, 1991).

Germany is particularly well known for its history of romanticism,
with its focus on individual feelings and even *Schwärmerei*, or
somewhat unrealistic, idealistic imaginings and yearnings. The
romantic vision was not always well-balanced. But it laid the basis
for individual self-reflection on feelings in relation to significant
attachments.

The Beginning Search for One's Inner Life—
"Anton Reiser: A Psychological Novel"

A direct link between romanticism and modern psychological writing can be found in the work of Karl Philipp Moritz (1757–93), most
especially in his pseudonymous autobiography-cum-self-analysis,
which appeared in installments between 1785 and 1790. Moritz
named the protagonist of his autobiographical reflections Anton
Reiser (Moritz, 1987). In the text, which bespeaks a poignant sense
of inner futility, Anton continually reflects on his psychologically
miserable life in search of a reason for his deplorably low self-
esteem. Nothing quite like these reflections had ever been published
before. It was the Age of Enlightenment, of the new state-philoso-
phies of human rights manifested in the U.S. Constitution of 1776
and the French Revolution of 1789. Likewise, it was a romantic age,
among its cultural highlights the famous Mozart and Da Ponte operas
with their lively individual characters struggling for autonomy and
romantic love in confrontation with reality.

The author, Karl Philipp Moritz, was born in 1756 in the city of
Hameln—where the Pied Piper of Hameln organized his musical

kidnapping. In 1783, he founded the world's first psychological journal, the *Magazine for Experiential Knowledge of the Soul for All Devoted to and Supportive of Knowledge and Science of General Utility, and for All Observers of the Human Heart Who in Each Rank and Condition Wishes to Actively Further Truth and Happiness among Mankind.* In ten volumes over the next decade Moritz published materials written by himself and others in pursuit of psychological knowledge of the life of individuals. "What is," he asked, "our moral life if it is not abstracted from individuals? It would be nothing but the outline of a building drawn on sand, destroyed by a tender wind, a casual sketch without inner content, like old education not grounded in special observations and experience of its own." A single observation in the real world, Moritz asserted, often had more practical value than a thousand ones collected from books, and he demanded "facts and no moral chatter" (Moritz, 1783–93, Hh 3ff). His journal inspired more than a century of diarists writing on infant and child development, from Dieterich Tiedemann, Jean Paul, Bronson Alcott, Charles and Emma Darwin, and E. Willard, to William Thierry Preyer, Charlotte Bühler, and Hildegard Hetzer. These collections of observations, in fact, were the beginnings of continuous research in child psychology, but for a long time there was no means to make systematic use of them (Bühler and Hetzer, 1929, p. 208).

In the autobiography, Anton Reiser describes himself as "suppressed from the cradle on," both in terms of his self-regard and in his craving for loving closeness. Exploited by a contemptuous hatmaker, he made a suicide attempt at 13 years of age. Moritz, the author, was himself a gifted learner, but he tried to escape from the coercions of formal schooling several times. He eventually became a teacher at a famous Berlin gymnasium, but the life of continual enforced subordination made him think of emigration and, once again, suicide. On becoming a professor some years later at the same school, the Graue Kloster, he began his career as a writer on manifold topics, including education, language, and poetry, and he composed a travelog, "Travels of a German to England in 1782." These, of course, were in addition to the life story of Anton Reiser and the psychological journal.

Moritz traveled often, and on one such trip to Italy he fulfilled his most extravagant dream by meeting Goethe. In 1774 Goethe had exposed to public gaze a novel entitled *The Sorrows of Young Werther*, which depicts Werther's enduring, ultimately fatal passion for one Charlotte Buff, a young married woman safely out of reach from the start. The novel took the old world by storm because, as Thomas Carlyle observed, it gave expression to a nameless unrest and longing discontent then agitating every bosom. The book was not just a sentimental tear-jerker; Goethe was moved by formal considerations of a high aesthetic nature as well as by a personal, individualized passion. The effect was overwhelming. Henceforth, individuality, romantically cast in terms of passionate fantasies and deeply felt suffering, was established as a topic of enlightened interest. To be sure, both the passion and the sense of suffering had been voiced in the love-poetry of countless ages before, but the self-consciousness, the sense of interiority, had not.

In 1791 Moritz became professor of fine arts in Berlin and a member of the Berlin Academy of Sciences, but his psychological problems remained. Periods of activity continued to alternate with periods of hypochondriacal passivity, moments of exaggerated self-importance were followed by moments of self-doubt, clear rationality cycled with depressing delusion. In 1792 he married Friederike Matzdorff, then divorced her only to remarry her again within a few months; for this he was ridiculed by the public. A biographer has commented on the marriage: "It was a desperate attempt to attach closely with another human being, while at the same time he was incapable of doing it in the way prescribed by bourgeois society" (Wieckenberg, 1987). Moritz died one year later, in 1793, from tuberculosis.

Anton Reiser constituted Moritz's attempt to escape from his own most unlucky attachment history and, at the same time, to understand it and thereby to find meaning in his life. As Anton Reiser, Moritz repeatedly recounts his suppression by his parents, their rejection and coldness. His only moving memory from an otherwise miserable childhood was when "his mother wrapped him in a coat and carried him through storm and wind." He felt entirely dependent on his environment, he writes, not autonomous at all. Both his self-worth and the repeated breakdowns in his self-esteem were triggered by external events. "The forces of the soul were paralyzed" when things went wrong: he would lapse into a condition of inactivity and become obsessed by an anxiety that made any reasonable self-control impossible and pushed him toward self-destruction. At times, the attempt at biographical understanding becomes a litany of self-recrimination: Anton feels only contempt from others, he neglects his physical appearance, and he develops a moral indifference. He hovers on the verge of becoming an outsider and a delinquent, and he still thinks of himself as low and mean (*niederträchtig*). Yet, he also has fantasies of grandeur as well as of aggression, while he occupies himself destroying plants and paper figures, cracking stones of cherries and plums, and burning paper houses. His brother wrote in a letter to Jean Paul that Karl Philipp

Moritz entertained himself with such destructive games ("*Zerstö-rungsspiele*"; Wieckenberg, 1987, p. 390) even as an adult.

At eight years of age, Anton Reiser asks: "Where, by all means, should this passionate longing for loving care come from since he (Anton) had never experienced anything like it, and therefore would not have had any perceptions of it?" He longed for a friend but was afraid of approaching one: "the dejected feeling of contempt which he had suffered from his parents, and the shame about his poor, dirty, and torn clothes kept him back" (Moritz, 1785–90, Part 1 [1785], p. 14).

Anton had no sense of value of his own: he was uncritically at the mercy of others' judgments. There was little sense of a personal boundary (Boszormenyi-Nagy and Spark, 1973). He felt a general antipathic rejection from others. One reason for this, he wrote, was his stupid looks: a mistrusting, mean expression disclosing slavish fear (p. 145). Anton reports at length about his insecurity in using socially appropriate language to establish relationships with other human beings. He is yearning for a deeper understanding of their nature. Even his attempts to measure up to this or that ideal put him "out of time with reality" (p. 47). When, for example, he tries to become an actor, he does not learn to act out interpretations of the roles, but, instead, he struggles to find a psychological existence of his own in an artificial world of make-believe.

Anton is, as should be enormously clear by now, permanently afraid of rejection, without any self-esteem, and at a constant risk for demoralization. Yet, his courage in describing the misery of his psychological situation was, until then, unheard of. Anton understands his social disqualifications as nonetheless aspects of human nature, and he retains a strong desire for self-fulfillment. He never thinks of changing society by revolution, a dimension well perceived by Mozart and DaPonte and many others at that time. Anton's thoughts center, rather, around psychological security as an individual human right. He writes emphatically about the possibilities of cure for a damaged ego, not about a better political future (Wieckenberg, 1987, p. 400). In the final analysis, Anton Reiser is capable of moving, if futile, cognitive reflection about his early rejection and the subsequent crippling of his emotional development, but he remains incapable of coping with the demands of life by rising above them. Ultimately, he is unable to liberate himself from neurosis by his attempts at self-enlightenment (Wieckenberg, 1987, p. 405). Nor, despite the empirical bent implicit in his writing, can he find a way of anchoring his personal narrative in a domain of inquiry that extends beyond himself. In the end, as Moritz wrote in his psychological journal (vol. 7), everything must be explained naturally, because, to be sure, it cannot be otherwise than natural. But how can a single person, he goes on to ask, comprehend nature with his own single thoughts, when nature has yet to be comprehended by *all* men's thoughts (cit. Wieckenberg, 1987, p. 410)?

Attachment theory as a vehicle for achieving the kind of balance between personal experience and scientific enlightenment that Karl Philipp Moritz sought came only 180 years after Anton Reiser and some 80 years after Freud. Indeed, one could argue that perhaps the first scientist in history to truly grasp the universal relevance of maternal sensitivity to individual development on an empirical basis was Mary Ainsworth, during the time she worked in Uganda in the mid-1950s. At that time even she believed more in theories of social learning and reinforcement than in what Bowlby was arguing about attachment! Recognizing this makes one sympathize with what Moritz was searching for in himself when he wrote his biographical psychology of a strangulated ego. His failed attempt to harness reason in the service of self-understanding initiated 200 years of similarly futile attempts to understand the developmental conditions for a better or worse life. In view of this long tradition, Ainsworth's breakthrough cannot be overestimated.

I cannot close my account of the romantic paradigm without recognizing that it constituted an important shift in our cultural history: in romanticism the quality of individual life became proclaimed as a human right. Like the study of infancy through diaries, psychoanalysis was a descendant of the romantic tradition; and, like some of its predecessors within romanticism, it erred through emphasizing the unrealistic and fantastic side of emotional life, to the detriment of studying actual developmental experiences. More generally, the problem facing all the descendants of the romantic tradition, diarists of infancy and psychoanalysts alike, was to find a way of uniting the emphasis on the quality of individual life with the rigors of scientific research. It took nearly 180 years after Karl Philipp Moritz before a way was found to anchor their concerns and their hypotheses "in a coherent theory as well as in a tested body of evidence" (Bowlby, 1988b).

PSYCHOLOGY OF ATTACHMENT IN HISTORICAL PERSPECTIVE

By combining scientific rigor with a concern for the quality of lived experience, the work of Ainsworth and Bowlby constitutes a unique historical breakthrough in our own understanding of Anton Reiser's desperate craving—and that of people like him—for psychological freedom in the real world. In my final section I examine this development within the context of the history of academic psychology, before concluding with some remarks about the broad prescriptive significance that attachment theory possesses in regard to modern society.

Attachment—A New Psychological Paradigm

Moritz's *Anton Reiser* was the first profound self-reflection of romanticism with its new perspective of a democratic society that honored human rights for self-determination and self-fulfillment. During the past 200 past years, autobiographical narratives, diaries about child development, and uncounted written and unwritten attempts at self-analysis conducted under the psychoanalytic signification of imagination and fantasies have been authored by bright and sophisticated people attempting to understand human psychological development with an enlightened mind. But with all these efforts, including child diaries, a method of scientific analysis was missing. Attachment theory has attempted to provide a basis for that method of analysis by appealing to empirically derived knowledge about the universal necessity for sensitive caretaking by significant attachment figures for the development of emotional integration, as reflected in Bowlby's (1951) report "Maternal Care and Mental Health." Moritz's old questions remain the same, but the answers have begun to give way to testable hypotheses (see Bretherton, 1991). For this, a revolution in psychology as a discipline was required.

For early academic psychology, the main goal was to search for universal laws. The method of choice was experimental, because physics achieved its great breakthrough, so we were told, by experimentally testing hypotheses deduced from mathematically formulated theories. This has been referred to as the "Galilean style" by the German phenomenologist Edmund Husserl, who was not against the scientific description of the world per se. Indeed, he wished to revitalize the natural sciences against what he perceived to be the rising tide of irrationalism in philosophy (which he took to be symptomatic of the "crisis" of European life in general). The equation of the Galilean style with all of science obscured the relation between science and the life-world and so made impossible any philosophical grounding of the claims of the empirical sciences. The task for Husserl as a phemonenologist was to indicate the "essential relation between consciousness, experience, and this life-world" (Vatela, Thompson, and Rosch, 1991, p. 17).

The Galilean revolution in physics pushed academic psychology so far in the direction of mimicking physics that, as a discipline, psychology almost completely forgot biological considerations and virtually ignored the domain of individual life experiences as a main determinant of personal development. To be sure, Darwin (1809–82), who lived 240 years after Galileo Galilei (1564–1642), did capture the attention of some prescient psychologists. Yet, although Darwin paved the way for more stringent observation and systematic interpretation, his concepts of selection and adaptation were not framed in a way that could easily be appropriated for the study of individual development. This required a new way of thinking, or a new "paradigm," in Kuhn's (1962) terms.

Assisted by Robert Hinde, Bowlby (1969, 1990) took his cue from Darwin, Lorenz, Tinbergen, and early systems theorists in fashioning that new paradigm. The dilemma of psychology as a science ("Naturwissenschaft") is that its subject matter makes history (Boesch, cited in Eckensberger, 1993). Human behavior is biologically adapted both to one's kinship and to one's culture (Eibl-Eibesfeldt, 1989), because, as Lorenz (1973) has put it, man is adapted to culture by nature. John Bowlby was fascinated by the possibilities of an ethological approach that might yet be capable of analyzing individual histories—important for clinicians—with the tools of behavioral biology.

Bowlby's reality-oriented concept of inner working models and of goal-corrected behavior constituted a new psychological basis that was flexible enough to be adapted to different historical and cultural settings. One's attachment history is as much natural history as it is cultural and individual history (Grossmann, 1993). Following Bowlby, Ainsworth reflected further on the phylogenetic, ontogenetic, and mental health usages of the term "adaptation." The mental health usage of the term "adaptation," she noted, is, for all intents and purposes, synonymous with the term "adjustment" and therefore clearly evaluative (Ainsworth, 1984).

A proper understanding of adaptation in both its descriptive and evaluative dimensions requires that we fill the frame of the human universality of inner working models with ideographic or biographic knowledge about the development of qualitative differences between individuals. Only both perspectives taken together allow an efficient and mutually beneficial interchange between researchers and clinicians. The paradigmatic difference between attachment theory and the Galilean behavioristic model of reinforcement is reflected in fairly stark terms in the research strategy adopted by Ainsworth and Bell (1977). They were challenged by Gerwitz and Boyd (1977) for asserting that maternal responsiveness reduced infant crying. Why should mothers who "reinforce" their babies by appearing when their babies cry have infants who at the end of the first year actually cry less (Bell and Ainsworth, 1972; Grossmann et al., 1985), instead of more, if one assumes that crying itself had been rewarded?

Ainsworth and Bell (1977), however, decided it would be fruitless to attempt to anticipate such criticisms of their research based on a strict reinforcement paradigm. Disputes between advocates of different paradigms, as Kuhn has noted, tend to be sterile. Thus, keeping to their new attachment paradigm, Ainsworth and Bell avoided direct, Galilean-style experimentation framed by the reinforcement model. Instead, they selected measures appropriate for use in naturalistic studies and concentrated extensively on individuals and their relationships during developmental segments of their life span, for example, 16 hours per infant-mother dyad over the first year in the case of infant crying (Ainsworth et al., 1978). Mothers' consolations of crying infants were a priori predicted to end the infants' distress and to further more differentiated communications skills and were not seen as reinforcement of crying at all. Ainsworth and Bell (1977) dismissed the need to investigate such putative reinforcement on the basis that it "cannot be identified until after it has been found to change systematically the rates of the response(s) upon which it is contingent" (p. 1212). In this interpretive context, it was actually the infants' signaling behaviors that were reinforced: "Thus, a baby whose experience has been that his mother responds with fair consistency and promptness to his signals learns to expect that signalling—and later communication—is effective, and not merely that crying will be responded to" (p. 1213). The emphasis on the actual developmental context of an infant in a family and the nature of the goals originating within that context constitute the cutting edge of the essential difference between the two paradigms. As for the possibility of a rival study based on an operant-learning analysis, Ainsworth and Bell pointedly noted that they hoped that "whoever is moved to undertake such a study first conducts a pilot study to ascertain how mother and babies behave in the real world" (p. 1214).

My own and my colleague's data analysis has also clearly shown that qualitative differences in communicative ability can be detected in infants whose mothers responded more or less promptly to their crying from early on and were otherwise more or less sensitive to their babies' signals. Tender and vocally "contingent" mothers had babies at ten months who vocalized more in terms of richly "narrative" babbling sounds (Grossmann and Grossmann, 1985).

More generally, the attachment paradigm offers a perspective in which one can view the development of psychological freedom in a life course unfettered by anxious, paralyzing, or empty emotional appraisals of oneself and of others. Main, Kaplan, and Cassidy

(1985), with their "move to the level of representation," have
opened up this domain by providing a tool for penetrating
hermeneutical analysis of *present-day* attachment representations of
past events (Main et al., 1985; Grossmann et al., 1988; Main and
Goldwyn, in press). Introspection thereby becomes scientifically
manageable. Where psychoanalytic investigations emphasized fantasy, as opposed to real-life events (Bowlby, 1988a, b), the new
techniques allow thorough analyses of real separations and losses, as
well as of reflections on early attachment experience, and show
how these are capable of disturbing, disorganizing, and impairing
emotional and motivational appraisals, as well as cognitive understanding, of past and present reality. It seems to me that Moritz was
intuitively searching in an Adult Attachment Interview-like fashion
for an evaluation of his present inner working model and for an
interpretation of his past attachment experiences. In this context,
it is enlightening to compare Moritz's (1785–1790) futile psychological self-analysis with Bowlby's (1990) sophisticated attachment
biography of Charles Darwin or with Mary Main's technique of
analyzing Adult Attachment Interviews to assess present attachment
representations.

Mothers at Work and Children Elsewhere?

If we are to believe our historians of childhood (Ariès, Badinter,
deMause, Imhof) and of the family (Shorter), then the fate of today's
children has dramatically improved. There is still reason to be concerned about childhood maltreatment, abuse, and neglect; likewise,
there is reason to be concerned about easing the stresses on the
modern family. These issues finally have become a matter of public
policy as well as of intensive research.

In two main issues within public policy in Western societies
today, our newly acquired knowledge of the importance of early
attachment must be clearly voiced. The first concerns the issue of
out-of-family child care. The second, related to the first, is the issue
of finding a desirable balance between individual freedom from psychological constraints and sympathetic commitment to others. The
first is a hotly debated issue; particularly thorny is the implicit question of whether the newly acquired rights of children are being
sacrificed in favor of the rights of their mothers and fathers for
exclusive self-determination. The second, related issue brings us into
the realm of social philosophy. In line with Ainsworth's notion that
"adaptive" means to be well adjusted, and "maladaptive" means to
be maladjusted, to the environments in which we live, the findings
of attachment research potentially bear on our overall notion of

what constitutes mental health and what must be provided by others if it is to be achieved. That is, attachment research has clearly shown and emphasizes that adaptive development requires care, concern, availability, and sensitivity from reliable attachment figures. Thus, though it is concerned with the emotional development of individuals as individuals, attachment theory nonetheless stands far removed from approaches that emphasize egoistic "independence" or even "self-reliance," the virtues of a social-Darwinist perspective.

Mothers from the mid-17th century on were overloaded with children. Imhof's example of Gabelsbach provides a case in point of how child care potentially suffers under the impact of an exaggerated birthrate—and Gabelsbach is by no means the exception from a historical viewpoint. All of the historians mentioned (Ariès, deMause, Imhof, and Shorter) have documented widespread negligence and even abandonment of "surplus" infants. At first glance, today's child-care debate seems to be far removed from the lessons to be learned from Gabelsbach or from the Gemeinhardt family in Regensburg of 280 years ago. In much of the contemporary literature on infant day care, however, the discussion is clearly guided by the sheer economic necessity of both parents' contributing to the family income. Obviously, this necessity is most pressing in lower-class families, but it is also felt in middle-class families eager to ensure for themselves and for their offspring a better quality of life. Then, too, as one moves up the economic ladder, economic motives become supplemented by psychological ones as women claim the right to learn skills and pursue professions, both as a vehicle for their own self-realization and as a means of guaranteeing their own economic independence. In this context, children again seem to be a burden to their parents.

But how plastic is the adaptability of the infant to day-care regimes set up by economic motives and by the goals of the women's movement? Anton Reiser potentially reveals that two rather incompatible ends to the story may occur in the next generation: psychological freedom and individual independence as adults and, at the same time, crippling consequences for children arising from early parental neglect, unavailability, and indifference. Attachment research provides a new frame of reference for understanding the development of the sense of self-esteem in children and adults; by the same token, it also provides a frame of reference for intervening in society's present struggle about in- and out-of-family rearing of infants (Scarr and Eisenberg, 1993).

Unquestionably, there is good child care available outside the home. In particular, studies of Israeli kibbutzim have shown that good day care can be compatible with secure attachment status and with good emotional adjustment. Van IJzendoorn, Sagi, and Lambermon (1992) show that combined scores of qualities of attachment to mother, father, and caretaker indicate that children are overwelmingly secure in those kibbutz day-care centers which take the children from from 7 A.M. to 4 P.M. To be noted, moreover, is that the three attachment relationships combined also predict the child's quality of adjustment better than each of them alone. This implies that the caretaker in the infant day-care center becomes a truly significant figure in the child's emotional development. Matters were quite otherwise for infants in other kibbutzim, however, where the regime used to call for the infant to be taken to the infant house during the night. These infants, by contrast, were overwhelmingly so disorganized, disoriented, and insecurely-ambivalently attached that their attachment relationships became poor predictors of differences in subsequent adjustment (Sagi et al., in preparation). These practices have since been terminated by the mothers, during the Gulf War, and have not been resumed since (Sagi, personal communication 1994).

The fierce discussion in the United States about day-care policy in relation to the findings of attachment research has been vividly described in Robert Karen's (1994) book in a chapter entitled "A Rage in the Nursery: The Day-Care Wars." From a European persepctive, there are many peculiar aspects to this debate. In particular, the deplorable lack of concern within the social sector for parents and the inadequate resources provided for family maintenance and day care, even in the restricted realm of public health care, are noteworthy. Other industrialized countries have passed laws on appropriate maternity leaves, standards of day care, mother's leave of absence around a child's illness, and so on. Consequently, there is no such "rage" in or about the "nursery," nor has there been in recent decades. Rather, there have been continuous public concern and discussion, leading fairly directly to timely social changes. For example, after James Robertson's film *Laura Goes to Hospital*, major changes were made in both British and Continental hospital care for children. From the European perspective, the intemperate nature of the American debate suggests a startling, almost inexplicable lack of consensus about the relation of public policy to the family. When one American researcher characterizes Jay Belsky's views on attachment as "bunkum," or another one sees attachment theory as a "backlash against the women's movement" while maintaining that "children's brains are Jell-O and their memories akin to those of decorticated rodents" (Karen, 1994, pp. 331–332), these statements seems to be indications of an unresolved public consensus about child rearing in present-day United States. From a research point of view, such arguments cannot possibly be taken seriously. Historically, they are reminiscent of the highly conflictual and controversial arguments once made against Bowlby's original (1951) World Health Organization report on the fate of children following the upheavals of World War II.

Are we, albeit in a lessened degree, returning to the practice of giving infants away as our foreparents did 200 years ago? Certainly not. But new psychological knowledge and values have developed in the interim, and our attitude toward day care should be informed by them. If we now understand the necessity for a secure base in early development, if we grasp that the quality of primary attachment relationships has a direct relation to the development of self-esteem and of the feeling that one is worthy of love, at least in childhood, do we not want to make such an understanding the broad basis for our policy decisions regarding infant care? Instead, the bitter U.S. day-care feud has reached the point where researchers fight over small differences in numbers of secure versus insecure attachment classifications in the Strange Situation, of day-care versus non-day-care infants. It reminds one ominously of similar intolerant arguments in the former German Democratic Republic and in other East European countries in the 1970s in favor of day care and against decadent, bourgeois views on mother-infant attachment (e.g., see Schmidt-Kolmer, Tonkowa-Jampolskaja, and Atanassowa, 1979). There appears to be still a long way to go before the new psychological ideals of ego-resiliency, freedom of choice, sympathy, and openness—and all the other axes of self-fulfillment—can be seen not just as adults "consumer" rights but in meaningful juxtaposition with the rights of the weaker children for care (Grossmann and Grossmann, in preparation). Only when such a broad social consensus is present will the effects of day care, good and bad, be investigated thoroughly, in an unprejudiced and integrative manner. Until then attachment theory and research will probably be forced to play the role of a culprit in the day-care debate rather than the role of a competent provider of unique scientific instruments based on an elegant and highly integrative theory.

Quality of Child Rearing and Mental Health

Separation from attachment figures is stressful for infants. Repeated stress in monkeys leads to greatly disturbed behavior, including pathology (Harlow, 1971; Hinde and Spencer-Booth, 1971). In humans, avoidance of mothers by 12-month-old infants during reunions in the Strange Situation, such as is typical of the insecure-avoidant classification, does *not* constitute mature independence.

The heart rates of these children go up like those of all children when their mothers leave the laboratory. In avoiding their mothers during reunion, moreover, they behave rather like rhesus monkeys who have been deprived of the means to communicate with their mothers through physical isolation (Levine and Wiener, 1988). The sense of psychological isolation in these children, the result of an inability to organize attachment feelings and behavior around the secure base of a responsive attachment figure, causes both stress and maladaptation. In fact, the cortisol level of avoidant infants increases significantly 15–30 minutes after the Strange Situation, even though they appear to be much calmer during the separation episodes as compared with secure infants, who often cry and organize vital behavior of protest and search for their mothers (Spangler and Grossmann, 1993).

In attachment theory the interpersonal, systemic aspect is as important as the ethological. This dimension still lacks the methodological precision it ought to have, but conceptually there is little disagreement. In the process of forming a highly individualized attachment, a baby learns to organize his expressions of emotions and, subsequently, his behaviors around people. First he or she is oriented to all people, then to familiar people, and then, when developing a goal-corrected partnership, he or she starts considering the feelings, intentions, and interests of particular, significant others when making his or her own plans. The developing child is practicing a flexible balance of interests and thereby slowly overcomes sociobiological selfishness (Trivers, 1974). The child thus establishes the beginnings of an esteemed membership in his or her own culture of "con-science" along at least two moral dimensions: justice in Kohlberg's sense and care in Gilligan's sense. The development of a goal-corrected organization of emotions, motives, cognition, and conscience is a central principle of attachment theory. Persons who can integrate negative and positive emotions, be they derived from past memories or present events, into an overall strategy of goal-corrected behavior are better off in many ways. A point that is frequently misunderstood (e.g., Oatley and Jenkins, 1992) is that Main's "coherency and integration of emotion" as a measure of adults' inner working models (Main et al., 1985) differentiates adults' *present* narrative reports about past events and does not pertain to the past events themselves. (Methodologically, there is currently no other alternative.) Such goal-corrected "integrative systems" are of a higher order than less integrated and less coherent attachment representations; they contain, in terms of systems theory, more elements and clearer relations between elements. In addition, the secure-autonomous inner working models reveal an organizing principle of self-trust in the context of an ability to accept help; persons having such present-day working models have learned to pursue goals worth pursuing, in Minsky's (1987) sense, that is, by following the experienced values of attachment learning.

The development of a goal-corrected behavioral organization adapted to actual reality as the infant experiences it has become the focus of theoretical and empirical research. It starts early: between four and seven months babies of highly insensitive mothers already show elevated cortisol response while playing in their mothers' presence; these infants seem to experience more stress than infants of sensitive mothers (Spangler et al., 1994). Stress symptoms associated with insecure behavior in the Strange Situation have also been shown by heightened cortisol levels (Spangler and Grossmann, 1993). At age 3½ and again at age six, children whose mothers have helped organize their behavior at home without intrusive interference are both more concentrated on tasks and more enthusiastic in test situations (Loher, 1988; Schildbach, 1992). This was also true for Ainsworth's securely attached children when they were observed by Main at age two (Main, 1973) and in our sample, both when observed at age two by Karin Grossmann (Grossmann, 1984) and when observed at age five in preschool (Suess et al., 1992). By age six, children previously classified as secure show much more open communication and access to sad feelings on many levels, as well as higher stability in their attachment classification (Main et al., 1985; Wartner et al., 1994).

At ten years significantly more secure children from the North German sample were well adapted (Scheuerer-Englisch, 1989). Even in old age, the elderly grandparents of our Regensburg sample who remembered supportive attachment figures during their own childhoods made better use of their supportive networks. They reported more active participation, received more help, and enjoyed more reliable helping persons. They also reported a signficantly higher degree of subjective life satisfaction. In contrast, elderly people with an insecure attachment representation were more rigidly self-reliant, and some had no perspective of their future at all (Grossmann et al., 1993; Wensauer, 1994; Wensauer & Grossmann in press).

CONCLUSION

In my review of the evolution and history of attachment research and theory I have adopted a broad cultural-historical perspective. I chose this path partially out of necessity, because the specific history of attachment theory and research has been well presented by Inge Bretherton (Bretherton, 1992; this volume). The historically reported frequently harsh, and even cruel, treatment of many infants and children in the past constituted an additional challenge, however, because it is in utter contrast to the human values behind attachment theory.

Individuality has been known, of course, throughout history. To grasp this, one has only to consider the high degree of intellectual organization of the great minds who, from ancient times down to the present, have been among the founders of our modern, enlightened Western tradition. The onset of romanticism, however, created a new public concern for one's inner world; and psychology was a long time catching up. Wilhelm Wundt, the founder of the first German psychological laboratory in Leipzig in 1879, tried to assess individuals' psychological functioning by conscious introspection, but this method failed to provided "objective" results. Individuality, as a consequence, was much less investigated than universality. Freud, who greatly upset academic psychology by focusing on the unconscious motives behind individual behavior, tried to use bits and pieces from patients' fantasies, and pieced them together like a Sherlock Holmes (see Eco and Sebeok, 1983). But, as Bowlby repeatedly emphasized, Freud failed to relate his detections to reality.

The stream of unverifiable or unfalsifiable psychoanalytic speculations was bound to cause a huge backlash in the science of the human mind, with behaviorism finally declaring the mind as only a fancy fiction. The chasm continues to exist in our day, with artificial intelligence research standing in sharp contrast to the contentions of humanistic psychologists like Bruner that we organize our experience and our memory of human affairs mainly in the form of narratives (Bruner, 1991). According to this latter line of reasoning, our vision of reality is dictated by convention and "narrative necessity" rather than by logical requirements and empirical verification (Bruner, 1990; Fiske, 1993). Yet, ultimately, this way of thinking only perpetuates the Cartesian separation of the cultural world as subjective and thus distinct from the world of objective proof, without addressing the fact that in the life sciences, especially the human life sciences, the two worlds belong together (Riedl, 1985; Grossmann, 1986; Varela et al., 1991).

Interest in the psychological relevance of individual experience for the development of one's own feelings, motives, and perceptions of the world and of other people has never waned, but rather steadily increased. It has been prematurely declared as unscientific by academic psychology. Two psychologies have existed side by side for more than a hundred years, and the shakiness of the bridges between them has ever so often been deplored. Charlotte Bühler and Hildegard Hetzer reviewed the history of child psychology up to 1929 for a *Festschrift* for Karl Bühler's 50th birthday (Bühler and Hetzer, 1929). They stated then:

> The less one believes that the pursuit of life goals is imma-nent in life itself and part of its natural developmental course, the greater, in most people's opinion, is the role of prescription and commands. In periods when the goals of life are dislocated into eternity, there is no room for psychological considerations. Likewise there is no room at the opposite end, when an unre-flective biological determinism prevails. Both extremes were indicative of historically immature epochs: Consideration for the individual in his own right was practiced only when it appeared useful [Bühler and Hetzer, 1929, p. 205].

John Bowlby was 20 years old when this passage was written. His concept of a goal-corrected partnership did not limit itself to the utilitarian outlook scored by Bühler and Hetzer. Rather, it sought to capture the psychological necessities of modern, self-directed indi-vidual life and its cultural integration within attachment relation-ships. In a unique symbiosis, Ainsworth and Bowlby opened the door for empirically grounding man's never waning interest in him-self. Considering the thousands of strange situations performed all over the world, rightly or wrongly (Karen, 1994, p. 323), and the hundreds of young scientists and clinicians who devote long and tedious hours to the assessment and understanding of inner working models, of attachment representations, and of goal-corrected behav-ior, the attachment paradigm has firmly established itself. Bowlby's regret that many developmental researchers, but only few clinicians, found attachment theory useful is no longer justified. The historical breakthrough has been made: "subjective" psychology, once resting on psychoanalytic speculations and therefore despised by "objective" academic psychology, has become a subject of enor-mous combined academic, empirical, and clinical interest.

From an academic research perspective, individual differences, temperament, genetic endowment, environmental variables, intel-lectual training, developmental shifts, and many other issues will continue to be important areas of research. It seems to me, how-ever, that only an attachment perspective is able to integrate these issues at the level of the individual's feelings, goals, persistence, care for others, and sense of coherence. Attachment is *not* one relation-ship among others; it is the very foundation of healthy individual development. More, it is the precondition for developing a coherent mind, even if it is, finally, insufficient by itself for understanding the whole mind. Scientifically, attachment theory has done nothing less than bridge the gap between individual experience and objective research.

On the societal level, child rearing in the future can no longer be critically seen without attachment theory. Robert Karen (1994), in looking back on Ainsworth's work and on the work that has grown out of it, quotes her saying in an interview in 1988: "It's more a matter of faith than anything else, but I do think it has great relevance to the well-being and happiness of mankind. It sounds corny, and I don't go around shouting it from the rooftops, but that's what's behind the whole thing as far as I'm concerned" (p. 440). Bowlby likewise saw the lasting value of attachment theory in "the light it throws on the conditions most likely to promote healthy personality development. Only when those conditions are clear beyond doubt will parents know what is best for the children and will communities be willing to help them provide it" (p. 440).

For a researcher such as myself it is extremely rewarding to see the concept of attachment prove so useful for integrating clinical and prospective developmental research. The two domains, together with the concepts, can, in Bowlby's words, be "likened to a trilothon made up of two stout pillars of evidence and a cross-piece of theory" (Bowlby, 1988b, p. 2), the pillars being individual development and developmental psychopathology, and the crosspiece, of course, being attachment theory. But it is even more rewarding, from a cultural-historical perspective, to see its unrivaled integrating power for bringing together developmental psychology and developmental psychiatry in a way that sheds light on the prerequisites for the development of autonomous, freely related selfhood, no matter whether one lives in the United States, Europe, or Israel (Sagi et al., in prep.), Japan (Benedict, 1946; Watanabe, 1994), or elsewhere. I, too, should like to shout it from the rooftops.

REFERENCES

Ainsworth, M. D. S. (1967), *Infancy in Uganda*. Baltimore, MD: Johns Hopkins University Press.
—— (1984), Adaptation and attachment. Presented at the International Conference on Infant Studies, New York, April.
—— (1985), Patterns of infant–mother attachments: Antecedents and effects on development. *Bull. New York Acad. Medicine*, 61:771–791.
—— & Bell, S. M. (1977), Infant crying and maternal responsiveness: A rejoinder to Gewirth and Boyd. *Child Devel.*, 48:1208–1216.
—— Blehar, M. C., Waters, E. & Wall, S. (1978), *Patterns of Attachment*. Hillsdale, NJ: Lawrence Erlbaum Associates.
—— & Bowlby, J. (1991), An ethological approach to personality development. *Amer. Psychol.*, 46:333–341.

Ariès, P. (1975), *Geschichte der Kindheit* [History of childhood]. Munich: Carl Hanser Verlag. (*History of Childhood*, trans. from the second French edition of *L'enfant et la vie familiale sous l'ancien régime*, 1973.

Badinter, E. (1984), *Die Mutterliebe. Geschichte eines Gefühls vom 17. Jahrhundert bis heute* [Motherlove: History of an Emotion from the 17th Century until Today]. München: Deutscher Taschenbuch Verlag. (Orig.: *L'amour en plus*, 1980).

Bell, S. M. & Ainsworth, M. D. S. (1972), Infant crying and maternal responsiveness. *Child Devel.*, 43:1171–1190.

Benedict, R. (1946), *The Chrysanthemum and the Sword*. Tokyo: Tuttle, 1954.

Boszormenyi-Nagy, I. & Spark, G. M. (1973), *Invisible Loyalties*. New York: Harper & Row.

Bowlby, J. (1946), Forty-four juvenile thieves: Their characters and home life. *Internat. J. Psycho-Anal.*, 25:19–52, 107–127.

—— (1951), Maternal care and mental health. *Bull. World Health Organ.*, 3:355–534.

—— (1969), *Attachment and Loss, Vol. 1: Attachment*. London: Hogarth Press. (Deutsch: Bindung, München: Kindler, 1975).

—— (1973), *Attachment and Loss, Vol. 2: Separation*. New York: Basic Books. (Deutsch: *Trennung*. München: Kindler, 1976).

—— (1980), *Attachment and Loss, Vol. 3*. New York: Basic Books (Deutsch: *Verlust*. Frankfurt: Fischer, 1983).

—— (1988a), *A Secure Base*. London: Tavistock/Routledge.

—— (1988b). Developmental psychiatry comes of age. *Amer. J. Psychiat.*, 145:1–10.

—— (1990), *Charles Darwin*. London: Hutchinson.

—— (1991), Ethological light on psychoanalytic problems. In: *The Development and Integration of Behavior*, ed. P. Bateson. Cambridge: Cambridge University Press, pp. 301–313.

Bretherton, I. (1991), Pouring new wine into old bottles: The social self as internal working model. In *Self Processes and Development*, ed. M. R. Gunnar & L. A. Sroufe. Hillsdale, NJ: Lawrence Erlbaum Associates, pp. 1–41.

—— (1992), The origins of attachment theory: John Bowlby and Mary Ainsworth. *Devel. Psychol.*, 28:759–775.

Bruner, J. S. (1990), *Acts of Meaning*. Cambridge, MA: Harvard University Press.

—— (1991), The narrative construction of reality. *Crit. Inq.* 18:1–21.

Bühler, C. & Hetzer, H. (1929), Zur Geschichte der Kinderpsychologie [On the history of child psychology]. In: *Beiträge zur Problemgeschichte der Psychologie*. Festschrift zu Karl Bühlers 50. Geburtstag. Jena: Verlag von Gustav Fischer, pp. 204–224.

Bühler, K. (1925), *Abriß der geistigen Entwicklung des Kindes [An Outline of the Mental Development of the Infant]*. Leipzig: Quelle & Meyer.

de Mause, L. (1974), The evolution of childhood. In: *The History of Childhood*, ed. L. de Mause. New York: Psychohistory Press, pp. 41–73.

Dunn, J. (1993), *Young Children's Close Relationships*. Newbury Park, CA: Sage.

—— & R. Plomin (1990), *Separate Lives*. New York: Basic Books.

Eckensberger, L. M. (1993), Kulturvergleichende Entwicklungspsychologie: Mehr als eine Forschungsstrategie [Culture-comparative developmental psychology: More than a research strategy]. *Newsletter Entwicklungspsychologie*, 2:22–44.

Eco, U. & Sebeok, T. A., ed. (1983), *The Sign of Three: Dupin, Holmes, Peirce*. Bloomington: Indiana University Press.

Eibl-Eibesfeldt, I. (1989), *Human Ethology*. New York: Aldine de Gruyter.

Fiske, S. T (1993), Social cognition and social perception. *Ann. Rev. Psychol.*, 44:153–194.

Fox, N. A. (1995), On the way we were: Adult memories about attachment experiences and their role in determining infant-parent relationships. *Psychol. Bull.*, 117:404–410.

Fremmer-Bombik, E. & Grossmann, K. E. (1993), Über die lebenslange Bedeutung früher Bindungserfahrungen [About the life-long meaning of early attachment experiences]. In: *Frühe Schädigungen–späte Folgen? Psychotherapie und Babyforschung*, ed. H. G. Petzold. Band 1., Paderborn: Junfermann Verlag, pp. 83–110.

Gewirtz, J. L. & Boyd, E. (1977), Does maternal responding imply reduced infant crying? A critique of the 1972 Bell and Ainsworth report. *Child Devel.*, 48:1200–1207.

Grossmann, K. (1984), Zweijährige Kinder im Zusammenspiel mit ihren Müttern, Vätern, einer fremden Erwachsenen und in einer Überraschungssituation: Beobachtungen aus bindungs- und kompetenztheoretischer Sicht [Two-year-olds in interaction with their mothers, fathers, a stranger and in a surprise situation: Observations from an attachment and a competence point of view]. Unpublished doctoral dissertation, Universität Regensburg.

—— Fremmer-Bombik, E., Rudolph, N. J. & Grossmann, K. E. (1988), Maternal attachment representations as related to patterns of infant-mother attachment and maternal care during the first year. In: *Relationships within Families*, ed. R. A. Hinde & J. Stevenson-Hinde. Oxford: Oxford Science, pp. 241–260.

—— & Grossmann, K. E. (1991), Newborn behavior, early parenting quality and later toddler-parent relationships in a group of German infants. In: *The Cultural Context of Infancy, Vol. 2*, ed. J. K. Nugent, B. M. Lester & T. B. Brazelton. Norwood, NJ: Ablex, pp. 3–38.

—— —— Spangler, G., Suess, G. & Unzner, L. (1985), Maternal sensitivity and newborns' orientation responses as related to quality of attachment in northern Germany. In: *Growing points in Attachment Theory and Research*, ed. I. Bretherton & E. Waters. *Monographs of the Society for Research in Child Development*. Serial No. 209, Vol. 50, Nos. 1–2, pp. 233–256.

—— —— (in prep.), Bindungstheoretische Überlegungen zur Krippenbetreuung und ihre Anwendung auf berufsbegleitende Supervision [Child day care from an attachment theory perspective and its application in training supervision]. Unpublished manuscript and video demonstration, Universität Regensburg.

Grossmann, K. E. (1986), From idiographic approaches to nomothetic hypotheses: Stern, Allport, and biology of knowledge, exemplified by an exploration of sibling relationships. In: *The Individual Subject and Scientific Psychology*, ed. J. Valsiner. New York: Plenum Press, pp. 37–69.

—— (1993), Universalismus und kultureller Relativismus psychologischer Erkenntnisse [Universalism and cultural relationism of psychological knowledge]. In: *Einführung in die kulturvergleichende Psychologie*, ed. A. Thomas. Göttingen: Hogrefe Verlag, pp. 53–80.

—— & Grossmann, K. (1985), Die Entwicklung von Konversationsstilen im ersten Lebensjahr und ihr Zusammenhang mit der mütterlichen Feinfühligkeit und der Beziehungsqualität zwischen Mutter und Kind [The development of conversational styles between mother and child during the first year as related to maternal sensitivity and quality of attachment]. In: *Bericht über den 34. Kongreß der Deutschen Gesellschaft für Psychologie in Wien, 1984*, ed. D. Albert. Göttingen: Verlag für Psychologie, pp. 394–397.

—— —— (1990), The wider concept of attachment in cross-cultural research. *Human Devel.*, 33:31–47.

—— Grossmann, K., Loher, I., Grossmann, K., Scheuerer-Englisch, H., Schildbach, B., Spangler, G., Wensauer, M. & Zimmermann, P. (1993), The development of inner working models of attachment and adaptation beyond infancy Presented at meeting of Society for Research in Child Development. New Orleans, March.

Harlow, H. F. (1971), *Learning to Love*. San Francisco: Albion.

Hazan, C. & Shaver, P. (1987), Romantic love conceptualized as an attachment process. *J. Per. Soc. Psychol.*, 52:511–524.

Hewlett, S. A. (1991), *When the Bough Breaks*. New York: Basic Books.

Hinde, R. A. & Spencer-Booth, Y. (1971), Effects of brief separation from mother on rhesus monkeys. *Sci.*, 173:111–118.

Imhof, A. E. (1981), Die gewonnenen Jahre [The gained years]. Von der Zunahme unserer Lebensspanne seit dreihundert Jahren oder von der Notwendigkeit einer neuen Einstellung zum Leben und zum Sterben. Ein historisches Essay. Munich: Beck.

—— (1984), Wandel der Säuglingssterblichkeit vom 18. bis 20. Jahrhundert [Changes in infant mortality from the 18th to the 20th century]. In: *Gesundheitspolitik. Historische und zeitkritische Analyse*, ed. H. Schaefer, H. Schipperges & G. Wagner. Köln: Deutscher Ärzte-Verlag, pp. 1–35.

Johnson, F. A. (1993), *Dependency and Japanese Socialization*. New York: New York University Press

Karen, R. (1994), *Becoming Attached*. New York: Warner Books.

Kuhn, T. S. (1962), *The Structure of Scientific Revolutions*. Chicago: University of Chicago Press.

Levine, S. & Wiener, S. G. (1988), Psychoendocrine aspects of mother–infant relationships in non-human primates. *Psychoneuroendocrinol.*, 13:143–154.

Loher, I. (1988), Intellektuelle und soziale Erfahrungen im vierten Lebensjahr und ihre Beziehung zur Kompetenz im Alltag und in einer Belastungssituation [Intellectual and social experience in four-year-old children and its relationship to everyday competence and in a challenging situation]. Unpublished doctoral dissertation, Universität Regensburg.

Lorenz, K. (1973), *Die Rückseite des Spiegels. Versuch einer Naturgeschichte menschlichen Erkennens [Behind the Mirror: A Search for a Natural History of Human Knowledge]*. Munich: Piper.

Main, M. (1973), Exploration, play, and cognitive functioning as related to child-mother attachment. Unpublished doctoral dissertation, Johns Hopkins University.

—— & Goldwyn, R. (in press), Interview based adult attachment classifications: Related to infant–mother and infant–father attachment. *Devel. Psychol.*

—— & Hesse, E. (1990), Parents' unresolved traumatic experiences are related to infant disorganized attachment status: Is frightened and/or frightening parental behavior the linking mechanism? In: *Attachment in the Preschool Years*, ed. M. T. Greenberg, D. Cicchetti & E. M. Cummings. Chicago: University of Chicago Press, pp. 161–182.

—— Kaplan, N. & Cassidy, J. (1985), Security in infancy, childhood, and adulthood: A move to the level of representation. In: *Growing Points in Attachment Theory and Research*, ed. I. Bretherton & E. Waters. *Monographs of the Society for Research in Child Development*, Serial No. 209, Vol. 50, Nos. 1–2, pp. 66–106.

Minsky, M. (1987), *The Society of Mind*. London: Heinemann.

Montada, L. (1987), Entwicklung der Moral. (Development of morality) In: *Entwicklungspsychologie. 2. völlig neu bearbeitete und erweiterte Auflage*, ed. R. Oerter, & L. Montada Munich: Urban & Schwarzenberg, pp. 738–766.

Moritz, K. P. (1783–1793), *Magazin zur Erfahrungsseelenkunde als ein Lesebuch für Gelehrte und Ungelehrte. Mit Unterstützung mehrerer Wahrheitsfreunde herausgegeben. [Magazine for Experiential Knowledge of the Soul as a Reader for Scholars and Laymen* (1987) edited with support of several truth lovers]. Berlin: August Mylins.

—— (1987). *Anton Reiser. Ein psychologischer Roman.* München: C. H. Beck Verlag (Original: 1785–1790). [*Anton Reiser. A Psychological Novel*] London: Humphrey Milford, 1926.

Musham, H. V. (1979), *The Demographic Transition.* Liège: Ordina Editions.

Nyssen, F. (1984), *Die Geschichte der Kindheit bei L. de Mause.* [The History of Childhood in L. de Mause]. Frankfurt: Peter Lang.

Oatley, K. & Jenkins, J. M. (1992), Human emotions. Function and dysfunction. *Ann. Rev. Psychol.,* 423:55–85.

Parkes, C. M., Stevenson-Hinde, J. & Marris, P. (1991), *Attachment across the Life Cycle.* London: Tavistock.

Plato (1953), *Sämtliche Werke,* [*Collected Works*] Vol. 6. Nomoi. Hamburg: Rowohlt.

Portmann, A. (1956), *Zoologie und das neue Bild des Menschen. Biologische Fragmente zu einer Lehre vom Menschen.* [*Zoology and the New Image of Man. Biological Fragments towards a Study of Man*]. Hamburg: Rowohlt.

Riedl, R. (1985), *Die Spaltung des Weltbildes.* [*The Schism of the World Image*]. Berlin: Paul Parey.

Sagan, L. A. (1987), *The Health of Nations.* New York: Basic Books.

Sagi, A., van IJzendoorn, M., Scharf, M., Joels, T., Koren-Karie, N., Mayseless, O. & Aviezer, O. (in preparation), Ecological constraints for intergenerational transmission of attachment: In search of determinants of transmission failures.

Scarr, S. & Eisenberg, M. (1993), Child care research: Issues, perspectives, and results. *Ann. Rev. Psychol.,* 44:613–644.

Scheuerer-Englisch, H. (1989), Das Bild der Vertrauensbeziehung bei zehnjährigen Kindern und ihren Eltern: Bindungsbeziehungen in längsschnittlicher und aktueller Sicht [Representations of trust-relationships in ten-year-olds and their parents: Attachment relationships in longitudinal and present perspectives]. Unpublished doctoral dissertation, Universität Regensburg.

Schildbach, B. (1992), Die Bedeutung emotionaler Unterstützung bei der Bewältigung von intellektuellen Aufgaben. [The significance of emotional support in coping with intellectual tasks]. Unpublished doctoral dissertation, Universität Regensburg.

Schmidt-Kolmer E., Tonkowa-Jampolskaija, R. Atanassowa, A. (1979), *Die soziale Adaption der Kinder bei der Aufnahme in Einrichtungen der Vorschulerziehung.* [The Social Adaption of Children During Introduction in Institutional Preschool]. Berlin: VEB Verlag, Volk und Gesundheit

Schmuck, C. (1993), Die Gemeinhardtin oder Mutterliebe im Pestjahr 1713. Mittelbayerische Zeitung, May 8–9, (Mrs Gemeinhardt or motherlove in the year of pestilinee 1713).

Schuster-Keim, U. & Keim, A. (1988), *Zur Geschichte der Kindheit bei Lloyd de Mause.* [On the history of childhood in Lloyd de Mause]. Frankfurt: Peter Lang.

Shorter, E. (1975), *The Making of the Modern Family.* New York: Basic Books [*Die Geburt der modernen Familie.* Reinbek: Rowohlt Verlag, 1977].

Spangler, G., Fremmer-Bombik, E. & Grossmann, K. (in press), Social and individual determinants of attachment security and disorganization. *Infant Ment. Health J.*

—— & Grossman, K. E. (1993), Biobehavioral organization in securely and insecurely attached infants. *Child Devel.,* 64:1439–1450.

—— Schieche, M., Ilg, U., Maier, U. & Ackermann, C. (1994), Maternal sensitivity as an external organizer for biobehavioral regulation in infancy. *Devel. Psychobiol.,* 27:425–437.

Sroufe, L. A., Egeland, B. & Kreutzer, T. (1990), The fate of early experience following developmental change: Longitudinal approaches to individual adaptation in childhood. *Child Devel.,* 61:1363–1373.

Suess, G., Grossmann, K. E. & Sroufe, L. A. (1992), Effects of infant attachment to mother and father on quality of adaptation in preschool: From dyadic to individual organization of self. *Internat. J. Behav. Devel.*, 15:43–65.

Tinbergen, E. A. & Tinbergen, N. (1972), *Early Childhood Autism*. Fortschritte der Verhaltensforschung 10. Berlin: Parey Verlag.

Trevarthen, C. (1987), *Brain Development*. In *The Oxford Companion to the Mind*, ed. R.L. Gregory. Oxford: Oxford University Press, pp. 101–110.

Trivers, R.L. (1974), Parent-offspring conflict. *Amer. Zool.*, 14:249–264.

van IJzendoorn, M. (1995a), Adult attachment representations, parental responsiveness, and infant attachment. A meta-analysis on the predictive value of the Adult Attachment Interview. *Psychol. Bull.*, 117:387–403.

—— (1995b), On the way we are: On temperament, attachment and the transmission gap. A rejoinder to Fox. *Psychol. Bull.*, 117:411–415.

van IJzendoorn, M., Sagi, A. & Lambermon, M. W. E. (1992), The multiple caretaker paradox: Data from Holland and Israel. In: *Beyond the Parent*, ed. R. C. Pianta. San Francisco: Jossey-Bass, pp. 5–24.

Vatela, F. J., Thompson, E. & Rosch, E. (1991), *The Embodied Mind*. Cambridge, MA: MIT Press.

Wartner, U., Grossmann, K., Fremmer-Bombik, E. & Suess, G. (1994), Attachment patterns at age six in South Germany: Predictability from infancy and implications for preschool behavior. *Child Devel.* 65:1014–1027.

Watanabe, H. (1994), The applications of attachment and amae to clinical problems in Japan. In: *The Clinical Application of Ethology and Attachment Theory*, ed. J. Richer. London: Association for Child Psychology and Psychiatry, pp. 36–43.

Wensauer, M. (1994), Die Bedeutung internaler Abreitsmodelle für erfolgreiches Altern [The meaning of inner working models for successful aging]. Unpublished doctoral dissertation, Universität Regensburg.

—— & Grossmann, K. E. (in press), Qualität der Bindungsrepräsentation, soziale Integration und Umgang mit Netzwerkresssourcen im höheren Erwachsenenalter [Quality of attachment representation, social integration, and coping with social networks in senior people]. *Zeitschrift für Gerontologie.*

Wieckenberg, E. P. (1987), *Nachwort zu Anton Reiser von Karl Philipp Moritz* [*Postcript to Anton Reiser by Karl Philipp Moritz*]. Munich: C. H. Beck, pp. 379–410.

5

The Developmental Perspectives of Attachment and Psychoanalytic Theory

MORRIS EAGLE

In a certain sense, distinguishing too sharply between attachment theory and psychoanalytic theory can be somewhat misleading insofar as attachment theory can be understood as a particular kind of contemporary psychoanalytic theory or, more specifically, as a particular kind of object relations theory. Despite their close links, however, there are sufficient differences between attachment theory and contemporary psychoanalytic theory in a generic sense—in influences, methods, and traditions—to make it useful to compare them. This comparison furthermore can facilitate focusing on more specific issues that are worth pursuing in their own right.

In reacting against central aspects of classical Freudian theory, both attachment theory and contemporary psychoanalysis end up sharing certain basic assumptions and conclusions. Both attachment theory and contemporary psychoanalytic theories (i.e., object relations theory and self psychology) have in common their rejection of certain core assumptions and formulations of Freudian drive theory— for example, the ideas that the infant's attachment to mother is secondary to the latter's role in gratification of the infant's hunger drive; that the vicissitudes of the sexual drive are primary determinants of personality development; and that reduction of excitation is a superordinate motive underlying a wide range of behaviors. They also share the alternative views that infant–mother attachment is an autonomous motivational system rather than one subservient to other instinctual drives and that, in important ways, personality is shaped by early attachment experiences. (See Eagle, 1984, for a fuller discussion of the differences between classical Freudian theory and contemporary psychoanalytic theories.) Thus, quite frequently points of *divergence* between classical psychoanalysis and attachment theory constitute points of *convergence* between contemporary psychoanalysis and attachment theory. In that sense, attachment theory becomes, in part at least, a mirror of contemporary psychoanalysis.

CONVERGENCES BETWEEN ATTACHMENT THEORY AND CONTEMPORARY PSYCHOANALYTIC THEORY

The Formative Role of Early Maternal Experiences

An obvious point of convergence between attachment theory and contemporary psychoanalytic views is the etiological emphasis given to early infant–mother experiences. Although Freud had much to say regarding the general formative role of early maternal experiences—for example, he maintained that these experiences put their indelible stamp on object choice—according to classical theory, the primary determinant of health versus neurosis lies in how one resolves the later and triadic oedipal situation. Both attachment theory and contemporary psychoanalysis deemphasize the significance of the oedipal complex and, at the same time, place correspondingly greater stress on earlier developmental periods. In the context of attachment theory, the emphasis on the determinative role of early experiences is expressed in the assumption that attachment styles established early in life are relatively stable throughout one's life.

In both the psychoanalytic and attachment theory contexts, skepticism regarding this assumption has taken pretty much the same form. In the psychoanalytic literature, Mitchell (1988), for example, makes the point that what is taken to be the determinative effect of early experiences is often likely the cumulative consequence of repeated experiences of a similar form throughout the life of the child. In the attachment context, Thompson, Lamb, and Estes (1982), for example, raised the similar question of whether stability in attachment style reflects stability primarily of parental care and life circumstances. This issue certainly warrants further investigation.

Relatedness and Autonomy

Another obvious commonality or point of convergence between attachment theory and contemporary psychoanalysis is a clear deemphasis of sex and aggression and the primacy of drive gratification, and a correspondingly strong emphasis on the two broad developmental trends of relatedness and autonomy. Although different terms are used, and different nuances are stressed, in both literatures one finds the basic assumption that a critical factor in personality development is how one manages the interplay between relatedness and autonomy. In the attachment literature the terms are attachment and exploration. In the early psychoanalytic literature,

Angyal (1941, 1965) referred to homonymy and autonomy; Hermann (1936) referred to clinging and going-in-search—an obvious precursor to attachment and exploration. In Mahler's (1968) work the dimensions are symbiosis and separation-individuation. For Fairbairn (1952) they are primary identification and separation, and for Blatt (e.g., Blass and Blatt, 1992; Blatt, 1992) the key dimensions are relatedness and self-definition and attachment and separateness. Winnicott (1965) links the introjection of an ego-supportive environment to the capacity to be alone.

Whatever the differences among these theorists (and they do not take identical positions) and the different terms used, there seems to be a convergence on the common assumption that, in order to experience oneself as a separate and individuated person who is comfortable exploring the world, one must have experienced adequate early caring and have been able to internalize these early experiences. The common assumption in the attachment and contemporary psychoanalytic literatures is that lives are made or broken not primarily on the basis of conflict in relation to libidinal or aggressive wishes or on the basis of fixation at different psychosexual stages but rather as a function of balancing relatedness and autonomy.

Representations

Contemporary psychoanalytic theories are also characterized by a shift in the conceptualization of the unconscious—from a repository of repressed instinctual wishes, a "cauldron of seething excitations," to a structure comprising *representations* of self, of object, and of prototypic interactions between the two. This reconceptualization is seen, for example, in Sandler and Rosenblatt's (1962) writings on the representational world, Fairbairn's (1952) theory of internalized objects, Stern's (1985) representations of interactions generalized (RIGs), Weiss, Sampson, and the Mt. Zion Psychotherapy Research Group's (1986) unconscious pathogenic beliefs, Kernberg's (1976) self–object affect units, and role-relationship models and self and object schemata. In attachment theory, the emphasis on unconscious representations is most clearly expressed in the centrality of the concept of *internal working models* (e.g., Bowlby, 1973; Bretherton, 1990).

Accuracy of Representations

In addition to a common emphasis on the concept of representations, there is a marked agreement regarding the nature of these

representations. That is, in attachment theory and in at least some of
the psychoanalytic literature, representations, particularly of self–
other interactions, are understood as relatively *accurate* accounts of
actual events.[1] For example, Stern (1985) writes that early representations of interactions generalized (RIGs) are free of distortion and
represent abstractions (what Nelson and Gruendel [1981] refer to as
general event representations) of frequent and prototypic self–
object interactions. Similarly, according to Bowlby (1973), internal
working models generally represent relatively accurate accounts of
actual interactions between the child and the caregiver. Bowlby's
position was partly a reaction to what he thought was the excessive
Kleinian emphasis on fantasy and reflected his desire to balance that
emphasis with a sharp reminder that real traumatic events (loss,
separation, threats of separation, and rejection) happen to children
and that these real events exert a strong developmental influence.

Endogenous Factors Versus Environmental Failure

The conception of representations as relatively accurate accounts of
actual events and interactions is but one expression of what appears
to be a general shift in psychoanalytic theories of etiology, from an
emphasis on *endogenous factors* in the production of pathology to
the increasing recognition of the role of purported *environmental
failure*. This shift is quite apparent in the object relations theories of
Fairbairn (1952) and Winnicott (1965) and in Kohut's (1971, 1977,
1984) self psychology. In spite of differences among these theories,
they all appear to converge on the proposition that pathology is
largely the consequence of marked deficiencies in early caregiving–
deficiencies that include rejection and deprivation, impingements,
absence of "good-enough mothering," and traumatic failures to provide empathic mirroring and opportunities for idealization. In the
attachment literature, the role of maternal failure is discussed largely
in the context of the caregiver's rejecting, unresponsive, and inconsistent behavior, with emphasis on the consequent insecure attachment and the corresponding internal working models that render
one especially susceptible to pathology and to maladaptive patterns
of behavior. Although the avoidant and resistant patterns of attachment that result from maternal failures are less optimal than secure
attachment, they are nevertheless within the range of normality.
That is, rather than representing forms of pathology, these less than

---

[1] Not all psychoanalytic theorists make this assumption. For example, Sandler does
not appear to assume that representations are generally accurate accounts of the self-
object interactions. Also, in this volume, Bretherton observes that internal working
models model meaning rather than objective reality.

optimal patterns of attachment render the individual more *vulnerable* to various forms of maladaptive behavior and pathology.

We can see, then, that the related ideas in attachment theory that representations are relatively accurate accounts of actual interactions and that insecure attachment is largely the product of environmental failure constitute both points of divergence from classical Freudian theory and points of convergence with contemporary psychoanalytic theories, most especially object relations theory and self psychology.

In emphasizing the accuracy of representations and the overriding etiological role of environmental failure, both contemporary psychoanalytic formulations (particularly self psychology) and attachment theory seem to have left little room for the influence of wishes, conflict, fantasy, and idiosyncratic construals of meanings on personality development. They also seem to leave little room for the consideration that young children's immature cognitive and affective structures may contribute to idiosyncratic construals and fantasy elaborations of events. Interestingly enough, this seems less true for attachment theory—particularly in the light of some recent work—than for self psychology. Thus, the concept of "multiple working models," work on the avoidant pattern of attachment, and recent research with the Adult Attachment Interview point to the operation and importance of defensive and fantasy-like processes.

With regard to the concept of multiple working models, Bowlby (1973, p. 205) notes that people may have more than one internal working model and suggests that different working models may conflict with each other. Furthermore, some working models may represent idealized representations that reflect the operations of defense and the fantasy of what the child would have liked the relationship with caregiver to be, rather than the actual early caregiving experiences. By the same token, however, the postulation of multiple and even conflicting working models of the same figure and of defensive and idealized representations seems to mitigate the claim that internal working models are essentially accurate representations. Bowlby never explored the range of implications embedded in this idea of multiple working models.

The work of Main and Goldwyn (1984), however, with the Adult Attachment Interview Schedule, supports and elaborates upon Bowlby's concept of multiple working models. According to their findings, some adults who, according to other indirect evidence, were likely to be insecurely attached in childhood tend to report idealized accounts of their early attachment figure and of early attachment experiences. If Bowlby is correct, these conscious and idealized representations may coexist with an earlier model that, to use Bowlby's words, "is constructed on fairly primitive lines, but that the person himself may be relatively, or completely, unaware of." This more primitive model, in Bowlby's formulation, is "radically incompatible" with conscious and later representations (Bowlby, 1973, p. 205).

The work of Main and her colleagues further suggests a possible rapprochement between the polarities of an emphasis on actual interactional experiences and the conception of internal working models as accurate records of such experiences, on one hand, and an emphasis on the role of intrapsychic individual construals and meanings, on the other. That is, the stance one takes later in life toward one's early experiences—how one construes and evaluates them—plays a determinative role in the developmental consequences of these experiences. Main's work also suggests that, although early representations may accurately reflect early interactions, these representations are constantly worked over and revised, not only in the light of new experiences but also as a consequence of metacognitive and meta-affective processes such as remembering, reflecting upon, working through, coming to terms with, and so on. In accordance with this work, Fonagy et al. (this volume) also present evidence that in successful psychotherapy (with borderline patients) there is an increase in what they refer to as "reflective self-function."

Contemporary psychoanalytic literature has tended to focus strongly on the "corrective emotional experience" provided by the therapeutic relationship. For example, in self psychology the primary therapeutic vehicle is the empathic mirroring provided by the therapist—which presumably leads to repair of self-defects and structure building (Kohut, 1984). From an attachment theory perspective, however, the therapist as an attachment figure provides not only a corrective emotional experience but also a *secure base* from which exploration can occur. In the therapeutic context, the most important kind of exploration one can engage in is self-exploration. It is easy to forget that, according to attachment theory, the importance of secure attachment lies not only in the feeling of well-being and security it provides but also in its facilitation of exploration of the world and of oneself. Thus, attachment theory and research suggest an obvious integration between the therapeutic factors of insight and understanding, and the therapeutic relationship. The safe base provided by the therapist and the therapeutic setting is not only directly therapeutic— through its contribution to a sense of security and well-being—but also indirectly (and perhaps more important) therapeutic through its facilitation of exploration and understanding.

In this context, it is worth noting that, so many years after Freud's (and Santyana's) claim that those who do not remember are destined to repeat the past, the best systematic evidence for that assertion comes not from psychoanalytic research but from attachment research that investigates the intergenerational transmission of maternal patterns of behavior that are associated with insecure attachment. Furthermore, attachment research also provides support for the corollary idea that those who do remember and attempt to confront and come to terms with their early unsatisfactory attachment experiences are less likely to repeat these patterns (Fraiberg, Adelson, and Shapiro, 1975; Main and Goldwyn, 1984). It is ironic that during a period in psychoanalytic history in which the therapeutic value of insight, awareness, and remembering has been radically deemphasized, attachment research reminds us of their value and relevance.

Temperament, Representations, and Psychic Reality

The issue of accuracy of a representation or working model of the mother–infant interaction has embedded within it the temperamental and dispositional predilection of the infant. Because individual differences in infant temperament may influence the nature of subjective experience, it is unlikely that representations or working models can be understood as accurate in any simple way. What constitutes sensitive responsiveness for an infant with one kind of temperament will be experienced differently by an infant with a different kind of temperament. One infant may wait patiently while waiting to be fed, while another may go into a rage at even a brief delay. Each infant is likely to form a different representation of objectively similar events, a representation that corresponds to his or her own experiences. Indeed, particularly in the areas that we are discussing, representations are always likely to reflect the nature of the idiosyncratic experience. If temperament influences the nature of idiosyncratic experience, it would necessarily also influence the nature of representations. In short, temperamental factors may influence *how* maternal behavior is experienced and, therefore, the nature of the representations of maternal behavior.

If temperamental factors can influence subjective experience and the nature of the representations of these experiences, they are also likely to influence attachment style—even if in an indirect, rather than a direct, manner. As Belsky, Rosenberger, and Crnic (this volume) note, however, there is a good deal of controversy regarding the relationship between security of attachment and infant temperament. Thus, on one hand, in a number of recent studies (e.g., Goldsmith and Alansky, 1987; Vaughn, et al., 1992) in which the results of different samples are subject to statistical meta-analysis or discursive summary, there is evidence for a modest but significant relation between temperament and security of attachment. Indeed, in the Goldsmith and Alansky (1987) paper, in which the single temperamental factor of proneness to distress is related to resistant infant behavior (which is one aspect of insecure attachment), the effect size for temperament is comparable to the effect size for maternal responsiveness.

On the other hand, a number of findings cited in the Belsky et al. chapter in this volume appear to contradict the claim of a direct relationship between temperamental differences and variations in security of attachment. For example, Belsky, Fish, and Isabella (1991) found that almost 25% of 148 infants studied changed their relative level of negativity over a six-month period and that personality and marital characteristics of both parents, as well as quality of parenting observed when babies were three months of age, accounted for the observed changes. As another example cited by Belsky, Rosenberger, and Crnic (this volume), van den Boom (1990) found that an intervention designed to heighten maternal sensitivity not only did, in fact, succeed in doing so, but increased the number of infants classified as secure relative to a control group that received no intervention.

As Belsky et al. (this volume) note, the relationship between infant temperament and attachment—as well as the relationship between attachment and such other factors as psychological health of mother, quality of marriage, and social support—is likely to be mediated "by impacting more proximal processes of parent–child interaction." Indeed, there is evidence that temperament does exert such a mediational influence. For example, Lee and Bates (1985) found that temperamentally difficult infants elicited more confrontations, including more conflictual ones, with mother. In accord with these findings, Rutter (1987) found that temperamentally difficult children were more likely to be the target of parental criticism, and Hinde and Stevenson-Hinde (1986) reported that children with more negative moods were more likely to have irritable mothers with hostile features. As Goldsmith, Bradshaw, and Rieser-Danner (1986) note, temperamental fearfulness might influence the number of opportunities the infant has for experiencing the mother as a secure base for exploration. That negative parental behavior is, at least in part, elicited by the child's cues is suggested by the finding that when the child's behavior changed—in one case, through beneficial drug effects on hyperactivity (Barkley, 1981) and in another case through behavioral training (Brunk and Henggeler, 1984)—the parental behavior changed.

It seems to me that the most reasonable conclusion one can draw regarding the influence of infant temperament on attachment is the one drawn by Belsky et al. in this volume—namely, that it is not a main effect, but rather one mediated by its impact on the proximal processes of infant–mother interaction. After all, maternal sensitivity entails sensitivity to a particular infant with a particular set of characteristics and demands. Hence, it is likely that proper maternal responsiveness to a very difficult infant will enable that infant to become securely attached. As the evidence suggests, however, a very difficult infant also makes greater demands on maternal responsiveness, demands that may not be successfully met. The additional consideration I am suggesting is that maternal behavior that, to an outside observer, may be viewed as adequately responsive may be experienced and represented differently by infants endowed with different temperaments.

If endogenous temperamental factors influence the nature of infant–mother interactions, as well as how these interactions are experienced by the infant, they surely influence the nature of representations and working models. Hence, representations and working models do not reflect, in any simple way, what actually happened but incorporate the infant's individual and perhaps idiosyncratic experience of infant–mother interactions. The role given to the endogenous factor of drive in classical psychoanalytic theory parallels the role of temperamental factors in nonpsychoanalytic theories. In some instances drives are treated essentially as a temperamental variable. For example, Kernberg (1976) speculates that borderline patients are constitutionally endowed with a high level of aggression and hence, as infants, are likely to react with oral rage to even moderate degrees of frustration. I am not suggesting that Kernberg's theory is necessarily correct, but it illustrates well how some psychoanalytic theories treat so-called drive factors essentially as temperamental variables.

Both classical and contemporary psychoanalytic theories put a great deal of emphasis on the role of fantasy and psychic reality in influencing behavior. A characteristic point made by psychoanalytic theorists is that whereas nonpsychoanalytic theories focus on the role of external events, psychoanalysis emphasizes personal meanings and fantasies, that is, psychic reality. This was the primary reason given for dismissing attachment theory as a *psychoanalytic* theory or even as relevant to psychoanalytic theory in one of the early assessments of attachment theory by A. Freud (1960). She wrote in response to Bowlby's (1960) paper, "We do not deal with the happenings in the external world as such but with their repercussions in the mind, i.e., with the form in which they are registered by the child" (A. Freud, 1960, p. 54). The fact is, however, that, although personal meanings and fantasies—the patient's psychic reality—are undoubtedly and understandably emphasized in the clinical situation, as I noted earlier, in their etiological formulations contemporary psychoanalytic theories, in fact, stress the role of external events, primarily maternal failures of various kinds. This discrepancy between clinical practice and theory notwithstanding, the fact remains that an emphasis on personal meanings and fantasies, or idiosyncratic psychic reality, immediately raises the question of how to account for the individual differences in personal meanings that people give to events and for the individual differences in fantasies generated by these events. If there are marked individual differences in people's psychic reality, in how different people experience and construe similar events, including the fantasies generated by these events, then one must look somewhere to account for them. One wants to understand and identify the multiplicity of determinants of these individual differences in psychic reality. Put another way, a particular psychic reality is itself a developmental product whose determinants need to be understood. I am reminded of the philosopher Max Black's (1967) comment regarding explanation of human behavior from the point of view of the individual's motives and reasons. He writes, "As soon as reasons for action have been provided, an inquiring mind will want to press on to questions about the provenance and etiology of such reasons" (p. 656). In short, differences in temperament represent one possible source in accounting for individual variability in fantasy and in the provenance and etiology of reasons and motives. That is, temperamental variables may help account for individual differences in the representation of events that seem objectively similar or even identical.

METHODOLOGICAL AND CLINICAL IMPLICATIONS

Let me turn now to the implications of attachment research and theory for psychoanalytic development and etiological theories. My main point here is that the latter tend to be excessively simplistic and linear and have a good deal to learn from attachment research and theory. As a specific illustration of this claim, I discuss the question of how people perpetuate maladaptive patterns.

Developmental and Etiological Theories

Bowlby (1988) contrasts the concept of *developmental pathways*–a concept that he claims is central to attachment theory's perspective on development–with the traditional psychoanalytic emphasis on such notions as fixation and regression to earlier specific phases of development. I would add the general contrast between a conception of developmental pathways and a somewhat simplistic linear causal model that is characteristic of some contemporary psychoanalytic etiological theories.

It seems highly unlikely that either normal personality development or the development of psychopathology would follow so simple and linear a course as suggested by contemporary psychoanalytic theories. Consider, for example, the etiological theories of Fairbairn's (1952) object relations theory and Kohut's (1971, 1977, 1984) self psychology. With regard to the former, however complex, convoluted, and interesting Fairbairn's metapsychology of internalized objects may be, his etiological theory is remarkably simple and essentially limited to a simple factor–early deprivation, frustration, and rejection. The situation is similar for Kohut's etiological theory, which states that narcissistic disorders and self defects are attributable to traumatic parental failures in empathic mirroring, in the provision of opportunities for idealization, or both. This is an example of a linear theory in which the relationship between the purported causal factor of empathic failure and presumed self defects is formulated in a simple "A causes B" linear form. One moves from parental failures rather directly to psychopathology, with few intervening, modulating variables or influences.[2] Little consideration is given to such complicating factors as individual differences in thresholds for experiencing certain interactions as empathic failures, the role of synergistic or protective variables, the factors that, so to speak, "transform" personality or behavioral dispositions into clinical pathology, and so on. Of course, no systematic evidence is provided for these etiological claims. The only evidence cited is the productions of adult patients in treatment.

In addition to the pitfalls of employing clinical data from adult patients for etiological purposes, there is the larger problem of relying primarily on what Kohlberg, LaCrosse, and Ricks (1970) call *follow-back* data–which is contrasted with *follow-up* data–to make etiological claims. Let me illustrate the importance of this distinction with one actual and one hypothetical example.

---

[2] Kohut (1977, p. 7) does discuss the modulating role of "compensatory structures." But these compensatory structures are ways of dealing with defects that have already occurred.

In a study on the relationship between childhood difficulties (of sufficient concern so that the children were referred to a child guidance clinic) and adult adjustment, Robins (1966) reported that 11% of childhood truants became adult alcoholics, a figure not much different from the 8% of all the adults in the study (including the control group) who were alcoholics. When one looks at the adult alcoholics in the study, however, one finds that 75% of them had been childhood truants, compared with 26% for the adults who showed no diagnosable pathology. The former *follow-up*, or prospective, data suggest quite a different picture regarding the nature and strength of the relationship between childhood truancy and adult alcoholism than do the *follow-back* data.

Let me now turn to a hypothetical example that cogently illustrates the different conclusions one might draw from follow-back and follow-up data. Imagine that being sexually abused is a necessary, but not sufficient, condition for becoming a borderline personality as an adult and that 10% of all children who were sexually abused warrant the diagnosis as adults of borderline personality. This would mean that *all* people diagnosed as adults as borderline personality were sexually abused as children but that 90% of children who were sexually abused do *not* become a borderline personality as adults. Note the striking difference between follow-back and follow-up data. In the follow-back data 100% of adults diagnosed as borderline personality were sexually abused as children. In the follow-up data 10% of children who were sexually abused develop borderline personality disorder as adults. Consider the strikingly different etiological conclusions that one would be likely to draw from the two different sets of data.

Let us take this hypothetical example a step further. Imagine that all the adults who are diagnosed as borderline personality enter treatment and that very few of the 90% who had been sexually abused and were not given a clinical diagnosis enter treatment. The therapists who treat the former 10% subgroup and who never come into contact with the remaining 90% of the group would all find a history of sexual abuse in their adult patients. On the basis of these follow-back data, they would likely develop an etiological theory seriously distorting and exaggerating the nature and strength of the relationship between childhood sexual abuse and adult personality disorder. Insofar as virtually all case studies and other clinical data rely exclusively on follow-back data, they represent a very flimsy, potentially seriously misleading, basis for etiological theories if they are approached uncritically and are not supplemented by follow-up data. Here is another area, then, in which attachment research and theory, with their emphasis on longitudinal studies, have much to contribute to psychoanalytic theorizing.

Although, as noted, Bowlby contrasts the concept of developmental pathways with typical psychoanalytic conceptions of development, the work of Rutter and his colleagues (e.g., Rutter, 1990), as well as work of Garmezy (1985) and Masten and Garmezy (1985) on the resilient child, most clearly illustrates and implements the approach to understanding development and psychopathology in terms of developmental pathways. Rutter (1989) notes that development is characterized by discontinuities as well as continuities, and his work suggests that something like a decision tree, with different choice points and indirect connections, rather than a linear causal model, is more appropriate to understanding the nature of development and adaptation. To illustrate with a specific example (Rutter, Quinton, and Hill, 1990), for a group of women who grew up in an orphanage, school success emerges as an important "choice point" in the direction that their lives took. Thus, doing well at school appears to give these women confidence in their ability to plan and to make choices in regard to work and marriage, an ability that, in turn, serves them well in choosing a supportive mate, a choice that, in turn, has a major impact on their general adaptation and adjustment. The complexity of the "indirect linkages" between childhood and adulthood is indicated in a number of other ways in Rutter's findings. For example, the protective factor of planning that was so important for the institution-reared women had little effect on the noninstitution-reared control group.

A "decision tree" model of development is also implied in the research of Main and Goldwyn (1984) discussed earlier. This work suggests that, although a woman may have been rejected as a child and may have therefore developed an insecure attachment style, the ability to remember, confront, and work through these early experiences in some way "transforms" her internal working model and interactive style so that she does *not* transmit a pattern of rejection and consequent insecure attachment to her own infant. One of the most important questions in this area is what kinds of events and experiences lead to crucial modifications in internal working model in one case and perpetuation of an early working model in another case. That there is no simple linearity between early events and subsequent personality development is also implied in Belsky's et al.'s (this volume) observation that a risk factor may not have a measurable effect on development unless it is taken together with other risk factors.

As noted, contemporary psychoanalytic etiological theories generally do not address these kinds of questions—although therapists undoubtedly do in clinical work with individual patients. Perhaps this is partly a function of the follow-back nature of clinical data. That is, patients seen in treatment are more likely to be those in whom the etiological trajectory has taken the predictable path, for example, from presumed parental failures to adult pathology. Those whose developmental pathway has not gone the predictable way are less likely to be seen in treatment and therefore less likely to contribute data that would be disconfirming or, at least, modulating. This selective factor may then lead to the partly spurious confirmation by the clinical data of the etiological theories. It seems to me that psychoanalytic theorizing, particularly in the area of etiological formulations, has much to learn from attachment research as well as from work in the other related areas.

BEHAVIORAL CUES AND PERPETUATION OF MALADAPTIVE PATTERNS

Contemporary and classical psychoanalytic theory has paid remarkably little attention to what people actually *do* to perpetuate their pathology, particularly their maladaptive relationship patterns. The focus has been almost exclusively on intrapsychic factors. Attachment research and theory, by contrast, suggest ways in which people actively perpetuate maladaptive patterns. The concept of the internal working model suggests that people come to new relationships with a set of interactional expectations that exerts a strong influence on their behavior and the cues they emit to others.

Consider the study by Jacobson and Willie (1986), who report that, although insecurely attached three-year-olds make as many social overtures as securely attached children, they are *selected* less frequently as playmates by other children. Why is this so? Surely, other children do not say to themselves: "Oh, he is insecurely attached. I don't want him as a friend." It must be the case that insecurely attached children emit cues that lead to their less frequent selection.

Sroufe (1990) reports that teachers who were blind to the attachment history of securely and insecurely attached preschool children behaved differently toward them. They tended to be warm, uncontrolling, and positive toward, and expect age-appropriate behavior from, securely attached children; by contrast, they scored significantly higher on control/negative expectations for compliance, and anger in their behavior toward avoidant children. Sroufe remarks that this behavior on the part of teachers is "quite reminiscent of what these children had experienced with their caregivers" (p. 299). For anxious/resistant children, similarly, teachers "were

unduly nurturant and tolerant of rule violations, but again controlling and with low expectations" (p. 299). As Sroufe notes, this pattern of teacher response was "in remarkable accord with patterns of
adaptation shown by the children and therefore confirmed the children's working models of self" (p. 299). On what basis do teachers
behave differently toward the children? Some clues are provided by
the findings that the teachers judged the children with a history of
secure attachment to be more independent and resourceful than
children with a history of an avoidant attachment pattern. It is likely
that a child experienced as more independent and resourceful is
likely to elicit different behavior than a less independent and
resourceful child.

The findings from these studies suggest that both children and
adults not only distinguish the behavior of secure and insecure children but also behave differently toward them. An investigation of
the differential cues emitted by children with different attachment
patterns, as well as the different behaviors they elicit from others
and the role these elicited behaviors play in maintaining attachment
styles, is an important and neglected research area. A plausible
scenario is that the insecurely attached child enters new situations
with a set of expectations (e.g., afraid that he or she will be
rejected) and then behaves in a way that strengthens and confirms
them. Thus, a vicious circle is set up in which a dysfunctional working model becomes a self-fulfilling prophecy (see Wachtel, 1982,
1987). I am not suggesting that this is the whole story but, rather,
that it is an important aspect of maladaptive relationship patterns.

As long as analytic neutrality was interpreted in terms of the
"blank screen" role assigned to the analyst, it was difficult to identify
and provide a role in the psychoanalytic situation for the kinds of
interactions I am describing—despite the centrality of the concept of
transference. If the analyst was a "blank screen," surely there was
little he or she could be doing that would serve to confirm (or
disconfirm) the expectations with which the patient entered the
situation. In addition, little or no attention was paid to the impact of
the patient on the analyst's behavior and how the analyst's behavior
might, in turn, serve to perpetuate a particular working model and
associated expectations. Any serious impact the patient had on the
analyst was usually understood as an expression of countertransference—something the analyst needed to work out intrapsychically.

As we all know, the meaning of the concepts of transference and
countertransference, as well as the general conceptualization of the
analytic situation, has changed dramatically. Under the impact of the
writings of people like Gill (1982) and Racker (1957) and, of course,
the earlier work of Sullivan (1953) and others from the interpersonal

school, the analytic clinical situation came to be conceptualized as increasingly interactional in nature, and it became permissible to look at what patients do, the impact these doings have on the analyst, and the ways in which the analyst's reactions to this impact, as well as his or her own general style, strongly influence the patient's experiences and perceptions of both the analyst and himself or herself. If one wanted to view all these developments from the perspective of attachment theory, one could say that a primary goal of psychoanalytic treatment became the alteration of the patient's working model of his or her self- and object representations, including the intense and conflictual affects with which they are linked.

The clearest discussion of the patient's impact on the therapist is provided by Strupp and his colleagues (e.g., Strupp and Binder, 1984; see also Sandler, 1976; Wachtel, 1987). Their formulation is quite simple and compatible with the attachment research referred to earlier. They note that patients' behaviors "pull for" certain responses from the therapist, similar to those "pulled for" in other relationships, particularly important and intimate ones. Among the most important functions of the therapist in the treatment situation are (1) the need to be aware of the responses "pulled for" from him or her; (2) the importance of *not* responding to the patient in accord with these demands; and (3) bringing these demands to the patient's awareness and examining the sequence of event and interactions that has occurred.

Let me provide a simple, concrete example of this sequence. A patient behaves in a provocative and hostile manner, which normally elicits in others the "complementary" reaction of dislike and counterattack or rejection. The therapist experiences these reactions but, instead of acting on them (which, of course, would likely strengthen and perpetuate the patient's provocativeness and hostility), makes the nature of the interaction explicit and opens it for further examination and exploration. In this very simple and eminently commonsensical way, Strupp and Binder (1984) combine the "corrective emotional experience" with the insight and understanding aspects of psychodynamic treatment. But note that insight and understanding are not limited to the patient's intrapsychic life but are also directed to the ways in which his or her interpersonal behaviors—including those that emerge in interaction with the therapist—perpetuate maladaptive schemata, expectations, and relationship patterns.

Research and theory on attachment style and internal working models can elucidate the specific ways in which people behave that tend to perpetuate their maladaptive relationship patterns. Although suggested by attachment research, the issue of the interactional cues emitted by people with different attachment styles is an important area in need of full exploration.

Sex and Attachment as Motivational Systems

Quite understandably, attachment theory has little to say regarding other motivational systems, such as sex and aggression. There are undoubtedly important and complex relationships between attachment and sex and aggression. The unexpected findings of severe disturbances in the areas of sex and aggression in the monkeys raised by a surrogate mother (Harlow, 1958) suggest such important links. On the human level, Shaver and Hazan (1992) found that subjects who were rated as ambivalent on a self-report attachment questionnaire reported greater sexual attraction toward the opposite sex and a shorter period of engagement prior to getting married. Perhaps ambivalently attached people feel a greater insecurity about "reaching the object" and hence experience both greater sexual intensity and a greater urgency to secure and finalize the relationship through marriage. In any case, this study is one of the few that attempts to relate attachment and sexual patterns.

In current psychoanalytic relational theories there is a tendency to consider the psychological significance of sexuality entirely as a route to the object, that is, to view sexuality as entirely in the service of meeting object relational and attachment needs (e.g., Mitchell, 1988). This strikes me as replacing Freudian reductionism, in which the primary significance of the object lies in its role in drive gratification, with what might be called relational reductionism. It would be a mistake for attachment theory to subsume or attempt to assimilate other motivational systems to the attachment instinctual system. As Stern (1985) notes, the concept of motivation "clearly will have to be reconceptualized in terms of many discrete, but interrelated motivational systems. . . . [Further study] will be hampered if these motivational systems are assumed a priori to be derivative of one or two basic, less definable instincts rather than more definable separate phenomena" (p. 238).

There may also be important differences among different instinctual and motivational systems with regard to the degree of fixedness versus looseness of connection between the instinctual system and the ideas and objects that are linked to that system. For example, water and food, as well as the ideas of water and food, have obvious motivational properties in relation to thirst and hunger. One of Freud's most interesting and original claims is that, with regard to the sexual system, there is enormous latitude in the range of ideas that can serve as "instinctual representative." Given the processes of displacement, condensation, and symbolization, ideas and objects that are manifestly remote from sex can nevertheless serve as their "instinctual representatives." As is indicated, for example, by the phenomena of fetishism and perversions, virtually any idea or object, according to Freud, can represent or become linked to sexual aims. Thus, objects ranging from shoes (as in a shoe fetish) to dead bodies (as in necrophilia) can serve to gratify sexual aims for some people (Freud, 1905). Even the "normal" behavior of delivering a paper at a professional meeting can serve sexual exhibitionistic aims.

The looseness of connection between the instinctual drive and its corresponding idea or object permits an enormous range of possibilities regarding the ideas that can serve as "instinctual representatives" and the objects that can serve the aim of drive gratification. One concrete, clinically relevant implication of the looseness of connection between drive, on one hand, and idea and object, on the other, is the virtually limitless possibilities for drive-related wishing and fantasy, for what one can wish, desire, and fantasize about. It also means there are virtually limitless possibilities regarding the ideas and objects that can trigger sexual wishes and fantasies. Thus, in Freud's instinct theory, the working of sexual drives in the mind is characterized by the odd combination of fixedness and rigidity of *aim* (i.e., discharge) and an almost limitless flexibility of mental contents that can serve this aim. Virtually anything can be passionately desired. It may well be that, for the attachment instinctual system, there is, in contrast to the sexual system, a rather tight, biologically programmed connection between the instinct and the object.

One need not assume that all instinctual systems operate the same way, either physiologically or psychologically. Thus, there would seem to be good biological reasons for a more rigid and fixed connection between the instinct and the object in the case of the attachment instinctual system than in the case of the sexual instinct. There is little room for variation or flexibility in the operation of the biological "rule" that the infant becomes attached to the early caretaker. It may also be the case that the attachment instinctual system —particularly in view of the more fixed connection between the instinct and the object—affords less opportunity for florid and varied wishes and fantasies than does the sexual instinct. Or it may be that this aspect of the attachment system has simply not been explored by attachment researchers and others. Certainly, there is clinical evidence of *some* range of variability in fantasies related to the attachment system—for example, fantasies of merging, of total self-sufficiency, and so on.

Pleasure and Attachment

According to attachment theory, the need for felt security is the primary proximal motivational variable involved in attachment; however, there are likely other motives and factors implicated in attachment, including those involving the experience of pleasure. As Slade and Aber (1992) note in a recent chapter, Bowlby did not explicitly discuss the role of pleasure, probably because of its centrality in Freudian theory, where it is defined primarily in terms of drive discharge and excitation reduction. Surely, however, attachment is associated with, and influenced by, the experiences of pleasure and well-being that accompany caregiving—including the homeostatic regulation and sensual gratifications provided by the caregiver. This issue was raised by A. Freud (1960), who wrote that Bowlby's attachment theory "is paralleled in our way of thinking by the conception of an inborn readiness to cathect with libido a person who provides pleasurable experiences" (p. 55). She also writes that "in both theories [that is, attachment and psychoanalytic theories] . . . the mother is not chosen for attachment by virtue of her having given birth to the infant but by virtue of her ministering to the infant's needs" (p. 55)—and the pleasure that such ministering provides.

The work of Hofer (e.g., 1983, 1984, 1990) suggests that, prior to the kind of attachment described in attachment theory, the infant becomes attached—"addicted" is the term that Hofer uses—to the caregiver through the wide range of physiological functions she regulates. One also recalls Dowling's (1977) report of seven infants with esophageal atresia who, when fed by a stomach bypass without simultaneous mouth stimulation, developed a tenuous attachment to mother and showed little motivation, vitality, and intentionality. This and other work suggest as an important area for future investigation the effects on attachment of physiological and affect regulation functions and pleasures provided by object relations.

Attachment and Repetition

Clinical, impressionistic evidence suggests that people maintain deep and persistent psychological ties to early attachment figures (as well as stand-ins for these figures) for complex motives that may be related to the need for felt security but that go beyond that single motive. For example, Fairbairn (1952) writes about the strange loyalties people feel toward depriving and rejecting early figures and ultimately understands such loyalties in terms of the need for inner objects—even malevolent inner objects—and the avoidance of an empty inner world devoid of objects. Weiss et al. (1986) describe certain maladaptive patterns that are perpetuated by the "unconscious pathogenic belief" that to change these patterns entails harming or destroying early parental figures. Hence, for people holding these pathogenic beliefs, loyalty and guilt toward early figures represent particularly important motives in maintaining ties to them.

Attachment theory, through its concepts of internal working models and need for felt security, helps account for repetition of behavior, a phenomenon that so intrigued and puzzled Freud and led to concepts that were not especially useful, such as the repetition compulsion and, ultimately, the death instinct (see Eagle, in press). Very briefly, the stability of relationship patterns is partly accounted for by the idea that early established working models guide expectations, strategies, and perceptions and serve as a template for future relationships. It is also partly accounted for by the consideration that one may unconsciously seek out objects who resonate with early attachment figures and patterns of relating that, however unsatisfactory they may have been, provided the only felt security one experienced. As Sroufe and Fleeson (1986) note, an important motivational factor in the perpetuation of attachment patterns is the desire to reproduce a familiar relationship pattern, one known and understood.

Attachment and Mental Health

An area worthy of investigation is the relationship between attachment style and mental health versus psychopathology. Secure attachment appears to be a protective factor and is associated with a wide range of "healthier" personality variables, such as lower anxiety (Collins and Read, 1990), less hostility, greater ego resilience (Kobak and Sceery, 1988), and greater ability to regulate affect through interpersonal relatedness (Vaillant, 1985; Simpson, Rholes, and Nelligan, 1992). Insecure attachment appears to be a risk factor and is associated with such "sick" personality characteristics as greater degree of depression (Armsden et al., 1990), anxiety, hostility, and psychosomatic illness (Hazan and Shaver, 1990) and less ego resilience (Kobak and Sceery, 1988). Despite these and other similar findings, it would be precipitous to equate secure attachment with mental health and insecure attachment with clinical pathology.

The relationship between attachment pattern and pathology is likely to be quite complex. Thus, in one recent study (Schaffer, 1993), although the author replicated many of the previously cited findings demonstrating "healthier" characteristics for securely versus insecurely attached adult individuals, among a group of people in psychotherapy there were no significant differences in *diagnosis* between the securely and insecurely attached groups. The fact that securely attached people—at least, securely attached as measured by available instruments—are well represented in a group seeking treatment clearly indicates that security of attachment does not immunize one against experiencing difficulties of sufficient intensity and magnitude to warrant seeking professional help. Clearly, many different aspects of personality, other than security of attachment, determine one's overall level of functioning. These are likely to include specific ego functions, the nature of one's wishes, conflicts, and defenses, and, of course, life circumstances.

To complicate the picture even further, these variables are probably not independent and additive but, rather, are likely to interact in a complex and bidirectional manner. Suggestive and converging evidence, however, that security of attachment is related to certain aspects of ego functioning, particularly metacognitive processes such as capacity for self-reflection, is provided by Main (1991) and Fonagy et al. (this volume). It appears that secure attachment facilitates and provides a safe base for exploration not only of the external world but also of one's inner world. Hence, to the degree that security of attachment is linked to the capacity for self-exploration and self-reflection, it serves as an additional protective factor in contributing to one's overall level of mental health.

Attachment and Defense

In recent years, psychoanalytic formulations on repression as a psychic defense have been complemented and, to some extent, modified by a new area of personality research on what has come to be called "repressive style." There are, interestingly, some striking similarities in descriptions of the repressive style as a personality trait and the avoidant pattern of attachment. The person with a repressive style, as a general personality style, tends "to keep painful, unpleasant experiences out of consciousness or awareness" (Davis, 1990, p. 388), whereas the avoidant attachment pattern is characterized by the tendency to keep painful affect and ideas specifically linked to attachment experiences out of awareness. A researchable question that arises, therefore, is whether the avoidant attachment pattern becomes generalized to a repressive avoidant style in which virtually *all*—not just those linked to attachment experiences—painful experiences tend to be kept out of awareness.

Another researchable and important question that arises is whether an avoidant attachment pattern is associated with the kinds of psychological and physiological "costs" that accompany the repressive style. Thus, the low anxiety and low distress reported by the individual employing a repressive style are belied by the relatively high levels of physiological arousal shown, particularly during stress (e.g., Weinberger, 1990). Furthermore, there is a good deal of evidence that repressive style is associated with a number of maladaptive characteristics, including greater susceptibility to certain physical illness (e.g., hypertension) and poorer immune response. Would one find similar "costs" exacted by an avoidant pattern of attachment?

In a related vein, Bonanno (1993) has identified a group of people who, in contrast to the repressors, experience a great deal of emotion and distress yet attempt to suppress their behavioral expression. These people cannot shut out distressing thoughts and feelings and instead try not to show how distressed they are. In certain respects, their pattern seems to parallel an enmeshed/preoccupied pattern of attachment. Bonnano suggests that this group's defensive pattern is more maladaptive than the repressive pattern—a finding that parallels Adam's (this volume) report that the avoidant pattern of attachment is a protective factor and the enmeshed pattern a risk factor in relation to suicide attempts. It would be interesting and perhaps fruitful to link research on attachment patterns to research on general defense and coping styles. Are attachment patterns lawfully related to defense and coping styles in nonattachment areas? Do they show a similar profile of adaptive and maladaptive features? These are only some of the questions that such a program of research would generate.

Attachment and Object Love

One final important area for investigation is the relationship between attachment style and what is referred to in classical psychoanalytic theory as object love. Most of the emphasis in attachment theory, as well as in contemporary psychoanalytic theorizing, is on what the infant needs from the caregiver. This orientation is often extended to include adult behavior, where the emphasis is also on what one requires from the object. To be sure, some attempts have been made in the contemporary psychoanalytic literature to distinguish the "complementarity" characteristics of the infant–parent relationship from the "reciprocity" of mature peer love relationships (Gerwitz, 1972; Weiss, 1974; West and Keller, 1994). More work is needed in this area. As I have elaborated elsewhere (Eagle, 1993), in the contemporary psychoanalytic literature there is remarkably little written about object love—about the factors and motives that account for providing for the object as well as requiring from the object. It is ironic that, although he was rightly criticized for assigning object relations a derivative status and for defining the object as "the thing in regard to which the instinct achieves its aim" (Freud, 1915, p. 122), Freud (1914) insists on the crucial importance of object love and writes that "in the last resort we must begin to love in order not to fall ill" (p. 85).

Recent work on adult attachment suggests that attachment styles are related to what one might call styles of loving as well as conceptions of love, marriage, and intimate relationships (e.g., Hazan and Shaver, 1987; Weiss, 1982). In any case, it seems to me that the concepts of attachment and internal working model, as well as research in these areas, should focus not only on the individual's expectations regarding the availability of the other but also on an inner sense of one's own capacity and motivation to love the object in intimate peer relationships. It is likely that security of attachment is related to capacity for object love, in the context of both the parent–child relationship and peer love relationships.

Undoubtedly, other aspects of the relationship between attachment theory and psychoanalysis bear comment and discussion. I hope, however, that I have identified at least some important and interesting issues that emerge in the interface between these two theoretical approaches to human behavior.

As noted at the very beginning of this chapter, along with much contemporary psychoanalytic theorizing, attachment theory, to a large extent, developed as a reaction against classical psychoanalytic theory. In contrast to contemporary psychoanalytic theories, however, attachment theory is grounded in a sturdy scientific tradition that has been able to generate new research methods, an extensive and continuing program of research, and important and relatively rigorous empirical data. Attachment research also serves as an exemplar of how extra-clinical findings can inform clinical sensitivity and clinical theories (see, e.g., the chapters by Adams, Keller, and West; Fonagy et al.; and Liotti in this volume). These achievements alone should serve as important guides and inspirations in the development of psychoanalytic theorizing.

It is also likely that clinical data and psychoanalytic theories can enrich attachment theory and research. In this chapter, I have addressed certain areas, highlighted by psychoanalytic theory—for example, the role of fantasy and wishes and the idiosyncratic construal of events—that can be more adequately addressed by attachment researchers and theorists. I have also suggested, as an area for future work, research on the complex interaction between the sexual and attachment motivational systems. For example, what is the relationship among early attachment status, style and adequacy of resolution of oedipal conflicts, and capacity for heterosexual intimacy? What are the relative roles of sexual conflict and attachment style in maladaptive intimate relationships? How do sexual and attachment dysfunctions interact with each other in the generation of psychopathology? Bacciagaluppi (1989) suggests that, in an attachment dysfunction in which the parent inverts the parent–child relationship, "the redirection of sexual strivings of children onto alternative peer relationships is particularly threatening for needy parents" (p. 316). These are only some of the questions and issues that are generated by a psychoanalytic perspective on attachment research and theory. Undoubtedly, there are many others.

Bowlby always viewed himself as a psychoanalyst and attachment theory as a reaction against and a correction of certain aspects of classical psychoanalytic theory. Recently, strong voices within psychoanalysis have urged a radical separation between psychoanalytic theory and a scientific tradition and have argued for a purely hermeneutic construal of psychoanalysis. Bowlby (e.g., 1979) was always opposed to such trends and argued strongly for the necessity of a rigorous scientific basis for psychoanalytic theorizing. Quite apart from specific research findings, perhaps the most important metacontribution that attachment research and theory can make to psychoanalysis is a strengthening of the scientific foundations for psychoanalytic theorizing.

REFERENCES

Angyal, A. (1941), *Foundations for a Science of Personality*. New York: Commonwealth Foundation.

—— (1965), *Neurosis and Treatment*. New York: Wiley.

Armsden, G. C., McCauley, E., Greenberg, M. T., Burke, P. M. & Mitchell, J. R. (1990), Parent and peer attachment in early adolescent depression. *J. Abn. Child Psychol.*, 18:683–697.

Bacciagaluppi, M. (1989), Attachment theory as an alternative basis of psychoanalysis. *Amer. J. Psychoanal.*, 49:311–318.

Barkley, R. A. (1981), The use of psychopharmacology to study reciprocal influences in parent–child interaction. *J. Abn. Child Psychol.*, 9:303–310.

Belsky, J., Fish, M. & Isabella R. (1991), Continuity and discontinuity in infant negative and positive emotionality: Family antecedent and attachment consequences. *Devel. Psychol.*, 27:421–431.

Black, M. (1967), Review of A. R. Louch's "Explanation and Human Action." *Amer. J. Psychol.*, 80:655–656.

Blass, R. B. & Blatt, S. J. (1992), Attachment and separateness: A theoretical context for the integration of object relations theory with self psychology. *The Psychoanalytic Study of the Child*, 47:189–203. New Haven, CT: Yale University Press.

Blatt, S. J. (1992), Relatedness and self definition. In: *Interface of Psychoanalysis and Psychology*, ed. J. Barron, M. Eagle & D. Wolitzky. Washington, DC: American Psychological Association, pp. 399–428.

Bonanno, G. A. (1993), Repression, accessibility, and dispositional threat avoidance. Presented at American Psychological Association Annual Convention, Toronto, Canada.

Bowlby, J. (1960), Grief and mourning in infancy and early childhood. *The Psychoanalytic Study of the Child*, 15:9–52. New York: International Universities Press.

—— (1973), *Attachment and Loss, Vol. 2*. London: Hogarth Press.

—— (1979), Psychoanalysis as art and science. *Internat. Rev. Psycho-Anal.*, 6:3–14.

—— (1988), Developmental psychiatry comes of age. *Amer. J. Psychiat.*, 145:1–10.

Bretherton, I. (1990), Open communication and internal working models: Their role in attachment relationships. In: *Socioemotional Development (Nebraska Symposium 1987)*, ed. R. Thompson. Lincoln: University of Nebraska Press, pp. 57–113.

Brunk, M. A. & Henggeler, S. W. (1984), Child influence on adult controls. An experimental investigation. *Devel. Psychol.*, 20:1074–1081.

Collins, N. L. & Read, S. J. (1990), Adult attachment, working models and relationship quality in dating couples. *J. Per. Soc. Psychol.*, 58:644–663.

Davis, P. G. (1990), Repression and the inaccessibility of emotional memories. In: *Repression and Dissociation*, ed. J. L. Singer. Chicago: University of Chicago Press, pp. 387–403.

Dowling, S. (1977), Seven infants with esophageal atresia: A developmental study. *The Psychoanalytic Study of the Child*, 32:215–256. New Haven, CT: Yale University Press.

Eagle, M. (1984), *Recent Developments in Psychoanalysis*. Cambridge, MA: Harvard University Press.

—— (1993), Freud's concept of narcissism: Its relationship to self psychology and object relations theory. Presented at Toronto Psychoanalytic Society, Toronto, Canada.

—— (in press), Why don't people change?: A psychoanalytic perspective. In: *Why Don't People Change?*, ed. H. Askowitz. New York: Guilford Press.

Fairbairn, W. R. D. (1952), *Psychoanalytic Studies of the Personality*. London: Tavistock.

Fraiberg, S., Adelson, E. & Shapiro, V. (1975), Ghosts in the nursery: A psychoanalytic approach to the problems of impaired infant–mother relationships. *J. Amer. Acad. Child Psychiat.*, 14:387–421.

Freud, A. (1960), Discussion of Dr. John Bowlby's paper. *The Psychoanalytic Study of the Child*, 15:53–62. New York: International Universities Press.

Freud, S. (1905), *Three Essays on the Theory of Sexuality. Standard Edition*, 7:125–243. London: Hogarth Press, 1953.

—— (1914) On narcissism. An introduction. *Standard Edition*, 14:73–102. London: Hogarth Press, 1957.

—— (1915), Instincts and their vicissitudes. *Standard Edition*, 14:117–140. London: Hogarth Press, 1957.

Garmezy, N. (1985), Stress resistant children: The search for protective factors. In: *Recent Research in Developmental Psychopathology*, ed. J. Stevenson. Oxford: Pergamon Press, pp. 213–233.

Gewirtz, J. L. (1972), *Attachment and Dependency*. Washington, DC: Winston.

Gill, M. M. (1982), *Analysis of Transference, Vol. 1*. Madison, CT: International Universities Press.

Goldsmith, H. H. & Alansky, J. A. (1987), Maternal and infant temperamental predictors of attachment: A meta-analytic review. *J. Consult. Clin. Psychol.*, 55:805–816.

—— Bradshaw, D. L. & Rieser-Danner, L. A. (1986), Temperamental dimensions in potential developmental influences on attachment. In: *New Directions for Child Development*, ed. J. V. Lerner & R. M. Lerner. San Francisco: Jossey-Bass, pp. 5–34.

Harlow, H. F. (1958), The nature of love. *Amer. Psychol.*, 13:673–685.

Hazan, C. & Shaver, P. (1987), Romantic love conceptualized as an attachment process. *J. Per. Soc. Psychol.*, 52:511–524.

—— & —— (1990), Love and work: An attachment-theoretical perspective. *J. Pers. Soc. Psychol.*, 59:270–280.

Hermann, I. (1936), Sichanklammern-Auf-suche-gchen. *Int. Z. für Psa.*, 22:349–370.

Hinde, R. A. & Stevenson-Hinde, J. (1986), Relating childhood relationships to individual characteristics. In: *Relationships and Development*, ed. W. W. Hartup & Z. Rubin. Hillsdale, NJ: Lawrence Erlbaum Associates, pp.

Hofer, M. A. (1983), On the relationship between attachment and separation processes in infancy. In: *Emotion, Vol. 2*, ed. R. Plutchik & H. Kellerman. New York: Academic Press. pp. 199–219.

—— (1984), Relationships as regulators: A psychobiologic perspective on bereavement. *Psychosom. Med.*, 46:183–197.

—— (1990), Early symbiotic processes: Hard evidence from a soft place. In: *Pleasure beyond the Pleasure Principle*, ed. R. A. Glick & S. Bone. New Haven,: CT Yale University Press, pp.

Jacobson, J. L. & Willie, D. R. (1986), The influence of attachment pattern on developmental changes in peer interaction from the toddler to the preschool period. *Child Devel.*, 57:338–347.

Kernberg, O. (1976), *Object Relations Theory and Clinical Psychoanalysis*. New York: Aronson.

Kobak, R. R. & Sceery, A. (1988), Attachment in late adolescence: Working models, affect regulations and representations of self and others. *Child Devel.*, 59:135–146.

Kohlberg, L., LaCrosse, J. & Ricks, D. (1970), The predictability of adult mental health from childhood behavior. In: *Handbook of Child Psychopathology*, ed. B. Wolman. New York: McGraw-Hill.

Kohut, H. (1971), *The Analysis of the Self*. New York: International Universities Press.

—— (1977), *The Restoration of the Self*. New York: International Universities Press.

—— (1984), *How Does Analysis Cure?* Chicago: University of Chicago Press.

Lee, C. & Bates, J. (1985), Mother child interaction at age two years and perceived difficult temperament. *Child Devel.*, 56:1314–1325.

Mahler, M. (1968), *On Human Symbiosis and the Vicissitudes of Individuation, Vol. 1*. New York: International Universities Press.

Main, M. (1991), Metacognitive knowledge, metacognitive monitoring, and singular (coherent) vs. multiple (incoherent) model of attachment: Findings and directions for future research. In: *Attachment Across the Lifecycle*, ed. C. M. Parks, J. Stevenson-Hinde & P. Morris. London: Tavistock, pp.

—— & Goldwyn, R. (1984), Predicting rejection of her infant from mother's representation of her own experience: Implications for the abused-abusing intergenerational cycle. *Child Abuse Neglect*, 8:203–217.

Masten, A. & Garmezy, N. (1985), Risk, vulnerability, and protective factors in developmental psychopathology. In: *Advances in Clinical Child Psychology, Vol. 8*, ed. B. B. Lahey & A. E. Kazdin. New York: Plenum Press, pp. 1–52.

Mitchell, S. A. (1988), *Relational Concepts in Psychoanalysis*. Cambridge, MA: Harvard University Press.

Nelson, K. & Gruendel, J. (1981), General event representations: Basic building blocks in cognitive development. In: *Advances in Developmental Psychology, Vol. 1*, ed. M. E. Lamb & A. Brown. Hillsdale, NJ: Lawrence Erlbaum, Associates, pp. 131–158.

Racker, H. (1957), The meanings and uses of countertransference. *Psychoanal. Quart.*, 26:303–357.

Robins, L. N. (1966), *Deviant Children Grown Up*. Baltimore: Williams & Wilkins.

Rutter, M. (1987), Temperament, personality and behavior disorder. *Brit. J. Psychiat.*, 150:443–458.

—— (1989), Intergenerational continuities and discontinuities in serious parenting difficulties. In: *Child Maltreatment*, ed. D. Cicchetti & V. Carlson. Cambridge: Cambridge University Press, pp. 317–348.

—— (1990), Psychosocial resilience and protective mechanisms. In: *Risk and Protective Factors in the Development of Psychopathology*, ed. J. Rolf, A. S. Masten, D. Ciccheti, K. H. Neuchterlein & G. Weintraub. Cambridge: Cambridge University Press, pp. 181–214.

—— Quinton, D. & Hill, J. (1990), Adult outcome of institution-reared children: Males and females compared. In: *Straight and Devious Pathways from Childhood to Adulthood*, ed. L. N. Robins & M. Rutter. Cambridge: University of Cambridge Press, pp. 135–157.

Sandler, J. (1976), Countertransference and role-responsiveness, *Internat. Rev. Psycho-Anal.*, 3:43–47.

—— & Rosenblatt, B. (1962), The concept of the representational world. *The Psychoanalytic Study of the Child*, 17:128–145. New York: International Universities Press.

Schaffer, C. E. (1993), The role of attachment in the experience and regulation of affect. Unpublished doctoral dissertation, Yale University.

Shaver, P. & Hazan, C. (1992), Adult romantic attachment: Theory and evidence. In: *Advances in Personal Relationships*, ed. D. Perlman & W. Jones. London: Kingsley, pp. 29–70.

Simpson, J. A., Rholes, W. S. & Nelligan, J. S. (1992), Support seeking and support giving within couples in an anxiety-provoking situation: The role of attachment styles. *J. Per. Soc. Psychol.*, 60:434–446.

Slade, A. & Aber, J. L. (1992), Attachment, drives and development: Conflicts and convergences. In: *Interface of Psychoanalysis and Psychology*, ed. J. Barron, M. Eagle & D. Wolitzky. Washington, DC: American Psychological Association, pp. 154–185.

Sroufe, L. A. (1990), An organizational perspective on the self. In: *The Self in Transition*, ed. D. Cicchetti & M. Beeghly. Chicago: University of Chicago Press, pp. 281–307.

—— & Fleeson, J. (1986), Attachment and the construction of relationships. In: *Relationships and Development*, ed. W. W. Hartup & Z. Rubin. New York: Cambridge University Press, pp. 51–72.

Stern, D. N. (1985). *The Interpersonal World of the Infant*, New York: Basic Books.

Strupp, H. & Binder, J. (1984), *Psychotherapy in a New Key*. New York: Basic Books.

Sullivan, H. S. (1953), *The Interpersonal Theory of Psychiatry*. New York: Norton.

Thompson, R. A., Lamb, M. E. & Estes, D. (1982), Stability of infant-mother attachment and its relationship to changing life circumstances in an unselected middle class sample. *Child Devel.*, 53:144–148.

Vaillant, G. E. (1985), Loss as a methaphor for attachment. *Amer. J. Psychoanal.*, 45:59–67.

van den Boom, D. (1990), Preventive intervention and the quality of mother–infant interaction and infant exploration in irritable infants. In: *Developmental Psychology behind the Dikes*, ed. W. Koops et al. Amsterdam: Eburon, pp. 249–270.

Vaughn, B. E., Stevenson-Hinde, J., Waters, E., Kotsaftis, A., Lefever, G. B., Shouldice, A., Trudel, M. & Belsky, J. (1992), Attachment security and temperament in infancy and early childhood: Some conceptual clarifications. *Devel. Psychol.*, 28:463–473.

Wachtel, P. L. (1987), *Action and Insight*. New York: Guilford Press.
—— ed. (1982), *Resistance*. New York: Plenum Press.
Weinberger, D. A. (1990), The construct validity of the repressive coping style. In: *Repression and Dissociation*, ed. J. L. Singer. Chicago: University of Chicago Press, pp. 337–386.
Weiss, J., Sampson, H. & the Mount Zion Psychotherapy Research Group (1986), *The Psychoanalytic Process*. New York: Guilford Press.
Weiss, R. S. (1982), Attachment in adult life. In: *The Place of Attachment in Human Behaviour*, ed. C. M. Parkes & J. Stevenson-Hinde. New York: Basic Books, pp. 171–184.
West, M. L. & Keller, A. E. R. (1994), *Patterns of Relating in Adults*. New York: Guilford Press.
Winnicott, D. (1965), The capacity to be alone. In: *The Maturational Processes and the Facilitating Environment*. Madison, CT: International Universities Press, pp. 29–36.

Part II

Contemporary Research

6

The Origins of Attachment Security

"Classical" and Contextual Determinants

JAY BELSKY, KATE ROSENBERGER, AND KEITH CRNIC

More than two decades of intensive research on the infant–parent attachment relationship (for reviews, see Colin, 1991; Belsky and Cassidy, 1994), particularly in concert with the more recent application of attachment theory to the study of close relationships in adulthood (Hazan and Shaver, in press), make it clear that Bowlby's (1969–1982) seminal ideas have had a major impact on the thinking of psychologists and on the care of children. The legacy of Bowlby that we address in this chapter derives directly from Mary Ainsworth. This is because Ainsworth transported Bowlby's ideas across the Atlantic and further developed the theory to explain the origins of individual differences in attachment security during infancy and early childhood—and that is the focus of this chapter.

Why do some children develop secure relationships with their primary caregivers, but others do not? Whereas Bowlby's (1944, 1958) original thinking on the roots of security/insecurity was organized around the development of serious disorders (e.g., those of juvenile thieves) and led to a focus on major separations from parents early in life, Ainsworth (1973) addressed the issue of variation in the normal population both theoretically and empirically. Central to Ainsworth's elaboration of Bowlby's theory of attachment was the proposition that a sensitive, responsive caregiver is critically important to the development of a secure, as opposed to insecure, attachment bond during the opening years of life. Such a person understands the child's individual attributes, accepts his or her behavioral proclivities, and is thus capable of orchestrating harmonious interactions between self and infant, especially those involving the soothing of distress.

Not long after Ainsworth (1973) first advanced these ideas and generated data from a small, but intensively investigated, sample of 26 middle-class mother–child dyads in Baltimore (Ainsworth et al.,

1978), what might be regarded as a "cottage industry" developed within the field of developmental psychology that sought to replicate—or refute—her findings. Child temperament was the major focus of those seeking to disconfirm Ainsworth's theory and evidence. According to those theorists and investigators, the source of security and insecurity lay not in the caregiver's ministrations but in the constitutional attributes of the child. Those like the child psychiatrist Stella Chess viewed the Ainsworth-Bowlby view as little more than refurbished psychoanalysis that attributed far too much influence to parents and "blamed" them for difficulties inherent in the child (Chess and Thomas, 1982). In the first half of this chapter we examine research on these two different, "classic" determinants of attachment security, contrasting evidence that highlights the role of the mother with evidence that highlights the role of the infant. This topic motivated much of the early attachment research.

More recently, however, Bronfenbrenner's (1979) ecological perspective has drawn attention to the broader context of human development beyond the confines of the mother–child relationship, and many of those attracted to the ideas of Bowlby and Ainsworth have begun to ask questions not only about the mother as a psychological agent but about her relationship with her spouse or partner and her social support. In the second half of this chapter, accordingly, work on this broader psychological and social context of attachment is examined.

Reflection on the ways in which the ecological perspective and attachment theory have come together reveals two reasons this integration has taken place. First, and perhaps most obvious, is that whereas attachment theory is essentially a theory of the microprocesses of development that emphasizes the daily interactional exchanges between parent and child and the developing internal working model of the child, the ecological/social-contextual perspective draws attention to the contextual factors and processes likely to influence these microdevelopmental processes. In essence, then, the ecological perspective turns an independent variable in attachment theory—patterns of mother–infant interaction—into a dependent variable, something itself to be explained. It must be emphasized that this ecological or contextual view of classical attachment theory and research in no way violates the premises of the theory or research traditions it has spawned; rather, it is our view that it enriches it while preserving its strengths.

The second reason an ecological perspective, with an emphasis on the life course and psychological attributes of adults, meshes so well with attachment theory is that each underscores the importance of the lifespan and the developmental makeup of the parent providing care to the child. In research strictly derived from attachment theory and as promulgated most originally by Mary Main (herself a student of Ainsworth), this concern is manifested in attention paid to the parent's internal working model or current representation of his or her own developmental history and childhood relations with parents (as revealed in the Adult Attachment Interview). In the work of those influenced by Bronfenbrenner's (1979) ecological perspective (e.g., Belsky, 1984), as well as other theoretical orientations, this concern focuses on the study of the psychological attributes or personality of parents of secure and insecure children. While not unrelated to the classical concept of "internal working models," the traditions that guide investigators to study and measure personality traits are quite different from those that have led investigators to study adults' representations of attachment. Moreover, even though the work of Main and her colleagues (Main and Goldwyn, 1984, in press; George, Kaplan, and Main, 1985) dealing with this latter topic merits consideration in a chapter dealing with classical and contextual determinants of attachment theory, it is excluded from this chapter because thorough coverage is provided in the separate contributions of Mary Main and Peter Fonagy to this volume. What are included, however, are data from an ongoing study of some 135 middle- and working-class families rearing first-born sons during the second and third year of life. Because this investigation, designed to examine the so-called terrible twos and identify factors and processes that make this developmental period more difficult for some families than others (Belsky and Crnic, 1990), included measurements of attachment security (with mothers when infants were 12 months of age and with fathers when infants were 13 months) together with many of the correlates of attachment to be considered in this chapter, we have chosen to supplement the literature reviewed with a reporting of findings from the first 75 families included in the larger research project. In what follows, then, we first examine the classical determinants of attachment security and then turn attention to ecological correlates, and we highlight findings from our ongoing work where appropriate.

"CLASSICAL" DETERMINANTS OF ATTACHMENT SECURITY

We begin this review of the "classical" determinants of attachment security by considering the relative importance of characteristics of the infant (particularly his or her temperament) and the role of the mother in determining whether a child develops a secure or insecure attachment to the caregiver.

Infant Temperament

The study of infant temperament and particularly its influence on infant development remains a source of heated debate among developmentalists (Chess and Thomas, 1982; Sroufe, 1985). With regard to temperament-attachment associations, there are two general schools of thought concerning the role that temperament plays in the development and assessment of individual differences in infant–mother attachment relationships. Some contend that temperament does not directly influence the quality of attachment that develops between infant and mother, because even a difficult infant, given the "right" care, can become secure—there being multiple pathways to security. It is recognized, nevertheless, that some infants are more difficult than others to care for in a sensitive, security-promoting manner and that even infants with "easy" temperaments, if provided insensitive care, can develop insecure relationships. This line of argument suggests, of course, that temperament does not exert a "main" effect in determining attachment quality (Sroufe, 1985). Consistent with this view are Crockenberg's (1981) findings that highly irritable infants are more likely to develop insecure attachment relationships principally when their mothers experience low levels of social support.

Even though temperament does not determine whether an infant will be securely or insecurely attached, it remains possible that it shapes the "kind" of secure or insecure attachment that develops between infant and mother. One reasonable hypothesis is that temperamentally less irritable babies, if cared for in a sensitive manner, will display secure attachments in the Strange Situation that are classified as B1 or B2 and involve limited overt distress on separation and greeting across a distance on reunion (e.g., smile, wave, show toy; whereas, if cared for in an insensitive manner, these babies will develop insecure-avoidant attachments. Children classified B1 or B2, like those classified insecure-avoidant, evince little distress in the Strange Situation (Frodi and Thompson, 1985). Those who fail to establish psychological contact upon reunion, however, are labeled avoidant. In contrast, babies characterized by high levels of irritability would be expected to display B3- or B4-type secure attachments when cared for sensitively and to develop insecure-resistant attachments when they receive insensitive care. Common to each of these relationship types is a greater susceptibility to distress on separation (Frodi and Thompson, 1985). Belsky and Rovine's (1987) finding that one-year-olds classified in the Strange Situation as avoidant (A1 or A2) differed from those classified as B3 or B4 or resistant (C1 or C2) on early indices of temperament (e.g., autonomic instability as neonates; perceived difficulty at three months) is consistent with this interpretation (see also Frodi and Thompson, 1985).

The second school of thought regarding the temperament-attachment association contends that an infant's temperament, particularly his or her susceptibility to distress, directly affects the development of the attachment relationship via its impact on mother–infant interaction and is the principal determinant of behavior used to evaluate attachment security in the Strange Situation (Chess and Thomas, 1982; Kagan, 1982). The claim is advanced, moreover, that infants classified as securely attached are simply less upset by separation in the Strange Situation, whereas those infants classified as insecurely attached are simply more distressed—despite the fact that both secure *and* insecure infants display the same kinds of discrete behaviors (e.g., crying) in the Strange Situation assessment. A meta-analysis of some 18 studies nonetheless provides some support for the assertion that insecurity is a direct function of an infant's proneness to distress (Goldsmith and Alansky, 1987). Resistant behavior measured in the Strange Situation (e.g., kicking legs, pushing away on reunion) was found to be reliably, though weakly, associated with proneness to distress as measured by both questionnaire and observational measures.

The most extensive investigation done to date, however, on the topic of temperament/irritability and attachment security challenges this view. In a sample of economically at-risk families in the Netherlands, van den Boom (1990, 1995) longitudinally followed 100 infants who scored very high on irritability on two separate neonatal examinations. Contrary to the Goldsmith and Alansky (1987) findings, more than three of every four of those distress-prone infants whose mothers received no intervention services (n = 50) and who were classified as insecure were categorized as insecure-avoidant, not insecure-resistant. As van den Boom (1990) noted, these "data directly challenge the assumption of Chess and Thomas (1982) and Kagan (1982) who have contended that variation in security of attachment is a product of temperamental differences among babies" (p. 241).

Recent research from our own laboratory also poses serious problems for the notion that temperament—especially, distress proneness —is a major determinant of attachment security. First, in our ongoing investigation of toddlers, we find little evidence for direct temperament-attachment linkages. When temperament reports of positive and negative emotionality are examined (Rothbart, 1981, Infant Behavior Questionnaire), and positive and negative emotionality when elicited in the laboratory (apart from the Strange Situation) is considered, only one of eight tests reveals a relation between temperament/emotionality and attachment security: infants classified as insecure-resistant with father expressed more negative emotion in the laboratory at 13 months than other infants. This association was not replicated with mothers, nor did attachment to mother or father correlate with other temperament report data.

Before even these limited findings linking irritability with insecure-resistant infant–father attachment can be embraced, attention must be directed to our work with a separate cohort of children studied longitudinally through the first year of life. In this related work, Belsky, Fish, and Isabella (1991) discovered that almost 25% of their 148 subjects changed substantially in their relative level of negativity over a six-month period. In fact, 11% of infants who were highly negative at nine months scored low on negativity six months earlier, and 12% who scored very high on negativity at three months scored very low at nine months. This discontinuity in negative emotionality was not random. Personality and marital characteristics of both parents measured *before* their infants were born, as well as the quality of parenting observed when babies were three months of age, accounted for the observed changes. Such data not only lead nicely to a consideration of the role of parenting and family ecology in fostering security but also alert us to the fact that associations between temperament and attachment such as those chronicled by Goldsmith and Alansky (1987) may themselves reflect (earlier) parental influence on temperament and attachment security rather than effects of a child's inborn constitution, as is often presumed (see Thompson, Connell, and Bridges, 1988).

The Role of the Parent/Caregiver

As noted already, central to Ainsworth's (1973) elaboration of Bowlby's (1969) theory of attachment is the proposition that the day-to-day care that the mother provides the child, particularly the sensitivity of that care, is of critical importance to the development of secure attachments. In this section we review evidence pertaining to the contribution of caregiving, first by focusing on investigations of caregiving by mothers and then by considering research on the caregiving of nonmaternal child-care providers, including fathers.

The quality of maternal care. A critical review of the data available a decade ago led Lamb and his colleagues (1984) to conclude that the evidence pertaining to Ainsworth's (1973) proposition that the quality of mothering was the primary determinant of the child's attachment security was not particularly strong. Although Lamb et al.'s (1984) critique of the limits of the original Ainsworth study

(Ainsworth et al., 1978) was harsher than necessary and certainly insufficiently appreciative of the contributions of her groundbreaking work, it is difficult, from an objective view, to fault the final conclusion. Not only was Ainsworth's sample far from representative and particularly small (n = 26), but a good deal of the other evidence available at that time and pertaining to the impact of mothering on attachment could be interpreted as either consistent or inconsistent with Ainsworth's ideas regarding maternal sensitivity in promoting security (for a more detailed analysis, see Belsky and Isabella, 1988). Nevertheless, as Clarke-Stewart (1988) astutely noted with regard to the evidence in question, we are "doomed to frustration . . . if we demand complete consistency across different studies and different measures" (p. 51). We should not expect exact duplication among our results, she further observed, concluding that "the problem is probably with the measure not with the hypothesis about maternal sensitivity" (p. 51).

If we look at the data now, it is ever more apparent that Clarke-Stewart (1988), like others, was correct about maternal sensitivity. Even though the evidence is still not perfectly uniform (see Schneider-Rosen and Rothbaum, 1993), there can be little doubt that with more and better current data, the contribution of caregiving behavior is clear. Consistent with Clarke-Stewart's appraisal, ratings of maternal sensitivity in the first year are linked to security in the Strange Situation in samples of middle-class American families (Ainsworth et al., 1978; Cox et al., 1992; Isabella, 1993) and German families (Grossmann et al., 1985), as well as economically disadvantaged, often single-parent ones (Egeland and Farber, 1984). Furthermore, security is associated with prompt responsiveness to distress (Crockenberg, 1981; Del Carmen et al., 1993), moderate, appropriate stimulation (Belsky, Rovine, and Taylor, 1984), and interactional synchrony (Isabella, Belsky, and von Eye, 1989; Isabella and Belsky, 1991), as well as warmth, involvement, and responsiveness (Bates, Maslin, and Frankel, 1985; O'Connor, Sigman, and Kasasi, 1992). In contrast, insecure-avoidant attachments are related to intrusive, excessively stimulating interactional styles and insecure-resistant attachments to an unresponsive, underinvolved approach to caregiving (Belsky et al., 1984; Smith and Pederson, 1988; Isabella et al., 1989; Lewis and Feiring, 1989; Malatesta et al., 1989). It should be noted that, in addition to such associations in studies using the Strange Situation procedure, similar contemporaneous and time-lagged relations have emerged in research relying on Waters and Deane's (1985) Q-sort measures of attachment security (Pederson et al., 1990; Moran et al., 1992). Thus, as Clarke-Stewart (1988) observed, "there does seem to be a significant degree of predictability from parents' behavior to infants' attachment classifications" (p. 51).

This is not to say that the strength of associations is large. As Goldsmith and Alansky (1987) observed in their meta-analysis of 15 studies carried out between 1978 and 1987 (thus excluding many more recent investigations just cited), "the effect [of maternal interactive behavior on attachment security] that has enjoyed the confidence of most attachment researchers is not as strong as was once believed" (p. 811). Nevertheless, we are aware of no study that has found high maternal sensitivity to be reliably associated with *in*secure attachment.

The modesty of the association between maternal behavior and attachment security, coupled with the logical possibility that this reliably discerned association could be a product of the effect of infant characteristics on maternal functioning, continues to provide grounds for skeptics to question the role of maternal care in fostering security or insecurity. Fortunately, van den Boom's (1990) aforementioned longitudinal study of 100 irritable Dutch infants from economically at-risk families puts the issue to rest. In her study design she included an experimental manipulation to heighten maternal sensitivity and evaluated its effects on attachment security. Fifty mothers randomly assigned to an experimental group received three home visits during which behavior toward their infants was monitored, and individualized feedback was provided to foster "contingent, consistent and appropriate responses to both positive and negative infant signals." The home-visitor/intervenor "aimed to enhance mothers' observational skills . . . assisted mothers to adjust their behaviors to their infant's unique cries" (p. 208). Control-group mothers were simply observed in interaction with their babies.

Not only did *pre*intervention home observations indicate the two groups to be equivalent in terms of maternal behavior, and postintervention observations reveal that maternal sensitivity was greater in the experimental group, but results of Strange Situation evaluations four months after the termination of the intervention were strongly consistent with predictions derived from attachment theory: whereas a full 68% (34 out of 50) of the infants in the control group were classified as insecure, this was true of only 28% (14 out of 50) of the experimental subjects. No doubt these findings resulted from the fact that "experimental mothers respond[ed] to the whole range of infants' signals (during post-intervention home observation), while control mothers mainly focus[sed] on very negative infant signals" (van den Boom, 1990, p. 236). More specifically, in the insecurity-producing control group, mildly negative infant behaviors like fussing are ignored for most of the time or are responded to ineffectively. Positively toned attachment behaviors, on the contrary, are ignored for the most part. And infant exploration is either ignored or interfered with.

The program mothers' infants' negative actions boost maternal positive actions. Maternal anger is not observed. . . . Positive social infant behaviors are also responded to in a positive fashion. And program mothers are attentive to the infant's exploration, but they do not interfere in the process [van den Boom, 1990, p. 236].

It is noteworthy, but by this time no longer surprising, that a recent meta-analysis of a number of attachment studies that include infants or mothers with problems and disorders considered to increase the probability of insecurity is strongly consistent with these compelling experimental findings. An analysis of 34 clinical studies indicates that

groups with primary identification of maternal problems show attachment classification distributions highly divergent from the normal distribution, whereas groups with a primary identification of nonpsychiatric child problems such as prematurity and deafness show distributions that are similar to the distributions of normal samples [van IJzendoorn et al., 1992, p. 840].

More specifically, whereas groups characterized by maternal problems such as mental illness and child maltreatment evince rates of security of 49% (clearly lower than the normative average of 67%), groups with child problems have rates of security of 66%. Consistent with the nonclinical data previously reviewed, "in clinical samples, the mother appears to play a more important role than the child in shaping the quality of the infant–mother attachment relationship" (p. 840).

The quality of nonmaternal care. Although attachment theory is often cast as a theory of the infant–*mother* relationship, most attachment theorists and researchers actually consider attachment to be involved in close child–*adult* relationships in general. Indeed, Bowlby made it clear that in writing about mother, he was assuming that mothers were usually the primary caregivers. If, as is now widely recognized, infants and young children can establish relationships with more than a single individual (neither Bowlby nor Ainsworth argued otherwise), a theoretically important question is whether the interactional processes highlighted as important to the development of secure relationships with mothers also operate in other cases. The few available studies of fathers and of nonparental caregivers indicate that this is, indeed, the case.

In one of two published studies of the interactional origins of infant–father attachment security, Cox and her colleagues (1992) found that men who related to their three-month-olds in a more positive, sensitive, and reciprocally playful manner had infants who evinced more security in the Strange Situation with them nine months later. It is notable that these data are strikingly similar to those reported a decade earlier by Chibucos and Kail (1981), who endeavored to measure security at age 7 1/2 months and found that infants who engaged in more proximity-seeking and contact-maintaining behavior and less proximity-avoidance and physical resistance (i.e., infants who might be judged to be more secure) had fathers who, when the infants were two months old, were more sensitive toward, and playful with, them.

Work in the United States by Howes and her associates (1988) using the attachment Q-sort reveals that 12–24-month-olds are more likely to score low on security to a nonparental caregiver if the caregiver frequently ignores them and if the caregivers care for many children. Additional evidence from the Netherlands indicates that infants classified in the Strange Situation as securely attached to their caregivers have caregivers who provide more sensitive care (Goosens and van IJzendoorn, 1990). In sum, then, interactional processes similar to those delineated in studies of mothering appear relevant to the development of secure relationships with others with whom the child is expected to develop a close, affectional bond.

Conclusion

When considered in its entirety, the evidence summarized in this section pertaining to the "classical" determinants of attachment security provides compelling support for Ainsworth's (1973) extension of Bowlby's theory of attachment. Individual differences in attachment security, whether measured with the laboratory-based Strange Situation or the home-based Q-sort procedure, are systematically related to the nature of the care that an infant or toddler experiences with a particular caregiver. What makes the evidence particularly convincing is that it is both correlational and experimental in nature; it is longitudinal as well as cross-sectional; it involves samples of so-called normal mother–child dyads as well as more clinical samples; and it applies to fathers and day-care providers as well as to mothers. Even though infant temperamental characteristics may contribute to the quality of interaction between caregiver and child, the evidence that such attributes are the primary determinants of attachment security is weak.

PSYCHOLOGICAL AND SOCIAL-CONTEXTUAL DETERMINANTS OF ATTACHMENT SECURITY

Through this point we have reviewed evidence pertaining to what we have described as "classical" determinants of attachment security, that is, those factors and forces addressed primarily by attachment theorists and researchers: infant temperament and quality of caregiving. In the second part of this chapter we move beyond the confines of contemporary attachment theory and consider the social-ecological context of attachment. Thus, we examine, first, more general parental personality and psychological-resource correlates of attachment security. After focusing on what might be regarded as the psychological attributes of the parent, attention is turned to the broader context of child–parent attachment relationships and thus to social-contextual sources of stress and support (marital relationship, social support).

Parental Psychological Resources/Personality

In the light of the fact that the hallmark of security-producing, sensitive care is considered to involve the accurate reading of, and timely and empathic responding to, the child's affective and behavioral cues so as to affirm the experience of the child, there is every reason to expect that psychological attributes of the caregiver would be related to the security of attachment that the child develops. After all, much theory and evidence suggest that a parent's psychological health and well-being are related to the quality of care that she or he provides (Belsky, 1984; Belsky and Vondra, 1989; Gelfand and Teti, 1990). A thorough review of evidence involving both normal samples and clinical ones and pertaining to the relation between parental personality/psychological well-being and infant–parent attachment security reveals, in the main, that psychologically healthier parents are more likely to have infants who are securely attached to them than are less psychologically healthy parents.

Normal Samples. Both cross-sectional studies (Ricks, 1985; Benn, 1986) and longitudinal investigations (in which personality is measured prior to attachment security, Belsky and Isabella, 1988) indicate that in nondisturbed populations, secure attachment relationships are more likely to develop among psychologically healthier mothers than ones who might be considered psychologically less healthy. One large-sample project (n = 160) found, for example, that mothers whose infants were classified as securely attached to them scored higher on a series of personality subscales measuring nurturance, understanding, autonomy, inquisitiveness, and dependence than did mothers of infants subsequently classified as insecure, yet lower on a subscale assessing aggressiveness (Maslin and Bates, 1983). More recently, Del Carmen and colleagues (1993) reported that mothers who scored higher on prenatal anxiety were more likely to have infants classified as insecure at age one than those scoring lower on anxiety. It is notable that such findings are not restricted to economically well-off families but also emerge in research on high-risk, low socioeconomic-status (SES) households (Jacobson and Frye, 1991). In addition, evidence presented by Egeland and Farber (1984) shows that even though measures of personality were unrelated to attachment security at 12 months, systematic links existed between stability of attachment (from 12 to 18 months) and maternal personality; in contrast to those who remained secure, infants who changed from secure to insecure had mothers who scored higher prenatally and/or at three-months postpartum on personality measures of aggression and suspicion.

Not all relevant investigations, however, provide evidence of the anticipated associations between personality and attachment security (Levitt, Weber, and Clark, 1986; Barnett et al., 1987; Zeanah et al., 1993). Indeed, data from our ongoing toddler study show no significant relations in the case of mothers or fathers between attachment security and four different measures of personality, as well as a composite measure scaled to reflect well-being (extroversion + agreeableness + interpersonal affect − neuroticism). Perhaps more noteworthy, however, is the fact that no evidence, to our knowledge, suggests that parents of secure infants are *less* psychologically healthy than other parents. As we turn to research on clinical samples, a similar pattern is evident.

Clinical Samples. Depression in its variety of manifestations—unipolar and bipolar—has been the clinical disorder most studied with regard to its relation to attachment security. A quick perusal of the available evidence reveals rather inconsistent findings. Whereas some research fails to discern the expected association between maternal psychological disorder and elevated rates of insecurity (Sameroff, Seifer, and Zax, 1982; Lyons-Ruth et al., 1986 [12-month data]), other investigations discover a relation (Gaensbauer et. al., 1984; Radke-Yarrow et al., 1985; D'Angelo, 1986; Lyons-Ruth, 1988 [18-month data]; Spieker and Booth, 1988; DeMulder and Radke-Yarrow, 1991; Radke-Yarrow, 1991; Campbell et al., 1993; Teti and Gelfand, 1993). Yet, more careful consideration of the entire corpus of evidence highlights some underlying consistencies that may help to reconcile this seemingly erratic pattern.

The age when attachment is assessed seems to distinguish investigations that discern higher rates of insecurity among infants with depressed parents. Of nine studies that reported a significant effect of maternal depression on infant attachment, two-thirds (six of nine) involved samples with infants 15 months of age or older (Gaensbauer et al., 1984; Radke-Yarrow et al., 1985; Lyons-Ruth, 1988; DeMulder and Radke-Yarrow, 1991; Radke-Yarrow, 1991; Teti and Gelfand, 1993), raising the possibility that amount of exposure to a depressed caregiver may explain inconsistency in the available evidence. This interpretation receives its strongest support from two longitudinal studies in which absence of an effect of depression at 12 months became a significant effect by 18 months (Gaensbauer et al., 1984; Lyons-Ruth, 1988).

Four independent lines of evidence are consistent with the interpretation that amount of exposure to a depressed parent may reconcile some inconsistency in the database. The first is evidence indicating that the quality of parenting is compromised among depressed mothers, who exhibit greater degrees of intrusive/hostile or detached/unresponsive caregiving relative to nondepressed mothers (for a review, see Gelfand and Teti, 1990). The second is that Cicchetti and Barnett (1991) reported a strikingly similar pattern in the case of maltreated children, with those classified as secure at an earlier age being more likely to be classified as insecure subsequently than nonmaltreated children originally classified as insecure. The third is that Cohn, Campbell, and Ross (1991) found that infants of depressed mothers were less likely to be insecurely attached when cared for during their first year in a nonmaternal care arrangement while their mothers worked outside the home than when cared for primarily by their (depressed) homemaker mothers. The fourth and final piece of evidence comes from other depression-attachment findings pertaining to the severity and chronicity of maternal disturbance.

Five different studies directly draw attention to the issues of severity and chronicity in the case of depression and attachment security (Radke-Yarrow et al., 1985; Lyons-Ruth et al., 1986; Radke-Yarrow, 1991; Campbell et al., 1993; Teti and Gelfand, 1993). This body of work indicates, first, that a greater number of insecure attachments are found among mothers with bipolar depression than among those with unipolar depression (Radke-Yarrow et al., 1985; Radke-Yarrow, 1991). Comparing the infants of 99 mothers with unipolar or bipolar depression or no history of depression, Radke-Yarrow et al. (1985)

observed significant differences among bipolar, unipolar, and well mothers, such that 71% of infants with bipolar mothers were insecurely attached, compared with 55% with unipolar mothers and 25–30% with well mothers. Furthermore, mothers of infants classified as disorganized had histories that revealed significantly more serious depression than those of other attachment groups. These mothers of disorganized infants were more chronically ill during the life of the child, had more severe depression as rated by the Global Assessment Scale (GAS), and were more likely to have been hospitalized, medicated, or in psychotherapy. In fact, in this study, disorganized infants were found exclusively with mothers who had major affective illness.

Although these data buttress a cogent argument pertaining to extent of exposure to a disturbed parent, it must be noted that one study contradicts these findings. DeMulder and Radke-Yarrow (1991) discovered no effect of chronicity of depression on attachment. Nevertheless, the preponderance of evidence lends weight to the thesis that a disorder diagnosis alone does not explain linkages between depression and attachment security. Severity, chronicity, and thus the nature and extent of exposure to a psychologically disturbed parent must be taken into account. This makes good sense in light of the fact that the presumption underlying this entire chapter, as well as being central to attachment theory more generally, is that distal factors like maternal personality, marital quality, and social support are presumed to exert their influence by affecting actual mothering behavior (i.e., the mediational hypothesis). The more psychologically disordered a mother, the more her caregiving behavior is expected to be compromised.

The exact form of such compromised mothering may well be of critical importance. Indeed, recent work by Radke-Yarrow (1991) suggests that depressed mothers' sadness and anxiety, rather than their anger and irritability, likely have the most profound effect, as she found that depressed women displaying the former affective pattern were more likely to have insecure children. The reason for this, conceivably, is that anxiety and sadness may be more enduring affective conditions, and irritability and anger may be more transient, leading, fundamentally, to differential exposure of the child to compromised care.

Perhaps the best evidence that the effect of a mother's psychological condition on her actual parenting explains how personality/ psychological well-being factors relate to attachment security is to be found in Benn's (1986) study of nondisordered women. When a composite index of emotional integration (drawn from clinical interview ratings of competence, emotional responsivity, warmth, and acceptance of motherhood) was statistically controlled, a previously discerned and significant association between maternal sensitivity and attachment security was substantially attenuated. Such data clearly support the aforementioned mediational hypothesis linking distal factors—in this case, involving maternal personality—with attachment security via the more proximal mediating processes of parenting.

Contextual Sources of Stress and Support

Although both parent and child contributions to attachment security have now been considered, an ecological perspective on this topic requires consideration of the *social context* of the infant–parent relationship. For this purpose, we turn to evidence that highlights the generally beneficial impact of social support on both psychological and physical health (e.g., Mitchell and Trichett, 1980). Of particular significance is research showing that parents who experience more social support are more psychologically healthy than parents who are relatively unsupported (Nuckolls, Cassel, and Kaplan, 1972; Colletta and Gregg, 1981; Colletta, 1983). But even more important is research demonstrating that, probably as a consequence of the positive impact of social support on psychological well-being, such support is positively related to parental functioning (for reviews of literature, see Belsky, 1984; Belsky and Vondra, 1989; Belsky, 1990). Such a surmise is certainly consistent with the preceding evidence pertaining to parental psychological resources and infant–parent attachment security. In line with the extensive literature on social support, it is likely that support from spouses, friends, relatives, and neighbors, as well as from professionals (e.g., physicians, community workers), influences infant–parent attachment security by influencing the quality of care parents provide.

The Marital Relationship. Numerous investigations provide evidence that supportive spousal relations during the infancy and toddler years are correlated with the very kinds of parenting theorized (and found) to predict attachment security (for review of relevant literature, see Belsky, 1984, 1990). In fact, such findings emerge when observed parental behavior serves as the dependent variable, as in studies where the focus is on middle-class parents rearing healthy children in this country (Goldberg and Easterbrooks, 1984; Oates and Heinicke, 1985; Dickie, 1987; Jouriles, Pfiffner, and O'Leary, 1988; Cox et al., 1989) and in Japan (Durrett et al., 1986), Israel (Levy-Schiff and Israelashvili, 1988), and Germany (Engfer, 1988; Meyer, 1988); where the focus is on middle-class parents caring for premature infants (Crnic, Greenberg, et al., 1983); or where the focus is on impoverished, inner-city mothers rearing premature infants (Feiring et al., 1987). Indeed, some of this work even substantiates Belsky's (1981) speculative assertion that their marriage might be the most important source of support for most mothers (see Crnic, Greenberg, et al., 1983).

In view of such evidence linking marital quality with many of the same facets and features of parenting implicated in the study of the interactional origins of attachment security, there are grounds to expect lawful relations between marital functioning and infant–parent attachment security. In the main, the data gathered to date tend to support this expectation. That is, children growing up in families with better-functioning marriages are more likely to establish secure attachments to their parents than those growing up in households where spouses are less happy in their marriages. Such evidence appears in cross-sectional analyses carried out in the United States (Goldberg and Easterbrooks, 1984; Crnic, Greenberg, and Slough, 1986; Howes and Markman, 1989; Jacobson and Frye, 1991) and in Japan (Durrett, Otaki, and Richards, 1984). Perhaps more noteworthy, though, are the findings from several longitudinal studies. In one such investigation, Howes and Markman (1989) found that wives who reported higher levels of marital satisfaction and lower levels of spousal conflict prenatally had preschoolers who scored higher on the Q-sort measure of attachment security when one to three years of age (Q security). Tracking similar middle-class families across a somewhat shorter time period, Lewis, Owen, and Cox (1988) reported that one-year-old daughters (but not sons) were more likely to be securely attached to their mothers when marriages were more harmonious during pregnancy. Furthermore, marital quality declines more precipitously across the transition to parenthood in the case of infants classified as insecurely attached to their mothers (but not to their fathers) in the Strange Situation than it does in the case of infants classified as secure in their attachments to their mothers (Belsky and Isabella, 1988). Also noteworthy is Spieker's (1988; Spieker and Booth, 1988) research on high-risk mother–infant dyads, which indicates that the lowest levels of spousal support measured prenatally and at three months postpartum characterize the marriages in families in which infants develop the most insecure form of attachment relationships with their mothers, that is, disorganized attachments.

Despite the seeming persuasiveness of all this cross-sectional and longitudinal data, it would be a mistake to selectively cite only the aforementioned research and leave the impression that all studies of marriage and attachment present such positive results. Not only do a number of investigations discern no direct association between some index of marital quality and infant–parent attachment security (Levitt, et al., 1986; Teti et al., 1991; Zeanah and associates, 1993), including our ongoing toddler research, but one study actually reports results directly contrary to those just presented. In this research on an unusual sample of upper middle-class Japanese mothers temporarily living in the United States as a result of their husband's employment, higher levels of marital quality were associated with less Q-security (Nakasawa, Teti, and Lamb, 1992). Although this contrary result is difficult to reconcile with the remainder of the evidence, the null findings just reported present less severe obstacles to interpretation.

In fact, two recent studies draw attention to the possibility that null findings may reflect the limits of inquiring into direct effects only, rather than the absence of a relation between marital quality and attachment security. In one important piece of work, Isabella (1994) found that even though no direct relation between marital quality (measured prenatally) and attachment security (one year) could be discerned, an indirect pathway of influence did appear to exist. As indicated in Figure 1, higher levels of marital quality predicted greater maternal role satisfaction at four months postpartum, which itself predicted greater maternal sensitivity (labeled "maternal interaction" in Isabella's work) five months later and, thereby, attachment security (at age one).

Whereas the work of Isabella (1994) underscores an indirect–and typically unstudied–process by which marital quality might impact on the infant–mother attachment bond, new work by

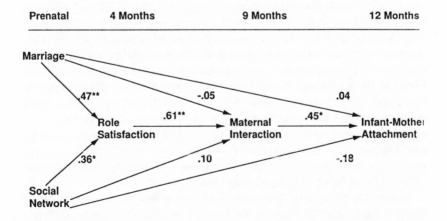

Figure 1 Path-Analytic Results Linking Marital Quality and Social Network Support with Infant–Mother Attachment. Isabella (1994).

Das-Eiden, Teti, and Corns (1993) draws attention to the need to study marital quality in context. Although Das-Eiden et al. found that higher levels of marital quality were related to higher levels of Q-security, further analyses revealed that this relation was restricted to those families in which mothers were classified as insecure on the Adult Attachment Interview. What is fascinating about these data are not only that they are consistent with other research showing that a mother with a risky developmental history is less likely to mother poorly if she has a supportive marriage (see Belsky and Pensky, 1988, for a review), but also that they suggest that in order to fully understand the impact of the marital relationship on the development of secure or insecure attachment bonds, additional information about the family is useful. We return to this theme of multiple determinants in the concluding section of this chapter. For now it suffices to point out, again, that acceptance of null findings may be premature when only direct effects are examined. Developmental influences do not operate only directly; thus, there is a need to take into consideration mediational processes (e.g., via role satisfaction and mothering) and moderational ones (e.g., interactions with maternal state of mind) when considering linkages between marriage and attachment.

Of course, it is important to note that, although much of this discussion has assumed that the marital relationship exerts a direct, indirect, or moderated influence on the development of secure and insecure attachment bonds, none of the data presented really demonstrate such a causal process. Because of the correlational nature of all findings, the possibility cannot be precluded that the positive associations discussed are simply a by-product of third-variable processes. Perhaps, for example, what transpires in the marriage has no impact on the infant–parent attachment relationship; rather, some other factor such as parental personality may influence both marital quality and the infant–parent relationship, so that associations between the latter two constructs simply reflect correlations masquerading as causal processes. Until experimental work with marriages chronicles an effect on attachment security, this alternative explanation to the marriage-attachment linkages under consideration must be seriously entertained. As we see when we consider *nonspousal* social support, however, correlational evidence *is* buttressed by experimental findings.

Social Support (Nonspousal). Not just relations with spouse or partner are systematically related to what transpires between parents and their children. Consistent with the theorizing of Cochran and Brassard (1979), a number of investigations now provide evidence that the amount and nature of contact and support that parents, especially mothers, experience from significant others in their lives affect the way they interact with their infants. For example, mothers with more community support have been observed to interact more positively with their four-month-olds (Crnic, Ragozin, et al., 1983); those with frequent negative interactions with significant others evince less sensitivity with their premature six-month-olds (Zarling, Hirsch, and Landry, 1988); and poor Hispanic women who receive more material resources from friends and relatives engage in more proximal (touch, kiss, hold) and distal (vocalize, look) interaction with their three-month-old premature infants (Feiring et al., 1987). Findings such as these, given the mediational process central to this chapter (i.e., social context→mother– infant interaction→attachment security), lead to the expectation that (nonspousal) social support should be positively associated with attachment security. In this subsection, we examine correlational evidence bearing on this issue and experimental data coming from studies in which support has been provided to parents to determine its influence on the infant–parent attachment relationship.

Correlational Evidence. Ten studies pertaining to the relation between nonspousal social support and infant–mother attachment security have been reported. Four of these provide positive evidence that support provided by someone other than a mate is related to attachment security. Three of these four investigations involve populations at some degree of risk for developing an insecure attachment. Crockenberg's (1981) research on a low-risk population showed that low social support predicted insecure attachment only in infants who were highly irritable. Crockenberg considered an irritable infant as a stressor and thus as having an "at-risk" status due to his temperament. Crnic et al. (1986), studying a high-risk premature infant population, found that an index of total support, which included intimate, friendship, and community support, was positively correlated with attachment security. Professional support, defined as assistance from physicians, nurses, and other social service providers, which was treated separately, was unrelated to security of attachment.

In Crittenden's (1985) investigation of a high-risk sample of infants with abusive and/or neglecting mothers, low social support did predict insecure attachment, but only when actual quality of maternal care (maltreatment or neglect) was not included in regression analyses. Such findings are consistent with the proposition that social support influences attachment security by influencing the quality of daily care that the mother provides. By controlling for the putative mediator of support effects, these otherwise discernible influences should attenuate, if not disappear entirely.

The final correlational investigation to be considered produced positive findings consistent with such reasoning. On employing path analytic techniques, Isabella (1994) observed that although social network support (like marital quality) did not exert a direct influence on infant–mother attachment security, it did exert an indirect influence (see Figure 1). In fact, even though social support did not directly predict maternal interactive behavior (at nine months), which itself did directly predict attachment security (at one year), high social support significantly forecast high maternal role satisfaction and, thereby, quality of maternal care and attachment security. Thus, while the contribution of social support to attachment security was neither overwhelming nor direct, a process of influence postulated by Isabella—and consistent with the mediational-process argument developed throughout this chapter—was confirmed.

The fact that Isabella could discern the influence of social support on attachment only by examining complex mediational processes may help to account for why five other studies, including our own ongoing toddler investigation—of both low risk (Crnic et al., 1986; Levitt et al., 1986; Belsky and Isabella, 1988; Zeanah et al., 1993) and high-risk families (Spieker, 1988; Spieker and Booth, 1988)—failed to uncover a significant association between indices of social support and attachment security. After all, Isabella, too, failed to discern any direct effects, clearly raising the prospect that the contribution of social support to attachment security may be more indirect than direct. In fact, in light of conflicting results across studies, as well as the fact that mediational processes may be a more appropriate venue for understanding the effects of social support on attachment security, it seems entirely inappropriate to embrace the null hypothesis of no relation between social support and infant–mother attachment.

Experimental Evidence. Whatever conclusions are drawn regarding the just reviewed data linking social support and attachment security, it must be acknowledged that because of the correlational nature of the findings, the possibility cannot be discounted that effects of social support, just like effects of marital quality, might be an artifact of a third variable, such as parental personality, that directly affects support received and attachment security (presumably via parenting). Indeed, evidence consistent with such a proposition can be found in research on social support that indicates that the nature and amount of support received are not randomly assigned but, rather, are, in part, a function of characteristics of the persons receiving the support (Sarason, Sarason, and Shearin, 1986). Fortunately, several experimental programs have been conducted to examine the effect of supportive services on infant–mother attachment security. Of course, investigations that randomly assign families to treatment condition overcome the methodological limits of correlational research. Two such programs that failed to discern effects on attachment security are not considered because differential attrition in experimental and control groups compromised the internal validity of the research (Barnard et al., 1988; Beckwith, 1988).

In the first experimental study of the effects of social support to be considered, Lyons-Ruth, Connell, and Grunebaum (1990) provided economically disadvantaged and often depressed mothers with weekly home visits when their infants were between 9 and 18 months, to (1) provide an accepting and trustworthy relationship, (2) increase the family's competence in accessing resources to meet basic needs (including social, financial, legal, health, and educational), (3) model and reinforce more interactive, positive, and developmentally appropriate exchanges between mother and infant (with emphasis on the mother's dual role as teacher and source of emotional security for her infant), and (4) decrease social isolation from other mothers through encouraging weekly participation in a drop-in social hour. At 18 months of age, infants of 28 treated mothers were studied in the Strange Situation and compared with ten infants of high-risk, untreated mothers; the rate of insecurity among the control infants was 80%, whereas that for the experimental infants was much lower, 43%.

In a second, social-support-oriented intervention study, using a federally subsidized prenatal nutrition program, Jacobson and Frye (1991) randomly assigned a group of mostly uneducated and unmarried mothers-to-be to a treatment or control group. The intervention continued through the first postpartum year and again involved a multidimensional service focused on maternal and infant needs, as well as strategies for obtaining support. Rather than relying on the Strange Situation, attachment security was assessed at 14 months with Waters and Deane's (1985) Q-sort, completed by observers blind to the experimental condition after a single three- to four-hour observation period in the home. In this study, too, it was found that infants whose mothers received extensive social support were rated more securely attached than controls on two subscales (differential responsiveness to attachment figure, attachment/exploration balance), though not on the overall security index.

The third and final intervention evaluation differed from those just described in that it offered psychotherapy to a group of mostly Spanish-speaking immigrant mothers from Mexico and Central America whose infants were evaluated as insecure in the Strange Situation at 12 months of age (Lieberman, Weston, and Pawl, 1991).

Unstructured, home-based, weekly sessions lasting approximately 1½ hours were provided for a period of a year. The main focus of the intervention was to respond to the affective experiences of mother and child, both as reported by the mother and as observed through the mother–child interaction. In contrast to the other interventions, there was no didactic teaching:

> In attachment theory language, this intervention approach . . . provide[d] the mother with a corrective attachment experience. The intervenor spoke for the mother's affective experience, addressing the legitimacy of her longings for protection and safety both when she was a child and currently as an adult, and enabled her to explore unsettling feelings of anger and ambivalence toward others [p. 202].

When randomly assigned experimental and control infants were compared on the basis of their behavior in a laboratory free-play situation (which included a separation and reunion) at 18 months, it was discovered that the experimental infants evinced less angry behavior during free play and less resistant and less avoidant behavior during reunion than did control infants. Quite conceivably, this was a function of their mothers' greater empathic responsiveness and initiation of interaction. Even though no significant effects of the intervention were discerned when the Q-sort procedure was employed to evaluate attachment security at 18 months, Lieberman et al. (1991) considered it noteworthy that when Strange Situations were readministered at 24 months, most of those experimental subjects who had been earlier classified as avoidant now were classified as resistant or even disorganized, whereas the originally classified insecurely attached control infants remained avoidant. Thoughtful speculation led the investigators to hypothesize that the intervention served to break down—via changes in their mothers' caretaking—the avoidant defensiveness of the infants in the experimental group but that the full effects of such a process were not sufficiently internalized by 24 months so as to be reflected in increased rates of security in the experimental group.

Conclusion. Although the results of the various experimental studies are by no means entirely uniform, there are certainly enough data, particularly when coupled with data emanating from correlational inquiries, to indicate that social support provided to parents—either by spouse, friends, relatives, and neighbors or by formal community services—contributes to the development of a secure attachment relationship. The specific elements of social support most likely to foster the development of a secure relationship are yet to be articulated, but there is reason to believe that the effect of support on the process of parent-infant interaction is central to the process. Not only do Lieberman et al.'s (1991) findings pertaining to maternal behavior in the lab when infants were 18 months point in this direction, but so, too, do the results of the path analysis carried out by Isabella (1994, see Figure 1).

INTEGRATION AND CONCLUSIONS

In this chapter we have examined the origins of individual differences in attachment security during infancy and early childhood by reviewing evidence pertaining to what we termed "classical" and "contextual" determinants of attachment security. We first discussed evidence highlighting the role of maternal care in fostering secure and insecure attachments and drew the strong conclusion that there are insufficient grounds for concluding that temperament exerts a direct impact on attachment security. In the second part of this chapter, determinants of attachment suggested by an ecological perspective were examined. Central to our discussion of psychological and contextual factors, as well as of classical factors, was the assumption that so-called distal influences—be they less distant, like personality, or more distant, like social support—exert their influence by impacting on more proximal processes of parent–child interaction. This is because it is principally via the child's direct experiences with his or her caregiver that the quality of the attachment bond is presumed to take shape.

Although there was certainly ample evidence presented to highlight the role played by all the factors examined in shaping the development of a secure or insecure attachment bond, we repeatedly highlighted inconsistency in the evidence, as well as more general trends. What we have not as yet done is put the many factors themselves, especially the so-called distal ones, "in context." By organizing the chapter around various factors, even while emphasizing mediational processes of influence, we risk leaving the impression that these sources of influence on the parent–child relationship, and thus on the child's attachment to his or her parent, operate in isolation. Nothing could be further from the truth.

Indeed, theorizing by the authors and others draws attention to the need to consider stresses and supports simultaneously (Belsky, 1984; Belsky and Isabella, 1988)—in terms of developmental psychopathology, risk, and protective factors (Cicchetti, 1983; Sroufe and Rutter, 1984). Central to both of these theoretical orientations is the assertion that risks can be balanced by strengths and, moreover, that risks of problematical developmental outcomes, including attachment insecurity, are more likely to be realized as risk factors accumulate and are not balanced by supports or compensatory factors.

In an earlier report on a sample different from the toddler sample we are now following, Belsky and Isabella (1988) presented data on this issue with respect to the probability of a secure attachment developing by the time infants were 12 months of age. By compositing data on three different sets of factors—maternal personality, infant temperament, and marital quality—we discovered a powerful relation between degree of risk and rate of insecurity. Simply put, the more vulnerability that was discerned, as indexed by a psychologically less healthy mother, an infant becoming more difficult over time, and a marriage deteriorating in quality, the more likely the child was to be classified as insecure at one year of age (Belsky and Isabella, 1988).

Figures 2 and 3 represent the results of a somewhat similar analysis run on the toddler sample mentioned throughout this chapter. After compositing measures of adult personality (extroversion + agreeableness + interpersonal affect − neuroticism), infant tempera-

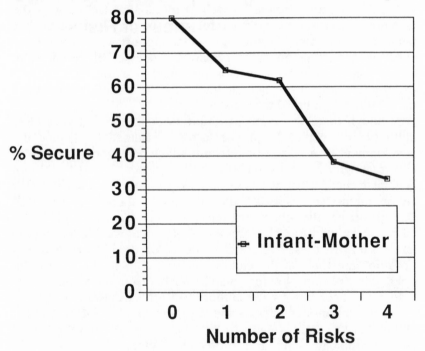

Figure 2 Infant–Mother Attachment Security as a Function of Cumulative Risk

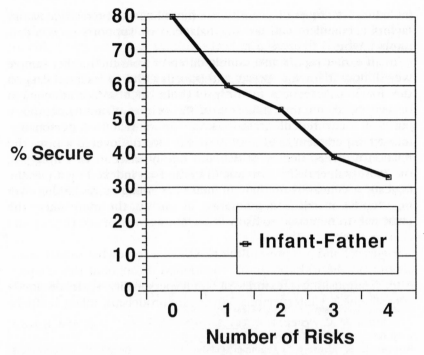

Figure 3 Infant–Father Attachment Security as a Function of Cumulative Risk

ment (positive emotionality – negative emotionality), marital quality (positive composite + satisfaction – negative composite), and social support (satisfaction with support) and splitting these composites at the median, we examined the rate of infant–parent attachment security among those subgroups of mothers and fathers who received higher and lower risk scores. (Risk was defined as scoring below the median on each composite variable.) What is noteworthy, is the pattern in each graph for rate of security to decline as number of risk factors increase (see Figures 2 and 3). In fact, in the case of both infant–mother and infant–father attachment security, insecurity is significantly more likely when three of four risks are present relative to when only two or fewer risks are present (I–M: $x^2[1] = 4.75$, $p < .05$; I–F: $x^2[1] = 3.77$, $p < .05$). Recall, as mentioned in various parts of this chapter, that not a single one of the components of the multiple risk score by itself differentiated secure and insecure attachment relationships; only in combination does such an effect emerge.

This observation underscores the closing point to be made in this chapter: to understand how psychological and social contexts influence the development of the child–parent attachment relationship, multiple factors must be considered simultaneously. Having a mother who is depressed is likely to have a dramatically different effect if a marriage is also conflicted and an infant is temperamentally difficult than if a spouse is supportive and an infant is easy to care for. In other words, not only do processes of mediation need to be central to our understanding of the origins of individual differences in attachment (distal factors→parent–child interaction→ attachment security), but so, too, do moderational ones, as the impact of one source of influence is highly likely to be contingent on another. As Bronfenbrenner (1979) so astutely noted, in the ecology of human development—and thus with respect to the etiology of secure and insecure infant–parent attachment bonds—"the principal main effects are likely to be interactions" (p. 38).

REFERENCES

Ainsworth, M. D. (1973), The development of infant–mother attachment. In: *Review of Child Development Research, Vol. 3*, ed. B. M. Caldwell & H. N. Ricciuti. Chicago: University of Chicago Press, pp. 1–94.

—— Blehar, M. C., Waters, E. & Wall, S. (1978), *Patterns of Attachment*. Hillsdale, NJ: Lawrence Erlbaum Associates.

Barnard, K. S., Magyary, D., Summer, G., Booth, C., Mitchell, S. K. & Speikers, S. (1988), Prevention of parenting alterations for women with low social supports. *Psychiat.*, 51:248–253.

Barnett, B., Blignault, I., Holmes, S., Payne A. & Parker, G. (1987), Quality of attachment in a sample of 1-year-old Australian children. *J. Amer. Acad. Child Adol. Psychiat.*, 26:303–307.

Bates, J. E., Maslin, C. A. & Frankel, K. A. (1985), Attachment security, mother–child interaction, and temperament as predictors of behavior-problem ratings at age three years. In: *Growing Points in Attachment Theory and Research*, ed. I. Bretherton & E. Waters. *Monographs of the Society for Research in Child Development*. Serial No. 209, Vol. 50, Nos. 1–2, pp. 167–193.

Beckwith, L. (1988), Intervention with disadvantaged parents of sick preterm infants. *Psychiat.*, 51:242–247.

Belsky, J. (1981), Early human experience: A family perspective. *Devel. Psychol.*, 17:3–23.

—— (1984), The determinants of parenting: A process model. *Child Devel.*, 55:83–96.

—— (1990), Parental and nonparental care and children's socioemotional development: A decade in review. *J. Marr. Fam.*, 52:885–903.

—— & Cassidy, J. (1994), Attachment: Theory and evidence. In: *Developmental Principles and Clinical Issues in Psychology and Psychiatry*, ed. R. Rutter, D. Hay & S. Baron-Cohen. Oxford: Blackwell, pp. 373–402.

—— & Crnic, K. (1990), Family stress and conflict: The "terrible twos." Grant funded by the National Institute of Mental Health, Penn State University.

—— Fish, M. & Isabella, R. (1991), Continuity and discontinuity in infant negative and positive emotionality: Family antecedent and attachment consequences. *Devel. Psychol.*, 27:421–431.

—— & Isabella, R. (1988), Maternal, infant, and social-contextual determinants of attachment security. In: *Clinical Implications of Attachment*, ed. J. Belsky & T. Nezworski. Hillsdale, NJ: Lawrence Erlbaum Associates, pp. 41–94.

—— & Pensky, E. (1988), Developmental history, personality and family relationships: Toward an emergent family system. In: *Relationships within Families*, ed. R. Hinde & J. Stevenson-Hinde. Oxford: Clarendon Press, pp. 193–217.

—— & Rovine, M. J. (1987), Temperament and attachment security in the strange situation: An empirical rapprochement. *Child Devel.*, 58:787–795.

—— Rovine, M. & Taylor, D. G. (1984), The Pennsylvania Infant and Family Development Project, III: The origins of individual differences in infant–mother attachment: Maternal and infant contributions. *Child Devel.*, 55:718–728.

—— & Vondra, J. (1989), Lessons from child abuse: The determinants of parenting. In: *Current Research and Theoretical Advances in Child Maltreatment*, ed. D. Cicchetti & V. Carlson. Cambridge: Cambridge University Press, pp. 153–202.

Benn, R. K. (1986), Factors promoting secure attachment relationships between employed mothers and their sons. *Child Devel.*, 57:1224–1231.

Bowlby, J. (1944), Forty-four juvenile thieves: Their characters and home life. *Internat. J. Psycho-Anal.*, 25:19–52, 107–127.

—— (1958), The nature of the child's tie to his mother. *Internat. J. Psycho-Anal.*, 39:350–373.

—— (1969), *Attachment and Loss, Vol. 1*. New York: Basic Books, 1982.

Bronfenbrenner, U. (1979), *The Ecology of Human Development*. Cambridge, MA: Harvard University Press.

Campbell, S. B., Cohn, J. F., Meyers, T. A., Ross, S. & Flanagan, C. (1993), Chronicity of maternal depression and mother–infant interaction. Presented at meeting of the Society for Research in Child Development, New Orleans.

Chess, S. & Thomas, A. (1982), Infant bonding: Mystique and reality. *Amer. J. Orthopsychiat.*, 52:213–222.

Chibucos, T. & Kail, P. (1981), Longitudinal examination of father–infant interaction and infant–father attachment. *Merrill-Palmer Quart.*, 27:81–96.

Cicchetti, D. (1983), The emergence of developmental psychopathology. *Child Devel.*, 55:1–7.

—— & Barnett, D. (1991), Attachment organization in maltreated preschoolers. *Devel. Psychopathol.*, 3:397–412.

Clarke-Stewart, K. A. (1988), Parents' effects on children's development: A decade of progress? *J. Appl. Devel. Psychol.*, 9:41–84.

Cochran, M. & Brassard, J. (1979), Child development and personal social networks. *Child Devel.*, 50:601–616.

Cohn, J., Campbell, S. & Ross, S. (1991), Infant response in the still face paradigm at 6 months predicts avoidant and secure attachment at 12 months. *Devel. Psychopathol.*, 3:367–376.

Colin, V. (1991), *Human Attachment* (Contract No. HHS-100-90-0035). Washington, DC: U.S. Dept. Health & Human Services.

Colletta, N. D. (1983), At risk for depression: A study of young mothers. *J. Genet. Psychol.*, 142:301–310.

—— & Gregg, C. H. (1981), Adolescent mothers' vulnerability to stress. *J. Ner. Ment. Dis.*, 169:50–54.

Cox, M., Owen, M., Lewis, J. & Henderson, V. (1989), Marriage, adult adjustment, and early parenting. *Child Devel.*, 60:1016–1024.

—— Owen, T., Henderson, V. & Margand, N. (1992), Prediction of infant–father and infant–mother attachment. *Devel. Psychol.*, 28:474–483.

Crittenden, P. M. (1985), Social networks, quality of child rearing, and child development. *Child Devel.*, 56:1299–1313.

Crnic, K. A., Greenberg, M. T., Ragozin, A. S., Robinson, N. M. & Basham, R. B. (1983), Effects of stress and social support on mothers and premature and full-term infants. *Child Devel.*, 54:209–217.
—— Greenberg, M. T. & Slough, N. M. (1986), Early stress and social support influences on mothers' and high-risk infants' functioning in late infancy. *Infant Ment. Health J.*, 7:19–33.
—— Ragozin, A., Greenberg, M., Robinson, N. & Basham, R. (1983), Social interaction and developmental competence of pre-term and full-term infants during the first year of life. *Child Devel.*, 54:1199–1210.
Crockenberg, S. B. (1981), Infant irritability, mother responsiveness, and social support influences on the security of infant–mother attachment. *Child Devel.*, 52:857–869.
Crowell, J. & Feldman, S. (1991), Mothers' working models of attachment relationships and mother and child behavior during separation and reunion. *Devel. Psychol.*, 27:597–605.
D'Angelo, E. J. (1986), Security of attachment in infants with schizophrenic, depressed, and unaffected mothers. *J. Genet. Psychol.*, 147:421–422.
Das-Eiden, R., Teti, D. & Corns, K. (1993), Maternal working models of attachment, marital adjustment, and the parent–child relationship. Presented at the biennial meetings of the Society for Research in Child Development, New Orleans.
Del Carmen, R., Pedersen, F., Huffman, L. & Bryan, Y. (1993), Dyadic distress management predicts security of attachment. *Infant Behav. Devel.*, 16:131–147.
DeMulder, E. K. & Radke-Yarrow, M. (1991), Attachment with affectively ill and well mothers: Current behavioral correlates. *Devel. Psychopathol.*, 3:227–242.
Dickie, J. (1987), Interrelationships within the mother–father–infant triad. In: *Men's Transitions to Parenthood*, ed. P. W. Berman & F. A. Pederson. Hillsdale, NJ: Lawrence Erlbaum Associates, pp. 113–144.
Durrett, M. E., Otaki, M. & Richards, P. (1984), Attachment and the mother's perception of support from the father. *Internat. J. Behav. Devel.*, 7:167–176.
—— Richards, P., Otaki, M., Pennebaker J. W. & Nyquist, L. (1986), Mother's involvement with infant and her perception of spousal support, Japan and America. *J. Marr. Fam.*, 48:187–194.
Egeland, B. & Farber, E. A. (1984), Infant–mother attachment: Factors related to its development and changes over time. *Child Devel.*, 55:753–771.
Engfer, A. (1988), The interrelatedness of marriage and the mother–child relationship. In: *Relationships within Families*, ed. R. Hinde & J. Stevenson-Hinde. Oxford: Oxford University Press, pp. 104–118.
Feiring, C., Fox, N. A., Jaskir, J. & Lewis, M. (1987), The relation between social support, infant risk status and mother–infant interaction. *Devel. Psychol.*, 23:400–405.
Frodi, A. & Thompson, R. (1985), Infants' affective responses in the Strange Situation. *Child Devel.*, 56:1280–1291.
Gaensbauer, T. J., Harmon, R. J., Cytryn, L. & McKnew, D. H. (1984), Social and affective development in infants with a manic-depressive parent. *Amer. J. Psychiat.*, 141:223–229.
Gelfand, D. & Teti, D. (1990), The effects of maternal depression on children. *Clin. Psychol. Rev.*, 10:329–353.
George, C., Kaplan, N. & Main, M. (1985), Adult Attachment Interview. Unpublished manuscript, Dept. Psychology, University of California, Berkeley.
Goldberg, W. A. & Easterbrooks, M. A. (1984), The role of marital quality in toddler development. *Devel. Psychol.*, 20:504–514.
Goldsmith, H. H. & Alansky, J. A. (1987), Maternal and infant temperamental predictors of attachment: A meta-analytic review. *J. Consult. Clin. Psychol.*, 55:805–816.

Goosens, F. & van IJzendoorn, M. (1990), Quality of infants' attachment to professional caregivers. *Child Devel.*, 61:832–837.

Grossmann, K., Grossmann, K. E., Spangler, G., Suess, G. & Unzner, L. (1985), Maternal sensitivity and newborns' orientation responses as related to quality of attachment in northern Germany. In: *Growing Points in Attachment Theory and Research*, ed. I. Bretherton & E. Waters. *Monographs of the Society for Research in Child Development*, Serial No. 209, Vol. 50, Nos. 1–2, pp. 233–257.

Hazan, C. & Shaver, P. (in press), Attachment as an organizational construct for research on close relationships. *Psychol. Inq.*

Howes, P. & Markman, H. J. (1989), Marital quality and child functioning: A longitudinal investigation. *Child Devel.*, 60:1044–1051.

Howes, C., Rodning, C., Galluzzo, D. C. & Myers, L. (1988), Attachment and child care: Relationships with mother and caregiver. *Early Childhood Res. Quart.*, 3:403–416.

Isabella, R. A. (1993), Origins of attachment: Maternal interactive behavior across the first year. *Child Devel.*, 64:605–621.

―― (1994), Origins of maternal role satisfaction and its influences on maternal interactive behavior and infant–mother attachment. *Infant Behav. Devel.*, 17:381–388.

―― & Belsky, J. (1991), Interactional synchrony and the origins of infant–mother attachment: A replication study. *Child Devel.*, 62:373–384.

―― ―― & von Eye, A. (1989), Origins of infant–mother attachment: An examination of interactional synchrony during the infant's first year. *Devel. Psychol.*, 25:12–21.

Jacobson, S. W. & Frye, K. F. (1991), Effect of maternal social support on attachment: Experimental evidence. *Child Devel.*, 62:572–582.

Jouriles, E., Pfiffner, L. & O'Leary, S. (1988), Marital conflict, parenting and toddler conduct problems. *J. Abn. Child Psychol.*, 16:197–206.

Kagan, J. (1982), *Psychological Research on the Human Infant: An Evaluative Summary.* New York: W. T. Grant Foundation.

Lamb, M. E., Thompson, R. A., Gardner, W. P., Charnov, E. L. & Estes, D. (1984), Security of infantile attachment as assessed in the "strange situation": Its study and biological interpretation. *Behav. Brain Sci.*, 7:127–172.

Levitt, M., Weber, R. & Clark, M. (1986), Social network relationships as sources of maternal support and well-being. *Devel. Psychol.*, 22:310–316.

Levy-Shiff, R. & Israelashvili, R. (1988), Antecedents of fathering: Some further exploration. *Devel. Psychol.*, 24:434–440.

Lewis, M. & Feiring, C. (1989), Infant, mother, and mother–infant interaction behavior and subsequent attachment. *Child Devel.*, 60:831–837.

―― Owen, M. T. & Cox, M. J. (1988), The transition to parenthood: III. Incorporation of the child into the family. *Fam. Press*, 27:411–421.

Lieberman, A. F., Weston, D. R. & Pawl, J. H. (1991), Preventive intervention and outcome with anxiously attached dyads. *Child Devel.*, 62:199–209.

Lyons-Ruth, K. (1988), Maternal depression and infant disturbance. Presented at the International Conference on Infant Studies, Washington, DC.

―― Connell, D. B. & Grunebaum, H. U. (1990), Infants at social risk: Maternal depression and family support services as mediators of infant development and security of attachment. *Child Devel.*, 61:85–98.

―― Zoll, D., Connell, D. & Grunebaum, H. (1986), The depressed mother and her one-year-old infant: Environmental context, mother–infant interaction and attachment. In: *Maternal Depression and Infant Disturbance*, ed. E. Tronick & T. Field. San Francisco: Jossey-Bass, pp. 61–82.

Main, M. & Goldwyn, R. (1984), Predicting rejection of her infant from mother's representation of her own experience. *Child Abuse Neglect*, 8:203–217.

—— & —— (in press), Interview-based adult attachment classifications: Related to infant–mother and infant–father attachment. *Devel. Psychol.*

—— Kaplan, N. & Cassidy, J. (1985), Security in infancy, childhood, and adulthood: A move to the level of representation. In: *Growing Points Attachment Theory and Research*, ed. I. Bretherton & E. Waters. *Monographs of the Society for Research in Child Development*. Serial No. 209, Vol. 50, Nos. 1–2, pp. 66–104.

Malatesta, C., Culver, C., Tesman, J. & Shepard, B. (1989), *The Development of Emotion Expression During the First Two Years. Monographs of the Society for Research in Child Development*. Serial No. 219, Vol. 54, Nos. 1–2.

Maslin, C. A. & Bates, J. E. (1983), Precursors of anxious and secure attachments: A multivariant model at age 6 months. Presented at the biennial meeting of the Society for Research in Child Development, Detroit.

Meyer, H. J. (1988), Marital and mother–child relationships: Developmental history, parent personality and child difficulties. In: *Relationships within Families*, ed. R. A. Hinde & J. Stevenson-Hinde. Oxford: Clarendon Press, pp. 119–142.

Mitchell, R. & Trichett, E. (1980), Task Force Report: Social networks as mediators of social support. *Comm. Ment. Health J.*, 16:27–44.

Moran, G., Pederson, D., Pettit, P. & Krupka, A. (1992), Maternal sensitivity and infant–mother attachment in a developmentally delayed sample. *Infant Behav. Devel.*, 15:427–442.

Nakasawa, M., Teti, D. M. & Lamb, M. E. (1992), An ecological study of child–mother attachments among Japanese sojourners in the United States. *Devel. Psychol.*, 28:584–592.

Nuckolls, C. G., Cassel, J. & Kaplan, B. H. (1972), Psychological assets, life crises and the prognosis of pregnancy. *Amer. J. Epidem.*, 95:431–441.

Oates, D. S. & Heinicke, C. (1985), Prebirth prediction of the quality of the mother–infant interaction: The first year of life. *J. Fam. Issues*, 6:523–542.

O'Connor, M., Sigman, M. & Kasasi, C. (1992), Attachment behavior of infants exposed prenatally to alcohol. *Devel. Psychopathol.*, 4:243–256.

Pederson, D., Moran, G., Sitko, C., Campbell, K., Ghesqure, K. & Acton, H. (1990), Maternal sensitivity and the security of infant–mother attachment. *Child Devel.*, 61:1974–1983.

Powell, D. B. (1980), Personal social networks as a focus for primary prevention of child maltreatment. *Infant Ment. Health J.*, 1:232–239.

Radke-Yarrow, M. (1991), Attachment patterns in children of depressed mothers. In: *Attachment across the Life Cycle*, ed. C. M. Parkes, J. Stevenson-Hinde & P. Maras. London: Tavistock/Routledge, pp. 115–126.

—— Cummings, M. E., Kuczynski, L. & Chapman, M. (1985), Patterns of attachment in two- and three-year olds in normal families and families with parental depression. *Child Devel.*, 56:884–893.

Ricks, M. H. (1985), The social transmission of parental behavior: Attachment across generations. In: *Growing Points Attachment Theory and Research*, ed. I. Bretherton & E. Waters. *Monographs of the Society for Research in Child Development*. Serial No. 209, Vol. 50, Nos. 1–2, pp. 211–227.

Rothbart, M. (1981), Measurement of temperament in infancy. *Child Develop.*, 52:569–578.

Sameroff, A. J., Seifer, R. & Zax, M. (1982), Early development of children at risk for emotional disorder. *Monographs of the Society for Research in Child Development*, Vol. 47, No. 7.

Sarason, I., Sarason, B. & Shearin, E. (1986), Social support as an individual difference variable. *J. Per. Soc. Psychol.*, 50:845–855.

Schneider-Rosen, K. & Rothbaum, F. (1993), Quality of parental caregiving and security of attachment. *Devel. Psychol.*, 29:358–367.

Smith, P. B. & Pederson, D. R. (1988), Maternal sensitivity and patterns of infant–mother attachment. *Child Devel.*, 59:1097–1101.

Spieker, S. J. (1988), Patterns of very insecure attachment found in samples of high-risk infants and toddlers. *Topics Early Childhood Spec. Ed.*, 6:37–53.

—— & Booth, C. (1988), Maternal antecedents of attachment quality. In: *Clinical Implications of Attachment*, ed. J. Belsky & T. Nezworski. Hillsdale, NJ: Lawrence Erlbaum Associates, pp. 95–135.

Sroufe, L. A. (1985), Attachment classification from the perspective of infant-caregiver relationships and infant temperament. *Child Devel.*, 56:1–14.

—— & Rutter, M. (1984), The domain of developmental psychopathology. *Child Devel.*, 55:17–29.

Teti, D. M. & Gelfand, D. M. (1993), Attachment security among infants and toddlers of depressed mothers: Association with maternal depression and mother–child behavior. Presented at meeting of Society for Research in Child Development, New Orleans.

——; Nakasawa, M., Das, R. & Wirth, O. (1991), Security of attachment between preschoolers and their mothers: Relations among social interaction, parenting stress, and mothers' sorts of the attachment Q-Set. *Devel. Psychol.*, 27:440–447.

Thompson, R., Connell, J. & Bridges, L. (1988), Temperament, emotion, and social interactive behavior in the strange situation. *Child Devel.*, 59:1102–1110.

van den Boom, D. (1990), Preventive intervention and the quality of mother–infant interaction and infant exploration in irritable infants. In: *Developmental Psychology behind the Dikes*, ed. W. Koops et al. Amsterdam: Eburon, pp. 249–270.

—— (1995), The influence of temperament and mothering on attachment and exploration. *Child Devel.* 65:1449–1469.

van IJzendoorn, M., Goldberg, S., Kroonenberg, P. & Frenkel, O. (1992), The relative effects of maternal and child problems on the quality of attachment. *Child Devel.*, 63:840–858.

Waters, E. & Deane, K. E. (1985), Defining and assessing individual differences in attachment relationships: Q-methodology and the organization of behavior in infancy and early childhood. In: *Growing Points in Attachment Theory and Research*, ed. I. Bretherton & E. Waters. *Monographs of the Society for Research in Child Development*. Serial No. 209, Vol. 50, Nos. 1–2, pp. 41–65.

Zarling, C. L., Hirsch, R. & Landry, S. (1988), Maternal social networks and mother–infant interactions in full-term and very low birthweight, preterm infants. *Child Devel.*, 59:178–185.

Zeanah, C., Benoit, D., Barton, M., Rega, C., Hirschberg, L. & Lipsitt, L. (1993), Representations of attachment in mothers and their one-year-old infants. *J. Amer. Acad. Child Adolesc. Psychiat.*, 32:278–286.

7

Influence of Attachment Theory on Ethological Studies of Biobehavioral Development in Nonhuman Primates

STEPHEN J. SUOMI

Although John Bowlby was a psychoanalyst by formal training, he was a true ethologist at heart. His love for the out-of-doors and his keen eye for observation made him naturally responsive to the basic tenets of classical ethological theory and methodology. Indeed, he readily recognized certain common features of psychoanalytic and ethological theorizing, for example, a belief in the biological basis of fundamental behavioral tendencies and an interest in the long-term consequences of specific early experiences. But Bowlby also argued frequently and passionately that many basic features of human development could be better understood by focusing on external relationships rather than on internalized psychic struggles among the id, ego, and superego. He treasured the insights that he believed direct observation of behavior in naturalistic contexts could provide over and above any analysis of an individual's unconscious memories and desires. When Bowlby first articulated these views, they were considered heretical, but today his original insights are widely accepted across a broad range of disciplines, including both ethology and psychoanalysis.

Bowlby began reading the classical ethological literature in the early 1950s and soon became fascinated with the notion of imprinting (Bowlby, 1957). He was especially influenced in his development and elaboration of attachment theory by the work of contemporary primatologists studying mother–infant relationships in rhesus monkeys and other nonhuman primate species. He had a long-standing friendship with Robert Hinde, the Cambridge ethologist who had switched his primary research interest from studies of birds to studies of rhesus monkeys in the late 1950s and 1960s. These studies focused on the normative development of mother–infant relationships in rhesus monkeys (e.g., Hinde and Spencer-Booth, 1967), providing convincing demonstrations of secure-base phenomena, an essential feature of secure attachment relationships.

Hinde also introduced Bowlby to the work of Harry Harlow at the very time Bowlby was writing his seminal attachment paper "The nature of the child's tie to his mother" (Bowlby, 1958), and Bowlby included in that paper a footnote describing Harlow's not-yet-published classic study of cloth-covered and wire-covered "surrogate mothers" (Harlow, 1958). Bowlby was delighted by Harlow's clear demonstration of the importance of clinging contact with the mother, not only as a behavioral prerequisite for the infant that was at least as salient as nursing but also as the basis (for monkey infants, at least) for the development of a secure base for subsequent exploration of the environment (Harlow and Zimmermann, 1959). In the 1960s both Hinde and Harlow carried out studies of mother-infant separation in rhesus monkeys that informed and solidified crucial aspects of Bowlby's characterizations of separation reactions as predictable evolutionary adaptations, as well as providing telling signs of the specific nature of an individual infant's tie to its mother (e.g., Seay, Hansen, and Harlow, 1962; Hinde, Spencer-Booth, and Bruce, 1966).

Not surprisingly, Bowlby invited noted primatologists to each of his four biennial Tavistock Seminars on Mother–Infant Interaction (Foss, 1961, 1963, 1965, 1969), which preceded the publication of the first volume in his classic attachment trilogy (Bowlby, 1969). In subsequent years he followed the nonhuman primate literature closely, and he continued to cite it extensively throughout the rest of his career.

Given that Bowlby's ideas about attachment were clearly influenced by ethological principles in general and by studies of primate behavioral development in particular, it seems fitting that the reverse has also been true—over the past 30 years Bowlby's ideas about attachment have had a major influence on numerous studies of primate biobehavioral development in general and mother–infant attachment in particular. Three major areas of research especially stand out in this respect: descriptive studies of the development of mother–infant attachment and other social relationships in monkeys and apes, experimental and naturalistic studies of mother–infant and other forms of social separation or loss, and investigations of the long-term developmental consequences of differences in the nature of early attachment relationships (e.g., secure versus insecure early attachments).

DESCRIPTIVE STUDIES OF THE DEVELOPMENT OF ATTACHMENT AND OTHER SOCIAL RELATIONSHIPS IN MONKEYS AND APES

In the years immediately following Bowlby's seminal monograph on the nature of the child's tie to mother, studies of mother–infant relationships in nonhuman primates began to appear in the literature. During the 1960s and 1970s, investigators working both in laboratory and in field settings carried out descriptive, longitudinal studies of mother–infant interactions in a variety of primate species. While many of these early studies had been originally conceived and designed without explicit consideration of attachment theory, the data that emerged were frequently analyzed and discussed from an attachment theory perspective.

Most of these classic longitudinal studies were carried out with Old World monkeys and apes. These primate species are our closest phylogenetic relatives, sharing approximately 88–94% (for Old World monkeys) and 96–99% (for apes) of the same genes with Homo sapiens (Lovejoy, 1981). By way of comparison, the next closest primate taxa–New World monkeys, whose lineages separated from those of Old World monkeys, apes, and hominids approximately 40–50 million years ago–share approximately 80–85% of our genes. The most primitive primates–the prosimians (lemurs, lorises, tarsiers, and aye-ayes)–diverged genetically even earlier and more completely.

The general developmental picture from these early studies of Old World monkeys and apes was remarkably similar from study to study and from species to species. Virtually all infants in these species spend their initial days, weeks, and (for apes) months in almost continuous physical contact with their biological mothers and typically cling to their mother's ventral surface for most of their waking and all of their sleeping hours each day. These young infants clearly and consistently display four of the initial five "component instinctual responses" in Bowlby's (1958) list of universal human attachment behaviors–sucking, clinging, crying, and following (the fifth, smiling, is universally seen in chimpanzee but not monkey infants). In subsequent weeks and months virtually all infants in both laboratory and field settings use their biological mothers as a "secure base" to explore their immediate physical and social environment. Mothers, in turn, expand their range of infant-directed behavior to include extensive grooming bouts, on one hand, and occasional physical punishment, especially around the time of weaning, on the other. In sum, the basic behavioral components and developmental course of mother–infant interactions and relationships seem to be highly congruent across these different primate species and settings–and highly consistent with the basic tenets of Bowlby's theorizing for humans.

The research that followed these pioneering descriptive studies of mother–infant relationships has both broadened the range of primate species examined and looked for systematic variation among mothers and infants within species. As before, most of these studies have focused on Old World monkeys and apes, and the consistent picture of strong mother–infant attachment as a universal feature of social development in these primates has been sustained and elaborated considerably. For example, Hinde (Hinde and Atkinson, 1970) developed an objective metric for determining the relative contribution of both mother and infant rhesus monkeys to the maintenance of mutual contact and close proximity, and he and his students were able to demonstrate normative developmental changes in this metric that effectively tracked the development of secure-base behavior by the maturing infant. Other primate researchers have used this metric in analyzing mother–infant relationships in numerous other Old World monkey and ape species, and the universal finding has been that mothers are at first primarily responsible for maintaining contact/proximity but that infants take over that role as they grow older, albeit with a predictable fluctuation around the time of weaning. While there are clear differences among mother–infant dyads in the exact timing of this developmental shift, the differences appear to be as much a function of differences in the infant's gender, the mother's parity and status within her social group, and the nature of the dyad's physical and social environment as they are a function of species differences (cf. Higley and Suomi, 1986).

The same principle seems to hold for other aspects of the mother–infant relationship, such as infant nursing schedules, maternal grooming bouts, or maternal punishment—the amount of within-species variance in any one measure is usually as great or greater than between-species variance, and the patterns of within-species variance seem similar across different Old World monkey and ape species. For example, male infants in all these species tend to spend more time in physical contact with their mothers during the first month but less time after weaning than females, while mothers across the species tend to punish male infants more frequently, especially if they are primiparous (Rasmussen and Suomi, in prepation). Thus, the consistent finding throughout the history of this research area has been that mother–infant relationships in Old World monkeys and apes involve common behavior patterns, follow similar sequences of developmental change, and appear to be subject to the same set of influences, all of which provide empirical support for the basic tenets of Bowlby's attachment theory.

This picture of cross-species consistency in attachment phenomena is not completely shared by the rest of the primate order. Infant prosimians and New World monkeys are also highly dependent on their mothers and spend much, if not all, of their time in mutual physical contact during their initial days and weeks of life. In most of these "lower" primate species, however, the nature of the mother–infant contact is different (predominantly dorsal-ventral rather than ventral-ventral), the diversity and frequency of mother-infant interactions are reduced, and the existence of basic features of Bowlby-like attachment, for example, secure-base phenomena, is less obvious or dramatic than in Old World monkeys, apes, or humans (cf. Higley and Suomi, 1986).

Consider the case of capuchin monkeys (*Cebus apella*), a highly successful species of New World monkeys whose natural habitat includes much of South America. These primates are remarkable in many respects, not the least of which is an amazing capacity for the spontaneous manufacture and use of a wide range of tools (E. Darwin, 1794; Visalberghi, 1990). In this respect they clearly surpass all Old World monkeys and most likely all of the apes except chimpanzees. Nevertheless, mother–infant relationships in capuchin monkeys seem somewhat primitive by rhesus or other Old World monkey standards. Capuchin monkey infants spend virtually all of their first three months of life clinging to their mother's back, swinging around to her ventral surface only during nursing bouts (Welker et al., 1987; Fragaszy, Baer, and Adams-Curtis, 1991; Byrne and Suomi, 1995). Consequently, during this time there is very little visual, vocal, or grooming interaction with the mother. In contrast, rhesus monkey infants begin to use their mother as a secure base by 3–4 weeks of age, when they start exploring their immediate environment, and by this time they are already participating in extensive one-on-one interactions with their mothers that involve a wealth of visual, auditory, tactile, and vestibular stimulation.

When capuchin monkeys finally get off their mother and begin physically exploring their environment during their third and fourth months, the transition is much more abrupt and complete than it is for rhesus infants, such that capuchin infants spend long periods of time (i.e., more than 30 minutes) away from their mother with little apparent upset or concern. If frightened, they are almost as likely to seek protective contact with another group member as with their own mother (Bryne and Suomi, 1995). At this age and thereafter capuchin monkey youngsters have far fewer and briefer interactions with their mother than do comparably aged rhesus monkeys (e.g., they spend only a third as much time in grooming bouts with mother as do rhesus), and the specific behaviors of these interactions are not markedly different from those characterizing interactions with other group members, for example, siblings, peers, or unrelated adult females (Welker et al., 1990; Byrne and Suomi, 1995). In contrast, mother-infant relationships in rhesus monkeys involve a unique set of behaviors that are seldom, if ever, seen in other types of social relationships, for example, those with peers (Suomi, 1979). All in all, capuchin monkey infants seem far less "attached" to their biological mothers than are rhesus monkeys (and other Old World monkeys and apes) in terms of the primacy and prominence of the relationship, the relative uniqueness of the constituent behavior patterns comprising the relationship, and the relative paucity of secure base behaviors in the context of environmental exploration. One wonders how Bowlby's attachment theory might have looked had Hinde and Harlow been studying capuchin, rather than rhesus, monkeys!

Most other New World monkey species have mother–infant relationships that more closely resemble those of capuchin monkeys than those of rhesus monkeys (for example, Fragaszy et al., 1991), while in marmoset and tamarin species the mothers are not even the primary caregivers. Prosimian infants seem even less "attached" to their mothers than New World monkey infants (cf. Higley and Suomi, 1986). To be sure, infants in all these primate species appear to become "imprinted" on their mothers, as do most other social mammals and many avian species (Immelmann and Suomi, 1981). Nonetheless, atttachment involves considerably more developmental complexity and reciprocity than classical notions of imprinting (actually, it represents a special case of imprinting), and it seems clear that attachment phenomena are most apparent in humans and their closest phylogenetic kin—and thus may represent a relatively recent evolutionary adaptation among primates.

FACTORS FACILITATING THE ESTABLISHMENT AND MAINTENANCE OF ATTACHMENT RELATIONSHIPS

What sort of behavioral, cognitive, and emotional processes are involved in the establishment and maintenance of these attachment relationships? To begin, certain neonatal predispositions have evolved in these primate species. Newborn Old World monkeys, apes, and humans are born with strong behavioral propensities, clear-cut perceptual biases, and a host of physical and social features that make them highly attractive to any caregiver. For example, rhesus monkey neonates possess numerous physical features that clearly distinguish them from older conspecifics and appear to serve as releasing stimuli for potential caregivers. These neonates share many of the "babylike" physical and physiognomic characteristics that contribute to the distinctive appearance of human neonates, including a head that is large in proportion to the body, a protruding forehead that is large in proportion to the rest of the face, and large eyes that are seated below the midline of the head (Brooks and Hochberg, 1960; Sternglass et al., 1977; Alley, 1981). In addition, rhesus monkeys are born with an unusually dark pelage and bright red facial coloration, features that begin to fade noticeably around the time of weaning (Higley et al., 1987).

Rhesus monkey neonates also exhibit behavioral propensities that serve to promote essential contact with their mother or other care-givers. Within minutes of delivery they are able to sustain ventral contact with their mother, without her support, via powerful grasp-ing and clasping reflexes and to locate and suckle from their mothers' nipples via rooting and sucking reflexes (e.g., Mowbray and Cadell, 1962; Schneider and Suomi, 1992). These neonatal reflexes serve to ensure prolonged tactile stimulation from the mother via ventral-ventral contact, providing what Harlow (1958) deemed "contact comfort" and what subsequent research has linked to stimulation of growth hormone (Champoux et al., 1989). Such extensive tactile communication between mother and infant helps cement the emerging attachment relationship between the pair.

In addition to these reflexive behavioral propensities, rhesus monkey infants are born with visual and auditory preferences for stimuli associated with their most likely caregiver, their mother. They prefer female to male adult conspecifics, and they prefer conspecific females to females of different species within the genus (Sackett, 1970; Suomi, Sackett, and Harlow, 1970). Additionally, newborn rhesus monkeys are blessed with facial, vocal, and postural expressions that not only denote distinctive emotional states but also serve as powerfully salient stimuli for conspecifics within sight and sound. Darwin (1872) was among the first to argue that humans do not have a monopoly on emotional expressions, if not emotional states. There are compelling parallels between specific facial expres-sions universally displayed by rhesus monkey infants and those expressed by human infants and young children and universally interpreted as indicative of basic emotional states (cf. Suomi, 1984).

These various features, propensities, and preferences serve to channel a newborn primate's attention and effort toward establish-ing and maintaining an attachment relationship with its mother—or, in her absence, whatever potential substitute might be available. Infant rhesus monkeys reared away from their biological mother have readily formed attachments to unrelated adult females, adult males, peers, dogs, hobbyhorses, and Harlow's classic, cloth-covered, inanimate "surrogate mothers" (but not wire-covered surrogates; cf. Harlow, 1958; Harlow and Suomi, 1970). Such exper-imental findings are clearly in keeping with Bowlby's (1958, 1969) notion of infant-initiated attachment behavior representing an adaptive product of primate evolution. There can be little question that infants of advanced primate species are highly prepared, if not actually programmed, to establish attachments to caregivers in their initial days, weeks, and months of life. In nature, of course, the overwhelming likelihood is that those attachments will be formed with the biological mother.

Moreover, the attachment relationships that these young primates establish with their mothers are unique, differing in several fundamental respects from all other social relationships that each individual develops during its lifetime. For example, both laboratory and field studies have consistently shown that rhesus monkeys typically develop distinctive relationships with siblings, peers, and adults—both kin and nonkin—of both genders as they are growing up; some of these relationships even persist throughout adulthood. But the initial attachment relationship each rhesus monkey forms with its mother is different from all other relationships in terms of primacy, constituent behaviors, nature of receprocity, and pattern of developmental change (cf. Suomi, 1979).

Perhaps Bowlby was not entirely correct (at least for rhesus monkeys) when he argued that an infant's attachment relationship with its mother provides the prototype for all subsequent social relationships. Rather, the consistent lesson from the primate literature is that mother–infant attachments are truly different from all other relationships that advanced primates inevitably develop. On the other hand, Bowlby was absolutely correct when he argued that the nature of the relationship an infant develops with its mother—and what happens to that relationship—can profoundly affect present and future relationships the infant might develop with others in its social sphere. On this issue, the nonhuman primate literature is highly supportive, as demonstrated later in this chapter.

STUDIES OF SOCIAL SEPARATION IN NONHUMAN PRIMATES

A second area of primate research in which Bowlby's ideas have had widespread influence concerns social separation phenomena. A prominent feature of Bowlby's attachment theory is its emphasis on the nature and consequences of an infant's experiencing separation from its mother (or other primary attachment figure). From early on Bowlby recognized the ethological, psychological, and potential clinical significance of mother–infant separation, and he devoted a substantial portion of his writing to consideration of separation phenomena (e.g., Bowlby, 1960, 1973).

Experience with social separation is not unique to human primates. Mother–infant and other forms of social separation are ubiquitous across most species of nonhuman primates in nature. For example, virtually every rhesus monkey infant born into a wild troop experiences repeated short-term separations from its mother at approximately seven months of age, when she consorts with different adult males during the troop's annual breeding season (Berman et al., 1994). Virtually all adolescent male rhesus monkeys experience permanent separation from all female kin (including their biological mothers) when they emigrate from their natal troop and join other social groups, never to return. Thus, frequent experience with social separation of one form or another is the norm for nonhuman primates in the wild, just as it is the norm for human primates in both ancient and modern cultures (cf. Suomi, 1994).

Experimental studies of social separation in captive nonhuman primates have been carried out under a variety of laboratory conditions for over 30 years. Most of these studies have focused on mother–infant separation in macaque monkeys, although a wide range of species, ages, and types of separation has been examined in the extensive nonhuman primate separation literature (cf. Mineka and Suomi, 1978; Suomi, 1991).

Studies of mother–infant separation have consistently found that infant monkeys and apes initially respond to separation with behavioral agitation, characterized by dramatic increases in locomotor activity and "coo" vocalizations, and a cessation of exploratory and play behaviors. These behavioral responses clearly resemble Bowlby's description of initial "protest" in human children experiencing involuntary maternal separation (Bowlby, 1960, 1973). Maternal separation also typically activates the hypothalamic-pituitary-adrenal axis, as indexed by sharp increases in levels of plasma cortisol and corticotrophin (ACTH), and increased turnover of the noreadrenergic system, as indexed by decreased cerebral spinal fluid levels of norepinephrine (NE) and increased levels of the NE metabolite MHPG, as well as elevated heart rate, indicating sympathetic arousal.

While most infants in these monkey studies began to return to preseparation levels of behavioral and physiological functioning within a few hours, some individuals continued to display profound behavioral and physiological reactions for several days, if not longer. Behaviorally, these young monkeys became passive and withdrawn, largely failing to respond to social initiations from other group members, and many exhibited a fetal-like posturing that appeared strikingly depressive in nature. This aspect of the separation response seems akin to Bowlby's description of the "despair" phase of separation response in young humans (Bowlby, 1960, 1973). Virtually all of these young monkeys separated from their mothers essentially showed spontaneous recovery when reunited with their mothers, although physical contact with the mother remained elevated, and social play reduced, relative to preseparation levels, for days or even weeks following reunion.

Many investigators have noted the parallels between these reactions to separation and Bowlby's characterizations of prototypical separation reactions in human infants and young children. Parametric studies have demonstrated that numerous factors can influence various features of reaction to maternal separation in nonhuman primates, including species, age at separation, nature of the attachment relationship with mother prior to separation, duration of separation, nature of the separation (and reunion) environment, and availability of substitute caretakers during the time away from the mother (for a comprehensive review of these studies see Mineka and Suomi, 1978).

There have also been many studies of the reactions of young nonhuman primates to separation from individuals or objects other than their biological mothers, including peers and surrogates. In general, the more the infants' relationships to such individuals or objects prior to separation resemble that of a typical mother–infant attachment, the more closely their separation reactions follow the prototypical patterns previously described. In addition, studies of the reactions of juvenile, adolescent, and adult monkeys to separation from their respective social groups have often reported similar patterns of physiological response, although the nature of the behavioral reactions is typically not the same as that exhibited by infants separated from their mothers (Suomi, 1991).

Recent studies have documented dramatic individual differences in both behavioral and physiological reactions to separation among rhesus monkeys of similar age, rearing background, and separation paradigm. For example, only about 20% of most young rhesus monkeys react to maternal separation with despairlike behavioral withdrawal and passivity. These dramatic differences between monkeys are remarkably consistent across repeated separations and reunions, and they remain strikingly stable throughout major periods of development, perhaps the entire life span. Thus, individuals who exhibit extreme reactions to maternal separation as infants are likely to display extreme reactions to separation from familiar conspecifics as juveniles, adolescents, or even adults, while individuals who exhibit mild reactions to maternal separation as infants are likely to display mild reactions to subsequent separations throughout their lifetimes.

Both heritable and experiential factors contribute to these dramatic and developmentally stable differences in biobehavioral response to separation. Significant heritability has been demonstrated for measures of hypothalamic-pituitary-adrenal reactivity, as well as for the major monamine metabolites—although the precise pattern of heritability is somewhat different for each of those measures (Higley et al., 1993). On the other hand, an increasing body of longitudinal data clearly indicates that certain early experiences can alter both behavioral and physiological developmental trajectories of individual monkeys.

LONG-TERM CONSEQUENCES OF DIFFERENTIAL EARLY ATTACHMENTS IN RHESUS MONKEYS

A third area of primate research that has been inspired and informed by Bowlby's observations and ideas concerns the long-term outcomes for individuals who differ in the nature of their early attachment relationships. From the outset Bowlby believed that problems in an infant's developing attachment relationship with the mother would translate into problems in other social relationships later in life, a principle not inconsistent with classical psychoanalytic theory. He developed a theoretical model for the process by which infant attachment experiences become internalized during later childhood and adolescence. Termed "working models," these internal conceptions emerging from early attachment experiences are thought to affect the initiation and maintenance of social relationships with others, including one's parents as well as one's offspring, later in life.

Bowlby's account of the process(es) by which early attachment experiences ultimately influence later relationship behavior requires cognitive capabilities not usually ascribed to rhesus monkeys (of any age). On the other hand, impressive empirical evidence of early experience effects on juvenile, adolescent, and adult monkey behavior and physiology suggests that complex cognitive imagery and projection need not be a prerequisite for complex behavioral and physiological consequences of differential early social experience to occur. At one extreme, classic studies of early isolation of rhesus monkeys carried out in the 1960s demonstrated profound and largely permanent social deficits and extreme behavioral abnormalities in individuals denied the opportunity to form attachments with conspecifics throughout at least the first six months of life. These studies clearly showed that preventing the formation of early attachment relationships via rearing in isolation severely compromises the formation of subsequent social relationships throughout development in rhesus monkeys (cf. Suomi, 1991).

More recent studies have examined the consequences of much less extreme early social privation. In these studies rhesus monkeys have been reared apart from their biological mother but in social settings where the formation of attachment bonds with other conspecifics, for example, foster mothers or peers, is possible. In general, monkeys reared under such circumstances develop relatively normal behavioral repertoires and clearly do not display the extreme behavioral abnormalities characteristic of isolation-reared monkeys. In some cases, however, the attachment relationships that they form with these other conspecifics are not entirely normal— indeed, such relationships can be characterized as clearly "insecure" —and long-term problems often appear throughout development in these individuals (cf. Suomi, 1991).

For example, several recent studies have demonstrated that rhesus monkeys reared for the first six months of life in the company of same-age peers, but no adults, clearly develop strong attachment bonds to these peers. Because peers, however, are not nearly as effective as a typical monkey mother in providing a secure base for exploration or in reducing fear under conditions of novelty or stress, the attachment relationships formed with these peers are "anxious" in nature. As a consequence, while the peer-reared monkeys exhibit species-normative motor development and complex social repertoires, they appear to be timid in the face of novelty, they are less likely to initiate play bouts with strangers than are their mother-reared counterparts, and they tend to be lower in social dominance hierarchies when grouped with mother-reared agemates. Nevertheless, in familiar physical and social settings most peer-reared rhesus monkeys are largely indistinguishable from their mother-reared counterparts in most aspects of their social and nonsocial behavior as they pass through adolescence and enter adulthood.

Peer-reared rhesus monkeys, however, generally display much more severe biobehavioral reactions to social separations than do mother-reared monkeys. As infants and juveniles, peer-reared monkeys exhibit higher levels of self-directed behavioral withdrawal, greater and more prolonged elevation of plasma cortisol and ACTH, and higher concentrations of cerebrospinal fluid (CSF) MHPG. These behavioral and physiological differences persist throughout development, even when the peer-reared and mother-reared monkeys are living in the same social groups (Suomi, 1991).

Follow-up studies comparing peer-reared with mother-reared monkeys later in life have demonstrated other long-term deficits resulting from peer-rearing during the first six months of life. For example, peer-reared adolescents display higher levels of aggression toward strangers, along with lower CSF levels of serotonin metabolite 5-HIAA, than their mother-reared counterparts. Peer-reared adolescents are also more likely to be expelled from their social group. Finally, peer-reared mothers are more likely to show inadequate care of their firstborn offspring than are their mother-reared counterparts (although the vast majority of peer-reared mothers are competent maternally). Thus, although peer-reared monkeys develop sophisticated social repertoires and in most circumstances appear to be highly similar to mother-reared monkeys in most aspects of their behavior, they show clear-cut deficiencies in coping with novelty and stress throughout development (see Suomi, 1994).

Other recent studies have examined the consequences of foster-rearing rhesus monkey infants with unrelated multiparous females who differ systematically in their characteristic maternal "styles." Foster-reared infants readily establish attachment relationships with these foster mothers, and in most cases they develop species-normative social and nonsocial behavioral repertoires. Different matches between infant temperament and characteristic foster-mother maternal "style," however, yield differential short- and long-term developmental outcomes. Of special interest is the finding that infants with "behaviorally inhibited" or physiologically "reactive" temperaments who are reared by unusually "nurturant" foster mothers develop "secure" early attachments and appear to have optimal long-term developmental outcomes. In particular, reactive infants cross-fostered by these nurturant females become especially adept at recruiting and retaining other group members for support in subsequent agonistic interactions. In turn, these monkeys tend to rise to the very top of their social group's dominance hierarchy in spite of their temperamental status as infants. In contrast, infants with similarly reactive temperaments who are reared by more punitive foster mothers develop "insecure" attachments and subsequently are likely to display extreme reactions to environmental novelty and stress throughout development —and end up at the bottom of their group's dominance hierarchy. On the other hand, rhesus monkey infants who have less reactive (uninhibited) early temperaments seem relatively unaffected by the type of foster mother who rears them; that is, such youngsters appear to have similar long-term outcomes whether their foster mothers were unusually nurturant or not. Taken as a whole, these findings suggest that specific types of attachment experiences may have quite different long-term consequences for monkeys with different temperamental predispositions (Suomi, 1994). An emerging body of human longtitudinal data is providing increasing support for similar conclusions regarding temperament-attachment interactions and their differential long-term consequences.

Among the most intriguing aspects of long-term effects of different early attachment experiences is the apparent cross-generational transfer of certain features of maternal behavior. Several studies involving Old World monkeys in both laboratory and field settings have demonstrated strong continuities between the type of attachment relationship a young female develops with her mother (or mother substitute) and the type of relationship she develops with her own offspring when she grows to adulthood and becomes a mother herself. In particular, the pattern of ventral contact a female infant has with her mother (or mother substitute) during her initial months of life is a powerful predictor of the pattern of ventral contact she will exhibit with her own infants during their first six months of life (e.g., Fairbanks, 1989; Champoux et al., 1992). Such predictions seem to be equally strong whether the young female's early attachment experience was with her biological mother or with an unrelated conspecific, and imply that the mode of cross-generational transmission of maternal behavior in this case must necessarily involve nongenetic mechanisms (Suomi, 1994). What those nongenetic mechanisms might be—and the developmental processes through which they might act—remains largely a mystery at this time.

Recent theoretical and empirical work on long-term consequences of differential early attachment relationships in humans has also begun looking at possible cross-generational continuities in attachment styles. The findings from the initial empirical studies (some of which are described in more detail in other chapters in this volume) suggest the existence of strong cross-generational continuities; for example, mothers who experienced secure attachments as infants and young children tend to develop secure attachments with their own infants, while those who experienced avoidant or ambivalent attachments with their mothers tend to promote avoidant or ambivalent attachments as mothers themselves.

These and other findings demonstrate that different patterns of early attachment are associated with predictable long-term developmental outcomes. In the case of humans, current attachment theorizing attributes these infancy-to-parenthood continuities in attachment type to internalized "working models" initially based on early memories and periodically transformed by more recent experiences. Most of the support for such continuities is based on comprehensive interviews retrospectively probing memories of events and experiences. On the other hand, the most powerful empirical support for apparently parallel continuities in attachment behavior in the primate literature comes from prospective longitudinal observations and physiological recordings, both in controlled experimental settings and in naturalistic habitats. One suspects that the ethologist in Bowlby would approve of this research strategy—after all, he often argued that direct observation in naturalistic contexts could provide insights over and above any analysis of an individual's unconscious memories and motivations.

One insight that the primate data bring to discussions about long-term consequences of early attachment experiences is that such developmental continuities can unfold in the absence of language or complex human imagery. What cognitive, emotional, and mnemonic processes in monkeys and apes might underlie these continuities—and do they have parallels in human nonverbal mental processes? These questions await future research. It is comforting to realize that such research will be securely based in the compelling behavioral and physiological documentation of primate attachment continuities.

As Bowlby (1988) himself said, "All of us, from cradle to the grave, are happiest when life is organized as a series of excursions, long or short, from the secure base provided by our attachment figure(s)" (p. 62). Thanks, in part, to Bowlby's work, the primate attachment literature provides its own secure empirical base for embarking on future research excursions in this area.

REFERENCES

Alley, R. (1981), Head shape perception of cuteness. *Devel. Psychol.*, 17:650–654.

Berman, C. M., Rasmussen, K. L. R. & Suomi, S. J. (1994), Responses of free-ranging rhesus monkeys to a natural form of social separation: I. Parallels with mother–infant separation in captivity. *Child Devel.*, 65:1028–1041.

Bowlby, J. (1957), An ethological approach to research in child development. *Brit. J. Med. Psychol.*, 30:230–240.

—— (1958), The nature of the child's tie to his mother. *Internat. J. Psycho-Anal.*, 39:1–24.

—— (1960), Separation anxiety. *Internat. J. Psycho-Anal.*, 51:1–25.

—— (1969), *Attachment*. New York: Basic Books.

—— (1973), *Separation*. New York: Basic Books.

—— (1988), *A Secure-Base*. New York: Basic Books.

Brooks, V. & Hochberg, J. (1960), A psychological study of "cuteness." *Percept. Motor Skills*, 11:205–210.

Byrne, G. D. & Suomi, S. J. (1995), Development of activity patterns, social interactions, and exploratory behavior in tufted capuchins (*Cebus apella*). *Amer. J. Primatol.*, 35:255–270.

Champoux, M., Byrne, E., Delizio, R. & Suomi, S. J. (1992), Motherless mothers revisited: Rhesus maternal behavior and rearing history. *Primates*, 33:251–255.

—— Coe, C. L., Shanberg, S., Kuhn, C. & Suomi, S. J. (1989), Hormonal effects of early rearing conditions in the infant rhesus monkey. *Amer. J. Primatol.*, 19:111–117.

Darwin, C. (1872), *The Expression of Emotions in Man and Animals*. New York: D. Appleton.

Darwin E. (1794), *Zoonomia, or the Laws of Organic Life*. London (St. Peter's Church-yard): Johnson.

Fairbanks, L. A. (1989), Early experience and cross-generational continuity of mother–infant contact in vervet monkeys. *Devel. Psychobiol.*, 22:669–681.

Foss, B. M., ed. (1961), *Determinants of Infant Behaviour, Vol. 1*. London: Methuen.

—— (1963), *Determinants of Infant Behaviour, Vol. 2*. London: Methuen.

—— (1965), *Determinants of Infant Behaviour, Vol. 3*. London: Methuen.

—— (1969), *Determinants of Infant Behaviour, Vol. 4*. London: Methuen.

Fragaszy, D. M., Baer, J. & Adams-Curtis, L. (1991), Behavioral development and maternal care in tufted capuchins (*Cebus apella*) and squirrel monkeys (*Saimiri sciureus*) from birth through seven months. *Devel. Psychobiol.*, 24:375–393.

Harlow, H. F. (1958), The nature of love. *Amer. Psychol.*, 13:673–685.

—— & Suomi, S. J. (1970), The nature of love-simplified. *Amer. Psychol.*, 25:161–168.

—— & Zimmermann, R. R. (1959), Affectional responses in the infant monkey. *Sci.*, 130:421–432.

Higley, J. D., Hopkins, W. D., Hirsch, R. M., Marra, L. & Suomi, S. J. (1987), Preferences of female rhesus monkeys (*Macaca mulatta*) for infantile coloration. *Devel. Psychol.*, 20:350–357.

—— & Suomi, S. J. (1986), Parental behaviour in primates. In: *Parental Behaviour*, ed. W. Slukin & M. Herbert. Oxford: Blackwell, pp. 152–207.

—— Thompson, W. T., Champoux, M., Goldman, D., Hasert, M. F., Kraemer, G. W., Scanlan, J. M., Suomi, S. J. & Linnoila, M. (1993), Paternal and maternal genetic and environmental contributions to CSF monoamine metabolites in rhesus monkeys (*Macaca mulatta*). *Arch. Gen. Psychiat.*, 50:615–623.

Hinde, R. A. & Atkinson, S. (1970), Assessing the roles of social partners in maintaining mutual proximity, as exemplified by mother–infant relations in rhesus monkeys. *Animal Behav.*, 18:169–176.

—— & Spencer-Booth, Y. (1967), The behaviour of socially living rhesus monkeys in their first two and a half years. *Animal Behav.*, 15:169–196.

—— Spencer-Booth, Y. & Bruce, M. (1966), Effects of 6-day maternal deprivation on rhesus monkey infants. *Nature*, 210:1021–1033.

Immelmann, K. & Suomi, S. J. (1981), Sensitive phases in development. In: *Behavioral Development*, ed. K. Immelmann, G. W. Barlow, L. Petrinovich & M. Main. New York: Cambridge University Press, pp. 75–96.

Lovejoy, C. O. (1981), The origins of man. *Sci.*, 211:341–350.

Mineka, S. & Suomi, S. J. (1978), Social separation in monkeys. *Psychol. Bull.*, 85:1376–1400.

Mowbray, J. B. & Cadell, T. E. (1962), Early behavior patterns in rhesus monkeys. *J. Comp. Physiol. Psychol.*, 55:350–357.

Rasmussen, K. L. R. & Suomi, S. J. (in prep.), Social relationships in nonhuman primates.

Sackett, G. P. (1970), Unlearned responses, differential rearing experiences, and the development of social attachments by rhesus monkeys. In: *Primate Behavior, Vol. 1*, ed. L. A. Rosenblum. New York: Academic Press, pp. 112–140.

Schneider, M. L. & Suomi, S. J. (1992), Neurobehavioral assessment in rhesus monkey neonates (*Macaca mulatta*): Developmental changes, behavioral stability, and early experience. *Infant Behav. Devel.*, 15:155–177.

Seay, B. M., Hansen, E. W. & Harlow, H. F. (1962), Mother–infant separation in monkeys. *J. Child Psychol. Psychiat.*, 3:123–132.

Sternglanz, S. H., Gray, J. L. & Murakami, M. (1977), Adult preferences for infantile facial features: An ethological approach. *Animal Behav.*, 15:108–115.

Suomi, S. J. (1979), Differential development of various social relationships by rhesus monkey infants. In: *The Child and Its Family*, ed. M. Lewis & L. A. Rosenblum. New York: Plenum Press, pp. 219–244.

—— (1984), The development of affect in rhesus monkeys. In: *The Psychobiology of Affective Development*, ed. N. A. Fox & R. J. Davidson. Hillsdale, NJ: Lawrence Erlbaum Associates, pp. 119–160.

—— (1991), Early stress and adult emotional reactivity in rhesus monkeys. In: *The Childhood Environment and Adult Disease*, ed. D. Barker. Chichester, Eng.: Wiley, pp. 171–188.

—— (1994), Social and biological pathways that contribute to variations in health status: Evidence from primate studies. *Proceedings of the Honda Foundation Symposium on Prosperity, Health, and Well-being*, pp. 105–112.

—— Sackett, G. P. & Harlow, H. F. (1970), Development of sex preferences in rhesus monkeys. *Devel. Psychol.*, 3:326–334.

Visalberghi, E. (1990), Tool use in *Cebus*. *Folia Primatol.*, 54:146–154.

Welker, C., Becker, P., Hohman, H. & Schafer-Witt, C. (1987), Social relations in groups of the black-capped capuchin (*Cebus apella*) in captivity: Interactions of group-born infants during their first 6 months of life. *Folia Primatol.*, 49:33–47.

—— —— —— —— (1990), Social relations in groups of the black-capped capuchin (*Cebus apella*) in captivity: Interactions of group-born infants during their second half-year of life. *Folia Primatol.*, 54:16–33.

8

Hidden Regulators

Implications for a New Understanding of
Attachment, Separation, and Loss

MYRON A. HOFER

"I emphasize ... my belief ... that ethology will prove a fruitful approach to psychoanalytic problems. ... [My] reason for preferring it to other approaches is the research which it suggests. With ethological concepts and methods it is possible to undertake a far-reaching programme of experimentation into the social responses of the preverbal period of infancy, and to this I attach much importance."
                                                                    —Bowlby, 1958, p. 365

I did not consciously recall these words when I embarked on the "programme of experimentation" that I am about to describe, but Bowlby's early papers and later trilogy (Bowlby, 1969, 1973, 1980), were a great inspiration to me during the early years of my research.

As I began using ethological concepts and methods to study the responses of infant animals to separation from their mothers, I was soon confronted with a series of puzzling and unexpected results. One by one, these surprises forced me to reexamine my assumptions about how separation responses occur and even about the "nature of the child's tie to its mother." For gradually these experiments revealed the existence of an extensive layer of biological processes underlying the behavioral and psychological constructs of attachment theory. Hidden within the observable interactions of the mother and her offspring we found multiple sensorimotor, thermal-metabolic, and nutrient-based events that had unexpected regulatory effects on the behavioral and biological systems of the infant. I use the word "regulatory" to convey the sense that individual systems of the infant were found to be controlled in their level, rate, or rhythm by particular components of the ongoing social interaction with the mother. This chapter tells how these hidden regulators were discovered in laboratory rats, what we now know about them, and how

203

this knowledge can be applied to our understanding of attachment, separation, and loss in humans.

Our experiments showed that when these sources of regulation are all withdrawn at once by separation of the mother from the infant, a pattern of changes ensues over the next minutes and hours that is the result of release of each of the infant's individual systems from the regulatory effect of the previous interaction. This release from regulation represents a novel mechanism by which the experience of separation can be translated into widespread effects on infant behavior and physiology. It provides an explanation for the temporal unfolding of behavioral responses to separation that does not depend on an inferred emotional bond and provides a novel mechanism for the physiological changes that are known to follow loss in humans as well as in other mammals.

It is likely that during the early mother–infant relationship in humans, these hidden regulatory interactions come to be experienced by the infant as synchrony, reciprocity, and warmth or as dissonance and frustration, depending on variations in their timing, contiguity, or patterning. With the maturation of learning and memory, the traces of these early regulatory interactions become organized into mental representations and emotional states that are thought to constitute the "internal working model" of attachment theory. But some hidden regulators may continue to operate independently, within close relationships throughout life.

The discovery of these hidden regulatory processes provides new insights into the relationship of attachment to separation, the genesis of protest and despair patterns in response to loss, and the developmental processes whereby qualitative differences in early relationships may shape personality and future vulnerability to stress. They promise to afford a bridge between biology and psychology in the study of early development and of social relationships later in life.

SERENDIPITY AND SURPRISE IN THE DISCOVERY OF HIDDEN REGULATORS

When I began research in the late 1960s, I thought it unlikely that rat pups would show much response to maternal separation. Monkeys perhaps, but not rats. After all, the separation response, I thought, depends on the ability of the infant to conceive of an object as something that exists independent of itself. Furthermore, were rat pups capable of the complex emotions thought to be required for the formation of attachment bonds and necessary for a response to their rupture? More basic still, how could we even imagine that an infant rat knows its mother is gone? These are still good questions, but, looking back, I realize how little we then knew about the capabilities of very young mammals. Twenty-five years ago even human newborns were thought to be simple bundles of primitive reflexes. Now we know that within a day of birth, infant rats are capable of learning to press a pad with a particular scent in order to receive milk through a tube in its mouth (Johanson and Hall, 1979), that by two weeks of age, pups will avoid an odor previously associated with separation from their mother (Smith, Kucharski, and Spear, 1985), and that between 2½ and 4 weeks, a slow weaning process takes place that is the result of a complex interplay between maturational changes in the pups' behavior and physical characteristics and changes in the mother's response repertoire over time since giving birth (Cramer, Thiels, and Alberts, 1990).

Rat pups are born in an even more immature state than human infants: hairless, deaf, eyes closed, and unable to maintain body temperature against even a mild challenge. The mother spends most of her time crouching over them, nursing and vigorously licking them, leaving for only five to ten minutes every hour or two to drink and eat. The pups' sense of smell and their tactile sense in the area of their lips and mouth are already well developed. If artificially reared and not allowed to suckle for the first day or two, they will show no interest in the lactating mother's nipples. Even if they are passively placed on nipples each day for short periods of time, they fail to nurse. But if they are allowed to search out and find teats for themselves on only six five-minute occasions on each of two days, they will be able to attach and suckle normally (Stoloff et al., 1980). This complex learning depends on their highly discriminating olfactory sense. Pups will choose to approach their own mother rather than another lactating female within a few days of birth, a preference that depends, in part, on olfactory cues present in the amniotic fluid during the pups' fetal period (Hepper, 1986a, b).

By the first week of age, pups' fur begins to grow, ears open, and the pups are capable of vigorous burrowing and locomotion. After two weeks, their eyes open, and they look like miniature adults with big heads, about the size of adult mice. At this age they begin to eat solid food, drink water, and make increasing forays outside the nest. They are capable of life without their mother if food is available but will continue to nurse at least occasionally until 25–30 days of age, during which time rough-and-tumble play, climbing, exploration, and other juvenile behaviors become dominant.

The age at which most of our studies have been done is two weeks following birth, when weaning is first possible, but pups are still engaged in active nursing, grooming, and other interactions with their mothers for bouts of 15–40 minutes duration every one to two hours, throughout the day and night. The rest of the time the mother leaves the pups in the home nest while she feeds, grooms herself, and rests at some distance from her litter (Grota and Ader, 1969). Thus, rat pups, like human infants in modern societies, experience repeated short separations from their mothers every day throughout infancy and the early juvenile period. Unlike nonhuman primate infants, which are virtually always in contact with their mothers, rat pups experience repeated short separations every day. In this particular, rats are a better model for studies of attachment and separation than are monkeys or apes, a point that is not generally appreciated. Motorically more advanced and visually far behind human infants, the two-week-old rat pup is in the early stages of natural weaning and, from the point of view of its attachment system, is roughly comparable to a 6–12-month-old human infant.

Little of this information about the early development of rat pups was known 25 years ago, and although adult rats were confidently studied as models for human learning, the capacity of this species for responses such as those involved in early attachment, separation, and loss seemed extremely unlikely. With these preconceptions, I set out to use rat pups for studies on the early development of cardiac rate responses to various forms of direct stimulation, until a fortunate accident occurred.

One day I came into the laboratory to find that a dam had escaped from her cage overnight. When I took the pups' heart rates, they were only half their normal resting level. In addition, the pups were relatively unresponsive; they moved slowly and seemed depressed, and their body temperatures were 2 or 3°C below normal (36°C). These initial findings were borne out in more systematic studies (Hofer, 1973a) in which pups in a series of litters were left in their home cage nests in natural groups of four littermates for 24 hours without their mothers. The next day, pups were tested for their response to being placed in a novel test chamber. They were considerably less active in the chamber than their littermates that had been left with their mother, as measured by an automated movement detector. They showed less self-grooming and rising behavior. In addition, we found a mean loss of 3.5°C in their rectal temperatures. Resting cardiac rates at the end of five minutes in the test box were 250 beats/minute while those of their mothered littermates were 500 beats/minute.

These results made a perfect case for some sort of despair response, and for a while I thought I had discovered anaclitic depression in the rat. But soon I realized there might be a simpler explanation: the pups' low body temperatures caught my attention, and I thought this physical change might have caused both the cardiac and the behavioral changes simply by cooling the cardiac pacemaker and slowing nerve conduction and muscle contraction. So I arranged to supply a source of artificial heat and found to my surprise that even when the separated pups were kept warm, their resting heart rates fell to the same extent as those of the pups separated at room temperature. This seemed to rule out a simple physical cause for the lowered heart rates and pointed to an alteration in the autonomic nervous system controlling cardiac function. Through the use of autonomic blocking drugs such as atropine and propranolol, which selectively interrupt parasympathetic and sympathetic nerve pathways, Herbert Weiner and I (1971) showed that heart rates of separated pups were low because autonomic balance was shifted toward a withdrawal of the sympathetic component, rather than an increase in parasympathetic activity. This also tended to exclude the possibility that intrinsic cardiac rates were abnormally depressed by some metabolic process induced by separation.

Not until we studied the behavior of the pups that had been kept warm during separation did I realize that something very unusual was going on. When provided with artificial heat to maintain their normal body temperature, the separated pups, instead of being depressed, were *more* responsive to handling than normal pups and were *hyper*active when placed alone in a novel test chamber. The separated pups now moved across more floor areas, rose up against the sides of the test chamber more frequently, and scored significantly higher on the automated activity detector than their normally mothered littermates (Hofer, 1973a). It thus emerged that while the pups' cardiac rate was not affected by a fall in body temperature, the behavior of separated pups could be either depressed or hyperactive depending on how much warmth was provided during separation.

At this point I began to ask the right question—exactly what is lost in separation? It looked as if each of the several responses to separation might be linked to loss of a different component of the infant's relationship with its mother, such as the provision of milk, body heat, and stimulation of the infant's tactile and olfactory senses through licking and handling pups with her paws. By using nonlactating foster mothers (Hofer, 1973b), we found clues to the kinds of losses that might be related to the slowly developing behavioral hyperactivity and the dramatic fall in heart rate. After interacting with their dam but not receiving any milk for a period of hours, pups had normal activity responses, but their resting heart rates were as low as if they had been separated.

This suggested that the decrease in heart rate was related to loss of milk, while hyperactivity was related to loss of some aspect of the

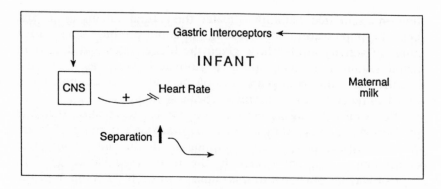

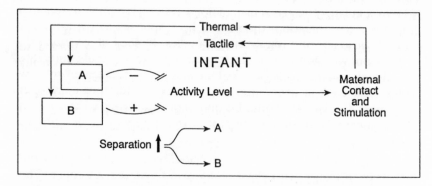

Figure 1 Diagrams illustrating the regulation of infant heart rate (upper box) and activity level (lower box) by components of the mother–infant interaction (maternal milk, contact, or stimulation). The particular sensory systems of the infant engaged during the interaction (gastric interoceptors, thermal, tactile) project to the infant's central nervous system (CNS, A, B) and result in an ongoing level of activation (+) or inhibition (–) of infant systems (heart rate, activity level). The resulting regulation of infant systems maintains them at their characteristic levels. When these regulatory influences are withdrawn by separation (↑), the levels of these functions slowly rise or fall to new levels over a period of a few hours after separation (curving arrows), constituting the responses to loss of these specific regulators. Note that activity level is down-regulated by maternal tactile stimulation (A) but up-regulated by her warmth (B), the outcome of separation depending on relative levels of these two regulators.

behavioral interaction with their dams. This is just what we found when we supplied these individual components of the mother–infant relationship to separated pups. Pups given milk infusions through an indwelling gastric tube could be made to have almost any resting heart rate we wanted by varying the rate at which we infused milk during 24 hours of separation, but behavioral hyperactivity developed equally in all groups despite the nutrient infusions (Hofer, 1973c). If, instead, we provided intermittent tactile stimulation on a schedule that approximated the natural nursing cycles and kept the pups warm (Hofer, 1975), we could produce pups with a range of activity levels, those given the higher rates and density of tactile stimulation having the more normal, lower rates of activity. But the fall in the basal heart rates of the same pups continued as if they had received no intervention during separation.

The results of these experiments made me realize that the mother–infant interaction might be *regulating* a number of infant systems. Apparently, each component of the interaction was controlling a different system in the infant (see Figure 1). This control was proportional to the intensity of each component of the interaction and could either increase (up-regulate) or decrease (down-regulate) the particular biological or behavioral system. The responses to separation, then, must be responses to withdrawal or loss of these specific regulating processes. Instead of assuming that separation was like other stress responses (a centrally integrated emotional and physiological response to a perceived event), we could now look at separation as a pattern of different component responses to loss. We could be quite specific about what was lost. This concept is illustrated for the infant systems just described in Figure 1.

HIDDEN REGULATORS IN AN ATTACHMENT SYSTEM

How do these novel processes fit in with Bowlby's attachment system? Certainly, they give us a new way to understand the more slowly developing responses to separation—what Bowlby referred to as the "despair" phase and the disturbed biological homeostasis that was thought to accompany "despair." But what of the "protest" phase? For that matter, do rat pups show attachment behaviors? Are these activated by sudden separation from the dam?

Work by developmental psychobiologists has revealed a wide array of behaviors by which rat pups can recognize and find their mothers from a distance by using their remarkable early maturing olfactory systems to detect her scents. Pups utilize tactile, thermal, and olfactory gradients on their mother's body to maintain contact and to locate and attach to her nipples. They vigorously attempt to maintain contact with their dam when she moves and rapidly learn to negotiate mazes in order to renew this contact (Rosenblatt, 1983). Peter Hepper (1986) has shown that rat pups have an extraordinary ability to discriminate close relatives using the exquisite specificity of olfactory cues. They not only choose to follow and remain close to their own mother in preference to other lactating mothers but can be shown to discriminate and prefer their own littermates to unfamiliar pups of the same age.

But the most remarkable attachment behavior of the young rat, the separation cry, was not recognized for years. This is because it is ultrasonic, far above the human hearing threshold. A few years after Pierce and Griffen (1938) discovered the echolocating signals of bats, similar electronic equipment was used by a European ethologist, Wolfgang Schleidt, to discover that infant mice produced pulses of ultrasound when they were displaced from their home nests and that these calls seemed to help their mothers find and retrieve them (Zippelius and Schleidt, 1956). For some years, these sounds remained a curiosity, and it was not clear how the pups produced them.

Since initial research had shown that cold temperatures and rough handling increased detectable ultrasounds and that home cage bedding reduced them (reviewed in Hofer and Shair, 1978), I reasoned that ultrasonic calls might possibly be elicited by separation from familiar companions. So I obtained a bat ultrasound detector from England. Harry Shair and I gently removed the mother and then the littermates one by one from a litter of pups asleep in their home cage nest. When only a single pup was left, and not until then, we began to hear ultrasound. This last isolated pup awoke after a few moments and started moving around the cage, raising its head, sniffing, and calling in ultrasound repeatedly. We have since learned that pups make these ultrasounds by using the same patterns of respiratory and laryngeal muscle contraction that produces crying in other mammals and humans (Roberts, 1975; Hofer and Shair, 1993). Shair and I (1978) went on to show that these isolation distress calls were produced at even higher rates if the pup was alone in an unfamiliar place and that if the pup was then given a littermate or a dam, he rapidly stopped crying and kept close contact with the companion— a contact comfort response (Hofer and Shair, 1978).

These ultrasonic calls, together with the searching, following, and huddling previously described, constitute the typical repertoire of attachment behaviors that, as Bowlby pointed out, exist in infants of other mammalian species and even in young birds. These attachment behaviors are activated at high intensity in rat pups that are alone in unfamiliar surroundings, just as Bowlby described for primate infants. The separation cry is the most salient of these "protest" responses, has a powerful effect on the rat mother's behavior, and elicits search and retrieval of pups to the nest (Smotherman et al., 1978). Adult rats and mice have been shown to have specialized auditory adaptations providing an island of heightened sensitivity to sound in the specific frequency range (40 Khz) of rat pup ultrasonic calls (Ehret, 1983). Once activated, pup calling can be rapidly terminated when proximity to the mother or littermate is regained, and sensory feedback from this contact is reestablished.

Thus, the rat pup has an effective "proximity maintenance" system, as Bowlby has termed it, and a typical mammalian separation response with searching and vocalization that is terminated by contact with the dam. Two-week-old pups follow a departing dam and use her as a base from which to begin to explore. Recently, we found evidence that pups of this age will vary their rate of crying according to whether they perceive cues that their dam is near, crying more when she may be near (Hofer, Brunelli, and Shair, 1994). This is evidence for the development of a "goal-corrected" capability in the system for maintaining proximity, a relatively advanced stage in the ontogeny of attachment that Bowlby (1969) describes: "And then his attachment to his mother-figure is evident for all to see" (p. 267).

A question can be raised, however, as to the specificity of the rat pup's attachment. The element of specificity in attachment has sparked considerable argument, particularly as young families increasingly turn to day care and careers. Some of the issues involved may be clarified by the comparative approach used in the present research. Many children today grow up with multiple attachment figures and thus are very different from the exclusive mother–infant dyads of the post-World War era described by Robertson and Bowlby (Bowlby, 1969). How much of the apparent specificity of attachment in humans and in some species of birds and monkeys may be the result of restricted early experience with attachment figures and the early development of fear of strangers in these species? Stranger anxiety is a different behavioral system from attachment and develops much later than attachment in some children, in other primate species, and in dogs and rats. The fear of strangers, more than a rigid specification of attachment behavior to a unique figure, produces the child (or duckling) that will approach and be comforted only by its own mother.

Infant rodents direct their approach behaviors with as great specificity as any species and recognize, approach, and follow their own mother in preference to other lactating dams (Leon, 1975; Gurski and Scott, 1980; Hepper, 1986a). Furthermore, they can discriminate and prefer their own kin (e.g., biological fathers or siblings reared apart), something that is impossible for humans. This is accomplished through the young rodents' extraordinary sense of smell, which is capable of molecular memory and "phenotype matching" that far exceeds the primarily visual discrimination used by humans (Hepper, 1986b). But rat pups are not afraid of strangers until about 25 days of age and, if isolated in an unfamiliar place when two weeks old, derive similar contact comfort from dam, littermates, and even artificial surrogates that share olfactory and other cues with their familiar social companions (Hofer and Shair, 1980). In their natural environment, however, they are always seen in the company of their own dam, rather than other lactating females, and continue to sleep with their natural family until well into adolescence (Calhoun, 1962). Thus, analysis of the capabilities of infant rats can teach us something about the existence of unforeseen subcomponents within our own human attachment system and suggest processes that may mediate different "qualities" of attachment in children raised under a variety of conditions.

Can we peer within the workings of our model attachment system to discern the sensory pathways and component stimuli within the contact experience that mediate the feedback effect that terminates crying? If we can do so, is it possible that specific stimuli, acting over discrete sensory pathways, serve to regulate the levels of ultrasonic vocalization in the way that warmth, nutrient, and tactile stimuli were found to regulate heart rate and general activity levels in the previous studies? We devised a series of artificial surrogates, each presenting one or more modalities present in the familiar littermate: warmth, texture, scent, contour, and movement (Hofer and Shair, 1980). We found that only two modalities, when presented singly, had any significant effect on the call rate of an isolated rat pup in an unfamiliar test box: texture (a flat piece of synthetic fur) and thermal warming. Neither of these stimuli alone was very effective, but the more modalities that were combined, the greater the effect. A combination of texture, warmth, home cage scent, and contour was as effective as a littermate in reducing the call rate, whereas a warm but smooth, soft plastic model was totally ineffective. In this system, a graded down-regulation of ultrasonic calling is achieved through the additive effect of several different, specific sensory modalities normally presented by the pup's social companions. The amount of contact time elicited by the surrogates correlated closely with their effectiveness in reducing calling rate.

Which of the pups' sensory systems are responsible for mediating this regulatory effect? By lesioning the olfactory system and the sensory nerves innervating the sensitive vibrissal hair regions of the pup's snout, we found out that pups showed normal comfort responses if either one of these sensory systems was left intact, although contact time was significantly reduced (Hofer and Shair, 1991). But if both sensory pathways were interrupted, the companion was not at all effective in reducing the lesioned pups' ultrasonic (USV) call rate, although pups still showed a normal level of calling in response to isolation in the test chamber. These experiments show that the contact comfort response is under different sensory control than the isolation distress response—an interesting result that sheds new light on the mechanisms of attachment and separation responses.

Thus, we have identified the stimuli presented by the social companion and the sensory pathways over which these stimuli act to suppress ultrasonic calling in the normal litter situation. A graded control of calling rate is evident in the additive effect of these component processes, and the overall effect of the mother and littermates is to powerfully down-regulate calling so that cries are seldom heard in the home nest. Withdrawal of the several component regulatory processes at once, by separation, releases high rates of calling and other proximity-maintenance or attachment behaviors. Here again, analysis of the fine structure of behavioral control within the social interaction revealed the operation of multiple regulators of ultrasonic calling and contact maintenance that had not been evident before.

Working with this isolation distress response, we and others have been able to go further, to begin to specify the central neural systems responsible for both down- and up-regulation of ultrasonic calling (Blass and Fitzgerald, 1988; Carden and Hofer, 1990; Carden, Barr, and Hofer, 1991; Insel and Winslow, 1991; Miczek, Tornatzky, and Vivian, 1991). These neuromodulator systems are listed in Figure 2. It is noteworthy that compounds known to produce anxiety in humans (the beta-carbolines, pentylenetetrazol, and serotonin 1B, and Kappa opiate receptor agonists) greatly increase the calling rates of rat pups, regardless of whether they increase or decrease general activity. Clinically effective antianxiety drugs (benzodiazepines, serotonin 1A and Mu receptor opiate agonists, and selective serotonin reuptake inhibitors) powerfully reduce calling rates. Since the pharmacology of the rat pups' vocal response to isolation is so similar to the pharmacology of human (and adult rat) anxiety states, this response would appear to be mediated by a set of neural systems that have been highly conserved in evolution. This biological evidence suggests a parallel between infant separation states and adult anxiety, an idea put forward by Freud (1926) and placed in an evolutionary perspective in a recent publication (Hofer, 1995).

Furthermore, Susan Carden and I (1990) have shown that the comfort provided to an isolated rat in an unfamiliar test chamber by its familiar littermate or dam is prevented by prior administration of an opiate receptor blocking drug, naltrexone. This strongly suggests that comfort is mediated by release of the rat pup brain's own opiate

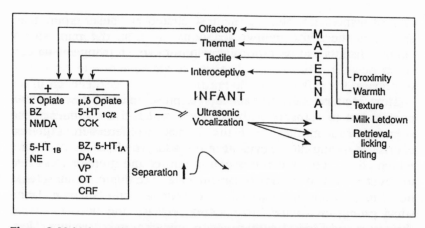

Figure 2 Multiple regulators of infant crying (ultrasonic vocalization) by components of the mother–infant interaction (proximity, warmth, texture, and milk letdown), each acting over particular sensory systems (olfactory, thermal, tactile, oral, and gastric interoceptive) projecting to a number of different central neuromodulator systems. The receptor subtypes at which pharmacologic receptor agonists increase infant vocalization rates are listed on the left (+), and those which mediate decreased rates are on the right (–). Those for which there is evidence (using specific receptor antagonists) for a physiologic role of endogenous ligands either in separation or comfort responses are listed toward the top of each column. The net effect of changes in activity of these two sets of antagonist systems determines the rate at which the infant vocalizes. When maternal cues are present, vocalizations are inhibited, as indicated by the curved line with the (–) beneath. When maternal (and littermate) cues are withdrawn by separation (↑), this down-regulation is removed, and vocalization ensues in a steep curve of rising rates. Finally, infant vocalization initiates retrieval of the pup by the dam, reduces the latency to the next milk ejection, elicits licking, and inhibits maternal biting.

Abbreviations of Receptor Classes: BZ = benzodiazepine; NMDA = N-methyl d aspartate; 5HT = serotonin; CCK = cholecystokinin; NE = norepinephrine; DA = dopamine; VP = vasopressin; OT = oxytocin; CRF = corticotropin releasing factor

and serves to link attachment with the central reward system defined in studies of drug addiction (Gardner and Lowinson, 1993).

Thus, activation of attachment behaviors such as crying can be understood as release from the regulation previously exerted by sensorimotor interactions within the relationship of the infant and its social companions. We can begin to specify the central and peripheral sensory mechanisms for this regulation. The protest response to separation now emerges as one of several relatively independent processes that occur during separation and also represents the release from (or loss of) specific regulators. It can readily be shown to be independent of the more slowly developing despair type of response. If littermates are separated in a small group, such as occurs when the mother abandons the nest, the pups slowly become listless and unresponsive without ever showing any protest response.

Because the infant's attachment behaviors are also elicited in the context of an ongoing relationship (albeit at relatively low levels in comparison to separation levels), they can, and do, influence the behavior of the mother (see Figure 2). This is different from the regulated physiological systems of the infant, such as cardiac rate, which are far less perceptible to the mother and therefore less able to affect her behavior toward the infant. For example, nuzzling, licking, and huddling by pups elicit maternal nursing behavior. Ultrasonic calling, in addition to eliciting retrieval and nest relocation (Brewster and Leon, 1980), facilitates maternal milk letdown (Deis, 1968), elicits maternal licking of pups (Brouette-Lalou, Vernet-Maury, and Gigouroux, 1992), and also inhibits maternal biting or stepping on pups (Noirot, 1972). Thus, infant regulation by the mother is complemented by regulation of maternal behavior by the infant; together these processes regulate the relationship.

OTHER REGULATORS AND THEIR ROLE IN DEVELOPMENT

The number and variety of infant systems known to be regulated by components of the mother–infant interaction in the rat are now quite extensive. Evidence is accumulating for the presence of similar regulation in other species, including humans. The different time courses of the various different responses to separation in the rat, insofar as is currently known, are illustrated in Figure 3. I will describe three examples.

Infant sucking patterns, both nutritive and nonnutritive, are increased in rate and force by separation (reviewed in Brake, Shair, and Hofer, 1988). We found that nonnutritive sucking is down-regulated by the orosensory stimulation provided by the maternal teat while nutritive sucking is down-regulated by feedback from gastric fill resulting from the ingestion of maternal milk (see Figure 4, top). Thus, the two different patterns of sucking that increase greatly following separation are the result of withdrawal (by separation) of two different forms of maternal regulation, both involving the nursing interaction. Bottle-fed human infants also show clear-cut nutritive and nonnutritive sucking patterns (Wolff, 1968), and increased oral behavior is a hallmark of the human infant separation response (Heinicke and Westheimer, 1965). The well-known differential effects of nonnutritive nipples and of feeding in babies strongly

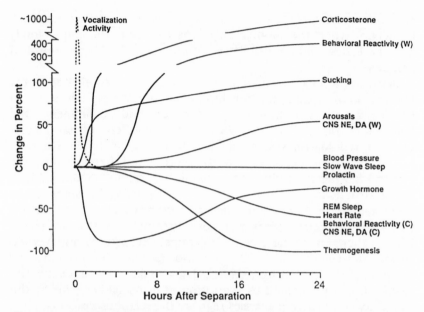

Figure 3 Schematic representation of the time course of changes in physiology and behavior during 24 hours following separation of infant rats from their mothers. Percent change from baseline in levels of the measures are plotted over time. The dotted lines at the extreme left show the immediate response to isolation of a single pup in a novel environment; the solid lines, the slower developing responses to removal of the dam from pups left together in a litter group in the home cage. (W) and (C) refer to whether pups are kept warm at nest temperature or allowed to cool in a room temperature environment during separation. NE = norepinephrine; DA = Dopamine.

suggest that regulatory processes could be elucidated for humans as well.

Using some of our methods for detecting regulatory interactions, Saul Schanberg, Cynthia Kuhn, and their associates (reviewed in Kuhn and Schanberg, 1991) have described a fall in growth hormone (GH) following separation in rat pups that can be reversed by brief periods of interaction with a nonlactating dam and prevented by vigorous tactile stimulation of the separated pup. A concomitant fall in ornithine decarboxylase (ODC), a rate-limiting enzyme involved in cell protein synthesis, accompanies these changes in growth hormone but appears to depend on a different central mechanism (see Figure 4, bottom). For although growth hormone usually elicits ODC activity in normal rat pups, after six hours of separation it no longer does so, due to a block in the peripheral transduction system. This peripheral biochemical block is rapidly

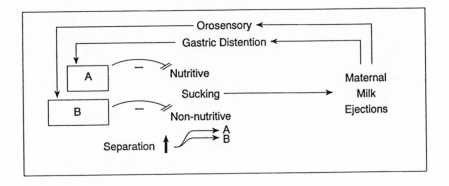

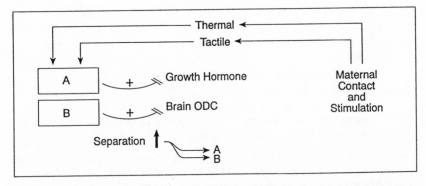

Figure 4 Separate and independent pathways for regulation of infant nutritive and nonnutritive sucking (upper box), and for growth hormone secretion (GH), and for induction of brain ornithine decarboxylase (ODC), the rate-limiting enzyme for purine synthesis in rapidly developing tissue (lower box). The rhythmic pattern of sucking during periods surrounding maternal milk ejections (nutritive) is inhibited by gastric distention by ingested milk, and this pattern of sucking is elicited more readily and at greater rates as gastric fill levels subside following maternal separation (A). The arrhythmic sucking pattern (nonnutritive), characteristic of time periods between milk ejections, is normally inhibited by the orosensory stimulation of periodic sucking on the maternal teat and is augmented by periods of loss of the opportunity for "dry" sucking following separation (B). The lower box illustrates the regulation of infant growth hormone and ODC, which are maintained at relatively high levels by the tactile and thermal stimulation provided by active interaction and contact with their dam. Following separation and loss of this up-regulation, levels of both fall precipitously but can be maintained by artificial provision of the two modalities of sensory stimulation (see text).

reversed by a period of interaction with a nonlactating dam. Thus, GH and ODC are normally up-regulated by tactile interaction with the dam; following withdrawal of this regulation by separation, their levels fall.

I mention the peripheral transduction block because a similar failure of growth hormone to affect peripheral tissues occurs in the human syndrome of psychosocial dwarfism, and growth hormone levels are often similarly low initially. Clinical examples have been reported of infants in chaotic and/or neglectful families who failed to grow, even in the hospital and despite adequate nutrition, until nurses took the time to interact warmly and playfully with these children.

A more systematic example of the operation of hidden regulators of growth processes in humans is the study by Field, Schanberg, and coworkers (reviewed in Kuhn and Schanberg, 1991). Based on their animal model work, they studied 40 premature infants (less than 36 weeks and 1,500 grams), half of whom were given three, 15-minute periods of tactile and kinesthetic stimulation each day for two weeks. The control and stimulated groups were virtually identical in starting weight and age and in number, volume, and total caloric content of feedings. The stimulated babies, however, averaged 25 grams of weight gained per day while the controls gained only 16 grams per day (p<.001). Furthermore, the stimulated group showed significant improvement in Brazelton and Bayley scores and left the hospital six days earlier, at an average savings of $3,000 per child! This is just one example of how an appreciation for the role of hidden regulators can lead to simple and effective intervention in cases of enforced social deprivation or dislocation.

A final example is the sleep disturbance that we discovered in maternally separated infant rats (Hofer, 1976; Hofer and Shair, 1982). After 24 hours of maternal separation, the pups left in their home cage nest show disturbed sleep-wake cycles, with many more frequent short awakenings, a marked reduction in time spent in REM sleep, and an increased frequency of shortened slow-wave sleep periods. Providing continuous warmth to the litter partially reduced the size of some of these effects, but providing periodic stimulation or periodic gastric infusions of milk was most effective in preventing the fragmentation of sleep-wake states. Apparently, the temporal organization of sleep is entrained (a form of temporal regulation) by the regularly occurring periodic events provided by the ongoing interaction of infants with their mothers.

There is evidence that similar forms of social entrainment are also present in adult relationships in humans. When small groups of people are isolated from daylight cues in specially protected environments, each group develops its own circadian period (usually somewhere between 23- and 25-hour days) to which all members of the group become entrained. If one person is moved between groups, he or she gradually resynchronizes biologic rhythms to the new group's period (Vernikos-Danellis and Winget, 1979). Another example is the menstrual synchrony of women (and female rats) who live together (McClintock, 1983; Graham, 1991). This may be mediated by a pheromone present in axillary secretions, but evidence for other factors is suggested by the finding that best friends synchronize more closely than roommates in a college dormitory (Goldman and Schneider, 1987).

The fact that many of the infant's physiological systems, as well as her behaviors, are regulated by specific components of interaction with the caretaker extends our concept of homeostasis in early life. In this view, Bowlby's "inner" and "outer rings of homeostatic control" are condensed into a single system. The mutual regulation that has been found to take place gives substance to the use of the word "symbiosis" as applied to this phase of our lives (Hofer, 1990).

Hidden regulators also provide a plausible set of mechanisms for explaining a crucial role of attachment: how early relationships shape development. For qualities of relationships consist of individual differences in the balance of specific interactive components that create a different pattern in regulation of the biological systems of the developing infant. Maintained over time, this results in individual differences in the patterns of physiological responses and behaviors of the mature organism. Thus, different qualities of early interaction may eventually lead to different long-range outcomes for biological, as well as behavioral, development. There is already substantial evidence for the long-term regulation of biological systems (e.g., hypertension in a genetically susceptible strain of rat, Myers, Shair, and Hofer, 1992) and of emotional development in surrogate-reared monkeys (Mason and Berkson, 1974) by specific components of early interactions.

Early, permanent separation of the infant rat from its mother also can produce long-term changes in the rat pups' vulnerability to stress later in life. Ackerman, Weiner, and I (Ackerman, Hofer, and Weiner, 1975) found a major increase in the incidence and severity of immobilization-induced gastric ulceration in 30-day-old (early adolescent) rats separated from their mothers at 15 days instead of the routine 21 days of age. This vulnerability was not present in the days following the separation (day 17), nor were early separated rats more vulnerable as older adults, so that an age-specific vulnerability resulted from the early separation. Studies on the psychobiological mechanisms involved (summarized in Ackerman, 1981) revealed that early separated rats responded to the stress with a disturbance of sleep and of temperature regulation, which were both related to levels of gastric acid secretion. Thus, withdrawal of maternal regulators in infancy had produced a predisposition to widespread regulatory disturbance under stress in early adolescence.

Taken together, these results encourage us to believe that hidden regulators are present in early human relationships as well as in other animals, that some may continue to operate in adult relationships, and that they form an important mechanism by which interaction with the environment, in this case the social environment, shapes the development of biological systems and behavior.

THE NATURE AND DEVELOPMENT OF SEPARATION RESPONSES

The discovery of these regulatory processes has given us a new understanding of the dynamics of early social relationships during what is described as the "preattached phase" and provides a mechanism for early separation responses that does not depend on attachment theory. The fact that separation involves a withdrawal of specific regulatory processes allows us to understand more precisely what is lost during early maternal separation and provides us with an explanation for the pattern of separation responses that does not depend on the complex mental and emotional processes we once thought were necessary to mediate the transition from protest to despair.

There are two previously puzzling aspects of early separation responses that the discovery of hidden regulatory processes has helped us to understand. The first is the widespread character of the changes following separation, involving a number of different behavioral and physiological systems. The second is the magnitude and heterogeneity of the responses in respect to latency, direction, peak time, and form (altered *patterns* of function). In particular, the magnitude and variety of biological changes seem inconsistent with the uniformity and apparently innocuous nature of the separation event. We are accustomed to biological responses that are elicited by obviously strong stimuli, whereas the *absence* of stimuli seems to elicit separation responses. Attachment theory, the powerful underlying motivational system that Bowlby inferred, and the psychological construct of a "bond" with its prominent affective involvement provided a conceptual basis for understanding the powerful effects of separation on children and adults. But this theory has been less successful in accounting for the more slowly developing biological changes of the despair and detachment phases and in explaining the vigorous behavioral "protest" response in the young of species, such as the rat, that have not yet shown evidence of attachment in the sense described by Bowlby for human infants 8–12 months of age.

How does withdrawal of a specific maternal regulator produce a specific component of the separation response? Regulation is apparent at all levels of biological organization within individuals, ranging from molecules to organ systems. The sudden loss of one of these regulators, by its nature, leads to a rebound response in the opposite direction, to altered patterns of function, or both. For example, the increase in blood sugar and the disordered metabolic state underlying diabetes mellitus are a response to loss of insulin and its regulatory effects on carbohydrate metabolism. Another example would be an addict's sudden loss of narcotic drugs, which causes an evolving series of changes that we call "withdrawal." These responses are generally opposite in direction to the effects of the narcotic, and they subside over time—like the effects of separation due to withdrawal of regulatory interactions. These withdrawal symptoms are known to be caused by the unopposed activity of the brain's long-term adaptation to the pharmacologic regulatory effects of the drug, now suddenly no longer present. In the case of separation responses, the source of regulation is in the interaction with the mother, but the principle of response activation is the same. In each of the infant's systems, the response to withdrawal of its particular regulator is an escape or release effect within that system. The overall result of the loss of all the component regulators at once by maternal separation is the pattern of dysregulation illustrated in Figure 3.

Although loss of regulators appears to be the primary mechanism for separation responses in very early development, when we consider older children—and even older rats—responses begin to occur to *signals* of *impending* separation without requiring the actual loss of the interaction to elicit responses. What appears to happen is that development gradually brings individual regulatory processes under higher integrative control through the repeated associative experiences that lead to the formation of mental structures such as those postulated, for example, in the "internal working model" of attachment theory. The component regulatory processes of infancy thus become bound together into larger units in which the mother, as a highly specific, dynamic stimulus complex, becomes linked with regulation of integrated patterns in the infant's behavioral and biological systems, patterns that we call behavioral or emotional states. For example, we ordinarily think of the mother as a regulator of the infant's *affective* states, with these conceived of as part of the infant's internal world. These higher forms of regulation are currently a focus of much research interest.

Thus, the transition from the "preattached" phase to the "attached" phase, as these are currently conceptualized, depends on a transition from hidden physiological regulation to learned responses, from particular maternal interactions that regulate specific neural systems to maternal behavioral signals that are associated with that regulation. The transition from maternal loss to psychological loss is the transition from the loss of hidden regulators to the loss of the objects of expectations stored in memory as a part of the mental representations that were built originally on these regulatory interactions.

But there is evidence that hidden regulators continue to operate, to some extent, in losses throughout life. For example, some of the symptoms of grief may be due to the withdrawal or loss of numerous physical and temporal interactions with the person who is now dead, as well as to the inner psychological loss of the expectancies built up around the mental representation of the other person and of the self (Hofer, 1984). Several of the cognitive and physical changes seen in bereavement are strikingly similar to those seen in acute sensory deprivation (Solomon et al., 1961). Others involve changes in cardiovascular regulation, sleep-wake states, appetite, and muscular energy, not to mention bouts of crying, which are all reminiscent of the dysregulation we have observed in young rats after prolonged separation from their dams. The role of early regulators in the development of mental representations and their role in the inner experience of grief are briefly discussed in the final section.

REGULATORY INTERACTIONS, REWARD, AND THE FORMATION OF ATTACHMENT

The area we know the least about, despite its obvious importance, is the process by which attachment is formed. Bowlby described the progression of infant behaviors that take place from the first reflex responses along tactile and thermal gradients, to the final operation of a "goal-corrected system," but what developmental processes account for the formation of this motivational system? Bowlby believed that something similar to imprinting probably occurred in mammals, but he pointed out that there was little evidence for this at the time.

Although the specific interactions that are most important for the formation of the several different patterns of attachment are not yet well established, the evidence gathered thus far points to (1) frequent and sustained physical contact, (2) active reciprocal interactions, (3) timing of contact and interaction that is based on the infant's own rhythms and behavioral signals, and (4) activation of the full range of infantile sensory systems. It is perhaps no accident that these are precisely the interactional principles we have found at work in the hidden regulatory processes that I have described in this chapter. Indeed, I believe that these early regulatory interactions are the machinery by which the attachment system is formed. Two lines of thinking lead me to this hypothesis (reviewed in Hofer, 1990).

First, a number of recent experimental studies have revealed a set of interactional processes that are capable of inducing at least some of the key features of attachment in young rats. Pups learn to approach, select, and remain close to the source of a previously neutral odor that has been repeatedly associated with either warmth, nonnutritive sucking, maternal contact, or several different kinds of tactile stimulation that mimic maternal interactions such as licking, grooming, and even being stepped on (Alberts and May, 1984; Sullivan, Hofer, and Brake, 1986; Sullivan et al., 1986). Localized changes in olfactory bulbs have been identified in these animals (Leon, 1987). The selective approach and proximity-maintenance behaviors so induced have been shown to promote huddling with a specific group of littermates or attaching to the teats of a specific dam, if these were scented with conditioned odors. Since simple forms of stimulation (e.g., tail pinching) are capable of inducing these learned associations and since a wide variety of tactile and thermal stimuli is more effective in this regard than standard reinforcements such as milk, these learning processes would appear to resemble imprinting. Thus, the same mother–infant interactions that we have found to regulate the infant's physiology have also been shown to be reinforcing and to induce selective preference and proximity maintenance behaviors toward cues associated with them. In the natural life of pups, these would be the cues possessed by their own dam and would therefore mediate attachment to her.

A second way in which hidden regulators may participate in the formation of attachment is that collectively they maintain a physiological state that is homeostatic for infants, as described in the early portions of this chapter. This comes to be experienced by the infant as an optimal state and may form the basis for the affective state we refer to as "security" or "contentment" later in development. Thus, the state of being actively regulated and, in turn, regulating the dam's maternal behavior is likely to constitute the complex affective core of the attachment system (Hofer, 1990).

One of the systems likely to play an important role in this aspect of attachment is the brain's own opiate network, which acts on the central "reward" system in the midbrain and mediates the intensely reinforcing effects of electrical brain stimulation and the drugs that commonly figure in human substance abuse (Gardner and Lowinson, 1993). In a previous section, I described evidence that interaction with familiar companions engages the pup's endogenous opioid systems and that these mediate the separation cry. Drugs such as morphine and heroin act at the same receptors that receive the brain's own opioids (e.g., endorphins, enkephalins). Habitual use of these drugs is known to induce intense feeling states that we describe in the same terms as those that figure in attachment: "need," "craving," "dependence." Response to separation from the source of supply causes "withdrawal" symptoms, but the craving can persist for months or years and is intensified by cues reminding the individual of his former habit.

In summary, the regulatory interactions we have described appear to be capable of inducing the searching and proximity-seeking behavior directed toward an increasingly specific object that is the hallmark of attachment behavior. They also provide a physiological basis for development of the affective state of "security." This, in turn, forms the emotional base for the infant's ventures into the larger world outside this first relationship. Finally, regulation of endogenous opioid peptides by the mother–infant interaction provides a link between attachment processes and the powerful reward system of the brain that appears to mediate intense affects of pleasure and need.

FROM MATERNAL REGULATORS TO MENTAL REPRESENTATIONS

Thus far, I have been concerned primarily with the role of hidden regulators in the genesis of the motivational behavioral control system that underlies the internal working models of attachment theory. Mental representations operate at a different level of organization from the regulators described in this chapter, and involve cognitive-emotional structures gradually established through the experiences of learning and the memory of past interactions. Daniel Stern (1989) has described a way of conceptualizing the units of these representations ("moments" and "scenarios") and how they become organized in early development into "internal working" and "narrative" models. The regulatory interactions at work in early infancy become the building blocks out of which mental representations and related inner, affective experiences of children and adults are built. A diagram illustrating how these systems interact in attachment and separation is presented in Figure 5.

As soon as associative memories begin, infants begin to function at a symbolic level as well as the sensorimotor level at which regulatory processes originate. In infants of species with the necessary cognitive capacities, mental representations of caretakers are formed out of the individual units of their experience with the regulatory interactions I previously described. Once formed, these organized

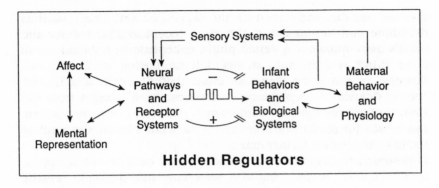

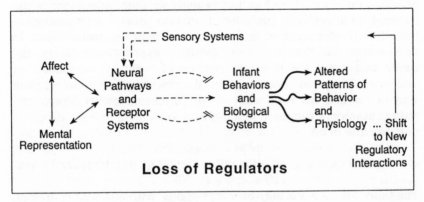

Figure 5 Diagram at the top illustrates the dynamics of the hidden regulatory processes inherent in the interaction of the infant with the mother as these, in turn, influence maternal behavior and physiology (on the right) and shape the development of the infant's affective systems and mental representation of the relationship, the "internal working model" (on the left). Regulatory processes operate over different sensory systems to set the levels of continuous functions (+ or –) and the timing of repetitive events and rhythmic transitions between states (square wave arrow). The lower diagram illustrates the effects of maternal separation that results in loss of all the hidden regulators at once, resulting in decreases in functions previously up-regulated (+), increases in those previously down-regulated (–), and shifts to new patterns of periodic rhythmic functions. Finally, at the far right, the shift to new environmental (or social) regulatory interactions is depicted.

mental structures probably come to act as superordinate regulators of biological systems underlying motivation and affect and gradually supplant the sensorimotor, thermal, and nutrient regulatory systems found in younger infants. Maternal warmth, patterns of touch, smell, rocking, and nursing are associated with the infant's clinging, reaching, and sucking. If these interactions have the capacity to regulate powerfully many of the infants' biological homeostatic systems, this may add a phenomenological dimension to these early experiences that warrants further consideration. Biological systems would thus be linked with internal object representations and would account for the remarkable emotional and cognitive upheavals that take place in bereavement and that can be elicited simply on hearing of a death, for example, by telephone (Hofer, 1984). Thus, in older children and adults, the regulation inherent in an important social relationship may be transduced not only by the sensorimotor and temporal patterning of the actual interactions but also by the internal experience of the relationship in the form of an internal working model or mental representation.

Maternal regulators control neural systems mediating reward, arousal, and sleep, as well as motivational states such as thermoregulation and hunger. This could be a major reason that early caretakers arouse such intense feelings of need and pleasure and could help explain many of the "primitive" elements in dreams, fantasies, and bodily delusions. Likewise, the actions of early hidden regulators and their incorporation into mental representations may explain why separation involves such deeply intense feelings of anxiety, anger, and despair, even in adults.

Insofar as mother–infant relationships differ in quality and consequently involve different levels of regulation in a variety of systems, these differences will be reflected in the nature of the mental representations constructed by individual children as they grow up. The emotions aroused during the early crying response to separation, during the profound state changes associated with the loss of regulators as previously described, and during the reunion of a separated infant with its mother are clearly intense. They have commanded our attention, they are what everyone knows about attachment and separation, and they are the essence of what we feel about the people to whom we are close. They occur at a different level of psychobiological organization than do the changes in autonomic, endocrine, and neurophysiological systems we have been able to study in rats and monkeys, as well as in younger human infants.

The discovery of regulatory interactions and the effects of their withdrawal allows us to understand not only the responses to separation in young organisms of limited cognitive-emotional capacity but also those in which the familiar emotions and mental representations can be described to us by the child or inferred from higher-order behavioral capabilities. It is not that rat pups respond only to loss of regulatory processes while human infants respond only to emotions of love, sadness, anger, and grief. Human infants, as they mature, can respond both at the symbolic affective level and at the behavioral-physiological level of regulatory processes. The two levels appear to be organized as parallel but complementary response systems. Even adult humans continue to respond at the sensorimotor-physiological level in some aspects of their social interactions, separations, and losses, continuing a process begun in infancy (Hofer, 1984).

Insofar as mutual homeostatic regulation characterizes our first relationship, and insofar as mental representations are built on this experience, some of the characteristics of later mental derivatives from this preverbal stage may be more readily understood. For example, affect states associated with the experience of separation later in life involve sensations of fragmentation and loss of control that may derive from the early experience of regulation of so many infant systems by the first relationship. The biological, symbiotic aspects of the early mother–infant interaction may also help us understand the power of some of the many bodily sensations—the sensations in heart and stomach so familiar in everyday speech—that are experienced in connection with memories associated with important people in our lives.

Bowlby hoped that ideas from ethological experiments would build a bridge between psychoanalysis and the expanding world of modern neurobiology. The work discussed here indicates that this hope is being realized and that research on the first relationship can be a meeting ground where the infant's psychological world is closest to its biological origins.

REFERENCES

Ackerman, S. H. (1981), Premature weaning, thermoregulation and the occurrence of gastric pathology. In: *Brain, Behavior and Bodily Disease*, ed. H. Weiner, M. A. Hofer and A. J. Stunkard. New York: Raven Press, pp. 67–86.

—— Hofer, M. A. and Weiner, H. (1975), Age at maternal separation and gastric erosion susceptibility in the rat. *Psychosom. Med.*, 37:180–184.

Alberts, J. R. & May, B. (1984), Nonnutritive, thermotactile induction of filial huddling in rat pups. *Dev. Psychobiol.*, 17:161–181.

Blass, E. M. & Fitzgerald, E. (1988), Milk-induced analgesia and comforting in 10-day-old rats: Opioid mediation. *Pharmacol. Biochem. Behav.*, 29:9–13.

Bowlby, J. (1958), The nature of the child's tie to his mother. *Internat. J. Psycho-Anal.*, 39:350–373.

—— (1969), *Attachment and Loss, Vol. 1*. New York: Basic Books, 1982.

—— (1973), *Attachment and Loss, Vol. 2*. New York: Basic Books.

—— (1980), *Attachment and Loss, Vol. 3*. New York: Basic Books.

Brewster, J. & Leon, M. (1980), Relocation of the site of mother-young contact: Maternal transport behavior in Norway rats. *J. Comp. Physiol. Psychol.*, 94:69–79.

Brouette-Lalou, I., Vernet-Maury, E. & Gigouroux, M. (1992), Role of pups' ultrasonic calls in a particular maternal behavior in Wistar rat pups anogenital licking. *Behav. Brain Res.*, 50:147–154.

Calhoun, J. B. (1962), *The Ecology and Sociology of the Norway Rat*. Washington, DC: U.S. Dept. Public Health Service, Pub. No. 1008.

Carden, S. E., Barr, G. A. & Hofer, M. A. (1991), Differential effects of specific opioid receptor agonists on rat pup isolation calls. *Devel. Brain Res.*, 62:17–22.

—— & Hofer, M. A. (1990), Socially mediated reduction of isolation distress in rat pups is blocked by naltrexone but not by RO 15–1788. *Behav. Neurosci.*, 104:457–463.

Cramer, C. P., Thiels, E. & Alberts, J. R. (1990), Weaning in rats. I. Maternal behavior; II. Pup behavior patterns. *Devel. Psychobiol.*, 23:479–510.

Deis, R. P. (1968), The effect of an exteroceptive stimulus on milk ejection in lactating rats. *J. Physiol. (London)*, 197:37–46.

Ehret, G. W. (1983), Psychoacoustics. In: *The Auditory Psychobiology of the Mouse*, ed. J. F. Willott. Springfield, IL: Charles C. Thomas, pp. 33–56.

Freud, S. (1926), *Inhibitions, Symptoms and Anxiety. Standard Edition*, 20:87–172. London: Hogarth Press, 1959.

Gardner, E. L. & Lowinson, J. H. (1993), Drug craving and positive/negative hedonic brain substrates activated by addicting drugs. *Seminars Neurosci.*, 5:359–368.

Goldman, S. E. & Schneider, H. G. (1987), Menstrual synchrony: Social and personality factors. *J. Soc. Behav. Per.*, 2:243–250.

Graham, C. A. (1991), Menstrual synchrony: An update and review. *Hum. Nature*, 2:293–311.

Grota, L. J. & Ader, R. (1969), Continuous recording of maternal behavior in Rattus Norvegicus. *Animal Behav.* 17:722–729.

Gurski, J. C. & Scott, J. P. (1980), Individual vs. multiple mothering in mammals. In: *Maternal Influences and Early Behavior*, ed. R. W. Bell and W. P. Smotherman. Holliswood, NY: Spectrum Press, pp. 403–438.

Heinicke, C. M. & Westheimer, I. (1965), *Brief Separations*. New York: International Universities Press.

Hepper, P. G. (1986a), Parental recognition in the rat. *Quart. J. Exper. Psychol.*, 38B:151–160.

—— (1986b), Kin recognition: Function and mechanisms. *Biol. Rev.*, 61:63–93.

Hofer, M. A. (1973a), The effects of brief maternal separations on behavior and heart rate of two-week-old rat pups. *Physiol. Behav.*, 10:423–427.

—— (1973b), Maternal separation affects infant rats' behavior. *Behav. Biol.*, 9:629–633.

—— (1973c), The role of nutrition in the physiological and behavioral effects of early maternal separation on infant rats. *Psychosom. Med.*, 35:350–359.

—— (1975), Studies on how early maternal separation produces behavioral change in young rats. *Psychosom. Med.*, 37:245–264.

—— (1976), The organization of sleep and wakefulness after maternal separation in young rats. *Devel. Psychobiol.*, 9:189–205.

—— (1984), Relationships as regulators: A psychobiological perspective on bereavement. *Psychosom. Med.*, 46:183–197.

—— (1990), Early symbiotic processes: Hard evidence from a soft place. In: *The Role of Affect in Motivation, Development and Adaptation, Vol. 1*, ed. R. S. Glick & S. Bone. New Haven, CT: Yale University Press, pp. 55–80.

—— (1995), An evolutionary perspective on anxiety. In: *Anxiety as Symptom and Signal*, ed. S. Roose & R. A. Glick. Hillsdale, NJ: The Analytic Press, pp. 17–38.

—— Brunelli, S. A. & Shair, H. N. (1994), Potentiation of isolation-induced vocalization by brief exposure of rat pups to maternal cues. *Devel. Psychobiol.*, 27:503–517.

—— & Shair, H. N. (1978), Ultrasonic vocalization during social interaction and isolation in 2-week old rats. *Devel. Psychobiol.*, 11:495–504.

—— & —— (1980), Sensory processes in the control of isolation-induced ultrasonic vocalizations by 2-week-old rats. *J. Comp. Physiol.*, 94:271–299.

—— & —— (1982), Control of sleep-wake states in the infant rat by features of the mother–infant relationship. *Devel. Psychobiol.*, 15:229–243.

—— & —— (1991), Trigeminal and olfactory pathways mediating isolation distress and companion comfort responses in rat pups. *Behav. Neurosci.*, 105:699–706.

—— & —— (1993), Ultrasonic vocalization, laryngeal braking and thermoregulation in rat pups: A reappraisal. *Behav. Neurosci.*, 105:699–706.

—— & Weiner, H. (1971), Development and mechanisms of cardiorespiratory responses to maternal deprivation in rat pups. *Psychosom. Med.*, 33:353–362.

Insel, T. R. & Winslow, J. T. (1991), Rat pup ultrasonic vocalizations: An ethologically relevant behaviour responsive to anxiolytics. In: *Animal Models in Psychopharmacology*, ed. B. Olivier, J. Mos & J. L. Slangen. Basel: Birkhauser Verlag, pp. 15–36.

Johanson, I. B. & Hall, W. G. (1979), Appetitive learning in 1-day-old rat pups. *Sci.*, 205:419–421.

Kuhn, C. M. & Schanberg, S. M. (1991), Stimulation in infancy and brain development. In: *Psychopathology and the Brain*, ed. B. J. Carroll & J. E. Barrett. New York: Raven Press, pp. 97–111.

Leon, M. (1975), Dietary control of maternal pheromone in the lactating rat. *Physiol. Behav.*, 14:311–319.

—— (1987), Plasticity of olfactory output circuits related to early olfactory learning. *Trends in Neurosci.*, 10:434–438.

Mason, W. A. & Berkson, G. (1974), Effects of maternal mobility on the development of rocking and other behaviors in rhesus monkeys: A study with artificial mothers. *Devel. Psychobiol.*, 8:197–211.

McClintock, M. K. (1983), Pheromonal regulation of the ovarian cycle: Enhancement, suppression, and synchrony. In: *Pheromones and Reproduction in Mammals*, ed. J. Vandenbergh. New York: Academic Press, pp. 113–149.

Miczek, K. A., Tornatzky, W. & Vivian, J. (1991), Ethology and neuropharmacology: Rodent ultrasounds. In: *Animal Models in Psychopharmacology*, ed. B. Olivier, J. Mos & J. L. Slangen. Basel: Birkhauser Verlag, pp. 410–427.

Myers, M. M., Shair, H. N. & Hofer, M. A. (1992), Feeding in infancy: Short- and long-term effects on cardiovascular function. *Experientia*, 48:322–333.

Noirot, E. (1972), Ultrasounds and maternal behavior in small rodents. *Devel. Psychobiol.*, 5:371–387.

Pierce, G. W. and Griffen, D. R. (1938), Experimental determination of supersonic notes emitted by bats. *J. Mammol.*, 19:454–455.

Roberts, L. H. (1975), Evidence for the laryngeal source of ultrasonic and audible cries of rodents. *J. Zool. (London)*, 175:243–257.

Rosenblatt, J. S. (1983), Olfaction mediates developmental transition in the altricial newborn of selected species of mammals. *Devel. Psychobiol.*, 16:347–376

Smith, G. J., Kucharski, D. & Spear, N. E. (1985), Conditioning of an odor aversion in preweanling rats with isolation from home nest as the unconditioned stimulus. *Devel. Psychobiol.*, 18:421–434.

Smotherman, W. P., Bell, R. W., Hershberger, W. A. & Coover, G. D. (1978), Orientation to rat pup cues: Effects of maternal experiential history. *Animal Behav.*, 26:265–273.

Solomon, P., Kubzansky, P. E., Leiderman, P. D., Mendelson, J. H., Trumbull, R. & Wexler, D., eds. (1961), *Sensory Deprivation*. Cambridge, MA: Harvard University Press.

Stern, D. N. (1989), The representation of relational patterns: Developmental considerations. In: *Relationship Disturbances in Early Childhood*, ed. A. J. Sameroff & R. N. Emde. New York: Basic Books.

Stoloff, M. D., Kenney, J. T., Blass, E. M. & Hall, W. G. (1980), The role of experience in suckling maintenance in albino rats. *J. Comp. Physiol. Psychol.*, 94:847–856.

Sullivan, R. M., Brake, S. C., Williams, C. L. & Hofer, M. A. (1986), Huddling and independent feeding of neonatal rats can be facilitated by a conditioned change in behavioral state. *Devel. Psychobiol.*, 19:625–635.

—— Hofer, M. A. & Brake, S. C. (1986), Olfactory-guided orientation in neonatal rats is enhanced by a conditioned change in behavioral state. *Devel. Psychobiol.*, 19:615–623.

Vernikos-Danellis, J. and Winget, C. M. (1979), The importance of light, postural and social cues in the regulation of the plasma cortical rhythms in man. In: *Chronopharmacology*, ed. A. Reinberg & F. Halbert. New York: Pergamon, pp. 101–106.

Wolff, P. H. (1968), The serial organization of sucking in the young infant. *Pediatrics*, 42:943–945.

Zippelius, H.-M. & Schleidt, W. M. (1956), Ultraschall-laute bei jungen mausen [Ultrasonic vocalization in infant mice]. *Naturwissenschaften*, 43:502.

Part III

Clinical Significance and Applications of Attachments

✧ 9 ✧

Attachment, the Reflective Self, and Borderline States

The Predictive Specificity of the Adult Attachment Interview and Pathological Emotional Development

PETER FONAGY, MIRIAM STEELE, HOWARD STEELE,
TOM LEIGH, ROGER KENNEDY,
GRETTA MATTOON, AND MARY TARGET

Nothing can be loved or hated unless it is first known.
—Leonardo da Vinci, *Notebooks*

BOWLBY'S MODEL AND MODERN PSYCHOANALYSIS

Modern psychoanalysis and the emerging field of developmental psychopathology (Cicchetti, 1990) have in common the purpose to which John Bowlby's life was devoted: to uncover the developmental course of psychological disorders of childhood and adulthood. As Jeremy Holmes (1993) reminded us in his inspiring contribution to this volume, Bowlby (1980, 1988), to the very end of his life, maintained his identity as a psychoanalyst. He saw his scientific mission as preserving what he saw as the most valuable aspect of psychoanalytic views: its emphasis on the critical role of parent–child relationships in the evolution of the mental world of the child. It remains a core assumption of psychoanalytic models and practice that parents respond to their children's behavior and characteristics with expectations based on past experiences with their own primary caregiving figures (Freud, 1940; Fraiberg, Adelson, and Shapiro, 1975, Fraiberg, 1980). Bowlby (1987) also saw himself as a conduit for ideas from disciplines on the borders of psychoanalysis (ethology, control

The work reported in this chapter was supported by generous grants from the Economic and Social Research Council of Great Britain, the Köhler-Stiftung and Lord Ashdown Trust.

systems theory, cognitive science) with the potential to inform psychoanalysts and educate them about the wider scientific context of their ideas. Epistemologically, he had no time for behaviorism but bravely embraced cognitive ideas, even in the early days when these were still tainted with notions specific to the learning theory framework from which they originated. It is at the confluence of the psychoanalytic and cognitive lines of discovery that this contribution is located.

In this chapter we review our work on the predictive power of the Adult Attachment Interview (AAI), the remarkable achievement of one of the great pioneers of the attachment field, Mary Main. The studies bear on two related areas: (1) the effect of the parent's representation of interpersonal relationships on the child's attachment and (2) the intergenerational effects of maltreatment and abuse on attachment-related representational systems. Thus, our aim is identical to that of John Bowlby: to identify aspects of normal developmental process that might be of value in our understanding of clinical problems and to inspire effective modes of intervention.

A greatly oversimplified appraisal of the model that resulted from John Bowlby's fruitful collaboration with Mary Ainsworth might identify two powerful organizing constructs: (1) the evolutionary significance of proximity seeking and the "secure base phenomenon" and (2) the unconscious belief system into which early experiences are integrated and that, under favorable circumstances, reflects the individual's confidence in the significant other's availability, understanding, and responsiveness. Our presentation leans heavily on Bowlby's theory of "internal working models" or latent cognitive structures, which, as he saw them, arise out of social experiences and, once present, filter these experiences in a way that minimizes the likelihood of spontaneous change (e.g., Sroufe and Fleeson, 1988; Dodge, 1991).

Central to work with the AAI is John Bowlby's (1973) notion of internal working models (see Figure 1), a notion derived from psychoanalytic object relations theory, particularly as formulated by British object relations theorists (e.g., see Bretherton, 1987, 1990, 1992). Attachment researchers assume that, on the basis of repeated experiences of characteristic patterns of interaction, children develop expectations regarding the nature of interactions between themselves and the attachment figure. For example, the repeated experience of being nonintrusively picked up by the caregiver after falling over leads to the expectation that distress will be met by reassurance and comforting. These expectations are embodied in mental representations, or internal working models (IWM), that have the capacity to aggregate past experience (Bowlby, 1980). Integrated

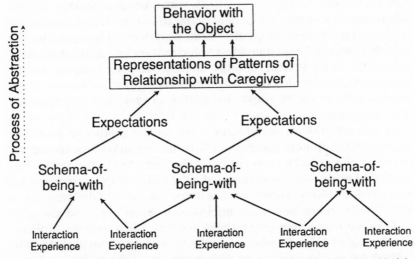

Figure 1 The Relationship of Experience, Expectations and Internal Working Models of Attachment Relationships

with, and perhaps integrating (see Stern, 1993), these expectations are the emotional experiences associated with these interactions.

Daniel Stern (1993) detailed the building blocks of internal working models: "schemata-of-a-way-of-being-with," which are temporal segments or "sound bytes" of mental life. Internal working models are the superordinate structures that combine numerous schemas "of-being-with" (see Figure 1). They regulate the child's behavior with the attachment figure and, in due course, come to organize behavior in all significant relationships, including, eventually, the relationship with one's own child.[1]

TRANSGENERATIONAL STUDIES OF ATTACHMENT

Bowlby's model has provided the background for transgenerational studies that have demonstrated a strong association between the child's security of attachment and an assessment of the caregiver's internal working model. These studies were made possible by Main and her colleagues' work on a structured assessment instrument, the

---

[1] Stern's (1993) elaboration of the IWM model concept leans heavily on connectionist theories of neural nets (Rumelhart and McClelland, 1986) and Edelson's (1987) concept of neural Darwinism. Such exciting, speculative explorations indicate the possibility of productive and genuine interdisciplinary dialogues between cognitive scientists and psychodynamic clinicians to stimulate a comprehensive overhaul of our notions concerning the mental representation of relationships (Fonagy, 1994a).

Adult Attachment Interview (AAI) (George, Kaplan, and Main, 1985; Main and Goldwyn, 1991), which provided an indication of the functioning of the internal working model. The interview is designed to elicit the individual's account of his or her childhood attachment and separation experiences, together with his or her evaluations of the effects of those experiences on present functioning. It asks questions about the quality of childhood relationships with caregivers (e.g., happy, loving) and memories that might justify this. Interviewees are asked to describe their childhood experiences of separation, illness, injury, punishment, loss, and, most important, abuse. Ratings of emotional and cognitive features of the individual's representational world as revealed in the transcripts constitute the basis of a fourfold classification scheme (Main and Goldwyn, 1991; Bakermans-Kranenburg and van IJzendoorn, 1993). This classification scheme parallels the well-known fourfold typology avoidant/ secure/resistant/disorganized of infant–caregiver attachments (after Ainsworth et al., 1978; Main and Solomon, 1986; Main and Hesse, 1990). Individuals classified as *secure* (F) on the AAI are able to describe both pleasant and painful aspects of their lives in a coherent manner that neither minimizes nor maximizes the emotional qualities and consequences of past relationship experiences. By contrast, the *insecure-preoccupied* (E) group's narratives are incoherent, and these people appear still angry as if they were entangled in their past experiences with attachment figures; the *insecure-dismissing* (Ds) group is characterized by incoherence because of the lack of detail; they have few memories and a highly restricted range of emotions to attachment experiences. Individuals classified as *unresolved-disorganized* (U) also show incoherence. This is seen in relation to memories of loss and abuse; these individuals will always be given a second, alternate classification. The broad distinctions among the four types of interviews are summarized in Table 1.

These major categories have dominant or common themes, but individual responses may vary considerably within each group. For example, the insecure-preoccupied (E) category contains interviews that indicate a passive stance regarding an ill-defined experience of childhood (E1), others that are filled with current anger concerning past experiences (E2), and yet others that are characterized by preoccupation with traumatic events (E3). While the reliability of major categories is excellent (Bakermans-Kranenburg and van IJzendoorn 1993), much less is known of the test-retest and interrated reliabilities of the subcategories.

In psychoanalytic terms, broadly speaking, security is indicated by "undistorted" free/autonomous cognitive and emotional processes; insecurity, on the other hand, is indicated by significant interference

	Secure 'F'	Dismissing 'D'	Entangled 'E'	Unresolved 'U'
Value attachments	+	-	+	+/-
Defensive distortions	-	+	+	+/-
Detailed memories	+	-	+	+/-
Current anger	-	-	+	+/-
Profound disorganization	-	-	-	+
Approximate percentage	60%	25%	15%	10%

Table 1 Main and Goldwyn's (1992) Classification of AAI Interviews

with cognitive or affective aspects of mental representations of self and other, including splitting, derogation, and denial. Secure individuals demonstrate what Jeremy Holmes (1992) has aptly termed "autobiographical competence." Trauma (whether abuse or loss) has a tendency to distort the internal working model. In the fourth group classified by the AAI, *unresolved mourning* (U) connected to abuse or loss is indicated by interviews where signs of continuing disorganization appear when the attachment figure is discussed (e. g., through inappropriate guilt about experiences of having been maltreated or continued fear of the abusive parent). These signs of disorganization indicate a breakdown of psychic defenses.

Many studies bridging diverse linguistic, cultural, and economic contexts have confirmed a transgenerational link between AAI assessments of caregivers and Strange Situation assessments of children. The studies carried out to date were recently reviewed by van IJzendoorn (1994), who found that the correspondence between infant and parent classification across studies was consistently 70–80%. In the London Parent–Child Project[2] (Fonagy, Steele, and Steele, 1991; Fonagy, Steele, Moran et al. 1991; H. Steele, M. Steele, and Fonagy, in press; M. Steele, H. Steele, and Fonagy, in prep. a), we administered the Adult Attachment Interview,[3] along with a range of instruments to assess self-esteem, marital satisfaction, personality, attitudes to the pregnancy and the future infant, to 100

---

[2] The project was the initiative of Miriam Steele. Howard Steele and Peter Fonagy joined the project at the late design stages.

[3] Four of us independently classified the 200 interviews, and the level of agreement was high (Kappa=.7–.9).

mothers and 100 fathers expecting their first child, in the last trimester of pregnancy. As in the studies we aimed to replicate and extend (Main, Kaplan, and Cassidy, 1985; Grossmann et al., 1988), the participating families formed a predominantly middle-class group and were relatively easy to follow up at 12 and 18 months after the birth of the child (attrition rate < 5%). The Strange Situation gave us a window on the nature of the developing attachment relationship between child and mother at 12 months and between child and father at 18 months.

The analysis of the interview data powerfully confirmed the existence of an intergenerational relationship (see Fonagy et al., 1991; H. Steele, M. Steele, and Fonagy, in press). When the mother's prenatal interviews indicated either dismissal or preoccupation, almost three-quarters of the children responded to their mothers in an insecure (avoidant or resistant) way on their return following the brief episodes of separation in the Strange Situation at one year of age. This contrasted with autonomous (F) mothers' children, 80% of whom responded on reunion by openly attending to their mothers or approaching them with visible reductions of their anxiety. Only 27% of the children of dismissing or preoccupied mothers responded this way. A somewhat weaker, yet statistically still highly significant, pattern of concordance emerged for fathers. Only 18% of children of autonomous (F) fathers behaved in an insecure manner toward them on reunion, while half the children of the fathers classified as detached/dismissing (D) or entangled/preoccupied (E) did so. For both parents the associations between a detached adult interview pattern and insecure child behavior and between free/autonomous interview and secure infant behavior were the strongest. A classification of preoccupied on the AAI was only slightly more likely to be linked to infant behavior indicating insecurity rather than security. It particularly impressed us that none of the wide range of control measures we used (including personality, verbal fluency, marital satisfaction, and psychopathology screening measures) achieved statistically significant levels of prediction from pregnancy to infant attachment security (H. Steele, M. Steele, and Fonagy, in preparation b).

These global findings do no more than add to the accumulating body of data that confirms that there is a form of intergenerational transmission of both security and insecurity (Main et al., 1985; Grossman et al., 1988; Haft and Slade, 1989; Ainsworth and Eichberg, 1991; van IJzendoorn et al., 1991, 1992; Bus and van IJzendoorn, 1992; see review by van IJzendoorn, 1995) and that this latter risk may be assessed before the birth of the child (see also Ward et al., 1991; Radojevic, 1992; Benoit and Parker, 1993).

Eighteen studies covering 853 parent–child dyads summarized in Marinus van IJzendoorn's (1995) meta-analysis yielded a combined effect size comparable to a correlation coefficient of .47 for the autonomous-to-secure (F–B) link, .45 for the dismissing-to-avoidant (D–A) link, and .42 for the preoccupied-to-ambivalent (E–C) link. Taken together, these results suggest that the AAI can account for approximately one-quarter of the variance in infant behavior in the Strange Situation.

CAREGIVER-SPECIFIC PREDICTIONS OF STRANGE SITUATION BEHAVIOR

The parent's internal working model of relationships influences or at least prefigures the child's security of attachment. To demonstrate unequivocally its transmission, a *direct* relationship between the child's and parent's internal working models needs to be established. As part of this, we need to show that the transmission of security to the infant is caregiver-specific, not the artifact of constitutional factors, temperament, assortative mating, or the generalizing of security from one caregiver to the other.

To test this, we reanalyzed our data using log-linear analysis.[4] Each child was assigned two Strange Situation classifications: secure versus insecure with mother (SS_M) and with father (SS_F). Each child was further categorized on the security status of mother's (AAI_M) and father's (AAI_F) AAI transcripts, creating a 2 x 2 x 2 x 2 (AAI_M x AAI_F x SS_M x SS_F) matrix when all the possible two-way interaction terms were introduced. Only terms relating to the association between mother's AAI and infant–mother attachment ($p < .0001$) and father's AAI and infant–father attachment ($p < .0005$) were statistically significant (see M. Steele et al., in press). There was no indication that the security status of either parent affected the child's relationship with the other parent. Father's security appeared to have no observable influence on the infant–mother relationship, and

---

[4] Log-linear analysis is a model-fitting procedure for categorical data such as Strange Situation (SSN) on AAI classifications. In a manner analogous to other linear model analyses (such as analysis of variance), the researcher can introduce terms to account for an observed distribution until the distribution predicted on the bases of the terms introduced no longer differs significantly from the observed distribution. The statistical significance of a term is indicated by the contribution the inclusion of the term makes to the closeness of fit (the reduction of the difference) between observed and predicted distributions. In the hierarchical version of this procedure, all terms are introduced first individually and then in two-way, then three-way interactions. For example, the two-way interaction between mother's AAI classification and infant–mother Strange Situation classifications represents the association between these classifications.

the influence of mother's security on the infant–father dyad was also negligible.

It follows from this model that when there is congruence between the Strange Situation classifications of the child with each parent, we would expect congruence in parental classifications as well. This was, in fact, the case. Seventy-seven percent of the 56 parental interviews were concordant (i.e., both secure or both insecure) when the infant received the same classification in the Strange Situation with mother and father. This contrasts with only 23% of the 34 couples receiving the same classification for their interviews when the infants were discordant across the two Strange Situations ($\chi^2 = 7.41$, $df = 1$, $p < .007$). These data, together with the results of the log-linear analysis, offer clear support for the independent influence of the two parental internal working models on the security of infant–parent relationship in the first 18 months of life. The strong association suggests that each parent "transmits" his or her internal working model independently of the actions of the other parent. We assume that, on the basis of manifestations of the parent's working model in the relationship, the child develops and maintains distinguishable sets of expectations in relation to each of his or her primary caregivers. We do not yet know if, how, and when such separate internal working models are combined to determine the child's general stance toward attachment relationships. Taking a developmental approach akin to that of Heinz Werner (1948), we assume that all earlier structures are retained and, though not directly modified, are built on or integrated into developmentally more sophisticated organizations. In later development these earlier structures may be activated by changed circumstances, new relationships, or acute stress (Sroufe, 1989).

The specificity of each parent's influence on the child, at least for the first two years, may be highly adaptive. The insulation of the internal working models of young children allows for the creation of a secure internal working model alongside one or more highly insecure ones. We may speculate that this is the case for the resilient maltreated child. This supposition plays a critical part in the attachment theory account of why the presence of even a relatively remote, but stable and responsive, figure in the child's early life can be a protective factor, fostering a secure internal working model of relationships and contributing to the child's resilience to hardship (e.g., Hunter and Kilstrom, 1979; Werner and Smith, 1982; Brown, Harris, and Bifulco, 1986; Quinton and Rutter, 1988; Werner, 1989; Braithwaite and Gordon, 1991). It appears that the small child has the capacity to encode, differentiate, and isolate the internal working models of primary caregivers independently. Eventually, in ways we do not yet understand, she or he will show preference for one caretaker over others and choose to be guided by what may be termed the preferred or dominant model.

THE PROCESS OF TRANSMISSION:
A ROLE FOR SENSITIVE RESPONSIVENESS

The predictive validity of the AAI begs the key psychological question of the process of transmission. Genetic and temperamental accounts (see Belsky, this volume, for a review) of infant security and insecurity do not seem strong contenders as an alternative explanation insofar as Strange Situation classifications appear to be specific to each parent's AAI classification (H. Steele, M. Steele, and Fonagy, in press).

Many attachment researchers appear to adhere to a model of the transgenerational process originating in Bowlby's work that may be said to involve four stages: (1) the parent's attachment-related experiences in childhood are embodied within a working model (Bowlby, 1973, 1980; Bretherton, 1985) that (2) is thought to affect the development of the mental representation of the child in the caregiver's mind (see Bretherton et al., 1989), which (3) determines parenting functions underlying sensitive caregiving behavior (Bowlby, 1969), which then (4) constitutes the primary determinant of the child's quality of attachment to the parent (Ainsworth et al., 1978). Thus, the best candidate for a process through which parental mental representations influence the infant's behavior in stressful situations has been widely regarded as the sensitive responsiveness of the caregiver (Bowlby, 1973).

The role of sensitive responsiveness was empirically established by Ainsworth et al. (1978), and a number of studies have since replicated this finding, linking the sensitivity of early care to the child's reunion behavior (Belsky, Rovine, and Taylor, 1984; Grossman et al., 1985; Solomon, George, and Silverman, cited in Waters et al., 1993). Studies in Holland (van IJzendoorn et al., 1991; Bus and van IJzendoorn, 1992), in Germany (Grossman et al., 1989), and in the United States (Ward and Carlson, 1993) have further linked high sensitivity on Ainsworth's rating scale for parental sensitivity in home interactions to parental security as measured by the AAI. Similarly, a number of laboratory-based studies, using structured interactions, have shown parents who are secure on the AAI to be more responsive to their infants than insecure ones (Crowell and Feldman, 1988; Crowell et al., 1991; Cohn et al., 1992; Das-Eiden, Teti, and Corns, 1993). A separate group of studies has demonstrated that expectant parents classified as free-autonomous on the AAI are more likely to develop

representations of the child over the first 18 months that are characterized by loving acceptance and coherence and by a relative
absence of ambivalence (Steele et al., 1992).

Thus, there is considerable experimental support for the central
role of sensitive responsiveness; nevertheless, this construct falls
short of offering a complete account. The studies of sensitivity
previously cited yield relatively modest effect sizes; parental sensitivity ratings account for only 7% of the variance in infant security (van
IJzendoorn, in press). Furthermore, with the odd exception, these
studies have not yet examined whether sensitivity ratings actually
account for *that* portion of the variability in the Strange Situation
classification that is predicted by the AAI. Similarly, although secure
individuals appear to develop more coherent representations of
their child, this quality of the mental representation of the child in
the parents' minds seems to be statistically unrelated to the propensity of free-autonomous parents to raise infants who are secure with
them (Steele et al., 1992). Thus, the caregiver's representation of the
child and her or his rated sensitivity may not be on the causal path
between AAI and Strange Situation classification, and even if they
are part of a mediating process, the correlations are too small to
corroborate their unique involvement. The field therefore appears to
have come up against what van IJzendoorn (1995) has aptly termed
a "transmission gap." Sensitivity may account for some, but not all,
of the AAI→Strange Situation correlation. Current conceptualization
and operationalisation of the sensitive parenting model need to
become more sophisticated and perhaps more dynamic.

BRIDGING THE TRANSMISSION GAP THROUGH THE STUDY OF DEFENSIVE PROCESSES

What we believe to be crucial to caregiving sensitivity is the extent
to which parents are inclined to be defensive about their own negative emotional experiences. In our view such defensiveness may
lead to a lack of understanding (dismissal) or to incomplete understanding of their infants' states of anxiety (preoccupation). Parents
preoccupied by past experiences may misconstrue their child's
affective state, and this misconstrual may lead to a persistence of
distress observed on reunion. The parent's preoccupations may be
exaggerated by conflicts surrounding becoming a parent; thus,
parents judged secure before the birth of the child may not invariably rear secure children. At other times, however, becoming a
parent may trigger an adaptive reorganization of the inner world;
thus, dismissing or entangled interviews are not inevitable indicators
of insecure infant–parent attachments.

The Kleinian analyst Wilfred Bion (1962) discussed the significance of the mother's capacity to mentally "contain" the baby and respond to the infant emotionally and in terms of physical care in a manner that modulates unmanageable feelings and acknowledges the child's "intentional stance" (Dennett, 1983). Ideally, the mother will "reflect" to the infant her understanding of *both* the cause of the distress and her appreciation of the affective state of the child. This goes beyond "mirroring" (Meltzoff, 1993), as the caregiver reflects appreciation of the infant's emotional state, *in combination* with her own adult mastery of it. Going beyond "mirroring", her response implies her capacity not to be overwhelmed by, but to deal with, the distress; this we believe is the central and potentially measurable aspect of Bion's (1962) containment concept.

For instance, we predict preoccupied mothers to be strong on the mirroring of affect but poorer on conveying coping with the affect. Conversely, dismissing mothers might fail to mirror affects accurately but transmit to the child a sense of stability and coping. It should also be noted that sensitivity is not invariably coterminous with mirroring, which implies contact in the visual modality. In our Western cultures, visual and verbal modalities have considerable primacy, but in other cultures where the infant is carried on the mother's body, contact through different channels (tactile, kinesthetic, auditory) may be more important. Many channels allow caregivers to communicate containment. One potentially fruitful line of inquiry concerns so-called complex intonation patterns. Fonagy and Fonagy (1987) demonstrated that expressive emotional communication, as, for example, in the artistic rendition of poetry, frequently involves the combination or superposition of two or more conventional intonation contours. Sensitive caregivers may be able to combine a mimicking of the emotional communication of the child with the communication of a normally incompatible affective states; thus, for example, the intonation contours of tenderness or joy may be combined with the mimicking of fear. The envelope of the emotional messages that contradict distress may function to "contain" the infant.

From this perspective *secure attachment is the outcome of successful containment*, while insecure attachment is a defensive compromise (Fonagy et al., 1992; Holmes, 1993) in which either intimacy (avoidant/dismissing) or autonomy (resistant/preoccupied) appears to be sacrificed for the sake of retaining physical proximity to the caregiver incapable of containing the infant's affect. We believe that the mother's failure to understand the infant's distress and reflect this in a controlled way forces the infant to adapt, using what Selma Fraiberg (1982) termed "defensive behaviors." These serve to restrict contact with (avoidant), or distract (resistant), the caregiver. Behaviors characteristic of the avoidant pattern are defensive because they permit the infant to disengage from a painful situation; the resistant pattern may be adaptive in distracting an emotionally preoccupied individual, for example, making a somewhat depressed or withdrawn mother "come to life." The defensive behaviors may be specific to the adult and frequently appear to be "borrowed" from the caregiver, or, in psychoanalytic jargon, adopted by a process of identification/internalization.

When we adopt an idiographic, rather than nomothetic, approach to our data, we find some remarkable instances of correspondence between aspects of the child's behavior in the Strange Situation and inferences that could be made about the caregiver's habitual ways of coping with painful attachment experiences (Fonagy et al., 1992). The convergence of the parents' and infants' modes of defense, as reflected in the parents' interviews and the child's behavior in the Strange Situation, was striking in a large number of cases. For example, one mother, whose little boy was disturbed by the separation, vigorously bounced the one-year-old on her knee shortly after they were reunited. Her response to the child showed an excess of (positive) affect incompatible with his anxiety and thus a striking lack of mirroring. The child responded to the reunion with his mother with eventual giggling, laughing off his sense of hurt and turning his initially visible anger and upset (or at least trying to do so) into apparent pleasure at the mother's behest. At the end of the three-minute period, however, when the bouncing stopped, he was still tearful.

When we turn to this mother's memories as elicited by the AAI interview, we find that she blatantly denies emotional conflict and bolsters her denial by inappropriate laughter.

She was clearly under pressure to remember her childhood as happy. Asked, *"How would you describe your relationship to your parents during your childhood?"* she said, "I wasn't unhappy, I wasn't. I was never unhappy in my childhood at all, I was blissfully happy."

The same tendency to avoid unpleasure through denial and idealization seemed apparent at many levels of conflict. For example, she said:

I am the apple of my father's eye and come first and he absolutely, I mean he does absolutely idolize me. . . . and I think it's amazing that my mother has never been remotely jealous of that in any way at all!. . . . and she's just genuinely never held that against me at all and is fantastic!

Her answers give evidence of some insight into how she uses laughter as a protection against sadness. Asked, *"Do you think your childhood experiences have affected your adult personality?"* she said:

> I still find one of the most important things in my relationships with people, with, with my husband and friends, I think that if I, if I pointed to one thing, I think, that laughter is, is one of the key things that I think's important because it, it, er . . . it just, it just makes you see the, the, the bright side of everything, and I don't see any point in not seeing the bright side of things.

The observations illustrate how the mother unconsciously forces the child into the adaptive strategy which she finds most reassuring. The child's distress signals anxiety to the mother and brings forth a minimalizing strategy of forced jollity. At the moment of the observation, the strategy has not yet been internalised by the child but the beginnings of the process are evident.

In another case we observed, a little girl who displayed very marked avoidance in the Strange Situation reunion, averted her eyes from mother's gaze throughout, and failed to seek proximity. She had been visibly upset by the separation but, throughout the period on her own, struggled hard to maintain an illusion of independence. She manifested fierce, almost defiant, independence and showed with all her movements and actions that she did not "need" the mother and was more comfortable left to her own devices. She actively distanced herself from her mother, even when the mother drew the child to her. She clearly wished to continue to play on her own after the mother's return; as soon as the mother joined one of her games, she purposefully moved on to another toy. The mother mirrored the child's distressed affect but did not initiate an incompatible emotional response to her anxiety and wariness so as to help the child contain the feelings.

It is striking how the daughter's self-sufficiency in the Strange Situation is prefigured by the mother's comments on her childhood experiences. This mother had an appalling history. Both of her parents were rejected from their respective family homes. The parents were prone to violent quarrels, and the father's physical abuse of his pregnant wife caused this mother to be born with a crippled foot, which needed subsequent surgical correction. She was abnormally isolated in her childhood, and from the age of five she was forced to look after herself: "I was a latchkey kid, you know; I'd come home and knock on the door next door and they'd give me the key and let, and I'd let myself in so I'd be on my own for about an hour and a half till my mother got in from work."

The most striking feature of the interview is the extent to which this mother is able to avoid the sadness of her past and to refer to her relationship with her father as characterized by pride and loving despite the fact that he was profoundly disappointed in his only child's not being a boy. She recalls overhearing him say, "Well, if she'd been a lad we'd have never lost, never have left the farm." Yet, characteristically, the memory is not associated with an affect: "As a child I'm sure I never felt rejected."

Repression appears to permeate the interview. She could not remember being upset as a child, let alone being comforted. What she called "small" upsets were apparently minimized. When the interviewer asked her if she really had no early memories of being upset, she replied "No, because nobody died."

> I think it's made me very independent, um, probably a little too independent. . . . it's very fortunate that I. . . . Dick [her spouse], Dick's a lone wolf and so am I, um, it's very fortunate that we managed to, to get along so well seeing really quite little of each other. . . . I can see that could be, in some house-holds, very, er, very much a source of discontent. . . . so it's made me very fiercely independent. It's made me just very self-reliant.

Such observations led us to the conclusion that the infant's pattern of relating to the parent in the Strange Situation may reflect the parent's habitual pattern of dealing with the infant's communica-tion of unpleasurable states. This is, of course, consistent with the more general proposition advanced by Cramer and Stern (1988), Lebovici and Weil-Halpern (1989), and others working in the field of infant–mother psychotherapy. It is claimed that pathological features of the infant's mental representations of relationships derive from the internalization of enactments of maternal conflicts observ-able in microscopic aspects of the infant–caregiver interchange. Fraiberg's (1982) observations of the genesis of defensive behaviors in the second year of life are also consistent with this point of view.

How can we explain the intergenerational transmission of habit-ual modes of defense? Normally, the infant turns to his mother when threatened with loss or when in states of physical distress. The mother bases her intervention on what she perceives to be the qual-ity of the affective signals emanating from the infant. Within Bowlby's (1973) theory, the activation of the attachment system in the mother accounts for a more or less coordinated response.

Attachment theory recognizes that the signals of distressed affect are biologically rooted in unpleasure and are therefore inwardly as well as externally directed. The unpleasurable phenomenal experience associated with the signal initiates a quasi-amplificatory process. We are all familiar with the sight of the child who falls and is okay, unless someone gives the "have a real cry" signal. Thus, the act of giving such signals serves to intensify further the helpless infant's subjective distress. The mother aims to reduce the baby's heightened state of arousal, sometimes unconsciously, through taking appropriate action on the infant's behalf. In carrying out her ministrations, the empathic mother acts on her ideas about the source of the infant's distress. She is also unconsciously attuned to the emotional distress engendered by the infant's experiences of the state of being anxious or angry (see Figure 2a).

With a secure/autonomous (F) mother, the baby learns to associate emotional distress with the possibility of its alleviation and learns that future moderate distress will not lead to the mobilization of extreme defensive maneuvers. Thus, repeated encounters with a mother capable of reflecting, containing, and alleviating distress strengthen the child's capacity to tolerate negative affect and increase confidence that the need for auxiliary support in regulating affect will not go unmet.

This simple model helps us to distinguish three common forms of failure in the mother–infant relationship (see Figure 2b). First, the

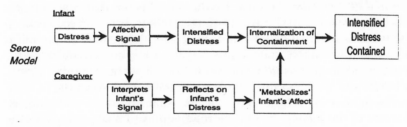

Figure 2a. Transmission of Secure IWMs

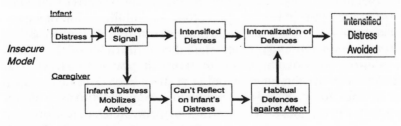

Figure 2b. Transmission of Insecure IWMs

mother may fail to recognize negative affective signals. There are a variety of reasons why mothers fail to respond adequately to their infants' distress. These range from external factors, such as socio-economic pressures that may reduce the mother's attentiveness, to internal psychological states, such as mental illness (deMulder and Radke-Yarrow, 1991), that preclude adequately attuned emotional responsiveness. Second, the mother may locate the source of the child's distress but fail to attend to the quality of the distressing affect and fail to reflect a combination of congruent affect and mastery in her response. Third, there may be a more subtle failure to respond empathically to the intentional stance of the infant toward the caregiver's mental state and to an existential anxiety that surrounds it, by which we mean early manifestations of individuation, intentionality, and ownership of one's body representation or states of mind in contrast, and often in opposition, to the object. We feel that the third category, the mother's intuitive understanding of the young child's emerging "intentional stance" (Dennett, 1978), may be most important in maximizing the likelihood of the child's forming a secure attachment. In all three cases the mother reduces her own unconscious discomfort by adopting one of a number of common strategies of attenuating painful experience. These include mental maneuvers that are manifest in the mother's interaction with the child.

If the child cannot rely on the mother to respond to the signals of his negative affective states and to reduce them, he or she must find alternative ways to diminish them. With an immature and as yet unstructured psychic apparatus, the infant has no recourse to repression, and a behaviorial strategy must be evoked. As he is deprived of auxiliary ego support to alter the physical source of his distress, defensive efforts will be restricted to the modification of the affective state signaling unpleasure, rather than its cause.

What behavioral responses can the child invoke to achieve this? Closest to hand must be the internalization of behavioral manifestations of the mother's defenses to ward off the child's affect. In other words the child internalizes perception of the mother's reaction to his own affective signals. Fraiberg's (1982) observations of the genesis of defensive behaviors in the second year of life are, we propose, consistent with this point of view. *The child's behavior in the Strange Situation may then be a direct function of the child's cumulative experience of the maternal behavior in response to distress.* This view is an elaboration of Anna Freud's (1965) conception of the early period in childhood wherein conflicts with the environment shape developmentally acquired tendencies, prefiguring the more psychologically complex mechanisms that eventually come to regulate conflict.

METACOGNITIVE MONITORING: FURTHER CLUES TO THE TRANSGENERATIONAL PROCESS

A compelling model for the transmission of secure attachment that has moved the field beyond a simple view of caregiver sensitivity is suggested by Mary Main (1991) in her seminal chapter on metacognitive monitoring and singular versus multiple models of attachment in her manual for the AAI. She proposes that differences in attachment organizations during childhood are strongly linked to the quality of metacognition in the parent and that incoherent adult narratives indicating poorly structured multiple models of attachment relationships may be a key cause of the child's insecure pattern of attachment. Main (1991) further argues that the absence of metacognitive capacity, the inability to "understand the *merely* representational nature of their own (and others') thinking" (p. 128), makes infants and toddlers vulnerable to the inconsistency of the caregiver's behavior. They are unable to step beyond the immediate reality of experience and grasp the distinction between appearance and reality, between immediate experience and the mental state that might underlie it.

Considerations based on psychoanalytic theory would lead us to very similar conclusions concerning the importance of metacognitive monitoring on the part of the caregiver in attachment relationships. Psychoanalysts have long distinguished between the mother's attitude and behavior toward the child independent of the child's current mental state, and the mother's inferred capacity to envisage the infant as a mental entity, as a human being with relatively sophisticated feelings, beliefs, and desires (e.g., Winnicott, 1956, 1967, 1971; Bion, 1962, 1967b, 1970; Stern, 1985; Fonagy, Moran, and Target, 1993).

Main's model of transgenerational transmission and its psychoanalytic elaboration implies that ratings of *observable* maternal sensitivity and caregiving are not necessarily reliable predictors of the quality of the parent–child relationship. The mother's metacognitive capacity, her understanding of mental states, and her readiness to contemplate these in a coherent manner should provide a powerful and clear prediction of the likelihood of the child's developing a secure relationship with her. Main and Goldwyn's (1992) manual provides a pioneering rating procedure for metacognitive control. Main's coding is based primarily on reflective self-awareness. It focuses on the individual's capacity to monitor his output in the course of the interview and to bear in mind the mental state of the listener. It does not encompass the extent of the interviewee's concern with mental states in general nor with his or her own and the object's mental states in particular. She warns of the danger of mistaking genuine concern with the state of mind of the object with "canned," rote-learned phrases of apparent interest. Our contribution in this field builds on Main's discoveries and attempts to refine our understanding of individual differences in metacognitive capacity and extend it to the subject's awareness of the mental states of his attachment objects, as well as the clarity of his representation of his own mental states in the past and present.

REFLECTIVE SELF-PROCESSES:
AN ELABORATION OF METACOGNITIVE MONITORING

We attempted to operationalize Main's (1991) notion of individual differences in adults' metacognitive capacities. This led to a variation on this important theme that we believe has the potential to contribute to filling the "transmission gap." We were curious to know whether the pervasiveness of self-reflective observations about the mental states of self and others in AAI narratives could predict infant security. We chose the term "reflective self-scale" (as opposed to "self-reflection scale") to underscore that we were concerned about the clarity of the individual's representation of the mental states of others as well as the representation of his own mental state. The term "reflective" derives from William James (1890), who used it in his description of the point in the evolution of a self-structure when the mental state of the individual becomes a subject of thought ("to think of ourselves as thinkers," p. 296).

Our operationalization was based on the rich literature on the evolution of metacognitive knowledge (Flavell, Green, and Flavell, 1986), as well as more recent contributions under the heading of "a theory of mind" (see Astington, Harris, and Olson, 1988; Butterworth et al., 1991; Frye and Moore, 1991; Whiten, 1991; Baron-Cohen, Tager-Flusberg, and Cohen, 1993). Our formulation was based on the assumption that the psychological process variously labeled "metacognitive monitoring" (Main, 1991) or "mentalization" (Fonagy, 1989, 1991; Morton and Frith, 1995) or, more narrowly, "theory of mind" (Premack and Woodruff, 1978; Bretherton, McNew, and Beeghley-Smith, 1981; Whiten, 1991; Baron-Cohen, 1992) or "reflective self-function" (Fonagy, Moran, and Target, 1993; Fonagy et al., 1994) is an intrapsychic and interpersonal developmental achievement that emerges *fully* only in the context of a secure attachment relationship. It is subject to the vicissitudes of conflict and anxiety and consequent defensive disruption, along with many other high-level cognitive processes. We assumed that in the narratives of their attachment histories of the defended, nonreflective group of parents, a number of categories of mentalization would be less frequently found and less explicitly invoked. We have noted how the defensive style of the parent is communicated to the child and that this was most evident in the cases of children with insecure classifications. This part of our work focused on the role mentalization plays in making parents vulnerable to such intergenerational transmission or how mentalization may circumvent the need to repeat our own past in our relationship with our children. This led us to take a special interest in those parents who were scoring low on our new measure of mentalization. We asked raters to note the frequency of statements in AAI narratives in a number of categories that were not intended to be mutually exhaustive and each of which subsumed several different types of observations:

1. *Special mention of mental states*
   a. *Representing self or other as thinking and feeling.*
   The statement "I was angry" is nonreflective, whereas the statement "At the time I often felt very angry" is considered reflective.

   b. *Explicit statements concerning the source of interpersonal knowledge as inference, observation, or information transmission.*
   "I assume that she must have felt angry because she would try to hide her feelings, but I never saw her actually expressing it to anyone."

   c. *Anticipation of the reaction of another that takes into account the other's perception of the mental state of the self.*
   "He probably thought that we didn't really love him, so he tried to avoid disappointment by being sometimes a bit short with us."

2. *Sensitivity to the characteristics of mental states*
   a. *Recognizing the fallible nature of knowledge.*
   One mother describing her reactions to her manic-depressive father commented: "You can easily mistake depression and withdrawal for rejection. I still find it hard to tell the difference."

   b. *Explicit recognition of the limited power of wishes, thoughts, and desires with respect to the real world.*
   "Most people must want things they can't have. I always wanted a mother who would come and pick me up from school and it took me a long time to accept that she was not going to be that mother for me."

c. *Acknowledgment of the opaqueness of the mental world of others while retaining the principle of psychic causation.*

"I couldn't tell what she had in mind. She might react to things and it would leave me feeling confused and frustrated. Afterwards, sometimes I understood [that it was] because she had an argument with Dad or something, but not at all always."

3. *Sensitivity to the complexity and diversity of mental states*
   a. *Explicit recognition of the possibility of diverse perspectives and points of view of the same event.*

"People might say that she was caring and attentive to us, but to my sister and I it just felt [as if] she was constantly wanting to be in control, and that's why she was such a disciplinarian."

b. *Recognition of the complexity of causation in the social world and that the world of physical causality is a poor model for the mental world.*

"I don't know why he behaved as he did. In part it had to do with his sense of inadequacy, because of the job he had, but also he was disappointed by us and he was angry because he felt we had let him down. There is no simple reason and it would be facile to pretend that there is just one simple explanation."

c. *Recognition that social roles interact and the same person can maintain sometimes contradictory attitudes in the context of different relationships.*

"She is a lovely, generous, almost selfless woman in the confines of her family, but she is quite constrictive [sic] and resents people outside and can be quite mean to them."

4. *Special efforts at linking mental states to observed behaviors*
   a. *Recognition that observed behavior may be determined by an underlying mental state and that the latter can serve as a satisfactory account of the former.*

"I would say he behaved very badly, but he was very worried about his job and being unemployed again."

b. *Understanding that people may express different emotions from those they feel.*

"She was always kind and generous but we knew that underneath it she was suffering. It must have been terribly difficult for her to cope on her own."

c. *Recognition that people may intentionally wish to deceive by presenting themselves in self-serving ways.*

"He needed to be liked, so he was careful to make a good impression on all the people who came to visit us."

5. *Appreciation of possibility of change in mental states, with implications for corresponding changes in behavior*
   a. *Acknowledging the possibility of change between the ideas of a child and those of an adult.*
   "As a child you see your parents as being able to do everything. It's sad when you realize that they are just human."

   b. *Acknowledging the possibility of changing attitudes in the future.*
   "I want him to be happy with what he has. I would be content just if he was content but I know, once he is born, I will probably want him to be prime minister."

The interviews rated in the lower third of the scale were quite different in style from those in the middle or upper third. Interviews in the "poor reflective function" group did not represent either self or the others as "intentional" (i.e., seen as governed by beliefs and desires) and gave banal, generalized, "sociological" (rather than psychological) accounts of interpersonal events. Reference is made to others' affects and cognitions, but this is grounded in the immediate reactions of others to external circumstances ("They were constantly tired because there was a war on at that time"; "Everyone then had rather Victorian attitudes"). Interviews in the middle third tended to have some psychological attributions, but these lacked specificity; perceptions of the mental world appeared to be either inaccurate or extended way beyond the behavioral data (in psychoanalytic terms, dominated by projection). For example, in response to the question, "Were there any setbacks in your development?" one subject classified in this group replied: "I mean, ever since the concept of maturity, you know, formed in my consciousness I have always been aware of being some distance from it. It's easy to rationalize, you come out with trite . . . er . . . er . . . half-baked . . . er . . . psychological interpretations." The top third of the interviews reflected the most consistent ability on the part of the interviewees to understand psychological states. They included many examples of reasoning about actions in terms of mental states, they evidenced assumptions concerning the impact of psychological conflict, and thus they showed awareness of the limited power of consciousness to monitor all aspects of mental activity. These were also the scripts most likely to underscore a developmental dimension to mental states indicating awareness that adults' thinking was often different in quality and content from the beliefs and desires of children.

Consistent with our expectation, reflective self-ratings were reliable and provided a good prediction of the Strange Situation behavior of the child (Fonagy et al., 1991). Both fathers and mothers who were rated to be high in this capacity were three or four times more likely to have secure children than parents whose reflective capacity was poor. Although the power of prediction from this scale was only slightly below that of the AAI classification, significant numbers of caregivers had secure children despite low ratings; the number with insecure children among those with the highest ratings was relatively small. This led us to think in terms of a vulnerability/resilience model.

RESILIENCE AND REFLECTIVE OR METACOGNITIVE CONTROL

Main (1991) proposes that the capacity for metacognitive control may be particularly important when the child is exposed to unfavorable interaction patterns, in the extreme, abuse or trauma (see also Fonagy et al., 1994). For example, in the presence of the capacity to represent ideas qua ideas, the child is not forced to accept the implication of parental rejection and adopt a negative view of himself. A child who has the capacity to conceive of the mental state of the other can also conceive of the possibility that the parent's rejection of him or her may be based on false beliefs, and therefore the child can moderate the impact of negative experience. We can therefore expect that this interpersonal form of metacognitive capacity would be particularly important for individuals who experienced social stress in the course of their upbringing.

Eighteen months after they had completed the Adult Attachment Interview, we examined this issue by administering to parents a brief structured interview, concerning a number of simple indicators of family stress and deprivation that had been reported in past studies to increase dramatically the probability of adverse outcome for the child (Rutter, Cox et al., 1975; Rutter, Yule et al., 1975; Shaw and Emery, 1988; Blanz, Schmidt, and Esser, 1991; Sanson et al., 1991). In a recent study, family stress was shown to increase the likelihood of insecure infant attachment (Shaw and Vondra, 1993). Our indicators included single-parent families residing separately, overcrowding, paternal unemployment, chronic or acute life-threatening illness of father or mother, parental criminality, psychiatric illness of the parents, major illness in childhood, prolonged separation from parents before the age of 11, and boarding school before the age of 11. Previous studies indicated that such stressors were cumulative (see Rutter, Cox et al., 1975; Rutter, Yule et al., 1975), and thus we divided our sample into those who had reported significant experience of social stress and deprivation (more than two items) and those who had not. Our prediction, on the basis of Main's hypothesis, was that mothers in the highly stressed, deprived group would be far more likely to have children securely attached to them if their reflective self-rating (metacognitive capacity) was high.

Ten out of 10 of the mothers in the highly stressed, deprived group with high reflective self-ratings had children who were secure with them, whereas only 1 out of 17 of highly stressed, deprived mothers with low ratings did so. Reflective-self function seemed to be a far less important predictor for the nondeprived group. This difference is statistically reliable. When mother's history of deprivation and reflective-self function are simultaneously introduced as predictors of infant security, the three-way interaction remains significant in the hierarchical log-linear analysis (p < .001). These results confirm the prediction that the capacity to reflect on ideas related to attachment serves a protective, resilience-enhancing function, reducing the likelihood of intergenerational transmission of insecurity.

Metacognitive monitoring completes one aspect of the intergenerational cycle (see Figure 3). Not only are parents who are high in reflective capacity more likely to promote secure attachment in the child, notwithstanding adverse experience, but also secure attachment may be a key precursor of robust reflective capacity. Main (1991) provided preliminary data on the association between secure attachment in infancy and efficient metacognitive monitoring in six-

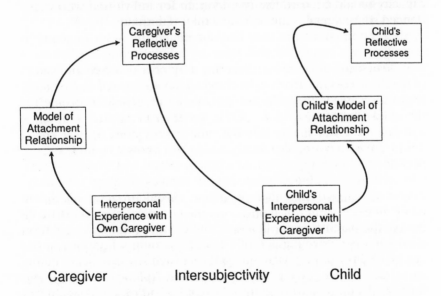

Caregiver   Intersubjectivity   Child

Figure 3 The Role of Reflective Processes in the Intergenerational Transmission of Attachment

and ten-year-old children. In a pilot investigation, we have observed the relationship between attachment security in three- to four-year-olds measured by separation-anxiety test (SAT) and measures of the child's theory of mind that were independent of verbal IQ and general sociability measured on the Vineland. Also in London, we are in the process of collecting cross-sectional data from three- to five-year-olds that appear to indicate a strong correlation between secure attachment in the parents (AAI) and in the child (Strange Situation) and the early development of a theory of mind; we use a task that requires the child to recognize that the other's behavior may be determined by an inaccurate perception (false belief task). We are also in the process of collecting longitudinal data to test the hypothesis that children who were securely attached at one year will be developmentally advanced in the acquisition of first- and second-order theory of mind (an appreciation of the influence of others' beliefs and of the influence of others' beliefs about beliefs, respectively). Throughout these studies we assume that a secure attachment relationship provides a congenial context, a "secure base" (Bowlby, 1969) for the child to explore the mind of the caregiver and that only through getting to know the mind of the other can the child develop full appreciation of the nature of mental states (Hegel, 1807; Wittgenstein, 1953, 1969; Davidson, 1983; Cavell, 1988, 1991). The process is intersubjective: the child gets to know the caregiver's mind as the caregiver endeavors to understand and contain the mental state of the child. To quote Hegel's (1807) elegant statement of this general principle:

> Self-consciousness exists in and for itself when, and by the fact that, it so exists for another; that is, it exists only in being acknowledged. This has a twofold significance: first, it (the self) has lost itself, for it finds itself as an other being; secondly, in doing so it has superseded the other, for it does not see the other as an essential being, but in the other sees its own self [p. 111].

Our acceptance of a dialectical perspective of self-development shifts the traditional psychoanalytic emphasis from internalization of the containing object to the internalization of the thinking self from within the containing object (see Figure 4). Traditionally, psychoanalytic theories assume that the child internalizes the image of the caregiver who is capable of emotional containment. Through this internalisation, given adequate capacities within the caregiver, the child will acquire a self-structure capable of containing conflict and distress.

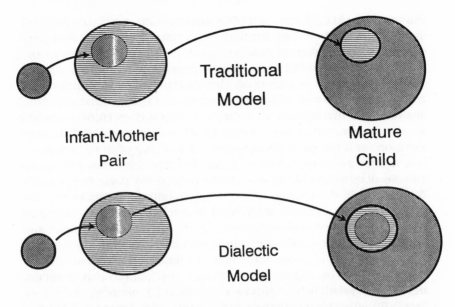

Figure 4 Traditional Object Relations Model and Dialectical Model of the Formation of the Soothing/Containing Object.

The traditional model assumes that the sensitive caregiver is internalized to provide internal control of affect; by contrast, the dialectic model assumes that the caregiver's image of the intentional infant comes to be internalized and to constitute the core of the child's mentalizing self.

Our view is somewhat different and is illustrated in Figure 4. The child not only perceives in the caregiver's behavior her mentalizing stance, which he has to assume in order to account for her behavior, but, in particular, perceives the caregiver's stance vis-à-vis an image of him as mentalizing, desiring, and believing. This representation is internalized. If the caregiver's reflective capacity enables her accurately to picture the infant's intentional stance, the infant has the opportunity to "find himself in the other" as a mentalizing individual. If the caregiver's capacity is lacking in this regard, the version of itself that the infant encounters is an individual conceived of as thinking in terms of physical reality rather than mental states. If the child finds no alternative interpersonal context where he is conceived of as mentalizing, his potential in this regard will not be fulfilled. In cases of an abusive, hostile, or simply totally vacuous relationship with the caregiver, the infant may deliberately turn away from the mentalizing object because the contemplation of the object's mind is overwhelming, as it harbors frankly hostile or dangerously indifferent intentions toward the self. This may lead to a widespread disavowal of mental states by the child that further reduces the chance of identifying and establishing intimate links with an understanding object.

To summarize, we assume that the quality of the infant's attachment to the parent is intrinsically linked to two factors both present and measurable before the birth of the child: (1) the parent's internal working model; and (2) the parent's capacity to reflect on the current mental state of the child and to reflect on, and exert control over, his or her own expectations of relationships as these influence his or her behavior toward the child. Both these aspects of the parental mental world can be operationalized and assessed using the AAI, the former primarily through attachment classification, the latter in terms of the manifestations of the parent's ability to reflect on mental states in self and other in the context of her or his own attachment relationships. The child is likely to be securely attached if *either* the parent's internal model of relationships is benign, dominated by favorable experiences, *or* if the parent's reflective function is of sufficient quality to forestall the activation of working models based on adverse experiences inappropriate to the current state of the relationship of child and caregiver.

Secure attachment experiences create a favorable context for the acquisition of the sociocognitive capacity that has been operationalized in developmental research as the "theory of mind," the mental operations that we believe underpin mentalizing, metacognitive monitoring, or the reflective self-function. As studies of resilient children suggest, even a single secure/understanding relationship may be sufficient for the development of reflective processes. Metacognitive monitoring is biologically prepared and spontaneously emerges unless its development is inhibited by the dual disadvantage of the absence of a safe relationship and the experience of maltreatment in the context of an intimate relationship. We do not anticipate that trauma outside the context of an attachment bond would have pervasive inhibitory effects on mentalizing. Because the theory of mind and reflective self-function evolve in the context of intense interpersonal relationships, the fear of the mind of another can have devastating consequences on the emergence of social understanding. To illustrate the clinical relevance of this model, it may be helpful to consider borderline personality disorder from the point of view of attachment theory.

BORDERLINE PERSONALITY DISORDER AND ATTACHMENT

The borderline patient provides the testing ground for much modern psychoanalytic theory and, in that sense, is probably the paradigmatic patient of our time. Although the breadth of psychiatric problems to be diagnosed as borderline remains controversial (Rutter, 1987; Zanarini et al., 1990; Tyrer et al., 1990; see Higgitt and Fonagy, 1993, for a review), it is generally agreed that somewhere between 15% and 20% of patients seen in the average clinical practice would be included in this group (Gunderson and Zanarini, 1987). To those working with borderline patients, two in ten may seem an underestimate, as it does not capture the impact of these difficult patients on the therapist's life and work. It takes but one patient with severe borderline pathology to shatter the equilibrium of the therapist's life with unending demands for "special" treatment, round-the-clock availability, physical and sometimes sexual contact, perfect attunement, heroic efforts to prevent self-injury or suicide, and all the therapist's efforts are repaid only by contempt, reproach, hostility, and, at times, outright physical attack.

Kernberg (1967, 1975, 1976, 1984) conceives of borderline personality organization in terms of *level of psychic functioning*. In this respect he continues Melanie Klein's and Herbert Rosenfeld's emphasis on personality organization (see Spillius, 1988). The borderline personality organization, according to Kernberg, includes: (1) nonspecific manifestations of ego weakness reflecting (2) the predominance of developmentally less mature psychological defenses such as splitting, projection, and projective identification, leading to (3) identity diffusion and the related specific pathology of internal object relations, such that mental representations of important others are fragmented and strongly charged as either good or bad. Thus, Kernberg's concept of the borderline includes a range of personality disorders such as infantile personalities, narcissistic personalities, antisocial personalities, as-if personalities, and schizoid personalities.

Gunderson (1984) offered a useful set of specific criteria to limit further the range of individuals diagnosed with this personality disorder; these criteria include impulsivity, low achievement, heightened affectivity, manipulative suicide attempts, mild psychotic experiences, and disturbed interpersonal relations.

Perhaps the most frequently noted characteristic of individuals considered borderline is an impairment of attachment relationships (intrapsychic as well as external), identified within and outside the therapeutic relationship. The attachment relationships they evince appear fundamentally disordered, short-lived, chaotic yet extremely intense. They do make attachment bonds, including a strong relationship with their therapist, yet the attachment is never without problems, discord, complaint, disarray, destruction, and damage. They manifest an interpersonal hypersensitivity that leads to dramatic alterations in their relationships, a fragmentation of their sense of identity, an overwhelming affective response, and mental disorganization. These features are particularly evident in the transference. Their submissiveness can suddenly turn to disparagement and rage of remarkable intensity. The trigger may be the mildest criticism or the slightest rebuff in the face of what appear to the therapist to be unreasonable demands for understanding or gratification.

THE ASSOCIATION OF ATTACHMENT STATUS AND BORDERLINE STATES

The Adult Attachment Interview has been helpful to us in our attempts to explore the intergenerational nature and origins of borderline personality disorder and its association with experiences of childhood maltreatment. In an ongoing study, we administered AAIs to a sample of 85 consecutively admitted nonpsychotic inpatients at the Cassell Hospital in London, which is run along the principles of a psychoanalytic therapeutic community. About 40% of the patients met DSM III-R criteria for borderline personality disorder (BPD) on the basis of a structured interview (SCID-II). Thirty-three percent met Gunderson's criteria for BPD on the basis of assessments using the Diagnostic Interview for Borderlines (DIBS).

The distribution of AAI classifications, arrived at totally independently of the diagnostic process, did not distinguish borderline personality disorder (BPD) from other DSM III-R personality disorder (Axis II) diagnoses, although the number of entangled (particularly E3) classifications was above the expected number. A previous study by Peter Hobson and colleagues (Patrick et al., 1992), which contrasted 12 dysthymic patients with 12 BPD individuals, found that all patients in the latter group fell into the E3 category.

Borderline patients' interviews were, however, differentiated by a combination of three characteristics: (1) higher prevalence of sexual abuse reported in the AAI narratives (92% versus 40%), (2) significantly lower ratings on the reflective self-function scale ($\bar{x}_{BPD}$ = 2.3 versus $\bar{x}_{Non-BPD}$ = 4.1), and (3) a significantly higher rating on the lack of resolution of abuse, but not loss, scale of the AAI ($\bar{x}_{BPD}$ = 5.2 versus $\bar{x}_{Non-BPD}$ = 2.8).

These findings are consistent with our assumption that individuals with experience of severe maltreatment in childhood who respond to this experience by an inhibition of reflective self-function are less likely to resolve this abuse, and are more likely to manifest borderline psychopathology (see Figure 5).

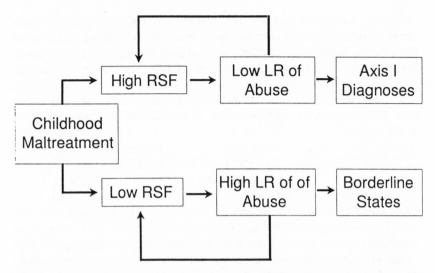

Figure 5 A Hypothetical Model of the Relationship of Childhood Maltreatment and Borderline States.

RSF = reflective self-function; LR = lack of resolution.

Childhood maltreatment may or may not have long-term sequelae, and the determinants of the outcome are only partially understood (Brown and Finklehor, 1986; Cahill, Llewelyn, and Pearson, 1991; Dewberry and Ussher, in press). Here we propose that if children are maltreated but have access to a meaningful attachment relationship that provides the intersubjective basis for the development of mentalizing capacity, they will be able to resolve (work through) their experience, and its outcome will not be one of severe personality disorder. We do not expect that their reflective processes will protect them from episodic psychiatric disorder, such as depression, and epidemiological data suggest that victims of childhood maltreatment are at an elevated risk for many forms of Axis-I disorder (e.g. Mullen et al., 1988; Burnham et al., 1988; Palmer et al., 1993).

If, however, the maltreated child has no social support of sufficient strength and intensity for an attachment bond to develop that could provide the context for the acquisition of a reliable capacity to envisage the psychological state of the other, even in intense interpersonal relationships, then the experience of abuse will not be reflected on or resolved. Naturally, the unresolved experience of abuse diminishes the likelihood of meaningful relationships, which, in a self-perpetuating way, further reduces the likelihood of a satisfactory resolution of the disturbing experience through the emergence of reflective processes. In fact, a pattern may be established whereby suspicion and distrust generalize and lead to a turning away from the mental state of important objects and thence to an apparent "decoupling" of the "mentalizing module," and ultimately the person is left bereft of a meaningful inner experience of human contact. This may account for the "neediness" of borderline personality individuals. Yet, as soon as they become involved with an other, the malfunctioning of their disavowed mentalizing capacity leads them into terrifying interpersonal confusion and chaos. Within intense relationships, their inadequate mentalizing function rapidly fails them; they regress to the earliest stages in the intersubjective development of mental representations, and they are no longer able to differentiate clearly their own mental representations from those of others and both of these from actuality. These processes combine and interact, leaving the individual terrorized by his or her own thoughts about the other experienced *in the other*, particularly their aggressive impulses and fantasies. The interpersonal complications rapidly become crippling, and, most commonly, borderline individuals reject or arrange to be rejected by their object. In treatment, their relation to their therapist reflects this fragmentation, and their transference may be appropriately described as "transitional-object transferences" (Modell, 1984). Psychotherapy can break the vicious cycle by providing a reinforcement for their strained reflective capacity, but this is not the only route to remission. Michel Stone's (1990) follow-up studies of borderline patients remind us that a significant proportion of these patients improve substantially in later life if and when they find themselves in an attachment relationship with an understanding other (Fonagy, 1994).

A TRANSGENERATIONAL MODEL OF
BORDERLINE PERSONALITY DISORDER

Although accurate figures are hard to come by and vary across studies, considerable evidence has accumulated to support the contention that child abuse is transmitted across generations. Oliver (1993), in his recent review of 60 studies, mainly from the United States and the United Kingdom, concludes that approximately one-third of child victims of abuse grow up to continue a pattern of seriously inept, neglectful, or abusive child rearing as parents. A further third are at risk of becoming abusive when exposed to intense psychosocial stress, but the remainder are resilient and appear to escape the repetition of this pattern (e.g., Wright and Lunn, 1971; Oliver, 1985, 1988). Poor parental care plays a major role in the etiology of severe emotional disorder (see Sheldrick, 1991; Birtchnell, 1993). This has been shown in both hospital and community samples in the United States (Burnham et al., 1988) and the United Kingdom and elsewhere (Mullen et al., 1988; Palmer et al., 1993). Research has documented that a specific link exists between the history of childhood maltreatment and borderline personality disorder (e.g., Herman, 1986; Herman, Perry, and Kolk, 1989); sexual abuse is especially implicated (e.g., Westen et al., 1990; Stone, 1992; Paris and Zweig-Frank, 1992). In brief, as infants and children, borderline individuals frequently have caretakers who are themselves within the so-called borderline spectrum of severely personality-disordered individuals. The social inheritance aspect of BPD may be an important clue to our understanding of the disorder.

George Moran, ex-director of the Anna Freud Centre, and Peter Fonagy have put forward an attachment theory formulation of severe narcissistic and borderline states based on epidemiological findings of the association of severe personality disorder and a history of childhood maltreatment and sexual abuse (Fonagy, 1989, 1991; Fonagy and Higgitt, 1989; Fonagy and Moran, 1991). We propose that borderline individuals are those victims of childhood (sexual) abuse who coped by refusing to conceive of the contents of their caregiver's mind and thus successfully avoided having to think about their caregiver's wish to harm them. They go on defensively to disrupt their own metacognitive monitoring processes in all subsequent intimate relationships. They unconsciously, but deliberately, limit their capacity to depict feelings and thoughts in themselves and in others.

The parents' abuse undermines the child's theory of mind, so that it is no longer safe for the child, for example, to think about wishing, if this implies the contemplation of the all too real wishes of the parent to harm the child. The secondary representation of mental events may thus become permanently inhibited. Such inhibition may turn out to have substantial benefits for the individual because it enables him to circumvent intolerable psychic pain. Individuals whose primary objects are unloving and cruel may find the contemplation of the contents of the mind of the object unbearable. Overwhelmed by intolerable aggression from within and without, the individual desperately seeks comfort in a regressive fusion with the object, "a rescuing parent" who, however, is also, in reality or in phantasy, the mental vehicle of his sadistic wishes and all too often in reality the actual instigator of his torment (Shengold, 1985). The abandonment of the capacity for secondary representation thus becomes an adaptive, if extreme, measure, enforcing a vital separation [Fonagy, 1991, pp. 650–651].

This restriction of capacity leaves them to operate on inaccurate and schematic impressions of thoughts and feelings, and they are thus immensely vulnerable in all intimate relationships.[5]

Many of the symptoms of BPD individuals may be understood in terms of a defensive strategy of disabling mentalizing or metacognitive capacity.

1. Their failure to take into consideration the listener's current mental state makes their associations hard to follow.
2. Their desperate dependence may reflect their difficulty in retaining a representation of their therapist as a thinking caregiver, as opposed to just a physical figure. They therefore depend on his or her physical presence to be able to keep them in mind as a mentalizing object.
3. The absence of concern for the other, which may manifest as extreme violence and cruelty, arises because of the lack of a compelling representation of suffering in the mind of the other. A key moderator of aggression is therefore absent. The lack of reflective capacity, in conjunction with a hostile worldview, may predispose individuals to child maltreatment.
4. Their fragile sense of self or identity diffusion, to use Kernberg's (1984) term for borderline patients, may be a consequence of their failure to represent their own feelings, beliefs, and desires with sufficient clarity to provide them with a core sense of themselves as a functioning mental entity. This leaves them with overwhelming fears of mental disintegration and a desperately fragile sense of self (Kernberg, 1975; Giovacchini, 1979; Searles, 1987).
5. Such a patient's mental image of the object remains at the immediate, context-dependent level of primary representations. He or she needs the object to stay as it is and experiences substantial difficulties when confronted with change.
6. An "as if" quality is not prominent in the transference. Genuine transference requires metarepresentations, the capacity to entertain a belief while, at the same time, knowing it to be

---

[5] Although our theory focuses on BPD, the defensive strategy of disrupted metacognitive monitoring may be observed in a wide range of severe psychopathology. In paranoid states, for example, the faulty capacity to mentalize leads to an overactivity of the reflective function; there is no check on the accuracy of mental state attributions, and the patient is in a perpetual state of terror because of his beliefs about others' beliefs. In affective disorder, individuals' capacity to monitor their own mental states may be dysfunctional. John Kerr (personal communication, 1994) has pointed to the tendency in some of these patients to avoid mentalizing their affect because these are felt to be either overwhelming and humiliating or potentially disruptive of important attachment relationships.

false. Psychotherapy requires such pretense, and its absence manifests as so-called "acting out" of the transference.

Broadly speaking, we believe that the widespread failure of "symbolization" in borderline individuals and their predilection for "concrete thinking" noted by British Kleinian psychoanalysts (Segal, 1957; Bion, 1962, 1963, 1965, 1967a) derive from their incapacity to appreciate that ideas merely "represent" external reality. We are in agreement with the basic formulation that this massive defensive structure arises as a consequence of the caregiver's failure to "contain" the primitive and overwhelming feelings of the infant by accepting (recognizing and reflecting on) the infant's emotional communications. The latter are "reasonably calculated to arouse in the mother feelings of which the infant wishes to be rid" (Bion, 1962). As we have seen, capable caregivers are likely to experience and transform these feelings into a tolerable form that probably combines mirroring of intolerable affect in combination with emotional signals indicating that the affect is "contained," that is, is under control (Bion's "alpha function"). The infant can then cope with, accept, and reinternalize what was projected, thus creating a representation of these emotional moments of interaction with the caregiver as tolerable in place of original experiences that were not. The nonverbal nature of this process implies that physical proximity of the caregiver is essential for this. This is perhaps the sociobiological root of the infant's need for proximity to the psychological caregiver, the adult mind. It is also the basis of vulnerability to adults who are incapable of understanding through experience and therefore provide inhumane care.

ATTACHMENT CLASSIFICATION AND THE OUTCOME OF PSYCHOTHERAPY

In the Cassell Hospital study, we were able to assess the outcome of one year's intensive inpatient psychotherapy. Although psychotherapy is not the sole component of the treatment offered, it is regarded by both patients and staff as its critical component. At the current stage of our analysis of the data, we can speak of the outcome of only 35 of the 85 patients, yet several important findings have already emerged.

A significant minority (40%) of the patients were assigned secure-autonomous classification on discharge, whereas all their initial classifications were "insecure." The increase in the proportion of secure classifications is already statistically highly significant $(\chi^2 = 11.8, df = 2, p < .001)$.

When individual scale ratings were examined, ratings of the experiences described by these individuals on admission and discharge did not shift significantly between the two times of testing. Interestingly, there was a slight tendency for childhood experience to be rated in follow-up interview as somewhat less loving and more characterized by neglect and rejection than in the intake Adult Attachment Interviews. This difference is unlikely to become significant because of the floor and ceiling effects (many of the patients' backgrounds were very extreme); however, the frequency of attachment histories that gave a bland or idealized picture of parents appeared to have been reduced during their treatment (Hotelling's $T = .48$, $df = 4.32$, $p < .01$). A pattern of pervasive memory blockages was more characteristic of intake interviews than of AAIs on discharge. This pattern of repression, splitting, and idealization is highly characteristic of the presentation of adults who were abused as children and who go on to abuse in their caregiving capacity (see Hunter and Kilstrom, 1979; Egeland, Jacobovitz, and Papatola, 1987; Egeland, Jacobovitz, and Sroufe, 1988).

In attempting to predict the outcome of treatment, we have already obtained some indication that the Adult Attachment Interview may be able to make a unique contribution to identifying individuals who are most likely to benefit from psychoanalytic psychotherapy. Thus far, we are unable to predict outcome on the basis of either Axis I or Axis II diagnoses, initial ratings of severity based on a symptom checklist (SCL-90), or a rating of general social adaptation (GAS). Nonetheless, a median split separating those most improved from those least improved finds somewhat more detached/dismissing individuals in the group manifesting greater improvements ($\chi^2 = 3.6$, $df = 2$, $p < .05$).

The AAI may be even more useful in identifying those who are likely to drop out early from treatment. In another study, comparing the effectiveness of intensive and nonintensive psychoanalytic treatment for a group of severely personality-disordered young adults, we used the Adult Attachment Interview as one of our important predictors of outcome (Fonagy and Tallandini, 1993). Although the sample size is small, we have been fascinated to note that patients who prematurely dropped out of treatment were all from the preoccupied-entangled group, in particular, the passive subcategory (E2). These interviewees were quite confused, lacking in objectivity, and preoccupied with past relationships; their responses were characterized by passivity, fearfulness, and a *vague, inchoate negativity*. There was an absence of the structure that would have been provided by anger—an indication that the struggle for autonomy had been particularly limited.

The interview in one patient's case particularly clearly prefigured the patient's premature departure from analysis. In the treatment she was unwilling to represent her male analyst as a transference object and dreaded the possibility of the sexualization of her relationship with him. The patient's AAI interview identified a lack of internal structure in the narrative. This may link to the patient's sense that her mental structure would not be able to withstand analytic scrutiny. The patient's negativity manifested most frequently in the treatment as an indulgence in reverie states and derealization; these states nonetheless may have served as self-structuring experiences that were profoundly threatened by the regressive pull of the psychoanalytic process.

The response to treatment matched her interview, which was particularly characterized by the tendency to seem lost in thought, with unfinished questions, flatness of affect, and dependence on the interviewer to retrieve her concentration, which was then readily lost again. It is tempting, but perhaps premature, to conclude that the E2 classification points to a fragility of the self-structure that makes patients in this group poor candidates for a treatment primarily based in self-reflection.

The extent of symptomatic improvement in psychodynamic treatment was associated with the improvement of reflective self-function (metacognitive monitoring). Clinical psychoanalysis inevitably deals with individuals whose past experience has left them vulnerable to current stress and the repetition of adverse early experiences. The treatment imposes a nonpragmatic elaborative, mentalistic stance. This enhances the development of reflective self-function and may, in the long run, enhance the psychic resilience of individuals in a generic way and provide them with improved control over their system of representation of relationships. The development of this function equips them with a kind of self-righting capacity in which, through being able to operate on their internal working models, the latter can become an object of review and change. Such gradual and constant adjustments and readjustments facilitate the development of an internal world where the behavior of others may be experienced as understandable, meaningful, predictable, and characteristically human. This reduces the need for splitting of frightening and incoherent mental representations, and new experiences of other minds can more readily be integrated into the framework of past relationship representations.

Psychotherapy maintains a rigorous focus on the mental world of self and other through clarifications and interpretations, as well as through the experience of the therapist's mind as a "secure base" (Bowlby, 1988). This enhances metacognitive control and makes the entire attachment system more available for adaptation. Ultimately, the patient in treatment comes to experience his or her mind as a secure base from which self-understanding emanates.

DIFFICULTIES IN BREAKING THE CYCLE OF ABUSE, OR "THERE IS SAFETY IN EVERY CHILD–CAREGIVER RELATIONSHIP"

We would not want to minimize the enormous difficulties facing this clinical population and any sample of adults who experienced significant abuse during their childhood if they seek to foster a secure attachment in their children. Resistance to change is powerful and may be better understood in light of modern psychoanalytic theory. Specifically, clinical experience indicates that safety does not arise only out of relationships that are characterized by availability and responsiveness of the caregiver (see also Sandler, 1960, 1985). Some individuals seem to feel safest when re-creating an early, but familiar, experience of being neglected and overlooked and repeatedly manipulate interpersonal situations to achieve this. Such apparently insecure patterns of relationships counterintuitively seem to be able to generate an internal sense of security.

The apparent paradox is resolved if we assume that attachment occurs to mental representations of the other (i.e., as we wish or believe them to be, not how they actually are) and that the experience of being appropriately responded to (i.e., understood by the caregiver) lies at the root of the phenomenon of attachment (Bowlby, 1969, 1973). Human understanding, as we have seen, at least in the early years, presumes physical proximity. Attachment to neglecting or abusive figures is the expectable response of the child whose experience of security arises out of the sense of being understood by a cruel and destructive caregiver, who, in reality, may show very little human understanding. The need to be "recognized" and "understood" is, of course, greatest when the individual's fragile sense of self is under direct threat from the perpetrators of abuse. The subjective moment of understanding may be one in which the child masochistically submits to the caregiver's groundless attacks or criticisms and internalizes the blame. He or she feels profound guilt and becomes deeply attached to the persecutor as the only path to a sense of security achieved through the experience of being understood by an understanding other, that is, understanding that submitting to the caregiver is the safest "way-of-being-with" the parents.

Similar considerations may also underpin the use of elaborate strategies such as provocative or sadomasochistic behaviors that have the goal of maintaining a familiar relationship system through which the individual can achieve subjective closeness (union) to the maltreating caregiver. The biological need to feel understood, even if only in fantasy, takes precedence over almost all other goals, sometimes even the survival motive itself. In this way, the need for relatedness to a caregiver and the corollary psychological wish to be perceived as a mental entity may be severely constrained, available solely through the re-creation of relationships marked by inequity, persecution, and malevolence. The normal processes of development malfunction for the abused child and unremittingly compel him to seek closeness through violence or suffering.

CONCLUSION

To sum up the complex model we propose: first, we assume that the quality of the infant's attachment to the specific parent is intrinsically linked to two prenatal factors: (1) the parent's predominant internal representation of relationships and (2) the parent's capacity to reflect on the current mental state of the child. The cognitive underpinning of the latter aspect of emotional development may be operationalized as the parent's having a theory of the child's mind. A robust theory enables the caregiver to "contain" (reflect and cope with) the child's unmanageable affects and limits the extent to which the child needs to protect himself or herself from the psychological presence of the caregiver. Insecure attachments are formed when the infant is forced habitually to employ defensive behaviors to afford herself or himself protection from a caregiver with an insufficient grasp of the child's mental state. In such cases the caregiver confronts the child with his or her own habitual defenses, which the child then internalizes. The child is likely to be securely attached if (1) the parent's internal model of relationships is benign, dominated by favorable experiences, *or* (2) if the parent's reflective function is of sufficient quality to prevent the activation of internal working models based on adverse experiences inappropriate to the child's mental state and to the current state of the relationship between child and caregiver.

Second, secure attachment experiences create a favorable context for the acquisition of a "theory of mind," the sociocognitive capacity that we believe underpins reflective self-function. Even a single experience of a secure/understanding relationship may be sufficient for the development of reflective processes. Positive intimate life experiences, if sufficiently intense, are likely to be able to reverse this developmental anomaly in later childhood and probably even in adulthood. The intergenerational transmission of secure attachment patterns may, in part, be explained by the cultural transmission of reflective or mentalizing capacity. Secure parents high in reflective function provide better containment of the child's affect and engender security in the child and thus create a more stable basis for the child's development of mentalizing function, which, in turn, facilitates that individual's capacity to develop secure relationships with others, including his or her own child.

We are not suggesting that early experiences determine reflective capacity. There is probably no one pathway to borderline personality functioning, but weakness of reflective function may be a precondition for BPD. Trauma, usually repeated and unrelenting, is probably a necessary condition to the pervasive inhibition of mentalizing observed in such individuals. If the nature of experience changes from adverse to favorable at later stages, the inhibition of mentalizing may be lifted, and BPD will not develop. Longitudinal studies as well as psychopathological investigations confirm that adolescents and adults with BPD tend to have histories of unremitting negative experiences as well as isolated instances of trauma.

Limited mentalizing capacity may be seen as a cause as well as a consequence of traumatic experience. Lack of mentalizing capacity makes the young child developmentally vulnerable to mentally vacuous, or cruel treatment, as he or she is unable to create the distance between physical and mental experience that full appreciation of the appearance/reality distinction provides (Flavell et al., 1986). Observed thoughts and feelings are experienced as real, not merely as representations. The young child does not have the efficient control over internal representations of relationships to aid him or her in reconstruing social situations in safe and secure ways, even when the immediate danger has passed.

The abused child, evading the mental world, never acquires adequate metacontrol over the representational world of internal working models. Unhelpful models of relationship patterns emerge frequently, and the internal world of the child and adult comes to be dominated by negative affect. As a direct consequence, the world of people can become stripped of meaning and may remain profoundly bewildering and forbidding for the developing child. The individual's enhanced suspiciousness of human motives reinforces his or her strategy of forgoing mentalizing, thus further distorting the normal development of a reflective function. Caught in a vicious cycle of paranoid anxiety and exaggerated defensive maneuvers, the individual becomes inextricably entangled in an internal world dominated by dangerous, evil, and, above all, mindless objects. He or she has abnegated the very process that could extract him from his predicament, the capacity to reflect on mental states.

Psychotherapeutic treatment in general and psychoanalytic treatment in particular compel the patient's mind to attend to the mental state of a benevolent other, the therapist. The frequent and consistent interpretation of the mental state of both analyst and patient (i.e., the interpretation of the transference in the broadest sense) is then desirable, if not essential, if the inhibition on this aspect of mental function is to be lifted. Over a prolonged time period, diverse interpretations concerning the patient's perception of the analytic relationship would enable him or her to attempt to create a mental representation both of self and of the analyst as thinking and feeling. This could then form the core of a sense of self with a capacity to represent ideas and meanings and create the basis for the bond that ultimately permits independent existence.

As Tennessee Williams put it far more eloquently than we could:

> I don't ask for your pity
> But just your understanding—
> Not even that—no.
> Just for your recognition of me in you,
> And the enemy, time, in us all.
> —Tennessee Williams,
> *Sweet Bird of Youth*

REFERENCES

Ainsworth, M. D. S., Blehar, M. C., Waters, E. & Wall, S. (1978), *Patterns of Attachment*. Hillsdale, NJ: Lawrence Erlbaum Associates.

—— & Eichberg, C. (1991), Effects on infant–mother attachment of mother's unresolved loss of an attachment figure, or other traumatic experience. In: *Attachment across the Lifespan*, ed. C. Parkes, J. Stevenson-Hinde & P. Marris. London: Tavistock/Routledge, pp. 160–183.

Astington, J., Harris, P. & Olson, D. (1988), *Developing Theories of Mind*. New York: Cambridge University Press.

Bakermans-Kranenburg, M. J. & van IJzendoorn, M. H. (1993), A psychometric study of the Adult Attachment Interview: Stability and discriminant validity. *Devel. Psychol.*, 29:870–879.

Baron-Cohen, S. (1993), The development of a theory of mind: Where would we be without the intentional stance. In: *Developmental Principles and Clinical Issues in Psychology and Psychiatry*, ed. M. Rutter & D. Hay. Oxford: Blackwell.

—— Tager-Flusberg, H. & Cohen, D. J. ed. (1993), *Understanding Other Minds*. Oxford: Oxford University Press.

Belsky, J., Rovine, M. & Taylor, D. G. (1984), The Pennsylvania Infant and Family Development Project, III: The origins of individual differences in infant–mother attachment: Maternal and infant contributions. *Child Devel.*, 55:718–728.

Benoit, D. & Parker, K. (1994), Stability and transmission of attachment across three generations. *Child Devel.*, 65:1444–1456.

Bion, W. R. (1962), Learning from experience. In: *Seven Servants*. New York: Aronson, 1977.

—— (1963), *Elements of Psycho-Analysis*. London: Heinemann.

—— (1965), *Transformations*. London: Heinemann.

—— (1967a), *Second Thoughts*. London: Heinemann.

—— (1967b), A theory of thinking. In: *Second Thoughts*. London: Heinemann, pp. 110–119.

—— (1970), *Attention and Interpretation*. London: Tavistock.

Birtchnell, J. (1993), Does recollection of exposure to poor maternal care in childhood affect later ability to relate? *Brit. J. Psychiat.*, 62:335–344.

Blanz, B., Schmidt, M. H. & Esser, G. (1991), Familial adversities and child psychiatric disorders. *J. Child Psychol. Psychiat.*, 32:939–950.

Bowlby, J. (1969), *Attachment and Loss, Vol. 1*. New York: Basic Books.

—— (1973), *Attachment and Loss, Vol. 2: Separation*. London: Hogarth Press.

—— (1980), *Attachment and Loss, Vol. 3*. New York: Basic Books.

—— (1987), Attachment. In: *The Oxford Companion to the Mind*, ed. R. Gregory. Oxford: Oxford University Press, pp. 56–58.

—— (1988), *A Secure Base*. London: Routledge.

Braithwaite, R. L. & Gordon, E. W. (1991), *Success Against the Odds*. Washington, DC: Howard University Press.

Bretherton, I. (1985), Attachment theory: Retrospect and prospect. In: *Growing Points of Attachment Theory and Research*, ed. I. Bretherton & E. Waters. *Monographs of the Society for Research in Child Development*, Serial No. 209, Vol. 50, Nos. 1–2, pp. 3–35.

—— (1987), New perspectives on attachment relations: Security, communication and internal working models. In: *Handbook of Infant Development* (2nd ed.), ed. J. Osofsky. New York: Wiley, pp. 1061–1100.

—— (1990), Open communication and internal working models: Their role in attachment relationships. In: *Nebraska Symposium on Motivation: Vol. 36 Socioemotional Development*, ed. R. Thompson. Lincoln: University of Nebraska Press, pp. 57–113.

—— (1992), Internal working models: Cognitive and affective aspects of attachment representations. Presented at Rochester Symposium on Developmental Psychopathology, Rochester, NY.

—— Biringen, Z., Ridgeway, D., Maslin, C. & Sherman, M. (1989), Attachment: The parental perspective. *Infant Ment. Health J.*, 10:203–221.

—— McNew, S. & Beeghley-Smith, M. (1981), Early person knowledge as expressed in gestural and verbal communication: When do infants acquire a "theory of mind"? In: *Infant Social Cognition*, ed. M. E. Lamb & L. R. Sherrod. Hillsdale, NJ: Lawrence Erlbaum Associates, pp. 333–373.

Brown, A. & Finklehor, D. (1986), Impact of child sexual abuse: A review of the research. *Psychol. Bull.*, 99:66–77.

Brown, G. W., Harris, T. O. & Bifulco, A. (1986), Long-term effects of early loss of parent. In: *Depression in Young People*. ed. M. Rutter, C. E. Izard & P. B. Read. New York: Guilford Press.

Burnam, M. A., Stein, J., Golding, J. M., Siegel, L. M., Sorenson, S. B., Forsythe, A. B. & Tellus, C. A. (1988), Sexual assault and mental disorders in a community population. *J. Consult. Clin. Psychol.*, 56:843–850.

Bus, A. G. & van IJzendoorn, M. H. (1992), Patterns of attachment in frequently and infrequently reading mother–child dyads. *J. Genet. Psychol.*, 153:395–403.

Butterworth, G., Harris, P., Leslie, A. & Wellman, H. (1991), *Perspectives on the Child's Theory of Mind*. Oxford: Oxford University Press.

Cahill, C., Llewelyn, S. P. & Pearson, C. (1991), Long-term effects of sexual abuse which occurred in childhood: A review. *Brit. J. Clin. Psychol.*, 30:117–130.

Cavell, M. (1988), Interpretation, psychoanalysis and the philosophy of mind. *J. Amer. Psychoanal. Assn.*, 36:859–879.

—— (1991), The subject of mind. *Internat. J.Psycho-Anal.*, 72:141–154.

Cicchetti, D. (1990), An historical perspective on the discipline of developmental psychopathology. In: *Risk and Protective Factors in the Development of Psychopathology*, ed. J. Rolf, A. Masten, D. Cicchetti, K. Nuechterlein & S. Weintraub. New York: Cambridge University Press, pp. 2–28.

Cohen, D. A., Cowan, P. A., Cowan, C. P. & Pearson, J. (1992), Mother's and father's working models of childhood attachment relationships, parenting styles, and child behavior. *Devel. & Psychopathol.*, 4:417–431.

Cramer, B. & Stern, D. N. (1988), Evaluation of changes in mother–infant brief psychotherapy: A single case study. *Infant Ment. Health J.*, 9:20–45.

Crowell, J. A. & Feldman, S. S. (1988), Mothers' internal models of relationships and children's behavioral and developmental status: A study of mother–child interaction. *Child Devel.*, 59:1273–1285.

Crowell, J. A., O'Conner, E., Wollmers, G. & Sprafkin, J. (1991), Mothers' conceptualizations of parent–child relationships: Relation to mother–child interaction and child behavior problems. Special Issue: Attachment and developmental psychology. *Devel. & Psychopathol.*, 3:431–444.

Das-Eiden, R., Teti, D. M. & Corns, K. M. (1993), Maternal working models of attachment, marital adjustment, and the parent–child relationship. Presented at 60th Meeting of the Society for Research in Child Development, New Orleans.

Davidson, D. (1983), *Inquiries into Truth and Separation.* Oxford: Oxford University Press.

de Mulder, E. & Radke-Yarrow, M. (1991), Attachment and affectively ill and well mothers: Concurrent behavioral correlates. *Devel. & Psychopathol.* 3:227–242.

Dennett, D.C. (1978), *Brainstorms*, Cambridge, MA: MIT Press.

—— (1983), Styles of mental representation. In: *Proceedings of the Aristotelian Society*. London: Aristotelian Society, pp. 213–226.

Dewberry, C. & Ussher, J. M. (in press), A survey of the long-term effects of child sexual abuse on adult women. *Brit. J. Clin. Psychol.*

Dodge, K. (1991), The structure and function of reactive and proactive aggression. In: *The Development and Treatment of Childhood Aggression*, ed., D. Pepler & K. Rubin. Hillsdale, NJ: Lawrence Erlbaum Associates, pp. 201–218.

Edelson, G. M. (1987), *Neural Darwinism*. New York: Basic Books.

Egeland, B., Jacobovitz, D. & Papatola, K. (1987), Intergenerational continuity of child abuse. In: *Child Abuse and Neglect*, ed. J. Lancaster & R. Geiles. New York: Aldine De Gruyrer.

—— —— & Sroufe, L. A. (1988), Breaking the cycle of abuse. *Child Devel.*, 59:1080–1088.

Emde, R. N. (1988a), Development terminable and interminable. 1. Innate and motivational factors from infancy. *Internat. J. Psycho-Anal.*, 69:23–42.

—— (1988b), Development terminable and interminable 2. Recent psychoanalytic theory and therapeutic considerations. *Internat. J. Psycho-Anal.*, 69:283–286.

Flavell, J. H., Green, F. L. & Flavell, E. R. (1986), Development of knowledge about the appearance-reality distinction. *Monographs of the Society for Research in Child Development, Serial No. 212.*

Fónagy, I. & Fónagy, J. (1987), Analysis of complex (integrated) melodic patterns. In: *In Honour of Ilse Lehiste*, ed. R. Channon & L. Shockey. Dordrecht, The Netherlands: Foris, pp. 75–98.

Fonagy, P. (1989), On tolerating mental states: Theory of mind in borderline patients. *Bull. Anna Freud Centre*, 12:91–115.

—— (1991), Thinking about thinking: Some clinical and theoretical considerations in the treatment of a borderline patient. *Internat. J. Psycho-Anal.*, 72:1–18.

—— (1994a), Mental representations from an intergenerational cognitive science perspective. *Infant Ment. Health J.*, 15:57–68.

—— (1994b), Discussant of Michel Stone's paper "The Long-Term Follow-Up of Borderline Patients in Hospital and in Private Practice: Implications for Therapy." Presented at IPA Research Conference, London.

—— & Higgitt, A. (1989), A developmental perspective on borderline personality disorder. *Revue Internationale de Psychopathologie*, 1:125–159.

—— & Moran, G. S. (1991), Understanding psychic change in child analysis. *Internat. J. Psycho-Anal.*, 72:15–22.

—— Moran, G. S., Steele, M. & Steele, H. (1992), The integration of psychoanalytic theory and work on attachment: The issue of intergenerational psychic processes. In: *Attaccamento E Psiconalis*, ed. D. Stern & M. Ammaniti. Bari, Italy: Laterza pp. 19–30.

—— Moran, G. S. & Target, M. (1993), Aggression and the psychological self. *Internat. J. Psycho-Anal.*, 74:471–485.

—— Steele, M. & Steele, H. (1991), Maternal representations of attachment during pregnancy predict the organization of infant–mother attachment at one year of age. *Child Devel.*, 62:880–893.

—— —— —— Higgitt, A. & Target, M. (1994), The theory and practice of resilience. *J. Child Psychol. Psychiat.*, 35:231–257.

—— —— Moran, G., Steele, H. & Higgitt, A. C. (1991), The capacity for understanding mental states: The reflective self in parent and child and its significance for security of attachment. *Infant Ment. Health J.*, 13:200–216.

—— & Tallandini, M. (1993), On some problems of psychoanalytic research in practice. *Bull. Anna Freud Centre*, 16:5–22.

Fraiberg, S. (1980), *Clinical Studies in Infant Mental Health*. New York: Basic Books.

—— (1982), Pathological defenses in infancy. *Psychoanal. Quart.*, 51:612–635.

—— Adelson, E. & Shapiro, V. (1975), Ghosts in the nursery: A psychoanalytic approach to the problem of impaired infant–mother relationships. *J. Amer. Acad. Child Psychol.*, 14:387–422.

Freud, A. (1965), *Normality and Pathology in Childhood*. Harmondsworth, Eng.: Penguin Books.

Freud, S. (1940), An outline of psycho-analysis. *Standard Edition*, 23:137–207. London: Hogarth Press, 1964.

Frye, D. & Moore, C. (1991), *Children's Theories of Mind*. Hillsdale, NJ: Lawrence Erlbaum Associates.

George, C., Kaplan, N. & Main, M. (1985), *The Adult Attachment Interview*. Privileged communication. Dept. Psychology, University of California at Berkeley. (To appear in *Assessing Attachment Through Discourse, Drawings and Reunion Situations*, ed. M. Main & R. Goldwyn. New York: Cambridge University Press.)

Giovacchini, P. L. (1979), *Treatment of Primitive Mental States*. New York: Aronson.

Grossmann, K. Fremmer-Bombik, E., Rudolph, J. & Grossmann, K. E. (1988), Maternal attachment representations as related to patterns of infant–mother attachment and maternal care during the first year. In: *Relationships within Families*, ed. R. A. Hinde, & J. Stevenson-Hinde. Oxford: Oxford University Press, pp. 241–260.

—— Grossmann, K. E., Spangler, G., Suess, G. & Unzner, L. (1985), Maternal sensitivity and newborns' orientation responses as related to quality of attachment in northern Germany. In: *Growing Points of Attachment Theory and Research*, ed. I. Bretherton, & E. Waters. *Monographs of the Society for Research in Child Development*, Serial No. 209, Nos. 1–2 Vol. 50, pp. 233–256.

Gunderson, J. G. (1984), *Borderline Personality Disorder*. Washington, DC: American Psychiatric Press.

—— & Zanarini, M. C. (1987), Current overview of borderline diagnosis. *J. Clin. Psychiat.*, 48:5–11.

Haft, W. & Slade, A. (1989), Affect attunement and maternal attachment: A pilot study. *Infant Ment. Health J.*, 10:157–172.

Hegel, G. (1807), *The Phenomenology of Spirit*, trans. A. V. Miller. Oxford: Oxford University Press, 1977.

Herman, J. L. (1986), Histories of violence in an outpatient population. *Amer. J. Orthopsychiat.*, 56:137–141.

—— & —— (1993), Psychotherapy in borderline and narcissistic personality disorder. In: *Personality Disorder Reviewed*, ed. P. Tyrer & G. Stein. London: Gaskell, pp. 225–261.

—— Perry, C. & Kolk, B. (1989), Childhood trauma in borderline personality disorder. *Amer. J. Psychiat.*, 146:490–495.

Holmes, J. (1992), *Between Art and Science*. London: Routledge.

—— (1993), Attachment theory: A biological basis for psychotherapy? *Brit. J. Psychiat.*, 163:430–438.

Hunter, R. & Kilstrom, N. (1979), Breaking the cycle in abusive families. *Amer. J. Psychiat.*, 136:1320–1322.

James, W. (1890), *Principles of Psychology*. New York: Holt.

Kernberg, O. (1967), Borderline personality organization. *J. Amer. Psychoanal. Assn.*, 15:641–685.

—— (1975), *Borderline Conditions and Pathological Narcissism*. New York: Aronson.

—— (1976), *Object Relations Theory and Clinical Psychoanalysis*. New York: Aronson.

—— (1984), *Severe Personality Disorders*. New Haven, CT: Yale University Press.

Lebovici, S. & Weil-Halpern, F. (1989), *Psychopathologie du Bebe*. Paris: Presses Universitaires de France.

Main, M. (1991), Metacognitive knowledge, metacognitive monitoring, and singular (coherent) vs. multiple (incoherent) models of attachment: Findings and directions for future research. In: *Attachment across the Lifecycle*, ed. P. Harris, J. Stevenson-Hinde & C. Parkes. New York: Routledge, pp. 127–159.

—— & Goldwyn, R. (1991), Adult Attachment Classification System. Version 5. Unpublished manuscript, University of California, Berkeley.

—— & —— (1992), Interview-based adult attachment classifications: Related to infant–mother and infant–father attachment. *Devel. Psychol.*

—— & Hesse, E. (1990), Parents' unresolved traumatic experiences are related to infant disorganized attachment status: Is frightened and/or frightening parental behavior the linking mechanism? In: *Attachment in the Preschool Years*, ed. M. Greenberg, D. Cicchetti & E. M. Cummings. Chicago: University of Chicago Press, pp. 161–182.

—— Kaplan, N. & Cassidy, J. (1985), Security in infancy, childhood and adulthood: A move to the level of representation. In: *Growing Points of Attachment Theory and Research*, ed. I. Bretherton & E. Waters. *Monographs of the Society for Research in Child Development*, Serial No. 209, Vol. 50, Nos. 1–2, pp. 66–104.

—— & Solomon, J. (1986), Discovery of an insecure-disorganized/disoriented attachment pattern. In: *Affective Development in Infancy*, ed. T. B. Brazelton & M. W. Yogman. Norwood, NJ: Ablex, pp. 95–124.

Meltzoff, A. & Gopnik, N. (1993), The role of imitation in understanding persons and developing a theory of mind. In: *Understanding Other Minds*, ed. S. Baron-Cohen, H. Tager-Flusberg & D. Cohen. New York: Oxford University Press, pp. 335–366.

Modell, A. (1984), *Psychoanalysis in a New Context*. New York: International Universities Press.

Morton, J. & Frith, U. (1995), Causal modelling: A structural approach to developmental psychopathology. In: *Manual of Developmental Psychopathology*, ed. D. Cicchetti & D. J. Cohen. New York: Wiley. pp. 357–390.

Mullen, P. E., Romans-Clarkson, S. E., Walton, V. A., et al. (1988), Impact of sexual and physical abuse on women's mental health. *Lancet*, 1(8,590):841–845.

Oliver, J. E. (1985), Successive generations of child maltreatment: Social and medical disorders in the parents. *Brit. J. Psychiat.*, 3:484–490.

—— (1988), Successive generations of child maltreatment: The children. *Brit. J. Psychiat.*, 153:543–553.

—— (1993), Intergenerational transmission of child abuse: Rates, research, and clinical implications. *Amer. J. Psychiat.*, 150:1315–1324.

Palmer, R. L., Coleman, L., Chaloner, D., Oppenheimer, R. & Smith, J. (1993), Childhood sexual experiences with adults: A comparison of reports by women psychiatric patients and general-practice attenders. *Brit. J. Psychiat.*, 163:499–504.

Paris, J. & Zweig-Frank, H. (1992), A critical review of the role of childhood sexual abuse in the etiology of borderline personality disorder. *Canadian J. Psychiat.*, 37:125–128.

Patrick, M., Hobson, R. P., Castle, P., Howard, R. & Maughan, B. (1994), Personality disorder and the mental representation of early social experience. *Devel. Psychopathol.*, 94:375–388.

Premack, D. & Woodruff, G. (1978), Does the chimpanzee have a theory of mind? *Behav. Brain Sci.*, 4:515–526.

Quinton, D. & Rutter, M. (1988), *Preventing Breakdown.* Aldershot, Hants: Avebury.

Radojevic, M. (1992), Predicting quality of infant attachment to father at 15 months from pre-natal paternal representations of attachment: An Australian contribution. Presented at the 25th International Congress of Psychology, Brussels Belgium.

Rumelhart, D. E. & McClelland, J. L. [and the PDP Research Group] (1986), *Parallel Distributed Processing*, Vol. 1. Cambridge, MA: MIT Press.

Rutter, M. (1987), Psychosocial resilience and protective mechanisms. *Amer. J. Orthopsychiat.*, 57:316–331.

—— Cox, A., Tupling, C., Berger, M. & Yule, W. (1975), Attainment and adjustment in two geographical areas: 1. The prevalence of psychiatric disorder. *Brit. J. Psychiat.*, 126:493–509.

—— Yule, B., Quinton, D., Rowlands, O., Yule, W. & Berger, W. (1975), Attainment and adjustment in two geographical areas: 3. Some factors accounting for area differences. *Brit. J. Psychiat.*, 126:520–533.

Sandler, J. (1960), The background of safety. In: *From Safety to Superego*. London: Karnac, 1975, pp. 1–8.

—— (1985), Towards a reconsideration of the psychoanalytic theory of motivation. *Bull. Anna Freud Centre*, 8:223–243.

Sanson, A., Oberklaid, F., Pedlow, R. & Prior, M. (1991), Risk indicators: Assessment of infancy predictors of pre-school behavioral maladjustment. *J. Child Psychol. Psychiat.*, 32:609–626.

Searles, H. F. (1987), The development in the patient of an internalised image of the therapist. In: *The Borderline Patient, Vol. 2*, ed. J. S. Grotstein, M. F. Solomon & J. A. Lang. Hillsdale, NJ: The Analytic Press, pp. 25–40.

Segal, H. (1957), Notes on symbol formation. *Internat. J. Psycho-Anal.*, 38:391–397.

Shaw, D. S. & Emery, R. E. (1988), Chronic family adversity and school-age children's adjustment. *J. Amer. Acad. Child Adoles. Psychiat.*, 27:200–206.

—— & Vondra, J. I. (1993), Chronic family adversity and infant attachment security. *J. Child Psychol. Psychiat.*, 34:1205–1215.

Sheldrick, C. (1991), Adult seqealae of child sexual abuse. *Brit. J. Psychiat.*, 158:55–62.

Shengold, L. (1985), The effects of child abuse as seen in adults: George Orwell. *Psychoanal. Quart.*, 54:20–45.

Spillius, E. B. (1988), General Introduction. In: *Melanie Klein Today, Vol. 1*, ed. E. B. Spillius. London, Routledge. pp. 1–7.

Sroufe, L. (1989), Relationships and relationship disturbances. In: *Relationship Disturbances in Early Childhood*, ed. A. Sameroff & R. Emde. Hillsdale, NJ: Lawrence Erlbaum Associates, pp. 3–17.

—— & Fleeson, J. (1988), The coherence of family relationships. In: *Relationships within Families*, ed. R. A. Hinde & J. Stevenson-Hinde. Oxford: Clarendon Press, pp. 27–47.

Steele, H., Steele, M. & Fonagy, P. (in press), Associations among attachment classifications of mothers, fathers and their infants. *Child Devel.*

Steele, M., Steele, H. & Fonagy, P. (in prep. a), A snapshot of the internal working model of attachment: The factor structure of the Adult Attachment Interviews.

—— —— —— (in prep. b), A path-analytic model of determinants of infant–parent attachment: Limited rather than multiple pathways.

—— —— —— & Higgitt, A. (1992), Stability and change in maternal models of attachment across the transition to parenthood, and their association to the quality of the infant–mother attachment. Presented to the Eighth International Conference on Infant Studies.

Stern, D. N. (1985), *The Interpersonal World of the Child*. New York: Basic Books.

—— (1994), One way to build a clinically relevant baby. *Infant Ment. Health J.*, 15:9–25.

Stone, M. H. (1990), *The Fate of Borderline Patients*. New York: Guilford Press.

—— (1992), Incest, Freud's seduction theory, and borderline personality. *J. Amer. Acad. Psychoanal.*, 20:167–181.

Tyrer, P., Seivewright, N., Ferguson, B., Murphy, S., Darling, C., Brothwell, J., Kingdon, D. & Johnson, A. L. (1990), The Nottingham Study of Neurotic Disorder: Relationship between personality status and symptoms. *Psychol. Med.*, 20:423–431.

van IJzendoorn, M. (1994), Intergenerational transmission of attachment. State of the art in psychometric, psychological, and clinical research. Presented at the Clarke Conference on Attachment and Psychopathology, Toronto, Canada.

—— (1995), Adult attachment representations, parental responsiveness, and infant attachment: A meta-analysis on the predictive validity of the Adult Attachment Interview. *Psychol. Bull.*, 117:387–403.

—— Goldberg, S., Kroonenberg, P. M. & Frenkel, O. J. (1992), The relative effects of maternal and child problems on the quality of attachment: A meta-analysis of attachment in clinical samples. *Child Devel.*, 59:147–156.

—— Kranenburg, M. D., Zwart-Wordstra, H. A., Van Busschbach, A. M. & Lambermon, M. W. E. (1991), Parental attachment and children's socio-emotional development: Some findings on the validity of the Adult Attachment Interview in the Netherlands. *Internat. J. Behav. Devel.*, 14:375–394.

Ward, M. J., Botyanski, N., Plunket, S. & Carlson, E. (1991), The concurrent and predictive validity of the Adult Attachment Interview for adolescent mothers. Presented at the meeting of the Society for Research in Child Development, Seattle.

—— & Carlson, E. A. (1995), Associations among Adult Attachment representations, maternal sensitivity, and infant-mother attachment in a sample of adolescent mothers. *Child Devel.*, 66:69–79.

Waters, E., Posada, G., Crowell, J. & Lay, K.-L. (1993), Is attachment theory ready to contribute to our understanding of disruptive behavior problems? *Devel. Psychopathol.*, 5:215–224.

Werner, E. E. (1989), Children of the garden island. *Sci. Amer.*, 106–111.

—— & Smith, R. S. (1982), *Vulnerable, But Invincible*. New York: McGraw-Hill.

Werner, H. (1948), *Comparative Psychology of Mental Development*. New York: International Universities Press.

Westen, D., Ludolph, P., Nisle, B., Ruffins, S. & Block, J. (1990), Physical and sexual abuse in adolescent girls with borderline personality disorder. *Amer. J. Orthopsychiat*, 60:55–66.

Whiten, A., ed. (1991), *Natural Theories of Mind*. Oxford: Blackwell.

Winnicott, D. W. (1956), Primary maternal preoccupation. In: *Collected Papers*. New York: Basic Books, 1958, pp. 300–305.

—— (1967), Mirror-role of the mother and family in child development. In: *The Predicament of the Family*, ed. P. Lomas. London: Hogarth Press, pp. 26–33.

—— (1971), *Playing and Reality*. London: Tavistock.

Wittgenstein, L. (1953), *Philosophical Investigations*. Oxford: Blackwell.

—— (1969), *The Blue and Brown Books*. Oxford: Blackwell.

Wright, C. H. & Lunn, J. E. (1971), Sheffield problem families: A follow-up study of their sons and daughters. *Community Med.*, Nov: 301–307; Dec.: 315–321.

Zanarini, M. C., Gunderson, J. G., Frankenburg, F. R. & Chauncey, D. L. (1990), Discriminating borderline personality disorder from other Axis II disorders. *Amer. J. Psychiat.*, 147:161–167.

✧ 10 ✧

Child Maltreatment and Attachment Organization

Implications for Intervention

DANTE CICCHETTI AND SHEREE L. TOTH

In recent years, John Bowlby's (1969–1982) attachment theory has had a major impact on efforts to provide a framework within which to conceptualize, treat, and understand the etiology and transmission of some forms of risk for developmental maladaptation and psychopathology. This is a fitting legacy for a theorist whose professional life course was influenced by volunteer work at a school for maladjusted children while formulating his career goals (Bretherton, 1992). Despite his training as an analyst and Melanie Klein's influence on his development, Bowlby held steadfastly to his belief in the importance of early family relationships for personality development. Although not as frequently recognized, he also emphasized the importance of societal support in fostering the bond between parent and child.

> Just as children are absolutely dependent on their parents for sustenance, so in all but the most primitive communities, are parents, especially their mothers, dependent on a greater society for economic provision. If a community values its children it must cherish their parents [Bowlby, 1951, p. 84].

The failure of society to achieve this requisite support for parents (Carnegie Corporation, 1994; Leach, 1994) has contributed to the

---

We acknowledge grants from the Prevention Research Branch of the National Institute of Mental Health (MH 45027) and the Spunk Fund, Inc. for support of this work. We thank the children and families who have helped us to formulate our views on intervention. We also have benefited from our discussions with colleagues and interns at Mt. Hope Family Center. We appreciate Jeanne Ledtke's assistance with manuscript preparation. Although therapy vignettes are based on actual clinical cases, all names and identifying information have been changed to protect confidentiality.

reality addressed by the current chapter, namely, child maltreatment and its assault on development. Bowlby himself clearly recognized the existence of harsh parenting and addressed its implications for theory and intervention. Specifically, he tried to explain why a child would form a bond to a maltreating parent and how the relationship with a maltreating parent might differ from that formed with a more nurturing parent. Of note was Bowlby's emphasis on psychological unavailability rather than the presence of more concrete economic, medical, or housing difficulties as the source of social problems (Bowlby, 1951). Bowlby also reported on the success of home-based interventions for young families and stated that "in a field that is both deeply troubling and notoriously difficult, these findings give hope" (Bowlby, 1988, p. 98). We believe that the legacy of John Bowlby can continue to guide intervention efforts and to combat the sequelae and perpetuation of child maltreatment.

HISTORICAL CONSIDERATIONS

Despite Bowlby's consistent exposition of the utility of attachment theory for contributing to the understanding of the varied pathways that lead to mental health and psychopathology, as well as for informing therapeutic interventions with a number of clinical disorders (Bowlby, 1977a, b, 1988), the influence of attachment theory on empirical work was initially restricted to nondisordered populations from middle socioeconomic backgrounds (Ainsworth and Wittig, 1969), to impoverished, nondisordered groups (Vaughn et al., 1979; Egeland and Farber, 1984); and to cross-cultural examination of attachment (Ainsworth, 1967; Grossman et al., 1985; Miyake, Chen, and Campos, 1985; Sagi et al., 1985). In fact, in his preface to *A Secure Base*, Bowlby (1988) stated that he found it somewhat "unexpected that, whereas attachment theory was formulated by a clinician for use in the diagnosis and treatment of emotionally disturbed patients and families, its usage . . . has been mainly to promote research in developmental psychology" (p. ix).

Fortunately, in the past decade, the field of developmental psychopathology (Cicchetti, 1984, 1993), with its focus on the interface between normal and atypical development, has fostered a return to Bowlby's original goals (Cicchetti et al., 1990; Cicchetti and Greenberg, 1991). Research on attachment, risk, and psychopathology has been evident in a range of clinical conditions, including Down syndrome (Cicchetti and Serafica, 1981; Thompson et al., 1985; Vaughn et al., 1994), autism (Capps, Sigman, and Mundy, 1994), substance abuse (O'Connor, Sigman, and Brill, 1987;

Rodning, Beckwith, and Howard, 1991), conduct disorder (Greenberg and Speltz, 1988), maternal depression (Radke-Yarrow et al., 1985; Lyons-Ruth et al., 1986), and bipolar disorder (Radke-Yarrow et al., 1985).

Not surprisingly, in view of the extreme disruption in caregiving that it entails, considerable attention has been directed toward attachment organization in children who have been maltreated. In this chapter we discuss research on child maltreatment and attachment within a developmental framework. We then examine implications of these findings for attachment-informed approaches to intervention at various periods of the life span.

ATTACHMENT AND CHILD MALTREATMENT

An Organizational Perspective on Development

Child maltreatment imposes serious risks on the developing child, not only during the period when maltreatment occurs, but across the life course. Even prior to the emergence of psychopathological conditions, deviations in the developmental process of maltreated children are present. An organizational perspective (Werner and Kaplan, 1963; Cicchetti and Sroufe, 1978) that conceptualizes development as a series of qualitative reorganizations among and within biological and behavioral systems can be utilized to understand the impact of maltreatment on development. As growth proceeds, reorganization occurs at many levels, including the biological, behavioral, psychological, environmental, and sociological. Within each domain, processes are in dynamic transaction. The resulting developmental reorganizations proceed in accord with the orthogenetic principle that the developing organism moves toward increased differentiation and hierarchic integration of domains (Werner and Kaplan, 1963; Sroufe and Rutter, 1984). Because this process involves the incorporation of earlier patterns of adaptation into successive reorganizations at subsequent periods in development, continuity of functioning can be maintained over time. Changes in the developmental course, however, are always possible as a function of new experiences and reorganizations. While this implies that development is not immutable, it is important to recognize that early competence facilitates future adaptation, while incompetence poses significant challenges to successful adjustment at later stages and may eventuate in psychopathological outcomes.

In this regard, the emergence of stage-salient tasks and their influence across the life span can be understood. Although specific tasks are of primary importance during circumscribed periods of development, their influence transcends their period of apogee as a result of the hierarchic integration and reorganization that occur. In the context of an "average expectable environment" (Hartmann, 1958) development proceeds adaptively among genetically normal individuals; however, because maltreatment involves serious failure of the caregiving environment, the child's ability to negotiate tasks of development successfully is severely challenged.

Due to the extreme relational dysfunction that occurs in maltreating families, we examine the attachment relationship, an important task during the period of infancy. Moreover, in accord with the organizational perspective, we consider the development of this early adaptational failure throughout the life course. We believe, along with many others, that attachment dysfunction exerts a substantial effect on the development of the psychopathological disorders and symptoms that have been associated with child maltreatment. We therefore review work in this area over the life course. Although, in studies of maltreatment, the mother is often named as the primary perpetrator of maltreatment, this information is not consistently specified in research investigations. Even when efforts are made to specify the perpetrator, often *both* parents or the biological mother *and* her significant other are involved in maltreatment. Therefore, current studies reviewed in this chapter do not allow for clear specification of the perpetrator, even though this information is important from an attachment theory perspective.

Infancy and Toddlerhood

In the 1980s, investigators began to study the attachment organization of maltreated infants and toddlers and utilized the Ainsworth and Wittig (1969) Strange Situation paradigm. While maltreated infants and toddlers were found to form attachments to their caregivers, approximately two-thirds were insecurely attached (Egeland and Sroufe, 1981; Schneider-Rosen & Cicchetti, 1984; Crittenden, 1985; Lamb, et al., 1985; Schneider-Rosen, et al., 1985). This contrasted markedly with the patterns of attachment in nonmaltreated comparisons, where approximately two-thirds of the infants and toddlers evidenced secure attachments (Youngblade and Belsky, 1989). Additionally, Schneider-Rosen et al. (1985) found that maltreated infants and toddlers with insecure attachments evidenced greater stability of attachment than did maltreated infants and toddlers with secure attachments. This finding differs from the conclusions reached by Lamb, et al. (1985), who found greater stability of secure, than of insecure, attachments in normal populations.

In addition to the increase of insecurity among maltreated infants and toddlers, researchers also detected patterns of behavior in maltreated samples that were not easily captured by the then-extant three-category attachment coding system. Specifically, maltreated infants and toddlers evidenced a mix of strategies: they appeared avoidant of their mother at some times and resistant or secure at others. Crittenden (1988) labeled this pattern A/C. Atypical behaviors such as stereotypies, stilling and freezing, and fear reactions in response to the caregiver were also noted. These unusual behaviors in the Strange Situation led to the identification of the disorganized-disoriented or Type D pattern (Main and Solomon, 1986, 1990). Main and Hesse (1990) also discussed the etiological role that the introjection of fear into the caregiving relationship exerts on the emergence of Type D attachments.

The incorporation of the D and A/C atypical attachment patterns into the traditional A-B-C coding system resulted in a dramatic increase in the percentage of maltreated infants and toddlers who were classified as insecure, with rates averaging around 90% (Lyons-Ruth et al., 1987; Crittenden, 1988; Carlson et al., 1989). The majority of the insecure attachment classifications in maltreated infants and toddlers have been found to be Type D (Lyons-Ruth et al., 1987; Carlson et al., 1989). Findings of stability of Type D attachments in infancy and toddlerhood also have been reported (Barnett, Ganiban, and Cicchetti, 1992).

Prior to the availability of the expanded coding system, maltreated infants and toddlers were often incorrectly classified as secure, thereby clouding the validity and predictive capability of the attachment classification system for use with maltreated children. Although appearing to evidence positive attachments to caregivers, closer examination of the attachments of maltreated youngsters often revealed problems. One such pattern of anomalous interaction is captured by Crittenden and DiLalla (1988). In an examination of mother-child interaction in youngsters ranging in age from 1 to 36 months, they found interesting differences between adequately reared and maltreated children. Specifically, maltreated youngsters displayed "compulsive compliance," a behavioral pattern marked by hypervigilance to parental demands and quick compliance. Although maltreated infants prior to one year of age responded to maternal control with passivity, with increased age they inhibited negative signals and exhibited positive behavior. The increase in compulsive compliance between 12 and 30 months of age in maltreated children differed markedly from the "independent" and "difficult" behavior typically associated with normal development in two-year-olds. Thus, a pattern that could easily be interpreted as nonproblematic and asymptomatic actually reflects the emergence of a style whereby the child's interpretation of reality is distorted. Though adaptive within a maltreating context, this style and the associated representational models of relationships portend poorly for future development. Of significance for intervention purposes was the finding that compulsive compliant infants and toddlers were able to modify their behavior when with a less controlling adult (Crittenden and DiLalla, 1988). This finding underscores the importance of providing intervention before maladaptive relationship models become entrenched and less easily modifiable.

Preschool

To date, the majority of work on the attachment relationships of maltreated children has focused on the period of infancy and toddlerhood. A number of investigators, however, have examined attachment in maltreated preschoolers. The preschool period is important from an attachment theory perspective because the enhanced cognitive, linguistic, representational, social-cognitive, and emotional capabilities of preschoolers allow the relationship between parent and child to become more interpersonally connected, while the child's increased autonomy results in a decreased need for proximity (Cicchetti and Barnett, 1991).

In examining attachment relationships in maltreated youngsters as old as 48 months of age, Crittenden (1988) utilized the A/C classification in conjunction with the other standard classification patterns. The A/C pattern was found to be present in the older (25–48 months) and more severely maltreated children, especially in those who had been both physically abused and neglected. Crittenden (1988) also noted that the older maltreated children did not evidence a goal-corrected partnership by 48 months, an achievement thought to be present in adequately reared preschoolers (Bowlby, 1969–82; Marvin, 1977).

In a cross-sectional/longitudinal examination of attachment organization in maltreated preschoolers, Cicchetti and Barnett (1991) found that a greater proportion of maltreated than nonmaltreated children in each of the three age groups studied (30, 36, and 48 months) evidenced insecure attachments. These findings also were noteworthy for the smaller percentage of atypical patterns (A/C and D combined) found in the maltreated preschoolers (i.e., 36.4% at 30 months, 36.4% at 36 months, and 27.8% at 48 months) than would be expected based on an extrapolation from the infant and toddler results. Additionally, only 30-month-olds differed significantly from

nonmaltreated comparisons with regard to the percentage of atypical attachments. Of note also was the tendency for maltreated Type
D children to manifest a controlling pattern with their mothers, a
finding consistent with Main, Kaplan, and Cassidy's (1985) finding
that infants who were coded Type D developed a controlling relationship with their caregivers at age six (Cicchetti and Barnett,
1991).

More generally, the longitudinal data obtained in this investigation
also revealed that maltreated children with insecure attachments
evidenced stability over the assessment period, while the attachments of maltreated preschoolers who were classified as secure
tended to be unstable (Cicchetti and Barnett, 1991). This finding of
greater stability of insecurity in maltreated preschoolers is consistent
with the findings of Schneider-Rosen et al. (1985) on attachment
stability during infancy and toddlerhood.

School Age

As the examination of attachment moves beyond the early years of
life, it becomes increasingly necessary to utilize assessments of the
internalized representation of the caregiving relationship. Thus,
investigators are less likely to be able to examine the parent–child
relationship directly but, rather, must rely on assessments that are
thought to tap the mental model of the attachment relationship.

One recent method that has emerged to assess attachment-based
constructs in school-aged children involves the use of a self-report
measure, the Relatedness Scales (Connell and Wellborn, 1991; Lynch
and Cicchetti, 1991). On these scales the child is asked to rate the
quality of his or her relationship to various relationship partners,
including mother, teacher, and peers. Research with normative
populations has demonstrated that children's responses to these
scales form patterns that are consistent with attachment and self-
system theory (Lynch, 1990; Connell and Wellborn, 1991). Specifically, it is believed that by measuring feelings of positive affect in
conjunction with felt needs for increased psychological closeness to
various relationship figures, patterns are revealed that reflect an
internal representational model of the relationship figure and of the
self in relation to that figure.

Lynch and Cicchetti (1991) administered the Relatedness Scales to
7–13-year-old maltreated and nonmaltreated children. These investigators found that maltreated youngsters described more "confused"
and less "optimal" patterns of relatedness with a number of relationship partners, including their mothers, teachers, peers, and best

friends, than did nonmaltreated comparison children. Approximately 30% of maltreated children reported "confused" patterns of relatedness with their mothers, a pattern thought to be consistent with the atypical classifications of the infancy, toddlerhood, and preschool periods (Lynch and Cicchetti, 1991). Moreover, children's patterns of relatedness with their mothers were highly concordant with patterns reported with other relationship figures, a result suggesting the influential role of caregiving history on relationships with peers and nonparental adult figures (Lynch and Cicchetti, 1991).

In a recent examination of the possible role of nonoptimal patterns of relatedness in contributing to depression among maltreated and nonmaltreated comparison school-aged children, Toth and Cicchetti (in press) found that maltreated children exhibiting nonoptimal patterns of relatedness with their mothers evidenced elevated depressive symptomatology and lower perceived competence, while maltreated children who had achieved optimal/adequate patterns of relatedness evidenced less depressive symptomatology and higher competence. This study is important in suggesting that achieving a capacity for relatedness at later ages may mitigate against the adverse effects of maltreatment; it is consistent with research that has found that resilient individuals frequently report a positive relationship history with a significant adult during childhood (Masten, Best, and Garmezy, 1990).

In yet another approach to assessing the mental representations of relationships among school-age maltreated children, a projective storytelling task was administered (McCrone et al., 1994). Children who had been maltreated told stories that revealed relationships characterized by negative interpersonal expectations and difficulty resolving relationship problems. The stories told by maltreated children also reflected a focus on the negative dynamics of relationships to the exclusion of positive relationship components. These results are discussed in terms of attachment theory, which posits the contribution of maltreatment to the development of internal working models of self as unworthy and of others as unavailable.

Findings such as these suggest that the distortions in maltreated children's relationships with others may continue into the school-age years and that, when present, they may exacerbate the occurrence of maladaptive functioning. Although the rates of atypical attachments among maltreated children appear to decrease after infancy and toddlerhood (Cicchetti and Barnett, 1991; Lynch and Cicchetti, 1991), the continued prevalence of attachments that are insecure in nature underscores the risk that maltreated children face in achieving adaptive outcomes.

Adulthood

Although there are similarities between adult and childhood attach-ment, a number of important differences also exist (Hazen and Shaver, 1994). While childhood attachment is typically complemen-tary, with a child seeking but not providing security, adult attach-ments are more commonly reciprocal. Additionally, over the course of development, attachment progresses from the level of observable interactions to internally represented conceptualizations about rela-tionships. While this shift is gradual and begins in childhood, it culminates in the adult years. Adult attachment and childhood attachment also differ with respect to the attachment figure, typi-cally a parent in infancy and early childhood and a peer or sexual partner in adulthood. Events that initiate the attachment system also differ over the course of development. While some theoreticians view caregiving and mating as separate systems, we share Hazen and Shaver's (1994) view that caregiving and mating are added to the childhood motivators of anxiety and distress. Even if these two issues are viewed as separate systems, the anxiety that may accom-pany caregiving and mating could serve to activate the attachment system. Conceptually, attachment is thought to be transferred from caregivers to adult peers when peer relationships take on similar functions and meet needs for support and security historically fulfilled by parents (Hazen and Shaver, 1994). Although childhood models continue to exert an effect on relationship formation due to the expectations of relationship figures that are carried forward, their salience in the attachment hierarchy may decrease in adult-hood (Hazen and Shaver, 1994). The relative impact of early attach-ment experiences, however, may be a function of the extent of caregiver dysfunction experienced during childhood. Preliminary support for this view can be garnered from the previously described research that has revealed greater stability of insecure attachments among maltreated than nonmaltreated children (Schneider-Rosen et al., 1985; Cicchetti and Barnett, 1991).

Attachment theory, with its focus on the development of repre-sentational models and the role of these models in affecting subse-quent relationships, suggests that individuals with maladaptive care-giving histories are likely to evidence a preponderance of insecure patterns of attachment in adulthood. In a sample of females who had been victims of incestuous abuse in childhood, Alexander (1993), using a self-report attachment style questionnaire, found that only 14% of the women rated themselves as securely attached, while 13%, 16%, and 58% described themselves as preoccupied, dismiss-ing, and fearful, respectively. This differs significantly from how subjects in normative samples rate their attachment organization (49% secure, 12% preoccupied, 18% dismissing, and 21% fearful; Bartholomew and Horowitz, 1991). The high rate of fearful, disorganized attachment in survivors of incest is especially interesting in view of the high rates of disorganized attachment reported in maltreated infants and toddlers. Moreover, it is compatible with Main and Hesse's (1990) discussion of disorganized attachment organization in infancy being the result of the introjection of fear into the caregiving relationship.

Alexander (1993) also reported that the absence of secure attachment was predictive of the avoidance of memories of abuse, as well as of a number of personality disorders, including avoidant, dependent, self-defeating, and borderline. These results are consistent with Main and Goldwyn's (1984) findings that mothers who had experienced maltreatment during childhood and who possessed dismissing or preoccupied adult attachment organizations were likely to engage in maladaptive parenting of their own children. Conversely, women who had processed their negative childhood histories have been shown to be unlikely to perpetrate maltreatment with their children (Hunter and Kilstrom, 1979; Egeland, Jacobvitz, and Sroufe, 1988). These studies suggest that childhood maltreatment exerts a significant impact on adult attachment organization, the combination of which, in turn, has implications for personality disturbances and subsequent parenting.

In an examination of the Adult Attachment Interview in a group of maltreating mothers and their partners, rates of dismissing or preoccupied-engaged attachment organizations exceeded 90% in both males and females (Crittenden, Partridge, and Claussen, 1991). Attachment organization in maltreating parents was found either to match, with both partners evidencing either dismissing or preoccupied attachments, or to mesh, with one partner being dismissing and the other preoccupied. In low-income, nonmaltreating families, secure adult attachment organizations were common, and both partners were likely to match on the presence of security. Secure attachment, even with only one partner evidencing security, was virtually absent in maltreating families.

Thus, in addition to a high percentage of insecure attachments in adults who have been maltreated during childhood, these individuals are likely to choose mates who bring their own negative attachment histories into the spousal dyad, with the result of extreme risk for dysfunctional parenting for any children who are brought into the union. Because research with normative populations has shown that a secure partner may act as a buffer against the negative effects of having an insecure spouse (Cohn, et al., 1992), the relative absence of secure-insecure matings in maltreating families most likely exacerbates family conflict and maladaptive functioning.

The Life Span Influence of Attachment

As the preceding developmental conceptualization suggests, the role of attachment in maltreating families far exceeds the boundaries of infancy and early childhood. The representational models that emerge from the caregiving matrix of maltreated children exert influences on their conceptualization of self, as well as on their responses to potential relationship partners. While representational models most likely contain information specific to a given relationship, these specific models may contribute information to more generalized models of relationships (Crittenden, 1990). Because the internal representational models of the early caregiving relationship are largely insecure in maltreated children, these children may be doomed to perpetuate the maladaptive relationship patterns of their childhoods. The fact that not all maltreated children do so lends hope to a potentially bleak scenario and also speaks to the potential benefit of theoretically grounded approaches for the prevention of maltreatment, as well as for the treatment of those who have experienced caregiving trauma.

IMPLICATIONS FOR INTERVENTION

Despite our knowledge base regarding the adverse effects that maltreatment exerts on attachment and the implications of this for development across the life span, intervention efforts grounded in attachment theory for maltreated populations are rare. While this may seem unusual, it becomes less surprising when one considers the relatively recent ascendance of attachment theory into the psychotherapeutic community. In fact, one of the first books to examine the clinical implications of attachment theory was published less than a decade ago (Belsky and Nezworski, 1988). The historical focus of intervention for maltreatment on parents to the exclusion of the child also has most likely contributed to the dearth of attachment-guided methods of treatment for victims of abuse and neglect (Mann and McDermott, 1983; Azar, Barnes, and Twentyman, 1988). While the importance of an intervention approach for individuals who have experienced maltreatment that is based on our knowledge of the consequences of maltreatment has been stressed (Cicchetti, Taraldson, and Egeland, 1978; Friedrich and Einbender, 1983; Cicchetti and Toth, 1987), progress in meeting this goal has been slow. In efforts to move a step closer to the realization of a theoretically informed approach to intervention for those who suffer from the consequences of maltreatment, we discuss the applicability of attachment theory for this purpose. Because research suggests that the attachment-related deficits associated with maltreatment may be felt throughout life, we explore interventions from infancy through adulthood.

Infancy and Toddlerhood

In recent years, a number of attachment-based therapeutic approaches have been developed that have relevance for addressing the deficits associated with maltreatment. In view of the salience of the attachment relationship during the 12–18-month period (Sroufe, 1979), it is somewhat expectable that the majority of attachment-driven approaches have focused on efforts to improve the very early mother–child relationship. Perhaps one of the most widely utilized approaches has its origins in the work of Selma Fraiberg. In "Ghosts in the Nursery," Fraiberg and her colleagues poignantly describe the pernicious influence that remnants of the parental past can have on the evolving parent-child relationship (Fraiberg, Adelson, and Shapiro, 1975):

> In every nursery there are ghosts. They are the visitors from the unremembered past of the parents, the uninvited guests at the christening. Under all favorable circumstances the unfriendly and unbidden spirits are banished from the nursery and return to their subterranean dwelling place. . . . But how shall we explain another group of families who appear to be possessed by their ghosts? . . . While no one has issued an invitation, the ghosts take up residence and conduct the rehearsal of the family tragedy from a tattered script [pp. 387–388].

Families "possessed by their ghosts" best describe the context in which maltreatment occurs, often exerting influence cross-generationally.

Although infant-parent psychotherapy has its roots in this early work, Lieberman and her colleagues (Lieberman and Pawl, 1988, 1993; Lieberman, 1991) have focused more extensively on the possible contributions of both parent and child to attachment dysfunction. By elaborating on the role that early parental history exerts on the caregiving context, infant-parent psychotherapy seeks to address disorders of attachment. The therapeutic sessions are structured to include the infant so that reciprocal influences between parent and child can be addressed directly.

Infant–parent therapy has not been used specifically with maltreating populations, but its success with a group of low Socioeconomic Status (SES) immigrant mothers and their offspring portends well for its potential efficacy (Lieberman, Weston, and Pawl, 1991). Because these women were considered to be at risk for disorders of attachment due to the presence of high rates of depression, anxiety, poverty, unemployment, and cultural issues related to their immigrant status, it is not difficult to expect similar stressors in a maltreating population. The intervention was initiated at the infant's age of 12 months and continued on a weekly basis for one year. Results revealed that the intervention was successful in enhancing maternal empathy and interaction with the child, increasing the goal-corrected partnership between mother and child, and decreasing child avoidance, resistance, and anger.

In considering the applicability of this mode of intervention to maltreating populations, a number of issues must be considered. Because maltreatment does not always surface during infancy, the utilization of this approach with older children needs to be evaluated. In fact, Lieberman (1992) has discussed the utility of this therapeutic modality with a toddler population. Due to the child's increased cognitive and language skills, some modifications are recommended. In our own work with toddlers who have depressed mothers, we have found that sessions often need to be alternated between dyadic and individual meetings. This is necessary because, at times, the mother's level of distress is not appropriate to address with her child present. Situations that require individual time typically have been related to maternal discussions of their own childhood abuse or to significant marital conflict. We have found that the opportunity to process such experiences individually enables the mother to deal more adaptively with the role of her early experiences in the current parent–child relationship and her resultant parenting behaviors when the child is reintegrated into sessions. We also have found that in women who have been maltreated, the capacity to trust and engage is often so damaged that the initial therapeutic goal must be to establish some basic level of trust.

While individual sessions or dyadic sessions that are devoted largely to the mother are sometimes necessary to achieve this goal, our work at Mt. Hope Family Center, University of Rochester, also revealed an interesting aspect associated with the presence of the child in sessions. For some women, having the child physically present actually decreases their avoidant stance and allows them to enter into a therapeutic relationship. A brief case vignette illustrates this situation.

Mary, a 35-year-old Caucasian female, entered therapy due to her concerns over the impact of her depression on her toddler. Dyadic interactions were generally positive, with Mary being very responsive to Jody and with Jody typically presenting as very happy and engaged with her mother. At times, however, Mary seemed to be overly engaged with Jody, and the therapist feared that Jody's emerging autonomy might suffer were this pattern of interaction to continue. The content of sessions was often vague, with Mary complaining of some diffuse and rather mundane concerns. She largely avoided direct communication with the therapist and chose, rather, to interact exclusively with Jody or to speak to the therapist through Jody. At times, the child seemed to be the mother's mouthpiece, voicing Mary's anxieties and fears.

After several months of meeting, Mary arrived for a session with Jody sound asleep. While Jody continued to sleep peacefully in her mother's arms, Mary haltingly began to tell her story of childhood physical abuse. Subsequent sessions varied, with active mother–child interaction interspersed with painful sessions during which a sleeping Jody was cradled in her mother's arms. As Mary began to feel more engaged with the therapist, she requested individual time for herself. Mary was increasingly able to examine her fears about the experiences of her own childhood on her parenting. One of her primary concerns was that Jody might also be abused unless she protected her. This seemed to account for some of the over-involvement that was present, and as Mary grappled with her own childhood issues, she began to modify some of the potentially maladaptive patterns between herself and Jody. Without the security that she experienced by having Jody present, Mary may not have been able to engage sufficiently to reveal her childhood abuse. As this case illustrates, although work with individuals who have experienced maltreatment poses some new challenges for infant–parent psychotherapy, it has great potential as a form of therapy that can address the attachment deficits associated with caregiving dysfunction.

Another intervention directed toward parent–child interaction was initiated at the University of Minnesota (Egeland and Erickson, 1990; Erickson, Korfmacher, and Egeland, 1992). Similar to the Lieberman sample, the target of the intervention was a group of mothers at risk for parenting difficulties due to the presence of a number of stressors, including poverty, limited education, social isolation, and stressful life circumstances. A number of services, including home visitation and parenting informational and support groups, were provided. The goal of modifying a maladaptive attachment relationship between mother and infant was consistent with that previously described. Services were initiated during the mother's second trimester of pregnancy and continued through the child's first birthday.

Although governed by the belief that the alteration of both parent and child working models of relationships was necessary if the maladaptive attachment was to improve, the multiservice nature of the program made it difficult to attribute therapeutic change to a specific factor. The influence of attachment theory, however, can be seen throughout the structure of the intervention, beginning with the efforts to address maternal representations of the unborn child, a factor shown to be a powerful predictor of the quality of postbirth attachment relationships (Fonagy, Steele, and Steele, 1991). The therapeutic relationship formed between the mother and the inter-venor also is viewed as important in helping the mother to develop new models of relationships. Toward this end, Erickson and her colleagues (1992) describe a number of important principles, includ-ing consistency with the mother, the identification and affirmation of strengths in mother and baby, maternal empowerment, com-munication directed at the alteration of working models, and elucidation of interactional patterns between the mother and the intervenor, with the goal of linking these styles with maternal relationship history.

Preliminary data on the effectiveness of this program are promis-ing and suggest that the intervention improved maternal understand-ing of infant needs and resulted in more appropriate home environ-ments and in a decrease in maternal emotional problems (Erickson et al., 1992). While differences in security of attachment were not found at the conclusion of the intervention, follow-up assessments revealed a trend for intervention dyads to move toward a more secure relationship during the infant's second year.

Yet another intervention designed to promote positive parent–child relationships in impoverished families with caregiving difficul-ties was initiated when infants were less than 9 months old (Lyons-Ruth, 1992). Two nonintervention groups also were assessed. Because 32% of this sample included mothers who had been identi-fied as maltreating, it is especially important for our purposes. Not surprisingly and in accord with attachment theory predictions, Lyons-Ruth (1992) found that mothers who had experienced more stable childhood environments provided more attentive, involved care to their infants than did mothers from less cohesive homes. Hostile-intrusive maternal behavior also was related to a history characterized by family conflict, severe punishment, lack of warmth, maternal psychopathology, and poor peer relationships. Interven-tion consisted of weekly home visitation designed to promote adequate parenting and to address the family's social service needs. Although a variety of interventions was provided, Lyons-Ruth conceptualizes and attributes the success of the intervention to its attachment focus. Improvements in mother–child interaction were noted when infants reached 12 months of age, with insecure-disorganized attachment being twice as high in infants of depressed mothers who did not receive intervention (54% versus 22%).

A compelling approach to the treatment of insecure attachment in infancy is proposed by Crittenden (1992), whose integration of attachment theory with ethological, psychodynamic, evolutionary, learning, and cognitive theories is extremely relevant to work with maltreated infants. Crittenden proposes that procedural models of the self and of attachment figures develop in infancy, are maintained across the lifecourse, and are accessed preconsciously to regulate behavior. Emphasis is given to memory systems, where procedural, episodic, and semantic memory are thought to contain information on behavior sequences, events, and verbal generalizations, respectively (Tulving, 1972, 1985).

Crittenden (1992) hypothesizes that each memory system and its associated model regulate behavior under different circumstances. Procedural models, present beginning in infancy, reflect expectations about the behavior of caregivers and of the self. Semantic models arise during the transition to preoperational intelligence, and these verbally encoded models contain linked generalizations about the self and the attachment figure. Unlike procedural models that operate without conscious thought, semantic models are believed to be initiated to facilitate problem solving. Due to the complex encoding, storage, and retrieval demands, episodic memory is thought to be the last memory system to develop, most likely around the age of four (Tulving, 1985). Episodic memory is associated with the recall of affectively arousing events, often of a traumatic nature.

According to Crittenden's conceptualization, inconsistency among models is believed to be related to both anxious attachment and risk for emotional disorders. For Crittenden, when experiences are encountered that are too complex to process, as in the case of maltreatment, a style of coping emerges that could lead to future relationship difficulties if it continues to be utilized (Crittenden, 1992). Thus, insecure attachment is seen not only as a reflection of current relationship dysfunction but also as the utilization of a processing style where the acquisition, integration, and evaluation of information occur in a skewed manner.

In view of possible processing permutations during infancy, a central goal of intervention is to help infants perceive and respond to their actual experiences rather than employing processing that obfuscates reality (Crittenden, 1992). Toward this end, Crittenden stresses the importance of directing intervention toward the infants' procedural models with the goal of keeping models open rather than closed. A number of strategies can be employed to attain this objective, including modifying the behavior of the caregiver, providing the infant with alternate positive relationship opportunities, and helping the infant to perceive attachment figures accurately. In view of the cognitive limitations of the infant, considerable effort needs to be directed toward modifying the caregiver or the caregiving context.

Preschool

In working with preschoolers who have experienced maltreatment, the parent–child relationship remains an important area of intervention. The child's evolving competencies, however, make it increasingly possible to direct efforts to the child. The conceptualization of intervention described by Crittenden for the period of the infancy continues to be relevant for preschoolers. The preoperational capacities of preschoolers, Crittenden believes, are appropriate for treatments that target the content of memory systems and models, the integration of various types of information, and the translation of processing into behavior.

Findings that confirm the existence of processing differences in maltreated children such as those discussed by Crittenden have been reported by Rieder and Cicchetti (1989). In examining the cognitive control functioning of maltreated preschool and school-age children, these investigators found that maltreated children were hypervigilant to aggressive stimuli. Rieder and Cicchetti hypothesized that the maltreating environment encouraged the development of hypervigilance as an adaptive coping strategy. Moreover, they noted that problems in the cognitive-affective balance of maltreated youngsters could result in the interpretation of ambiguous stimuli as threatening. Subsequently, this processing style could contribute to the emergence of difficulties in establishing positive relationships, a view compatible with conceptualizations of the effect of negative representational models on interpersonal relations (Bretherton, 1985; Rieder and Cicchetti, 1989).

In order to address the attachment-related difficulties of maltreated preschoolers, in our work at Mt. Hope Family Center we have found that an integrative approach to treatment is necessary. Often the maltreating caregiver has experienced childhood abuse and therefore possesses limited capacities to form relationships; thus, intervention becomes quite complex. In our experience of providing intervention to preschoolers who have experienced maltreatment, a comprehensive service system is offered to the families. Specifically, we provide a therapeutic preschool program that enables the children to begin to form relationships with individuals who are supplementing the caregiving provided at home. We often find that the children have models of relationships that are already quite entrenched. Consequently, considerable work must be done with the classroom staff to help them understand that the child's anger or avoidance is not specific to them but rather the only mode of interaction that the child knows. By helping classroom personnel to respond to each child in ways that cause the child to question the accuracy of his or her representational models, we are addressing a major goal, namely, helping the child to keep his or her models of relationships open to new and potentially positive experiences.

In view of the potential for intervention to influence the child's processing and integration of relationship experiences, we consider individual child therapy to be important, beginning in the preschool years. Therapists working with the maltreated preschool child often find that they, too, are the target of an established representational model. Therapy sessions often reveal the replay of well-rehearsed modes of interaction. In our work with a severely neglected five-year-old girl, we found that she consistently engaged her therapist in a manner that increased the likelihood that the therapist would reject her. For example, she avoided eye contact (with the therapist) and frequently contradicted the therapist's seemingly obvious observations or reflections. Overtly, the child appeared to have no investment in her relationship with the therapist and frequently stated that she missed her prior therapist or that she wished she could return to her teacher. The depth of her connection to the therapist surfaced more symbolically through her efforts to emulate the therapist's hairstyle or by assigning the therapist's name to dolls that she cared for lovingly. While, in truth, possible rejection was the child's worst fear, she had become so accustomed to her needs and feelings being ignored that the discrepancy between her prior experience and the therapist's acceptance and positive regard created disequilibrium and resultant anxiety. For her, the anxiety could be minimized only if the world responded in accord with her expectations. Thus, treatment focused on helping her to believe that not all adults would reject her, an intervention that sought to keep her models of relationships more open to the actual experiences that she encountered rather than expecting all situations to confirm the reality she had learned in her home.

We also have found that direct intervention with parents is critical in the preschool period. In our experience with an impoverished group of children, we have found that the majority reside in single-parent families primarily headed by a mother. Although the mothers may be involved with various father figures, these men are typically peripheral to the family (Howes and Cicchetti, 1993). Thus, our intervention most often targets single mothers. Again, the role of childhood experiences and the manner in which parenting is affected is striking. The neediness and isolation of the mothers we serve often preclude their willingness to "share" therapy time with their child. Therefore, parent–child conjoint therapy is not as viable as it is during infancy and toddlerhood. Because the mothers with whom we intervene have models of relationships that are often closed to new input, extraordinary effort must go into relationship formation if intervention is to be successful. Toward this end, we respond to the expressed needs of the mother, whether for concrete assistance with food and housing or for transportation to a medical appointment. Over time, we have found that this approach begins to form a foundation of trust upon which to build. Because the process can move quite slowly, we believe our child-focused interventions are critical if the child is to avoid repeating parental patterns of maladaptation with future relationship partners.

An example of the comprehensive nature of services that we believe to be necessary for addressing the attachment-related difficulties associated with maltreatment can be conveyed through the description of the issues that we encountered in the treatment of a three-year-old boy who was referred for treatment due to concerns associated with familial physical abuse. Carl was the third of four children, ages two, three, four, and five years, and the second male child born to Sandra. Both Carl and his older sibling had been named in a number of abuse reports, which had resulted in two separate foster care placements. Carl had just been returned to Sandra's care at the time of referral.

On presentation, Carl appeared to be a shy, withdrawn child. He made no eye contact when greeted but, rather, clung to his mother. In the Strange Situation, Carl evidenced a mix of attachment strategies, at one moment appearing to be avoidant of his mother, only subsequently to appear clingy and anxious. Perhaps most striking was Carl's fear response in his mother's presence, along with two episodes of looking dazed. Carl's attachment organization was judged to be consistent with a disorganized/disoriented classification.

During a clinical interview, Sandra was vague regarding her own childhood. She did share that she had been in a series of foster homes, beginning at age eight, but avoided providing further detail. Over the course of individual treatment, Sandra's therapist learned that Sandra had been both physically and sexually abused during her childhood. Although Sandra could verbalize anger over her early experiences, she more often viewed herself as damaged and deserving of abuse. Sandra's history of intimate relationships was characterized by brief involvements with abusive men. Each of her four children had a different father. In the case of her youngest, she denied knowledge of paternity.

During the Adult Attachment Interview (AAI), Sandra presented her childhood experiences in a global fashion, often stating that she could not recall her early childhood. Intense anger emerged as she described her mother, but when she was queried for specific memories, significant lapses occurred. Sandra denied any significant relationship with her father. When she perceived herself as being pressured by the interviewer's efforts to obtain specific memories of her relationship with her parents, rage was directed toward the interviewer. While generally coherent despite the lack of detailed recall, Sandra's reasoning deteriorated as she became affectively stressed around recollections of physical abuse. No mention of sexual abuse was made. With regard to classification, Sandra's AAI was consistent with a classification of dismissing. It also was assigned to the unresolved/disoriented-disorganized category.

Despite years of varied forms of treatment, including behaviorally based and psychoeducational methods, Sandra continued to abuse her children. Her controlling parenting was juxtaposed against her belief/hope that she could avoid repeating with her children the trauma that she had suffered. In fact, Sandra consistently denied abusing her sons and saw the system that sought to protect them as a threat. Paranoia frequently surfaced during treatment, but as Sandra came to trust her therapist more, the details of her history became clearer. Sandra viewed her sons as extensions of their fathers, and her powerlessness of childhood manifested itself as a need to dominate her male children. Interestingly, Sandra's two female children were not abused by her.

Although Sandra was a bright woman who was able to articulate appropriate child-rearing practices, she was not able to incorporate her knowledge into her actual parenting. Rather, her own unresolved feelings about her childhood abuse carried over into her choice of mates and her anger toward her young sons. It was clear that Sandra had a closed model of relationships that she generalized to all new situations that she encountered. Therefore, it was determined that continued didactic instruction and/or behavioral intervention alone would not effectively address the crux of Sandra's attachment-based difficulties. Rather, treatment needed to be directed toward helping her to rework her relationship models and ideally to help Carl retain an open representational model so as to be able to form positive relationships with alternative caregivers.

Cases such as this are among the most challenging and convey a clear sense of the devastating effects of early experiences on parenting, as well as the factors that perpetuate the intergenerational transmission of maltreatment. After extensive treatment, it was determined that Sandra was not responding sufficiently to therapy and that she was continuing to abuse her sons. Although she was making progress in her ability to relate with the therapist, her sons were continuing to be victimized. Foster placement was reinstituted, and continued individual therapy with Sandra contained the additional goal of helping her to free her sons for adoption.

Carl responded well to ongoing therapy, and as his capacity to realistically confront his anger toward his mother improved, his rageful behavior decreased. Carl's brother also appeared to benefit from outpatient therapy. Despite the tragedy of foster placement and Sandra's inability to improve sufficiently to care for her children adequately, the children's ability to respond to therapy and to continue to be receptive to new relationship experiences was a positive prognostic sign.

School Age

In considering intervention for school-age maltreated children, the fact that their world increasingly is centered outside the home must be addressed. Because the school environment becomes a major focus for social interaction, new opportunities, as well as challenges, confront the child who has experienced maladaptive caregiving. As research has demonstrated, maltreated children are at considerable risk for continuing the patterns of maladaptive social interactions that originated in the caregiving environment. Therefore, intervention efforts need to be directed toward helping the child to remain open to positive relationship experiences rather than approaching all new relationships with a preconceived negative bias (Lynch and Cicchetti, 1992). Specifically, it is imperative that a child who has been maltreated be helped to perceive situations accurately.

In view of the difficulties noted in the affective-cognitive balance of maltreated children (Rieder and Cicchetti, 1989), intervention needs to be directed toward this area. Cognitive control therapy (Santostefano, 1985) can be used to help work toward the integration of cognition, inner experience, and the external environment and thereby address possible peer difficulties associated with either an overly inner- or outer-directed style. The overarching goal of therapy is the facilitation of a reality-based view of the world, rather than reliance on preconceived and potentially invalid assessments of the environment. This approach is compatible with Crittenden's (1988) discussion of the importance of preserving representational models that are responsive to new experiences.

While individual child therapy continues to be indicated during the school-age years, increased emphasis needs to be given to facilitating positive peer interaction. Because the peer arena can provide the school-age child with a natural context within which to develop positive relationships, it is important that the child be receptive to relationship partners that may be discrepant with their own models of relationships. In the absence of intervention, maltreated children are prone to repeat negative patterns of interaction. Serious consideration should therefore be given to utilizing interventions that minimize the likelihood of perpetuating negative interactions.

Peer-pair counseling (Selman, Schultz, and Yeates, 1991) is a modality that can be applied toward helping the maltreated child to avoid a cycle of relational dysfunction. In this approach, children meet in pairs with an adult trainer. The overall goal of the intervention is to help children learn more mature strategies for interpersonal problem negotiation and to enable them to practice the new strategies in a supportive context. This intervention holds promise for helping to promote more positive peer interactions in maltreated children. In turn, this may help maltreated children remain more open to positive relationship experiences over time.

Recently, peer pairing has been directed toward early intervention and prevention with school-age children from low-income neighborhoods having high rates of violence and substance abuse (Selman et al., 1992). Children who participate in this program are referred by teachers due to their aggressive behavior or social withdrawal, and pairing combines children with opposing styles. Although not specifically identified as maltreated, some of the children who participated in the intervention probably come from violent homes. The effectiveness of this intervention for vulnerable youth is noteworthy, and it has potential for being applied to children who have experienced familial violence.

Although the school-age years may be especially challenging for addressing the relationship difficulties that have their origins in the early caregiving relationship, interventions directed toward the modification of representational models are possible. If a pattern of maladaptive parenting has continued from infancy through later childhood, emphasis must be placed on working with the child, either individually or in a peer context. An integration of individual and small group therapy may be necessary in order to achieve overt behavioral change while simultaneously helping the child to process the roots of relationship difficulties. This will be especially critical if dysfunctional parenting continues to assault the child's view of self and others. Of course, intervention efforts also must continue to target maltreating parents, with the goal of helping them to support the child's gains if the parent and child are to remain together.

Adulthood

Efforts to treat adults who suffered abuse during childhood pose significant challenges for the therapist. If little prior intervention has occurred, the therapist is likely to be faced with a patient who mistrusts others and who expects to be victimized. The resistance to change may be powerful due to the influence of existing representational models of relationships. In fact, the adult who was maltreated during childhood may feel least anxious when early childhood experiences, regardless of how negative, are re-created. Therefore, the challenge to therapy lies in how best to engage an individual in the therapeutic process.

An assessment of representational models prior to the initiation of therapy may provide insight on how best to intervene. Dozier (1990) found that patients with secure attachment relationships at the initiation of treatment were more compliant with therapy, while those with avoidant tendencies were less receptive to treatment. Fonagy and Tallandini-Shallice (1993) were able to relate attachment organization to the utilization of intensive versus nonintensive psychoanalytic therapy, with patients who dropped out of treatment possessing preoccupied-entangled attachments in the passive subcategory. Although links between adult attachment organization and treatment utilization and effectiveness are in their preliminary stages, results suggest that attachment organization may serve to inform the therapist as to which therapeutic modalities are likely to be effective. In view of the preponderance of insecure attachments in adults who were maltreated during childhood, the effects of insecurity on treatment efficacy must be considered. Efforts to utilize relationally based interventions may fail in some cases where a more directive, structured mode of intervention might have succeeded.

In considering how best to address the intergenerational transmission of maltreatment, we believe that both parent and child must be considered (Cicchetti, Toth, and Bush, 1988). As previously discussed, the developmental level of the child will determine the

relative emphasis placed on child- versus parent-focused intervention, with infancy requiring extensive parental participation. If
improved parenting is to be sustained, however, efforts must be
directed at modifying the representational model that the caregiver
has incorporated into the caregiving context. The success of these
efforts may well be limited by the type of attachment organization
that the caregiver possesses. Minimally, the therapist must be
empathic toward the patient and tolerant of the significant transference issues that will emerge during treatment if efforts to help the
individual rework representational models are to be effective (Toth
and Cicchetti, 1993).

When considering the spousal attachment patterns present in
maltreating families and the effects of the patterns on caregiving,
family therapy also emerges as a potentially effective mode of intervention (Minuchin, 1988; Marvin and Stewart, 1990; Stevenson-
Hinde, 1990; Howes and Cicchetti, 1993). In fact, family therapy
may be utilized in two-parent families where both members are willing to commit to treatment. Under these circumstances, intervention
can focus on the attachment organization of both parents, as well as
on the emerging representational models of the children. In mother-
headed households, however, or in situations where the mother
continues to repeat a history of victimization through her involvement with abusive mates, we have found individual treatment to be
necessary.

While the difficulties of providing treatment to adults who were
severely maltreated during childhood cannot be minimized, we
believe that the incorporation of attachment-based interventions
into treatment can be an effective mode of treatment for the individual as well as for improving the quality of caregiving provided. As
our developmental analysis suggests, however, prevention and
intervention that is provided in close proximity to the occurrence of
the traumatic insult, rather than the delayed provision of therapy,
are likely to minimize the lifelong consequences associated with
damaged attachment organization.

CONCLUSION

In this chapter we have examined research on the attachment relationships of individuals who were maltreated during childhood. Our
overarching goal has been to discuss the implications of dysfunctional attachment for development across the life span. Although we
posit links between attachment difficulties and psychopathology,
much more extensive research of a longitudinal nature will be nec-

essary before causality can be definitely ascertained. By understanding the problems that may emerge in individuals who have been maltreated as a function of attachment difficulties, preventive efforts can be implemented prior to the emergence of diagnosable disorders (Cicchetti, 1987; Zeanah, 1993). Moreover, recognition of the continued impact of attachment dysfunction can be used to inform psychotherapeutic intervention across the life course. Attachment-informed approaches to prevention and intervention for this vulnerable population must be developed, implemented, and evaluated if the potential value to be derived from John Bowlby's vision is to be realized.

REFERENCES

Ainsworth, M. D. S. (1967), *Infancy in Uganda: Infant Care and the Growth of Love.* Baltimore, MD: Johns Hopkins University Press.

—— & Wittig, B. A. (1969), Attachment and the exploratory behavior of one-year-olds in a strange situation. In: *Determinants of Infant Behavior, Vol. 4,* ed. B. M. Foss. London: Methuen, pp. 113–136.

Alexander, P. C. (1993), The differential effects of abuse characteristics and attachment in the prediction of long-term effects of sexual abuse. *J. Interper. Viol.,* 8:346–362.

Azar, S. T., Barnes, K. T. & Twentyman, C. T. (1988), Developmental outcomes in physically abused children: Consequences of parental abuse or the effects of a more general breakdown in caregiving behaviors? *Behav. Ther.,* 11:27–32.

Barnett, D., Ganiban, J. & Cicchetti, D. (1992), Temperament and behavior of youngsters with disorganized attachments: A longitudinal study. Presented at the International Conference on Infant Studies, Miami.

Bartholomew, K. & Horowitz, L. (1991), Attachment styles among young adults: A test of a four-category model. *J. Per. Soc. Psychol.,* 61:266–244.

Belsky, J. & Nezworski, T., ed. (1988), *Clinical Implications of Attachment Theory.* Hillsdale, NJ: Lawrence Erlbaum Associates.

Bowlby, J. (1951), *Maternal Care and Mental Health.* WHO Monogr. No. 2. Geneva: World Health Organization.

—— (1969), *Attachment and Loss, Vol. 1.* New York: Basic Books, 1982.

—— (1977a), The making and breaking of affectional bonds. *Brit. J. Psychiat.,* 130:201–10.

—— (1988), Developmental psychiatry comes to age. *Amer. J. Psychiat.,* 145:1–10.

Bretherton, I. (1985), Attachment theory: Retrospect and prospect. In: *Growing Points of Attachment Theory and Research,* ed. I. Bretherton & E. Waters. *Monographs of the Society for Research in Child Development,* Serial No. 209, Vol. 50, Nos. 1–2, pp. 5–38.

—— (1992), The origins of attachment theory: John Bowlby and Mary Ainsworth. *Devel. Psychol.,* 28:759–775.

Capps, L., Sigman, M. & Mundy, P. (1994), Attachment security in children with autism. *Devel. Psychopathol.,* 6:249–261.

Carlson, V., Cicchetti, D., Barnett, D. & Braunwald, K. (1989), Disorganized/disoriented attachment relationships in maltreated infants. *Devel. Psychol.,* 25:525–531.

Carnegie Corporation of New York (1994), *Starting Point.* New York: Carnegie Corp.

Cicchetti, D. (1984), The emergence of developmental psychopathology. *Child Devel.*, 55:1–7.
—— (1987), Developmental psychopathology in infancy: Illustrations from the study of maltreated younsters. *J. Consult. Clin. Psychol.*, 55:837–845.
—— (1993), Developmental psychopathology: Reactions, reflections, projections. *Devel. Rev.*, 13:471–502.
—— & Barnett, D. (1991), Attachment organization in preschool aged maltreated children. *Devel. Psychopathol.*, 3:397–411.
—— Cummings, M., Greenberg, M. & Marvin, R. (1990), An organizational perspective on attachment beyond infancy: Implications for theory, measurement, and research. In: *Attachment in the Preschool Years*, ed. M. Greenberg, D. Cicchetti & E. M. Cummings. Chicago: University of Chicago Press, pp. 3–49.
—— & Greenberg, M. T., ed. (1991), Attachment and developmental psychopathology. (special issue). *Devel. Psychopathol.*, 3:347–531.
—— & Serafica, F. C. (1981), Interplay among behavioral systems: Illustrations from the study of attachment, affiliation, and wariness in young children with Down's syndrome. *Devel. Psychol.*, 17:36–49.
—— & Sroufe, L. A. (1978), An organizational view of affect: Illustration from the study of Down's syndrome infants. In: *The Development of Affect*, ed. M. Lewis & L. Rosenblum. New York: Plenum Press, pp. 309–350.
—— Taraldson, B. & Egeland, B. (1978), Perspectives in the treatment and understanding of child abuse. In: *Perspectives for Child Mental Health and Education*, ed. A. Goldstein. New York: Pergamon Press, pp. 301–378.
—— & Toth, S. L. (1987), The application of a transactional risk model to intervention with multi-risk maltreating families. *Zero to Three*, 7:1–8.
—— —— & Bush M. (1988), Developmental psychopathology and incompetence in childhood: Suggestions for intervention. In: *Advances in Clinical Child Psychology, Vol. 11*, ed. B. Lahey & A. Kazdin. New York: Plenum Press, pp. 1–71.
Cohn, D., Silver, D., Cowan, C., Cowan, P. & Pearson, J. (1992), Working models of childhood attachment and couple relationships. *J. Fam. Issues*, 13:432–449.
Connell, J. P. & Wellborn, J. G. (1991), Competence, autonomy and relatedness: A motivational analysis of self-system processes. In: *Minnesota Symposia on Child Psychology, Vol. 23*, ed. M. Gunnar & L. A. Sroufe. Hillsdale, NJ: Lawrence Erlbaum Associates, pp. 43–78.
Crittenden, P. M. (1985), Maltreated infants: Vulnerability and resilience. *J. Child Psychol. Psychiat. Allied Disc.*, 26:85–96.
—— (1988), Relationships at risk. In: *Clinical Implications of Attachment Theory*, ed. J. Belsky & T. Nezworski. Hillsdale, NJ: Lawrence Erlbaum Associates, pp. 136–174.
—— (1990), Internal representational models of attachment relationships. *Infant Ment. Health J.*, 11:259–277.
—— (1992), Treatment of anxious attachment in infancy and early childhood. *Devel. Psychopathol.*, 4:575–602.
—— & DiLalla, D. (1988), Compulsive compliance: The development of an inhibitory coping strategy in infancy. *J. Abn. Child Psychol.*, 16:585–599.
—— Partridge, M. F. & Claussen, A. H. (1991), Family patterns of relationship in normative and dysfunctional families. *Devel. Psychopathol.*, 3:491–512.
Dozier, M. (1990), Attachment organization and treatment use for adults with serious psychopathological disorders. *Devel. Psychopathol.*, 2:47–60.
Egeland, B. & Erickson, M. F. (1990), Rising above the past: Strategies for helping new mothers break the cycle of abuse and neglect. *Zero to Three*, 11:29–35.
—— & Farber, E. (1984), Infant-mother attachment: Factors related to its development and changes over time. *Child Devel.*, 52:44–52.

———— Jacobvitz, D. & Sroufe, L. A. (1988), Breaking the cycle of abuse. *Child Devel.*, 59:1080–1088.

———— & Sroufe, L. A. (1981), Developmental sequelae of maltreatment in infancy. *New Dir. Child Devel.*, 11:77–92.

Erickson, M. F., Korfmacher, J. & Egeland, B. (1992), Attachments past and present: Implications for therapeutic intervention with mother-infancy dyads. *Devel. Psychopathol.*, 4:495–507.

Fonagy, P., Steele, H. & Steele, M. (1991), Maternal representations of attachment during pregnancy predict the organization of infant–mother attachment at one year of age. *Child Devel.*, 62:891–905.

———— & Tallandini-Shallice, M. (1993), On some problems of psychoanalytic research in practice. *Bull. Anna Freud Centre*, 16:5–22.

Fraiberg, S., Adelson, E. & Shapiro, V. (1975), Ghosts in the nursery: A psychoanalytic approach to impaired infant-mother relationships. *J. Amer. Acad. Child Psychiat.*, 14:387–421.

Friedrich, W. N. & Einbender, A. J. (1983), The abused child: A psychological review. *J. Clin. Consult. Psychol.*, 12:244–256.

Greenberg, M. T. & Speltz, M. (1988), Attachment and the ontogeny of conduct problems. In: *Clinical Implications of Attachment*, ed. J. Belsky & T. Nezworski. Hillsdale, NJ: Lawrence Erlbaum Associates, pp. 177–218.

Grossmann, K., Grossmann, K. E., Spangler, G., Suess, G. & Unzner, L. (1985), Maternal sensitivity and newborns' orientation responses as related to quality of attachment in northern Germany. In: *Growing Points of Attachment Theory and Research*, ed. I. Bretherton & E. Waters. *Monographs of the Society for Research in Child Development.* Serial No. 209, Vol. 50, Nos. 1–2, pp. 233–256.

Hartmann, H. (1958), *Ego Psychology and the Problem of Adaptation*. New York: International Universities Press.

Hazen, C. & Shaver, P. (1994), Attachment as an organizational framework for research on close relationships. *Psychol. Inq.*, 5:1–22.

Howes, P. & Cicchetti, D. (1993), A family/relational perspective on maltreating families: Parallel processes across systems and social policy implications. In: *Child Abuse, Child Development and Social Policy*, ed. D. Cicchetti & S. L. Toth. Norwood, NJ: Ablex, pp. 249–300.

Hunter, R. S. & Kilstrom, N. (1979), Breaking the cycle in abusive families. *Amer. J. Psychiat.*, 136:1320–1322.

Lamb, M., Gaensbauer, T. J., Malkin, C. M. & Schultz, L. A. (1985), The effects of child maltreatment on security of infant–adult attachment. *Infant Behav. Devel.* 8:35–45.

———— Thompson, R., Gardner, W. & Charnov, E. (1985), *Infant-Mother Attachment*. Hillsdale, NJ: Lawrence Erlbaum Associates.

Leach, P. (1994), *Children First*. New York: Knopf.

Lieberman, A. F. (1991), Attachment theory and infant–parent psychotherapy: Some conceptual, clinical, and research considerations. In: *Rochester Symposium on Developmental Psychopathology, Vol. 3*, ed. D. Cicchetti & S. L. Toth. Rochester, NY: University of Rochester Press, pp. 261–287.

———— (1992), Infant–parent psychotherapy with toddlers. *Devel. Psychopathol.*, 4:559–574.

———— & Pawl, J. H. (1988), Clinical applications of attachment theory. In: *Clinical Implications of Attachment*, ed. J. Belsky & Nezworski. Hillsdale, NJ: Lawrence Erlbaum Associates, pp. 325–351.

———— & ———— (1993), Infant–parent psychotherapy. In: *Handbook of Infant Health*, ed. C. Zeanah. New York: Guilford Press, pp. 427–442.

———— Weston, D. & Pawl, J. H. (1991), Preventive intervention and outcome with anxiously attached dyads. *Child Devel.*, 62:199–209.

Lynch, M. (1990), Children's relatedness to peers: Attachment beyond infancy and its organization across relationships. Unpublished master's thesis, University of Rochester.

———— & Cicchetti, D. (1991), Patterns of relatedness in maltreated and nonmaltreated children: Connections among multiple representational models. *Devel. Psychopathol.*, 3:207–226.

———— & ———— (1992), Maltreated children's reports of relatedness to their teachers. *New Dir. Child Devel.*, 57:81–107.

Lyons-Ruth, K. (1992), Maternal depressive symptoms, disorganized infant-mother attachment relationships and hostile-aggressive behavior in the preschool classroom: A prospective longitudinal view from infancy to age five. In: *Rochester Symposium on Developmental Psychopathology, Vol. 4*, ed. D. Cicchetti & S. L. Toth. Rochester, NY: University of Rochester Press, pp. 131–171.

Lyons-Ruth, K., Zoll, D., Connell, D. & Grunebaum, H. (1986), The depressed mother and her one-year-old infant. In: *Maternal Depression and Infant Disturbance*, ed. E. Tronick & T. Field. San Francisco: Jossey-Bass, pp. 61–82.

———— Connell, D., Zoll, D. & Stahl, J. (1987), Infants at social risk: Relationships among infant maltreatment, maternal behavior, and infant attachment behavior. *Devel. Psychol.*, 23:223–232.

Main, M. & Goldwyn, R. (1984), Predicting rejection of her infant from mother's representation of her own experience: Implications for the abused-abusing intergenerational cycle. *Child Abuse & Neglect*, 8:203–217.

———— & Hesse, E. (1990), Parents' unresolved traumatic experiences are related to infant disorganized attachment status: Is frightened and/or frightening parent behavior the linking mechanism? In: *Attachment in the Preschool Years*, ed. M. Greenberg, D. Cicchetti, & E. M. Cummings. Chicago: University of Chicago Press, pp. 161–182.

———— Kaplan, N. & Cassidy, J. C. (1985), Security in infancy, childhood and adulthood: A move to the level of representation. In: *Growing Points of Attachment Theory and Research*, ed. I. Bretherton & E. Waters. *Monographs of the Society for Research in Child Development*. Serial No. 209, Vol. 50, Nos. 1–2, pp. 66–104.

———— & Solomon, J. (1986), Discovery of a disorganized/disoriented attachment pattern. In: *Affective Development in Infancy*, ed. T. B. Brazelton & M. W. Yogman. Norwood, NJ: Ablex, pp. 95–124.

———— & ———— (1990), Procedures for identifying infants as disorganized/disoriented during the Ainsworth strange situation. In: *Attachment in the Preschool Years*, ed. M. Greenberg, D. Cicchetti & E. M. Cummings. Chicago: University of Chicago Press, pp. 121–160.

Mann, E. & McDermott, J. (1983), Play therapy for victims of child abuse and neglect. In: *Handbook of Play Therapy*, ed. C. Shaefer & K. O'Connor. New York: Wiley, pp. 283–307.

Marvin, R. (1977), An ethological-cognitive model for the attenuation of mother-child attachment behavior. In: *Advances in the Study of Communication and Affect, Vol. 3*, ed. P. Piner. New York: Plenum Press, pp. 25–60.

———— & Stewart, R. B. (1990), A family systems framework for the study of attachment. In: *Attachment in the Preschool Years*, ed. M. T. Greenberg, D. Cicchetti & E. M. Cummings. Chicago: University of Chicago Press, pp. 51–86.

Masten, A., Best, K. & Garmezy, N. (1990), Resilience and development: Contributions from the study of children who overcome adversity. *Devel. Psychopathol.*, 2:425–444.

McCrone, E., Egeland, B., Kalkoske, M. & Carlson, E. (1994), Relations between early maltreatment and mental representations of relationships assessed with projective storytelling in middle childhood. *Devel. Psychopathol.*, 6:99–120.

Minuchin, P. (1988), Relationships within the family: A systems perspective on development. In: *Relationships within Families: Mutual Influences*, ed. R. A. Hinde & J. Stevenson-Hinde. Oxford: Clarendon Press, pp. 7–26.

Miyake, K., Chen, S. & Campos, J. (1985), Infants' temperament, mothers' mode of interaction and attachment in Japan: An interim report. In: *Growing Points of Attachment Theory and Research*, ed. I. Bretherton & E. Waters. *Monographs of the Society for Research in Child Development*, Serial No. 209, Vol. 50, Nos. 1–2, pp. 276–297.

O'Connor, M. J., Sigman, M. & Brill, N. (1987), Disorganization of attachment in relation to maternal alcohol consumption. *J. Consult. Clin. Psychol.*, 55:831–836.

Radke-Yarrow, M., Cummings, E. M., Kuczynski, L. & Chapman, M. (1985), Patterns of attachment in two-and-three-year-olds in normal families and families with parental depression. *Child Devel.*, 56:884–893.

Rieder, C. & Cicchetti, D. (1989), An organizational perspective on cognitive control functioning and cognitive-affective balance in maltreated children. *Devel. Psychol.*, 25:382–393.

Rodning, C., Beckwith, L. & Howard, J. (1991), Quality of attachment and home environments in children prenatally exposed to PCP and cocaine. *Devel. Psychopathol.*, 3:351–366.

Sagi, A., Lamb, M. E., Lewkowicz, K. S., Shoham, R., Dvir, R. & Estes, D. (1985), Security of infant-mother, -father, and -metapelet among kibbutz reared Israeli children. In: *Growing Points of Attachment Theory and Research*, ed. I. Bretherton & E. Waters. *Monographs of the Society for Research in Child Development*, Serial No. 209, Vol. 50, Nos. 1–2, pp. 257–275.

Santostefano, S. (1985), *Cognitive Control Therapy with Children and Adolescents*. Elmsford, NY: Pergamon Press.

Schneider-Rosen, K., Braunwald, K., Carlson, V. & Cicchetti, D. (1985), Current perspectives in attachment theory: Illustration from the study of maltreated infants. In: *Growing Points in Attachment Theory and Research*, ed. I. Bretherton, E. Waters. *Monographs of the Society for Research in Child Development*, Serial No. 209, Vol. 50, Nos. 1–2, pp. 194–210.

—— & Cicchetti, D. (1984), The relationship between affect and cognition in maltreated infants: Quality of attachment and the development of visual self-recognition. *Child Devel.*, 55:648–658.

Selman, R., Schultz, L. H. & Yeates, K. O. (1991), Interpersonal understanding and action: A development and psychopathology perspective on research and prevention. In: *Rochester Symposium on Developmental Psychopathology, Vol. 3*, ed. D. Cicchetti & S. L. Toth. Rochester, NY: University of Rochester Press, pp. 289–329.

—— —— Nakkula, M., Barr, D., Watts, C. & Richmond, J. (1992), Friendship and fighting: A developmental approach to the study of risk and prevention of violence. *Devel. Psychopathol.*, 4. 529–558.

Sroufe, L. A. (1979), The coherence of individual development: Early care, attachment, and subsequent developmental issues. *Amer. Psychol.*, 34:834–841.

—— & Rutter, M. (1984). The domain of developmental psychopathology. *Child Devel.*, 54:17–29.

Stevenson-Hinde, J. (1990), Attachment within family systems. *Infant Ment. Health J.*, 11:218–227.

Thompson, R., Cicchetti, D., Lamb, M. E. & Malkin, C. (1985), The emotional responses of Down syndrome and normal infants in the strange situation: The organization of affective behavior in infants. *Devel. Psychol.*, 21:828–841.

Toth, S. L. & Cicchetti, D. (1993), Child maltreatment: Where do we go from here in our treatment of victims? In: *Child Abuse, Child Development, and Social Policy*, ed. D. Cicchetti & S. L. Toth. Norwood, NJ: Ablex, pp. 399–438.

—— & —— (in press), Patterns of relatedness, depressive symptomatology, and perceived competence in maltreated children. *J. Consult. Clin. Psychol.*

Tulving, E. (1972), Episodic and semantic memory. In: *Organization of Memory*, ed. E. Tulving & W. Donaldson. New York: Academic Press, pp. 382–402.

—— (1985), How many memory systems are there? *Amer. Psychol.*, 40:385–398.

Vaughn, B., Egeland, E., Sroufe, L. A. & Waters, E. (1979), Individual differences in infant-mother attachment at 12 and 18 months: Stability and change in families under stress. *Child Devel.*, 50:971–975.

—— Goldberg, S., Atkinson, L., Marcovitch, S. MacGregor, D. & Seifer, R. (1994), Quality of toddler-mother attachment in children with Down syndrome: Limits to interpretation of strange situation behavior. *Child Devel.*, 65:95–108.

Werner, H. & Kaplan, B. (1963), *Symbol Formation: An Organismic-Developmental Approach to Language and the Expression of Thought*. New York: Wiley.

Youngblade, L. & Belsky, J. (1989), Short- and long-term consequences. In: *Children at Risk*, ed. R. T. Ammerman & M. Herson. New York: Plenum Press, pp. 109–146.

Zeanah, C., ed. (1993), *Handbook of Infant Mental Health*. New York: Guilford Press.

❖ 11 ❖

Attachment Organization and Vulnerability to Loss, Separation, and Abuse in Disturbed Adolescents

KENNETH S. ADAM, ADRIENNE E. SHELDON KELLER,
AND MALCOLM WEST

"[T]he [developmental] pathway followed by each individual and the extent to which he or she becomes resilient to stressful life events is determined to a very significant degree by the pattern of attachment he or she develops during the early years."
—Bowlby, 1988, p. 172

The publication of "Forty-Four Juvenile Thieves" (Bowlby, 1944) was an important event in the history of psychoanalytic thinking about the relationship of trauma to psychopathology. In this study Bowlby selected a group of 44 "affectionless characters" showing serious difficulties in interpersonal relations. The life histories showed that 12 had been separated from their mothers in infancy or early childhood, a much higher proportion than in the rest of the thieves. The results of this study directed attention to the role of actual adverse family experiences in the determination of psychopathology and made clear Bowlby's belief that a range of traumatic early experiences (such as maternal deprivation and parental loss), which have always had etiological connotations in psychoanalysis, can be approached in terms of systematic investigation. This chapter is but one example that attachment researchers are meeting the challenge of Bowlby's approach.

This study was supported by Health and Welfare Canada, NHRDP Project 3 6606-4221-MH. The authors wish to thank Dr. Mary Owens of the C. M. Hincks Training and Resource Institute, Toronto, Ontario, who participated as one of the AAI raters in this study. The authors also recognize the contributions of Dr. Betty Kershner, Dr. Libby Goszer, and Dr. Mario Cappelli, who conducted the interviews; and Simon Larose, who assisted in the data analysis. We are grateful to Mary Main and Mary Jo Ward for consultations around coding of some of the adolescent AAI transcripts.

309

Psychiatric Contributions

The concept of trauma is included in DSM-IV classifications of post-traumatic stress disorder and acute stress disorder (American Psychiatric Association, 1994). Both disorders are defined by characteristic symptoms and clinical courses following exposure to psychologically distressing events. The events described as typical traumatic stressors within this schema are all extreme events external to the individual, for example, direct threat to life or physical integrity, witnessing such a threat directed toward others, and learning about the unexpected or violent death of family members or close associates. While DSM-IV assumes that the severity, duration, and proximity of exposure to these events are the most important factors leading to traumatic effects, there is explicit recognition that other variables, such as the availability of social support, childhood experiences, and personality variables, may affect risk of morbidity following trauma. The precise role of these variables, however, remains uncertain and controversial (McFarlane, 1990; Herman, 1992).

Within DSM-IV, stressful life experiences, such as marital breakdown, the termination of romantic relationships, or separation from the parental home, are considered precursors of adjustment disorders but not of acute stress disorders. The argument for this distinction within the DSM classifications has been that, in contrast to more extreme events, these events are commonplace, normally take a predictable course, and rarely produce long-term effects. Bereavement is considered separately as "other condition that may be a focus of clinical attention" (p. 684), although it is also acknowledged that under certain circumstances (violent, unexpected death) it may lead to posttraumatic stress disorder.

Unlike the psychiatric literature, which has focused on the impact of current traumatic events, psychoanalytic theories have been particularly concerned with early trauma and trauma inflicted upon the child by caretakers (Balint, 1969; Blum, 1986).

Psychoanalytic Contributions

In the theory of infantile seduction, Freud originally considered that events were traumatic for purely quantitative reasons; that is, trauma results from an influx of stimuli from without that overwhelm the child's stimulus barrier (Breuer and Freud, 1893–95; Freud, 1920). In 1926, Freud proposed a new formulation that defined trauma as a psychological experience of helplessness arranged around the danger situations of loss of the object, loss of the object's love, castration, and superego condemnation. In this revised model, a distressing experience is traumatic because of the way it impinges on the individual's state of mind, regardless of its source. Freud observed, "The essence of a traumatic situation is the experience of helplessness on the part of the ego in the face of an accumulation of excitation, whether of external or internal origin" (p. 81). Thus, Freud added the psychological meaning of the experience to his conception of trauma (Baranger, Baranger, and Mom, 1988). Because of this focus on the psychological meaning of the event, psychoanalytic writers have favored the terms "traumatic experience" and "traumatic situation" instead of "trauma" or "traumatic event."

Sandler, Dreher, and Drews (1991) differentiate between the immediate reactions to traumatic situations (such as posttraumatic stress disorder) and the later consequences (such as somatoform and personality disorders). The latter are viewed as adaptations or containments of traumatic experience involving defensive operations and integration of the experience at the representational level. Psychoanalytic developmental theory has been concerned with determining which early experiences are potentially traumatic and how they impinge upon developing internal structures to produce symptomatic or characterological manifestations. Major theoretical differences exist regarding the kind of events that are viewed as potentially traumatic, the extent to which traumatic experience is inherent in development, providing impetus for growth, and the extent to which it is a complication for development, threatening its progression.

Within both the Freudian and the Kleinian frameworks, specific developmental traumas are linked to specific developmental phases. In the traditional Freudian theory specific traumas (loss of the object, castration threat, and so on) are related to the stages of psychosexual development, each of which is held to have characteristic tasks, anxieties, and consequences for character development. In Kleinian theory the trauma of weaning is seen as contributing to a central developmental task, the move from the paranoid-schizoid to the depressive position. These positions are characterized by specific anxieties and internal object relations and are seen as dynamic constellations with structurelike properties, wherein the residue of traumatic experience resides (Segal, 1986). Within both the Freudian and Kleinian frameworks, traumatic experience is both an inevitable accompaniment of, and stimulus to, development. Resolution and integration of traumatic experiences are considered crucial developmental tasks.

Unlike traditional Freudian and Kleinian theorists, who conceptualize trauma in phase-specific terms, object relations theorists distinguish untraumatized normal development from development compromised by trauma. Winnicott (1960) viewed healthy personality development in touch with a true self as emerging from the experience of "good-enough" mothering. Maternal failures marked by traumatic impingements, on the other hand, could lead to false self-formation and personality disorder. For Fairbairn (1952), the self is, from the beginning, a whole that subsequently splits as a result of traumatization. According to Fairbairn's account, more or less durable psychic structures represent what has been internalized through traumatic interactions. Sutherland (1989) summarized Fairbairn's two central hypotheses as follows: psychic structures constitute a record of traumatic interactions between the child and its caregiver; and dissociative splits within the child occur as a result of these interactions. Similarly, for Guntrip (1969), psychopathology represents the structuring of "bad" traumatic experience that cannot be "metabolized," leading to a defensive schizoid retreat from the dangers of reexperiencing the traumatic situation.

In summary, the relational tradition within psychoanalysis has not seen the parent–child relationship as an inevitable source of traumatic experience. Instead, this relationship is viewed as a protective cocoon between the internal and external worlds that insulates the child from traumatic experience and allows development to proceed.

Empirical efforts to demonstrate causal links among childhood traumatic experience, developmental psychopathology, and adult psychiatric disorder have foundered on the complexity of these interactions and the lack of appropriate means for investigating them. The definition of traumatic events of interest has often been imprecise and arbitrary, with great variability across studies making comparison of findings a difficult exercise. The focus on linear relationships between putative traumatic events (such as parental death) and later psychopathology has produced many inconsistent findings, leading some to question both the strength and specificity of traumatic effects (Tennant, Bebbington, and Hurry, 1980, 1981; Lloyd, 1980). Furthermore, there has been a tendency to treat specific events, such as sexual abuse or parental loss, as independent variables with separate effects, rather than to examine the possibility that they might exert their effects on common developmental pathways (Adam, 1994). Finally, while there is general agreement that traumatic experiences may be internalized within the individual and actively influence thinking and behavior, adequate instruments for identifying traumatic residua and measuring their contemporary effects have been lacking. While a good deal is known about the external variables that influence traumatic response, such as the frequency and severity of trauma, much less is known about factors that predispose to individual vulnerabilty to trauma or those that promote resiliency.

Full understanding of these relationships must involve knowledge of the usual developmental pathways that might be affected and the effects of specific traumas in relation to these pathways. The growth of attachment theory, with its strong empirical base and the development of instruments devised to explore its specific concepts, opens the door to systematic exploration of these issues.

Attachment Theory

The development of attachment theory was shaped by Bowlby's conviction that both parental loss and prolonged separations from parents in childhood were potentially traumatic experiences. His early case studies and his extensive review of the literature on maternal deprivation for the World Health Organization convinced him that the stable presence of primary caretakers was essential to healthy personality development, while discontinuities in this care could have profound deleterious effects (Bowlby, 1940, 1944, 1951, 1969; Newcombe and Lerner, 1982). His search for evidence for his views took him in two diverging directions, each of which informed the other. The first was to a far-reaching theoretical reconsideration of the nature of the early mother–infant bond, and the second was to the fostering of systematic research on the effects of disruptions of this bond in children.

The early naturalistic studies of normal children following brief separations from their parents yielded a number of important findings: (1) dramatic responses to separation appeared to be universal in children; (2) children's responses to prolonged separation appeared to proceed regularly through a series of phases: a phase of protest in which the child's behavior is organized toward retrieving the lost parent; a phase of despair and disorganization when circumstances make this impossible; and finally a phase of detachment in which the child becomes closed off to feelings about the parent; and (3) certain conditions, such as adequate preparation, the presence of familiar alternative caretakers, and visits by the parents, altered the intensity and duration of the responses (Robertson and Bowlby, 1952; Robertson, 1952, 1953; Bowlby, 1953; Heinicke and Westheimer, 1966).

Bowlby was impressed by the similarity between children's responses to brief separations and descriptions of adult mourning and noted that the protest phase of the recently separated child resembled the yearning and pining of the adult in early grief and that the despair phase resembled the preoccupying sadness of adult mourning. He observed that, unlike the normal course of adult mourning, in which grief and despair give way to the acceptance of the reality of the loss and a reorientation toward new relationships, in children the premature onset of detachment often dominated the mourning process and produced a situation resembling pathological mourning in adults (Bowlby, 1960, 1961). Bowlby posited that an identical, but more extreme, process occurred when separation was permanent or when the parent died and that this often led to later psychiatric disturbance.

Ainsworth's experimental Strange Situation protocol provided methodological access to Bowlby's insight that separation was the key to understanding attachment (Ainsworth et al., 1978). Careful observation of a sequence of brief separations from, and reunions with, the parent confirmed separation to be a strong activator of the attachment system and enabled infants from 12 to 24 months of age to be classified into three patterns of attachment. Infants classified as secure (B category) attend to the mother with ease and interest, protest her departure during separations, and welcome her return and usually seek close contact. Insecure/avoidant infants (A category) appear uninvolved with the parent when present, are apparently untroubled by her departure, and ignore her on reunion and seldom seek or welcome contact. Insecure/ambivalent infants (C category) are anxiously oriented toward the parent, protest separations violently, tolerate them poorly, and show a mixture of angry contact seeking and rejection of the parent on reunion.

The differences in behavior observed in the Strange Situation correlate consistently with parent–child interactions in the home situation, and these interactions form the basis of the child's internal working models of attachment (Bowlby, 1973; Bretherton, 1985). Through repeated transactions with caretakers, these internal models become increasingly complex and organized into traitlike patterns or "structures" within the child's personality and inform expectations of caretakers and guide the child's behavior in relation to them. While it is the product of dyadic interactions between parent and child, with the growth of cognitive competence and symbolic function, the internal working model increasingly becomes "the property of the child" (Bowlby, 1988, p. 129). The process by which repeated interactions with the same caretaker or different interactions with several caretakers eventually become integrated into generalized internal models of attachment is at present, poorly understood but appears to involve the development of hierarchies and to be contingent on certain cognitive capacities that themselves are affected by the quality of parent–child interaction (Main, Kaplan, and Cassidy, 1985; Bretherton, 1985; Main, 1991).

In the third volume of his trilogy *Attachment and Loss*, Bowlby discussed the relationship of loss and pathological mourning to depression, anxiety, and other psychiatric disorders (Bowlby, 1980). Using clinical evidence and empirical studies of adult mourning, Bowlby (1977, 1980) delineated three personality types prone to pathological mourning: those who were anxious and ambivalent (anxiously attached), those who put others' attachment needs before their own (compulsive caregiving), and those who persistently maintained their independence from others (compulsive self-reliance). Although these deviant patterns of attachment clearly resemble the insecure patterns of attachment in infants described by Ainsworth, the role of early trauma and variations in attachment patterns to later vulnerability to trauma is not spelled out. Happily, two recent developments in attachment research have allowed these issues to be explored more directly: (1) the discovery of the insecure disoriented/disorganized (D) pattern among infants in the Strange Situation and (2) its relationship to the parent's own attachment pattern.

Several Strange Situation studies of children in high-risk samples identified atypical attachment patterns previously reported rarely in nonclinical studies. Crittenden (1985, 1988), Spieker and Booth (1988), and Radke-Yarrow et al. (1985) all described a mixed avoidant/ambivalent (A/C) pattern in maltreated children and children of severely depressed mothers. Simultaneously, Main and Solomon (1986) described a disorganized-disoriented (D) pattern after an extensive review of difficult-to-classify infants from several normative samples. Unlike the other three groups of children, who showed well-organized strategies for dealing with attachment-related stress, the disorganized-disoriented children showed a variety of unusual and contradictory behaviors in the reunion episodes (e.g., seeking, then avoiding, proximity to the parent or showing "freezing" and other stereotyped behaviors). Similar to the A/C pattern, the D pattern was found in a high percentage of maltreated infants (Lyons-Ruth et al., 1987; Carlson et al., 1989). The D pattern in children was subsequently found to be strongly associated with a parental history of unresolved loss of a close family member and suggested an intergenerational link between extremes of parental attachment experience and extremes of attachment insecurity in the child (Main, Kaplan, and Cassidy, 1985; Main and Hesse, 1990).

The Adult Attachment Interview was initially developed by George, Kaplan, and Main (1985) to provide a means of assessing parents' internal working models with respect to their early attachment relationships. Three patterns of parental attachment were initially described in the coding system developed by Main and Goldwyn (1985–94): an autonomous/secure pattern (F), corresponding to the infant secure pattern; a dismissing pattern (Ds), corresponding to the infant avoidant pattern; and a preoccupied pattern (E), corresponding to the infant ambivalent pattern. A fourth classification, lack of resolution of mourning (U), was later added, based on Bowlby's descriptions of normal and pathological mourning for parents who had experienced the loss of an attachment figure prior to adolescence (Main et al., 1985). Subsequently, this classification was expanded to include lack of resolution for trauma due to physical or sexual abuse and renamed the unresolved/disorganized-disoriented (Ud) pattern. The relationship between parental Ud classification and infant D classification has been confirmed in several studies (Ainsworth and Eichberg, 1991; Fonagy, Steele, and Steele, 1991; van IJzendoorn, 1992; Bakermans-Kranenburg and van IJzendoorn, 1993; Benoit and Parker, 1994; Ward and Carlson, in press). The ability to assess both the basic organization of attachment and the effects of traumatic attachment experience on this organization empirically now allows Bowlby's hypothesized relationship between attachment organization and loss to be tested directly (see also Cicchetti, this volume).

Present Study

Using a variety of attachment-related instruments, the present study is part of a larger study undertaken to explore the role of insecure attachment in adolescent suicidal behavior. Subjects consisted of 187 adolescents recruited to the study on admission to outpatient and residential treatment centers in three Canadian cities. Subjects with psychosis, organic brain disorder, mental subnormality, and severe physical illness were excluded; otherwise, the sample reflected a full range of emotionally and behaviorally disturbed adolescents. A subsample of subjects (those 13 and older) was given the Adult Attachment Interview. The final AAI sample consisted of 133 subjects between 13 and 19 years of age (mean age 15.3, S.D. 1.47) and included 74 males and 59 females. We report here the Adult Attachment Interview findings for these 133 subjects and focus on the subsample of subjects unresolved for traumatic attachment experiences (loss, separation, and abuse). The protocol for the overall study and other findings are described in related publications (Adam et al., 1994; Adam, Sheldon-Keller, and West, in press; Sheldon-Keller et al., submitted).

DATA COLLECTION AND RATING

All subjects were seen in two interviews. During the first they completed a variety of demographic and psychiatric questionnaires, and during the second they completed an adolescent version of the Adult Attachment Interview, with some questions slightly modified as suggested by Ward and Carlson (personal communication, 1990) to suit this population. The interviews were tape-recorded, the taped interviews transcribed, and the transcripts distributed between three trained raters for independent blind rating. All interviews were rated by at least two of the three raters, with final ratings arrived at by consensus following discussion. The mean concordance rate across the four major AAI classifications for all pairs of raters was 78.6%, and mean kappa for the unresolved/disorganized and primary AAI categories was .50. When order of assignment of the unresolved/disorganized category was ignored (e.g., a classification of Ud/F was considered equivalent to a classification of F/Ud) the kappa rose to .71. A full report of the AAI reliabilities can be found in Sheldon-Keller et al. (submitted).

Adult Attachment Interview (AAI)

The AAI explores the current state of mind with respect to attachment in a semistructured interview based on a series of questions exploring attachment-related themes. Interviews are rated from verbatim transcriptions by using a series of nine-point scales according to criteria outlined by Main and Goldwyn (1985–94). Five scales concern the subject's probable experience with parents in childhood, and a further five scales are concerned with his or her current state of mind with respect to these experiences. The final rating of the transcript is based on the overall coherence of the discourse and specific characteristics of the current state of mind as outlined in the classification system. Assignment is made to one of four major categories: secure/autonomous (F) with respect to attachment; dismissing (Ds) of attachment and/or attachment-related feelings; preoccupied (E) with or by early attachments; and unresolved/disoriented or disorganized (Ud) state of mind with respect to experiences of loss or abuse (sexual or physical). A fifth category, cannot classify (CC), is used where no single primary attachment category can be determined. Each of the primary categories has a number of subcategories, depending on specific characteristics of the interview discourse. For example, while all individuals in the E category have in common a marked preoccupation with past parental relationships, three different types of preoccupation can be discerned. The

E1 subgroup appear passively preoccupied with childhood experiences and speak about them at length while seeming unable to focus clearly on relevant themes. The E2 subgroup are angrily entangled with negative thoughts of their parents and unable to see any role they might play in their interactional difficulties. The E3 subgroup are preoccupied throughout the interview with frightening, often traumatic, attachment-related experiences. Subdivisions of the other primary categories follow specific characteristics outlined in the manual.

Where the unresolved/disorganized or cannot classify categories are assigned, the best-fitting F, Ds, or E category is also assigned to reflect the overall coherence of the transcript and the basic underlying attachment organization. For example, a classification of Ud/F indicates the subject is unresolved for loss or trauma, with an autonomous, underlying organization, while CC/Ds-E indicates the subject cannot be classified but shows a mixture of dismissing and preoccupied elements. We refer to the first three categories (F, Ds, and E) as "primary" to reflect the basic underlying organization and to "first" and "second" categories when the presence of Ud or CC requires a complex categorization such as Ud/F.

The Unresolved/Disoriented, Disorganized Scale

The unresolved (Ud) scale of the AAI is used to classify subjects who show lapses in the monitoring of reasoning or discourse when asked to describe potentially traumatic events such as important losses or parental abuse. This classification is based on Bowlby's idea that, as attention is continually focused on the attachment figure during periods of vital dependence, the loss of an attachment figure is a naturally disorganizing and disorienting experience (Main and Hesse, 1990). Continuing disorganization and disorientation indicative of lack of resolution of loss or trauma are manifest during the interview in (1) lapses in the metacognitive monitoring of reasoning, such as indications of disbelief that a person is dead, ideas of being causal in the death, indications of confusion between the dead person and self, and other psychologically confused statements; (2) lapses in the metacognitive monitoring of discourse such as prolonged, innappropriate silences, odd associations, unusual attention to detail, poetic or eulogistic phrasing of speech; (3) reports of extreme behavioral responses at the time of the trauma in the absence of convincing evidence that resolution has taken place (Main and Goldwyn, 1985–94).

The unresolved scale was empirically derived from the observation that the mothers of infants classified as disorganized/disoriented in the Strange Situation had a high incidence of unresolved loss (Main and Solomon, 1986; Main and Hesse, 1990). Subsequent observations revealed that similar evidence of disorganization in discourse and thinking was found in mothers describing incidents of sexual abuse. It is now recognized that other extreme events involving parents may lead to confusion, irrational thinking, and disorientation similar to what is associated with loss or sexual abuse. Severe physical abuse, bizarre punishments, and frightening parental behavior are now considered potentially traumatic events within the Ud category of the AAI (Main and Goldwyn, 1985–94). Other extreme experiences, such as being witness to extreme violence directed toward others or being the victim of extreme events not involving family figures, are not currently considered under the Ud scale within the AAI manual, although some workers are beginning to consider these and other extreme experiences as possible precursors of a Ud state of mind. Ainsworth and Eichberg (1991) reported several cases of disorganized infants whose mothers were not unresolved for loss but who showed disorganized thinking around other traumatic experiences. One mother had experienced a close brush with death, a second had a father with a serious drug addiction that affected her mother, and a third had been physically abused and placed in a foster home.

Unresolved Separation as an Attachment Trauma

In a number of pilot interviews, when subjects reported severe separation experiences, such as being unwillingly ejected from the home or placed in residential or foster care, we found many of the same indexes of disorganization described in the AAI manual for unresolved loss or abuse. This led us to feel that lack of resolution of separation ought to be considered as another potentially traumatic event under the Ud category. These Ud characteristics are best illustrated by examples drawn from transcripts of our subjects. (In these transcripts, some details have been altered to disguise the identity of the subjects.)

Lapses in the Metacognitive Monitoring of Reasoning

Example 1. Psychologically confused statement around discussion of separation from foster parents. "Um, I've been living with them since five years and it's like they'd been a different family when we went to court and that's the last time *they* saw each other so . . ."

Example 2. Disbelief following being extruded from home to the street. "Well, when they kicked me out that day, I thought holy, I'm going to be by myself, I'm not going to be with my family, that was the scariest time. I mean I didn't cry, well I cried when I got to [institution] and I was lying in bed, I did cry but when--I mean I thought, *how can my parents kick me out of my own house, how could they do that to their own daughter?---they said, "You have to leave tonight." Where am I going to go? It's like I'm all here by myself here, my family won't take me, my home won't take me, what the hell am I gonna do?*---but that was scary, you know you're on your own, woman, it's like, ah, that's scary you know. I can understand if you're older, like I was only 12, no 13, but I just turned 12 in March, so I was only like three months - four months being thirteen, I mean, God, I was like just an early teenager, still I mean, I was scared, you know I didn't know what I was going to do, never been on my own before, but when you're older, you know more things about living, the money---but when you're that young, you don't know that much, yet I mean, your body's only thirteen years old!"

Lapses in the Metacognitive Monitoring of Discourse

Example 1. Subject responding with unusual detail to a probe about the events leading up to his residential placement. "Okay, we drove down the 400 to the Gardner [expressway], across the Gardiner to Jarvis, up Jarvis to 440 Jarvis--we open the car door first, my dad opened his, then the front right one on the driver's passenger's side, then---took out the suitcases and walked in the door - it opens to the left - we walked through—sat in the chairs until the receptionist arrived, etc."

Example 2. Odd associations, sudden changes of topic, and disorientation following admission to hospital. "Oh, I was pissed and I was s—and I was sad, cause I mean, you know, I would, I would, I would see ahhh. . . . like I nev . . . I'd nap and stuff like that and one time, you just, *I'd scared me cause I thought that like ahh, Dad sent me some flowers for . . . my birthday and I woke up late and . . . right?* and I thought my dad had come into the hospital and I was sleeping through it . . . *we have a wasp, are you afraid of them?* Okay, anyway, and I hears the nurses coming and said your dad delivered these which was a mistake *cause I'm a little kid* and I had just woken up and I was like Christ! I missed my dad! and I started to cry and everything and . . . *it was a little plant, styrofoam type of thing of a bee. . . .* [laughs] *a lit. . . . nice touch of a little bee.*"

Reports of Extreme Disorganization of Behavior following Separation

Example 1. Subject was asked to describe how he reacted when taken to residential placement after his depressed mother had unexpectedly been admitted to hospital. "How did I react? *I burned the place down* [laughs]*—sakes I lit a fire to a curtain in one of the rooms there....* then I, I really can't, *that's one of the times that I can't really remember,* I was only real little. Hmmm, Hmmm was fooling around with matches and fuuuuuuun! [laughs]"

Example 2. This 16-year-old girl raised the subject of parental separation spontaneously in response to a general question regarding possible setbacks in her early life. "My mom told me when we were walking across the street one time. My mom said [name], 'I'm going to be splitting up with your dad for awhile. What do you think about that?'—and I went, *'Yeah!'* [loud voice], *I stuck my hand up in the air and starting yell, 'Yeah! Yeah! Yeeah!'* and don't ask me why I did that, and then and then *I use to hide in the closet when I got mad or something and I use to draw people with no arms* and I use to--but I kept it in that I fel—I didn't feel I didn't know if I felt bad or not I jus—*I can't remember.*"

We drew up criteria for rating lack of resolution for separation similar to the criteria for rating unresolved loss or abuse in the AAI manual and included this as one of our Ud categories. In view of the ubiquity of separations in childhood, we considered only separations that were clearly unwilling and unexpected, such as parental separation or divorce, parental illness leading to prolonged hospitalization, the child's being ejected from the home by the parents or uplifted for foster or residential placement. Fourteen subjects were rated Ud for separation alone, and a further 14 were rated Ud for separation in addition to either loss or trauma. As many of our subjects experienced more than one category of trauma, we were careful to note whether the Ud rating was for loss (UdLoss), separation (UdSeparation), or abuse (UdAbuse).

RESULTS

AAI Classifications for Overall Clinical Sample

Sixty-five of the 133 subjects (49%) were classified as unresolved for loss, separation, or abuse (Ud); 21 (16%) were autonomous (F); 35

Table 1 AAI Classifications Total Clinical Sample (N = 133)

AAI Classifications	First Category		Forced Second Category (Ud Subjects only)		Total	
	n	%	n	%	n	%
Ud	65	49	–	–	–	–
F	21	16	9	14	30	23
Ds	35	26	10	15	45	34
E	8	6	31	48	39	29
CC	4	3	15	23	19	14
Total	133	100	65	100	133	100

KEY
AAI = Adult Attachment Interview (Adolescent Modification)
Ud = Unresolved/Disorganized
F = Autonomous, free
Ds = Dismissing
E = Preoccupied
CC = Can't classify
STATISTICAL SIGNIFICANCE: Ud is significantly associated with the primary classification of preoccupied (E) and with "can't classify" (CC) (χ^2 = 38.57, df = 3, p < .001).

(26%) were dismissing; and 8 (6%) were preoccupied (E). A further 4 (3%) subjects were placed in the cannot classify category (CC) (see Table 1). These first category classifications show considerably more subjects unresolved and fewer autonomous than in nonclinical adolescent populations.

Van IJzendoorn and Bakermans-Kranenburg (in press), in their meta-analysis of AAI studies, report average figures of 20% for Ud (including cannot classify) and 48% for autonomous (F) in normative adolescent samples. Our findings for Ud are consistent with those of Allen and Hauser (1991) and Allen (1993), who found 52% of their sample of nonpsychotic inpatient adolescents to be Ud for loss or abuse, but not with those of Rosenstein and Horowitz (in press), who report an incidence of only 18% unresolved in another inpatient adolescent sample. The data from these latter three studies are not directly comparable to ours, as Allen and Hauser and Allen included cannot classify subjects with Ud subjects, and Rosenstein and Horowitz, using an earlier AAI manual, did not rate Ud for abuse. None of the other studies rated subjects for lack of resolution of severe separation.

These first category classifications, however, do not tell the whole story because, within the AAI system, all subjects classified as unresolved (Ud) are also force-classified into their best-fitting primary

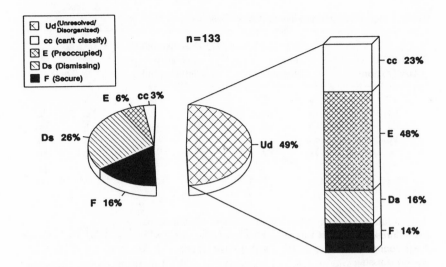

Figure 1 Adult Attachment Interview Classification

category, yielding the final complex categories of Ud/F (unresolved/
autonomous), Ud/E (unresolved/preoccupied), Ud/Ds (unresolved/
dismissing), and Ud/CC (unresolved/cannot classify). This markedly
increases the numbers of subjects in the sample with preoccupied
(E) and cannot classify (CC) elements. Figure 1 illustrates the relationship of Ud to the forced second-category classifications. The
first-category classifications including Ud subjects are indicated in
the circle on the left, and the Ud subjects are then shown redis-
tributed into each of the respective forced second categories in the
column to the right. There is a strong interrelationship between
unresolved/disorganized classification and forced second classification of preoccupied (E) and cannot classify (CC), which accounts for
the increase in these elements in the final complex categorizations.
Nearly half (48%) of the 65 subjects classified as Ud were assigned a
secondary classification of preoccupied (E), and a further 23%
subjects were assigned to cannot classify (CC). This represented 31
of the 39 (79.5%) subjects classified as E and 15 of the 19 (79%)
subjects classified as CC and pointed to a strong interrelationship
between these specific attachment categories and unresolved
attachment trauma.

Relationship of the Unresolved Category to the Preoccupied Subgroup

Although a majority of all preoccupied subjects were found to be
unresolved for loss, separation, or abuse, two subgroups stood out

Table 2 Unresolved/Disorganized (Ud) by Preoccupied (E) Subtype

PREOCCUPIED SUBTYPES	UNRESOLVED/DISORGANIZED STATUS					
	Ud		Non-Ud		Total	
	n	%	n	%	n	%
E1	6	19	5	63	11	28
E2	13	42	2	25	15	39
E3	12	39	1	13	13	33
Total	31	100	8	101	39	100

STATISTICAL SIGNIFICANCE: E1 is overrepresented in Non-Ud (Fisher's Exact two-tailed p = .03).

(see Table 2). Twelve of the 13 (92%) subjects classified in the E3 (traumatic preoccupation) subgroup were Ud, as were 13 of the 15 (87%) of E2 (angry preoccupation) subjects. Of the three subgroups, only the E1 (passive preoccupation) subgroup was overrepresented in the resolved/dismissed (non/Ud) group.

Not unexpectedly, in the E3 (traumatic preoccupation) subgroup, many subjects showed lapses in monitoring of reasoning or discourse in relation to more than one episode of traumatic experience. Ten of the 12 (83%) Ud/E3 subjects were classified as unresolved on more than one category of trauma, and both subjects classified as unresolved for all three categories of attachment trauma (loss, separation, and physical or sexual abuse) were classified Ud/E3. This contrasted with the other complex classifications; only 33% of Ud/E1, 31% of Ud/E2, 22% of Ud/F, and 26% of Ud/CC subjects were coded Ud for more than one category of attachment trauma. *None* of Ud/Ds were classified as unresolved (Ud) for more than one category of attachment trauma.

Effect of AAI Classification on Resolution of Loss, Separation, and Trauma

The criterion for classification of Ud is that subjects reporting loss, separation, or trauma must score 5 or more on the 9-point unresolved scale of the AAI. This requires specific evidence of disorganization or disorientation during discussion of potentially traumatic themes. Subjects not showing significant disorganization or disorientation around discussion of traumatic experiences are coded less than 5 on this scale and not assigned a Ud classification. While some of these subjects may have resolved the experience, others may have simply set it aside and dismissed it from active consideration. We have termed this group "resolved/dismissed" (non-Ud) to reflect this fact. In view of our interest in vulnerability to trauma, we were curious to see if adolescents coded unresolved for loss, separation, or abuse differed in their underlying primary classification from those who had either resolved or dismissed the experience.

Of the 133 young subjects completing the AAI, 109 (82%) reported at least one episode with a parent or other close figure meeting criteria for significant loss, separation, or abuse as set out in the AAI manual and our new criteria for traumatic separation. Sixty-five (60.0%) of these 109 subjects reached criteria for classification as unresolved (Ud), and the remainder were judged to be re-solved/dismissed (non-Ud) for the episode in question (see Table 3).

As noted earlier, subjects who were classified as unresolved were more likely to be coded as preoccupied (E) or cannot classify (CC) as a forced second category than were other subjects (see Figure 1). As can be seen in Figure 2, forced second-category classifications of autonomous (F) and dismissing (Ds) attachment strategies were given to fewer than one-third of the subjects classified as unresolved for loss, separation, or abuse. These relationships appear to hold for all unresolved subjects whether classified as unresolved for loss, separation, or abuse, although small numbers made statistical analysis impossible (see Figure 3).

Table 3 Loss, Abuse or Separation Experiences and AAI Primary Classification

Loss, Abuse or Separation	AAI Primary Classification									
	F		Ds		E		CC		Total	
	n	%	n	%	n	%	n	%	n	%
None	7	23	10	22	5	13	2	11	24	18
Resolved or Dismissed	14	47	25	56	3	8	2	11	44	33
Unresolved/ Disorganized	9	30	10	22	31	80	15	79	65	49
Total	30	100	45	100	39	101	19	100	133	100

KEY
AAI = Adult Attachment Interview (Adolescent Modification)
F = Autonomous, free
Ds = Dismissing
E = Preoccupied
CC = Can't classify
STATISTICAL SIGNIFICANCE: [None vs. Resolved/Dismissed] vs. Unresolved/Disorganized: χ^2 = 40.87, df = 6, p < .0001).
None vs. Resolved/Dismissed: χ^2 = 3.70, df = 3, p = .30
[None+Resolved/Dismissed] vs. Unresolved/Disorganized: χ^2 = 38.57, df = 3, p < .0001).

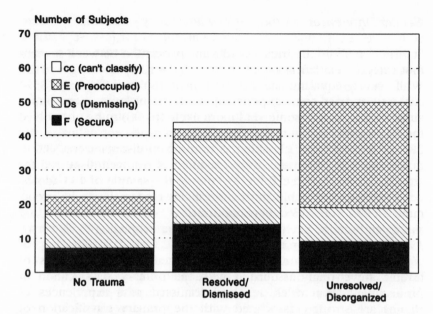

Figure 2 Resolution of Loss, Abuse or Separation Experiences in Relationship to Primary Classifications on the AAI

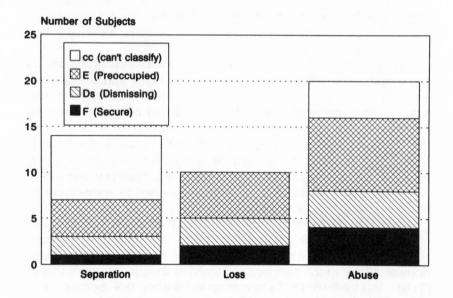

Figure 3 Type of Unresolved/Disorganized Trauma in Relationship to Primary Classifications on the AAI

Gender Differences

Statistical analysis confirms a significant association between sex and first category classification on the AAI (χ^2 = 12.9, df = 4, p = .012). While nearly equal numbers of both male (80%) and female (85%) subjects reported some experience of significant loss, separation, or abuse, females were somewhat more likely (p<.08) to be unresolved for these experiences than males. Forty-two percent of males and 58% of females were classified as unresolved/disorganized; 38% of males and 27% of females were classified as resolved/dismissed for attachment trauma (see Table 4). Among the sample of 133 adolescents, females are significantly more likely than males to be preoccupied (10% versus 3%; likelihood ratio = 3.763), while males are significantly more likely than females to be dismissing (35% versus 15%; likelihood ratio = 2.26).

For both sexes, unresolved/disorganized past experiences of trauma are strongly associated with the primary classification of preoccupied. For males, resolved/dismissed past experiences of trauma are strongly associated with the primary classification of dismissing; for females, resolved/dismissed past experiences of trauma are associated with both the primary classifications of autonomous and dismissing. For males, the absence of past experiences of trauma is associated with the primary classification of dismissing. For females, the absence of past experiences of trauma is approximately equally associated with autonomous, dismissing, and preoccupied (see Table 4).

Females were somewhat more likely to be classified as unresolved for sexual abuse than males (20% versus 11%), and males were somewhat more likely to be classified unresolved for separation than females (38% versus 26%), but these trends did not reach statistical significance. Unresolved sexual abuse accounted for a minority of the total unresolved traumatic abuse experiences in the sample overall (16.5%), and it was extremely rare for subjects to report sexual abuse in isolation. Only one subject was classified unresolved for sexual abuse alone, with all others classified as unresolved for physical abuse, loss, or separation as well.

While the numbers of subjects unresolved for more than one category of traumatic experience were too small for statistical analysis, it is interesting to note that of the 21 subjects coded unresolved for more than one category of trauma, 15 were female (71%), and only 6 (29%) were male. Within this context it is important to emphasize that when we refer to multiple traumas we refer to subjects who were unresolved for *more than one category* of trauma under the Ud scale of the AAI, not to repeated

Table 4 Loss, Abuse or Separation Experiences and AAI Primary Classifications by Sex

Loss, Abuse or Separation	AAI Primary Classification									
	F		Ds		E		CC		Total	
Males	n	%	n	%	n	%	n	%	n	%
None	4	31	8	26	1	6	2	17	15	20
Resolved or Dismissed	7	54	18	58	1	6	2	17	28	38
Unresolved/ Disorganized	2	15	5	16	16	89	8	67	31	42
Total	13	100	31	100	18	100	12	101	74	100
Females	n	%	n	%	n	%	n	%	n	%
None	3	18	2	14	4	19	0	0	9	15
Resolved or Dismissed	7	41	7	50	2	10	0	0	16	27
Unresolved/ Disorganized	7	41	5	36	15	71	7	100	34	58
Total	17	100	14	101	21	100	7	100	·59	101

KEY

AAI = Adult Attachment Interview
F = Autonomous, free
Ds = Dismissing
E = Preoccupied
CC = Can't classify
STATISTICAL SIGNIFICANCE:
Males: None vs. Resolved/Dismissed vs. Unresolved/Disorganized: χ^2 = 32.13, df = 6, p = .00002*; None vs. Resolved/Dismissed: χ^2 = .81, df = 3, p = .848*; None+Resolved/ Dismissed vs. Unresolved/Disorganized: χ^2 = 31.56, df = 3, p = .0000006; 2 x 2 table of (None+Resolved/Dismissed) vs. Unresolved/Disorganized by (Autonomous+Dismissing) vs. (Preoccupied+can't classify): Fisher's exact p < .0001; Odds ration = 21.14; 95% Confidence Interval for Odds Ratio = 5.55 to 87.41.

Females: None vs. Resolved/Dismissed vs. Unresolved/Disorganized: χ^2 = 14.42, df = 6, p = .0253*; None vs. Resolved/Dismissed: χ^2 = 3.35, df = 3, p = .188*; None+ Resolved/Dismissed vs. Unresolved/Disorganized: χ^2 = 11.42, df = 3, p = .099*; 2 x 2 table of (None+Resolved/Dismissed) vs. Unresolved/Disorganized by (Autonomous+Dismissing) vs. (Preoccupied+can't classify): Fisher's exact p < .003; Odds ratio = 5.8; 95% Confidence Interval for Odds Ratio = 1.60 to 22.05.

*Imprecise due to expected cell values < 5

experiences of the *same category* of trauma, although this could well be a variable in the inability to resolve such experiences. The number of reported episodes of significant loss, separation, or abuse did appear to be related to likelihood of being classified unresolved on at least one of them.

DISCUSSION

The finding that nearly 50% of this clinical sample were unresolved for attachment-related traumas provides some empirical support for Bowlby's general hypothesis linking traumatic experiences in childhood to later behavioral and psychiatric disorder. Bowlby's early theoretical work focused extensively on the pathogenic role of early parental loss and separation, in part, because he believed that these events posed the most immediate threat to the infant's survival and, in part, because such events seemed clear-cut and easy to define for research purposes, compared with more nebulous deficiencies in parenting (Bowlby 1960, 1961, 1973, 1980). While the idea that loss or separation from parents in itself leads to psychopathology has been challenged in recent years, research based on more complex causal models has shown that, when interactions with moderating and protective influences are taken into account, parental loss remains a significant risk factor for certain psychiatric disturbances (Brown and Harris, 1978; Adam, Bouckoms, and Streiner, 1982). Other recent research suggests that our ideas about the range of experiences that constitute attachment trauma need to be reconsidered. Various kinds of childhood maltreatment (including neglect and physical abuse) have, for some time, been identified as having clear effects on the attachment system and being important antecedents of both childhood and adult disorder (George and Main, 1979; Rutter, 1984a,b; Spieker and Booth, 1988; Cicchetti, this volume). Moreover, the full extent of childhood sexual abuse is only now coming to light (Finklehor, 1984; Robinson, 1992; MacMillan, MacMillan, and Offord, 1993).

We found that a sizable number of this sample of clinical adolescents showed disorientation/disorganization around discussion of severe separation experiences, a finding suggesting that unresolved separation may need to be considered as yet another attachment trauma within the AAI system. There is ample theoretical justification for taking this position. Separation is a prototypic activator of the attachment behavioral system (Bowlby, 1969, 1973), and even relatively brief separations can be disorganizing of behavior in younger children. The separations reported in our clinical subjects, who were often unwillingly and unceremoniously ejected or uplifted from their families, are particularly likely to be disorganizing of thinking and behavior. Such events usually occur without warning or preparation, often under frightening conditions, and frequently involve separations from siblings and other familiar figures as well as parents.

There are two possible ways that the disorganizing effects of separation may be understood from the perspective of attachment theory. Loss of the home as a familiar base toward which the child is naturally oriented is likely to lead to disorientation and confusion because of the generalizability of the attachment figure to his or her surroundings. Bowlby notes how this generalizability of security to a familiar environment is evident in the "home range" of many species of birds and mammals (Bowlby, 1973, p. 147) and argues that this concept undoubtedly applies to humans as well. The mechanism for disorganization/disorientation in this case is similar to that for death of a parent, where the attachment figure is lost as a principal point of orientation and security.

When the attachment figure is actively involved in ejecting the child from the home, the child is faced with a situation analogous to that hypothesized by Main and Hesse (1990) for disorganized/disoriented infants in the Strange Situation. It is hypothesized that frightening or frightened behavior on the part of the parent activates the child's attachment system and propels him or her toward the parent who, while representing a "haven of safety," is, at the same time, the "source of alarm" (p. 180). This presents the child with an unresolvable paradox that is inherently disorganizing of cognition and behavior. The conditions surrounding the separations we have described in this clinical sample of adolescents are, we believe, highly likely to provoke both these conditions for disorganization/disorientation.

While it is important to try to assess the effects of different types of trauma on attachment organization, this may prove to be an elusive goal, particularly in high-risk and clinical populations. Children from dysfunctional families are often exposed to a variety of attachment-related trauma whose effects may be cumulative. The death of one parent often leads to the absence or emotional withdrawal of the other (Harris and Brown, 1985), just as sexual abuse by a father almost always implies failure of maternal protectiveness. Furthermore, as Bowlby repeatedly pointed out, threats of separation or of physical violence in themselves may be profoundly frightening to the child, whether or not they are actually carried out. The real challenge to understanding the effects of traumatic experience is not in determining how much trauma high-risk and clinical samples have been exposed to or whether one type of traumatic experience is *worse* than another but in learning more about the developmental capacities that foster resilience and those that foster vulnerability to traumatic experience. The development of systematic approaches to the assessment of attachment organization and the serendipitous finding that this allows for assessment of attachment disorganization represent major steps in this direction.

Vulnerability to Trauma

The strong association between unresolved (Ud) status and the preoccupied (E) and cannot classify (CC) categories and the negative associations to the autonomous (F) and dismissing (Ds) categories raise important questions about the nature of these interrelationships and the directions of causality. Do the preoccupied and mixed attachment organizations increase vulnerability to attachment trauma, or does attachment trauma increase the likehood of preoccupied attachment or being unable to develop a consistent attachment strategy? To answer this complex question, we need to reach a clearer understanding of the structure of the AAI and how its classifications relate to the general assumptions of attachment theory.

Both the preoccupied attachment and the cannot classify groups represent current states of mind with respect to the entire history of the individual's attachment experience. The unresolved classification, on the other hand, is based on the state of mind with respect to a specific traumatic experience. While it is heuristically useful in considering complex categorizations, such as Ud/F, Ud/Ds, or Ud/E, to think of the autonomous, dismissing, and preoccupied elements as "primary" or "underlying" organizations influencing the vulnerability or resilience to trauma, the retrospective nature of historical inquiry in the AAI and its focus on current mental organization do not allow clear causal relationships to be established. In cases where a single traumatic event has been experienced within the context of an otherwise stable parent–child relationship, such as the unexpected death of a loving parent in later childhood, it seems reasonable to think of the experience as impacting on a preexisting or underlying attachment organization. In those cases, however, where traumas have been repeated, multiple and occurring over long periods throughout childhood, or both, traumatic experience does not simply impact on an existing structure but becomes part of the fabric out of which the structure is formed. In the first case one might consider a simpler, more unidirectional model of causality where trauma is the pathogenic "agent," and the underlying attachment organization is the "host," which receives and responds according to its capacities. In the second case one must consider a more bidirectional model or transactional model in which the agent and host interact more closely and insidiously, not only influencing each other but virtually causing each other (Bowlby, 1973). As

Sroufe (1988) points out, "the child seeks, creates, shapes and interprets experience" (p. 23). The complexities of such a model are well illustrated in the Ud/E group.

Preoccupied (E) attachment is associated with a reported childhood experience of intrusive or role-reversing parenting in which the child's attention is persistently focused on a parent who is described as incompetent, ill, overconcerned, or unduly critical of the child. Such parent–child relationships appear to be highly involving, intensely conflictual, and often accompanied by confusing or contradictory communications. Such interactions may severely compromise the child's sense of self and autonomy of thought and action. Bowlby (1973) has hypothesized that when parent–child interactions are markedly contradictory or when the child is given contradictory explanations for the same experience, multiple and incompatible models of self and attachment figure are liable to develop. Such incompatible models, which Bowlby suggests are often defensively excluded from awareness, are likely to interfere with the child's ability to comprehend and assess subsequent experience (Bowlby, 1973; Bretherton, 1985, 1990; Bretherton, Ridgeway, and Cassidy, 1992; Holmes, 1993). This is especially likely to be the case when such experiences are traumatic in nature and originate at the hands of caretakers. Furthermore, traumatic interactions with caretakers are often accompanied by just the kind of contradictory and distorted explanations that Bowlby believed were particularly likely to lead to multiple internal models, compounding the traumatic effects (Bowlby, 1973, 1988).

Main (1991) has suggested that a diminished capacity for metacognition, or the ability to think about ones' own and others' thoughts, may make a direct cognitive contribution to the development of multiple models. Main proposes that such deficits might be especially likely to occur in the insecure = ambivalent ≠ resistant (C) group of children because of their experience of extended interactions with an attachment figure whose behavior is unpredictable and highly conflicting. Direct continuity between ambivalent/resistant attachment in childhood and preoccupied attachment in adulthood has yet to be demonstrated in longitudinal studies. Several studies, however, have reported close correspondence between maternal preoccupied attachment on the AAI and ambivalent infant Strange-Situation classification, and, more recently, two studies have reported transgenerational correspondence between mothers and their adult daughters for preoccupied attachment on the AAI (Benoit and Parker, 1994; Rosenstein and Horowitz, in press).

It is also possible that the very intensity of the overinvolvement with parents described by preoccupied individuals may directly foster excessively hostile or intimate interactions with caretakers. This may well increase exposure to potentially traumatic situations such as physical or sexual abuse, further exacerbating the interaction between a preoccupied state of mind and traumatic experience. This may, in part, help to account for the interrelationship between Ud and the E2 category, in which angry preoccupation with caretakers predominates.

The cannot classify (CC) category is given when the transcript cannot clearly be categorized as dismissing, autonomous, or preoccupied but shows such a mixture of mental organizations that no single organized strategy is predominant. For example, the individual may show a complete shift from one state of mind midinterview (e.g., from preoccupied to dismissing) or completely different states of mind with respect to different people (e.g., preoccupied for mother and dismissing for father). Main, van IJzendoorn, and Hesse (1993) point out that individuals coded as cannot classify (CC) and those coded unresolved (Ud) and traumatically preoccupied (E3) share in common an inability to maintain a consistent and organized strategy for discussing and organizing information about relationships. They have presented preliminary evidence to suggest that the CC group, like the E3 group, may be overwhelmed with traumatic events but fail to exhibit a specific lapse in monitoring, which would give them a Ud classification. Our findings provide strong support for a link between trauma and the CC classification but indicate that, within this clinical population at least, a high percentage are also unresolved for a specific episode of trauma. We found no evidence to suggest they were overwhelmed with trauma as are the E3 subjects, since they were no more likely to be assigned a Ud classification for multiple traumas than were subjects in other primary categories. While the CC classification and its antecedents are incompletely understood, it would clearly appear to reflect the existence of multiple models of self and attachment figures, with all the implications previously noted for resolution of trauma.

The finding that unresolved status was not significantly associated with adolescents classified as F (autonomous) was not surprising and was in accord with Bowlby's assumptions regarding the protective effects of secure attachment. The fact that only 16% of the clinical sample overall were classified as autonomous (F), in contrast to the 50% found in nonclinical adolescent samples, provides further confirmation of this general hypothesis. The percentage of subjects classified as dismissing of attachment is not significantly different from that found in nonclinical or low-socioeconomic status adolescent samples, but it was somewhat surprising to see how few were unresolved for loss, separation, or abuse. Only 10 of the 45 subjects coded as dismissing were classified as unresolved, and, as noted before, *none* of these were classified unresolved for more than one type of attachment trauma. It would appear that the setting aside of attachment relationships, the feelings that accompany them, or both insulates the individual from at least the immediate effects of traumatic disorganization. It is important to bear in mind that dismissal of trauma carries no implication that the experience is resolved, only that the experience is neither preoccupying nor disorganizing of the individual's current state of mind. The AAI manual refers to this as "failed mourning."

The finding that both unresolved status and preoccupied attachment are overrepresented in females raises the possibility that vulnerability to trauma in females may, in part, be mediated through an increased likelihood to be preoccupied with attachments. The apparent male resiliency to the effects of trauma, on the other hand, may be mediated by an increased likelihood of being dismissing of attachment. An excess of preoccupied attachment in women and of dismissing attachment in men has previously been reported in two samples of nonclinical adolescents (Kobak and Sceery, 1988; Kobak, Sadler, and Gamble, 1991). Dozier (1990) and Dozier et al. (1991) found a similar distribution in two studies of adults with serious psychopathology. All these studies used the Kobak Q-sort procedure for scoring the AAI, which does not categorize for Ud, so that it is impossible to discern whether an interactive effect among Ud, E, and CC, such as we found, existed. A recent study in an inpatient adolescent population by Rosenstein and Horowitz (1994) found an excess of dismissing attachment in males and of preoccupied attachment in females, but no gender differences in those unresolved for loss. As mentioned earlier, they did not rate their subjects for either abuse or separation. The recent meta-analysis of AAI studies by van IJzendoorn and Bakermans-Kranenburg found no clear evidence of gender differences in AAI categories. Further research is clearly warranted.

Attachment Trauma and Psychopathology

The question of whether unresolved attachment trauma and particular attachment organizations as measured by the AAI are related to specific psychopathologies or only to an increased vulnerability to clinical disorder generally can be answered only by longitudinal studies. Important information, however, about the strength and specificity of the association between attachment categories and disorder can be gained by comparing symptom profiles and diagnostic groups within defined clinical populations. We have yet to complete intergroup comparisons of our data for symptom categories, but we have compared subjects reporting lifetime suicidal behavior with nonsuicidal subjects and found a highly significant relationship between the unresolved and preoccupied categories and suicidal behavior, with the Ud/E combination emerging as a particularly strong variable (Adam, et al., in press). Suicidal females were significantly more likely to be rated unresolved than males, regardless of the underlying primary AAI category. Loss, separation, and abuse have long been known to be correlates of suicidal behavior, and young females are known to be at particularly high risk for suicidal behavior, but the interrelationship of these attachment traumas to sex and to specific attachment organizations is a robust and previously unknown finding. It is of interest to note that Patrick et al. (1994) have recently found the E3 pattern in 10 of 12 patients with the diagnosis of borderline personality disorder, and 8 of them were Ud/E3. That female gender and suicidal behavior are both correlates of this disorder lends support to our findings. Fonagy's study (this volume) of nonpsychotic inpatients, however, did not confirm this finding, although the number of preoccupied subjects (particularly in the E3 group) in patients with borderline personality disorder was higher than expected.

Attachment theorists have cautioned against equating patterns of attachment derived from normative samples with psychopathology or expecting direct relationships between specific patterns and specific types of psychopathology (Cicchetti, 1984; Sroufe and Rutter, 1984; Sroufe, 1988). With the addition of the trauma-related categories derived from high-risk and clinical populations, however, greater specificity may be found than previously anticipated. Relatively few studies have been published to date reporting AAI findings in clinical populations, and some of these have employed the older three-category system of classification, which did not include the unresolved or cannot classify categories. Most of these studies have also employed relatively small numbers of subjects, limiting serious examination of subcategories and leading to collapsing of certain categories (such as unresolved with cannot classify) for statistical analysis. The findings of this study, in which we found the unresolved category to interact strongly with the E2 and E3 subtypes of preoccupied attachment but not the E1 subtype, is one example of the richness that may be contained in the full AAI classification. Similarly, the discovery that dismissing elements appear to moderate traumatic effects in both simple (Ds) or complex (Ud/Ds and Ud/CC[Ds-E]) categories would not have been discernible in a smaller sample.

We must also bear in mind that the categorical approach to attachment classification, as laid out in the Ainsworth system, does not claim to describe all possible patterns of attachment or to encompass every aspect of the attachment paradigm. The full significance of the more recent additions to the system, such as the disorganized/disoriented (D) and avoidant/ambivalent (A/C) infant categories and their adult equivalents, is yet to be determined (Main and Hesse, 1990; Main, van IJzendoorn, and Hesse, 1993 Crittenden, this volume). Full delineations of the relationships between attachment patterns and psychopathology may require their consideration along a number of attachment-relevant dimensions best considered on a continuum. Ainsworth (cited in Cummings, 1990) has stated that the Strange Situation patterns can usefully be considered along a continuum of felt security, and several workers have devised schemes for assessing this continuum (Crittenden, 1985; Main et al., 1985; Cummings, 1990). Main (1990) has suggested that the Strange Situation categories can be understood as contingent behavioral strategies mediating the activation of the attachment behavioral system within the context of specific parent–child dyads. Using this idea, Kobak (1989) has devised a Q-sort procedure for rating the AAI along both a security/insecurity dimension and an activation/deactivation dimension, where dismissing subjects are seen to be in a state of deactivation while preoccupied subjects are in a state of hyperactivation of the attachment system. The organization of attachment relationships has also been considered in relation to a flexibility/ adaptability dimension, with security of attachment considered highly flexible and adaptable and the insecure organizations being less so (Bowlby, 1969; Sroufe and Rutter, 1984).

We suggest, on the basis of the recent delineation of the D and Ud categories, that it might also be useful to think about attachment classification along an organization–disorganization continuum reflecting the greater or lesser proneness for given categories to disorganize in the face of trauma, particularly attachment-related trauma. If we use the adult system for illustration, at one extreme of this continuum might be the autonomous (F) categories, where high security of attachment is related to stability of organization and resilience in the face of stress. At the other extreme might be situated the preoccupied and cannot classify categories, where extreme insecurity is associated with instability of organization and proneness to disorganization in the face of stressful events. The placement of the dismissing group and all of the other groups in complex categories need to be determined empirically, but our data suggest that the most fragile organization of all along this continuum might well be the Ud/E3 combination.

SUMMARY AND CONCLUSIONS

This study has explored Bowlby's general hypothesis relating the quality of attachment to resilience or vulnerability to stressful life events and used the Adult Attachment Interview in a heterogeneous sample of clinical adolescents. A high percentage of these adolescents (82%) reported at least one episode of significant loss, separation, or abuse. Only 48%, however, exhibited cognitive lapses or reported extreme behavioral reactions in relation to these episodes, which qualified them for an unresolved/disoriented (Ud) designation, using AAI criteria. Subjects coded as preoccupied with attachment (E) and those showing mixed or inconsistent underlying attachment organization (CC) were significantly more likely to be unresolved/disoriented, as were females. Male subjects and all those with dismissing attachment were significantly less likely to be unresolved/disorganized for loss, separation, or abuse. A protective effect for security of attachment (autonomy) was not demonstrated in this study with respect to trauma, although the number of autonomous subjects overall in this clinical sample was rather small compared with the general population. This suggests they may be less prone to develop behavioral or psychiatric disorder than those who are insecurely attached, in line with Bowlby's predictions.

The AAI is a powerful instrument for exploring the role of trauma in clinical populations. By looking at the present organization of thinking around traumatic themes, it allows for assessment of how these experiences are currently construed, which may well be more relevant to current functioning and psychiatric disorder than the simple recording of past traumatic events. Furthermore, by allowing for the rating of disorganization/disorientation around the discussion of a variety of potentially traumatic events, the AAI, in effect, allows them to be assessed integratively in terms of their cumulative and qualitative effects, rather than as independent variables with unrelated effects, as is usually done. While separation and loss and physical and sexual abuse may seem, at first glance, to be rather different events, they all represent fundamentally unacceptable and, for the child, incomprehensible violations of the attachment system, with its inherent expectations of protection, safety, and security. By bringing the assessment of trauma within the context of overall attachment organization, the AAI allows for the assessment of traumatic effects on at least one central developmental system with known functions, variations, and developmental trajectories. This, in turn, allows for the testing, within a developmental framework, of hypotheses about the vulnerability to trauma.

REFERENCES

Adam, K. S., (1994), Suicidal behavior and attachment: A developmental model. In: *Attachment in Adults*, ed. M. B. Sperling & W. H. Berman. New York: Guilford Press, pp. 275–298.
—— Bouckoms, A. & Streiner D. (1982), Parental loss and family stability in attempted suicide. *Arch. Gen. Psychiat.*, 39:1081–1085.
—— Keller, A., West, M., Larose, S. & Goszer, L. (1994), Parental representation in suicidal adolescents: A controlled study. *Aust. N.Z. J. Psychiat.*, 28:418–425.
—— Lohrenz, J. G., Harper, D. & Streiner, D. (1982), Early parental loss and suicidal ideation in university students. *Canadian J. Psychiat.*, 27:275–281.
—— Sheldon-Keller, A. & West, M. (in press), Attachment and adolescent suicidality. *J. Consult. Clin. Psychol.*
Ainsworth, M., Blehar, M. C., Waters, E. & Wall, S. (1978), *Patterns of Attachment.* Hillsdale, NJ: Lawrence Erlbaum Associates.
—— & Eichberg, C. (1991), Effects on infant–mother attachment of mothers' unresolved loss of an attachment figure, or other traumatic experience. In: *Attachment across the Life Cycle.* ed. C. M. Parkes, J. Stevenson-Hinde & P. Marris. London: Routledge, pp. 160–183.
Allen, J. P. (1993), The relation of adolescent psychopathology to autonomy and relatedness in adolescent interactions, and attachment. Presented at the 60th Meeting of the Society for Research in Child Development, New Orleans.
—— & Hauser, S. T. (1991), Prediction of young adult attachment representations, psychological distress, social competence and hard drug use from family interactions in adolescence. Presented at the 59th Meeting of the Society for Research in Child Development, Seattle.
American Psychiatric Association (1994), *Diagnostic and Statistical Manual of Mental Disorders*, (4th ed.). Washington, DC: American Psychiatric Association.
Bakermans-Kranenburg, M. J. & van IJzendoorn, M. H. (1993), A psychometric study of the adult attachment interview: Reliability and discriminant validity. *Devel. Psychol.*, 29:870–880.
Balint, M. (1969), Trauma and object relationship. *Internat. J. Psycho-Anal.*, 50:429–435.
Baranger, M., Baranger, W. & Mom, J. (1988), The infantile psychic trauma from us to Freud: Pure trauma, retroactivity and reconstruction. *Internat. J. Psycho-Anal.*, 69:113–128.
Benoit, D. & Parker, K. C. H. (1994), Stability and transmission of attachment across three generations. *Child Devel.*, 65: 1444–1446.
Blum, H. P. (1986), The concept of the reconstruction of trauma. In: *The Reconstruction of Trauma*, ed. A. Rothstein. Madison, CT: International Universities Press, pp. 7–27.
Bowlby, J. (1940), The influence of early environment in the development of neurosis and neurotic character. *Internat. J. Psycho-Anal.*, 21:154–178.
—— (1944), Forty-four juvenile thieves: Their characters and their home life. *Internat. J. Psycho-Anal.*, 25:19–52, 107–127.
—— (1951), *Maternal Care and Mental Health.* Geneva: World Health Organization.
—— (1953), Some pathological processes set in train by early mother–child separation. *J. Ment. Sci.*, 99:265–272.
—— (1960), Grief and mourning in infancy and early childhood. *The Psychoanalytic Study of the Child*, 15:9–52. New York: International Universities Press.
—— (1961), Childhood mourning and its implications for psychiatry. *Amer. J. Psychiat.*, 118:481–497.

—— (1969), *Attachment and Loss, Vol. 1.* New York: Basic Books.

—— (1973), *Attachment and Loss, Vol. 2.* New York: Basic Books.

—— (1977), The making and breaking of affectional bonds. 1. Aetiology and psychopathology in the light of attachment theory. *Brit. J. Psychiat.*, 130:201–210.

—— (1980), *Attachment and Loss, Vol. 3.* New York: Basic Books.

—— (1988), The role of attachment in personality development. In: *A Secure Base*, ed. J. Bowlby. New York: Basic Books, pp. 158–180.

Bretherton, I. (1985), Attachment theory: Retrospect and prospect. In: *Growing Points of Attachment Theory and Research*, ed. I. Bretherton & E. Waters. *Monographs of the Society for Research in Child Development.* Serial No. 209, Vol. 50, Nos. 1–2, pp. 3–35.

—— (1990), Communication patterns, internal working models, and the intergenerational transmission of attachment relationships. *Infant Ment. Health J.*, 11:237–252.

—— Ridgeway, D. & Cassidy, D. (1992), Assessing internal working models of the attachment relationships: An attachment story completion task for 3 year olds. In: *Attachment in the Preschool Years*, ed. M. Greenberg, D. Cicchetti & E. M. Cummings. Chicago: University of Chicago Press, pp. 273–308.

Breuer, J. & Freud, S. (1893–1895), *Studies on Hysteria. Standard Edition* 2:167–174. London: Hogarth Press, 1955.

Brown, G. W. & Harris, T. (1978), *Social Origins of Depression.* London: Tavistock.

Carlson, V., Cicchetti, D., Barnett, D. & Braunwald, K. (1989), Disorganized/disoriented attachment relationships in maltreated infants. *Devel. Psychol.*, 25:4:525–531.

Cicchetti, D. (1984), The emergence of developmental psychopathology. *Child Devel.*, 55:1–7.

Crittenden, P. M. (1985), Maltreated infants: Vulnerability and resilience. *J. Child Psychol. Psychiat.*, 26:85–96.

—— (1988), Relationships at risk. In: *Clinical Implications of Attachment Theory*, ed. J. Belsky & T. Nesworski. Hillsdale, NJ: Lawrence Erlbaum Associates, pp. 136–174.

Cummings, E. M. (1990), Classification of attachment on a continuum of felt security: Illustrations from the study of children of depressed parents. In: *Attachment in the Preschool Years*, ed. M. Greenberg, D. Cicchetti & E. M. Cummings. Chicago: University of Chicago Press, pp. 331–338.

Dozier, M. (1990), Attachment organization and treatment use for adults with serious psychopathological disorders. *Devel. Psychopathol.*, 2:47–60.

—— Stevenson, A., Lee, S. & Velligan, D. (1991), Attachment organization and familial overinvolvement for adults with serious psychopathological disorders. *Devel. Psychopathol.*, 3:475–489.

Fairbairn, W. (1952), *An Object Relations Theory of Personality.* New York: Basic Books.

Finklehor, D. (1984), *Child Sexual Abuse.* New York: Free Press.

Fonagy, P., Steele, H. & Steele, M. (1991), Maternal representations of attachment during pregnancy predict the organization of infant–mother attachment at one year of age. *Child Devel.*, 62:891–905.

Freud, S. (1920), *Beyond the Pleasure Principle. Standard Edition*, 18:7–64. London: Hogarth Press, 1955.

—— (1926), *Inhibitions, Symptoms and Anxiety. Standard Edition*, 20:77–175. London: Hogarth Press, 1959.

George, C., Kaplan, N. & Main, M. (1985), Attachment Interview for Adults. Unpublished manuscript.

—— & Main, M. (1979), Social interactions of young abused children: Approach, avoidance and aggression. *Child Devel.*, 50:306–318.

Guntrip, H. (1969), *Schizoid Phenomenon Object Relations and the Self*. New York: International Universities Press.

Harris, T. & Brown, G. W. (1985), Interpreting data in aetiological studies of affective disorder: Some pitfalls and ambiguities. *Brit. J. Psychiat.*, 147:5–15.

Heinicke, C. & Westheimer, I. (1966), *Brief Separations*. New York: International Universities Press.

Herman, J. L. (1992), *Trauma and Recovery*. New York: Basic Books.

Holmes, J. (1993), *John Bowlby and Attachment Theory*. London: Routledge.

Kobak, R. (1989), *A Q-Sort for the Adult Attachment Interview*. Unpublished manuscript, University of Delaware, Newark.

—— Sadler, N. & Gamble, W. (1991), Attachment and depressive symptoms during adolescence: A developmental pathways analysis. *Devel. Psychopathol.*, 3:461–474.

—— & Sceery, A. (1988), Attachment in late adolescence: Working models, affect regulation and representations of self and others. *Child Devel.*, 59:135–146.

Lloyd, C. (1980), Life events and depressive disorders reviewed. 1. Life events as predisposing factors. *Arch. Gen. Psychiat.*, 37:529–535.

Lyons-Ruth, K., Connell, D., Zoll, D. & Stohl, J. (1987), Infants at social risk: Relations among infant maltreatment, maternal behaviour, and infant attachment behaviour. *Devel. Psychol.*, 23:223–232.

MacMillan, H., MacMillan, J. & Offord, D. (1993), Periodic health examination, 1993 update: 1. Primary prevention of child maltreatment. *Canadian Med. Assn. J.*, 148:151–163.

Main, M. (1990), Cross-cultural studies of attachment organization: Recent studies, changing methodologies, and the concept of conditional strategies. *Human Devel.*, 33:48–61.

—— (1991), Metacognitive knowledge, metacognitive monitoring, and singular (coherent) vs. multiple (incoherent) model of attachment: Findings and directions for future research. In: *Attachment across the Life Cycle*, ed. Colin M. Parkes, J. Stevenson-Hinde & P. Marris. London: Routledge, pp. 127–159.

—— & Goldwyn, R. (1985–94), Adult attachment scoring and classification system. Unpublished manuscript.

—— & Hesse, E. (1990), Parents' unresolved traumatic experiences are related to infant disorganized attachment status: Is frightened and/or frightening parental behaviour the linking mechanism? In: *Attachment in the Preschool Years*, ed. M. T. Greenberg, D. Cichetti & E. M. Cummings. Chicago: University of Chicago Press, pp. 161–182.

—— Kaplan, N. & Cassidy, J. (1985), Security in infancy, childhood and adulthood: A move to a level of representation. In: *Growing Points in Attachment Theory and Research*. ed. I. Bretherton & E. Waters. *Monographs of the Society for Research in Child Development*. Serial No. 209, Vol. 50, Nos. 1–2, pp. 66–104.

—— & Solomon, J. (1986), Discovery of a new, insecure-disorganized/disoriented attachment pattern. In: *Affective Development in Infancy*, ed. M. Yoqman & T. B. Brazelton. Norwood, NJ: Ablex, pp. 95–124.

—— van IJzendoorn, M. H. & Hesse, E. (1993), Unresolved/unclassifiable responses to the Adult Attachment Interview: Predictable from unresolved states and anomalous beliefs in the Berkeley-Leiden Adult Attachment Questionnaire. Presented at biennial meeting of the Society for Research in Child Development, New Orleans.

McFarlane, A. C. (1990), Vulnerability to post traumatic stress disorder. In: *Post Traumatic Stress Disorder*, ed. M. E. Wolf & A. D. Mosnaim. Washington, DC: American Psychiatric Press, pp. 2–20.

Newcombe, N. & Lerner, J. C. (1982), Britain between the wars: The historical context of Bowlby's theory of attachment. *Psychiat.*, 45:1–12.

Patrick, M., Hobson, R. P., Castle, D., Howard, R. & Maughan, B. (1994), Personality disorder and mental representation of early social experience. *Devel. Psychopathol.*, 6:375–388.

Radke-Yarrow, M., Cummings, E. M., Kuczynski, L. & Chapman, M. (1985), Patterns of attachment in two and three year olds in normal families and families with parental depression. *Child Devel.*, 56:884–893.

Robertson, J. (1952), *A Two Year Old Goes to Hospital* [film]. London: Tavistock.

—— (1953), Some responses of young children to loss of maternal care. *Nursing Times*, 49:382–386.

—— & Bowlby, J. (1952), Responses of young children to separation from their mothers. *Courrier Centre Internationale de l'Enfence*, 2:131–142.

Robinson, G. E. (1992), Adult survivors of sexual abuse. *Med. North Amer.*, 4:4232–4233.

Rosenstein, D. & Horowitz, H. (in press), Adolescent attachment and psychopathology. *J. Consult. Clin. Psychol.*

Rutter, M. (1984a), Psychopathology and development: 1. Childhood antecedents of adult psychiatric disorder. *Aust. N.Z. J. Psychiat.*, 18:225–234.

—— (1984b), Psychopathology and development: 2. Childhood experiences and personality development. *Aust. N.Z. J. Psychiat.*, 18:314–327.

Sandler, J., Dreher, A. N. U. & Drews, S. (1991), An approach to conceptual research in psychoanalysis illustrated by a consideration of psychic trauma. *Internat. Rev. Psychoanal.*, 18:133–141.

Segal, H. (1986), *Introduction to the Work of Melanie Klein*. London: Hogarth Press.

Sheldon-Keller, A., Adam, K. S., West, M. & Owens, M. (submitted), Attachment patterns in an adolescent clinical sample: Distribution and inter-rater reliability.

Spieker, S. J. & Booth, C. L. (1988), Maternal antecedents of attachment quality. In: *Clinical Implications of Attachment*, ed. J. Belsky & T. Nezworski. Hillsdale, NJ: Lawrence Erlbaum Associates, pp. 95–135.

Sroufe, L. A. (1988), The role of infant–caregiver attachment in development. In: *Clinical Implications of Attachment*, ed. J. Belsky & T. Nezworksi. Hillsdale, NJ: Lawrence Erlbaum Associates, pp. 18–38.

—— & Rutter, M. (1984), The domain of developmental psychopathology. *Child Devel.*, 55:17–29.

Sutherland, J. (1989), *Fairbairn's Journey into the Interior*. London: Free Association Books.

Tennant, C., Bebbington, P. & Hurry, J. (1980), Parental death in childhood and risk of adult depressive disorders: A review. *Psychol. Med.*, 10:289–299.

—— —— & —— (1981), The role of life events in depressive illness: Is there a substantial causal relation? *Psychol. Med.*, 11:379–389.

van IJzendoorn, M. H. (1992), Intergenerational transmission of parenting: A review of studies in nonclinical populations. *Devel. Rev.*, 12:76–99.

—— & Bakermans-Kranenburg, M. J. (in press), Attachment representations in mothers, adolescents and clinical groups: A meta-analytic search for normative data. *J. Clin. Consult. Psychol.*

Ward, M. J. & Carlson, E. A. (in press), Associations among adult attachment representations, maternal sensitivity, and infant–mother attachment in a sample of adolescent mothers. *Child Devel.*

Winnicott, D. W. (1960), Ego distortion in terms of true and false self. In: *The Maturational Processes and the Facilitating Environment*. New York: International Universities Press, 1965, pp. 140–152.

Disorganized/Disoriented Attachment in the Psychotherapy of the Dissociative Disorders

GIOVANNI LIOTTI

This chapter addresses an important aspect of John Bowlby's legacy, namely, the contribution of attachment theory to the understanding of the therapeutic relationship (Bowlby, 1979, pp. 143–160). Attachment theory holds that the behavioral/motivational system controlling attachment behavior is likely to become active "from the cradle to the grave," whenever a person is distressed, ill, or afraid (1979, p. 129). This activation results in the person's attaining or retaining physical or emotional proximity "to another differentiated and preferred individual, conceived as stronger or wiser" (p. 129). Patients engaged in a therapeutic relationship are likely to feel distressed, ill, or afraid while discussing their ailments with the therapist and to consider the therapist as wiser or stronger than themselves: the patients' attachment behavior, therefore, is directed, sooner or later, toward the therapist.

When the patient's attachment system is active within the therapeutic relationship, the internal working models of self and the early attachment figures are likely to influence the patient's attitude toward the therapist. These working models, we should remember, have been constructed from early experiences of attachment in infancy and usually have been consolidated during childhood and adolescence in relationship with parents (Grossmann and Grossmann, 1991). On the basis of these assumptions, attachment theory holds that some puzzling aspects of patients' reactions in the thera-

The author gratefully acknowledges the help provided by John Kerr and by Roy Muir in making this chapter readable. Precious reformulations, clarifications, and expansions of some ideas expressed in the first draft were suggested by John Kerr. Mary Main and Eric Hesse have generously supported, over the years, my efforts to apply the results of their empirical research and their theoretical formulations to my clinical practice. Without their friendly support, this chapter would never have been written.

peutic relationship may be interpreted in terms of their working models of attachment.

This is, of course, the topic of transference revisited in the context of attachment theory. One of the new contributions that attachment research brings to the study of transference is the knowledge of some basic patterns of early attachment. Psychotherapists may, on the basis of their knowledge of these patterns, figure out what type of working model the patient is using in construing the events of the therapeutic relationship (Liotti, 1991). A conceptually simple example comes from the study of the working model underlying avoidant attachment behavior. It is likely that a representation of the self as unlovable and of the attachment figure as rejecting constitutes the basis of the internal working model corresponding to avoidant patterns of early attachment (see, e.g., Ainsworth, 1982; Bretherton, 1985). Whenever patients seem paradoxically to avoid emotional proximity to the therapist when they are more distressed, the therapist may hypothesize that they are reenacting an old pattern of avoidant attachment. Therefore, the therapist may also assume that these patients, whenever they feel distressed, are prone to tacitly construe themselves as unworthy of attention and to expect to be rejected by the therapist if they ask for his or her attention.

In this chapter I concentrate on the disorganized/disoriented pattern of early attachment (Main and Solomon, 1990) as a tool for the understanding of some interpersonal dynamics that are often met with in the psychotherapy of adult patients suffering from dissociative disorders (Liotti, 1992, 1993). I first deal with the phenomenology of these dynamics and their possible relationship with disorganized attachment. A clinical case then illustrates how the knowledge of disorganized attachment may be instrumental in the psychotherapy of adult dissociative patients. (For a definition of the nosological category of the dissociative disorders, see American Psychiatric Association, 1987.)

DISORGANIZATION/DISORIENTATION IN THE THERAPEUTIC RELATIONSHIP

During the psychotherapy of the dissociative disorders, patients not infrequently become distanced from the dialogue; at these times, they assume a dazed expression and look as if they were absorbed in a trancelike state. While so absorbed, they may express anguish, sadness, or fear, without being able to report to the therapist the reason for these emotions. If asked directly why they are emotionally reacting in such a way to whatever the therapist may have said in that moment, patients fail to report any thought, mental image, memory, or process of attribution that may be meaningfully related to the concurrent events in the therapeutic relationship. A blank spell seems to have seized the patients' thought processes while they are estranged from the ongoing dialogue with the therapist and absorbed in the experience of a painful feeling (Liotti, 1993). When these trancelike states and blank spells occur, patients look disoriented both as to the meaning of their experience and in the relation with the therapist.

Besides being sometimes disoriented within the therapeutic relationship, dissociative patients often seem to construe the therapist according to multiple and incoherent representational models. They express different and incompatible attitudes toward the therapist, either across a few sessions or in quick succession during the same session—as if they were looking at their mental image of the therapist through the lens of a kaleidoscope. These different attitudes are more complex than those usually constituting the opposite poles of a simply ambivalent relationship. It is not that love and hate, or hope and despair, are expressed together; rather, a quick succession of multiple, incompatible, and ultimately incoherent views of self and the therapist is rattled off in sequence as though ambivalent feelings led straight away to profound fragmentation. Such is the case, for instance, with a patient who, in a single session (1) asks for the therapist's comforting attention; (2) states that she wishes to quit therapy; (3) expresses the hope of being loved by the therapist; (4) states that she may be dangerous to those who love her; (5) angrily remarks that the therapist has damaged her; and (6) reports being afraid of the therapist's possible reaction to her behavior, whether that reaction is acceptance or rejection. When these types of interactions with the therapist occur, it seems appropriate to state that the patient's relationship with the therapist is lacking in organization and coherence; beyond being disoriented, it is disorganized.

DISORGANIZED/DISORIENTED ATTACHMENT AND THE DISSOCIATIVE DISORDERS

It is tempting to compare these two types of patients' interpersonal behavior within the therapeutic relationship, the disoriented and the disorganized, to those types of children's behavior in the relationship with the caregiver observed by Main and Solomon (1990) and labeled, respectively, disoriented and disorganized attachment behavior. Some children classified as disorganized by Main and Solomon display contradictory behavior patterns toward the attachment figure, either sequentially or simultaneously, which is a sign of disorganization of attachment behavior. Children classified as disorganized may also show signs of disorientation, including a sudden "blind" look in the eyes, dazed facial expressions, mistimed movements, anomalous postures, or holding of movements and positions that suggest a lack of orientation to the present environment.

Might there be something more than a formal resemblance between Main and Solomon's observations of disorganization/ disorientation in the Strange Situation and the behavior of dissociated patients in the therapeutic relationship? In a first attempt to answer this question, Liotti, Intreccialagli, and Cecere (1991) tried to establish an indirect link between the two and suggested that a disorganized/disoriented pattern of early attachment may be a prelude to the dissociative disorders of adulthood.

One avenue for advancing a reasonable guess that an adult may have been disorganized/disoriented in his or her early pattern of attachment derives from a study of the state of mind of parents of disorganized children, conducted by Main and her collaborators (Main and Hesse, 1990). In their work, the transcripts of the Adult Attachment Interview of parents of children whose attachment was disorganized were rather consistently classified U (unresolved, i.e., these parents were suffering from unresolved traumatic experiences), whereas parents of other children seldom received this classification (Main and Hesse, 1990). Among unresolved traumas in the lives of parents of disorganized children, the loss through death of a significant other—a parent, a child, a sibling, a spouse—seems to be particularly frequent. This finding by Main and her collaborators was replicated by Ainsworth and Eichberg (1991). A major loss through death, one that plagued the life of a person's attachment figures when the person was still an infant, may then be considered an indirect, probabilistic index of that person's having been a disorganized baby. In other words, unresolved parental mourning linked to a major loss through death may be considered a significant risk factor for the development of disorganized attachment in the child.

This line of reasoning allows for the following hypothesis: if there is any relationship between disorganized attachment in childhood and instances of disorientation/disorganization in adult life, such as those observed in the dissociative disorders, then patients with dissociative disorders should be more likely than other psychiatric patients to be the offspring of parents who suffered unresolved grief secondary to a major loss when they were taking care of their children. To test this hypothesis, Liotti et al. (1991) asked 46 patients diagnosed as suffering from dissociative disorders and 109 patients with other psychiatric diagnoses the following question: "Did your mother suffer from the loss through death of one of her parents, another child, a sibling, or your father in the two years preceding your birth, or in the two years following it?" The question was limited to events in the mother's life because the mother, rather than the father or other caregivers, is usually the first and foremost attachment figure in infancy. The extension of the critical period to include the two years before the patient's birth was made on the basis that it seemed unlikely that mothers who suffered a major loss in that period of their life could have completed the mourning process to be truly available emotionally in the first two years of their children's life—the years in which the first pattern of attachment becomes established.

Significantly more often than all the other psychiatric patients interviewed, dissociative patients reported that, in the period from two years before to two years after their birth, their mothers had suffered a major loss through death: approximately 62% of the dissociative patients and only 13% of the controls were the offspring of mothers who had lost a parent, another child, a sibling, or their husband just before or shortly after the patient's birth (Liotti et al., 1991).

This finding supports the hypothesis that there may be developmental links between disorganization/disorientation in early attachments and disorganization/disorientation in adult dissociative patients engaged in relationships that activate attachment dynamics —such as the therapeutic relationship. The working model of self and the attachment figure is the mental structure that may link disorganization/disorientation in early attachments and disorganization/disorientation in adult relationships activating attachment. If this is the case, and if one grants that the similarity between the adult behavior and the infantile is more than superficial, then the question is raised whether or not the working model related to disorganized patterns of attachment is itself multiple, fragmented, and incoherent and portrays both the self and the attachment figure as frightened and frightening.

The Internal Working Model in Disorganized Attachment

Main and Hesse (1990) have advanced the hypothesis that frightening or frightened parental behavior is the causal mechanism linking unresolved traumas in the parent and disorganization/disorientation of attachment in the child; see also Main, this volume. If this is true, then disorganized children have reasons to construe the self as responsible for the fear expressed by the attachment figure while they are approaching him or her. Children with disorganized attachment also have reasons for attributing their own fear during the attachment relationship to the behavior of the frightened/ frightening parent. The representation of both the self and the attachment figure may then acquire negative connotations that "explain" the fear perceived in the self and in the caregiver. In extreme cases, one could imagine that these negative connotations, if confirmed throughout the subsequent development of the relationship between the child and the caregiver, may come to amount to an attribution of an evil, devilish hidden nature to the self, the attachment figure, or both.

It has also been argued that the working models of disorganized attachment are likely to become multiple and incoherent, while in secure patterns of attachment they are singular and coherent or at least more integrated (Main and Hesse, 1990; Liotti, 1992; Main, this volume). The disorganized attachment behavior, in other words, may be related to multiple and dissociated mental structures that control the child's actions. These structures may be related to incoherent, simultaneous representations of the self and the attachment figure. As to the nature and number of the multiple, simultaneous representations of self and others that may stem from disorganized attachments, one may note the following possible sequelae:

1. A representation of the attachment figure as frightening and of the self as frightened (self as "victim");
2. A representation of the self as frightening and of the attachment figure as frightened by the child (self as "persecutor," "bad," "evil");
3. A representation of the self as disoriented, linked to the subjective experience of altered states of consciousness (Liotti, 1992) during attachment interactions (self as "stupid," "incompetent," "confused");
4. A representation of the attachment figure as frightened by some unknown danger, not relatable to the child's behavior, and of the self as able to comfort her (self as the "rescuer" of the attachment figure). This last representation is related to reversing the roles in the attachment relationship, with the child trying to take care of, or to overcontrol, the frightened parent.

A CLINICAL ILLUSTRATION

The network of hypotheses that I have presented to this point, however plausible they may seem, necessarily must remain tentative until they have been tested on the workbench of science, most especially through controlled longitudinal studies. Here, however, I wish to test them on a different workbench, namely, in terms of their heuristic usefulness in psychotherapy with dissociated patients. In that context, the criterion for evaluating their worth is the extent to which they facilitate understanding of the patient's inner experience and help organize the therapist's observation of the patient's behavior in the relationship. The network of hypotheses that I now put to this test links together (1) unresolved parental traumas; (2) frightened/frightening interactions in the patient's early attachment relationship; (3) working models of self and the attachment figure that may be multiple, dissociated, and incoherent and convey an impression of intrinsic, frightening "evil" of the self, attachment figure, or both; and (4) disorientation or disorganization in the therapeutic relationship. I will illustrate the clinical usefulness of this network of hypotheses through the discussion of a clinical case.

The Diagnosis

Carla is a 28-year-old married woman who works part-time in a travel agency. She has an only daughter, now two years old. An obsessive-compulsive pattern of behavior has plagued Carla's life over the last year. The bedroom in her house is the object of compulsive rituals; Carla experiences an unbearable feeling of anguish and despair if anything in this room changes order and position. If something hinders her effort to reestablish the former order, Carla may reach such a climax of mental suffering as to consider committing suicide. Before entering the bedroom at night, both Carla and her husband must take a shower and wear clean pajamas. During the day, Carla allows no one besides herself to enter the bedroom. Before entering the bedroom, she changes her clothes.

Carla feels that only one reason justifies her entering the bedroom during the day: to clean it and to disinfect the floor, the walls, and the furniture. She devotes at least two hours a day to the ritualistic chore of disinfecting her bedroom. If Carla fails to perform her elaborate rituals of cleaning the bedroom—or if anything in the bedroom changes order and position—gloom, anguish, and despair seize her. What is notable in this compulsive pattern is that Carla is *not* afraid of germs and infections. The only reason for performing her compulsive rituals is the unbearable feeling of despair that seizes her if she fails to obey the compulsion. No mental image or thought related to germs, infections, or other forms of contamination emerges in Carla's consciousness while she is engaged in her rituals. More than that; no thought whatsoever is in her mind while she is cleaning and disinfecting her bedroom. Outside home, Carla feels at ease and is not prone to any form of phobic-avoidant behavior, compulsive hand washing, or disinfection. During holidays, for instance, she does not feel any need to clean or disinfect the hotel bedroom where she sleeps with her husband and daughter.

Carla remembers only vaguely how the compulsive pattern developed. It emerged from a period of distress related to her daughter's sleeping difficulties when the baby was eight months old. Carla is largely amnesic for that period of her life. This psychogenic amnesia, the lack of any mental content associated with the rituals (Carla described her mental state while she performed the rituals as a blank spell), and the unusual structure of the obsessive-compulsive pattern orient the diagnosis toward the category of the dissociative disorders rather than toward that of a clear-cut obsessive-compulsive disorder. (For a discussion of the overlap of dissociative disorders and some forms of obsessive-compulsive disorders, see Ross and Anderson, 1988.) The diagnosis of a dissociative disorder is also suggested by the different psychopathological syndromes that have followed one another in Carla's life. (Multiple psychopathological syndromes, either simultaneously present or following one another in the patient's life, may be a diagnostic cue pointing to a dissociative disorder; see Bliss, 1986, pp. 150–155; Ross, Norton, and Wozney, 1989.) During early adolescence, Carla suffered from a mild, atypical form of anorexia. While she was in high school, Carla suffered from psychogenic pain in her legs (a conversion disorder). When she was 24 years old, Carla began to suffer from a mice phobia that lasted for two years and then disappeared spontaneously.

Unresolved Parental Mourning and the Recovery of Memories of Abuse

The diagnosis of a dissociative disorder and the hypothesis that dissociative disorders may be linked to an early pattern of disorganized attachment, prompted me to inquire carefully about possible unresolved traumatic experiences in the life of Carla's parents before or immediately after her birth. Carla's maternal grandparents died during an air raid in World War II, when Carla's mother was five years old. The mother, now an orphan, was brought up in her aunt's house. This aunt died six months before Carla's birth. Carla's mother was still grieving over these losses when Carla reached adolescence; the painful feelings expressed by Carla's mother as she lingered over the death of her parents and her aunt—according to Carla's subsequent report—suggest lack of resolution of the mourning process.

At the beginning of the treatment, to be sure, Carla stated that she had no memory of her childhood. In fact, the reconstruction of the losses in her mother's life seemed to enable Carla to recover her childhood memories. Carla gradually began to report emotional and physical abuses she suffered from her mother when she was a little child. The reconstruction of her mother's losses seemed to constitute a frame for the attribution of a less unacceptable meaning to the memories of the abuses: Carla was now able to consider her mother's abusive behavior as the consequence of emotional suffering, rather than as the expression of sheer cruelty. It was, therefore, less painful for Carla to dwell upon episodes of her childhood when the mother had hit her head with a stick, humiliated her, or looked totally unmoved by Carla's desperate cry after a blow (dealt by the mother herself) that had caused her lips and nose to bleed profusely. "I understand now that my mother had had no mother, did not know what it means to be a mother," said Carla, and she added: "My mother had suffered too much as a child to be moved by her child's sufferings. She looked upon my pain as something of minor importance. After all, in her mind, I at least had a mother, while she had had none."

The retrieval of Carla's childhood memories offered the beginning of a possible explanation for the onset of the cleaning compulsion when Carla's daughter was eight months old. Carla had been afraid of her angry reactions to the baby's crying at night. She had feared she might treat her daughter as she had been treated by her mother. "To have to acknowledge that I am like my mother is the worst thing that could happen to me," said Carla. Since Carla's mother was completely indifferent to keeping the house tidy, Carla felt that she could reassure herself that she was not "like her mother" through repeated and careful operations aimed at keeping her own house neat and clean.

At this juncture, it may be noted how the idea of a connection between dissociation in adulthood, disorganized attachment in infancy and childhood, and unresolved traumas in the life of the patient's parents can facilitate the therapeutic process. The exploration of unresolved traumas in the life of the patient's parents can foster the patient's ability and willingness to develop new insights about her past relationship with the caregivers and allow for both the recovery of, and the reattribution of meaning to, traumatic memories related to these relationships.

The Activation of the Patient's Attachment System within the Therapeutic Relationship

The explanation of Carla's obsessive pattern in terms of her fear of identification with her frightening mother was accompanied by a *minor* reduction of Carla's compulsions to clean and disinfect her bedroom. Other aspects of her compulsive behavior were totally unaffected. Notably unaffected was the blank spell characterizing Carla's consciousness during the performance of the rituals. The most notable change following the elaboration of Carla's memories of childhood abuses and the construction of a possible explanation of the compulsive pattern was an important modification in the therapeutic relationship,

Carla had been rather uncooperative and emotionally distant at the beginning of the therapy. She refused to consider even the possibility of employing behavioral techniques aimed at reducing her compulsions. When she began reporting memories of her childhood, however, a notable change in her attitude toward the therapist took place. Carla started to cry during the sessions, and she now asked to be helped to give up her compulsions, even through behavioral techniques, if need be.

During one of these sessions, I asked Carla to try to observe the thoughts and feelings accompanying the silent tears that were pouring from her eyes and to try to report them to me. Carla reacted by entering a state of disorientation. She kept staring into a void for about five minutes, with a dazed expression, while her crying stopped. Then she abruptly looked frightened. Within a few seconds, her face again expressed sadness and despair. "What is going on?" I asked twice, very gently, while her facial expressions were changing. It looked as if she had not heard my voice.

After Carla had resumed a sad expression, however, she turned to me and said that she had been unable to notice any thought going on in her mind. Anguish and despair were the only feelings she was able to report. I told her that she had been crying and added that tears often accompany the tacit hope of being comforted or helped. She replied that she was unable to notice any such hope in herself. I said that a few minutes before, she had looked frightened. Carla replied that she did not remember having experienced any fear. Then she added that a memory of something she had read in a newspaper, or perhaps it was a novel, some years before was now surfacing: the story of an ugly, mentally retarded child and his grandfather. The grandfather loved the unfortunate child and searched for every possible medical help to foster the development of his mental capacities. The medical treatment had some success. The boy, as a consequence, became intellectually able to understand how different he was from his peers—how ugly, how stupid—and how desperate his situation was. The story ended with the boy's asking his grandfather to kill him in order to relieve him from the unbearable burden that his hard-won ability to understand his own life had placed on him. The grandfather killed his beloved grandson, as the grandfather perceived that this was now the only way of expressing his love for him.

How can we interpret these shifts in Carla's attitudes from an emotionally distant and uncooperative attitude, to asking for help and emotional closeness, to deep feelings of despair emerging in the context of a disoriented state of mind? Arguably, Carla's attachment system had gradually become activated within the therapeutic relationship, concurrently with the painful experience of reliving the harsh treatment to which she, as a child, had been subjected by her mother. As a tentative hypothesis, one might suppose that Carla's current working model of self and other was derived from an early disorganized/disoriented pattern of attachment. Such a working model is predicated on perceiving either the self or the attachment figure as frightened/frightening and is likely to reflect itself in multiple, incoherent representations of self and the attachment figure. Furthermore, when such multiple, incoherent, and dissociated models of self and other emerge simultaneously in a relationship, the person is likely to become disoriented and disorganized in that relationship. On the basis of this hypothesis, as soon as Carla became disoriented after having expressed a closer emotional attachment to me, I noticed carefully the emotions she was expressing and thought that each emotion could reflect a different aspect of a multiple working model of self and the attachment figure. Hope of being helped, sadness, fear, and then despair were the emotions expressed in sequence during the episode of disorientation. They were largely disconnected, or dissociated, from any thought process or mental representation of self and the therapist that Carla could cognitively monitor in herself, report to me, or both. The story that emerged in Carla's consciousness immediately after the episode of disorientation, however, provided hints as to the type of working model of self and the attachment figure underlying Carla's present way of construing the therapeutic relationship.

The Internal Working Model of the Attachment Relationship

If we equate the figure of the mentally retarded boy in the story with the representation of the self and equate the figure of the grandfather with that of the attachment figure, then the following structure of Carla's working model can be inferred:

1. Carla is loved and safe when she is unable to understand her own life and destiny (self as "incompetent" or "stupid").

2. Carla cannot enjoy the attachment figure's love anymore when she understands who she "really" is (a disgusting "monster").
3. Carla is potentially clever, even if she does not seem to be such at the moment.
4. The attachment figure's love is expressed by acknowledging Carla's potential capacities or hidden positiveness.
5. This expression of love is frightening (it is associated, in the story, with the idea that the attachment figure eventually kills the beloved grandson in order to protect him from unbearable pain).
6. If Carla asks for help and receives it, she becomes frightening to the attachment figure (association with the idea, in the story, of the boy's forcing his grandfather to kill him).

This reconstruction of Carla's working model of attachment, as it was now intervening within the therapeutic relationship, alerted me to the need to stop trying to help her understand the meaning of her compulsions. She had signaled to me that the relationship with an attachment figure could readily become dangerous and frightening, particularly so if she was induced to exceed her actual limits in understanding her own life. Thus, before resuming the attempt to reach a deeper joint understanding of why Carla had selected the bedroom as the center of her rituals, I needed to help Carla acknowledge and correct her working model of self and the therapist (perceived as an attachment figure). In order to approach this goal, I began to inquire, separately, about each of the elements that seemed to contribute to the complex structure of Carla's working model. Thus, some sessions after her reporting the story of the mentally retarded boy, I asked Carla to reflect on the idea that she might have undeveloped potentialities and that somebody, perhaps the therapist, could help her in developing them. In another session, I asked her what kind of risks she could foresee in a relationship where a well-meaning person was helping or comforting her. Both the positive and the negative expectations about both self and the therapist that thus emerged in Carla's talk were then related to past experiences with her caregivers.

After about one year of treatment, this therapeutic process somehow succeeded in making explicit (verbalizable) the elements of Carla's working model that were tacitly governing her mental processes within the therapeutic relationship. An episode among many others illustrates how Carla became able to reflect on her own working models of attachment.

One day, while we were dwelling on the meaning of the mice phobia that afflicted her when she was 24, Carla remembered a story she had read in a newspaper shortly before the onset of the phobia. It concerned a newborn baby assaulted by mice in her cradle. She was now able to see that the phobia expressed her feeling of having been neglected as a baby by her caregivers—left alone in the face of frightening danger, her situation symbolized by an infant assaulted by mice.

In this context, it was possible to consider in a new light how and why the phobia spontaneously disappeared. One day, Carla had found herself closed up in the bathroom of a country house, during a holiday, when a little mouse entered the bathroom through the window. She panicked and screamed—and noticed that the little mouse fled from her and tried to find a way out through the window. She then had an illuminating intuition: the mouse was frightened by her more than she was by the mouse. As a matter of fact, she was able to hurt the mouse much more than the mouse was able to hurt her. After this episode, her mice phobia vanished. When Carla and I examined this episode in the context of our newly acquired joint understanding of her working models, it became possible to figure out that an image of herself as frightened (as a consequence of serious neglect in her early attachment relationship) had been surfacing during the time when she developed the mice phobia. When another, complementary aspect of her complex working model of attachment—namely, the one portraying herself as frightening rather than frightened—was evoked by the meeting with the mouse, the phobia disappeared. Carla had switched from a representation of self as helpless, neglected, vulnerable, and frightened, to a representation of self as strong but also potentially frightening. This representation of the self as potentially frightening was likely to have greatly contributed, some two years later, to the feared identification with her frightening mother while Carla was taking care of her own eight-month-old daughter.

The Outcome of the Analysis of the Internal Working Models

After Carla became able to reflect on her representation of herself and the attachment figure as frightened/frightening, it finally became possible for her to start to face the meaning of her bedroom rituals. She was now able to decenter from the view of herself as the "persecutor" of those whom she loved and also from the view of herself as the "victim" of cruel, frightening attachment figures; as a consequence, she seemed prepared to give up the complementary view of herself as safe only insofar as she was "stupid," unable to understand the meaning of both her relationships and her own inner experiences. Her self-representation as "unable to understand," in turn, was linked to her entering into trancelike states when her multiple internal working model of attachment was activated (incompatible multiple representations of self and others, when simultaneously active, may exceed the integrative capacity of memory and consciousness and thereby facilitate the experience of an altered state of consciousness; to enter unwillingly into a trancelike state, subjectively experienced as a blank spell, may confirm the view of oneself as "unable to understand" one's own inner life). A dream marked the turning point of the treatment, when Carla gave up her dissociative defenses, that is when she both ceased to enter into trancelike states and began to understand the meaning of the bedroom rituals.

Carla resumed asking to be helped to give up her rituals concerning the bedroom. Feeling that by now she had somewhat distanced herself from the representation of self and the therapist as frightened/frightening—and was therefore prepared to react with less fear to direct attempts at helping her—I suggested that she just *imagine* violating one of her prohibitions by entering her bedroom dressed as she was after a walk in town and lying on the bed with those clothes on. (This confrontation with avoided situations in imagination is the first step in many cognitive-behavioral coping strategies, which are based on graded exposure to phobic or obsessive stimuli.) In response, she once again appeared to lose herself in a trancelike state. She remained silent, with a dazed expression, for some minutes, then replied that she could not see herself doing such a thing. She had been unable even to conjure up the mental image of what I had suggested. No particular emotion that she could report had accompanied her failed effort to conjure up that mental image. She had experienced a blank spell in response to my suggestion. My comment was that perhaps to accept my suggestion that she imagine herself breaking the self-imposed rules of her rituals still entailed some frightening expectation. I asked her if she had any idea about what risks might follow the acceptance of mental images such as the one I had suggested. Carla said that she was unable to see any risk in directing her attention to a mental image. In the following session, however, she reported a dream that she had had the night after our last session and that she felt was related to my question.

Carla dreamed that she was standing in her bedroom and that she noticed that the bedside table had been exchanged with another, ugly one. She was surprised and felt great anxiety at this sight: how could this change have taken place in her bedroom? Her husband now appeared in the dream, and he was astonished by the fact that Carla seemed to have *forgotten* that she herself had sold their bedside table and had bought this new one from an uncle, who was very poor. (This idea of "forgetting," as it now appeared in the dream, may suggest that Carla was beginning to consciously conquer her dissociative reactions and the accompanying psychogenic amnesias by recognizing, or metacognitively monitoring, the lapses related to dissociated memories.) Carla's husband, in the dream, said she had given the money earned by the sale to the same uncle (a character of the dream who does not exist in reality) from whom she had bought the ugly table. The relative, in this way, had been *helped* without being humiliated with a straightforward gift of money. (As I listened to the dream, I thought to myself that her helping a relative was the first hint that both her rituals and her dissociative defenses may be connected to one final aspect of Carla's working model of attachment that we had yet to examine: the inversion of the attachment roles and the view of herself as the "rescuer" of the attachment figures.)

In the dream, Carla felt an unbearable feeling of anguish and despair while she listened to her husband's explanation. She had the clear idea in her mind that the only way to get rid of that feeling was to disappear from that room and perhaps from the whole world. She contemplated, in the dream, committing suicide. At this point, the dream image changed: Carla turned toward her bed, which had been empty at the beginning of the dream, and saw that a little girl, perhaps ten years old, was lying on it, fast asleep. She did not know who the girl was but noticed that her posture in the bed was exactly the one she used to assume as a child while falling asleep. (This, the reader may notice, is an instance of multiple representations of the self—the self as composed of different and dissociated parts that, in extreme cases of dissociative disorders, can appear as "alter personalities." The issue of multiple personality disorder is a controversial one, and I am not implying that Carla is a multiple personality. According to DSM III-R categories, Carla might best be diagnosed, in my view, as a "dissociative disorder not otherwise specified." In the literature on the treatment of multiple personality, the first appearance of an "alter" may well take place during a dream (see, e.g., Putnam, 1989; Ross, 1989).

My hypothetical interpretation of this dream has been very elaborate. To date I have shared only a part of it with Carla. To summarize an aspect of it, I surmise that Carla, when about ten years old, may have experienced some dramatic change in her relationship with her father and may have then dissociated this experience, perhaps sexual in nature, from her conscious self. (The specifics of this experience have so far not been recovered by Carla, so that the possibility of its having been sexual remains my unspoken hypothesis.) The girl asleep in her bed may represent the dissociated self, prone to help her affectively deprived father (symbolized by the poor uncle, owner of the ugly table) by devoting herself to him, perhaps even to the point of approaching him in a way that he could have interpreted as sexual. But how could Carla have developed the view of herself as the "rescuer" of her attachment figures in the first instance?

Carla, as a child, intermittently perceived that her mother was the victim of adverse circumstances (particularly when the mother spoke of her losses) and thereupon tried to soothe her, to comfort her, and to help her by keeping the house tidy. Carla's mother, at times, actively invited her daughter to comfort her. On the basis of this inversion of roles in the attachment relationship, Carla tried to induce her mother to be more affectionate toward Carla's father, hoping that this would foster a warmer conjugal relationship and would make Carla's father happier. Carla perceived that her father, too, was affectively deprived; he, too, suffered from his wife's detached and harsh attitudes. Gradually, Carla came to feel that her mother was utterly unable or unwilling to love her father. (These reconstructions, but not the following ones, are based on Carla's memories.) Carla thereupon might have developed the fantasy of substituting for her mother in her father's sentimental life, in order to relieve his loneliness.

One may also wonder whether her father more or less explicitly asked for Carla's companionship and affection. Carla's father—I hypothesize—may have misinterpreted his daughter's way of approaching him in order to comfort him as a straightforward sexual overture, and perhaps he responded in some overtly sexual way when Carla was about ten years old. Carla then felt that her best strategy for coping with the difficulties in her relationship with her parents—to be strong, wise, self-reliant, loving, and able to take care of her parents—had led to a disastrous outcome. She experienced the utmost despair and felt like fleeing from home and killing herself (hence her feeling suicidal in the dream). Then, she dissociated the whole experience, *and her "rescuer" self, whom she held responsible for the tragedy*, from her conscious self. The dissociated "rescuer," however, was "summoned" again when Carla married, had a child, and tried to cope with the emergence of her "frightening" self in the relationship with her daughter. In order not to be "frightening," Carla had to function as the perfect caregiver (both to her daughter and to her husband, who was often ill), but to be a perfect caregiver meant to prime the dissociated memories related to the painful failure of her having tried to take care of her parents—memories that led to a dissociated feeling that she had to commit suicide. In the context of these self-representations, related to Carla's attachment history and reinvigorated by becoming a wife and a mother, Carla's rituals emerged. In the context of the therapeutic scrutiny of all the reciprocally dissociated aspects of her multiple working model of attachment—self as victim, self as persecutor, self as rescuer—Carla's rituals began gradually to disappear.

As I stated, I shared only part of this hypothetical reconstruction of Carla's childhood with her, and she provided confirmation only to some aspects of it. The reader may consider the following statements (uttered by Carla during the sessions that followed the report of the dream) as possible hints at the validity of my reconstruction:

"Yes, I thought of killing myself before I became a teenager; I remember I could not stand anymore the way my mother behaved, I remember how much I was suffering; I thought of fleeing from home and never returning—I should have been 10 or 11 years old—traveling to another city and letting me die there; I discovered that if I tried to ask for my father's help and affection, my mother became infuriated toward *him* . . . I decided—I think, just before my teens—not to show affection to my father anymore, or else my mother got into such a rage. After my baby was born, I became growingly annoyed with my husband's way of approaching me sexually. . . . at present we make love once in a month or less . . . just when I cannot repress my sexual wishes; there is more sadness than joy during intercourse."

During the last phase of the treatment, Carla and I developed a practical way of dealing with her different self-representations. As an outcome of the examination of Carla's dream, she and I agreed that the little girl asleep in the dream might represent a part of herself that had access to memories dissociated from her conscious self. We also agreed that Carla should try to establish contact with this dissociated part of herself in her inner dialogue. For instance, Carla could try to ask this part of herself whether or not she had any objection to her decision to give up some particular aspect of her rituals. Through the dialogue with the dissociated part, Carla's psychotherapy became much like the process of integrating alter personalities advocated by many therapists dealing with multiple personality disorders (see, e.g., Bliss, 1986; Putnam, 1989; Ross, 1989). It remains to be seen whether this similarity in treatment technique reflects an underlying similarity between multiple personality disorders and Carla's condition. My hypothesis (Liotti, 1992) is that the multiple models of self and the attachment figure that accompany the disorganization of attachment patterns in infancy underpin most developmental pathways that lead to adult dissociative disorders (and perhaps to borderline personality disorders). Further severe traumatic experiences in later childhood (e.g., incest) and serious omission, suppression, or falsification of information within family communications (Bowlby, 1973, Chap. 20; Bowlby, 1980, 1985) may foster the transformation of single aspects of the multiple internal working model of early disorganized attachment into the beginning construction of alter personalities. Aside from this case, the multiple working model of early attachment acts as a factor of vulnerability to dissociation throughout personality development (i.e., predisposing to the use of dissociative defenses in the face of interpersonal stressors). According to the extent and quality of dissociative experiences throughout development, the child who has been disorganized in attachment becomes either a normal adult or a dissociative personality (i.e., a person endowed with multiple, unintegrated, and shifting views of the self—a person thereby predisposed to various forms of dissociative disorders but not a true multiple personality).

Carla's treatment (under the influence of my view of the etiology of the dissociative disorders as possible sequelae of multiple working models of attachment) gradually turned into a joint investigation of her own history in terms of her multiple and shifting views of herself. This gradually enabled Carla to reincorporate parts of her past and to understand the appearance and disappearance of her various symptoms in different moments of her life as meaningfully related to shifts from one aspect of her multiple working model of attachment to another aspect of it (see, e.g., the disappearance of the mice phobia when Carla shifted from viewing herself as a helpless, frightened "victim" to viewing herself as somebody who may be frightening to others).

Under the pressure of environmental changes, mainly related to the vicissitudes of her attachment relationships, Carla switched from one representational model of self and others to a different one and preserved only a vague memory of the view of self and the other person she had before the switch. One of these representational models, the "rescuer," was related to such painful experiences that she did not dare remember it until after she considered the therapeutic relationship a secure enough base for the exploration of her inner world. Only then was she able to understand how the failure of the "rescuer" was related to suicidal ideation before adolescence—and to the reliving of hopelessness and despair, strenuously kept in check by the bedroom rituals, when (after the birth of her daughter and the fearful prospect of having to identify with the frightening "persecutor") the "rescuer" was summoned again.

CONCLUDING REMARKS

Are the four representational models of the self that have just been described–frightened in relationships implying attachment, frightening to the attachment figure ("bad"), strong and good when the attachment relationship is inverted, disoriented and "unable to understand" when it is not–invariantly present in patients suffering from dissociative disorders? My clinical experience suggests an affirmative answer to this question. My clinical experience also leads me to advance the following etiological hypothesis. When these self-representations are simultaneously present in a person, when they are feebly integrated or dissociated from one another, and when they are accompanied by anamnestic data suggesting unresolved parental mourning, frightened/frightening parental behavior, or both, then it is tempting to trace them back to an early pattern of disoriented/disorganized attachment.

Developmental psychologists have only recently begun to inquire more closely into the self-representations of children who have previously been observed as disorganized infants. The sparse data now available tend to support the hypothesis that children who have been disorganized infants tend to express excessively negative views of themselves and to be overcontrolling toward their parents (Cassidy, 1988). If these data are confirmed and refined, they lend support to the hypothesis that working models stemming from disorganized attachment are multiple, convey a view of the self as both frightened and bad/frightening, and allow for a positive view of the self only contingently upon the development of compulsive (overcontrolling) caregiving strategies toward the attachment figures.

For the time being, we should consider it only hypothetical that patients suffering from the dissociative disorders have multiple, incoherent working models of attachment, stemming from an early pattern of disorganized attachment and characterized by a nuclear representation of the self as both frightened and frightening. This working hypothesis, however, is extremely useful in guiding the therapist toward understanding what may underlie those moments in the therapeutic relationship with a dissociative patient when the patient appears disoriented and disorganized.

REFERENCES

Ainsworth, M. D. S. (1982), Attachment: Retrospect and prospect. In: *The Place of Attachment in Human Behavior*, ed. C. M. Parkes & J. Stevenson-Hinde. London: Tavistock, pp. 3–30.

————— & Eichberg, C. (1991), Effects on infant–mother attachment of mother's unresolved loss of an attachment figure, or other traumatic experiences. In: *Attachment Across the Life Cycle*, ed. C. M. Parkes, J. Stevenson-Hinde & P. Marris. London: Routledge, pp. 160–183.

American Psychiatric Association (1987),*Diagnostic and Statistical Manual of Mental Disorders, DSM III-R*. Washington, DC: American Psychiatric Press.

Bliss, E. L. (1986), *Multiple Personality, Allied Disorders andHypnosis*. New York: Oxford University Press.

Bowlby J. (1973), *Attachment and Loss, Vol. 2*. London: Hogarth Press.

————— (1979), *The Making and Breaking of Affectional Bonds*. London: Tavistock.

————— (1980), *Attachment and Loss, Vol. 3*. London: Hogarth Press.

————— (1985), The role of childhood experiences in cognitive disturbance. In: *Cognition and Psychotherapy*, ed. M. Mahoney & A. Freeman. New York: Plenum Press, pp. 181–200.

Bretherton, I. (1985), Attachment theory: Retrospect and prospect. In: *Growing Points of Attachment Theory and Research*, ed. I. Bretherton & E. Waters. *Monographs of the Society for Research in Child Development*, Serial No. 209, Vol. 50, Nos. 1-2, pp. 3–35.

Cassidy, J. (1988), The self as related to child–mother attachment at six. *Child Devel.*, 59:121–134.

Grossmann, K. E. & Grossmann, K. (1991), Attachment quality as an organizer of emotional and behavioral responses in a longitudinal perspective. In: *Attachment Across the Life Cycle*, ed. C. M. Parkes, J. Stevenson-Hinde & P. Marris. London: Routledge, pp. 93–114.

Liotti, G. (1991), Patterns of attachment and the assessment of interpersonal schemata: Understanding and changing difficult patient-therapist relationships in cognitive psychotherapy.*J. Cog. Psychother.*, 5:105–114.

————— (1992), Disorganized/disoriented attachment in the etiology of the dissociative disorders. *Dissociation*, 5:196–204.

————— (1993), Disorganized attachment and dissociative experiences: An illustration of the developmental-ethological approach to cognitive therapy. In: *Cognitive Therapies in Action*, ed. K. T. Kuehlwein & H. Rosen. San Francisco: Jossey-Bass, pp. 213–239.

————— Intreccialagli, B. & Cecere, F. (1991), Esperienza di lutto nella madre e facilitazione dello sviluppo di disturbi dissociativi nella prole: Uno studio caso-controllo [Unresolved mourning in mothers and development of dissociative disorders in children: A case-control study]. *Rivista di Psichiatria*, 26:283–291.

Main, M. (1991), Metacognitive knowledge, metacognitive monitoring, and singular (coherent) vs. multiple (incoherent) models of attachment: Findings and directions for future research. In: *Attachment Across the Life Cycle*, ed. C. M. Parkes, J. Stevenson-Hinde & P. Marris. London: Routledge, pp. 127–159.

————— & Hesse, E. (1990), Parents' unresolved traumatic experiences are related to infant disorganized attachment status: Is frightened and frightening parental behavior the linking mechanism? In: *Attachment in the Preschool Years*, ed. M. Greenberg, D. Cicchetti & M. Cummings. Chicago: University of Chicago Press, pp. 161–182.

————— & Solomon, J. (1990), Procedures for identifying infants as disorganized/ disoriented during the Ainsworth strange situation. In: *Attachment in the Preschool Years*, ed. M. Greenberg, D. Cicchetti & M. Cummings. Chicago: University of Chicago Press, pp. 121–160.

Putnam, F. W. (1989), *Diagnosis and Treatment of Multiple Personality Disorder*. New York: Guilford Press.

Ross, C. A. (1989), *Multiple Personality Disorder*. New York: Wiley.

—— & Anderson, G. (1988), Phenomenological overlap of multiple personality disorder and obsessive-compulsive disorder. *J. Nerv. Ment. Dis.* 176:295–299.
—— Norton G. R. & Wozney, K. (1989), Multiple personality disorder: An analysis of 236 cases. *Canadian J. Psychiat.* 34:413–418.

Part IV

New Directions in
Attachment Theory

✧ 13 ✧

Attachment and Psychopathology

PATRICIA MCKINSEY CRITTENDEN

In this chapter, I describe my thinking about the relations between quality of attachment and aspects of psychopathology from the perspective of mental processing of information. To do this, I retell the well-known story of attachment in infancy (Ainsworth, 1985) in terms of the process of learning to regulate mental and interpersonal functioning. Next I consider the effect of neurological maturation on the transition to preoperational functioning and sketch how this process may apply to later ages. Along the way, I integrate several theories, that is, evolutionary, learning, Piagetian, Vygotskyan, and information processing theories, theory regarding affect, and nonlinear probability theory, with attachment theory. I use these to generate a model of how the Ainsworth A/B/C patterns of attachment are differentiated with respect to mental functioning using two dimensions: (1) the source of information and (2) degree of integration of information. Lastly, I discuss the relation of this model to psychopathology.

LEARNING THEORY, VYGOTSKY, AND INTERNAL REPRESENTATIONAL MODELS IN INFANCY

Three Issues to Explore

The work of Ainsworth and her colleagues has shown that maternal sensitivity is the primary determinant of quality of attachment at 12 months: sensitive mothers have secure children, inconsistent mothers have ambivalent children, and interfering/rejecting mothers have avoidant children. The distribution of these patterns is about two-thirds secure, one-third avoidant, and a smidgen ambivalent (Ainsworth et al., 1978; Ainsworth, 1979). There are several interesting points about this situation.

I would like to thank John Bates, Julia Baumgarten, Angelika Claussen, and Nathan Szajnberg for their comments on earlier drafts and Beverley Fagot, Rene Geada, and Lotar Krappmann for access to observations and case histories that greatly informed the theory offered here.

1. How do these patterns develop? Although learning theory is often considered antithetical to attachment theory, it can both explain the process through which this distribution develops and also expand its implications into the realm of mental functioning. That is, although attachment is an unlearned, biologically based process, quality of attachment refers to learned understanding of the nature of specific attachment relationships. The principles of learning theory can explain how infants' interaction with attachment figures facilitates their learning to use their minds. For them to do so, however, I presume that some kinds of learning are "privileged"; that is, the nervous system is prepared to receive and attribute meaning preferentially to some kinds of information as opposed to others (Gallistel et al., 1991). In humans this includes information from and about humans, particularly attachment figures. Thus, the principles of learning are constant across species, although attention to specific information and the readiness with which specific associations are learned are not.

2. Why are there only three patterns of attachment when mothers are highly varied? Although mothers vary on a continuum of sensitivity, infants appear to dichotomize them as "good" or "bad" mothers. Indeed, inconsistent mothers are the least often identified (behaviorally) by infants, and yet most mothers are more or less inconsistent. It is as though the sensorimotor mind of infants could construct only one of two "pure" models of reality, even though few mothers truly fit either model. It is, therefore, important to discover how children revise models to bring them more in line with reality.

3. How does maturation change attachment relationships? The development of patterns of interaction and of attachment can be thought of, in Vygotskyan terms, as tasks in infants' zone of proximal development (Vygotsky, 1987). Mothers can then be considered in terms of *how* they support children's organization of these patterns, that is, the process by which their behavior provides a "scaffold" for children's learning. This perspective suggests that, as the zone of proximal development moves forward, attachment figures must adjust their functioning to continue to meet children's needs.

Learning to Interact

Let me describe the process of organizing patterns of interaction from the perspective of both evolutionary and learning theory.

Beginning at birth, humans behave in species-specific ways that reflect reflexes, the ability to learn associations, and feelings (Bowlby, 1969/1982; Papousek and Papousek, 1979). One way to think of these is to associate reflexive behavior that regulates essential life functions with the brain stem, the oldest brain structure.[1] The reptilian brain (the midbrain), as the next evolved structure, permits simple associative learning from experience. Human infants display an innate propensity to form temporally based mental associations. These are expressed as modifications to innate reflexive patterns and reflect actual, experienced contingencies of an operant (e.g., Skinner, 1938) sort.[2]

The limbic system, the next evolved brain structure, is associated with affective responses that regulate behavior in the absence of prior experience. As Bowlby (1969/1982) has pointed out, innate feelings of anxiety and comfort represent genetically encoded information relevant to survival. These feelings function so as to modify behavior in ways that reduce the probability of experiencing conditions that hold a high risk of being fatal in the first opportunity for experiential learning. For example, rapidly approaching loud noises and darkness both represent increased risk of life-threatening danger. The affective and behavioral responses of fight or flight (Selye, 1976) associated with such stimuli reduce that risk.

Thus, reflexive S→R patterns (in the brain stem), learned S→R patterns (in the reptilian midbrain brain), and affect (in the paleomammalian limbic system) are available and functioning at birth. Midbrain functioning provides the means for unique, individually learned information, whereas limbic functioning represents evolutionarily encoded information about danger. Neither, however, is conscious. The cerebral cortex, the last evolved structure, integrates information generated by the lower brain to yield more sophisticated knowledge. Unlike more primitive brain structures, the cortex develops primarily after birth. Moreover, this growth is both continuous and uneven (like evolution itself), with periods of rapid neurological change alternating with periods of steady incremental growth. The outcome is reflected in Piaget's theory of stages of

---

[1] The discussion of structure and brain function is based on work on the triune brain, particularly the work of Luria (1973), MacLean (1955, 1973, 1990), Ornstein and Thompson (1984), and Thompson (1985).

[2] The discussion of midbrain "cognition" refers specifically to the sensorimotor ability to learn modifications in behavioral sequences based on feedback. It is noteworthy that, even when the learning is tied to adverse outcomes, fear is neither displayed nor perceived without the involvement of the limbic system. Both phylogenetic and surgical procedures support this conclusion.

cognitive functioning in which, by the end of the sensorimotor period, mental functioning can sometimes be conscious.

These four characteristic types of functioning provide the basis for mastering the stage-salient task of establishing patterns of communication with caregivers (Stern, 1985; Tronick, 1989) *that provide meaningful information about future conditions.* When caregivers respond to infants' reflexive, conditioned, and affective behavior in ways that are comforting to infants, infants are reinforced and learn to display the behavior more predictably (Winnicott, 1958). In Vygotskyan terms, these mothers assist their children to learn both the communicative meaning of their behavior and the predictability of its effects on others. In attachment terms, they are securely attached (see Figure 1, B1–4).

On the other hand, when infants' signals result in interference or rejection, the effect is to punish infants for their behavior; consequently, they learn to inhibit the punished behavior. Infants who become avoidant by one year of age typically experience maternal rejection when they display affective signals indicative of a desire for closeness to their mothers (Ainsworth, 1979; Main, 1981). If infants protest this unpleasant outcome, they often experience maternal anger. Inhibition of affective signals both has the predictable effect of reducing maternal rejection and anger and also teaches infants that expression of affect is counterproductive.

If, in addition, the caregiver's own affective behavior is misleading, infants' task of learning the meaning of affect becomes even more difficult. Ironically, interfering and rejecting caregivers do use affective signals in misleading ways (Crittenden, 1981, 1988; Grossmann, Friedl, and Grossmann, 1987; Main and Cassidy, 1988; Grossmann and Grossmann, 1991). When their infants offer few

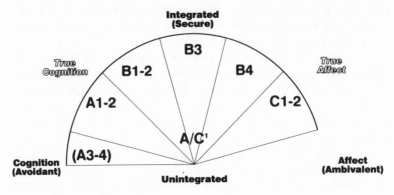

Figure 1 Infant Patterns of Attachment

affective signals, they often intrude with false positive affect as though signaling a desire for closeness. When, however, their infants reciprocate, these caregivers both inhibit their own negative affect and reject their infants. In Vygotskyan terms, these mothers create a situation in which infants (1) cannot discern the meaning of affective signals and (2) learn to inhibit their own signals of desire and anger (see Figure 1, A–2).

Other children have mothers who are clear in their affective communication but inconsistently responsive to infant signals. The inconsistency may involve either over- or underresponsiveness; in either case, infants find it difficult to learn to communicate effectively. When infants cannot predict their caregiver's response, they become anxious and angry. Expression of this anger leads to mixed outcomes: inconsistent mothers are sometimes comforting, sometimes angry, and sometimes ineffective. In learning theory terms, infants of such mothers are on a schedule of unpredictable, intermittent reinforcement. It is well known that such a reinforcement schedule maintains behavior at high rates, even in the context of intermittent negative outcomes. Because infants of inconsistent mothers are unable to make predictions, they are unable to organize their behavior on the basis of them. Cognition, in other words, fails them. They do, however, experience the temporal association of desire and its satisfaction with anger, uncertainty, and fear. By approximately nine months of age, infants are able to focus these feelings on the person responsible for eliciting or maintaining them; at this point anger can be expressed as aggression toward the attachment figure, and fear of abandonment by the attachment figure and desire for comfort from the attachment figure become "emotions," that is, integrated cognitive/affective structures. Without a strategy for changing the probabilities on caregiver behavior, however, these infants remain unorganized with regard to attachment (see Figure 1, C–2).

I argue, therefore, that, at the close of infancy, infants who are labeled secure have learned the predictive and communicative value of many interpersonal signals; they have made meaning of both cognition and affect. Avoidant infants, on the other hand, have learned to organize their behavior without being able to interpret or use affective signals; that is, they have made sense of cognition but not affect. Ambivalent infants have been reinforced for affective behavior but have not learned a cognitive organization that reduces the inconsistency of their mothers' behavior. Thus, secure infants are competent with both cognitive and affective models; that is, they are balanced with regard to source of information. Furthermore, they have developed *procedural* internal representational models that integrate both sorts of information into patterns of behavior that are predictive with regard to both children's actual safety and their felt security. Avoidant infants, on the other hand, are competent primarily with cognitive information whereas ambivalent infants are competent primarily with affective information (See Figure 1, A1–2, B1–4, C1–2).

By the end of infancy, this leads to three problems, whose resolution awaits the greater mental competence of preoperational functioning. First, both the secure and the avoidant representational models are overdrawn; they represent idealized positive and idealized negative caregivers when they are, in reality, relatively sensitive and relatively insensitive caregivers. Second, avoidant children have learned how to avoid punishing consequences but not how to elicit the caregiving that they desire. Third, because ambivalent infants have not learned how to change the contingencies on their caregivers' behavior, they are without strategy; that is, they are unorganized with respect to attachment.

MATURATION AND CHANGE IN INTERNAL REPRESENTATIONAL MODELS IN THE PRESCHOOL YEARS

Developmental Processes

Cognitive and affective maturation. Bowlby discusses the stages of the development of attachment in ways that are compatible with both Piagetian theory of cognitive maturation and current knowledge regarding periods of rapid neurological change (Piaget, 1952; Emde, Gaensbauer, and Harmon, 1976; Fischer, 1980; Klinnert et al., 1984). Both indicate that maturation changes the way in which the human mind functions. Emde and his colleagues have made the equally important observation that, in infancy, periods of cognitive maturation are accompanied by changes in affect. For example, the smile accompanies the two- to three-month cognitive shift and fear–wariness accompanies the seven- to nine-month shift (Bronson, 1972).

One way to think about these changes is to consider them increasingly sophisticated integrations of affect with cognition in which both the causal relation between other people's behavior and one's own feelings and also the communicative/predictive effect of affective signals on other people's behavior are recognized. Such integrations become possible as a result of maturational changes in the cortex of the brain. I propose that coy behavior reflects such an integration of previously discrete signals into a pattern of behavior that is used to regulate interpersonal behavior in particular contexts.

Coy behavior, disarming aggression, and hiding anger. Coy behavior, which becomes organized at the end of the second year of life, serves several functions. The meaning of these can be derived from ethological study of intraspecies conflict. When animals are in conflict, and one is clearly losing, the losing animal terminates the conflict before being destroyed. It does so by exhibiting a set of behaviors that function to acknowledge the dominance of the other animal and to elicit nurturance from the dominant animal (Eibl-Eibesfeldt, 1979). These signals include displaying the belly, offering the bared neck, opening the mouth while covering the teeth, and casting sideways glances toward the victor.

The first two signals make the animal vulnerable to destruction by the dominant animal; thus, they clarify the dominance hierarchy. But if the animal is merely submissive, it will either be attacked or forced out of the social group (Barnett, 1975). In either case, it is likely to perish. Signals are needed that reestablish the submissive animal in a social relationship with the dominant animal. In contrast to bared teeth, which signal aggression, and normal smiles, which signal friendly approach, an open mouth with covered teeth is a smile with both *exaggerated* evidence of lack of aggression (Eibl-Eibesfeldt, 1979) and also the infantile signal that elicits feeding. The fleeting eye contact signals the desire to maintain contact, but again with exaggerated effort to ensure that the signal cannot be mistaken for an aggressive stare. Both elicit nurturance from the dominant animal.

So, to anthropomorphize this a bit, consider two animals angry enough to fight. One is losing and displays a set of behaviors that terminate the other's aggression and reestablish the relationship in a dominance hierarchy. What is the true affective state of the loser? I propose that having fought, lost, and made itself vulnerable to destruction by the victor, it is both fearful and angry, even furious, at the turn of events.

Coy behavior in children functions similarly by integrating the same set of mammalian signals that disarm aggression and elicit nurturance within changing dominance hierarchies. Infants begin to show aggression at the end of the first year of life. At that time, infants are able to associate their feelings of anger with the person who is responsible for their condition. Their response is directed anger, that is, the affective/cognitive emotion of aggression (see Crittenden, 1994). The aggression of infants can be tolerated because it is harmless. Aggression from a two-year-old is not so harmless; it can easily engender aggression from parents. In order not to be killed (or sent away or hurt) by their angered parents, children need a way to stop parental aggressive behavior. Coy, disarming behavior serves this function. It also elicits nurturance from adults, including the increasing number of nonparental adults with whom preschoolers have contact. In the following sections, I describe how coy behavior is used by children who differ in quality of attachment.

Type C. All preschool-aged children use coy behavior to disarm others' anger and elicit nurturance. For children with inconsistent caregivers, however, this new behavior, combined with the greater cognitive competence associated with preoperational intelligence, presents the opportunity to organize a strategy with which to coerce inconsistently responsive caregivers to respond.

Imagine a two-year-old who signals her desire for her mother. Her mother is attending to other things and does not respond. The girl intensifies her demand. Then she screams angrily and throws a toy toward her mother. Her mother now probably responds. Her response, however, is a matter of uncertainty. She might recognize her oversight and respond soothingly to her child, or she might respond with anger. In the first case, the child is reinforced for heightening her affective signal; because the reinforcement is unpredictable and intermittent, the child's learned response will be more prompt and intense next time and very difficult to extinguish. In the second case, maternal anger, the girl is partly reinforced by achieving her mother's attention and partly punished by the anger. In response to the anger, however, she can display coy behavior. This both terminates her mother's aggression and elicits nurturance. Once she has terminated the mother's anger (and, thus, regained safety), the girl's anger can safely be expressed. She fusses, and her mother tries harder to soothe her; she makes new demands. This continues until her mother becomes fed up and angry, whereupon the child once again displays disarming behavior.

The outcome is that the girl learns to display, selectively and in alternation, her anger, on one hand, and her fear and desire for nurturance, on the other. Alternating these behavior patterns in response to changes in her mother's affective state results in a coercive strategy that maximizes the attention she receives from her mother and minimizes the risk. Behaviorally, she has learned to use coy behavior to cover anger at times when she feels both angry and vulnerable. Mentally, she has learned to split her feelings and to display them in a rapid and alternating escalation of intensity.

Caregivers usually feel frustrated and victimized by this coercive strategy (Patterson, 1980; Lieberman, 1993). The terrible twos are a challenge to many parents and very difficult for some. To gain control of their increasingly demanding and manipulative[3] children, many parents use their cognitive superiority to outwit their children. This includes threats, bribery, and trickery. The threats and bribes are simply an adult version of the children's behavioral threats and bribes. The trickery, however, deserves special attention.

Consider an example. In the Strange Situation, a mother starts to leave. Her son rushes up and clasps her leg while desperately demanding to go with her. "I go too, Mom! I go too!" His mother turns back into the room and says, with great enthusiasm, "Oh, look! There's the ball! Go get the ball!" Her son runs to get the ball, and she slips out the door. Another mother handles this by saying, "If you're good, I'll bring you back an ice cream cone." Her child acquiesces to her departure, but, when the mother returns, she has no ice cream. Her child demands the ice cream.

Each of these children is learning something very important about how to use information. Ambivalent infants discover that open expression of feelings and desires has little predictable effect on caregivers' behavior. Because they do not have a means for handing this, they are left with the highly arousing emotions of desire, anger, and fear. Preschool-aged children, however, learn that intense display of unambiguous affect motivates caregivers to attend to them. Moreover, judicious alternation of conflicting emotions disarms parental aggression and increases the probability that children's wishes are met. Finally, children learn not to be fooled by cognitive and verbal reasoning that purports to offer information about the predictable relations among behaviors. They learn that these are misleading. Sticking to affect, displayed at high intensity, leads to the most favorable outcomes. They now have an effective strategy of *coercion* that is based on keeping affect salient and defending against misleading cognition. The (1) *threatening* and (2) *disarming* behavior patterns are alternated so as to regulate the display of anger. The regulation is based on the children's judgment regarding the affective state of the caregiver. Moreover, because changing caregivers' behavior satisfies children's desires, there is the appearance that attachment figures are responsible for children's feelings. Consequently, coercive children tend to blame others for their problems.

---

[3] I use the term "manipulative" in a very precise way to mean that the manipulative person organizes his or her affective or cognitive behavior to lead others to inaccurate assumptions regarding the manipulator's feelings or intentions. Consequently, they respond to others' behavior in unexpected ways. This premeditated, unexpected outcome is resented by others and leads to distrust of manipulative people.

In response to extreme conditions, however, the balance between threatening and disarming behavior may shift, allowing one or the other pattern to become dominant and almost unregulated. In this case, threatening behavior escalates to obsession with revenge, that is, obsessively (3) *aggressive*, and disarming behavior becomes (4) an obsession with rescue, a feigned helpless pattern. In both cases, children behave as though blaming the attachment figure for their distress. Aggressive children and those who feign helplessness engage in massive risk taking, including the risks of retaliation, dangerous exhibitionist behavior, failure to protect themselves in dangerous situations, or any of these. More than threatening/disarming children, they demand that they be attended to and escalate their behavior without restraint until they are. This single-minded focus on their affective and interpersonal selves limits greatly the amount of cognitive/educational development they can undertake (see Figure 2, C1–4).

Every preschool-aged child discovers and tries out the coercive strategy. For many, it proves to be more effective than their infant pattern. Indeed, because most caregivers are inconsistent to some degree, most children experience some benefit from using the coercive strategy.

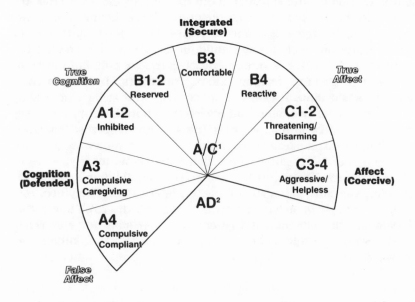

Figure 2 Preschool-Age Patterns of Attachment

Type B. On the other hand, caregivers who are very sensitive, especially those who are sensitive to their children's need to use their emerging mental and linguistic skills, neither reinforce this pattern nor create conditions that make its use probable. These caregivers recognize that the child's zone of proximal development has changed in quality and adjust their behavior accordingly. They engage in meaningful negotiations with their children, openly attend to their children's thoughts and feelings, and join with children to construct joint plans that they will honor (Marvin, 1977; Crittenden, 1992a). In other words, if the mother appears to accept the child's demand, she actually accepts it; in our example, when she says, "Go get the ball!" she stays and plays ball. If she offers a reward for compliance, she supplies the reward. Children of such forthright mothers try the coercive strategy but can be expected to find the secure strategy of open and direct communication more satisfactory.

Type A. Avoidant infants face different challenges as they enter the preschool years. A central issue is learning how to elicit positive attention. In addition, although work with middle-class samples has identified mothers of avoidant children as interfering and rejecting, studies of low income and troubled samples indicate that some mothers of type A children are openly hostile, whereas others are withdrawn and unresponsive (Crittenden, 1985, a,b; Erickson, Sroufe, & Egeland, 1985; Carlson et al., 1989; Lyons-Ruth et al., 1991). Because the outcomes of the preoperational shift may be different for each group, each must be described. Because type A preschoolers develop several different defensive patterns of behavior, I label this group "Defended" (see Crittenden, 1990, for a discussion of nomenclature).

Children who use avoidance to prevent rejection by interfering mothers face two problems in the preschool years. First, as Cassidy and Marvin (1991) point out, avoidance itself comes to be interpreted by adults as openly rude behavior. Consequently, it elicits angry responses from caregivers. Preschool children need a less obvious way of avoiding their mothers' intrusions. Therefore, they replace behavioral avoidance with psychological inhibition. They look at, and speak to, the attachment figure without signaling desire for closeness. Without being rude, they keep the interchange between themselves and their caregivers cool, proper, and polite.

Using this more sophisticated behavior, they can tolerate, in the context of activities with defined and impersonal roles, considerable physical closeness with their caregivers. For example, an inhibited preschooler can stand quite close to his mother to work on a puzzle or read a book but seeks to evade hugs or other affective exchanges. Mothers of type A children generally feel most comfortable with such role-defined, cognitive activities and feel pride in their children's achievements. Their inhibited children learn that, although affect misleads, cognition and cognitive activities can be trusted to yield reinforcing outcomes (see Figure 2, A1–2).

Children whose caregivers are withdrawn have a more complex problem. Without more attention from the parent, they can neither be safe nor feel secure (Bowlby, 1969/1982). Consequently, something must be done to elicit the attention of the parent. Direct bids for parental support have failed to achieve this end. As David DiLalla and I (Crittenden & DiLalla, 1988) have shown, the falsification of affect is well under way in the latter half of the second year of life. By the end of the preschool years, children are quite competent at displaying emotions that they do not feel (Dunn, Bretherton, and Munn, 1987). Children with withdrawn mothers learn both to inhibit display of their own feelings and also to substitute false positive affect. It is as though the child were reassuring the caregiver that everyone is happy, that nothing bad will happen (and no demands will be made) if the caregiver attends to the child. Such behavior is, of course, role-reversing in nature (Bowlby, 1980). Functionally, however, it results from an elaboration of the mental processes used in infants' avoidance and preschoolers' inhibition. That is, the child inhibits expression of true feelings. In addition, the *compulsive caregiving* (A3) child substitutes false, bright affect in order to draw the parent closer psychologically (Main and Cassidy, 1988) (see Figure 2, 43).

The falseness of the displayed feelings can be determined in two ways. First, the expressions themselves are incomplete: Duchenne smiles, crooked smiles, smiles while turning away, and so on (Ekman, 1992). In addition, their flow in the exchange of affect is atypical in that it is too sudden, very brief, and out of context. Indeed, "noncontextual joy" is a good term for this false positive affect. Second, when the caregiver responds with attention, the child suddenly becomes inhibited and evades contact. Such a child appears to want to be close, but not too close. As with all defended children, intimacy is uncomfortable (Crittenden, 1992a, 1994).

Finally, avoidant infants whose caregivers show hostile and demanding behavior learn, in the preschool years, to inhibit their own desires and to do exactly what is demanded of them (Crittenden and DiLalla, 1988). Because their environment is dangerous, *compulsively compliant* (A4) children maintain a wary vigilance and monitor caregivers' behavior in order to anticipate their desires. They comply immediately with these; intensive efforts to please in every detail, to do everything exactly right, may be the basis of compulsive behavior. In addition, however, in their effort to identify every predictor of parental anger, they are likely to err in favor of treating some random associations as causal. This "superstitious" learning may be the basis of "irrational" compulsions.

The compulsively compliant pattern is often accompanied by overachievement, especially when mothers seek evidence of children's obedience and intellectual performance (see Figure 2, A4). Nevertheless, the underlying mental process is inhibition of self-affect and substitution of behavior and affect perceived as desired by the parent. Because all defended children, especially compulsively compliant children, discover that modifying their own behavior reduces the threat from their attachment figures, defended children tend to accept responsibility for parental behavior; when parents are angry or rejecting, defended children tend to feel shame (Crittenden, 1994).

Type A/C. In addition to Ainsworth's three basic patterns, some children whose environments are very complex and variable may combine the defended and coercive strategies into an A/C pattern (Crittenden, 1985a; Radke-Yarrow et al., 1985). This pattern is best conceptualized as statelike shifts between extremes in which the child is in the defended or coercive "mode"; the lack of integration of affective thinking with cognitive thinking is denoted by the solidus (see Figure 2). An alternative perspective is to view A/C as a blend or variable function that covers the whole gradient from entirely defended, to somewhat defended with a bit of coerciveness, and so on to entirely coercive. Although such variability may characterize older children, it seems unlikely that it appears as early as the preschool years. Among preschool A/Cs, however, there may be different ways of integrating the subpatterns, for example, A3/C2.

Outcomes in the Preschool Years

Change in the distribution of patterns of attachment. This review leads to four main points. The first is the importance of maturation in the development of attachment relationships. Current research emphasizes continuity from infancy to later ages (Main, Kaplan, and Cassidy, 1985; Fonagy et al., this volume). Indeed, most assessment procedures have been developed and validated on the assumption of continuity from infancy to later ages (Main et al., 1985; Cassidy and Marvin, 1991).

Maturation, however, may lead to change in quality of attachment. For example, the prior discussion suggests that the "sliver" of ambivalent infants may become a substantial number of coercive children early in the preschool years, when most children try out the new strategy. Later, the number of Cs may decrease, possibly resulting in an equal distribution of the patterns among four- to six-year-olds. Data from two of my samples of two- to four-year-olds (Crittenden and Claussen, 1990, 1994), as well as two studies of 21-month-olds (Rauh and Ziegenhain, 1993; Teti et al., in press), two studies of 30-month-olds (Fagot, 1994; Moore, Crawford, and Lester, 1994), and one of 36-month-olds (Heckman, 1994) all suggest such a trend.

One might ask whether quality of attachment really changes or whether only surface behavior changes. Two things suggest that relationships are qualitatively different. The first is "folkloric." Mothers commonly complain that two-year-olds are especially troublesome, suggesting that the quality of the relationships actually deteriorates. The second is the fit between the coercive strategy and the behavior of inconsistent mothers; preschool-aged children appear to have organized an effective strategy that is too mentally and behaviorally demanding for infants. With the availability of this strategy, children are better able to reflect the full continuum of maternal sensitivity. Consequently, the distribution of qualities of attachment would be expected to change.

Change in internal representational models of attachment. A second reason for considering attachment from the perspective of processing information is to throw light on the notions of organization, reorganization, and disorganization (see Crittenden, 1992a, for an elaboration of this issue). One of the most exciting things about the changes resulting from maturation is the potential of children to form more accurate internal representational models of attachment relationships and more effective behavioral strategies for managing them. Certainly, preoperational functioning helps children whose mothers are inconsistent, unresponsive, and hostile to develop more effective strategies than were possible in infancy.

In addition, by producing new mental skills, periods of maturational shift create the conditions that facilitate reorganization of representational models that can be used to predict future conditions more accurately. By this, I mean that the mind functions in two ways (Lashley, 1958/60). First, it looks for regularities, for patterns. The secure and avoidant patterns represent such regularities as they are identified by infants. Second, the mind seeks discrepancies between what is expected and what occurs. With preoperational intelligence, children discover discrepancies between their models of "good" or "bad" mothers and their mothers' actual behavior (Fischer, 1980). These discrepancies reflect more accurate perception and interpretation of the meaning of mothers' behavior. This new information must be reconciled with children's existing representational models. For children in supportive environments, this should facilitate the development of more differentiated, complex, and accurate models.

When the models of anxiously attached children fail to represent and predict reality accurately in critical situations, the children face a challenging task. Not only must a wide gap between model and reality be resolved, but they have less experience than secure children with the process of integration. This may lead to further efforts to discard conflictual information in order to maintain the inaccurate model. This may delay the process of revision until a higher threshold of discrepant information finally propels the mind toward reconsideration of its functioning and reorganization of information (Lashley, 1958/60). Thus, for anxiously attached children, the process of revising models is likely to be jerky and uncomfortable. Both mental activity and behavior may stutter until the integration of the new and discrepant information is complete (Crittenden, 1992a).

On the other hand, each discrepancy provides an opportunity for self-correction of inaccurate models and for the generation of more effective interpersonal strategies. Periods of rapid maturation, more than other times, may be expected to yield numerous discrepancies. With each such period, there is the possibility that the discrepancies will reach a threshold that forces mental attention and initiates integrative activity.

In the process, children may look confused and uncertain. Whether this should be considered disorganization (Main and Solomon, 1986, 1990) is not a simple matter. If circumstances have changed drastically, and a formerly adequate model represents a no longer extant reality (e.g., in death), disorganization seems like an appropriate construct to describe the change under way (Main and Hesse, 1990). In addition, if the period of uncertainty results in a model that is less well suited to the child's context than the earlier model, disorganization may be the appropriate construct. If, however, the child is becoming aware of previously overlooked information and is in the process of revising his model to bring it more in line with reality, I prefer that we recognize the developmental accomplishment of this activity by labeling it reorganization. Unfortunately, such a perspective does not provide classificatory guidelines that can be applied unequivocally to a laboratory observation.

Anger. A third central point is that preschool-aged children learn to encode, access, and display anger in different ways that have implications for their development and the quality of their relationships. Anger is among the most powerful of attachment behaviors. Consequently, its use by both attachment figures and attached individuals is of great import. Indeed, patterns of attachment can be viewed, in part, as strategies for managing anger. From this perspective, secure dyads are sufficiently in synchrony that anger is not felt frequently. In addition, its expression elicits prompt responses that tend to be comforting. Thus, for secure dyads, anger functions as a signal of important issues requiring dyadic attention.

Anxiously attached children, on the other hand, experience substantial frustration of their desires; this leads to frequent feelings of intense anger. Both type A and type C children learn to regulate expression of this anger on the basis of caregiver responses. Defended children expect rejection when they display anger or when their parents feel angry; consequently, they inhibit expression of their own anger and watch warily for evidence of parental anger, which they then attempt to soothe. When they are older, they may learn to "contain" anger in nominalized words that do not refer to either the angry person or the recipient of the anger.

Coercive children, however, experience anger concurrently with fear and desire for comfort. Consequently, they may be unable to accurately identify and label their feelings. This can lead to extreme and rapid mood swings and an inability to achieve sufficient mental distance for the integration of cognitive and affective integration. Nevertheless, coercive children have learned that both threatening and disarming expression of anger increases the probability of parental attention. Consequently, many of their interactions with attachment figures have an angry quality. Ironically, for both defended and coercive dyads, anger loses some of its communicative power; that is, important occasions and issues cannot be differentiated from less important ones.

Attachment and the mental processing of information. As the fourth reason for this review of infant and preschool attachment, the strategies used by preschool-aged children and the conditions under which they are learned suggest a two-dimensional representational model for describing quality of attachment.

On one hand, the patterns differ in the kind of information used. Defended children find that cognitive activity provides a predictable and relatively satisfying basis for interaction with their caregivers and a suitable basis for representing their caregivers' behavior. Consequently, they learn to depend on cognition to regulate their behavior and defend against affect. Coercive children have learned the opposite. They emphasize affect and disregard, or defend against, cognition. Securely attached children have access to, and use, both affect and cognition; for this reason, they can be considered *balanced* with regard to mental and behavioral functioning. Children classified as A/C also have access to both affect and cognition.

They differ from secure/balanced children in that they are unable to access and use both sorts of information simultaneously.

The patterns also differ in how information is used. Secure/balanced children integrate affective and cognitive information. Discrepancies between feelings and cognition lead to mental activity that often yields more elaborated understanding of self and reality, that is, more elaborate internal representational models. Thus, secure/balanced children automatically and preconsciously use new and discrepant information to revise existing internal representational models to yield progressively more accurate models. Although, at any given moment, the changes are likely to be minor and nondisruptive, the sum of this activity is the ongoing reorganization of internal representational models (Bowlby, 1980).

Defended and coercive children, on the other hand, engage in much less integration and reorganization (Crittenden, 1992b). Because much information is discarded as unreliable, defended and coercive children often fail to identify discrepancies. Under such circumstances, integration does not often occur (see Figure 2).

MENTAL REPRESENTATION AND INTEGRATION IN THE SCHOOL YEARS AND ADOLESCENCE

Memory Systems

In the final volume of his trilogy, Bowlby (1980) explored the potential of the constructs of internal representational models and memory systems to explain distortions of mental functioning and behavior. This perspective has proven fertile within attachment theory and has enriched it with exciting accomplishments in cognitive science. In the following sections, I discuss three memory systems and associated models (procedural, semantic, and episodic memory/models).

The notion of *procedural* internal representational models of relationships (Tulving, 1979; Crittenden, 1990, 1992b) functions well to describe behavior in infancy and the preschool years. In the preschool years, the two memory systems (semantic and episodic) of which Bowlby wrote begin to develop. *Semantic* memory encodes the generalized "rules" about how life (and relationships) work; for example, "good children obey their parents" (and, therefore, are not punished). Semantic memory, in other words, provides generalized and verbalized cognitive predictions, especially predictions relevant to staying safe. Initially, however, it is biased to reflect the values articulated by parents; these may or may not represent actual parental behavior. Autobiographical *episodic* memory encodes information about specific experiences, for example, the time you refused to come when your mother called you and she got very angry. Because most experiences are ordinary and inconsequential, they are not remembered on an occasion-by-occasion basis. Consequently, memories encoded to episodic memory and its associated internal representational model are biased to reflect affectively arousing and unsettling experiences, particularly those with threats of danger. When the affect is sufficiently unpleasant or forbidden, the memory may be stored unconsciously.

Using Memory Systems to Regulate Behavior

These three memory systems regulate human behavior under different conditions. Specifically, procedural memory/models regulate everyday, preconscious behavior throughout our life span. When procedurally regulated behavior fails to result in expected outcomes, the mind may focus consciously on the situation. By accessing information and models associated with semantic memory, the individual may try to solve the problem by consciously constructing a new and potentially more sophisticated behavioral solution. Thus, semantic memory regulates problem-solving behavior. If the situation is affectively very arousing, however, such reasoned thought may not be possible. Instead, episodic models that encode similar feeling states may be activated and used to regulate behavior. Because the accessed memory reflects prior behavior, the outcome may be less mature than current, procedurally regulated behavior and much less mature than semantically regulated behavior. This "regressive" bias is augmented by the tendency of affect to reflect genetically transmitted behavioral biases. Nevertheless, because evolution provides solutions that have passed the test of millennia, it is not clear that the resultant behavior is less adaptive (MacLean, 1990). Nor does it seem necessary to presume that the individual's developmental course had been reversed.

In the school years and adolescence, children learn to integrate information from all three memory systems to construct increasingly accurate representations of reality. By doing so, they reduce the effect of the biases in each system/model. There may, however, be individual differences in opportunity to integrate memory systems and models.

Individual Differences in Integration across Memory Systems

Secure/balanced individuals are likely to experience the fewest discrepancies among the memory systems, to experience the greatest parental support in exploring discrepancies, and, therefore, to find it least difficult to revise and update models. Mental analysis of perceived discrepancies, that is, metacognition (Main and Goldwyn, in press), parental highlighting of discrepancies between children's behavior and explanations for their behavior, and new experience may each be the impetus to such reorganization. The reorganization itself is expected to result in more finely differentiated and contingency-based representations of reality, for example, "When my mother is relaxed, she is usually supportive of me, but when she is angry about something else, she might take it out on me if I get in her way."

Defended individuals, on the other hand, are likely to find many discrepancies between semantic models of what ideally should be the case and what is, procedurally and episodically, the case. They are also likely to have learned that there are unfortunate consequences for articulating awareness of these discrepancies or for displaying affect and emotions associated with activation of the attachment system. Consequently, defended individuals may be expected to have elaborate and idealized semantic models that are readily accessed and presented verbally. These idealized semantic models maintain the overdrawn and dichotomized representations that are typical of early childhood. Nevertheless, the behavior of defended children and adolescents may be regulated by procedural and episodic models (especially unconsciously held episodic models) that are unarticulated or verbally denied.

Coercive individuals, on the other hand, may depend excessively on episodic models. Because they have learned to distrust cognitive reasoning, their semantic memory system may be both limited and confusing in content. For example, at various times the child of inconsistent parents may be told, "Did I give you permission to do that?" and "Can't you do anything for yourself?" The semantic conclusions underlying these statements are opposites and, thus, fail to provide the child with a semantic guide to behavior. Episodic models of what to do under highly arousing, conflictual circumstances may provide a better guide. This guide, however, like the semantic models of defended children, presents the world too starkly as good or bad.

Thus, defended individuals have ready access to logically organized, idealized, and internally coherent semantic memory but little access to (affective) episodic memory, little ability to integrate episodic with semantic memory, or both. Often, then, they would be unable to provide true explanations for their behavior. This closely reflects Main's thinking regarding dismissing (type A) adults in the *Adult Attachment Interview* (Main and Goldwyn, in press). In contrast, coercive individuals have an affective organization in episodic memory as well as limited access to semantic models and limited ability to integrate semantic with episodic memory. If this is so, then many preoccupied adults should show "lack of recall" when asked to provide (semantic) adjectives regarding their attachment relationships and when asked to access episodic memory through these semantic adjectives. Once in episodic memory, however, there should be little evidence of failure to recall. The run-on episodic speech of preoccupied (type C) adults may reflect "affective logic" regarding danger. The absence of either affective or cognitive logic in individuals' discourse may be a key indicator of unresolved trauma, that is, disorganization, in adolescence and adulthood (Crittenden, in press). In offering this model, I continue the perspective of the A and C patterns as mental and behavioral inverses of one another.

Mental Distortions in Affect and Cognition

This model of variation in patterns of attachment suggests an interface between attachment and psychopathology. As can be seen in Figure 2, the defended pattern is defined by accurate cognition, but defense against affect. In the compulsive caregiving and compulsive compliant subpatterns, affect is not merely inhibited; it is falsified.

Similarly, coercive children heighten affect and defend against cognition. By the school years, when children learn to use concrete logical operations, some coercive children use the illogical cognition with which their parents outwitted them in the preschool years. They learn to hide truth behind the appearance of logic and reason; that is, they rationalize. False cognition involves the surface appearance of logic, when, in fact, the actual relation among events is not as it appears to be. For example, a child playing "doctor" with her mother may hit the mother painfully hard with the hammer, then disarmingly say, "I only meant to check your reflexes!" Such arguments mislead adults (and the children who utter them) as to children's actual (affective) motives and thus mislead them also with regard to children's future behavior.

Coercive children who use aggressiveness or feigned helplessness to coerce caregivers are likely to distort cognitive logic further into devious, twisted logic based on ulterior motives. They mislead others with crafty and deceptive arguments like those that their attachment figures used to trick them. Their logic, in other words, is inverted logic in which arguments are constructed to obscure the truth and to lead to hidden ends that are often harmful to others. Consequently, the outcome of the logical sequence is different from, and often in opposition to, the predicted outcome. Such arguments function to coerce attachment figures into complying with children's plans when, if they fully understood, they would not accept the plans. Indeed, such plans are often punitive (C5) in that they reflect an obsession with revenge and the use of false cognition to achieve it. Less aggressive children are more likely to be seductive (C6), that is, with false cognition they seduce others into accepting their malicious plans. Often caregiving is used to achieve this (see Figure 3, C5–6). In addition, many coercive children respond to others with the assumption that they, too, are devious; this creates the potential for "mind games" in relationships. False cognition is the parallel of false affect among defended children, however, because it is dependent on logical thinking, it develops later than false affect.

Consider an example. The setting is a board game played by a ten-year-old girl and her mother. In the game, the players must move together around the board, stopping at various activities. Some of the activities appeal to children; some, to adults. Mothers and children each get points when they convince the other to go to their

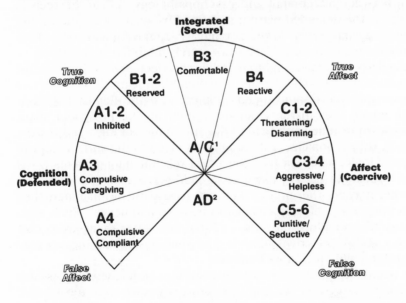

Figure 3 School-Age Patterns of Attachment

activity. Unfortunately, the convinced person also loses points. In this example, the mother promised that, if the child first accompanied her to the church, she would then accompany the child to the swimming pool. The child doubted this and wanted to go to her choice first. So the mother promised, by holding up three fingers (as in Scout's honor), that she really would go to the pool after the church. Her daughter responded, "But your legs are crossed!" (a sign that would nullify the promise). Clearly, this girl had learned that cognition can deceive, and she expected deception of her mother. It is noteworthy that, in this case, the daughter ultimately won the game by pretending to help her mother, that is, seducing her while actually leading her into fatal moves that cost her victory.

When it is unclear to an observer how an individual learned behavior, such as this daughter's suspicion, it may be attributed to "projection." It is possible, however, that such behavior is learned on the basis of accurately understood experience and represents the best prediction based on prior outcomes. The applicability of this experience to new situations and its amenability to modification based on new information are, of course, of direct relevance to mental health and psychopathology.

AFFECT, COGNITION, AND PSYCHOPATHOLOGY

Complexity and Variability

I have created a developmental model in which variations in experience lead to variations in mental functioning and corresponding variations in behavior. These, in turn, are repeatedly integrated with maturation-based changes in mental competence and thus create the potential for change in patterns of mental functioning. Patterns of attachment are used to define four patterns of mental functioning (A, B, C, A/C). Repeated periods of change and reintegration can lead to nonlinear variations in developmental pathways.

One of the advantages of this model over linear prediction based on infant patterns of attachment is its responsiveness to maturation. In addition, the use of two dimensions (i.e., source of information and degree of integration) creates a more complex framework with which to describe human variability than a three-category structure. In the two-dimensional structure, the categories identify areas on the dimensional framework; that is, they "tack down" points defined by the dimensions. Whether any individuals exactly fit these points, especially the extreme points, is not critical to the argument regarding the dimensions.

In spite of these improvements to the conceptualization of developmental pathways, there are several reasons that it is insufficient to define personality and risk for psychopathology. First, development is multidimensional, with factors other than species-specific behavior, maturation, and maternal caregiving affecting variation in developmental pathways. Of course, everyone knows this, but when it is not said explicitly, there is a tendency to presume that theories are limited to their central constructs. Second, individuals differ in mental capacity to integrate information. Third, in every life, there is a substantial element of luck or chance regarding what events occur.

Temperament. Among the other factors affecting development is individual-specific genetic variation, that is, temperament. Like many discussions of attachment, this chapter has been written as though infants arrived in their mothers' arms identically ready to be influenced by maternal sensitivity. This is obviously not the case. Each infant has a unique genetic endowment and a varied potential for expression of this endowment over the life span. The potential that is actually expressed in any given case is an interaction of genetic endowment, caregiver behavior, maturation, circumstances, and feedback.

Differences in individual-specific characteristics affect caregivers' response to children as well as children's response to caregivers' behavior (Bell and Harper, 1977; Vaughn, Stevenson-Hinde, and Waters, 1992). Put another way, one that is more typical of attachment theory, maternal sensitive responsiveness is defined by attachment figures' success in fitting their own response patterns to those of their offspring in ways that are mutually satisfying. Anything else must, by definition, be considered insensitive. From this perspective, there would be few traits that are inherently undesirable. Instead, traits can be evaluated as fitting more or less well with caregivers' traits and as enabling caregivers to shape them more or less effectively into personal advantages for children. For example, greater than average sensitivity to sensory stimuli could either facilitate or impede interpersonal relationships, depending on how a child learned to use this characteristic.

Thus, genetically based characteristics do not determine quality of attachment, but, in the context of different sorts of parental behavior, they are expressed differently. To take an extreme example, high activity level in the context of caregiver sensitivity may be displayed as liveliness whereas, in the context of inconsistency, it may lead to hyperactivity and conduct disorder. In the context of consistent rejection, depending on exactly what is punished, it may lead to athletic prowess or severe motor inhibition. The argument, in other words, is that it is not temperament that creates quality of attachment, nor the reverse, but rather that their interaction creates personality.

Furthermore, this interaction is not static; it does not occur at some specific time (say, infancy) and remain fixed thereafter. To the contrary, the interaction of biological endowment and circumstance is a dynamic process open to influence from all the relationships and experiences available to individuals, over the life span.

Self-organization and feedback. Humans are not merely passive recipients of conditions; their characters are not shaped blindly by unknown genetic information interacting with external persons and events. Rather, individuals select relationships, respond to influences, and pick niches within which to develop (Scarr and McCartney, 1983). Possibly most important, humans make these selections on the basis of feedback regarding their behavior, from others and from themselves. Furthermore, there are many sources of feedback. Like perceptions, some are selected and attended to whereas others are ignored or otherwise set aside. In making these selections, the human mind appears to be self-organizing; it functions to make coherence out of the greatest amount of reliable information.

There are individual differences in the effective use of feedback to attune behavior to circumstances. Some are tied to age; some, to prior experience. Greater maturity and breadth of information improve the ability to use feedback to achieve functional organizations. Children of type B caregivers have several advantages with reference to realizing their genetic potential. First, sensitive caregivers are more likely to transform children's attributes into advantages. Second, with more information available to their minds, secure/balanced children are better able to use feedback. Third, the opportunity to discuss puzzling experiences openly with caregivers enables type B children to benefit from the knowledge of caregivers. Of course, these are not all-or-none attributes, but, on the whole, *given a safe environment*, they favor children with balanced caregivers.

Intelligence. Intelligence is a particularly important source of individual variation. Although we associate intelligence with cognition, I differentiate these constructs by considering intelligence to refer to the ability (of the mind) to use information. This information may be cognitive (generated by the midbrain) or affective (generated by the limbic system). The ability of the mind to use this information and, particularly, to integrate information from different sources is the function of more recently evolved portions of the brain, that is, the cerebrum and cortex. This ability I think of as intelligence. In taking this approach, I reflect a notion of general intelligence, although I presume that individual-specific characteristics influence its display and lead to differences in intelligence with reference to various areas of functioning (Spearman, 1927).

Intelligence changes as a function of maturation (Piaget, 1952); these changes both enable humans to manage information in increasingly sophisticated ways and also reflect the functioning of the cerebrum and cortex (Ornstein and Thompson, 1984). From birth on, the value of information increases to the extent that (1) more information can be encoded, retrieved, and integrated (2) under an increasing variety of conditions (3) to yield more finely tuned knowledge and more adaptive behavior. Differences in intellectual ability interact with experience to yield variations in rigidity of patterns and success in implementing and modifying strategies.

Chance. The third reason predictability from early to later ages is limited is that life involves unforeseeable events that affect development (Lerner and Kauffman, 1986; Crittenden, 1994). Because these events are not tied to prior developmental history, they are not predictable from it. Consequently, the developmental pathways described here are best conceptualized as pathways with changing probabilities of outcome rather than fixed continuities or specific outcomes. Thus, the model becomes multidimensional, with unique points for each potential individual. Moreover, on the two-dimensional model that I have offered, one point has many, even an infinite number of, expressions in a population; each of these, however, has in common the two characteristics defined by the point.

In addition, however, it may be that human characteristics are neither evenly nor normally distributed within the population. Instead, they may tend to clump in a nonlinear fashion. Moreover, this clumping may be regular in nature, though not necessarily predictable for any given individual. The distribution of matter through space provides an analogy. Every point in space is specifiable with dimensional coordinates, but the actual distribution of matter is both uneven and patterned (in stars, galaxies, and so on.) Both the analogy and the line of thinking are amenable to conceptualization through "chaos" theory (Gleick, 1987; Waldrop, 1992). If so, the notion of turbulence, wherein the smooth flow of a substance, say, water, is broken into eddies, swirls, and rivulets after some velocity is exceeded is intriguing. Applied to humans, this suggests that, in relatively unstressed circumstances, all kinds of human attributes coalesce into highly varied personalities, whereas under substantial stress the smooth distribution breaks up, creating regular patterns and (depending on the level of analysis) subpatterns. If this is correct, both dimensions and classifications would be useful in describing personality. That is, attachment-relevant characteristics may be described dimensionally, but distributed in a patterned manner that is better described categorically. Moreover, the importance of recognizing the patterns, as opposed to the dimensions, may increase as the behavior reflects greater stress or, in attachment terms, greater perception of danger.

A butterfly's wing. To conclude this section, I offer an example of developmental change that illustrates most of the previous points. At home, eight-year-old Anne was a caregiver to her childlike and frightened mother and coyly compliant with her withdrawn, seductive, and sarcastic father. At school, she was extremely shy, immature, and withdrawn. In spite of having well-educated parents and no birth or developmental anomalies, she functioned academically in the dull-normal range and earned a solid D average in her subjects as she daydreamed through the school days. Teachers, sensing her fragility and feeling tender toward her, treated her gently, never chastised her, and continued to promote her, although she was always placed in the lowest sections.

This situation did not change until junior high school. There, at the end of her first year, a new classmate, the "brain" of the class, to whom she had never before spoken, asked Anne why she did so poorly when she was, in fact, the smartest kid in the class. Although Anne never saw this classmate again, her behavior changed dramatically. She began to study for long hours and, in her schoolwork and class reports, there appeared evidence of the wide reading she had used to occupy her long and lonely days. Soon the intelligence that had always been genetically available became characteristic of her behavior. To the schoolmates of her adolescence, intelligence became one of her defining characteristics. In adulthood, it became the key that freed her from the isolation of her childhood.

Several points are important about this anecdote. First, in the context of a distorted caregiving environment, Anne's genetic intellectual potential was not realized until she was mature enough to make use of verbal feedback. This probably could not have occurred before adolescence. Second, the source of the feedback was random, an unlikely and chance event, no more than the flutter of a butterfly's wing (Lorenz, 1979). Indeed, Anne, like all children, received a great deal of feedback, most of it more consistent with her observable behavior than this one comment. This one bit of feedback was so small, so unpredictable, and so isolated that it is almost impossible to believe that it could have had such a profound developmental effect. After all, the classmate was hardly an attachment figure! The importance of this discrepant bit of information may hinge on its having been consistent, in some not yet articulate way, with Anne's inner, privately experienced, intelligent self. Thus, a very minor perturbation in the flow of events came to have wide-ranging and unpredictable effects that increased as they were concatenated through successive developmental transitions (Lorenz, 1963). Third, timing may have been an important factor. Adolescence both gave Anne greater mental competence with which to organize change in her behavior and also created, in the outer world of school and family, a forum that valued academic achievement and fostered its development in nonsocial contexts. Finally, in elementary school, Anne's adaptation to her home environment would probably be described as a combination of the caregiving, compliant, and feigned helpless patterns of behavior (i.e., A/C) used to protect her from parental dysfunction. In discovering academic achievement, Anne found a productive means of eliciting approval. Some might view this as "compensation," and, of course, her mental and behavioral organization were defended. Nevertheless, this new-found competence increased greatly the adaptiveness of her functioning and could be expected to increase the probability of her ultimately, at some later developmental period, discovering the defense and reducing it. Such an achievement may be worthy of note without the devaluation implied by the term "compensation."

Developmental Pathways

Because this is only a chapter and not a text on developmental psychopathology, differences in outcome can only be sketched with broad brush strokes. The many and, ultimately, unique factors differentiating between one pathological outcome and another or between pathological outcomes and simple interpersonal discomfort (or even lack of problems) cannot be traced here. Nevertheless, the model offered lends itself to complexity and variation of outcome within a framework of predictable and lawful processes. With regard to mental health, the model implies that, with greater age, there is the potential for greater subtlety of adaptation as the mind moves from dichotomous classification to awareness of finer distinctions. Similarly, as one approaches balance in the integration of affect and cognition, mental and behavioral responses become more flexible and better adapted to unique circumstances. Together, increasing age and development within the context of supportive relationships maximize the potential of individuals for successful adaptation to varied situations. The risks for children who do not experience supportive relationships are now considered.

Behavior disorders in early and middle childhood. Coercive children can be expected to show disorders of behavior that draw attention to themselves and disorders of thought that both deflect responsibility away from themselves and also suggest that there are few causal relations. The disorders of behavior may emphasize either angry/threatening/fearless acting-out behavior or meek/submissive/fearful incompetent behavior. Similarly, the thought disorders may emphasize either one's own or others' hostility, power, and control, for example, grandiosity and paranoia, respectively, or, conversely, the vulnerability, victimization, and helplessness of the self. Both perspectives on disorder imply a vague, amorphous, "free-floating" anxiety that cannot be tied rationally to concrete experience. This is consistent with the argument that the anxiety has its origins in the evolution of protective affect in the limbic system. Bowlby emphasized the "helpless" form of the problem, for example, children with school phobia, fearfulness, and so on (Bowlby, 1973), whereas most current attention focuses on conduct disorders and other acting-out behavior (Achenbach et al., 1991).

Both the behavioral and mental forms of the type C pattern imply that others are responsible for the situation and that others must change to resolve it. In both cases, coercive children can be expected to form clinging, enmeshed (and often punitive) alliances with others, for example, gangs, jealous friendships. In addition, coercive children, more than defended children, are likely to demand immediate gratification as a substitute for true comfort; consequently, they may exhibit impatience, eating disorders tied to excessive intake, and immaturity. In addition, they may use risk-taking behavior that cannot fail to elicit protective attention, for example, careless hyperactivity, extreme refusal to eat, toleration of violent relationships. Irrational risk taking also implies disbelief in the contingencies that usually link events, a pattern first established in infancy with inconsistent parental responsiveness.

The majority of children who are referred for psychological services fit the coercive pattern of attachment and mental functioning (Achenbach, 1984). The majority are also boys; one theme of the approach offered here is that we may overlook a similar set of girls whose development is jeopardized by the risk taking of extreme feigned helplessness and the tolerance, even courting, of victimization. The previously offered example of Anne makes this point. By eliciting teacher nurturance in elementary school, Anne's disarming/immature behavior prevented her from receiving the academic help that she needed. Like many girls, she was overlooked in classrooms filled with children asking for assistance and boys, in circumstances not too different from her own, who displayed their distress with attention-grabbing behavior problems. Other disarming/vulnerable type C children may display physiological problems that demand adult attention. These range from colic in infancy to allergies, asthma, sickness, and extreme pickiness regarding food. All of these function to force adults to cater to children without the child's having to make reasoned arguments for the attention.

Among coercive children who are referred for service are those who cannot work independently and crave constant attention from attachment figures or substitute figures. Because they have learned that intense displays are necessary to attract their parents' attention, coercive children tend to be attention-seeking, loud, and disruptive in group settings, particularly school. The schedule of intermittent, unpredictable reinforcement used by their attachment figures leads to rapidly escalating behavior that does not cease in the face of either lack of response or punitive responses. Indeed, when adults such as teachers become angry, coercive children may be expected to display disarming behavior and thus make themselves appealing and reduce the power of adults' anger. Because they attend to others' affective displays to the (relative) exclusion of cognition and use affective display to attract attention to themselves, such children are also likely to appear to have attention deficit disorder and learning disabilities.

An example drawn from a sample of eight- to nine-year-old boys in a cooperative task with a peer demonstrates the point. Because Roger had no best friend, his teacher assigned him a companion. The task was to color jointly an outline of a figure to match a displayed real figure. As the boys began, Roger was fidgety, but his companion got right to work. The more concentration his companion showed, the more Roger fidgeted, until he was moving about the room and addressing comments to his companion. The "friend" generally ignored Roger, who was clearly unsatisfied. He made a few attempts to color, but no joint activity ensued. Finally, he leaned toward his companion and whispered, "I'll tell you the secret, if you're my best friend." The companion did not acknowledge this communication. Roger repeated it, this time more loudly. No response. Finally, Roger called out in a voice that was both angry and vulnerable, "Are you my best friend?" At this the other boy slowly turned to Roger, looked at him for a long moment, and said in an even tone of voice, "Not in your dreams." Roger slumped over, as though punched in the belly, his shoulders rose to protect his neck, and his head fell forward. Then he threw himself back, charged across the room toward the door, and leaned against the wall in a near fetal position. The room was silent for several long moments until Roger recovered. He then raced around the room, threw objects, tossed furniture aside, and yelled angry threats. He did not complete the picture.

Was he hyperactive? Yes, but for the functional purpose of drawing attention to his problems. Did he have attention deficit disorder?
Only if the researchers determine what children must attend to.
Roger at all times attended to the relationship with his companion.
Was he learning disabled? Yes and no. He was capable of learning,
but not when he needed to devote all of his attention to relationships and cope with unpredictable events and irrational cognition
from important adults. Yes, he was conduct-disordered, but for readily explained reasons. His parents, like other parents of coercive
children, puzzled professionals because they did not seem incompetent enough to explain Roger's extreme problems. A little inconsistent maybe, even a bit submissive as they begged for Roger's acceptance. Nevertheless, they really loved him and were very caring. Just
like parents of ambivalent infants and coercive preschoolers.

Roger represents both the coercive-threatening pattern and the
common pattern of conduct-disordered children. And he is a boy.
But what about girls? What about the children who display the coer-
cive-disarming pattern? I suspect that they experience identical
mental and interpersonal problems, but they are overlooked by
teachers who are content to nurture them and who are not threatened by their behavior (Sadker and Sadker, 1994).

A few defended children would be identified in the school years
as too withdrawn. A few others would be "teachers' pets" when
under the authority of adults but would display their anger as bullies[4] when there were no powerful adults nearby. Most defended
children, however, would be expected to please adults. They inhibit
negative affect, display positive affect, make few demands, and
struggle to comply with adults' demands. Some are likely to become
overachievers. Because defended children tend to be overcontrolled
and obedient, it may be difficult for most adults to perceive that they
inhibit feelings and desires or to recognize the sadness, isolation,
and anger of defended children. These, however, pose substantial
threats to children's ability to establish secure and supportive human
relationships.

Psychopathology and adolescence. Whereas the school years
present coercive children with problems of adjustment, adolescence
presents problems for defended children. Teenagers are expected to
develop several intimate, heterosexual relationships that are the
basis for ultimately choosing a mate (Erikson, 1950). Defended
adolescents find it very difficult to tolerate intimacy. Consequently,
they may find themselves alone and lonely (Sullivan, 1953; Erikson,

---

[4] Such bullies are context-specific. Others are indiscriminate bullies who challenge
everyone, including those who are hierarchically dominant; these bullies are more
likely to display type C functioning.

1968). Some children in the *inhibited* subgroup of the defended pattern may become the *isolated* (see Figure 4, A5), *compulsively self-reliant* individuals whom Bowlby described as adults (Bowlby, 1979). Others may cover this by using the sexual behavior system to mask the problem. They use *promiscuous* sexuality (Figure 4, A6) to provide physical intimacy while remaining psychologically distant. Others may hide behind overachievement, which brings some fame and approval, but not comfort. For all of these adolescents, the inability to use affect honestly jeopardizes their development and happiness. Unless access to affect is reclaimed or a preoccupying compensatory activity, such as academic achievement and sports, can be found, depression, substance abuse, and promiscuity become possibilities.

Among those who strive too compulsively for perfection, there is the risk that denied feelings of shame and failure may sometimes lead to suicide. Suicides of such defended individuals, unlike those of secure/balanced or coercive individuals, are rarely associated with signs and warnings that the individual felt desperate. To the contrary, suicidal defended individuals may appear to "have it all."

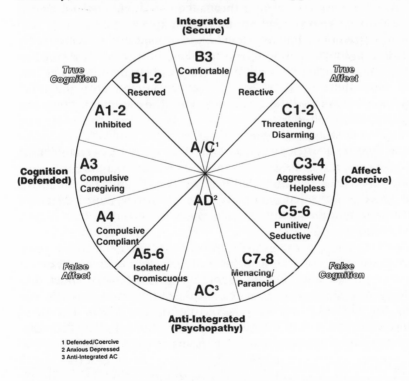

Figure 4 Adolescent and Adult Patterns of Attachment

Even after their deaths, family members and professionals often remain puzzled and unable to reconcile the now-apparent painful and secret life of the individual with his or her public appearance.

For coercive adolescents, there is the possibility that conduct disorders will escalate into truly dangerous and violent behavior, including delinquency and criminality. The attention-seeking behavior that typified school-aged coercive children will become more of an "in your face" threatening posture. The "attitude" of blaming others may expand to include retribution for slights and past offenses as motivation for entangling, grudge-generating disputes. In addition, territoriality becomes an issue in adolescence (possibly reflecting the hormonal effects of sexual maturity, Olweus, 1980, 1988). In this context, gang membership can fulfill the need to belong to an ever-present, always available, and responsive group that perceives relationships in coercive terms. Especially if they have learned the inverted logic of deception, coercive adolescents may engage in illegal activity. In addition, seductive and quarrelsome relationships are common; some of these become violent. Especially among girls, psychosomatic symptoms may be used to force others to offer nurturant attention; if that fails to satisfy, threats of suicide or suicide attempts may be used to express helplessness and demand attention from reluctant others. Desperate phone calls or suicide notes left for others tend to blame others for wronging the suicidal individual and for not protecting and saving him or her. For both boys and girls, there may be an obsession with maintaining relationships and punishing partners who threaten them. When the obsessive partner tends to use a submissive pattern, the anger may be expressed as passive-aggressive behavior.

A/C patterns of psychopathology. For some individuals, there may be a bi-polar alternation between behaving in a coercive manner and behaving in a defended manner. When actual environments vary so as to fit this pattern of adaptation, it may be maintained over great periods of time (Crittenden, in press; see Figure 4, A/C).

Depression. Depression is one form of psychopathology that appears to afflict humans with all patterns of mental functioning. Gut's proposition of a "basic depressed response" makes understanding this phenomenon easier. According to Gut (1989), when individuals experience circumstances for which their minds can find no solutions but that must be resolved before productive activity in other spheres of life can be undertaken, they display the basic depressed response. By that, Gut means that they withdraw into themselves and, show increasingly less interest in external conditions and ultimately even little interest in their own welfare. In this state, depressed individuals display behavioral indicators of depression. These function communicatively to elicit caregiving from others and thus reduce the risk of physiological dysfunction. Depressed individuals also ruminate on the problem. In doing so, all the individuals' energies and skills become focused, waking and sleeping, on the one central issue to be resolved. This intense focusing increases the probability that the mind will discover a new solution that will break the deadlock and thus release the individual from depression and free him or her to return to life's activities.

When the mind is healthy (in the sense that information is managed freely, creatively, and integratively), the probability of finding a solution is good. When, however, mental functions are constrained, there is risk that a solution will not be found. Clearly, individuals who defend against whole classes of information experience greater risk of "unproductive depression." Furthermore, those who falsify affect or cognition are expected to experience greater risk yet. Although depression may be experienced by anyone in response to self-disturbing events, for example, death of a loved one or knowledge of terminal disease, both the range and type of conditions that represent jeopardy for depression and also the way the depression is expressed may vary by pattern of mentally processing information.

Individuals who defend against affect (type A) are predicted to display depression with both increased affective distancing and increased compulsive behavior. Their behavior can be construed as seeking solutions through more careful management of protective contingencies and without admitting the shameful defeat of needing help (which, of course, would be expected to elicit rejection). In addition, like nondepressed defended individuals, they attempt to deflect attention away from the true problem.

On the other hand, those who defend against cognition (type C) are expected to manifest increased affective displays and impulsive behavior, that is, agitation (Patterson, 1990). In addition, when others attempt to reduce their distress by providing "rational" solutions, depressed coercive individuals are expected to show anger and suspicion and, to themselves, offer increasingly irrational solutions. Like other coercive individuals, they behave with an exaggerated presentation of their problem that holds others' attention.

Complete depression, that is, true helplessness, may result when individuals find that neither affect, nor cognition is helpful in resolving the problems of their lives (Seligman, 1975); some scraps of the strategies may be combined in a self-soothing intrapersonal strategy of depression (see Figure 4, AD).

This perspective on depression is consistent with empirical data on adolescent depression in which five subtypes were observed (Muratori, 1993). *Reactive depression* fits Gut's notion of event-elicited depression, which is resolved by mental reorganization to better match functioning to circumstances. As Muratori points out, the event may include adjustment to the maturational shifts from childhood to adolescence or from adolescence to adulthood. *Depression with neurotic symptoms* appears to represent a mild type A sort of depression in which severe social withdrawal, together with anxiety and compulsive mechanisms, functions to defend against feelings of anger and fear. *Depression with severe motor retardation* reflects a more severe form of defended depression typified by loss of self-esteem and feelings of guilt; loss of interest in activities is pronounced to the point of stupor. *Depression with disturbance of conduct* and *depression with severe thought disturbance* reflect two levels of Type C disturbance in which, in the less severe form, coercive, obsessive, acting-out behavior predominates and, in the more severe form, cognition is irrational, including persecutory delusions and influence delusions, that is, *menacing* (Figure 4, C7) and *paranoid* (C8).

Psychopathy (AC). In a few cases, the two processes of false affect and false cognition may coalesce in adolescence or adulthood to produce an inverted, anti-integration of affect and cognition. Because this implies integration, it is denoted as AC, without the solidus. In such cases, the individual may so distrust both affect and cognition that even discrepant information may not trigger the mind to reexplore reality. Instead, the mind may determine that this, too, is trickery and deception or that the risk of mistakenly responding as though it were true is too great to be tolerated. In such cases, the representation of reality is like a false, inverted mirror image in which good and bad, true and false are reversed. The image, however, is largely without flaw; it is whole cloth. Disarmingly seductive, but false, affect covers internal rage, and sharp intelligence applied to inverted cognition creates schemes beyond a normal person's imagination. Indeed, high intelligence may enable such psychopathic individuals to act with mental impunity on the intense anger and fear that all anxiously attached individuals feel when once again they are let down by loved caregivers. With enacted rage covered by charming seductiveness and fear hidden behind compulsive compliance and caregiving (Figure 4), this derivation of psychopathy has much in common with Bowlby's affectionless character (Bowlby, 1980). Using the perspective on the mental processing of information offered here, for psychopaths, the availability of truly supportive and protective humans is life's ultimate, cruel deception.

Symptoms, diagnoses, and theory. In outlining relations between psychopathology and the theory being developed here, I have had to rely on commonly used diagnoses and symptoms. DSM-IV diagnoses, however, are not organized on the basis of theory. Instead, they represent symptom clusters. Most clinicians would agree, however, that symptoms do not reflect directly the underlying disorder (Freud, 1933). That is, a single symptom or cluster of symptoms may have more than one etiology. This makes articulation of a new theory of psychopathology more difficult. Diagnostic labels are needed to express familiar ideas, and, yet, the diagnoses do not truly map the new distinctions being made.

Let me offer an example. On the surface, anorexia appears to be a disorder tied to inhibition of affect and rigid cognitive structuring of behavior that is often motivated by a component of shame that itself is exacerbated by the onset of sexuality. So it must be a problem tied to the defended pattern. Maybe. Refusal to eat can be an angry behavior when parents wish to express love through food-giving. This is not unusual either socially or ontogenetically. As a consequence, a very angry adolescent can draw attention to herself, can even control a family's activities, by refusing to eat; at the same time, she can express her rejection of parental love. When combined with willful twisting of parents' words and behavior so as to construe them falsely as hostile, the pattern fits the coercive-punitive strategy far better than the defended strategy. The point is that the diagnostic perspective being offered here depends on the *function of the behavior within relationships*, rather than its morphology within an individual.

SUMMARY AND CONCLUSIONS

To recap, I propose that Ainsworth's patterns of infant attachment be reconceptualized as patterns of mental processing of information that vary in the extent to which they integrate information based on cognition and affect to create models of reality. Attachment figures, then, are the individuals who both protect infants from harm and also provide the interpersonal context within which children learn to use their minds. Because maturation periodically changes the mind, attachment figures' roles must change accordingly. What remains constant, however, is the function of attachment figures to provide the attached person with the sense of a secure base from which to venture out into the unknown that, at one and the same time, beckons invitingly and threatens perilously.

In this model, type B children, who are called secure in infancy, are *balanced* with regard to the use of affect and cognition. Type A children, called avoidant in infancy, are *defended* against affect and depend heavily on cognition. Type C children, who are called ambivalent in infancy, use a *coercive* strategy based primarily on affect. In the extreme, some defended children develop false affect, and some coercive children develop false cognition. These mental and behavioral patterns leave children vulnerable to conduct and attentional disorders, disorders of intimate and sexual relationships, depression, and, in the extreme, addiction to substances and suicide. In a very few cases, the patterns lead to psychopathy.

Many of the ideas that I have expressed here go beyond the attachment theory that is familiar to us all. Have I strayed too far? How far should we stray from the secure base of Bowlby and Ainsworth? Maybe that depends on how secure we are. Bowlby and Ainsworth were both bold and integrative thinkers who conceptualized realities far beyond the range of the then familiar theories of human functioning. In that context, I like to think that Bowlby and Ainsworth would neither require, nor desire, that we retain unchanged all of their thinking. Indeed, I think we best honor them by emulating their method of wide, mental exploration and bold, integrative thought, particularly that which is clinically relevant to the relief of suffering of those who have experienced the least joy in human relationships (Bowlby, 1988). In this chapter, which I offer as a small gift to Bowlby and Ainsworth in exchange for their gift to us all of a magnificent and living theory and a powerful methodology, I have sought to follow that lead.

REFERENCES

Achenbach, T. M. (1984), The status of research related to psychopathology. In: *Development During Middle Childhood*, ed. W. A. Collins. Washington, DC: National Academy Press, pp. 370–397.

—— Howell, C. T., Quay, H. C. & Connors, C. K. (1991), *National Survey of Competencies Among Four- to Sixteen-Year-Olds: Parents' Reports of Normal and Clinical Samples. Monographs of the Society Research in Child Development*, Serial No. 225, Vol. 50, No. 3.

Ainsworth, M. D. S. (1979), Infant–mother attachment. *Amer. Psychol.*, 34:932–937.

—— (1985), Patterns of infant–mother attachment: Antecedents and effects on development. *Bull. NY Acad. Med.*, 61:771–791.

—— Blehar, M., Waters, E., & Wall, S. (1978), *Patterns of Attachment*. Hillsdale, NJ: Lawrence Erlbaum Associates.

Barnett, S. A. (1975), *The Rat*. Chicago: University of Chicago Press.

Bell, R. Q. & Harper, L. V. (1977), *Child Effects on Adults*. Hillsdale, NJ: Lawrence Erlbaum Associates.

Bowlby, J. (1969), *Attachment and Loss, Vol. 1*. New York: Basic Books, 1982.

—— (1973), *Attachment and Loss, Vol. 2*. New York: Basic Books.

—— (1979), The *Making and Breaking of Affectional Bonds*. London: Tavistock.

—— (1980), *Attachment and Loss, Vol. 3*. New York: Basic Books.

—— (1988), *A Secure Base*. New York: Basic Books.

Bronson, G. W. (1972), *Infants' Reactions to Unfamiliar Persons and Novel Objects. Monographs of the Society for Research in Child Development*, Serial No. 148, Vol. 37, No. 3.

Carlson, V., Cicchetti, D., Barnett, D. & Braunwald, K. (1989), Disorganized/disoriented attachment relationships in maltreated infants. *Devel. Psychol.*, 25:525–531.

Cassidy, J., & Marvin, R. S., with the Working Group of the John D. & Catherine T. MacArthur Foundation on the Transition from Infancy to Early Childhood (1991), Attachment organization in three- and four-year olds: Coding guidelines. Unpublished manuscript, University of Virginia.

Crittenden, P. M. (1981), Abusing, neglecting, problematic, and adequate dyads: Differentiating by pattern of interaction. *Merrill-Palmer Quart.*, 27:201–218.

—— (1985a), Maltreated infants: Vulnerability and resilience. *J. Child. Psychol. Psychiat.*, 26:85–96.

—— (1985b), Social networks, quality of parenting, and child development. *Child. Devel.*, 56:1299–1313.

—— (1988), Relationships at risk. In: *Clinical Implications of Attachment*, ed. J. Belsky & T. Nezworski. Hillsdale, NJ: Lawrence Erlbaum Associates, pp. 136–174.

—— (1990), Internal representational models of attachment relationships. *Infant Ment. Health J.*, 11:259–277.

—— (1992a), Quality of attachment in the preschool years. *Devel. Psychopathol.*, 4:209–241.

—— (1992b), Treatment of anxious attachment in infancy and early childhood. *Devel. Psychopathol.*, 4:575–602.

—— (1994), Peering into the black box: An exploratory treatise on the development of self in young children. In: *Rochester Symposium on Developmental Psychopathology, Vol. 5*, ed. D. Cicchetti & S. Toth. Rochester, NY: University of Rochester Press, pp. 79–148.

—— (in press), Individual differences in response to crisis: Effects on memory systems, internal representational models, and behavior. In: *Rochester Symposium on Developmental Psychopathology, Vol. 8*, ed. D. Cicchetti & S. Toth. Rochester, NY: University of Rochester Press.

—— & Claussen, A. H. (1990), Assessing attachment at two–four years. Presented at the Southeastern Conference on Human Development, Richmond, VA.

—— & —— (1994), Quality of attachment in the preschool years: Alternative perspectives. Presented at International Conference on Infant Studies, Paris.

—— & DiLalla, D. (1988), Compulsive compliance: The development of an inhibitory coping strategy in infancy. *J. Abn. Child. Psychol.*, 16:585–599.

Dunn, J., Bretherton, I. & Munn, P. (1987), Conversations about feeling states between mothers and their young children. *Devel. Psychol.*, 23:132–139.

Eibl-Eibesfeldt, I. (1979), Human ethology: Concepts and implications for the sciences of man. *Behav. Brain Sci.*, 2:1–57.

Ekman, P. (1992), Facial expression of emotion: New findings, new questions. *Psychol. Sci.*, 3:34–38.

Emde, R. N., Gaensbauer, T. J. & Harmon, R. J. (1976), *Emotional Expression in Infancy*. New York: International Universities Press.

Erickson, M., Sroufe, A. & Egeland, B. (1985), The relationship between quality of attachment and behavior problems in preschool in a high-risk sample. In: *Growing Points of Attachment Theory and Research*. ed. I. Bretherton & E. Waters. *Monographs of the Society for Research in Child Development*, Serial No. 209, Vol. 50, Nos. 1–2, pp. 147–166.

Erikson, E. H. (1950), *Childhood and Society*. New York: Norton.

—— (1968), *Identity, Youth, and Crisis*. New York: Norton.

Fagot, B. I. (1994), Attachment: Infancy to preschool. Presented at International Conference on Infant Studies, Paris.

Fischer, K. W. (1980), A theory of cognitive development: The control and construction of hierarchies of skills. *Psychol. Rev.*, 87:477–531.

Freud, S. (1933), *New Introductory Lectures in Psychoanalysis. Standard Edition*, 22:5–182. London: Hogarth Press, 1964.

Gallistel, C. R., Brown, A. L., Carey, S., Gelman, R. & Keil, F. C. (1991), Lessons from animal learning for the study of cognitive development. In: *The Epigenesis of Mind*, ed. S. Carey & R. Gelman. Hillsdale, NJ: Lawrence Erlbaum Associates, pp. 3–36.

Gleick, J. (1987), *Chaos*. New York: Penguin Books.

Grossmann, K., Friedl, A. & Grossmann, K. E. (1987), Preverbal infant–mother vocal interaction patterns as related to maternal sensitivity and the infant's attachment quality. Presented at the Second International Symposium, "Prevention and Intervention in Childhood and Youth: Conceptual and Methodological Issues," Bielefeld, Germany.

—— & Grossmann, K. E. (1991), Newborn behavior, the quality of early parenting and later toddler–parent relationships in a group of German infants. In: *The Cultural Context of Infancy, Vol. 2*, ed. J. K. Nugent, B. M. Lester & T. B. Brazelton. Norwood, NJ: Ablex, pp. 3–38.

Gut, E. (1989), *Productive and Unproductive Depression*. New York: Basic Books.

Heckman, P. D. (1994), Temperament, attachment, and toddler non-compliance styles: An account of salient identifying features. Unpublished doctoral dissertation, University of Notre Dame.

Klinnert, M. D., Sorce, J. F., Emde, R. N., Stenberg, C. & Gaensbauer, T. (1984), Continuities and change in early emotional life. In: *Continuities and Discontinuities in Development*, ed. R. N. Emde & R. J. Harmon. New York: Plenum Press, pp. 339–354.

Lashley, K. S. (1958/60), Cerebral organization and behavior. In: *The Neuropsychology of Lashley*, ed. F. A. Beach, D. O. Hebb, C. T. Morgan & H. W. Nissen. New York: McGraw-Hill, pp. 529–543.

Lerner, R. M. & Kauffman, M. B. (1986), The concept of development in contextualism. *Devel. Rev.*, 6:309–333.

Lieberman, A. F. (1993), *The Emotional Life of the Toddler*. New York: Free Press.

Lorenz, E. (1963), Deterministic, non-periodic flow. *J. Atmos. Sci.*, 20:130–141.

—— (1979), Predictability: Does the flap of a butterfly's wings in Brazil set off a tornado in Texas? Presented at the meeting of the American Association for the Advancement of Science, Washington, DC.

Luria, A. R. (1973), *The Working Brain*. London: Penguin Press.

Lyons-Ruth, K., Repacholi, B., McLeod, S. & Silva, E. (1991), Disorganized attachment behavior in infancy: Short-term stability, maternal and infant correlates, and risk-related subtypes. *Devel. Psychopathol.*, 3:377–396.

MacLean, P. D. (1955), The limbic system ("visceral brain") and emotional behavior. *Arch. Neurol. Psychiat.*, 73:130–134.

—— (1973), *A Triune Concept of Brain and Behavior*. Toronto: University of Toronto Press.

—— (1990), *The Triune Brain in Evolution*. New York: Plenum Press.

Main, M. (1981), Avoidance in the service of attachment: A working paper. In: *Behavioral Development*, ed. K. Immelmann, G. Barlow, L. Petrinovich & M. Main. New York: Cambridge University Press, pp. 651–693.

—— & Cassidy, J. (1988), Categories of response to reunion with the parent at age six: Predictability from infant attachment classifications stable across a one-month period. *Devel. Psychol.*, 24:415–426.

———— & Goldwyn, R. (in press), Adult attachment classification system. In: *A Typology of Human Attachment Organization*, ed. M. Main. Cambridge: Cambridge University Press.

———— & Hesse, P. (1990), Lack of resolution of mourning in adulthood and its relationship to infant disorganization: Some speculations regarding causal mechanisms. In: *Attachment in the Preschool Years*, ed. M. Greenberg, D. Cicchetti & E. M. Cummings. Chicago: University of Chicago Press, pp. 161–182.

———— Kaplan, N. & Cassidy, J. (1985), Security in infancy, childhood and adulthood: A move to the level of representation. In: *Growing Points of Attachment Theory and Research*, ed. I. Bretherton & E. Waters. *Monographs of the Society for Research in Child Development*, Serial No. 209, Vol. 50, Nos. 1–2, pp. 66–104.

———— & Solomon, J. (1986), Discovery of an insecure disorganized/disoriented attachment pattern: Procedures, findings, and implications for the classification of behavior. In: *Affective Development in Infancy*, ed. M. Yogman & T. B. Brazelton. Norwood, NJ: Ablex, pp. 121–160.

———— ———— (1990), Procedures for identifying infants as disorganized/disoriented during the Ainsworth strange situation. In: *Attachment in the Preschool Years*, ed. M. Greenberg, D. Cicchetti & E. M. Cummings. Chicago: University of Chicago Press, pp. 161–182.

Marvin, R. S. (1977), An ethological-cognitive model for attenuation of mother–child attachment behavior. In: *Advances in the Study of Communication and Affect, Vol. 3*, ed. T. M. Alloway, L. Kramer & P. Pliner. New York: Plenum Press, pp. 25–60.

Moore, L., Crawford, F. & Lester, J. (1994), Security of attachment at 30 months: Maternal, infant, and family variables. Presented at International Conference on Infant Studies, Paris.

Muratori, F. (1993), A clinical diagnostic classification for depression in adolescence. Presented at the Listening to Children: Yale/Italy Symposium, New Haven, CT.

Olweus, D. (1980), Testosterone, aggression, physical, and personality dimensions in normal adolescent males. *Psychosom. Med.*, 42:253–269.

———— (1988), Circulating testosterone levels and aggression in adolescent males: A causal analysis. *Psychosom. Med.*, 50:261–272.

Ornstein, R. & Thompson, R. F. (1984), *The Amazing Brain*. New York: Houghton Mifflin.

Papousek, H. & Papousek, M. (1979), Early ontogeny of human social interaction: Its biological roots and social dimensions. In: *Human Ethology*, ed. K. Foppa, W. Lepenies & D. Ploog. New York: Cambridge University Press, pp. 456–489.

Patterson, G. R. (1980), Mothers: The Unacknowledged Victims. *Monographs of the Society for Research in Child Development*, Serial No. 186, Vol. 45, No. 5. pp. 1–64.

———— (1990), A mediational model for boys' depressed mood. In: *Risk and Protective Factors in the Development of Psychopathology*, ed. J. E. Rolf, A. S. Masten, D. Cicchetti, K. H. Nuechterlein & S. Weintraub. New York: Cambridge University Press, pp. 141–163.

Piaget, J. (1952), *The Origins of Intelligence*. New York: International Universities Press.

Radke-Yarrow, M., Cummings, E. M., Kuczynski, L. & Chapman, M. (1985), Patterns of attachment in two- and three-year-olds in normal families and families with parental depression. *Child. Devel.*, 56:884–893.

Rauh, H. & Ziegenhain, U. (1993), Attachment classification procedures: Ainsworth, Main, and Crittenden in comparison. Presented at the Sixth European Conference on Developmental Psychology, Bonn, Germany.

Sadker, M. & Sadker, D. (1994), *Failing at Fairness*. New York: Scribner's.

Scarr, S. & McCartney, K. (1983), How people make their environments: A theory of genotype environment effects. *Child Devel.*, 54:424–435.

Seligman, M. E. P. (1975), *Helplessness*. San Francisco: Freeman.

Selye, H. (1976), *The Stress of Life*. New York: McGraw-Hill.

Skinner, B. F. (1938), *The Behavior of Organisms*. New York: Appelton-Century-Crofts.

Spearman, C. (1927), *The Abilities of Man*. New York: Macmillan.

Stern, D. (1985), *The Interpersonal World of the Infant*. New York: Basic Books.

Sullivan, H. S. (1953), *The Interpersonal Theory of Psychiatry*. New York: Norton.

Teti, D. M. & Gelfand, D. M., Messinger, D. S. & Isabella, R. (in press), Correlates of preschool attachment security in a sample of depressed and non-depressed mothers. *Develop. Psychol.*

Thompson, R. F. (1985), *The Brain*. W. H. Freeman.

Tronick, E. Z. (1989), Emotions and emotional communication in infants. *Amer. Psychol.*, 44:112–119.

Tulving, E. (1979), Memory research: What kind of progress? In: *Perspectives on Memory Research*, ed. L. G. Nilsson. Hillsdale, NJ: Lawrence Erlbaum Associates, pp. 19–34.

Vaughn, B., Stevenson-Hinde, J. M. & Waters, E. (1992), Attachment security and temperament in infancy and early childhood: Some conceptual clarifications. *Devel. Psychol.*, 28:463–473.

Vygotsky, L. S. (1987), *The Collected Works of L. S. Vygotsky*, ed. R. W. Rieber & A. S. Carlton (trans. N. Minick). New York: Plenum Press.

Waldrop, M. M. (1992), *Complexity*. New York: Simon & Schuster.

Winnicott, D. W. (1958), Psychoses and childcare. In: *Collected Papers*. London: Tavistock, pp. 219–228.

Recent Studies in Attachment

Overview, with Selected Implications for Clinical Work

MARY MAIN

The study of human attachment organization is founded on the work of John Bowlby and Mary Ainsworth, and takes among its topics several issues central to clinical work. This chapter begins with a history of the field, pointing first to Bowlby's early emphasis on the attachment figure as the infant's solution to experiences of fright and then to Ainsworth's discoveries regarding the three traditional forms of "organized" infant attachment—*secure, insecure-avoidant,* and *insecure-resistant/ambivalent*—together with their behavioral precursors and sequelae. Finally, the discovery of a fourth, *disorganized/disoriented* form of insecure infant attachment is described, together with the reappearance of these four forms of infant attachment status in discourse, narrative, and other representational processes during childhood and adulthood. I then discuss the "organized" insecure infant (avoidant and resistant) and adult (dismissing and preoccupied) attachment patterns in terms of defensive process, and I review earlier proposals that individuals disorganized with the primary caregiver in infancy may be more vulnerable than others to anxiety, phobia, and dissociative experiences. Finally, I consider potential links among adult attachment, mental suffering, and the therapeutic process.

The chapter opens with a consideration of three principal phases in the development of the field of attachment and is limited to those topics having the greatest relevance for clinicians. In the first phase,

This chapter was completed while I was a visiting professor at Leiden University, the Netherlands, sponsored by the Center for Child and Family Studies and by the Institute for the Study of Education and Human Development. I am grateful to Erik Hesse for his extensive critiques and comments, and to Kohler-Stiftung of Munich for its support of this project. Nino Dazzi and John Kerr provided helpful critiques with respect to earlier versions of this chapter.

drawing on evolutionary theory and observations of nonhuman primates, Bowlby (1969) called attention to the functioning of an "attachment behavioral system," which, having primary and immediate responsibility for regulating infant safety in man's original "environment of evolutionary adaptedness," unavoidably still acts to lead the infant to continually monitor the physical and psychological accessibility of its attachment figure(s). The development and organization of this instinctively guided system were used to explain the child's behavioral and emotional responses to separation and loss (Bowlby, 1973, 1980).

A second phase in the development of the field centered on individual differences in the one-year-old infant's behavioral response to separations from, and reunions with, the parent in an unfamiliar laboratory environment (Ainsworth et al., 1978). As previously noted, infant responses to the parent in the Ainsworth Strange Situation were categorized as secure, avoidant, or resistant/ambivalent. Precursors to each of these "patterns of attachment" were sought in mother–infant interaction, with secure infants repeatedly being found to have had the most sensitive and responsive mothering. Additionally, behavior was observed in settings in which mother was absent, and children secure with mother in infancy were found to exhibit the most favorable outcomes to 10 (Grossmann and Grossmann, 1991) and even 15 years of age (Urban et al., 1991).

The most recent phase in the study of individual differences in attachment organization has been described as a "move to the level of representation" (Bretherton and Waters, 1985; Main, Kaplan, and Cassidy, 1985). Here, children's narratives have been found significantly related to early attachment to the mother, with children exhibiting fearful, bizarre, or catastrophic fantasies being drawn almost exclusively from a new disorganized/disoriented category of infant Strange Situation behavior. There has also been considerable focus on the semistructured, hour-long Adult Attachment Interview, which calls for a description and evaluation of early relationships with each parent (George, Kaplan, and Main, 1985). As is the case with infant attachment status, there are four central classifications. Administered to parents, each state of mind as determined from this interview predicts a particular, corresponding pattern of infant response to the parent in the Ainsworth Strange Situation. Parents who are coherent and collaborative in discussing their histories (*secure/autonomous* parents) tend to have *secure* infants, parents *dismissing* of their own experiences tend to have *avoidant* infants, parents *preoccupied* by their own parents tend to have *resistant* infants, and parents suffering lapses in reasoning or discourse during the discussion of traumatic events (*unresolved/disorganized* parents) tend to have *disorganized/disoriented* infants. Perhaps the most striking result of these studies is that, even when the early history described within the interview is unfavorable, individuals who are coherent, consistent, and plausible have infants whose response to them in this semistressful situation is judged secure.

Spence (1987) has called for a "grammar" of early development that could trace the central forms of influence and their classification. With respect to the work of the last decade in the field of attachment, it would seem reasonable to say that such a grammar is presently emerging. This is because we have been able to use attachment status with mother at age one to predict both behavioral and representational processes at six years of age, and additionally we have been able to establish the influence of parental mental states on infant attachment organization. Finally, an individual's attachment status at age one predicts attachment status in adolescence and young adulthood. The import of these findings for clinical work is no doubt manifold. I discuss, however, only three selected implications:

1. I suggest that (a) the organized (avoidant and resistant) insecure infant attachment patterns may be conceived of as behavioral strategies for maintaining self-organization and for maintaining proximity to an insecure (dismissing or preoccupied) caregiver and (b) that, in the service of maintaining these behavioral strategies, children avoidant or resistant with the primary caregiver in infancy may actively attempt to maintain a particular attentional/representational state. These states— eventually experienced as a kind of "felt security" and held in place by anxiety—may later be maintained through discourse violations and transmitted to the infant through insensitivity to infant signals.

2. I review two proposals with respect to the sequelae to disorganized/disoriented infant attachment status: First, that infant disorganized attachment status may be associated with increased vulnerabilities to anxiety, phobia, and malignant self-concept (Main and Hesse, 1992; Hesse and Main, submitted); second, that it may be associated with increased vulnerability to dissociative disorders (Liotti, 1992; this volume). Systematic investigation of each of these proposals awaits longitudinal study.

3. Adult attachment interviews conducted with clinically distressed populations and the parents of clinically distressed children have shown that, even screening for thought disorder and organic disorders, only a small proportion are judged

secure-autonomous. I suggest some further relations that might be expected between adult attachment status and clinical status and the role that the attachment status of the therapist may play in therapy.

ATTACHMENT: THREE PHASES IN THE DEVELOPMENT OF THE FIELD

In this section of the present essay I trace three phases in the development of the field of attachment. I describe Bowlby's original theory of attachment, which focuses on the development and organization of an attachment behavioral system presumed to be present in all individuals raised in any but extremely anomalous circumstances; the discovery of individual differences in the organization of attachment behavior at one year of age, together with their behavioral precursors and sequelae; and, finally, the recent "move to the level of representation" in the study of individual differences in attachment. The lines of study to which these phases refer have not replaced one another in sequence; rather, each is being carried forward to the present time.

Bowlby's Ethological-Evolutionary Theory of Attachment

Bowlby proposed that maintenance of proximity to protective adult figures represents a primary mechanism for the regulation of infant safety and survival (Bowlby, 1969). In Bowlby's theory, behavior patterns having the predictable outcome of increasing proximity between infant and caregiver (such as crying, calling, pursuing, and clinging) are ascribed to the activity of a complex, instinctively guided but environmentally influenced control system termed the attachment behavioral system. This system is presumed to have evolved to serve the biological function of ensuring the protection of members of ground-living primate troops who are younger, weaker, or both. Once an attachment figure has been selected (usually, but not necessarily, the infant's biological mother), the infant closely monitors her whereabouts, and preserves proximity even under nonstressful conditions. If threatening conditions arise, the attachment behavioral system becomes highly activated, and the infant is led immediately to seek close proximity and contact. Bowlby refers to this specified individual as the infant's "primary" attachment figure, but two or three other attachment figures may also be selected, and, in some cases, the father, sibling, or a nonrelative may be selected as the primary figure.

Like the systems that serve survival and reproduction, attachment is understood to be closely coordinated with other behavioral systems, such as exploration, escape, and feeding. In contrast to earlier conceptualizations of instinct and in keeping with much of current psychoanalytic theory (Eagle, 1984), no buildup of psychic energy is presumed necessary to the activation of the behavioral system, nor is energy (other than physical energy) conceived as being released or spent following behavioral displays. Attachment behavior is presumed to be activated, modulated, and terminated by changes originating in the internal or external environment (threatened separation, actual separation, and reunion), and these changes are held responsible for the strongest of emotions, as joy, love, fear, anger, and despair (Bowlby, 1969, 1973). While most readily activated in younger individuals, attachment is presumed to remain influential throughout the lifetime and to account for central aspects of an individual's mental state.

The reader should note the following further points:

1. Specific or "focused" attachments appear by the third quarter of the first year of life in human infants and are presumed to be based on contingent social interactions (Ainsworth, 1969). There is no evidence that these interactions need be positive, and infants unquestionably take maltreating parents as attachment figures.
2. As must necessarily be the case if attachment represents the infant's chief mechanism for ensuring survival, the attachment behavioral system is conceived as continually active. This means that, whether or not attachment behavior is displayed at a given time, the attached individual is, at some level, monitoring the safety versus threat implicit in current conditions and attending to (monitoring) the physical location and accessibility of the attachment figure(s).
3. This continual monitoring (attention) cannot always be conscious. It is now widely recognized, however, that we have the capacity for attending to, processing, and drawing inferences from input that does not reach the usual levels of awareness (see Kihlstrom, 1987; Clyman, 1991).
4. The formation of an attachment to a specified individual signals a qualitative change in infant behavioral (and, no doubt, also brain) organization. This given, quantitative terms (such as "strongly" or "weakly" attached) are not used in describing differences among individuals (Ainsworth et al., 1978). Infants who have become attached to maltreating or simply insensitive

attachment figures are presumed no "less" attached than others, and virtually all infants become attached. Strong, continuing displays of attachment behavior in relatively safe circumstances or, conversely, the absence of attachment behavior in threatening situations in which it is expected is believed to signal interferences from other processes (e.g., fear, anger, their attempted inhibition) rather than quantitative differences in the "strength" of attachment (Ainsworth, 1969).

5. Although Bowlby originally proposed that the biological function of the attachment system in nonhuman primates was primarily protection from predation, the full import of the system is best understood by considering that it serves multiple survival functions (Main, 1981). In addition to protection from predation, proximity provides protection from starvation, from unfavorable temperature changes, from natural disasters, from the attacks of conspecifics, and from the risk of separation from the group. Maintenance of proximity should therefore predominate in the infant's response repertoire.

6. In sum, Bowlby's theory of attachment departs from most theories of object relations in that there is a return to an understanding of human behavior as shaped by instincts (now, behavioral systems or programs; see Hinde, 1982), with maintenance of proximity to protective individuals having a relation to survival more immediate than that of feeding or exploration. The infant's insistent concern with maintenance of relations to potentially protective attachment figures represents, then, not the working of a set of "quiet" ego instincts (e.g., see Modell, 1975), but rather the sine qua non of infant survival.

7. The attachment behavioral system in primates is therefore highly responsive to indications of danger. It is intimately related to fear and is activated by frightening conditions of any kind.

Ainsworth's Discoveries Regarding the Three Organized Patterns of Attachment in Infancy: Description, Precursors, and Sequelae

In emphasizing the immediacy of the tie between proximity-maintenance and survival in the environment of evolutionary adaptedness, Bowlby drew attention to two conditions of danger: (1) environmental or internal changes directly and immediately threatening to the infant's continuing survival and (2) any conditions intimating separation from the attachment figure, even in the absence of immediate threats from the environment. Any changes that signaled increased risk to the individual in the environment of evolutionary adaptedness—such as moving into an unfamiliar environment—were considered "natural clues" to danger and were also expected to activate the attachment behavioral system.

Following this line of reasoning, then, separation from the mother, conditions indicative of immediate threat, and conditions providing natural clues to danger were expected to activate attachment behavior. Exceptions were noted, however, in two- to three-year-old children undergoing prolonged, stressful separations from their parents in an unfamiliar setting in which no alternative caregiving figure was available. Separated for a long enough period, children of this age were observed to enter a state of detachment in which signs of concern with the mother were absent (Robertson and Bowlby, 1952; Bowlby, 1969, 1973). Detachment was considered indicative of the onset of repression; repression was considered an inevitable result of traumatic experience; and experiences of this kind were considered anomalous in terms of man's evolutionary environment. The onset of detachment was signaled by avoidance of the mother during visits to the separation setting.

In this light, we can well understand the initial impact of Ainsworth's discoveries regarding responses to extremely brief, laboratory-based separations from mother in 12-month-old, home-reared infants who had no experiences of major separation. As the reader will find, only (that majority of) infants whose mothers had been "sensitive and responsive to infant signals and communications" in the home showed the expected behavioral patterning. For infants whose attachment behavior had been consistently rejected, threatening conditions failed to activate attachment behavior. For infants whose mothers had been unpredictable, mother's presence failed to terminate it. Insecure infants, then, either failed to exhibit attachment behavior in threatening conditions and actively avoided the mother on reunion, or, remaining angrily or passively preoccupied with mother throughout the separation, failed to explore in conditions of safety. Ainsworth's work had illustrated, then, that behavior bearing a phenotypic resemblance to defensive processes could develop out of patterns of everyday interaction as well as in response to traumatic separations.

The Ainsworth Strange Situation The Ainsworth Strange Situation is a structured, observational procedure in which 12-month-old infants are observed responding to two separations from, and reunions with, the parent in a strange (laboratory) environment. This procedure constituted the final step in a year-long study of infant–mother interaction conducted in Baltimore. Each dyad was observed in the home for four hours approximately every three weeks, with interactions recorded in the form of narrative record

(66 to 80 hours of observation per dyad). As the first infants in the study reached one year of age, Ainsworth and Wittig devised the Strange Situation procedure with the intention of illustrating the effects on the infant of *combining* the two conditions expected to elicit propensities to exhibit attachment behavior—namely, separation from the attachment figure in circumstances providing a "natural clue to danger" (an unfamiliar setting). Twice separated from, and reunited with, the mother in the unfamiliar setting, then, all infants were expected to exhibit attachment behavior. Mother's presence was, however, generally expected to provide the basis for a return to play.

Unexpectedly, however, striking individual differences were observed, and the following discoveries were made:

1. While 13 of the 23 infants exhibited the expected pattern, in 6 infants attachment behavior was largely absent, while in 4 others attachment appeared completely preoccupying.
2. When attachment behavior was absent, it was replaced by exploratory behavior throughout the situation as a whole and active avoidance of the parent on reunion.
3. Where attachment behavior was continually focused on the parent, angry behavior was also present, exploration was absent, and the infant failed to settle down on the parent's return.
4. Each pattern exhibited was linked to a specific pattern of infant–mother interaction during the preceding year.

The Strange Situation is conducted in a pleasant, toy-filled room and consists of a very brief introductory episode, followed by seven three-minute episodes (separation episodes are terminated within 10 to 30 seconds if the infant is distressed). During the opening episodes of the Strange Situation, (1) mother and baby are briefly introduced to the room and (2) then left alone for three minutes, giving the baby the opportunity to explore the toys. (3) A stranger then enters the room and, after some time, speaks with the mother and then attempts to engage the baby in play. (4) Mother then leaves baby alone with the stranger and (5) then returns, after greeting the baby from the door (the stranger unobtrusively departs). After three minutes, (6) mother leaves again, leaving the baby entirely alone until (7) the stranger returns. The mother then returns (8), greeting the baby from the door and then picking him up. This is the final reunion episode. Throughout the situation, the mother is asked to respond to the infant as necessary but is otherwise not to direct his activities. (The female pronoun is used here for the mother, the male for the infant, for purposes of clarity.)

Ainsworth developed behavioral criteria by which each infant in her own and succeeding Strange Situation studies would be placed in one of three "attachment classifications." These three traditional classifications of the infant's attachment to a particular parent are now termed the *organized* classifications of infant attachment (Main, 1990). Additionally, Ainsworth developed coding systems for recording both crying and exploratory behavior and highly reliable scoring systems for the degree to which the infant avoided the mother, resisted the mother, sought the mother's proximity, and attempted to maintain physical contact.

In this chapter, I focus mainly on classification systems rather than continuous scoring systems. This is done both for heuristic purposes and because it is in these terms that most researchers have first attempted to understand the baby's behavior. The classification systems do, in fact, capture all the relevant continuous scoring systems, and, conversely, the scoring systems predict class membership (Ainsworth et al., 1978). In Ainsworth's view, however, creation of a classificatory system—while always alterable and always only an approximation of reality—constituted a first step necessary to the organization of complex behavioral data. Thus, she agrees with the behavioral biologist Robert Hinde (1974) that one must first describe and classify when one sets out to study natural phenomena:

> Description and classification may not seem very difficult tasks, but their neglect hampered many aspects of psychology for half a century. . . . This descriptive phase, essential in the development of every science, was bypassed by those experimental psychologists who attempted to model their strategies on classical physics. These workers overlooked the fact that classical physics was a special case in that its subject matter—falling apples, the apparent bending of sticks in the water, floating logs—were everyday events, so that the descriptive phase was part of common experience, and not especially a job for scientists. Of course, the way people behave is also part of everyday experience, but to describe behavior precisely is much more difficult than appears at first sight [p. 5].

While Hinde was referring to the classification of behavior patterns, Ainsworth found his comments relevant to the classification of relationships, specifically, to the classification of the infant's relationship to a particular parent as observed in a separation-and-reunion setting.

In the following I describe modal behavioral patterning throughout the Strange Situation for infants within each of the three traditional categories. There are subcategories for each of the three classifications, with some secure infants being, for example, somewhat
avoidant and with some avoidant infants being more extreme in
their avoidance than others. I describe here a prototypically secure
infant whose behavior would fall in Ainsworth's "very secure" (B3)
category and a highly (A1), as opposed to moderately (A2), avoidant
infant. There are two major subcategories of the resistant/ambiva-
lent classification, with some infants being actively and openly angry
(C1) and with some simply passive and preoccupied by the mother
(C2).   Together with a description of infant behavior leading to
category placement, I describe aspects of the mother's and infant's
behavior in the home as described in the Baltimore sample.

Group B: Secure.

Put down by mother, the baby creeps immediately to the
toys. His play is active, and he occasionally shows mother a toy,
smiling and vocalizing. When mother leaves, he shows signs of
missing her, perhaps by slowing in his play, or going to the
door. On reunion he greets mother actively, perhaps with a
smile and vocalization combined with raised arms or with
approach. If he has been distressed by this first absence, he is
readily comforted.

Left alone entirely in the second separation, the baby cries,
calling for mother. The stranger's return fails to console him,
and crying continues. When mother appears in the doorway,
he creeps to her and pulls himself up on her legs. Picked up, he
clings actively, and sinks into her body. While he may briefly
resist her attempted release, he soon returns to exploration of
the environment.

What is most striking within this behavioral sequence is the
immediacy with which the baby's distress is terminated (he
may cease crying immediately on seeing mother), the comfort
he takes in contact with her, and his readiness to return once
again to play. The observer has witnessed what appears to be a
miniature drama with a happy ending.

The mothers of secure infants had been "sensitive to the signals
and communications" of their infants (Ainsworth et al., 1978) during
the first year of life—responding promptly to crying, holding the
baby tenderly and carefully, and providing tactful, cooperative guidance or distraction in circumstances in which maternal and infant
desires conflicted (Ainsworth, Bell, and Stayton, 1971; Ainsworth et

al., 1978; see also Belsky, Rovine, and Taylor, 1984; Egeland and Farber, 1984; Grossmann et al., 1985; Smith and Pederson, 1988; Isabella, 1993). In addition to scoring systems devised to describe maternal behavior across several home visits, several kinds of "event" codings were undertaken, in which a given behavior pattern (e.g., each pickup of the baby) was described thoroughly on each occurrence. Event codings from the first 3 months of life showed that mothers of infants who would be judged secure with them at 12 months of age were tender and careful in handling the baby in a majority (53%) of pickup episodes, and they were only rarely inept in handling the baby (Ainsworth et al., 1978). Additionally, their behavior in face-to-face interactions was markedly contingent on the baby's and suggested early "attunement" to their infants (e.g., see Stern, 1985).

In the home, secure babies exhibited little anxiety. They did not cry in response to minor, everyday separations, such as mother moving downstairs to fetch the laundry (Ainsworth et al., 1971). Secure babies were far more compliant to the mother's commands and prohibitions than were insecure babies, a finding that was replicated in a separate Baltimore sample by Londerville and Main (1981) and in both an infant–mother and infant–father sample in Berkeley (Main, unpublished data). A coding of Ainsworth's narrative records undertaken by Sharon Slaton at Berkeley showed that little anger was displayed by secure babies in the home. Indeed, the extent to which the baby actively and immediately sought proximity and contact with the mother in the Strange Situation was highly negatively related to the extent to which anger had seemed to direct the baby's mood and activities between 9 and 12 months (r (23) = –.78; Ainsworth et al., 1978).

Group A: Insecure-Avoidant.
Introduced to the laboratory playroom, the baby begins exploration and play at once, but with little display of affect. He does not respond to mother's leavetaking when left alone with the stranger. Mother's second leavetaking also occasions no response. Left completely alone in this unfamiliar setting, he displays no distress, and continues to explore the room and/or the toys.

On both reunions, the baby immediately looks away and turns away from his mother, and indeed may bend over or reach for a toy immediately on hearing mother call from outside the door. Picked up by his mother, he may stiffen slightly but his affect remains neutral. Without expression, he lifts his arms away from mother's body, leans out, and points to a toy on the floor. Put down, he moves to a distance from the mother and renews attention to the environment. Signs of both distress and anger are absent throughout the situation. The baby appears competent but affectless, and in consequence, little appears to have happened within these 20 minutes.

Ainsworth drew attention to the presence of an "attachment-exploration balance" in secure babies, a balance observable not only in the Strange Situation but also in the home. This was observed in a relatively smooth alternation between exploration away from, and returns to, the mother and was also termed "secure base" behavior (Ainsworth et al., 1971, 1978). Note that attachment behavior is virtually absent throughout the Strange Situation in the avoidant baby and is replaced with active avoidance (looking away, moving away, turning away, and leaning out of arms) as well as a persistent attention to the inanimate environment.

As noted above, avoidance of the parent on reunion had been observed in two- to three-year-olds subjected to major separations from the parent (Robertson and Bowlby, 1952; Heinecke and Westheimer, 1966), but it was completely unexpected in home-reared infants who, never having undergone a major separation from the mother, were now being separated from her for only three to six minutes. In an examination of her narrative records, Ainsworth found avoidance of the mother in the Strange Situation linked specifically to maternal rejection of infant attachment behavior. Several mothers described themselves as disliking tactual contact or finding it aversive, and event codings showed them actively rebuffing the infants in response to bids for access (Ainsworth et al., 1971, 1978; replicated for two succeeding samples by Main and Stadtman, 1981). In free-play settings, mothers of avoidant infants were observed to withdraw from the infant specifically when the infant seemed sad (Grossmann and Grossmann, 1991).

The continual exploration of avoidant infants in the Strange Situation has been interpreted as an organized shift of attention or "diversionary activity" that ennables the infant to minimize responsiveness to fear-eliciting conditions and thus maintain the "deactivation" or repression of attachment behavior (Bowlby, 1980; Main, 1981). Physiological studies suggest, however, that this deactivation is incomplete: the heart rates of the apparently unconcerned avoidant infants have been found to be as elevated as those of secure infants during separation, and pre-to-post Strange Situation rises in cortisol are somewhat greater for avoidant than for secure infants (Sroufe and Waters, 1977; Spangler and Grossmann, 1993). In the home, the most avoidant of Ainsworth's babies not only expressed great distress on even minor, everyday separations but also exhibited the greatest anger toward the mother, with some striking her (Ainsworth et al., 1978). Angry mood as assessed in the home was, in fact, strongly correlated with avoidance of the mother during the Strange Situation (r (23) = .63). These findings suggest that avoidance of the mother in an inherently alarming setting may serve as a kind of strategy for maintaining self-organization, perhaps assisting the infant to inhibit expressions of anger as well as attachment (Main, 1981).

Group C: Insecure-Ambivalent/Preoccupied.

The baby may be fretful shortly following room entrance. He either fails entirely to engage in the toys, sitting passively by mother's feet (sub category C2), or else he may engage in some activity with the toys, while interrupting that activity frequently with fussing or with fretful returns to mother (C1). In either case, he seems preoccupied with his mother even prior to her leavetaking; he is fearful of or angrily resistant towards the stranger; and he exhibits great distress on each separation.

If he falls in Ainsworth's actively angry sub category (C1), he may seek the mother directly on room entrance, like a secure baby. After that, however, he will alternate bids for proximity with expressions of angry rejection, perhaps displaying tantrum behavior. If he falls in Ainsworth's passive sub-category of Strange Situation behavior (C2), he may barely raise his arms in greeting, appearing too distressed or incompetent to approach. Signs of resistance to the mother will then also be weak, but the baby will be unable to terminate his distress by the end of the episode.

For infants falling in both the angry and passive subcategories of the resistant group, mother's absence leads to exhibitions of marked distress, so that the separation episodes are very quickly terminated. Mother's return to the room fails to settle the baby, however, and consequently he is still crying, whining, or fussing at the end of the each reunion episode. To the observer, the behavior of resistant infants can be unsettling, since neither the baby's distress nor his preoccupation with the mother's whereabouts is affected by mother's actual return. In addition, as noted earlier, the baby may alternate between seeking to be held by the mother and angrily pushing away from her. In part for this reason, the alternative category title for the insecure-resistant baby is insecure-ambivalent.

Ainsworth's home records showed that mothers of the four resistant infants in her sample were unpredictable, discouraging of autonomy, and insensitive to infant signals and communications

(Ainsworth et al., 1971, 1978; see also a recent overview of this category by Cassidy and Berlin, 1994). Most displayed some warmth and involvement at times, however, and (as opposed to the mothers of avoidant infants) most considered themselves highly invested in mothering. The mothers of Ainsworth's four insecure-resistant infants were as insensitive to infant signals and communications as the mothers of the insecure-avoidant infants but differed from the latter in not rejecting their infants, either verbally or physically. In the first three months of life, the mothers of the infants who would later be resistant were inept in handling the baby in 41% of holding episodes and "tender and careful" in only 2% of episodes. Additionally, face-to-face interactions with their infants were marked by the absence of contingent pacing, suggesting that inept or unpredictable behavior existed in this as well as other areas.

Like an avoidant baby, a resistant baby may be said to be "organized" in the sense of having a singular attentional focus (Main, 1990). In contrast to the avoidant baby, who focuses exclusively on the toys, the resistant baby focuses insistently on his mother. The resistant baby is, in fact, often too distressed and preoccupied with his mother to attend to the toys at all, and in this sense he appears to be the "mirror image" of the avoidant baby. Like the avoidant baby and unlike the secure baby, however, his attention is not fluid, and he focuses on only one aspect of his surroundings.

The worldwide distribution of ABC attachment patterning is almost identical to that in Ainsworth's original sample, with a majority of infants in low-risk samples being judged secure, a substantial minority avoidant, and a small minority ambivalent (van IJzendoorn and Kroonenberg, 1988). The majority of middle-class babies from low-risk samples have been found to behave similarly toward the same parent at 12 and 18 months, so that ABC classifications over this time period have been found to have about 80% stability in such samples (Bretherton, 1985). As would be expected, however, if response to a given parent in the Strange Situation reflects the history of interaction with that parent, the *same* infant often *responds differently* to the Strange Situation with mother than with father. Thus, in our original Bay Area sample we found no relation between attachment classifications with the two parents (Main, 1983, unpublished data; see also Main and Weston, 1981), so that a baby could be secure with mother but avoidant with father or resistant with mother but secure with father. In a meta-analytic study of 672 families, however, a significant association between attachment classification to mother and to father was noted (Fox, Kimmerly, and Schafer, 1991).

The predictability of ABC patterning of reunion behavior to mother from one to six years is about the same as that across infancy, being 85% or above in two independent samples (Main and Cassidy, 1988; Wartner et al., 1994; see also Jacobsen et al., 1992). The stability observed in these low-risk samples is presumed to rest on stability in interaction as influenced by stability in life-circumstances. In samples in which there are major changes in mother's life-circumstances, there may also be substantial changes in infant attachment status (Vaughn et al., 1979).

The link between specific patterns of interaction in the home and the infant's response to the mother in a stressful situation suggests that differing internal structures may be developing out of differing patternings of dyadic regulation (e.g., see Stern, 1985; Sander, 1987). If so, differences in behavior should also be observable in mother's absence. Pioneered by Sroufe and Egeland at Minnesota, follow-up studies have confirmed that, whether from low- or high-risk samples, children secure with mother as infants show substantially greater concentration in play, more positive affect, greater social competence, and greater ego resilience than other children. When interactions with teachers unaware of attachment status were examined, children formerly avoidant of mother in infancy were found most likely to be angrily rejected, resistant children to be treated as though helpless, and secure children to be treated in a matter-of-fact manner (Sroufe and Fleeson, 1986). In addition, children who had been avoidant with mother as infants were found most likely to victimize others, while children who had been resistant were most likely to be their victims. As in a German sample, where children secure with mother in infancy exhibited skills at conflict resolution in preschool (Suess, Grossmann, and Sroufe, 1992), children secure with mother as infants were neither victimized nor victimizing (Troy and Sroufe, 1987). In the German preschool study, children secure with both as opposed to only one parent were found to have especially favorable outcomes (Suess et al., 1992).

Individual Differences in Attachment at the Level of Representation and the Discovery of a New Attachment Category

Although perhaps most closely identified with increasingly widespread interests in representational processes, the present phase in the study of attachment can also be understood in the light of (1) the move to a "realist" philosophy of classification, which suggests that, as applied to natural phenomena, classifications represent

provisional, albeit nonarbitrary approximations (Main and
Solomon, 1986, 1990) and (2) the use of a new semidialectical
method of hypothesis development and testing (Main and Cassidy,
1988; Main, 1993). These alterations in philosophy and methodology
have led to increased predictive power, with categorical matches
between infant and child attachment and between adult and infant
attachment reaching impressive levels. It should be emphasized,
however, that the predictive "matches" described in the following
studies inform us only regarding the way most children falling in a
particular attachment category in infancy are likely to behave, so
that, for example, some children avoidant with mother in infancy
may be found secure in sixth-year assessments. The term
"prediction," then, refers to probabilistic prediction across groups,
and not to individuals.

In this phase workers discovered:

- unclassifiable and "disorganized/disoriented" responses to the
  Strange Situation
- predictable relations between early attachment status to
  mother and children's fantasies (discourse, stories, and drawings)
- a relation between the parent's Adult Attachment Interview
  response and the infant's Strange Situation response to that
  parent, with significant prebirth prediction across the four
  categories being reported in four independent samples
- prediction of Adult Attachment Interview response from
  response to mother in the Strange Situation during infancy

*Disorganized/disoriented behavior in the Strange Situa-
tion.* Despite the fact that Ainsworth and Bell had observed "unclassifiable" Strange Situation behavior as early as 1970 (see Main and
Solomon, 1990, p. 125), for some years most workers continued to
attempt to classify every infant seen in the Strange Situation by
"fitting" the infant to A, B, or C category descriptors. During the
early 1980s, however, investigators working with maltreating and
psychiatrically distressed parents found that in using the ABC classification system (1) some maltreated infants were judged "secure," a
violation of the expected conjunction between the secure classification and sensitive responsiveness (Egeland and Sroufe, 1981; Gaensbauer and Harmon, 1982) and (2) some maltreated infants, as well as
infants of psychiatrically distressed mothers, simultaneously
exhibited characteristics of both the A and C attachment categories
(see especially the work of Crittenden, 1985; Spieker and Booth,
1985; Radke-Yarrow et al., 1985).

At the same time, working with our own large, low-risk Bay Area sample, we had found that about 13% of infants failed to respond to the Strange Situation in a manner that permitted fit to Ainsworth's classification directions (Main and Weston, 1981). We therefore undertook a review of 36 tapes from our sample with the aim of determining whether, among infants who could not readily be classifiable as A, B, or C, any new (e.g., D, E, F, and G) patterns of attachment would emerge (Main and Solomon, 1986). This review yielded no evidence for new, coherent patternings of response to separation from, and reunion with, the parent in a strange environment. A few years later, we had reviewed a total of 200 unclassifiable Strange Situation videotapes (100 drawn from high-risk samples), still without finding coherent new "patterns of attachment." Our analysis revealed, instead, that what these unclassifiable infants shared in common was bouts or sequences of behavior that seemed to lack a readily observable goal, intention, or explanation. Indeed, while avoidant, resistant, and secure infants can be seen as evidencing a "behavioral strategy" for dealing with separation from, and reunion with, the mother in the strange environment (Main, 1990), these infants could readily be seen as experiencing a collapse of strategy. Well over 90% of the previously "unclassifiable" infants were observed to show such behaviors and were assigned to a new category, termed disorganized/disoriented.

We suggested that infants should be considered disorganized/ disoriented if, in the parent's presence, their Strange Situation behavior included one or more of the following features:

1. *Sequential display of contradictory behavior patterns.* An example observed in a maltreated infant consisted of a strong display of attachment behavior (running crying to parent with arms outstretched) followed inexplicably by avoidance (infant suddenly stops, turns her back to the parent, silent).
2. *Simultaneous display of contradictory behavior patterns.* One infant sat on the parent's lap comfortably molded to the parent's body, while looking away, sullen and dazed. Another sat on the floor for several moments with her hand on mother's lap, leaning toward her mother but turned slightly away. Seemingly, these infants could neither respond to the parent, approach the parent, or fully shift attention away.
3. *Undirected, misdirected, incomplete, and interrupted movements and expressions, such as crying loudly at stranger leave-taking.* Review of our tapes of unclassifiable infants also showed an occasional very slow and seemingly "undirected" striking at the parent's face (often, the eyes), but in incom-

plete, weak movements that initially appeared innocuous. In several cases, we observed a change to a dazed, trancelike, yet faintly aggressive facial expression just prior to initiation of the slow aggressive movement. Some infants misdirecting their behavior seemed disoriented. Thus, turning and "greeting" the *stranger* was observed at the moment of reunion with the parent in several infants, as when an infant, immediately on door opening, turned to the stranger and, raising her arms as for a pickup, said, "Hi" brightly in a manner exactly fitting to a greeting to be made to the parent. Two maltreated infants pursued the parent to protest departure, then smiled immediately "at" the closed door. Some crept readily after the stranger and cried at her departure as though at the departure of the parent, which they ignored.

4. *Stereotypies, asymmetrical movements, mistimed movements, and anomalous postures.* Stereotypies and anomalous postures are observed in animals in conflict situations (Hinde, 1970). Within the Strange Situation, infants who had been unclassifiable with respect to the traditional three categories were observed adopting anomalies of posture such as head cocking; stereotypies such as rocking, ear pulling, hair pulling, and head banging; and mistimed movements. For example, one infant repeatedly raised both hands to her ears whenever she was hugged by her mother: the mother was later identified as abusive. Another infant, having begun a full approach to the mother on reunion, suddenly veered sharply away and rocked on hands and knees, facing the wall.

5. *Freezing, stilling, and slowed movements and expressions.* The infant of a clinically depressed mother stilled immediately on reunion and seemed disoriented. When mother entered the room in the first reunion episode, he rose, took two steps toward her, and then fell prone in a depressed, huddled posture. At mother's second entrance, he placed his hands over his mouth, bowed his head, and fell prone again, crying. Lifted and held on mother's lap, he again bowed his head and stilled completely for one minute.

6. *Direct indicators of apprehension regarding the parent.* Several maltreated infants seemed fearful of the parent and showed some apparent disorganization or disorientation in behavior, for example, smiling with an accompanying fear-face with arms outstretched. Some backed toward the parent with head averted.

7. *Direct indicators of disorganization or disorientation.* The seven thematic category headings are not mutually exclusive,

and direct indicators of disorientation often frequently involved the misdirection of behavior (see earlier). Additionally, however, directly on sighting (or even hearing) the approach of the parent, some infants exhibited confusion. We observed one infant hunch her upper body and shoulders at hearing her mother's call, then break into extravagant, laugh-like screeches with an excited forward movement. Her braying laughter became a cry and distress-face without a new intake of breath as she hunched further forward. Then, suddenly, her face lost all expression.

Some of these behavior patterns (such as stereotypies) are found in neurologically impaired infants. Disorganized attachment status may conceivably be influenced by heritable characteristics on the part of infants in normal samples,[1] but there are many reasons to suppose that the environmental contribution is far more substantial. In our Bay Area sample, for example, only 3 of 34 infants classified as disorganized with one parent were also disorganized with a second parent (Main and Solomon, 1990). Disorganization with each parent was related to unresolved/disorganized attachment status on the part of the parent as identified in the Adult Attachment Interview, and disorganization with the mother was associated with specific sequelae (e.g., role inversion). Similarly, in a recent study of 90 families conducted in London, no infant was judged disorganized with both parents (Steele, Steele, and Fonagy, in press).

Because "D" behavior consists, by definition, in an interruption of organized behavior, the disorganized/disoriented category is always assigned together with a best-fitting, alternative avoidant, secure, resistant, or "cannot classify" category (e.g., D/B, D/A, or D/CC). With most "unclassifiable" infants in low-risk samples now classified "disorganized/disoriented," the proportion of infants assigned to the disorganized/disoriented category ranges around 15% to even 35%. Bouts of disorganized/disoriented behavior sufficient for assignment to the category are often brief, not infrequently consisting in just one episode lasting 10–30 seconds. Such brief episodes are nonetheless highly significant. In the Spangler and Grossmann (1993) study cited earlier, for example, disorganized/disoriented infants—almost all of them otherwise fitting the behavioral descriptors for the

---

[1] By combining two independent, low-risk samples of infants and mothers, Spangler and his colleagues (Spangler, Fremmer-Bombik, and Grossmann, submitted) have uncovered a significant association between disorganized attachment status at one year and dysregulation during the newborn period. As Spangler and his colleagues point out, this finding could implicate intrauterine experience, interactions in the earliest days of life, heritable characteristics, or some combination of these factors.

secure attachment category—showed the sharpest increase in heart-
beat during the separation episode of the Strange Situation, and a
significantly greater rise in cortisol than secure infants across the
course of the Strange Situation.

Elsewhere, I have proposed that avoidant and resistant infants
have been able to develop indirect or "conditional" strategies for
dealing with stressful (mildly frightening) situations in the company
of a parent who—not frightening in herself—has historically been
either rejecting or unpredictably responsive (Main, 1990). The strategy developed by the avoidant infant seems to be one of *shifting
attention away* from potentially threatening conditions, while the
strategy developed by the resistant infant appears to be hypervigilance and preoccupation. Although they are inflexible rather than
fluid, both of these alternatives are organized and, in my view, may
be understood as representing a "working" behavioral and attentional strategy. We have reason to believe, then, that neither consistent, unalarming levels of rejection of attachment behavior nor
unpredictable responsiveness is likely in itself to lead to infant
disorganized attachment status (Main and Hesse, 1990, 1992), unless
the caregiver is also frightening.

What, then, are the conditions that should lead to the production
of disorganization and disorientation in Strange Situation behavior?
Elsewhere, I have argued that this outcome should be expected if
the attached infant has been alarmed *by the parent*, rather than
simply by the external situation (Main, 1981; Main and Weston,
1982; Main and Hesse, 1990, 1992; Hesse and Main, submitted).
Because the attached infant inevitably seeks the parent when
alarmed, any parental behavior that directly alarms an infant[2] should
place that infant in an irresolvable paradox in which it can neither
approach (the secure and resistant "strategies"), shift its attention
(the avoidant "strategy"), or flee (Main and Hesse, 1990, 1992). In
keeping with this hypothesis, the great majority of parentally
maltreated children (about 80%) in high-risk samples have been
found to fit the disorganized category, as compared with about 20%
to 40% of nonmaltreated children from the same population (Carlson
et al., 1989; Lyons-Ruth et al., 1991).

Battering parents are, of course, directly frightening. There is now
reason to believe, however, that like frightening parental behavior,
frightened parental behavior may also alarm an infant and leave him
without a strategy (Hesse and Main, submitted: Main and Hesse,

---

[2]When the parent indicates that something in the external environment is alarming, the parent is likely to behave in a comprehensible manner, and the environmental source of the alarm is usually clear. This source of alarm is not considered to stem
from the parent (Hesse and Main, submitted).

1990, 1992). This outcome seems especially likely if the parent withdraws from the infant as though the infant were the source of the alarm and/or appears to be in a dissociated or trancelike state. We have in fact informally observed dissociated, trancelike behavior and fearful behavior in some parents of disorganized infants who, as I will describe, often seem to suffer from still partially dissociated experiences of loss or abuse. In these cases disorganized behavior may appear as a second-generation effect of the parent's own traumatic experiences rather than as a direct effect of physical or sexual abuse.

Representational processes in childhood: Predicted from attachment to the mother during infancy. In keeping with an emerging interest in discourse and other representational processes, we conducted a follow-up study of 40 six-year-olds classified as avoidant, secure, resistant, or disorganized/disoriented with mother in infancy (Main et al., 1985). We have already observed that, in the stressful Strange Situation, attention is fluid in secure babies, restricted in avoidant and resistant babies, and liable to dysregulation or collapse in disorganized babies. The rationale for this sixth-year follow-up study lay in the supposition that not only attention but also memory, perception, and language might reflect differing patterns of infant–parent interaction (Main et al., 1985).

On the family's arrival at our offices, we took a Polaroid snapshot of the mother, father, and child. The children were then taken to the playroom for a 15–20-minute "warm-up" session to assist them in becoming comfortable with the examiner.[3] During this period, they were invited to draw anything they liked with colored marking pens and then to draw a picture of their families (Kaplan and Main, 1986). The family was then reunited to watch an abbreviated version of the separation film *Thomas* (Robertson and Robertson, 1967–1972, 1971). Following the film, refreshments were served, after which the parents left the room for individually conducted Adult Attachment Interviews. In the parents' absence, the children were presented with a series of six pictures depicting parent–child separations. The procedure was adapted by Kaplan (submitted) from Hansburg's Separation Anxiety Test for adolescents (Hansburg, 1972), with modifications for younger children made by Klagsbrun and Bowlby (1976). For each of the six pictures, the child was asked what the pictured child might *feel* and what the pictured child might *do* regarding the separation, and responses were transcribed

---

[3] A single, clinically sensitive examiner (Ellen Richardson) was used for all children. Use of a single examiner, together with a relatively long, pleasant, and task-free introductory session involving that examiner, may have influenced the success of our outcomes.

verbatim. Thereafter, the children were offered the photograph of
themselves with their parents that had been taken earlier. They were
then invited to participate in 15–20 minutes of unstructured sandbox play, to use any materials they wished, and to include the examiner in their play if they wished. Sandbox play was integrated into
the overall design of the study, in part, to alleviate any unsettling
feelings that may have arisen in conjunction with the Separation
Anxiety Test.

Reunions took place while the child was still engaged in sandbox
play, following a separation that had usually lasted about an hour.
Reunions were conducted in a casual, unstructured, and natural
manner, with parents returning to the room to sign consent forms,
collect their belongings, and say good-bye. No emphasis was placed
on this episode, but it was videotaped, and parent–child discourse
during these three to six minutes was later transcribed verbatim.
The prediction of the various aspects of sixth-year behavior and representations from first-year ABCD behavior to mother gathered in
this study ranged from 68% to 88%, while only reunion behavior and
discourse on reunion were significantly related to early Strange Situation behavior with the father. All assessments were conducted by
persons having no knowledge of the child's attachment to either
parent.

In the following, I summarize the work of our own laboratory and
the related work of others. The findings relating attachment status to
children's structured, separation-related narratives and fantasies are
the most thoroughly corroborated. At the time that Kaplan was first
comparing infant Strange Situation behavior to the structured questions of the Separation Anxiety Test (Main et al., 1985; Kaplan,
submitted), for example, Rosenberg (1984) at Minnesota was already
comparing infant Strange Situation behavior to unstructured fantasy
play in four-year-olds, and her comparisons of the free fantasies of
previously secure versus insecure infants yield the same overall
picture. These and other studies of fantasies and narratives are
therefore given the greatest weight in the following summary.

Our findings regarding children's family drawings have been
replicated and extended at the ABC level by Gail Fury for the large
Minnesota poverty sample (Fury, 1993) and at the B versus not-B
level by the Grossmann laboratory for the Regensburg sample
(Grossmann and Grossmann, 1991). There is one more unpublished
study that has found significant relations between children's family
drawings and attachment using the Kaplan and Main system at age
six, but I have also heard of three studies in which no significant
relationship to infant attachment status was found. Children's drawings should therefore be regarded only as *correlates* of early attach-

ment, and children's drawings should not be used in the assessment of attachment.

I am not aware of any completed attempts to replicate our studies relating the child's response to presentation of the family photograph and parent–child discourse to early Strange Situation behavior (except an as yet unsuccessful attempt using speakers of a nonwritten language). I describe the study of discourse processes in some detail (Strage and Main, 1985), because consideration of these may help to elucidate the strong relation between attachment processes and child and adult narrative. Nonetheless, the reader should remember that replication studies regarding discourse processes and response to the family photograph have yet to be undertaken.

Children secure with mother in infancy. On reunion at age six with a given parent, children secure in infancy with that parent remained calm and relaxed but expressed pleasure in the parent's return (Main and Cassidy, 1988). Many affectionately and confidently initiated conversation or interaction with the parent, and some made (usually subtle) physical contact with the parent. These results have been replicated in a South German study (Wartner et al., 1994).

Seen in our sixth-year follow-up study, children secure with mother in infancy described children depicted as undergoing separations from the parent as "probably feeling sad (or mad)" and then offered imaginative, constructive ideas regarding what the pictured child might do, for example, "try to get them to stay" or "find another relative to stay with—or maybe, he could go to a friend's house" (Kaplan, submitted; a replication and extension of Kaplan's study is reported by Grossmann and Grossmann, 1991). Kaplan termed these children *secure-resourceful.* Similarly, Bretherton and her colleagues presented three-year-olds with story stems potentially involving a crisis (e.g., hurt knees, parental departures, or monsters in the bedroom). Here, too, recognition of the affective implications of the situation, together with provision of constructive solutions was significantly (although modestly) related to security of attachment to the mother (Bretherton, Ridgeway, and Cassidy, 1990).

In a study using Main and Cassidy's sixth-year reunion procedures to identify ABCD attachment status to mother, Solomon and George (1991; Solomon, George, and DeJong, in press) engaged six-year-olds in doll play similar to that designed by Bretherton et al. but focusing especially on parent–child separations. As distinguished from avoidant and resistant children, secure children tended to invent what Solomon and George (1991) called "fairy tales"—for these children, a crisis frequently appeared during the parent–child separation but was followed by a happy ending. Similarly, Rosenberg (1984) found that the fantasy sandbox play of children secure with mother in infancy differed from that of other children in that they (1) invented a crisis and (2) then solved it with a happy ending. Note that these "classic" narrative structures produced by secure children reflect their Strange Situation response pattern, in that distressing experiences are recognized, described, or invented, then brought to resolution.

At six, the family drawings of secure children included well-individuated, well-grounded family members with open arms. The drawings often included real-world elements, like a house, bicycle, or car (Kaplan and Main, 1986; replicated for a Minnesota poverty sample by Gail Fury, 1993, and for a South German sample by Grossmann and Grossmann, 1991). Offered the family photograph, these children remained casual, smiling or making a comment and then returning it to the examiner.

The prediction of the properties of parent–child discourse following the one-hour separation was impressively strong, whether children were being reunited with mother or father (above 80% for both parents). The method of discourse analysis we utilized was devised by Amy Strage (Strage and Main, 1985). Previously secure dyads were *fluent* in their discourse at six years of age. Fluent discourse was identified on the basis of the following properties:

- *Fluidity.* Both partners answered one another directly and with little pause, and each individual spoke directly, with little apparent difficulty in directing speech or expressing information. Pauses occurred between, not within, bouts of conversation.
- *Dyadic balance.* Neither partner exclusively led or followed the other, and both addressed the other in a manner that invited further conversation. Questions were not rhetorical but invited "real" answers. Both partners moved the dialogue forward.
- *Breadth of focus.* Three types of discourse focus were distinguished: focus on objects, focus on activities with objects, and focus on relationships. Dyads in which the child had been secure with the parent in infancy were wide-ranging in their conversational topics.

Astonishingly, Strage had little difficulty in identifying subclass membership for secure mother–child and father–child dyads. Secure dyads in which the infant had been slightly avoidant of the parent (B1 and B2) or slightly preoccupied with the parent (B4) had stylistic characteristics that identified them (e.g., a tendency in B4 dyads for the partners to seek extra affirmation of their statements from the partner). Prototypically secure dyads were identified through their match to the general descriptors of the category and through the absence of an identifiable "style."

Children avoidant of mother in infancy. Reunited with the parent at age six, children who had been avoidant in infancy again avoided the parent (Main and Cassidy, 1988; replicated by Wartner et al., 1994). The form taken by avoidance, however, was now subtle, so that in moving away from the parent, the child appeared to be seeking a toy, and rather than being completely unresponsive to the parent, the child was minimally responsive.

In Kaplan's study, children who had been avoidant of the mother in infancy were described as *insecure-inactive* (Kaplan, 1987). In contrast to our expectations, most children did describe the child pictured as undergoing separation as sad. One said, "Sad . . . . He feels *sad*" (said loudly). Another said, "He feels sad because he doesn't know if his mom will come back or his dad will come back." A little girl highly avoidant of both parents in infancy (and again at age six) said passionately of the pictured child, "I don't think she feels very good at all. . . . She's kinda feeling that she . . . she's never going to see her fa- her friends again." However, like most children who had been judged avoidant of mother in infancy, this little girl was "inactive" with respect to solutions regarding what a child could "do" in response to a separation ("I don't know," "I don't know," "Run away"). A few of the avoidant children offered magical solutions or denied that a separation had occurred. Similarly, using the sixth-year classification system, Solomon and George (Solomon and George, 1991; Solomon et al., in press) found that for most avoidant six-year-olds, no crisis appeared or was invented during the separation, and concerns with separation were not expressed directly. In Rosenberg's (1984) study of unstructured fantasy play, children who had avoided the mother in infancy showed impoverished play themes in which people and social relations were notably absent.

Using the sixth-year classification system with a Charlottesville sample, Cassidy (1988) found that avoidant children tended to describe the self as perfect. At six, avoidant children in the Bay Area sample tended to draw smiling, nonindividuated family figures, not infrequently lacking arms (Kaplan and Main, 1986; Grossmann and Grossmann, 1991; Fury, 1993). Overall, we termed the drawings by these children *insecure-invulnerable.* The conventionally smiling figures were not grounded, and sometimes all members floated in the air, were distant from one another, and armless.[4] The figures were not individuated, and smiling faces drawn on family members by previously avoidant infants resembled the well-known "happy faces" of the 1970s. Presented with the family photograph, however, previously avoidant children typically turned away from it, refused it, turned it backward, or dropped it. Some did this casually, but one (avoidant of both parents in infancy) picked up the photograph by the corner and deliberately dropped it on the floor with a contemptuous expression.

In terms of the three discourse dimensions previously outlined, dyads in which the child had avoided the parent in infancy were termed *restricted* (Strage and Main, 1985). The conversation was not fluent, in that there were frequent (short) pauses between adult and child conversational turns, and minimal answers were given. Discourse topics were restricted to the impersonal perspective, such as inanimate objects, and topic elaboration was limited. Additionally, the conversation was not balanced, in that the parent took the lead. The parent's questions, however, were frequently rhetorical (no answer expected or required) or were yes-no questions (the child did not need to add anything new to the conversation in order to answer). In two cases, the parent did not address the child during the entire reunion episode and spoke, instead, with the examiner.

Children ambivalent with mother in infancy. Reunited with the parent at six, the few children who had been resistant as infants were found to exhibit continuing indications of ambivalence. Exaggerating or maximizing relatedness, as shown in putting the arm around the parent and looking toward the camera, speaking in a babylike voice, or sitting on the parent's lap, they were also likely to wriggle angrily away from their parents or to stab them with a toy (Main and Cassidy, 1988; Wartner et al., 1994).

Only two resistant children were available for Kaplan's follow-up study. One (whose Strange Situation behavior led to placement in the actively angry subcategory C1) suggested tossing a bow and arrow at the parents and shooting them, while the other (whose Strange Situation behavior led to placement in the passive-ambivalent subcategory C2) suggested buying the parents flowers but then hiding their clothing. Kaplan termed these children *insecure-ambivalent.* In the study conducted by Solomon and her colleagues (in press), ambivalent six-year-olds resembled avoidant six-year-olds

---

[4] In a later study, we investigated whether or not "armless" family figures as drawn by avoidant children could be explained by an overall lack of drawing ability: we found that a child who drew "armless" family figures at age six could, in fact, draw a very complete teddy bear (Kaplan and Main, unpublished data, 1988).

in that little happened during the overnight separation from the parents. Their stories, termed "Busy," characteristically featured busy activity and caregiving, with negative feelings displaced onto characters other than the self (e.g., the baby of the family, other siblings, or pets). Reunions were characterized by delay and distraction, and the narrative structure was digressive, with the storyline constantly interrupted by distracting, time-consuming, or irrelevant activities. For example, in one doll story, the child swept the floor on reunion before greeting the parents with a hug and a kiss. In fantasy play, Rosenberg had found that four-year-olds classified insecure-resistant with mother in infancy portrayed conflictual relationships (Rosenberg, 1984).

Drawings by the children resistant of mother in infancy were termed *vulnerable*. These children tended to draw either very large or very small family figures, placed unusually close together. One child drew extremely small figures crowded together in the upper left-hand corner of the page. Others drew very large figures, some emphasizing vulnerable or intimate body parts, such as round soft bellies with belly buttons (Kaplan and Main, 1986). These results were replicated by Fury (1993) at Minnesota. Recording equipment failure in our Bay Area sample left too few resistant children available for discourse analysis and for the analysis of the family photograph.

Children disorganized/disoriented with mother in infancy. Reunited with mother following a one-hour separation, children disorganized/disoriented with mother in infancy showed controlling, role-inverting behavior and were either punitive and directive or solicitous and caregiving (Main and Cassidy, 1988). Thus, one previously disorganized child ordered the father to sit down and close his eyes, then added, "And keep them closed! I said, keep them closed!" Another asked the parent what she had been doing and how she was feeling, then carefully invited her to play and reassured her that it would be fun for her. These children were respectively termed *controlling-punitive* and *controlling-caregiving*. The association between infant disorganized/disoriented attachment status to mother at age one and controlling/role-inverting behavior at age six found in the Bay Area sample was replicated in the South German sample (Wartner et al., 1994). Considered together, these studies suggest that children who were disorganized as infants attempt, in part, to "solve" the "irresolvable" paradox presented by the frightened/frightening attachment figure by stepping into the role of the caregiver (Main and Cassidy, 1988). As we see below, however, the parents of disorganized infants are often traumatized and may welcome or even seek this inversion of roles with the child.

In response to the pictured parent–child separations, previously disorganized children in the Bay Area study appeared fearful, as expressed in catastrophic fantasies, fearful silence and whispering, and (rare) overt indications of behavioral disorganization. These children were therefore termed *fearful/disorganized/disoriented* by Kaplan (submitted), who described them as "inexplicably afraid" and "unable to do anything about it." Fear was expressed most notably through catastrophic fantasies. For example, one six-year-old disorganized with mother in infancy imagined that the attachment figure would be seriously hurt or killed, while another imagined that the pictured child would lock himself in a closet and then kill himself. Finally, the responses of some of these children seemed to imply that actions occurred without an agent—that is, that things were done to them mysteriously. To Kaplan, such statements had an eerie quality and suggested "invisible actors who are unknown." Kaplan's findings were replicated in a study of Berlin children placed in day care (Jacobsen et al., 1992), and in an Icelandic longitudinal study Kaplan's fearful/disorganized separation anxiety test response was found to predict marked difficulties in verbally presented deductive reasoning tasks in adolescence (Jacobsen, Edelstein, and Hofmann, 1994).

Similarly, in doll play involving a parent–child separation in which the child was left alone in the house, Solomon and her colleagues (1991; Solomon et al., in press) found that *all eight* of their controlling six-year-olds either entered into catastrophic "nightmare" fantasies without solution or, like the previously disorganized children in Kaplan's study, seemed unable to speak and sat in frozen silence. In these imagined separations, the children were frequently depicted as helpless to get assistance from others, to control their behavior, or to control the events around them. Catastrophes arose without warning, and dangerous people or events were vanquished, only to surface again.[5] Like disorganized/disoriented behavior in infancy, then, the narratives produced by these children suggested experiences of fright that could not be prevented from arising and could not be resolved.

In her Charlottesville study, Cassidy (1988) found that controlling children tended to have a concept of the self as negative or bad. Children judged disorganized/disoriented in infancy in the Bay Area sample often scratched out parts of their family drawings, restarted a figure in another place, or asked to begin the drawing again on

---

[5] When pressed to describe the events taking place during the parent–child separation, the silent ("constricted/inhibited") children in this study also produced catastrophic fantasies. Violent/bizarre fantasies had also been noted in some controlling children by Cassidy (1986).

another sheet of paper (Kaplan and Main, 1986). Many added either ominous or overly-bright elements to their drawings (e.g., a family standing on a row of hearts with a small sun drawn directly over the mother's head, dismembered body parts, or skeletons).[6] Responses to presentation of the family photograph were also anomalous. One child, happily interacting with the examiner just previously, bent silently over the photograph for 12 seconds, then looked up, silent and depressed. Another looked into the photograph for some time, then murmured softly, "Where are you, Mama?" Another child handled the photograph tenderly, then set it on the table and patted it. For children who had been disorganized/disoriented with mother in infancy, then, the visual presentation of parent, self, or family presented within the photograph seemed to have an overwhelming and absorbing quality that drew attention away from the immediate situation.

In her blind analysis of discourse patterns, Strage was able to identify almost all dyads in which the child had been disorganized/disoriented with the parent with whom she or he was presently conversing and characterized the discourse of these dyads as *dysfluent*. Dysfluent discourse was marked by stumbling and false starts on the part of both partners, including stammering and restarts of sentences. In contrast to secure dyads, in which conversational topics were free-ranging, and avoidant dyads, in which topics were object- and activity-focused, the conversations of disorganized dyads appeared to be relationship-focused.[7] Additionally, unlike secure dyads, in which both partners moved the dialogue forward, and avoidant dyads, in which the parent dominated the conversation, in disorganized dyads the child took control of the conversation, provided the conversational lead, or both. In some cases, this was done by refusing response:

Parent: Hello.
Child: (silence)
Parent: Well, was, was it fun here?

---

[6] The reader should note that, in contrast to the family drawing configurations characterizing formerly secure versus insecure infants (replicated by Grossmann and Grossmann, 1991, and by Gail Fury, 1993), the relation between drawings of the kind described here and early disorganized attachment status has yet to be replicated. Further, in both the home and school setting, many secure children scratch out parts of their drawings, and many add hearts and flowers to their pictures.

[7] Many of the disorganized/disoriented children in this study had received an alternative insecure-resistant (D/C) classification. Therefore, it is possible that the relationship-oriented focus stemmed from the overall preoccupation with relationships seen in such children and their parents, rather than from disorganization and disorientation.

Child: (silence)
Parent: Whatcha, whatcha doing, can I watch?
Child: (silence)
Parent: Aren't, aren't you going to talk to me? You aren't talking to me?
Child (to examiner): Do we have any more of the green pens?

In other cases, the child provided direct orientation and assistance to the parent's conversational efforts, sometimes through linguistic "scaffolding":

Child: Where were you?
Parent: I was, I was, I forgot, I was with...
Child: You were with [interviewer], mommy.
Parent (to examiner): And, I'm sorry, I've forgotten your name?
Child: This is [examiner].
Parent: (12-second silence).
Child: See, here's the knight. He's a nice knight.
Parent: Oh, uh . . . where?

Using Strage's method of analysis, the prediction of dysfluent discourse from disorganized/disoriented infant attachment status was extraordinarily high (Strage and Main, 1985). The parent had just completed a set of queries in the Adult Attachment Interview regarding loss of beloved persons through death, and, as I will show below, the parents of most disorganized/disoriented infants in our sample appeared to be suffering from what we came to term unresolved/disorganized responses to loss. Queries regarding the nature of these losses, the parents' response at the time, their feelings at the time, and their present feelings regarding the loss were unquestionably disturbing to some of the parents of disorganized/disoriented infants, and at the moment of reunion, some parents appeared dazed and/or depressed. The parents' state at that specific moment may therefore have heightened the dysfluent nature of the conversation, especially by providing a necessity for the child to guide it.

The Adult Attachment Interview: Adult states of mind with respect to attachment as predictive of infant attachment classifications The Adult Attachment Interview is a structured, hour-long, semiclinical interview focusing on early experiences and their effects. Subjects are asked for five adjectives to describe their relationship to each parent during childhood and are then asked for memories that support each adjective. They are asked whether they felt closer to one parent and why; whether they had ever felt rejected; whether parents had been threatening or abusive; why parents may have behaved as they did; and how these experiences may have affected the development of their personality. Subjects are also asked about any major loss experiences. The interview technique has been described as "surprising the unconscious" (George et al., 1985), and a quick review of the interview protocol shows that it provides ample opportunities for a speaker to contradict, or fail to support, earlier or succeeding statements. For purposes of analysis, each interview is transcribed verbatim, and judges seeking to determine the speaker's "state of mind with respect to attachment" rely entirely on the discourse transcript.

In conjunction with our sixth-year follow-up study, we conducted Adult Attachment Interviews with both parents and ultimately identified four[8] major categories—*secure-autonomous, dismissing, preoccupied*, and (later) *unresolved/disorganized*. The classification and scoring system we developed relied primarily on the speaker's *language use* in the description of his or her experiences, and each classification was considered to represent a differing state of mind with respect to attachment (Main and Goldwyn, in press). The classification and scoring systems were constructed following a search for commonalities and differences among 44 transcripts of speakers whose infants had been, respectively, secure, avoidant, resistant (and later, disorganized/disoriented) with them in the Strange Situation five years previously. These 44 transcripts were then discarded, and a coder blind to infant attachment status continued through a succeeding 66 transcripts from the Bay Area sample.[9] Utilizing this latter set of transcripts, we found a substantial match between parent and infant with respect to the three organized attachment categories (75% for mothers and 69% for fathers: Main and Goldwyn, submitted).

Developed against the criterion of infant security of attachment as demonstrated within the Strange Situation, the Adult Attachment Interview permitted us to identify security in adulthood in terms of the speaker's empirically demonstrated ability to impart security to a young infant. As speakers, the parents of secure infants indicated that they valued attachment and regarded attachment-related experiences as influential, while appearing to be objective in the description of any particular attachment relationship. Transcripts fitting these criteria were termed *secure-autonomous* (Main and Goldwyn, 1985–95). The parents of avoidant infants typically provided generalized descriptions of their own parents as "excellent" or "very loving" but then either failed to support these descriptions

---

[8] Recently, a fifth category, "cannot classify," has been utilized. This is the equivalent of the infant Strange Situation "unclassifiable" category and is described at greater length below.

[9] A more complete description of this process is provided elsewhere (Main, 1993).

with specific memories or actively contradicted them. If any untoward experiences were presented, they were described as not having had much effect on the self, and many of the parents of avoidant
infants in fact insisted that they could not remember much about
their childhood. Ultimately, we called these parents *dismissing of
attachment*. The parents of resistant infants, in direct contrast,
seemed to be caught up in early memories regarding their own parents and spoke of past experience at great length, although in a confused and confusing manner. We therefore came to term the parents
of resistant infants *preoccupied by past relationships*.

As was the case for each of the three central or "organized" adult
attachment categories just described, linguistic features of the
interview transcripts of the parents of disorganized/disoriented
infants bore a striking resemblance to the Strange Situation behavior
of their infants and were therefore termed unresolved/disorganized/
disoriented (hereafter, *unresolved*; see Main and Hesse, 1990).
Adults were placed in the unresolved adult attachment category if
they exhibited marked disorganization and disorientation in thinking
or discourse processes during the attempted discussion of potentially traumatic experiences, as evidenced in one or several lapses in
the monitoring of reasoning or discourse. With the exception of
these lapses, interviews of this kind were often found to fit the
dismissing, secure, or preoccupied adult attachment categories.

*Secure, dismissing, preoccupied, unresolved, and "cannot clas-
sify" responses to the Adult Attachment Interview.* Coherence
versus incoherence in narrative was the central focus of our study of
the Adult Attachment Interview from the beginning of our investigations (Main and Goldwyn, 1984), so that the subject's presentation
of his or her "experiences" was considered relevant primarily as it
was judged to adhere to, or violate, the coherence of the overall
narrative. In continuing the process of formalizing this approach to
the analysis of the interview, we eventually turned to the work of
the linguistic philosopher Grice (1975). Grice identified coherent
discourse as following a cooperative principle and as requiring
adherence to four maxims:

- *quality* (be truthful and have evidence for what you say)
- *quantity* (be succinct, yet complete)
- *relation* (be relevant or perspicacious)
- *manner* (be clear and orderly)

The scoring systems on which the interview classifications rest were
found to have implicitly emphasized these principles. For example,

high scores for *idealization* had been assigned to transcripts in which the speaker had used only highly positive adjectives to describe the parent and then failed to support them (a violation of *quality* typical of the parents of avoidant infants). Additionally, high scores for *preoccupied/involving anger* had been assigned to speakers who angrily discussed the parent in inappropriate interview contexts (a violation of *relevance*) and in doing so spoke in confused, excessively long, and grammatically entangled sentences (violations of *manner* and *quantity*). These speakers were generally the parents of the angrily resistant infants. At present, our scale for overall coherence of transcript remains central to determining secure versus insecure attachment status and relies directly on adherence to, versus violation of, Grice's maxims.

Drawing on Grice, Hesse (submitted) has recently conceptualized the Adult Attachment Interview (AAI) as presenting the subject with two central tasks: (1) producing and reflecting on memories[10] involving early relationships as well as any potentially traumatic experiences *while simultaneously* (2) maintaining coherent, collaborative discourse. To participate most effectively in the interview, the speaker must respond to each question as relevant and then return the conversational turn to the interviewer. In order to be judged coherent in this context, speakers must be able to both access and evaluate memories while simultaneously remaining truthful (consistent) and collaborative. The joint execution of these tasks appears difficult for the parents of insecure infants.

Transcripts are classified *secure-autonomous* (F) when the presentation and evaluation of attachment-related experiences is coherent and internally consistent, and responses are clear, relevant, and reasonably succinct. For secure-autonomous speakers, the focus of attention appears to shift fluidly between interviewer queries and the memories that are called on. Notably, it is not only individuals whose experiences appear to have been supportive who are classified secure-autonomous. Many individuals who describe difficult backgrounds are coherent when discussing and evaluating the effects of their histories and are also therefore placed in this category.

Secure-autonomous speakers often leave the reader with the impression of an active and lively consciousness, as illustrated in elegance of narrative and a tendency to use the first person ("I"). At times, these speakers seem ready to examine past relationships, feelings, and statements afresh even while the interview is in progress, a

---

[10]Memory here is understood as an active and not necessarily veridical process of "recategorization"; see Edelman, 1989.

quality we describe as *metacognitive monitoring* (Main, 1991). Thus, wishes and facts may be spontaneously separated ("I know—and I, I also wish—that there is special place in his heart where he remembers me"), and the speaker may correct or comment on statements just made ("No. I never felt rejected. Even if I had I wouldn't have admitted it to myself. Well, actually yes. I did feel rejected).

Finally, more than other speakers, secure-autonomous speakers appear to take a "constructivist" position with respect to past interactions and their influences. During the interview, some indicate that their memories might be in error; that the person being discussed might have a different viewpoint; and that their present beliefs may later undergo, or may presently be the product of, representational change (Main, 1991). Fonagy and his colleagues (Fonagy, Steele, Steele, Moran et al., 1991) have developed a rating of "reflective-self" function for AAI transcripts, in which the individual's capacity to conceive of the wishes, intentions, and actions of others in terms of mental states is assessed. In parents, this scale has been found correlated with infant security of attachment (Fonagy et al., 1991).

Transcripts are classified *dismissing* (Ds) when discourse appears aimed at minimizing the import of attachment-related experiences. The interview responses of dismissing individuals are superficially collaborative, but internal contradictions render them apparently untruthful. Thus, typically, Grice's maxim of quality (be truthful and have evidence for what you say) is violated in that the parents tend to be described in highly positive terms ("excellent mother," "a wonderful, caring relationship") that are unsupported or actively contradicted by episodes recounted later ("I didn't tell her I broke my arm. She would have been really angry"). These contradictions normally go unnoticed. In part because of a frequently stated inability to recall childhood, responses to questions often also violate the maxim of quantity, by being excessively succinct ("I don't remember").

Note that the dismissing interview response pattern can be seen as representing a kind of resistance to the task presented by the inquiries of the interview. Overall, during the interview, dismissing speakers at once resemble the "rejecting" parents of avoidant infants and avoidant infants themselves. Dismissing speakers often show subtle to overt dislike of the interview topic, in part by cutting the interviewer and interview short with brief replies or insistence on lack of memory. In this way, these speakers appear to reject the interviewer. Additionally, like their infants, they appear, or attempt to appear, undistressed, invulnerable, and lacking in anger.

Speakers are classified *preoccupied* (E, for entangled) when their interviews indicate an excessive, confused, and either angry or passive preoccupation with attachment figures or attachment-related events, as shown in violations of manner, relevance, and quantity. Insofar as we can tell from linguistic manifestations within transcripts of this kind, this state of preoccupation with the parent or parents is not fully conscious[11] and is shown rather than stated. Violations of *manner* include use of psychological jargon ("I have a lot of material around that issue"); nonsense words ("She was just caring dadadada so much"); and addressing the parent as though present in recounting a childhood episode ("She was really mental, I mean, she just started caring when she saw my clothes on the floor, and why did you do that, why can't you ever act like the mother?"). Violations of manner also include childlike speech ("So I, I hided from the grownups at dinner") and nebulous phrases ("He would ask me to sit on his lap, and that. I would, and that."). In addition, preoccupied speakers often violate the maxim of relevance, as when they answer queries about childhood relations with parents by providing discussions of recent interactions. Finally, once started on a particular topic, these speakers frequently have difficulty—evidenced, for example, in long, grammatically entangled sentences—in "moving on" in a timely way through the interview format and thus violate quantity by producing interviews that are excessively long. Note that quality is not necessarily violated for such a speaker, since the negative characteristics attributed to the early relationship with the parent may be supported by specific incidents.

The interview responses of preoccupied speakers can, like those of dismissing speakers, be seen as representing a kind of resistance to the interview process, expressed in violations of Grice's maxims. Additionally, the interview responses of preoccupied individuals can be said at once to resemble the Strange Situation behavior of resistant infants and the behavior of their parents. Preoccupied individuals often overwhelm the interviewer by moving far beyond their conversational turn, in a confused/confusing manner that makes it difficult for the interviewer to keep track of answers, to respond, to reach the next question, and to close the interview in a timely manner. In this way, like the parents of resistant infants, preoccupied speakers appear overwhelming, unresponsive, and

---

[11]Indeed, when an ongoing state of mental preoccupation with the parents is described in a lucid manner, the speaker is likely to be judged secure-autonomous, and the infant is likely to be secure with the parent. This same principle holds, of course, for dismissing speakers, so that individuals who describe themselves as having set aside attachment relationships and attachment-related feelings to a greater extent than they would like are also likely to be judged secure-autonomous.

discouraging of autonomy (see Miyake, Chen, and Campos, 1985; Cassidy and Berlin, 1994). Preoccupied speakers can also be seen as inept and noncontingent in their interactions with the interviewer, characteristics which had been observed by Ainsworth in early interactions between resistant infants and their mothers (Ainsworth et al., 1978). Finally, once having begun their accounting of distressing or unfavorable events, these speakers, like resistant infants, express a heightened vulnerability and, additionally, fail to terminate this expression in a timely manner.

Interviews are placed in the *unresolved/disorganized* (U) category on the basis of indications of mental disorganization and disorientation occurring specifically during discussions of potentially traumatic events, such as loss of important persons through death or physical or sexual abuse. These indices of disorganization or disorientation are identified as lapses in the monitoring of reasoning or discourse. Lapses in the monitoring of reasoning include subtle indications that a deceased person is believed still alive in the physical sense *("So now she can get on with being dead, and I can get on with my schoolwork")*; indications that a person is believed to have died because of something the speaker thought or wished *("I promised to think about her every night, but I forgot to think about her that night, I was partying, and she died that night, so I always think that might be what killed her")*; or space-time confusions regarding when and where a person died, as when the speaker says in different portions of the interview that mother's death occurred when she was 9, 12, and 15 years of age or claims not to have been present when a loved one died, then describes the self as present. Lapses in the monitoring of *discourse* include eulogistic speech, as, *"She was young, she was lovely, and she was torn from us by that most dreaded of diseases, tuberculosis"* (an alteration from the speaker's previous discourse register); extremely prolonged silences, following which the speaker seems to have forgotten what was last said or discussed; and "absorbed" recountings involving extreme detail regarding loss or abuse experiences.

Note that an insistent series of questions regarding loss experiences such as appears within the Adult Attachment Interview may never previously have been encountered; may be disorganizing and disorienting; and may provide an occasion for revealing ideas or patterns of thought that have not attained the status of conscious process for many years. Lapses of the kind just described are usually brief and occur not infrequently in high-functioning professionals. As is the case in the system delineated for assigning disorganized/disoriented infant attachment status, transcripts assigned to unresolved status are also always placed in a second, best-fitting category

(Main and Goldwyn, in press). Thus, an unresolved speaker can otherwise fit well to any of the remaining categories, and an alternative secure-autonomous (U/F) assignment is by no means infrequent.

In our original Bay Area study, 11 out of 12 mothers (91%) identified as unresolved on the basis of their discussions of loss had disorganized/disoriented infants. In contrast, only 3 out of 19 mothers (16%) who had experienced loss, but showed no indications of unresolved/disorganized mental processes in discussing the loss, had disorganized infants (Main and Hesse, 1990). Ainsworth and Eichberg (1991) successfully replicated our findings in a sample of Charlottesville mothers and infants. In the Charlottesville study, not all disorganized infants had unresolved mothers, but all 8 mothers identified as unresolved on the basis of their discussions of loss had infants judged disorganized with them during the Strange Situation a few months previously. Loss as an event—even early loss of a parent—was not in itself associated with infant disorganized attachment status.

Elsewhere, we have suggested that lapses in the monitoring of reasoning or discourse may in various ways represent (a) interference from normally dissociated memory systems or else (b) unusual absorptions involving memories triggered by the discussion of traumatic events. Further, we have suggested that these alterations in normal consciousness may be mediated by associated lapses in working memory (Main and Hesse, 1992). Specifically, lapses in reasoning—that is, indications that a speaker believes a deceased person is both dead and not-dead (in the immediate, physical sense)—may indicate parallel, incompatible belief and memory systems regarding a traumatic event that have become dissociated. Lapses in the monitoring of discourse, such as sudden use of eulogistic speech, suggest the possibility of "state shifts" where the individual has entered a peculiar, compartmentalized state of mind involving a particular traumatic experience. Shifts of state involving intrusions from frightening, dissociated memories may result in frightened/frightening behavior on the part of the parent and hence be the mechanism linking the parent's unresolved state of mind to disorganized/ disoriented behavior on the part of the infant.

From this discussion it appears that, for speakers in both of the "organized" insecure attachment categories, transference-like patterns of interaction between interviewer and interviewee resembling the respective interactions of dismissing-avoidant or preoccupied-resistant dyads are recapitulated within the Adult Attachment Interview. In contrast, the intrusion of lapses of reasoning or discourse during the attempted discussion of potentially traumatic events that identifies unresolved speakers does not appear to me to be part of an interactive pattern or to represent a propensity toward a particular kind of relationship with the interviewer. The resemblance to infant Strange Situation behavior may then be said to consist in the fact that there has been an episode of disorganization or disorientation in reasoning or discourse that represents not so much an overall pattern of interaction as a collapse of patterning.

Finally, a small proportion of individuals are now assigned to the relatively new "cannot classify" category within the Adult Attachment Classification system. "Cannot classify" is assigned as a category placement when the speaker does not fit the "organized" secure, dismissing, or preoccupied adult attachment categories (Hesse, submitted). Speakers falling in this category either (1) alternate between the inherently incompatible preoccupied and dismissing states of mind with respect to attachment, being unable to maintain either strategy for discussing and evaluating past relationships, or else (2) appear globally incoherent but fail to manifest indices of preoccupation or dismissal sufficient for assignment to either of the corresponding categories (this latter category is especially rare). The "Cannot Classify" category is the adult equivalent of "unclassifiable" infant attachment status. Currently, 7% to 10% of individuals in low-risk samples are assigned to this category.

Psychometric properties of the Adult Attachment Interview: Stability and discriminant and predictive validity. Current studies utilizing the Adult Attachment Interview with adolescents, parents, and other adults yield about the same proportions of adults as infants across the four corresponding attachment categories, with a small majority of individuals being categorized as secure-autonomous. Thus, in a recent meta-analysis of several samples 55% of mothers were judged secure, 16% dismissing, 9% preoccupied, and 19% unresolved (van IJzendoorn and Bakermans-Kranenburg, in press). Distributions for fathers and for adolescents were comparable.

The dismissing, secure-autonomous, and preoccupied adult categories have been found remarkably stable, with 78% to 90% of subjects judged to fit the same classification at separate time periods. These studies have taken place over a 2-month period with 83 Dutch mothers (Bakermans-Kranenburg and van IJzendoorn, 1993, 78% stable); a 3-month period with 59 male and female Israeli college students (Sagi et al., 1994, 90% stable); and a 12-month period with 84 Canadian mothers (Benoit and Parker, 1994, 90% stable). Stability was 77% across four categories in the Canadian study, and it was 71% in the Dutch study when mothers experiencing a new loss within the testing interval were eliminated.

Despite the central role that coherence plays in determining adult attachment status, adult "state of mind with respect to attachment" in these and several other studies was not related to general intelligence or verbal fluency; subjects who were coherent in the description and evaluation of childhood experiences (secure-autonomous subjects) fared no better in tests of general intelligence than insecure subjects (Bakermans-Kranenburg and van IJzendoorn, 1993; Sagi et al., 1994; see van IJzendoorn, 1995, for review). In addition, despite the insistence on lack of recall for childhood seen during the Adult Attachment Interview in many dismissing subjects, tests of general memory skills and memory for nonattachment-related childhood events revealed no significant deficits in general memory or memory skills in dismissing subjects. In the Dutch and Israeli studies, interviewers were rotated across time, and the classification was found to have no relation to the person of the interviewer. Finally, Waters and his colleagues (1993) established that differences among subjects in responding to the Adult Attachment Interview did not simply reflect more general differences in narrative and discourse style.

Prior to 1991, most studies had compared the interview responses of parents to their child's Strange Situation response to them several months or even several years before. The first investigation demonstrating the power of the interview to predict infant Strange Situation behavior when administered prior to the birth of the first child utilized a white, middle-class sample of 100 London mothers and infants (Fonagy, Steele, and Steele, 1991). In a later investigation of this same sample that included fathers and infants, these investigators were able to demonstrate the specificity of the links between an adult's representational state and infant Strange Situation response (Steele, Steele, and Fonagy, in press). In brief, they showed that if the mother's prebirth interview was secure-autonomous, while the father's prebirth interview was dismissing, the infant would be found secure with her mother but avoidant of her father when seen in the Strange Situation.

Another critical prebirth study was conducted by Mary Jo Ward and Betty Carlson (1995), utilizing a sample of adolescent African-American and Hispanic mothers in inner-city New York. Here, the mother-to-infant category match was directly comparable to that obtained in middle-class studies, despite the harsh lives, low educational level, and slightly differing speech patterns of many of these young mothers. Two further prebirth studies, one conducted with Canadian mothers, the other with Australian fathers, have also found adult attachment status predictive of infant attachment status prior to the birth of the first child (Radojevic, 1992: Benoit and Parker,

1994). Thus, investigators in four countries have reported that the attachment status of a prospective, first-time parent assessed three months prior to the infant's birth predicts Strange Situation response to that parent 15 months later. van IJzendoorn's meta-analysis of these and other studies has shown that the ability of the Adult Attachment Interview to predict the first infant's attachment status *prior to birth* is equally as strong as when the interview is conducted succeeding the birth of the child (van IJzendoorn, 1995).

The adult-to-infant correspondence described above has been tested across 18 samples (van IJzendoorn, 1995). The overall correspondence between security versus insecurity in a parent's "state of mind with respect to attachment" and infant security versus insecurity of attachment across a combined sample of 661 dyads is 75%. Moreover, across studies there is a 70% correspondence between the three "organized" adult and infant attachment categories (dismissing/avoidant, secure-autonomous/secure, and preoccupied/resistant). When four categories are utilized, so that exact matches between the difficult-to-code unresolved adult and disorganized infant attachment categories are sought, 63% of dyads fall in the corresponding adult and infant attachment categories. The overall match between the unresolved and disorganized attachment categories is, however, substantial ($d = .65$) and is strongly positively related to the amount of training judges have had in coding disorganized/disoriented attachment (van IJzendoorn, 1995).

The strength of relation between the parent's Adult Attachment Interview classification and the infant's classification appears, in summary, remarkable. Expressed in terms of effect size, the 18 available samples examined by van IJzendoorn showed a combined effect size of $d = 1.06$ (equivalent to $r = .47$) in the expected direction for the secure-insecure split. Cohen (1988) suggested that $d = .20$ should be considered a small effect size; $d = .50$ would constitute a medium effect size; and $d = .80$ should be considered a large effect size.[12] This association, which compares representational states assessed through language use in the parent or prospective parent with nonverbal infant response to separation from, and reunion with, that parent is exceptionally strong for the behavioral sciences.

Prediction of the "organized" Adult Attachment Interview categories from the "organized" categories of infant Strange Situation behavior. Three reports of attempted prediction of Adult Attachment Interview status from infant Strange Situation behavior to

---

[12]Further, a sufficient number of studies have now yielded similar results so that the association between parental and infant attachment could not be reduced to insignificance in the next 1,087 studies, even if these 1,087 studies failed to find a significant association (van IJzendoorn, 1995).

mother have very recently become available. In one, a Q-sort method of Adult Attachment Interview analysis (Kobak, 1993) was utilized: in this study of German 16-year-olds, no relation was evident (Zimmerman et al., 1995). In two other studies the Adult Attachment Interview responses of both 17-year-olds (Hamilton, 1995) and 21-year-olds (Waters et al., 1995) were found predictable from Strange Situation behavior to the mother 16 and 20 years previously.

In both of the latter studies, coding for the disorganized/disoriented and unclassifiable infant attachment categories (an expected source of instability) had not been available in infancy, nor had participants been observed with father (an expected source of increased predictability). Comparisons were therefore made between secure, avoidant, and resistant attachment status with mother in infancy, and secure-autonomous, dismissing, or preoccupied attachment status in adolescence or young adulthood. In Hamilton's study of a Southern California sample of 30 adolescents from nontraditional families, 77% of adolescents retained their infant attachment status with respect to the secure versus insecure distinction, while 63% retained the specifically correspondent attachment category (i.e., secure/secure, avoidant/dismissing, resistant/preoccupied). In the Minnesota-based study of 50 young adults conducted by Waters and his colleagues, 70% retained their infant attachment status with regard to the secure versus insecure distinction, and 64% retained the precisely correspondent category. In the Waters et al. study, stability was markedly increased (78% for secure versus insecure attachment status) when subjects suffering severely negative life experiences were eliminated. Judges in both studies were, of course, blind to infant attachment status.

Issues of veridicality in the recounting of early experiences cannot yet be addressed by the preceding studies. The first (and simplest) conclusion to be drawn from these results is, that a majority of adolescents and young adults who were coherent and collaborative in recounting their life history had been secure with mother as infants, while a majority of those who were incoherent and noncollaborative had been insecure with mother. Moreover, we may conclude that (1) adolescents who were resistant with mother in the Strange Situation in infancy tended to violate manner, relevance, and quantity during the Adult Attachment Interview, while (2) adolescents who had avoided the mother in infancy tended to violate Grice's maxim of quality by providing unsupported or directly contradicted positive descriptors for her and to violate quantity by laying claim to a lack of memory. Notably, in another sample, dismissing (as opposed to secure and preoccupied) adolescents had had consistently unresponsive mothers as observed in the home in infancy and toddlerhood (Beckwith, Cohen, and Hamilton, 1995). The probable implication of this finding is that adolescents whose mothers had been consistently unresponsive during infancy tended to idealize the mother and to claim a lack of memory for early childhood.

These results had been partially anticipated in the follow-up studies of children's representational processes and parent–child discourse patterns at six years of age discussed earlier. They had also been anticipated in two studies that compared Adult Attachment Interview classifications for mothers and their adult children. In the first, the exact category match (secure/secure, dismissing/dismissing, preoccupied/preoccupied) for 77 Canadian mothers and their adult daughters was found to be 75%. The strongest match was from a secure mother to a secure daughter, with 45 of 51 (88%) daughters of secure mothers being also judged secure. The weakest match was from dismissing mothers to dismissing daughters, with only 5 out of 13 daughters of dismissing mothers being judged dismissing,[13] while 7 were judged autonomous (Benoit and Parker, 1994). Additionally, a study of the mothers of 27 psychiatrically hospitalized adolescents in the Philadelphia area yielded 81% (three-category) agreement between adolescent and maternal attachment classifications (Rosenstein and Horowitz, in press).

Finally, the results of both the study conducted by Hamilton (1995) and the study conducted by Waters and his colleagues (Waters et al., 1995) are in keeping with a theory advanced below, which suggests that attempts to maintain a particular insecure, organized representational state with respect to the original attachment to the parents should result in systematic violations of coherence and collaboration during the Adult Attachment Interview. The reader should note, however, that in each of these studies there is sufficient unpredictability to refute any claim to early determinism with respect to adolescent or adult attachment status.

ATTACHMENT AND CLINICAL STUDIES

As noted earlier Spence (1987) had called for a grammar of early development, a clearly defined system by which early experience

---

[13]These results bear an intriguing relation to a preliminary report regarding improvement in functioning across the course of long-term analytically oriented treatment for psychiatrically hospitalized patients (Fonagy et al., in press), In this report, patients whose initial status had been dismissing (rather than preoccupied) showed the greatest improvement across the course of treatment.

could be understood to be transformed into later behavior. Although the relations between infant attachment status and the onset of mental difficulties are as yet unknown, the studies reviewed earlier suggest that the grammar that Spence had called for is emerging and, correspondingly, that—as Emde (1989) had already suggested—the infant–caregiver relationship may conceivably influence early motivational structures in a unique way. Here I first discuss the organized (avoidant and resistant) insecure infant attachment patterns and suggest that they may be conceived of as conditional behavioral strategies for maintenance of proximity to an insecure (dismissing or preoccupied) caregiver. Dismissing and preoccupied adults may actively attempt to maintain a steady representational/attentional state with respect to their own parents, and I suggest ways in which such states may be (1) maintained through discourse violations, (2) held in place by anxiety, and (3) transmitted to the infant. I then discuss disorganized attachment status as a potential risk factor in anxiety and phobia and describe a hypothesis developed by Liotti (1992, 1993) connecting disorganized infant attachment status to increased vulnerability to the development of dissociative disorder. Finally, I consider potential links among adult attachment status, mental suffering, and the therapeutic process.

Organized Forms of Insecure Attachment Status: Maintenance of Steady Representational States with Respect to the Parent

Behavioral strategies, the control of attention, and the development of organized defensive processes. Earlier, I reviewed Ainsworth's original discoveries regarding the Strange Situation behavior of 12-month-old, home-reared infants who had no experiences of major separation. As the reader will remember, only (that majority of) infants whose mothers had been "sensitive and responsive to infant signals and communications" in the home had shown the expected behavioral patterning. For infants whose attachment behavior had been consistently rejected, threatening conditions (mother absence) failed to activate attachment behavior. For infants whose mothers had been unpredictable, in contrast, mother's presence failed to terminate it. Insecure infants, then, either failed to exhibit attachment behavior in threatening conditions and actively avoided the mother on reunion or else, remaining preoccupied with mother throughout the separation, failed to explore in conditions of safety.

Let us now consider these findings in the context of evolutionary biology, and specifically in the light of the concept of the "conditional behavioral strategy" (see Maynard Smith, 1979). Drawing on primate studies, Hinde (1982) questioned whether mothers will be optimally "sensitive" to their infants in all circumstances or whether, instead, variability in circumstances could produce substantial variability in maternal sensitivity and responsiveness. Specifically, he utilized the evolutionary concept of the conditional behavioral strategy to suggest that natural selection had operated to produce conditional maternal strategies, that is, to produce lability as opposed to stereotypy in the response repertoire. In certain environments, then, the mother's reproductive success may be optimized through behavior patterns that violate maximally sensitive caregiving. Under these conditions, she may be, for example, somewhat rejecting (perhaps promoting early infant independence) or somewhat unpredictably responsive (perhaps promoting a prolonging of dependence; Main, 1990). There is no implication that the mother's (or infant's—discussed later) selection of a particular strategy need be conscious. Moreover, as opposed to primary caregiving (or proximity-seeking) strategies, which are based on the activities of instinctively biased behavioral systems, conditional behavioral strategies are not presumed to rely on the operation of any particular behavioral system—as, for example, a "rejecting" or an "avoidance" behavioral system. They may, instead, simply involve manipulations of the output of the primary system by utilizing coexisting mechanisms.

Main (1981, 1990) proposed that insecure infants, as well as their parents, may be conceived as utilizing conditional behavioral strategies to meet with their circumstances—specifically, they may develop conditional strategies for maintaining proximity and/or self-organization under conditions of maternal rejection or unpredictable responsiveness. During infancy, maintenance of these behavioral strategies may rest on limiting or altering attentional patterning (see Allport, 1989; Main, 1993). The infant of the consistently rejecting mother is then conceived as shifting attention away from the mother and from threatening conditions and hence keeping the naturally occurring behavioral output of the attachment behavioral system at a minimum. In direct contrast, the infant of the unpredictably responsive mother is conceived as hypervigilant with respect to even minimally threatening conditions and thus keeping the behavioral output at a maximum. By serving ultimately to control the infant's behavior, these less flexible forms of attentional patterning may permit the maintenance of proximity and self-organization under conditions of maternal rejection or unpredictable responsiveness.

Because the attachment behavioral system is conceived as being continually alert and context-sensitive, however (Bowlby, 1969; Bretherton, 1985), at some level the primary propensity to seek proximity in response to threat and to terminate proximity-seeking in conditions of safety must still be active. In this conceptualization, then, the infant's conditional behavioral strategy (avoidance or preoccupation) is understood to be imposed on a still-active primary strategy. Maintenance of a "minimizing" (avoidant) or "maximizing" (resistant) behavioral strategy is therefore likely eventually not only to become dependent on the control or manipulation of attention but also eventually to necessitate overriding or altering aspects of memory, emotion, and awareness of surrounding conditions (Main, Kaplan, and Cassidy, 1985; see Cassidy, in press, for a discussion of emotion regulation in relation to attachment history). Although based on a behavioral program that serves protection as opposed to sexuality or aggression, this conceptualization is compatible with existing theories of defense.

Stability and intergenerational transmission of insecure-avoidant and insecure-resistant attachment patterns: The maintenance of organized attentional/representational states as related to felt security. We have now arrived at a proposal regarding the origins of defensive processes as related to attachment. Specifically, I have suggested (1) that infants whose mothers are rejecting or unpredictably responsive must learn either to limit the exhibition of attachment behavior in the presence of activating conditions or to heighten the exhibition of attachment behavior in the presence of terminating conditions and (2) that these particular behavioral patternings eventually come to be held in place by maintenance of a steady attentional/representational state. Note that because the parents of avoidant and resistant infants (as opposed to the parents of disorganized infants) have not themselves been a direct source of alarm, their conditional forms of responsiveness have permitted the infant to maintain behavioral organization. Thus, in the absence of inherently disorganizing, frightened/frightening parental behavior, a form of behavioral "compromise" on the part of the infant can be achieved.

If this conceptualization of the origins of defensive processes with respect to avoidant and resistant attachment status is correct, we can make the following further observations:

1. In the Strange Situation and elsewhere, the avoidant and resistant patterns of attachment are conceived as being held in

place by maintenance of a steady attentional/representational state. Challenges to, and violations of, these states—specifically, circumstances forcing shifts in attention toward threatening conditions and attachment figures in avoidant/dismissing individuals and conditions forcing attention away from attachment figures in resistant/preoccupied individuals—may eventually in themselves promote feelings of anxiety. Maintenance of these states may therefore subjectively be experienced as a kind of *secondary felt security* (see Main, Solomon, and Hesse, 1985), originating in the conditional strategy that the individual has utilized for maintaining proximity (and self-organization) in the face of repeated interactions with an insecure parent.

2. The similarities between the behavior of avoidant and resistant infants in the Strange Situation and the discourse of dismissing and preoccupied adults during the Adult Attachment Interview are remarkable. We may conceive of the Adult Attachment Interview (like the Strange Situation) as creating conditions that arouse and direct attention toward attachment. The Adult Attachment Interview, then, can be seen as directly challenging the "minimizing" attentional/representational state of dismissing individuals, by insisting repeatedly on recall, description, and evaluation of unfavorable relations and experiences. This challenge is met in an initially highly favorable presentation of the parent (which is unsupported or contradicted by the recounting of specific episodes) and by an insistent rejection of interview inquiries ("I don't remember"). For preoccupied individuals, in contrast, the interview appears to activate the speaker's state ("maximization" of attention to attachment figures), thereby producing noncollaborative discourse (e.g., excessive length, failure to address the question asked, failure to return the conversational turn to the interviewer at the appropriate time). For such individuals, violations of coherence and collaboration can be understood to result from difficulties in the ability to shift attention.

Within the Adult Attachment Interview, then, violations of Grice's maxims of quality, quantity, relevance, and manner may be conceived as acting to preserve a dismissing or preoccupied attentional/representational state. Within the framework provided by psychoanalysis, these discourse violations can also be understood as constituting resistance both to memory and to interaction.

3. Sander (1987) identifies states as consisting in a configuration of the values of variables representing the component subsys-

tems of an organism. Sander postulates that each state shows a profile that recurs, and can be recognized when it recurs. He further notes that every infant–caregiver system necessarily constructs its own unique configuration of regulatory constraint on the infant's access to awareness of his or her own states and inner experiences. Sander (1975) has shown that dyadic adjustments begin in the earliest weeks of infant life.

We may apply Sander's conceptualizations to the present context. Young infants express at once a need for protection by caregivers and an autonomous interest in exploration of the surroundings (Stern, 1985; Emde, 1989). The preservation of the insecure parent's state of mind with respect to attachment may initially be endangered by infant distress/proximity-seeking, infant autonomy/exploration, or both (e.g., in the case of a dismissing parent, distress/proximity-seeking may endanger state preservation). The parent can preserve a particular state of mind by failing to perceive, failing to interpret accurately, or failing to respond to those selected infant behaviors/ states that threaten to alter it. As an example, an infant's attempts to gain physical contact may threaten preservation of state for dismissing individuals whose "idealized" picture of their own early experiences is held in place, in part, through lack of active review of their own experiences of physical rejection. The proximity-seeking infant who could force awareness of deficiencies in the parent's experiences is then rejected in the service of maintaining a particular representational state with respect to the parent's parents. In response to these selective insensitivities, the infant then develops a conditional behavioral strategy for the maintenance of proximity and self-organization (e.g., in the infant of a dismissing parent, avoidance of the parent when distressed).

In summary, I suggest that the infant develops a defensive, conditional strategy for maintenance of proximity and/or self-organization in response to restrictions the parent has placed on proximity-seeking or on autonomous exploration. This conditional strategy, in turn, serves to assist the insecure parent in preservation of a particular state of mind with respect to his or her own parents. In later development, favorable relations with other or new attachment figures, favorable constitutional characteristics, and absence of intervening trauma may permit many insecure infants to become secure as adults; while, conversely, the intrusion of negative life events or changed interaction patterns with primary figures may lead secure infants to states of insecurity in adulthood. In the majority of cases, however, the organized forms of insecure attachment are likely preserved from infancy to adulthood (and transmitted from adult to infant) through this mechanism.

Disorganized Forms of Insecure Attachment: Implications of Disorganized Infant Attachment Status for Increased Vulnerability to Anxiety and Dissociative Disorders

With respect to forthcoming investigations of mental states as related to infant attachment, it seems likely that disorganized attachment status with the primary caregiver in infancy will be the form of early insecurity most frequently linked to significant mental difficulties (see Zeanah and Emde, 1993). This, of course, does not imply that more than a small proportion of individuals falling in this attachment category will later develop notable forms of psychopathology. Indeed, so long as direct maltreatment is not involved, many, perhaps most, are expected to have become "organized" by adulthood, being either secure, dismissing, or preoccupied.[14]

Disorganized/disoriented infant attachment status as a risk factor in the development of anxiety, phobia, and malignant self-concept. Disorganized/disoriented Strange Situation behavior has been observed in the great majority (80%) of maltreated infants in two independent samples (discussed earlier). In these samples, it has been presumed that lapses in behavioral/attentional strategy occuring during the Strange Situation reflect the infant's response to having repeatedly been presented with the paradox of threatening behavior on the part of an attachment figure who is also simultaneously the infant's haven of safety in times of alarm (Carlson et al., 1989; Main and Hesse, 1990; Lyons-Ruth et al., 1991). A substantial minority of infants in low-risk, middle-class samples (about 10% to 35%) are, however, also judged disorganized/disoriented. While maltreatment no doubt occurs within these samples, what appears most striking in studies of low-risk populations is the relation between infant disorganized attachment status and parental lapses in the monitoring of reasoning or discourse during attempted discussions of traumatic experiences (most often, loss of significant persons). As noted earlier, we have made the preliminary interpretation that these lapses may be indicative of states of absorption, and/or intrusion from normally dissociated memory systems, or both, occurring, in part, because of the frightening nature of the

---

[14]A small number of these individuals may, however, be found difficult to classify (i.e., may be "cannot classify" with respect to adult attachment status), having developed a tendency to shift between differing states of mind with respect to attachment.

experiences being described (Main and Hesse, 1992; Main and Morgan, in press).

With this in mind, we have recently begun to focus specifically on the possible consequences of interacting with parents who sporadically exhibit fright (alarm) in the presence of the infant in response to thoughts, events, or objects in the environment associated with their own overwhelmingly frightening experiences. Frightened/alarmed parental behavior that has no comprehensible relation to ongoing events in the immediate environment could place the infant in a conflict situation not unlike the one created by a directly threatening parent (see Hesse and Main, submitted). Thus, still-traumatized parents may sometimes react with fear to their own traumatic memories or to aspects of the environment somehow associated with those memories (e.g., when the memories themselves are not fully integrated into normal consciousness). Under such conditions, an infant interacting with a traumatized/frightened attachment figure (1) will be unable to identify the source of the attachment figure's alarm (i.e., what the parent is reacting to) and (2) may develop unexplained fears on this basis. Through diverse mechanisms elaborated on elsewhere, the infant may also (3) identify the *self* as the source of the alarm, (4) particularly if exposed to flight/retreat behavior on the part of the parent (Main and Hesse, 1990, 1992; Hesse and Main, submitted). We have, in fact, informally observed the parents of disorganized/disoriented infants in low-risk samples in trancelike states, and we have also observed them backing away from the infant as though frightened.

In keeping with a more general hypothesis examined earlier, then, it appears that frightened (alarmed) as well as frightening (maltreating) behavior may be a mechanism linking the parent's traumatized state of mind to the infant's disorganized/disoriented behavior in stressful situations. Parental behavior of this kind may then create vulnerabilities to the development of concept of self as inexplicably powerful, yet somehow bad or dangerous, particularly when the parent has repeatedly exhibited flight/retreat behavior in response to infant approaches, has repeatedly exhibited timid or deferential behavior, or has otherwise inadvertently identified the infant as the source of the parent's alarm (Hesse and Main, submitted).

We have also proposed that frightened behavior observed in a traumatized parent may lead to increased vulnerabilities to anxieties and phobias that, related to the *parent's* experiences, appear untraceable within the offspring to a direct experiential source. Specifically, a disorganized/disoriented infant could be vulnerable to anomalous, frightening ideation as a result of observing parents reacting in a frightened/frightening manner to their own partially dissociated, frightening memories or to objects in the environment that are not themselves intrinsically frightening but rather are linked to the parents' traumatic experiences (Main and Hesse, 1990, 1992; Hesse and Main, submitted). In some cases, the anomalous ideation of the offspring could have a general, rather than a specific, relation to the parent's experiences, as expressed in catastrophic fantasies having no specific repeating focus or form. In others, a phobia could develop, related to the parent's own traumatic experiences in a more specific way.

As an example, young parents and prospective parents do occasionally develop a fear of loss of a child through death that cannot be traced to a direct experiential source; that is, there is no knowledge of a previous loss within the family. One pathway to unexplained fears of this kind could then be early interactions with a parent who, having lost a previous infant, repeatedly became frightened/dissociated in circumstances reminiscent of her loss. In this way, a parent or prospective parent could acquire a pervasive fear that an infant might die (1) without the parent's having personally lost an infant and (2) without awareness that another child in the family of origin had been lost. In cases where direct experiences do not give rise to probable causal explanations, this line of reasoning may present a viable alternative to the presumption that an excessive fear for another person's welfare constitutes a reaction to an underlying wish to harm. Similar reasoning can be applied to the development of other anomalous forms of fear, and we advance this as a pathway to the development of phobias and anxiety that, to our knowledge, has not previously been explored (Main and Goldwyn, 1989; Hesse and Main, submitted).

Disorganized Attachment Status as a Risk Factor in the Development of Dissociative Disorders. Let us now examine a further proposal regarding vulnerabilities to mental suffering in individuals disorganized with the primary caregiver in infancy. Giovanni Liotti (1992) has suggested that—should traumatic circumstances intervene in later life—disorganized infants could be more vulnerable than others to the development of dissociative disorders. His reasoning takes its origins in descriptions of the trancelike states and behavior patterns observed in some disorganized/disoriented infants as described by Main and Solomon (1986, 1990) and in the likelihood that insofar as frightened/frightening behavior on the part of an attachment figure is tantamount to a "paradoxical behavioral injunction," it represents one form of trance induction and may lead to the onset of hypnotic states. We have been able to provide some tentative support for Liotti's hypothesis by drawing attention to phenotypic similarities among some disorganized/disoriented infant Strange Situation behavior, some lapses in discourse and reasoning observed in the Adult Attachment Interview, and dissociative phenomena (Main and Hesse, 1992; Main and Morgan, in press).

In this light, a case study presented by Liotti (1993) warrants consideration. Lisa, a patient subject to dissociative, trancelike states accompanied by fears that her infant would die by ingesting broken glass, had been informed that her fears represented death wishes for her infant. Questioning by her therapist regarding any frightened/frightening parental behavior revealed, however, memory for incidents to which she had previously made no connection—repeated experiences of being frightened as a young child by her mother's eerie recounting of the death of a sibling born when Lisa herself was still a toddler. Taken to the beach with her mother, the newborn had fallen out of her mother's arms and had lain with its face in the sand. Lisa's mother had attributed the baby's death a few days later to inhaling sand and to her own negligence. Lisa's trancelike states and pervasive fears that her own infant would die from inhaling small pieces of broken glass had arisen shortly following her infant's brief hospitalization for pneumonia.

Lisa had no previous awareness of this link between her mother's frightened/frightening recounting of her sibling's death through inhaling sand and her own fearful/dissociative states occasioned by fears that her infant would die by inhaling broken glass. In keeping with the preliminary communication regarding the case of Anna O (Breuer and Freud, 1895), Liotti suggested that, frightened by her attachment figure, Lisa may have listened to this story in a "hypnoid" state in which information is not processed normally and is later resistant to normal forms of access. He notes as well that Lisa's vulnerability may have been heightened in that she was, in the therapist's estimate, insecure with both her parents and additionally had suffered sexual abuse at the hands of a nonfamily member prior to maturity.

Liotti has also presented some anamnestic data respecting the relation between dissociative disorder and a patient's *mother's* loss experiences (Liotti, 1992). Because of the association established between infant disorganized/disoriented attachment status and (unresolved) loss, he queried 46 patients suffering from dissociative disorders and 119 other psychiatric patients as to whether mother had lost an important relative within two years of the patient's birth. About 62% of dissociative and only about 13% of remaining patients answered this question in the affirmative—a difference that is statistically highly significant. Because of the potentially traumatic impact of such an event, this implies increased likelihood that the mother may have been frightened/frightening in the patient's earliest years and hence that the patient may have been disorganized/disoriented in infancy. Similarly, Walsh (1978) cited an unpublished report by Orfinadis indicating that, within a given family, individuals suffering from schizophrenia were more likely than their nonschizophrenic siblings to have been born within two years of mother's loss of a parent. In the same publication, Walsh herself had reported similar findings.

We have at hand, then, two proposals regarding increased vulnerabilities to (1) anxiety and phobias and (2) dissociative disorders in individuals disorganized with the primary caregiver in infancy. It should be emphasized, however, that these proposals are still largely speculative. In addition, any relation uncovered among anxiety, phobia, dissociative disorders, and early disorganized attachment status is likely to be highly asymmetric. This means that while an impressive proportion of individuals suffering from a given form of mental difficulty in later life may, indeed, be found to have been disorganized with the primary caregiver as infants, among those individuals who are disorganized as infants, only a few are likely to develop the disorder (see Lyons-Ruth, in press, for a discussion of this asymmetry with respect to the relation between clinical levels of aggressive behavior at age seven and infant disorganized attachment status). Put another way, disorganized infant attachment may then approach the status of a necessary but not sufficient condition.

If this kind of asymmetrical relation between infant disorganized attachment status and varying forms of mental difficulty is found, we might presume that early disorganized status does not yield the outcome specified unless combined with other conditions, for example, genetically biased vulnerabilities or other life events. Additionally, this kind of outcome might mean that our predictive power had been reduced by a failure to record the specific kind of disorganized or disoriented behavior that had been exhibited. In fact, freezing and trancelike states might predict one unfavorable outcome, repeated slow strikes to the parent's face might predict a different outcome, and combined avoidance and resistance (D/A-C attachment status, see especially Crittenden, 1985; Main and Solomon, 1990) might predict a third (e.g., increased vulnerability to dissociative identity disorder, as proposed by Main and Hesse, 1992). For this reason we have recommended that the exact behavior leading to placement in the disorganized infant attachment category be recorded (Main and Solomon, 1990).

Adult Attachment Status in Relation to Clinical Work and Treatment Outcomes

The preceding proposals are, again, speculative and ultimately dependent on the outcome of long-term follow-up studies. Work regarding adult attachment status and clinical status in general is, however, currently in progress, and a recent meta-analysis of the Adult Attachment Interview as administered to psychiatrically distressed populations indicates a robust relation between secure versus insecure adult attachment status and clinical status in adult or child. Few hospitalized or previously hospitalized individuals and few mothers of clinically disordered children (excepting children suffering attention deficit disorder; see Crowell et al., 1991) were judged secure-autonomous, and both unresolved status and "cannot classify" attachment status were overrepresented in disordered populations (van IJzendoorn and Bakermans-Kranenburg, in press). Even when the data were analyzed in terms of secure, dismissing, and preoccupied categories only (with individuals originally assigned to unresolved and cannot classify attachment status reassigned to their best-fitting alternative category), few clinically distressed adults (12%) and few parents of clinically distressed children (14%) were judged secure (van IJzendoorn and Bakermans-Kranenburg, 1994).

As an example, in a study utilizing the five currently available Adult Attachment Interview categories, Allen, Hauser, and Borman-Spurrell (in press) followed up a sample of 142 upper-middle-class adolescents and compared Adult Attachment Interview responses at age 25 to psychiatric status 11 years earlier. At 14 years, 66 of these young adults had been psychiatrically hospitalized for problems other than thought disorder or organic disorder, while 76 had served as controls. The transcripts were blinded so that previous hospitalization could not be identified by the judge. Among 25-year-olds who had been psychiatrically hospitalized 11 years previously, only 8% were judged secure-autonomous, as compared with 45% of controls. Scores assigned to subjects for lapses in the monitoring of reasoning or discourse during the discussion of abuse experiences were strongly associated with previous hospitalization. Additionally, 26% of previously hospitalized subjects, but only 7% of control subjects, were placed in the cannot classify category.

To return to the previously mentioned meta-analysis combining several studies of psychiatrically distressed adults and children, the overall effect size associating security versus insecurity in adult attachment status to clinical versus nonclinical status in adult or offspring was remarkable (d = 1.03; N = 688; van IJzendoorn and Bakermans-Kranenburg, in press). Note again that this means that both substantially troubled adults and the parents of substantially troubled children are unlikely to be able to describe and evaluate childhood experiences with their parents consistently and collaboratively.

Adult attachment status related to mental difficulties. As the reader is aware, Bowlby proposed that a consideration of the infant's propensity to seek protection in times of alarm, together with the immediacy of the tie between maintenance of proximity and survival, could provide the clinician with an increased understanding of both the forms taken by certain mental difficulties and their origins. Separation, loss, and the insecure infant–mother interaction patterns identified by Ainsworth were considered capable of leading to the development of defensive processes detrimentally affecting the individual's "internal working model" or "representational state" (Bowlby, 1969, 1973, 1980).

Sexuality and aggression did not enter significantly into Bowlby's theorizing regarding the origin of mental difficulties. His exclusion of these aspects of human feeling and experience, together with that body of work that endeavored to understand their role in the development of psychopathology, has puzzled many clinicians. The reasons for this exclusion involve, in part, his focus on (1) immediate survival mechanisms (2) as affected by readily observable pathogens, such as major separations (3) in infancy.

In keeping with Bowlby's emphasis, researchers in attachment have continued to focus on the development of relationships and representational processes not directly related to sexuality or aggression. In future studies, systematic relations between differing patternings of attachment in infancy and the later management and expression of sex and aggression could well be uncovered, especially if attachment to both parents is considered in relation to sex of child.

In the South German follow-up study cited earlier, security of attachment to both mother and father predicted especially favorable outcomes in the preschool setting (Suess et al., 1992). I would also expect early security of attachment to both parents to act as a protective factor chiefly against an individual's developing major and repeating difficulties in those areas most closely related to attachment, namely, parenting, caregiving, and close relationships in adulthood. It should also provide a substantial, albeit incomplete, buffer against later difficulties associated with expressing and mastering sexual and aggressive impulses. Direct physical and sexual abuse, as well as interactions with still-traumatized but nonmaltreating parents who themselves have suffered physical or sexual abuse, is, of course, likely to unfavorably affect the development and management of aggression and/or sexuality, albeit to differing degrees and in differing ways. As a simple example, while a battered infant may be aggressive in untoward circumstances (George and Main, 1979; Main and George, 1985), the offspring of a battered but non-maltreating parent who fearfully withdraws from the infant may become inhibited with respect to later expressions of anger.

With respect to the relation between the presently recognized categories of adult attachment and the identification and treatment of patient difficulties, we may speculate as follows:

1. Some secure individuals will encounter circumstances leading to mental suffering, and a portion of these will no doubt seek some form of therapeutic intervention. The prospect for response to treatment should be favorable in such individuals, however, due to relative fluidity of attention and the capacity for metacognitive monitoring and for reflection on mental states of self and others (Fonagy, Steele, Steele et al., 1991; Main, 1991). Additionally, these individuals are likely to have the capacity for establishing relatively unambivalent relationships.

2. Earlier, I proposed that infants whose mothers are either rejecting or unpredictably responsive must learn either to limit the exhibition of attachment behavior in the presence of activating conditions or to heighten the exhibition of attachment behavior in the presence of terminating conditions. I proposed that the manipulation of attentional patterning plays a substantial role in the control and manipulation of attachment-related behavior for young infants[15] and that the continuing control of behavior would eventually involve distortions or limitations placed on memory, emotion, and perception. Thus, defensive processes with respect to attachment[16] were seen as serving to control or manipulate behavior in the service of permitting the infant to maintain proximity, maintain continuing self-organization, or both. Note that what is excluded in this conceptualization is not the memory of any particular traumatic experience but, rather, alternatives in attentional and behavioral patterning.

---

[15]See Allport's 1989 proposal that the selectivity of attention rests upon the control of behavior.

[16]Defense is, of course, organized. Disorganized/disoriented behavior is not defensive in the traditional sense, and, indeed, Freud conceptualized disorganization as the state to which defense is the alternative.

I have proposed, then, that the avoidant and resistant behavioral patterns can be conceived as held in place by maintenance of a steady attentional/representational state. Maintenance of these states may thereafter subjectively be experienced as a kind of secondary felt security, originating in the conditional behavioral strategy that the individual has utilized for maintaining proximity and self-organization. Feelings, memories, or interactions threatening to violate these states may then lead to the threat of anxiety (see Freud's [1926], signal anxiety), and individuals who are dismissing or preoccupied as a result of early interaction patterns may initially experience substantial anxiety in conjunction with efforts to alter this enduring patterning. Dismissing and preoccupied individuals may therefore present somewhat greater difficulties for therapy than secure-autonomous individuals (cf. Emde, 1989). In the absence of intervening trauma, however, such individuals may need less to recall specific early experiences than to alter attentional, emotional, and relational patternings through interactions with the therapist.

3. The phenotypic resemblance between dismissing and preoccupied strategies, and obsessive and hysteric states (especially as described by Freud, 1926) is marked. Dismissal and preoccupation appear, however, to represent working defensive strategies with respect to attachment, may more closely resemble "inhibitions" than neuroses (cf. Freud, 1926) and are not in themselves symptoms or disorders. These organized forms of insecure attachment status are therefore unlikely to be associated with the classic obsessional and hysteric disorders unless the individual is also unclassifiable (falls in the cannot classify category), is experiencing disorganized/disoriented responses to traumatic experiences (falls in the unresolved category), has been either unclassifiable or disorganized/disoriented with the primary caregiver in infancy, or any of these. Note that in each of these cases, the "working" defensive strategy has broken down.

4. Unresolved attachment status is found in combination with all other attachment categories (F, Ds, E, and CC), and difficulties presented by unresolved patients will no doubt differ in accordance with underlying alternative category (e.g., unresolved patients whose underlying state is secure may differ systematically from those whose underlying state is dismissing of attachment). Since, however, the lapses in monitoring of reasoning, discourse, or both used to identify this form of attachment status normally occur only during the discussion of

potentially traumatic experiences, it seems likely that, whatever the patient's underlying attachment organization, a joint exploration of feelings and ideas linked to these specific experiences will be necessary. These experiences are, again, those which overwhelm the patient's reasoning and discourse during attempted discussion.[17]

Favorable alterations in the patient's relation to the therapist and in the patient's emotional state are, of course, normally required to set the background for such explorations, especially when the individual's underlying attachment-related organization is insecure. In the case of patients with an underlying secure attachment organization, however, unresolved/disorganized responses to traumatic experiences and the difficulties that they cause for the patient may not lead to distorted interactions with the therapist or even to distortions in discourse surrounding other events and relationships. In this case, the origin of the patient's most central difficulties may be missed.

It would be unwise, of course, to presume that frightening experiences that appear to lead to disorganization in reasoning or memory would be all that troubles the unresolved but otherwise apparently secure patient. Many unresolved individuals frightened by a loss experience may have had repeated early interactions with parents who themselves had experienced a terrifying loss. In this case, even if largely secure in adulthood, such individuals will no doubt often have been disorganized/disoriented as infants and may unconsciously link their own current loss experience to those that had been frightening to the parent during infancy.

5. A recent paper concerning the few existing studies that include cannot classify status indicates that a significant proportion of individuals with the most severe psychological difficulties are unclassifiable with respect to adult attachment status, including individuals who have been psychiatrically hospitalized (Allen et al., in press), those who have criminally battered a spouse (Holtzworth-Monroe, Hutchinson, and Stuart, 1992), those who have been sexually abused (Stalker, in press), and psychiatrically hospitalized criminal offenders (van

---

[17]In a recent nonblind study of 18 mothers diagnosed with Axis I anxiety disorder and administered the Adult Attachment Interview, Manassis and her colleagues (1994) found 78% unresolved/disorganized with respect to traumatic experiences. Six were unresolved with respect to loss, two with respect to physical or sexual abuse, and six with respect to both.

IJzendoorn and Bakermans-Kranenburg, 1994). These findings
are in keeping with the notion that among individuals whose
mental states are most severely compromised, not only is
coherence of mind absent, but, in addition, defensive strategies have failed (see Hesse, submitted, for a review of the
emerging cannot classify category, and a brief overview of
these studies).

Attachment and the status of the therapist The demand that the
therapist should achieve a comparatively high degree of psychic
normality and correct adjustment as one of the qualifications for his
work was initiated by Freud (1937) and by Ferenczi (e.g., Ferenczi
and Rank, 1988). Their discussions implied that personal qualities of
the analyst, considered apart from technique, could be of import to
therapeutic success—an implication that has been given support in
recent years by Luborsky (1988, 1994), among others.

In considering the effect that the therapist may have on the
patient's state of mind with respect to attachment, we may return
once more to the theory cited earlier regarding the influence of
insecure parent on infant. Earlier, I interpreted the intergenerational
transmission of attachment in individuals falling in the "organized"
insecure attachment categories in terms of the insecure parent's
attempts to maintain a particular state of mind with respect to his or
her own history (Main, 1993). The development of a conditional
strategy by the infant was seen as ultimately assisting insecure
parents in preservation of their own particular state of mind.

Whether or not this theory provides an accurate account of the
intergenerational transmission of the organized forms of insecure
attachment status, the correspondence uncovered between parental
and infant attachment status underscores the recommendations of
those concerned with personal qualities of the therapist. Because
the infant brings no transfer from previous relationships to this first
relationship, the influence of parent on infant is, of course, stronger
than that of therapist on patient, and, unlike parents, therapists
preoccupied by their own past relationships may not engender a
preoccupied state of mind in their patients. Nonetheless, as Emde
(1989) argues, the empathic response of the therapist can be seen as
modeling the role of the caregiver's response. Secure-autonomous
therapists, who can be presumed able to provide security to a young
infant, should also be more likely than dismissing and preoccupied
therapists to be able to serve effectively as a "secure base" for their
patients (cf. Bowlby, 1988). Care provided by dismissing and preoccupied therapists, though equally well intentioned, may
indeliberately fail in providing the patient with full autonomy.

It is exceptions, however, which enable us to comprehend the underlying rules guiding apparent concordances among phenomena. Aspects of therapeutic training, the therapeutic process, or the recognized necessity of assisting others in distress, then, may permit some therapists to override an insecure state with respect to their own attachment histories when called on to provide caregiving to a troubled patient. This intriguing possibility is supported anecdotally by three cases I have observed in which insecure parents, as assessed by the Adult Attachment Interview, have had secure infants, as assessed by the Strange Situation. In each case, the infant had suffered a life-threatening illness in the year preceding the Strange Situation, and had been cared for at home. This preliminary finding suggests that what accounts for the relation between an adult's insecure state of mind with respect to attachment and the adult's "insensitive" caregiving is an inwardly directed attention that, serving to maintain a particular (dismissing or preoccupied) representational state, acts to preserve the original conditions of attachment to the parent.

Full caregiving, however, requires an outer-directed attention (see Stevenson-Hinde, 1994). Infants who reside in the home while experiencing life-threatening conditions will require, and therefore in many cases may evoke, the caregiver's full attention. Faced with these circumstances, some insecure caregivers may be able to override a dismissing or preoccupied state with respect to their own parents and direct attention fully and responsively to the infant. If this reasoning is correct, it is at least possible that some dismissing and preoccupied clinicians can also overstep their own states of mind with respect to attachment, in the service of providing care to a troubled individual.

SUMMARY

This clinically oriented overview of the field of attachment has had four primary objectives:

1. The first has been to emphasize the close and immediate tie between attachment behavior, survival, and fear. With this background in mind, it has been possible to illustrate the ways in which behavior and attention in attachment-related situations is both organized and flexible in individuals whose primary attachment figures have been considered likely to have been sensitive to their signals and communications throughout the first year of life; organized but inflexible in individuals whose attachment figures have been selectively

insensitive, but not frightening or maltreating; and disorganized in individuals whose attachment figures are considered
likely to have been maltreating or otherwise frightened/trau-
matized. The four patterns of behavior, discourse, and representational process associated with each of these patterns of
behavior on the part of the caregiver have been reviewed at
the level of infancy, childhood, and adulthood. At the adult
level, a secure pattern of response to the Adult Attachment
Interview has been found rare in individuals suffering from
psychiatric disorder, in the parents of psychiatrically disordered children, in criminal populations, in sexually abused
individuals, and in individuals who abuse others.

2. The second objective of this overview has been to point to an
extraordinary correspondence between individual differences
in attachment organization as observed in the infant's nonverbal responses to separation and reunion from a particular
parent and individual differences in both parent and child
discourse as observed in attachment-related settings. Here I
have described work at Berkeley illustrating the power of
infant Strange Situation behavior with a particular parent to
predict discourse on reunion with that parent at age six. I have
also shown how, in text analyses emphasizing Grice's maxims
for cooperative discourse, patterns of discourse used in
describing and evaluating one's attachment history during the
Adult Attachment Interview predict infant Strange Situation
behavior to the speaker even prior to the birth of the first
child. Additionally, when administered to the same individuals
16 to 20 years later, patterns of discourse usage during this
interview have recently been found predictable from the organization of the individual's early attachment to the mother, as
seen in infant Strange Situation behavior.

3. My third objective has been to point to some of the ways in
which concepts familiar to clinicians can be applied, albeit
carefully and with some alteration, to work currently taking
place within the field of attachment. Here, for example, I have
also suggested that discourse violations during the Adult
Attachment Interview as observed in dismissing and preoccupied speakers may represent a kind of resistance to the interview context. We may also speculate that, for such speakers,
caregiving of the infant represents a kind of transfer from the
early relationship to the speaker's own primary attachment
figure.

4. Finally, I have presented a developing theory respecting the
maintenance of the "organized" forms of insecure attachment.

Here I have suggested that, in the service of maintaining proximity and/or self-organization during interactions with an insecure attachment figure, individuals falling in these categories eventually develop and subsequently attempt to maintain a largely inflexible (i.e., dismissing or preoccupied) representational state. Successful maintenance of insecure representational states may be subjectively experienced in terms of a kind of secondary sense of "felt security" while events which threaten to alter these states may engender anxiety. In this case, both "insensitive" responses to infant signals and communications as observed in the home setting, and violations of Grice's maxims as observed within the Adult Attachment Interview may be seen as evidence for the speaker's active (although not necessarily conscious) attempt to maintain a particular representational state.

REFERENCES

Ainsworth, M. D. S. (1969), Object relations, dependency and attachment: A theoretical review of the infant–mother relationship. *Child Devel.*, 40:969–1025.

—— Bell, S. M. & Stayton, D. J. (1971), Individual differences in strange-situation behavior of one-year-olds. In: *The Origins of Human Social Relations*, ed. H. R. Schaffer. New York: Academic Press, pp. 17–57.

—— Blehar, M. C., Waters, E. & Wall, S., ed. (1978), *Patterns of Attachment*. Hillsdale, NJ: Lawrence Erlbaum Associates.

—— & Eichberg, C. G. (1991), Effects on infant–mother attachment of mother's unresolved loss of an attachment figure or other traumatic experience. In: *Attachment Across the Life Cycle*, ed. P. Marris, J. Stevenson-Hinde & C. Parkes. New York: Routledge, pp. 160–183.

Allen, J. P., Hauser, S. T. & Borman-Spurrell, E. (in press), Attachment theory as a framework for understanding sequelae of severe adolescent psychopathology: An eleven-year follow-up study. *J. Consult. Clin. Psychol.*

Allport, A. (1989), Visual attention. In: *Foundations of Cognitive Science*, ed. M. L. Posner. Cambridge, MA: MIT Press, pp. 631–682.

Bakermans-Kranenburg, M. J. & van IJzendoorn, M. H. (1993), A psychometric study of the Adult Attachment Interview: Reliability and discriminant validity. *Devel. Psychol.*, 29:870–879.

Beckwith, L., Cohen, S. E. & Hamilton, C. (1995), Mother–infant interaction and divorce predict attachment representation at late adolescence. Poster presented at the biennial meeting of the Society for Research in Child Development, Indianapolis, IN.

Belsky, J., Rovine, M. & Taylor, D. (1984), The Pennsylvania Infant and Family Development Project II: Origins of individual differences in infant–mother attachment: Maternal and infant contributions. *Child Devel.*, 55:706–717.

Benoit, D. & Parker, K. (1994), Stability and transmission of attachment across three generations. *Child Devel.*, 65:1444–1456.

Bowlby, J. (1969), *Attachment and Loss, Vol. 1*. London: Hogarth Press.

—— (1973), *Attachment and Loss, Vol II*. New York: Basic Books.

—— (1980), *Attachment and Loss, Vol. III*. New York: Basic Books.

—— (1988), *A Secure Base*. New York: Basic Books.

Bretherton, I. (1985), Attachment theory: Retrospect and prospect. In: *Growing Points of Attachment Theory and Research*, ed. I. Bretherton & E. Waters. *Monographs of the Society for Research in Child Development*, Serial No. 129, Vol. 50, Nos. 1–2, pp. 66–104.

—— Ridgeway, D. & Cassidy, J. (1990), Assessing internal working models of the attachment relationship: An attachment story completion task for 3-year-olds. In: *Attachment in the Preschool Years*, ed. M. T. Greenberg, D. Cichetti & E. M. Cummings. Chicago: University of Chicago Press, pp. 273–308.

—— & Waters E., eds. (1985), *Growing Points of Attachment Theory and Research. Monographs of the Society for Research in Child Development*, Serial No. 209, Vol. 50, Nos. 1–2.

Breuer, J. & Freud, S. (1895), Studies on hysteria. *Standard Edition*, 2. London: Hogarth Press, 1955.

Carlson, V., Cicchetti, D., Barnett, D. & Braunwald, K. (1989), Disorganized/disoriented attachment relationships in maltreated infants. *Devel. Psychol.*, 25:4, 525–531.

Cassidy, J. (1986), Attachment and the self at six. Unpublished doctoral dissertation, University of Virginia.

—— (1988), Child–mother attachment and the self in six-year-olds. *Child Devel.*, 59:121–134.

—— (1994), Emotion regulation: Influences of attachment relationships. In: *Emotional Regulation*, ed. N. Fox. *Monographs of the Society for Research in Child Development*, Serial No. 240, Vol. 69, pp. 228–249.

—— & Berlin, L. (1994), The insecure/ambivalent pattern of attachment: Theory and research. *Child Devel.*, 65:971–991.

Clyman, R. B. (1991), The procedural organization of emotions: A contribution from cognitive science to the psychoanalytic theory of therapeutic action. *J. Amer. Psychoanal. Assn.*, 39:349–382, supplement.

Cohen, J. (1988), *Statistical Power Analysis for the Behavioral Sciences*. Hillsdale, NJ: Lawrence Erlbaum Associates.

Crittenden, P. M. (1985), Maltreated infants: Vulnerability and resilience. *J. Child Psychol. Psychiat.*, 26:85–96.

—— (1988), Relationships at risk. In: *Clinical Implications of Attachment*, ed. J. Belsky & T. Nezworski. Hillsdale, NJ: Lawrence Erlbaum Associates, pp. 136–174.

Crowell, J., O'Connor, E., Wollmers, G., Sprafkin, J. and Rao, U. (1991), Mothers' conceptualizations of parent–child relationships: Relation to mother–child interaction and child behavior problems. *Devel. Psychopathol.*, 3:431–444.

Eagle, M. N. (1984), *Recent Developments in Psycho-Analysis*. New York: McGraw-Hill.

—— (1987), The psychoanalytic and the cognitive unconscious. In: *Theories of the Unconscious and Theories of the Self*, ed. R. Stern. Hillsdale, NJ: The Analytic Press, pp. 155–189.

Edelman, G. M. (1989), *The Remembered Present*. New York: Basic Books.

Egeland, B. & Farber, E. (1984), Infant–mother attachment: Factors related to its development and changes over time. *Child Devel.*, 55:753–771.

—— & Sroufe, A. (1981), Developmental sequelae of maltreatment in infancy. In: *Developmental Perspectives in Child Maltreatment*, ed. R. Rizley & D. Cicchetti. San Francisco: Jossey-Bass, pp. 77–92.

Emde, R. N. (1989), Mobilizing fundamental modes of development: Empathic availability and therapeutic action. *Internat. J. Psycho-Anal.*, 69:881–913.

Ferenczi, S. & Rank, O. (1988), The development of psychoanalysis: A historical critical retrospect. In: *Essential Papers on Countertransference,* ed. B. Wolstein. New York: New York University Press, pp. 25–35.

Fonagy, P., Leigh, T., Steele, M., Steele, H., Kennedy, R., Mattoon, G., Target, M. & Gerber, A. (in press), The relation of attachment status, psychiatric classification and response to psychotherapy. *J. Consult. Clin. Psychol.*

—— Steele, H. & Steele, M. (1991), Maternal representations of attachment during pregnancy predict the organization of infant–mother attachment at one year of age. *Child Devel.,* 62:891–905.

—— Steele, M., Steele, H., Moran, G. S. & Higgitt, A. C. (1991), The capacity for understanding mental states: The reflective self in parent and child and its significance for security of attachment. *Infant Ment. Health J.* 12:201–218.

Fox, N. A., Kimmerly, N. L. & Schafer, W. D. (1991), Attachment to mother/attachment to father: A meta-analysis. *Child Devel.,* 62:210–225.

Freud, S. (1926), *Inhibitions, Symptoms and Anxiety. Standard Edition,* 20: 87–172. London: Hogarth Press, 1959.

—— (1937), Analysis terminable and interminable. *Standard Edition,* 23:216–253. London: Hogarth Press, 1964.

Fury, G. F. (1993), The relation between infant attachment history and representations of relationship in school-aged family drawings. Poster session, biennial meeting of the Society for Research in Child Development, New Orleans.

Gaensbauer, T. J. & Harmon, R. J. (1982), Attachment behavior in abused/neglected and premature infants: Implications for the concept of attachment. In: *The Attachment and Affiliative Systems,* ed. R. N. Emde & R. J. Harmon. New York: Plenum Press, pp. 245–299.

George, C., Kaplan, N. & Main, M. (1985), The Berkeley Adult Attachment Interview. Unpublished protocol, Dept. Psychology, University of California, Berkeley.

—— & Main, M. (1979), Social interactions of young abused children: Approach, avoidance and aggression. *Child Devel.,* 50:306–318.

Grice, H. P. (1975), Logic and conversation. In: *Syntax and Semantics Vol. 3,* ed. P. Cole & J. L. Moran. New York: Academic Press, pp. 41–58.

Grossmann, K., Grossmann, K. E., Spangler, G., Suess, G. & Unser, L. (1985), Maternal sensitivity and newborn orienting responses as related to quality of attachment in Northern Germany. In: *Growing Points of Attachment Theory and Research.* ed. I. Bretherton & E. Waters. *Monographs of the Society for Research in Child Development,* Serial No. 209, Vol. 50, Nos. 1–2, pp. 233–256.

Grossmann, K. E. & Grossmann, K. (1991), Attachment quality as an organizer of emotional and behavioral responses in a longitudinal perspective. In: *Attachment Across the Life Cycle,* ed. C. M. Parkes, J. Stevenson-Hinde & P. Marris. London: Tavistock/Routledge.

Hamilton, C. E. (1995), Continuity and discontinuity of attachment from infancy through adolescence. Presented at biennial meeting of the Society for Research in Child Development, Indianapolis, IN.

Hansburg, H. G. (1972), *Adolescent Separation Anxiety.* Springfield, IL: Charles Thomas.

Heinecke, C. & Westheimer, I. (1966), *Brief Separations.* New York: International Universities Press.

Hesse, E. (submitted), Discourse, memory and the Adult Attachment Interview: A brief note with emphasis on the emerging Cannot Classify category.

—— & Main, M. (submitted), Frightened/dissociated behavior in traumatized but nonmaltreating parents: Risk factor in the development of anxiety and malignant self-concept?

Hilgard, E. R. (1977–1986), *Divided Consciousness*. New York: Wiley.

Hinde, R. A. (1970), *Animal Behavior*. New York: McGraw-Hill.

—— (1974), *Biological Bases of Human Social Behavior*. New York: McGraw-Hill.

—— (1982), Attachment: Conceptual and biological considerations. In: *The Place of Attachment in Human Behaviour*, ed. C. Parkes & J. Stevenson-Hinde. London: Tavistock.

Holtzworth-Monroe, A., Hutchinson, G. & Stuart, G. L. (1992), Attachment patterns of maritally violent vs. non-violent men: Data from the Adult Attachment Interview. Presented at meeting of Association for Advancement of Behavior Therapy, Boston.

Isabella, R. A. (1993), Origins of attachment: Maternal interactive behavior across the first year. *Child Devel.*, 64:605–621.

Jacobsen, T., Edelstein, W. & Hofmann, V. (1994), A longitudinal study of the relation between representations of attachment in childhood and cognitive functioning in childhood and adolescence. *Devel. Psychol.* 30:112–124.

—— Ziegenhain, U., Muller, B., Rottmann, U., Hofmann, V. & Edelstein, W. (1992), Predicting stability of mother–child attachment patterns in day-care children from infancy to age 6. Poster presented at the Fifth World Congress of Infant Psychiatry and Allied Disciplines, Chicago.

Kaplan, N. (submitted), Individual differences in six-year-olds' thoughts about separation: Predicted from attachment to mother at age one. Doctoral dissertation, Dept. Psychology, University of California, Berkeley.

—— & Main, M. (1986), A system for the analysis of children's family drawings in terms of attachment. Unpublished manuscript, Dept. Psychology, University of California, Berkeley.

Kihlstrom, J. F. (1987), The cognitive unconscious. *Sci.*, 237:1445–1452.

Klagsbrun, M. & Bowlby, J. (1976), Responses to separation from parents: A clinical test for young children. *Brit. J. Proj. Psychol.*, 21:7–21.

Kobak, R. R. (1993), The Attachment Q-Sort. Unpublished manuscript, University of Delaware.

Liotti, G. (1992), Disorganized/disoriented attachment in the etiology of the dissociative disorders. *Dissociation*, 4:196–204.

—— (1993), Disorganized attachment and dissociative experiences: An illustration of the developmental-ethological approach to cognitive therapy. In: *Cognitive Therapy in Action*, ed. H. Rosen & K. T. Kuehlwein. San Francisco: Jossey-Bass, pp. 213–239.

Londerville, S. & Main, M. (1981), Security of attachment, compliance and maternal training methods in the second year of life. *Devel. Psychol.*, 17:289–299.

Luborsky, L. (1988), *Who Will Benefit from Psychotherapy?* New York: Basic Books.

—— (1994), Therapeutic alliances as predictors of psychotherapy outcomes: Factors explaining the predictive success. In: *The Working Alliance*, ed. O. Adam, Leslie Horvath & S. Greenberg. New York: Wiley, pp. 38–50.

Lyons-Ruth, K. L. (in press), Attachment relationships among children with aggressive behavior problems: The role of disorganized early attachment strategies. *J. Consult. Clin. Psychol.*

—— Repacholi, B., McLeod, S. & Silva, E. (1991), Disorganized attachment behavior in infancy: Short-term stability, maternal and infant correlates, and risk-related subtypes. *Devel. Psychopathol.*, 3:397–412.

Main, M. (1981), Avoidance in the service of attachment: A working paper. In: *Behavioral Development*, K. Immelmann, G. Barlow, L. Petrinovitch & M. Main. New York: Cambridge University Press, pp. 651–693.

—— (1990), Cross-cultural studies of attachment organization: Recent studies, changing methodologies and the concept of conditional strategies. *Human Devel.*, 33:48–61.

—— (1991), Metacognitive knowledge, metacognitive monitoring, and singular (coherent) versus multiple (incoherent) models of attachment: Findings and directions for future research. In: *Attachment Across the Life Cycle*, ed. C. M. Parkes, J. Stevenson-Hinde & P. Marris. London: Routledge, pp. 127–159.

—— (1993), Discourse, prediction, and recent studies in attachment: Implications for psycho-analysis. *J. Amer. Psychoanal. Assn.*, 41:209–244, supplement.

—— (in press), Individual differences in attachment from infancy to adulthood: Four patterns seen in behavior, discourse and narrative. *Internat. J. Psychoanal.*

—— & Cassidy, J. (1988), Categories of response to reunion with the parent at age six: Predicted from attachment classifications and stable over a one-month period. *Devel. Psychol.*, 24:415–426.

—— & George, C. (1985), Responses of abused and disadvantaged toddlers to distress in agemates: A study in the daycare setting. *Devel. Psychol.*, 21:3, 407–412.

—— & Goldwyn, R. (1984), Predicting rejection of her infant from mother's representation of her own experience: Implications for the abused-abusing intergenerational cycle. *Internat. J. Child Abuse Neglect*, 8:203–217.

—— & —— (in press), Adult attachment scoring and classification system. Unpublished manuscript, Dept. Psychology, University of California at Berkeley. In: *Systems for Assessing Attachment Organization through Discourse, Behavior and Drawings*, ed. M. Main (working title). Cambridge: Cambridge University Press.

—— & —— (submitted), Interview-based adult attachment classifications: Related to infant–mother and infant–father attachment.

—— & Hesse, E. (1990), Parents' unresolved traumatic experiences are related to infant disorganized attachment status: Is frightened and/or frightening parental behavior the linking mechanism? In: *Attachment in the Preschool Years*, ed. M. T. Greenberg, D. Cichetti & E. M. Cummings. Chicago: University of Chicago Press, pp. 161–182.

—— & —— (1992), Disorganized/disoriented infant behavior in the Strange Situation, lapses in the monitoring of reasoning and discourse during the parent's Adult Attachment Interview, and dissociative states. In: *Attachment and Psycho-Analysis*, ed. M. Ammaniti and D. Stern. Rome: Gius, Laterza & Figli (translated into Italian).

—— Kaplan, N. & Cassidy, J. (1985), Security in infancy, childhood and adulthood: A move to the level of representation. In: *Growing Points of Attachment Theory and Research*, ed. I. Bretherton & E. Waters. *Monographs of the Society for Research in Child Development*. Serial No. 209, Vol. 50, Nos. 1–2, pp. 66–104.

—— & Morgan, H. (in press), Disorganization and disorientation in infant Strange Situation behavior: Phenotypic resemblance to dissociative states? In: *Handbook of Dissociation*, ed. L. Michelson & W. Ray. New York: Plenum Press.

—— & Solomon, J. (1986), Discovery of a new, insecure-disorganized/disoriented attachment pattern. In: *Affective Development in Infancy*, ed. T. B. Brazelton & M. Yogman. Norwood, NJ: Ablex, pp. 95–124.

—— & —— (1990), Procedures for identifying infants as disorganized/disoriented during the Ainsworth Strange Situation. In: *Attachment in the Preschool Years*. ed. M. T. Greenberg, D. Cichetti & E. M. Cummings. Chicago: University of Chicago Press, pp. 121–160.

—— —— & Hesse, E. (1985), Disorganized/disoriented attachment status: Its precursors and sequelae (working title). Unpublished manuscript, University of Virginia, Charlottesville.

—— & Stadtman, J. (1981), Infant response to rejection of physical contact by the mother: Aggression, avoidance and conflict. *J. Amer. Acad. Child Psychiat.*, 20:292–307.

—— & Weston, D. (1981), The quality of the toddler's relationship to mother and to father: Related to conflict behavior and the readiness to establish new relationships. *Child Devel.*, 52:932–940.

—— & —— (1982), Avoidance of the attachment figure in infancy: Descriptions and interpretations. In: *The Place of Attachment in Human Behavior*, ed. C. M. Parkes & J. Stevenson-Hinde. New York: Basic Books.

Manassis, K., Bradley, S., Goldberg, S., Hood, J. & Swinson, R. P. (1994), Attachment in mothers with anxiety disorders and their children. *J. Amer. Acad. Child Adol. Psychiat.*, 33:1106–1113.

Maynard Smith, J. (1979), Games theory and the evolution of behavior. *Proceedings Royal Society*, Series B, 205:475–488.

Miyake, K., Chen, S.-J. and Campos, J. H. (1985), Infant temperament, mother's mode of interaction, and attachment in Japan: An interim report. In: *Growing Points of Attachment Theory and Research*, ed. I. Bretherton & E. Waters. *Monographs of the Society for Research in Child Development*, Serial No. 209, Vol. 50, Nos. 1–2, pp. 276–297.

Modell, A. (1975), The ego and the id: 50 years later. *Internat. J. Psycho-Anal.*, 56:57–88.

Radke-Yarrow, M., Cummings, E. M., Kuczynski, L., & Chapman, M. (1985), Patterns of attachment in two- and three-year-olds in normal families with parental depression. *Child Devel.*, 56:884–893.

Radojevic, M. (1992), Predicting quality of infant attachment to father at 15 months from prenatal paternal representations of attachment: An Australian contribution. Presented at the 25th International Congress of Psychology, Brussels, Belgium.

Robertson, J. & Bowlby, J. (1952), Responses of young children to separation from their mothers. *Courrier Centre Internationale Enfance*, 2:131–142.

—— & Robertson, J. (1967–72), *Young Children in Brief Separations* (Film series). London: Tavistock.

—— & —— (1971), Young children in brief separation: A fresh look. *The Psychoanalytic Study of the Child*, 26:264–315. New Haven, CT: Yale University Press.

Rosenberg, D. M. (1984), The quality and content of preschool fantasy play: Correlates in concurrent social-emotional personality function and early mother–child attachment relationships. Unpublished doctoral dissertation, University of Minnesota.

Rosenstein, D. S. & Horowitz, H. A. (in press). Adolescent attachment and psychopathology. *J. Consult. Clin. Psychol.*

Sagi, A., van IJzendoorn, M. H., Scharf, M., Koren-Karie, N., Joels, T. & Mayseless, O. (1994), Stability and discriminant validity of the Adult Attachment Interview: A psychometric study in young Israeli adults. *Devel. Psychol.*, 30:771–777.

Sander, L. W. (1975), Infant and caretaking environment: Investigation and conceptualization of adaptive behavior in a system of increasing complexity. In: *Explorations in Child Psychiatry*, ed. E. J. Anthony. New York: Plenum Press, pp. 129–166.

—— (1987), Awareness of inner experience: A systems perspective on self-regulatory process in early development. *Child Abuse Neglect*, 11:339–346.

Smith, P. B. & Pederson, D. R. (1988), Maternal sensitivity and patterns of infant–mother attachment. *Child Devel.*, 59:1097–1101.

Solomon, J. & George, C. (1991), Working models of attachment of children classified as controlling at age six: Disorganization at the level of representation. Presented at the biennial meeting of the Society for Research in Child Development, Seattle.

—— —— & DeJong, A. (in press), Children classified as controlling at age six: Evidence of disorganized representational strategies and aggression at home and at school. *Devel. Psychopathol.*

Spangler, G., Fremmer-Bombik, E. & Grossmann, K. (submitted), Social and individual determinants of infant attachment security and disorganization.

—— & Grossmann, K. E. (1993), Biobehavioral organization in securely and insecurely attached infants. *Child Devel.*, 64:1439–1450.

Spence, D. P. (1987), *The Freudian Metaphor*. New York: Norton.

Spieker, S. J. & Booth, C. (1985), Family risk typologies and patterns of insecure attachment. Presented at symposium at biennial meeting of the Society for Research in Child Development, Toronto.

Sroufe, L. A & Waters, E. (1977), Heart rate as a convergent measure in clinical and developmental research. *Merrill Palmer Quart.*, 23:3–27.

—— & Fleeson, J. (1986), Attachment and the construction of relationships. In: *Relationships and development*, ed. W. Hartup & Z. Rubin. Hillsdale, NJ: Lawrence Erlbaum Associates, pp. 51–72.

Stalker, C. (in press), Attachment organization and adaptation in sexually abused women. *Canadian J. Psychiat.*

Steele, H., Steele, M. & Fonagy, P. (in press), Associations among attachment classifications of mothers, fathers and infants: Evidence for a relationship-specific perspective. *Child Devel.*

Stern, D. N. (1985), *The Interpersonal World of the Infant*. New York: Basic Books.

Stevenson-Hinde, J. (1994), Commentary to Hazan and Shaver's, "Attachment as an Organizational Framework for Research in Close Relationships." *Psychol. Inq.*, 5:62–65.

Strage, A. & Main, M. (1985), Attachment and parent–child discourse patterns. Presented at biennial meeting of the Society for Research in Child Development, Toronto.

Suess, G. J., Grossmann, K. E. & Sroufe, L. A. (1992), Effects of infant attachment to mother and father on quality of adaptation in preschool: From dyadic to individual organization of self. *Internat. J. Behav. Devel.*, 15:43–65.

Troy, M. & Sroufe, L. A. (1987), Victimization among preschoolers: The role of attachment relationship history. *J. Amer. Acad. Child Psychiat.*, 26:166–172.

Urban, J., Carlson, E., Egeland, B. & Sroufe, L. A. (1991), Patterns of individual adaptation across childhood. *Devel. Psychopathol.*, 3:445–460.

van IJzendoorn, M. H. (1995), Adult attachment representations, parental responsiveness and infant attachment: A meta-analysis on the predictive validity of the Adult Attachment Interview. *Psychol. Bull.*, 117:387–403.

—— & Bakermans-Kranenburg, M. J. (1994), Intergenerational transmission of attachment: State of the art in psychometric, psychological and clinical research. Presented at the Clarke Conference on Attachment and Psychopathology.

—— (in press), Attachment representations in mothers, fathers, adolescents and clinical groups: A meta-analytic search for normative data. *J. Clin. Consult. Psychol.*

—— Goldberg, S., Kroonenberg, P. M. & Frenkel, O. J. (1992), The relative effects of maternal and child problems on the quality of attachment: A meta-analysis of attachment in clinical samples. *Child Devel.*, 63:840–858.

—— & Kroonenberg, P. M. (1988), Cross-cultural patterns of attachment: A meta-analysis of the Strange Situation. *Child Devel.*, 59:147–156.

Vaughn, B., Egeland, B., Sroufe, A. L. & Waters, E. (1979), Individual differences in infant–mother attachment at 12 and 18 months: Stability and change in families under stress. *Child Devel.*, 50:971–975.

Wallerstein, R. S. (1986), Psycho-analysis as a science: A response to the new challenges. *Psychoanal. Quart.* 55:414–451.

Walsh, F. (1979), Concurrent grandparent death and birth of schizophrenic offspring: An intriguing finding. *Family Process*, 17:457–463.

Ward, M. J. & Carlson, E. A. (1995), The predictive validity of the adult attachment interview for adolescent mothers. *Child Devel.*, 66:69–79.

Wartner, U. G., Grossmann, K., Fremmer-Bombik, E. & Suess, G. (1994), Attachment patterns at age six in South Germany: Predictability from infancy and implications for preschool behavior. *Child Devel.*, 65:1014–1027.

Waters, E., Crowell, J., Treboux, D., O'Connor, E., Posada, G. & Golby, B. (1993), Discriminant validity of the Adult Attachment Interview. Poster presented at the 60th meeting of the Society for Research in Child Development, New Orleans.

—— Merrick, S. K., Albersheim, L. & Treboux, D. (1995), Attachment security from infancy to early adulthood: A 20-year longitudinal study. Presented at biennial meeting of Society for Research in Child Development, Indianapolis, IN.

Zeanah, C. H. & Emde, R. N. (1993), Attachment disorders in infancy. In: *Child and Adolescent Psychiatry*, ed. M. Rutter, L. Hersov & E. Taylor. Oxford: Blackwell.

Zimmerman, P., Fremmer-Bombik, E., Spangler, G. & Grossmann, K. E. (1995), Attachment in adolescence: A longitudinal perspective. Poster presented at biennial meeting of Society for Research in Child Development, Indianapolis, IN.

Index